Conservatives and the Constitution

Since the 1980s, a ritualized opposition in legal thought between a conservative "originalism" and a liberal "living constitutionalism" has obscured the aggressively contested tradition committed to, and mobilization of arguments for, constitutional restoration and redemption within the broader postwar American conservative movement. *Conservatives and the Constitution* is the first history of the political and intellectual trajectory of this foundational tradition and mobilization. By looking at the deep stories told either *by* identity groups or *about* what conservatives took to be flashpoint topics in the postwar period, Ken I. Kersch seeks to capture the developmental and integrative nature of postwar constitutional conservatism, challenging conservatives and liberals alike to more clearly see and understand both themselves and their presumed political and constitutional opposition. *Conservatives and the Constitution* makes a unique contribution to our understanding of modern American conservatism, and to the constitutional thought that has, in critical ways, informed and defined it.

KEN I. KERSCH is Professor of Political Science at Boston College. A noted scholar of American constitutional law and history and American political development and thought, he has won numerous awards for his work, including the American Political Science Association's Edward S. Corwin Award, the J. David Greenstone Prize from the American Political Science Association's Politics and History Section, and the Hughes-Gossett Award from the Supreme Court Historical Society.

Cambridge Studies on the American Constitution

Series Editors

Maeva Marcus, The George Washington University
Melvin I. Urofsky, Virginia Commonwealth University
Mark Tushnet, Harvard Law School
Keith Whittington, Princeton University

Cambridge Studies on the American Constitution seeks to publish works that embrace constitutional history, politics, law, and legal and political theory to better explain constitutional politics outside the courts, the determinants of constitutional change, the relationship between constitutional lawmaking and conventional politics, the nature of constitutional regimes, comparative approaches to constitutional systems, and the criteria for evaluating constitutional success and failure. Books in the series will explore these and similar issues within a variety of theoretical and methodological traditions, with special emphasis given to research using interdisciplinary approaches in innovative ways.

Titles in the Series

Conservatives and the Constitution

Imagining Constitutional Restoration in the Heyday of American Liberalism

KEN I. KERSCH
Boston College

CAMBRIDGE
UNIVERSITY PRESS

CAMBRIDGE
UNIVERSITY PRESS

University Printing House, Cambridge CB2 8BS, United Kingdom

One Liberty Plaza, 20th Floor, New York, NY 10006, USA

477 Williamstown Road, Port Melbourne, VIC 3207, Australia

314–321, 3rd Floor, Plot 3, Splendor Forum, Jasola District Centre, New Delhi – 110025, India

79 Anson Road, #06–04/06, Singapore 079906

Cambridge University Press is part of the University of Cambridge.

It furthers the University's mission by disseminating knowledge in the pursuit of education, learning, and research at the highest international levels of excellence.

www.cambridge.org
Information on this title: www.cambridge.org/9780521193108
DOI: 10.1017/9781139022491

First published 2019

Printed and bound in Great Britain by Clays Ltd, Elcograf S.p.A.

A catalogue record for this publication is available from the British Library.

Library of Congress Cataloging-in-Publication Data
NAMES: Kersch, Kenneth Ira, 1964– author.
TITLE: Conservatives and the constitution : imagining constitutional restoration in the heyday of American liberalism / Ken I. Kersch.
DESCRIPTION: Cambridge, United Kingdom ; New York, NY, USA : University Printing House, [2019] | Series: Cambridge studies on the American Constitution | Includes bibliographical references and index.
IDENTIFIERS: LCCN 2018056598 | ISBN 9780521193108 (alk. paper)
SUBJECTS: LCSH: Constitutional history – United States. | Conservatism – United States. | Law – United States – Christian influences. | Constitutional law – Religious aspects – Christianity. | United States – Politics and government – 1945–1989. | United States – Politics and government – 1989–
CLASSIFICATION: LCC KF4541 .K47 2019 | DDC 342.7302/9–dc23
LC record available at https://lccn.loc.gov/2018056598

ISBN 978-0-521-19310-8 Hardback
ISBN 978-0-521-13980-9 Paperback

Contents

Preface – Voices from the Political Wilderness

From the late nineteenth-century stirrings of Populism, to early twentieth-century progressivism, and on through Franklin Roosevelt's New Deal, Harry S Truman's Fair Deal, John F. Kennedy's New Frontier, and Lyndon Baines Johnson's Great Society, the modern American state was constructed on a base of liberal, reformist political suppositions, ideals, ideas, and institutions committed to active government advancing the common good. The "American Century" in this sense was the liberal century. Left-leaning and reformist social movements spearheaded by farmers, workers, women, African Americans, college students, and antiwar activists pioneered the goals and, as refracted through the stewardship of "vital center" liberals,[1] forged the institutions of this durably ascendant but perpetually unfolding governing order.[2] This liberalism found a home in the modern Democratic Party.

The liberal century, however, was bookended by predominantly conservative eras. The first, which in constitutional histories took its name from a 1905 US Supreme Court decision striking down a progressive-inspired New York State maximum hours law for bakery workers, was dubbed the "Lochner Era." This first conservative era was defined by a public philosophy holding a narrow conception of the powers of the national government; an expansive understanding of the powers of the states, where constitutionally protected rights were not involved; and a robust conception of rights and

---

[1] See Arthur M. Schlesinger Jr., *The Vital Center: The Politics of Freedom* (Boston: Houghton Mifflin, 1949).

[2] See, e.g., Elizabeth Sanders, *Roots of Reform: Farmers, Workers, and the American State, 1877–1917* (Chicago: University of Chicago Press, 1999); Ken I. Kersch, *Constructing Civil Liberties: Discontinuities in the Development of American Constitutional Law* (New York: Cambridge University Press, 2004); John Skrentny, *The Minority Rights Revolution* (Cambridge, MA: Belknap Press of the Harvard University Press, 2004).

prerogatives of private property owners, whether individuals or businesses.[3] The second conservative era, foreshadowed by the proud failure of Barry Goldwater's 1964 presidential campaign and the ideologically ambidextrous Richard Nixon's 1968 victory that ascended on the wings of a campaign promising law and order, a renewed patriotism, a "new federalism," and "strict construction" of the Constitution on behalf of the nation's "silent majority," triumphed with the election of Ronald Reagan at the beginning of the 1980s. This conservatism found a home in the modern Republican Party.

This tripartite developmental framework, to be sure, was not without anomalies. Republican President Dwight D. Eisenhower's two terms sit near the temporal heart of the regnant "consensus" New Deal liberalism of the 1950s, for example, just as Democratic Presidents Bill Clinton's and Barack Obama's two-terms sit squarely in the heart of late-century conservatism. As many have noted, Richard Nixon's truncated two terms in the White House did not challenge the fundamentals of the liberal New Deal order and in some respects extended it.[4] Other anomalies can be found in what in retrospect look like ideological mismatches between the period's causes, constituencies, and parties. For many of these years, conservative segregationists were unwavering Democrats. Virulent anticommunism – and anti-anticommunism – were as likely to be Democratic as Republican causes. Liberal, northeastern "Rockefeller Republicans" were a core Republican constituency and, in many respects, helped define the party until the 1980s. But, as the political scientist Walter Dean Burnham and others have long noted, these sorts of intraparty coalitions and tensions are common in party systems structured like that of the United States.

By 1980, however, a fundamental change was at hand. The conservative movement's staunch anticommunism, hostility to liberals and governmental bloat and overregulation, and conviction that civil rights and civil liberties, as defined by liberals, had been taken too far (or transmogrified, through corrupted understandings, into their opposites) came to define the core of a newly ideological Republican Party. At roughly the same time, the

---

[3] The era got its name from the case of *Lochner* v. *New York*, 198 US 45 (1905), a *bête noire* for progressives, in which the Supreme Court voided the New York baker's hours law on Fourteenth Amendment due process "liberty of contract" grounds. See generally Arnold Paul, *The Conservative Crisis and the Rule of Law: Attitudes of the Bar and Bench, 1887–1895* (Gloucester, MA: Peter Smith, 1976); Robert McCloskey, *The American Supreme Court* (Chicago: University of Chicago Press, 2000).

[4] By the lights of sophisticated models of "regime politics" advanced by political scientists, these ostensible aberrations do not undermine the core nature of the underlying governing order. See, e.g., Stephen Skowronek, *The Politics Presidents Make* (Cambridge, MA: Belknap Press of the Harvard University Press, 1997); Keith Whittington, *The Political Foundations of Judicial Supremacy: The Presidency, the Supreme Court, and Constitutional Law* (Princeton: Princeton University Press, 2007). See also David Plotke, *Building a Democratic Political Order: Reshaping American Liberalism in the 1930s and 1940s* (New York: Cambridge University Press, 1996).

Democratic Party realigned itself with ideological liberalism.[5] On the cusp of the twenty-first century, the country re-sorted itself and settled into its current ideological, partisan polarization, divided between "Red" and "Blue." In this new order, Democrats were liberal and Republicans were conservative. The formerly muttish and mongrel political order was re-launched in the form of a dogfight between snarling purebreds.[6]

Over time, it became clear to an increasing number of observers that the two parties had arrived at not only distinct sets of principles and policy preferences but also at very different intellectual and rhetorical frameworks for doing and talking about politics. Twentieth-century liberalism spoke the language of the "policy state"[7] it had created, which imagined politics as a meliorist, problem-focused practice in which political, social, and economic problems were first identified and then put on the path to solution through the formulation of government-initiated public policy aimed at the pragmatic, practical achievement of stated policy goals and objectives. Both the early and late twentieth-century conservatisms, by contrast, spoke the language not of pragmatic, meliorist policy, but of the foundational, constitutional rule of law.

These discourses operated no more independently of each other than did the contending parties themselves. Liberals had risen to power in significant part by arguing that the conservative preoccupation with strict adherence to the constitutional rules, as conservatives understood them, was leading to an unconscionable quietism in the face of a new set of massive – and addressable – social problems. For their part, late twentieth-century conservatives had risen to power in significant part by arguing that the liberal preoccupation with government problem solving through public policy had amounted to either an actual or *de facto* abandonment of the nation's foundational constitutional commitments, evincing not only a disregard of the

---

[5] See Bruce Miroff, *The Liberals' Moment: The McGovern Insurgency and the Identity Crisis of the Democratic Party* (Lawrence: University Press of Kansas, 2007); Eric Schickler, *Racial Realignment: The Transformation of American Liberalism, 1932–1965* (Princeton: Princeton University Press, 2016).

[6] See Alan Abramowitz, *The Disappearing Center: Engaged Citizens, Polarization, and American Democracy* (New Haven: Yale University Press, 2010); Matthew Levandusky, *The Partisan Sort: How Liberals Became Democrats and Conservatives Became Republicans* (Chicago: University of Chicago Press, 2009); Pietro Nivola and David Brady, editors, *Red and Blue Nation? Consequences and Correction of America's Polarized Politics* (Washington, DC: Brookings Institution Press, 2008); Barbara Sinclair, *Polarization and the Politics of National Policy Making* (Norman: University of Oklahoma Press, 2006); Thomas Mann and Norman Ornstein, *It's Even Worse Than It Looks: How the American Constitutional System Collided with the New Politics of Extremism* (New York: Basic Books, 2012); Matt Grossman and David Hopkins, *Asymmetric Politics: Ideological Republicans and Interest Group Democrats* (New York: Oxford University Press, 2016); Hans Noel, *Political Ideologies and Political Parties in America* (New York: Cambridge University Press, 2014).

[7] Karen Orren and Stephen Skowronek, *The Policy State: An American Predicament* (Cambridge, MA: Harvard University Press, 2017).

terms of the nation's social contract concerning the powers of government but
also of the substantive principles, such as limited, divided government and the
protection of rights that that contract had been instituted to protect.

The core argument of this book, *Conservatives and the Constitution*, is that
the defense of and restoration of the Constitution played a critical role, and
served as a politically effective rallying cry, for postwar twentieth-century
movement conservatives, many of whom angrily alleged that the Constitution
had been abandoned by liberals – first, they said, in the New Deal (1933–1939);
then by the liberal Warren Court (1953–1969); and, as conservatives have most
recently emphasized, even before that, in the Progressive Era (1890–1920),
when the progressive progenitors of modern liberalism had, they said,
substituted pure will, under the guise of (mere) politics or policy, for
a foundational, national commitment to the rule of law. While this critique in
many places echoed the conservative constitutional understandings of Lochner
Era constitutional conservatism, *Conservatives and the Constitution* argues,
moreover, that – many movement and scholarly understandings to the contrary
notwithstanding – postwar conservative constitutional argument was diverse,
multivocal, contested, mutable, and developmental: put otherwise, it was
perpetually constructed and reconstructed across time in response to
perpetually changing problems, contexts, and challenges posed by a changing
policy and political landscape. In this sense, conservative constitutional
argument in the postwar period extended well beyond what in time became
known as the (anti-modern, anti–New Deal) reactionary fringe of what has been
called the "Old Right."[8] By looking at the deep stories told either *by* identity
groups (Conservative Evangelical and Fundamentalist Christians, Conservative
Roman Catholics) or *about* what conservatives took to be flashpoint topics (free
markets, communism) in the postwar period that shaped and informed the
development of their constitutional understandings across time, I seek to
capture the developmental and, ultimately, integrative nature of postwar
constitutional conservatism. Perhaps most interestingly, and intriguingly,
these theories and stories within the movement – or, perhaps more accurately,
in conjunction with an incipient, inchoate, or forming movement – did not exist
on separate tracks, hermetically sealed off from one another or, for that matter,
from liberal constitutional theory and thought: the critical feature of this
developmental trajectory was that it involved a coalescing across time of
diverse and at time divergent theories, narratives, and memories in a way
that led these diverse strands and strains to imagine themselves as part of
a coherent community and identity, pursuing a common political (and
constitutional) cause. Over time, this "living" conservative constitutionalism –
to provocatively apply the epithet rule-of-law conservatives contemptuously

[8] See, e.g., Albert Jay Nock, *Memoirs of a Superfluous Man* (New York: Harper and Bros, 1943);
John E. Moser, *Right Turn: John T. Flynn and the Transformation of American Liberalism*
(New York: New York University Press, 2005).

hurled at their opponents – amounted to a robust, intellectually elaborated critique of the modern liberal American state, with constitutionalist visions to back it.

The variegation and sophistication of the postwar constitutionalist Right, however, did not last. *Conservatives and the Constitution* additionally argues that these features – one might even say virtues – proved to be luxuries of conservatism in its wilderness years during the heyday of mid-century American liberalism. As the prospect of actual political power loomed, constitutional theory on the Right was narrowed and weaponized for service in the mass mobilization of votes and the disciplining of Republican Party cadres. While it is fair to say that the right-wing constitutional theory of the wilderness years recurred frequently to arguments and achievements of the nation's Founders, the turn in the 1980s to "originalism" – helped along, to be sure, by a belated invitation to conservative constitutional theorists to become participating members of the formerly all but exclusively liberal professional legal academy, and party to its sometimes arcane debates – led conservative constitutional theory to harden into a relatively narrow orthodoxy and then, more recently, into a form of scholasticism – with all the attendant virtues and successes that orthodoxy allows for when enlisted in mass mobilizations, politics – and academic careers.

CREATING A CONSTITUTIONAL CONSCIOUSNESS

Conservatives and the Constitution makes what I believe is a unique contribution to our understanding of modern American conservatism in general, and conservative constitutional thought more specifically.[9] In recent years, there has been an outpouring of historical, sociological, psychological, political science, journalistic, and legal academic scholarship on modern American conservatism. This study could not have been written without that work. That said, however, something very important is still missing – an account that takes as its primary focus what conservatives themselves have repeatedly attested is the chief thematic touchstone of their movement: the US Constitution.

The claim that the championing of the principles and obligations of the Constitution – "the best arrangement yet devised for empowering government to fulfill its proper role, while restraining it from the concentration and the abuse of power"[10] – was not only one but *the* chief thematic touchstone of the

---

[9] There has been no shortage of books on originalism, and an entire subliterature is now devoted to "the history of originalism." See Logan Sawyer III, "Principle and Politics in the New History of Originalism," *American Journal of Legal History* 57 (2017): 198–222. But, as this book will make clear on virtually every page, that is parochial and anachronistic, and not at all the same thing.

[10] Young Americans for Freedom, "The Sharon Statement" (1960), in Isaac Kramnick and Theodore J. Lowi, editors, *American Political Thought: A Norton Anthology* (New York: W.W. Norton, 2009), 1281.

modern conservative movement, and, hence, the contemporary Republican Party, is far from idiosyncratic. Even the most casual glance at movement manifestos like Barry Goldwater's *The Conscience of a Conservative* (1960), "The Sharon Statement" of the Young Americans for Freedom (1960), Ronald Reagan's "A Time for Choosing" speech supporting Goldwater's presidential candidacy (1964), and, more recently, the rise of the Federalist Society and the Tea Party movement underline the centrality of the constitutional frame. To be sure, many contemporary scholars assume, if they do not state explicitly, that the constitutional frame is epiphenomenal – a stand-in for the "real" forces driving the American Right, be it racism, the advancement of the rich, or, more generally, the reinforcement of the hierarchies that promote the interests of society's "haves."[11] From this perspective, to focus on the Right's constitutional arguments and visions is to get distracted by the sideshow – to foreground the movement's *post hoc* rationalizations and self-justifications in place of the fundamental forces driving its politics.

Conservatives and the Constitution, by contrast, takes these arguments, frames, and rhetorics seriously as a major force in the postwar American conservative ascendency. It does so for the simple reason that movement members believe them and, hence, act on them in the public sphere. This is not to deny the dynamics of self-interest, rationalization, and self-justification. It is only to say that such self-conscious dissembling is relatively rare, and not enough on which to build a broad political movement – or, for that matter, to allow most members of that movement to maintain a positive self-conception of who they are and what they are doing. For conservatives, a constitutional consciousness served important personal and collective functions and, in many cases, rose to the level of a quasi-independent motivating force.

While this book glances backward to the Old Right's rejection of Franklin Roosevelt's New Deal and forward to the "Reagan Revolution" and the election of Donald Trump as president for a critical sense of antecedents and implications, its center of gravity is on the formative years of the modern Right's constitutional consciousness, its wilderness years between the beginning of the Warren Court to the Reagan election. These were the years in which the conservative movement built an infrastructure of idea incubators, disseminators, and forums in which, in essence, the movement created a new world in which its members, and members-to-be, could live – an alternative

---

[11] See, e.g., Corey Robin, *The Reactionary Mind: Conservatism from Edmund Burke to Sarah Palin* (New York: Oxford University Press, 2011); Nancy MacLean, "Neo-Confederacy Versus the New Deal: The Regional Utopia of the Modern American Right," in Matthew D. Lassiter and Joseph Crespino, editors, *The Myth of Southern Exceptionalism* (New York: Oxford University Press, 2009); Rick Perlstein, "I Thought I Understood the American Right: Trump Proved Me Wrong," *New York Times* (April 11, 2017), www.nytimes.com/2017/04/11/magazine/i-thought-i-understood-the-american-right-trump-proved-me-wrong.html.

intellectual and emotional universe, a counterculture, positioned outside of the era's predominating or, if you will, hegemonic liberalism. Chapter 1 provides an overview of the establishment of the financial and institutional architecture that worked to both generate and disseminate conservative constitutional ideas in the postwar period. Chapter 2 introduces readers to the rich world of constitutional theory on the Right in the postwar United States – a world that, until now, has been almost entirely unmapped by scholars, hidden in plain sight. It has been unmapped and hidden because during these years, legal academia, the home of academic constitutional theory, was entirely dominated by political liberals, and these liberals identified the constitutional theory that they did with the essence of constitutional theory itself. Excluded from this world, most serious conservative constitutional theory was undertaken outside legal academia, by political philosophers (along with scholars in a smattering of other disciplines and operating independently, high-level journalists, and independent intellectuals) rather than by legal academics. Only recently has this work assumed a broader public profile, where it is now poised to serve as the basis for the emergent constitutional understandings not only of movement conservatism and the Republican Party but also of the country itself. If this relatively sophisticated constitutional argument on the postwar Right is the movement's gemstone, the book's subsequent chapters take a step back and describe the various rings in which the gemstone of high-level constitutional theory was set – the stories that conservatives and proto-conservatives of diverse identities brought to the table that made them ripe for and receptive to these constitutional arguments, whether in their original or, most often, popularized forms. Fundamentalist and Evangelical Christians, right-wing Roman Catholics, fervent anti-communists, and anti-statist libertarians all told passion-laden and memory-drenched stories in their own ways about the country's history and trajectory and their place within it, which served as a motivation for, and prologue to, imagining the country's future, should they reclaim the power to direct it. These stories provided the frame within which they imagined constitutional restoration.

The constructivist approach I adopt in *Conservatives and the Constitution* emphasizes the ways in which each of the diverse communities and identities that converged to form the modern conservative movement did so while, and through, narrating America. Each forged narratives with the aim of arriving at both self- and collective understandings of who they and we were and are. These stories were actively fashioned and shaped discursively across time, in part in response to ongoing provocations and events. That fashioning was a complicated process, involving highly selective remembering and forgetting, spotlighting and minimizing, downplaying and ignoring, interpreting and reinterpreting, anathematizing and celebrating.

Tessa Morris-Suzuki has observed that the study of history has "affective dimensions" involving, to varying degrees, not simply the interpretation of events but also a bid for identification, implicating imagination, empathy, and other emotions.[12] As such, especially as enlisted by identity-forging political movements, history is told in a way designed to make target audiences "more conscious of certain historical periods and places [and events] than others, more readily able to identify with some fragments of the past than with others." This is the case, inevitably, even when all the facts are "true." History and historical facts are thus never simply one thing: they are heavily dependent on the narrative and choice.[13] Members of the diverse strands of the conservative movement, like others who live their politics, shaped their stories to suit their own agendas and needs, both personal and collective. As such, they both blamed and condemned, excused and exculpated. Through these stories, they coped, bonded, and inspired.

While I have described this process rather abstractly here, in its political guise – and implications – it is anything but. These stories underwrote – political scientists would say "cued" – the full slate of concrete reactions to real-world agendas, crises, and struggles.[14] They provided the framing impetus for extant and would-be legislation, judicial rulings, political and policy agendas and programs, and electoral campaigns, reminding, evoking, enraging, motivating, inspiring, and urging. Whereas each of the more intellectual constitutional arguments I survey in the book's first chapters set out a logic, the stories I subsequently describe, by contrast, are more aptly described as having *logics*. Considered as such, the goal of *Conservatives and the Constitution* is to set the logic within the logics.

THE MOBILIZATION OF MEMORY

In addition to making arguments, postwar American movement conservative elites mobilized history – that is, memory – "to support contending visions of the national identity."[15] Rogers M. Smith has argued that political elites play an important role in leading individuals toward a sense of their own identity and

---

[12] Tessa Morris-Suzuki, *The Past Within Us: Media, Memory, History* (London: Verso, 2005), 22–23, 24–25 ("[O]ur understanding of history is never just an intellectual matter; any encounter with the past involves feeling and imagination as well as pure knowledge. Since our knowledge of the past is something from which we derive personal identity, it also helps to determine how we act in the world.").

[13] Morris-Suzuki, *Past Within Us*, 43. See also Murray Edelman, *Constructing the Political Spectacle* (Chicago: University of Chicago Press, 1988), 6.

[14] See, e.g., Martin Gilens and Naomi Murakowa, "Elite Cues and Political Decisionmaking," *Political Decision Making, Deliberation and Participation* 16 (2002): 15–49. See also Rogers M. Smith, *Political Peoplehood: The Role of Values, Interests, and Identities* (Chicago: University of Chicago Press, 2015), 44–45, arguing that the stories of peoplehood he posits "are not natural ... [but] created by asymmetrical interactions between potential leaders and ... members." "[B]oth ... have agency" – are engaged in an "always ongoing" process of "people-building," which involves both an aspiration to power and efforts "to promote ways of life they regard as good" (pp. 44–45).

[15] Morris-Suzuki, *Past Within Us*, 4, 104–105.

their membership in political groups (forged, in part, through the creation of intragroup trust) by offering "people-making," "ethically constitutive stories." These stories are historically interpretive: they are rooted, that is, in interpretations of the group's (or nation's) past and offer shared readings of the group's mores, understood in light of where it has been in the past and where it is going in the future. Political elites fashion and endeavor to sell these people-making, ethically constitutive stories in the roiling political marketplace, where they are placed on offer against competing, rivalrous stories of peoplehood.

While it is often said that Americans have little interest in history, this has certainly not been true of the postwar American Right, whose politics has been saturated with historically-rooted, movement-making, ethically constitutive stories. Legions of books by conservative and mass circulation commercial publishers; magazine articles; and more recently cable television shows, websites, YouTube videos, newsfeeds, and podcasts have recurred extensively to American history, with a special interest in the American Founding, Civil War, and most recently the Progressive Era. Whether in the form of videos, online courses, or vetted bibliographies listing canonical works, conservatives currently offer hundreds if not thousands of instructional courses on American history and American constitutionalism on the web for interested ordinary citizens.[16] The narratives offered in these histories provide "a distinct perspective on responsibility" and "imagined landscapes" within which to live. Intergenerational stories about the nature of the nation's legal/constitutional order are perhaps the preeminent component of the postwar American Right's stories of peoplehood. These movement-making stories lend meaning to individuals' lives, associations, and identities. They rationalize, direct, motivate, and "provid[e] grounds or warrants" for political behavior.[17]

Since the 1980s, at least, the most familiar of such stories on the modern constitutionalist Right have been those associated with originalism, which,

---

[16] See, e.g., Bill O'Reilly and Martin Dugard, *Killing England: The Brutal Struggle for American Independence* (New York: Henry Holt and Co., 2017); Bill O'Reilly and Martin Dugard, *Killing the Rising Sun: How America Vanquished World War II Japan* (New York: Henry Holt and Co., 2016); Bill O'Reilly and Martin Dugard, *Killing Reagan: The Violent Assault that Changed a Presidency* (New York: Henry Holt and Co., 2015); Bill O'Reilly and Martin Dugard, *Killing Patton: The Strange Death of World War II's Most Audacious General* (New York: Henry Holt and Co, 2014); Bill O'Reilly and Martin Dugard, *Killing Jesus* (New York: Henry Holt and Co., 2013); Bill O'Reilly and Martin Dugard, *Killing Lincoln: The Shocking Assassination That Changed America Forever* (New York: Henry Holt and Co., 2011). The liberal Left seems much less interested in history; to the extent that the interest is there, it seems to be in the history of the civil rights movement. Hobsbawm once observed, "History is the raw material of nationalistic or ethnic or fundamentalist ideologies, as poppies are the raw material of heroin addiction." Eric Hobsbawm, *On History* (London: Weidenfeld and Nicolson, 1997), quoted in Morris-Suzuki, *Past Within Us*, 7.

[17] Morris-Suzuki, *Past Within Us*, 13–15, 17, citing and drawing upon Saul Friedländer, "Historical Writing and the Memory of the Holocaust," in Berel Lang, editor, *Writing and the Holocaust* (New York and London: Holmes and Meier, 1988).

generally speaking, holds that the nation was formed and defined by the fundamental law of the Constitution, as drafted and handed down by the nation's Founders – both the text's authors and the Founding generation of Americans who adopted it: that is, those who, through the exercise of popular sovereignty, made it law – and that modern liberals/progressives had abandoned that Founding anchor and sought to obliterate the faithful heritage layered upon it by succeeding generations of patriotic Americans. This book treats the arrival of originalism (in its modern sense, at least), perhaps the modern conservative movement's most significant ethically constitutive story, as a point in the line of its temporal development.[18]

While the Right's recent convergence on constitutional originalism suggests lockstep unity, most studies of modern conservatism have appropriately underlined the intellectual and political diversity of the modern conservative coalition composed of, among others, traditionalists, the "Religious Right," libertarians, neoconservatives, populists, and business conservatives. While much has been written about how, given their disagreements on important matters of principle, this coalition is fraught and fragile and on the verge of falling apart, much less has been written seriously reflecting on how, despite their disagreements on important matters of principle, this coalition has proved so enduring and, indeed, as I write, seems only to be expanding. On this durability, two main explanations have been offered, both from within the movement itself. The first, associated most prominently with the conservative intellectual Frank Meyer, argues that the movement developed a theoretical synthesis called "Fusionism" that reconciled traditionalism and libertarianism.[19] The second – not necessarily mutually exclusive – focuses on *National Review* editor William F. Buckley Jr.'s relatively early decision to expel the fringe elements of the Far Right (for Buckley, the conspiracy theorist John Birch Society, but also anti-Semites and other racists) from the postwar movement, the suggestion being that once these elements had been shut out, a core of principled agreement remained, capable of sustaining the movement long into the future.[20]

Conservatives and the Constitution offers a different explanation for the movement's strength and durability that speaks to the possibilities for its expansion. That explanation, I argue, is found in the power of stories – of memory-saturated, ethically constitutive stories of peoplehood that forge, motivate, and sustain movements in the face of disagreements (within limits, to be sure) over policy and principle. Indeed, as will become clear over the course of this book, disagreements over principle are often managed, if not

---

[18] See Smith, *Political Peoplehood*, 23–24.
[19] See George H. Nash, *The Conservative Intellectual Movement in America Since 1945* (New York: Basic Books, 1976).
[20] See George Hawley, *Right-Wing Critics of American Conservatism* (Lawrence: University Press of Kansas, 2016).

superseded, by stories. This process involves dynamics like the building – and destabilizing – of feelings of trust and worth, and the fashioning of constitutive stories about who the people being addressed are and should aspire to be across time. These dynamics are as likely to require ambiguity as clarity, contradiction as consistency, emotion as rationality.[21] Those tethered to the usual concepts and categories of political, legal, and constitutional theory will typically miss these important and influential dynamics.

The ethically constitutive story about original meaning and fundamental law that the Right eventually converged on at least since the 1980s worked by "establishing or symbolizing social cohesion or the membership of groups, real or artificial communities ... establishing or legitimizing [or delegitimizing] institutions, status or relations of authority" and had as its "main purpose ... socialization, the inculcation of beliefs, values systems, and conventions of behavior."[22] Despite their many disagreements and diverse preoccupations, by the time that the modern conservative movement converged on originalism as an "ism" and as its constitutional calling card in the early 1980s and sought to implement and enforce that originalism institutionally through the leadership provided by the Reagan Justice Department,[23] the diverse elements of conservative thinking about the Constitution and constitutional interpretation surveyed here came to understand themselves as tribunes of the American Founding and positioned themselves as locked in an epic battle with their faithless liberal (and, later, progressive) antagonists who were committed to unmooring the American polity from its Founding commitments and traditions.

CONCLUSION

Conservatives and the Constitution will set out a basic overview of my understanding of the development of conservative constitutional thought in its generative "wilderness" years – that is, its years out of power during postwar liberalism's heyday between 1954 and 1980 (with some contextualizing extensions backward to the Old Right and forward to Reagan and Trump). The book will canvas the development of the main lines of "big picture" conservative constitutional theory in these years and situate that theory within what I take to be the postwar conservative movement's major constitutive narratives. As such, this book is not a comprehensive history of postwar conservative constitutional argument on the Right. Absent, most notably, will be a sustained presentation of the constitutional argument on specific constitutional issues during those same years – civil rights and civil

---

[21] Smith, *Political Peoplehood.* [22] Hobsbawm, "Inventing Traditions," 9.
[23] James Fleming, *Fidelity to Our Imperfect Constitution: For Moral Readings and Against Originalisms* (New York: Oxford University Press, 2015); Steven Teles, "Transformative Bureaucracy: Reagan's Lawyers and the Dynamics of Political Investment," *Studies in American Political Development* 23 (2009): 61–83.

liberties; federalism; and legislative, executive, and judicial power. I will cover that subject, as it relates to the overarching framework, arguments, and constitutive movement narratives presented here, in two subsequent books, the first focused on the conservative confrontation with the consolidated modern American state through the advancement of arguments and framing stories about the constitutional structures of American government in these years, and the second focused on the conservative confrontation with arguments for modern civil rights and civil libertarian freedom. The first of these subsequent books will show the ways that, as it developed across time in response to both events and ongoing political competition with liberals and, in time, the Democratic Party, a broad and intellectually diverse conservative movement narrowed the focus of its constitutional vision to attacking an out-of-control, activist federal judiciary. It will then show how, as the movement moved from the wilderness to take the reigns of power, it expanded outward again to a more broad-ranging, substantive constitutional vision, de-centered once again off the judiciary, and relatively unconcerned with the aggressive exercise of judicial power. The second subsequent book on civil rights and civil liberties will depart from the usual claims about or characterizations of conservative racism and opposition to civil liberties and chart, through a developmental lens, how the contemporary conservative movement moved beyond opposition to civil liberties and civil rights to understand itself, at least, as the polity's most fervent champions of the twin causes of constitutional liberty and equality. Collectively, if not strictly speaking comprehensive, these three books, each of which I hope will be readable on its own, will present at least a rounded picture of the development of the conservative movement's constitutional argument in the postwar United States.

Acknowledgments

As this book has been gestating for the better part of a decade, my debts to individuals and institutions are countless: conversations, comments, criticisms, and suggestions by the hundreds informed, shaped, altered, and inspired my thinking along the way. Perhaps the most long-standing debt on the project is to my research assistant Matthew Karambelas, Boston College (BC) '10 – now a Boston lawyer – whose extensive original source research provided the backbone for both this and the two related books to follow. Additional research assistance was provided at BC by Michael Coutu, Heitor Goueva, Hillary Thomson, David Levy, John Louis, and Dustin Sebell. The hawk-eyed Ryan Towey, BC '16, generously copyedited the full manuscript in its late stages. My BC Political Science Department chair, Susan Shell, has been consistently supportive and accommodating. The department's administrator, Shirley Gee, helped in countless ways throughout.

Many institutions around the country graciously invited me to give lectures and presentations on various parts of this project at every stage of its development. These included the James Madison Program in American Ideals and Institutions; the Program in Law and Public Affairs (LAPA); and the American Studies Workshop at Princeton University (with particular gratitude to Brad Wilson, Kim Scheppele, Dirk Hartog, and Paul Frymer); the Princeton and University of Maryland Law School constitutional law "schmoozes" (directed by Kim Scheppele and Mark Graber, respectively); the Program on Science, Technology, and Society at Harvard's John F. Kennedy School of Government in conjunction with Harvard Law School's Institute for Global Law and Policy (Sheila Jasanoff and David Kennedy); Yale University's Institute for Social and Policy Studies; the Drake University Constitutional Law Center (Miguel Schor and Mark Kende); The New York Historical Society's Institute for Constitutional History; the Center for Political and Economic Thought at St. Vincent College (Bradley C. S. Watson); the University of Wisconsin Center for the Study of Liberal Democracy (Howard Schweber, Don Downs); the National Autonomous University of Mexico (UNAM) (Imer Flores); and Boston

College's Intersections Program, which supported my participation in a faculty writing retreat in York Beach, Maine.

A number of colleges and universities invited me to give public lectures which, in conjunction with the conversations surrounding them, allowed me to test out new ideas associated with the project. These included Brigham Young University; The University of Nevada, Las Vegas; the University of Montana; Drake University; the College of the Holy Cross; Union College; and Bates College. I also benefited by presenting work-in-progress at conferences and/or faculty seminars at the Harvard Law School, Yale Law School, UNLV's William S. Boyd School of Law, University of Texas at Austin Law School, Boston University Law School, Tulane University Law School, Drake University Law School, the University of Montana Law School, Syracuse University Law School, the University of Missouri, and Florida International University, as well as the Legal History Colloquia at the University of Virginia Law School, Boston University Law School, and Boston College Law School. I also benefited from presenting related papers at the meetings of a number of professional associations, including the American Political Science Association, the American Historical Association, the Law and Society Association, the New England Political Science Association, the Western Political Science Association, the Policy History Conference, and the Shawnee Trail Regional Conference on American Politics and Constitutionalism sponsored by the University of Missouri's Kinder Institute on Constitutional Democracy, with the assistance of the Political Science Department of the University of Colorado, Colorado Springs.

I owe a special debt to the University of Missouri's Kinder Institute on Constitutional Democracy under the founding directorship of Justin Dyer, which, in conjunction with Boston College, not only funded a year-long sabbatical that allowed me to bring this project to completion but also hosted a two-day book manuscript workshop that was of immense help in shaping the contours of both this book and the two related books to follow. Among the many who participated in that unusually productive conference – which drew upon Missouri's Political Science and History Departments, and Law School and Honors College – were Jack Balkin, Keith Whittington, Richard Izquierdo, Adam Seagrave, Carli Conklin, Janelle Beavers, David Golemboski, and Catherine Rymph. I received some early financial support for the project from Boston College's Clough Center. I am especially grateful for the sustained support, financial and otherwise, of Boston College's Political Science Department and BC's Morrissey College of Arts and Sciences.

Many individuals have been helpful and supportive along the way, who I will try to list rhythmically rather than alphabetically: Linda McClain, Kim Scheppele, Sheila Jasanoff, David Kennedy, Paul Frymer, Akhil Amar, Brad Hays, Nancy Scherer, Bruce Ackerman, Richard Bensel, Ron Kahn, Karen Orren, Steve Skowronek, Gary Jeffrey Jacobsohn, Nick Salvatore, Julie Novkov, Dan Carpenter, Mark Tushnet, Steve Griffin, Carol Nackenoff, Jeff

Pasley, Dan Geary, Steve Engel, Dirk Hartog, Shep Melnick, Richard Hamm, Greg Burnep, Sandy Levinson, Jim Fleming, Logan Sawyer, Tom Packer, Bob Faulkner, Kevin Kruse, Elizabeth Sanders, David Tanenhaus, Mary Bilder, Meg Jacobs, Amy Wallhermfechtel, Tim Fuller, Sophia Lee, Mary Ziegler, Joe Postell, Jeremy Rabkin, Steve Teles, Sot Barber, Mark Graber, Brad Wilson, Lisa Miller, Aziz Rana, Jesse Merriam, Justin Dyer, Intisar Rabb, Bradley C. S. Watson, Eldon Eisenach, Sean Beienburg, Barry Cushman, Larry Solum, Ted White, Paul Herron, Keith Bybee, Patrick Peele, Tom Keck, Miguel Schor, Mark Kende, Clem Fatovic, Emily Zackin, and Justin Crowe.

I remain profoundly grateful to Keith Whittington and Jack Balkin, who have been supportive of this project, and engaged interlocutors of my work more generally, from the beginning to now, which will soon tally as decades. The same goes, in a different way and even further back, to my Teagle Hall lifting partner Clem Fatovic (with spots on the neck scratcher and head popper ...), and, since sophomore year at Williams College, to Ted Holsten. I have also appreciated the ongoing support and friendship of Dan Peris, Jan van Eck, Carol Nackenoff, Linda McClain, Jim Fleming, and my parents Barbara and Robert Kersch.

At Cambridge University Press, I am grateful to Lew Bateman, who commissioned this project based on a short book proposal, but who retired before I belatedly submitted the manuscript. Lew's successor Sara Doskow skillfully shepherded that manuscript to publication. I am also grateful to the anonymous reviewers of both the initial book proposal for Cambridge and, later, of the completed manuscript, who were both supportive and brimming with criticisms and apt suggestions. Thanks to both Sara and those reviewers, this is a better book than it otherwise would have been.

The Intellectual Archipelago of the Postwar American Right

The Christian religion grew and developed and has been sustained by the constant reading of its sacred book, the Bible. In order to preserve our freedoms, it is necessary that similar attention be given to American history, especially American constitutional history.

Frank Holman[1]

Writing in the traditionalist *Modern Age* in the late 1960s, the conservative rabbi Will Herberg situated constitutional law within a much broader political and, indeed, theological framework. Herberg explained, "[T]he limited-power constitutional state recognizes, even if sometimes only implicitly and negatively, a majesty beyond itself, some limit intrinsically to its own pretensions, whether it be the natural law, the divine law, or whatever." By contrast, he instructed, "the totalitarian state normally espouses its own public conception of the 'good life' for man and society and proceeds to enforce this conception." Herberg continued, "[T]he constitutional state does not pretend to any such total conception of the 'good life' of its own: it strives merely to provide men, and groups of men, with sufficient freedom to follow their own, often diverse conceptions of the 'good life.'"[2]

Applying this to contemporary politics, Herberg observed that the conservatives of his day had retained their commitment to the foundational principles of liberal constitutionalism. Liberals, by contrast, had become proud anti-constitutionalists. They had engineered an entirely new understanding of American government and, over the course of the liberal century, had not only put it into practice but had also succeeded in institutionalizing it. The liberal

---

[1] Frank E. Holman, "The President's Annual Address: Must America Succumb to Statism?" *American Bar Association Journal* 35 (October 1949): 801–879, 878. This quotation is published as an epigraph by permission of the *American Bar Association Journal*.
[2] Will Herberg, "The Great Society and the American Constitutional Tradition," *Modern Age* 11:3 (Summer 1967): 232.

understanding was of a newly purposive government, directed not at protecting core constitutional principles (such as liberty) but rather at formulating an ever-changing list of policy goals with the aim of solving social problems.[3] Herberg explained to *Modern Age* readers as follows:

[T]he demand for a "sense of purpose" ... is ... a radical departure from our basic constitutional system. The federal government is not, and was never meant to be, a moral agency to give the people an inspirational lead ... [T]he sense of purpose, if it is to come at all, must come to each of us from the deepest sources – from our faith, from our "philosophy of life," from our religious and moral convictions. To look to the state to supply it to us is ... to "religionize" the state ... It is something never contemplated by the Founding Fathers and the makers of our constitutional republic as a function of the state.

"The state," he continued, "has no business having an official doctrine about the good life,"[4] adding for good measure that

it is an inseparable and inviolable part of our constitutional tradition that the government, while friendly and encouraging to the religion, or religions, of its citizens, may not itself become the object of religious devotion; it must on no account allow itself to be divinized and to engage the citizen's highest hopes and expectations. The government, to be constitutionally legitimate, must be content with being a power of the middle range, restricted to the rather prosaic functions proper to it, without pretending to be the seat of the citizen's highest values.[5]

While many contemporary scholars are familiar with some relatively crude, legalistic, and political benchmarks of conservative constitutionalism – a commitment to originalism and opposition to (at least liberal) "activist judges," for instance – they rarely appreciate the diversity of conservative constitutional thought in the postwar United States; the depth of its philosophical and ideological underpinnings; and, hence, of its political resonances; or the way in which that thought is, as the Herberg article illustrates, situated, often quite expressly, within larger political, theological, and civilizational frameworks. Lacking such an understanding, liberals have been repeatedly blindsided and bewildered by outbursts of right-wing rage that have appeared to form and structure contemporary conservatism.[6] A primary goal of this book is to make the arguments, associations, and emotions that help constitute the contemporary Right visible and legible. It is my conviction that chronicling and explaining the development of modern conservatism's

---

[3] See Ken I. Kersch, "The Gilded Age and the Progressive Era," in Mark Tushnet, Mark Graber, and Sanford Levinson, editors, *The Oxford Handbook on the U.S. Constitution* (New York: Oxford University Press, 2015).
[4] Herberg, "Great Society and the American Constitutional Tradition," 234.
[5] Herberg, "Great Society and the American Constitutional Tradition," 233.
[6] See, e.g., Arlie Russell Hochschild, *Strangers in Their Own Land: Anger and Mourning on the American Right* (New York: The New Press, 2016).

constitutional vision, so central to the modern movement, is an especially effective and novel way of doing that.

AN EMBEDDED CONSTITUTIONAL VISION

The best way to do so, I believe, is to understand conservative *constitutional* thought as integrated into broader and deeper currents of conservative *political* thought more generally. This is certainly how most conservatives – outside of the legal academy, at least – understand their constitutional thought and convictions. Only by approaching conservative constitutional thought as embedded within these larger frameworks can we hope to understand modern conservative constitutionalists as they understand themselves. One way to be led astray in this regard is to anachronistically conflate postwar conservative constitutionalism with contemporary originalism as initially formulated by its legal academic/judicial pioneers like Robert Bork and Antonin Scalia. While much of postwar conservative constitutional thought is originalist in a broad sense – placing a high value on the American Founding – it is not originalist in the sense that Bork, Scalia, and other conservative legalists have understood and continue to understand it today. Narrowly focusing on legalist originalism and its progenitors[7] as *the* foundational theory of conservative constitutionalism, if not approached in a relatively open spirit, can lead to distortion, misapprehension, and misunderstanding.[8]

This book will show that postwar conservative constitutional thought was actually much more diverse and contested than conventional originalism-centered understandings have recognized. It will show, moreover, that the conservative political thought that undergirded this constitutional thought was considerably more sophisticated and intellectually and ideologically rooted in other frameworks – philosophical, theological, historical – than is commonly understood. This more robust and filigreed backstory is, I believe, crucial to understanding why movement participants, particularly its intellectuals, including its ersatz intellectual judges, have long possessed a self-confidence, premised upon a conviction of their own seriousness and open-mindedness, that perpetually confounds and exasperates liberals, who tend to see little but shallowness, ignorance, emotionalism, rigidity, and selfishness ... if not worse.

Far from lacking any interest in history or ideas, the modern conservative movement has been, in significant respects, a movement of idea-drenched

---

[7] See, e.g., Johnathan O'Neill, *Originalism in American Law and Politics* (Baltimore: Johns Hopkins University Press, 2005).

[8] Nash, *Conservative Intellectual Movement in America*; Donald Critchlow, *The Conservative Ascendancy: How the GOP Right Made Conservative History* (Cambridge, MA: Harvard University Press, 2007); Patrick Allitt, *The Conservatives: Ideas and Personalities Throughout American History* (New Haven: Yale University Press, 2009).

autodidacts. Its denizens, including ordinary Republican voters, have been voracious readers and news junkies, with a lively interest in American history and political and constitutional theory.[9] As such, many understand themselves not as the ignorant and bigoted "deplorables" of Hillary Clinton's imagination but as having reflected seriously on the Western canon and the history of political thought in the West – or at least to have listened attentively to high-status conservative intellectuals, or ideamongers, who have. As lifelong learners, perpetually hungry to learn more about American history; the American Founders; and American ideals, institutions, and principles from what they are told are the most reliable sources, these same people have been primed and tutored – warned – again and again by conservative movement elites that they would be mercilessly stereotyped by the Left and liberals as ignorant, bigoted, closed-minded, and stupid, their endless reading, listening, and discussions notwithstanding. When this in fact happened, far from being chastened by the criticism, their worldview and self-regard was reinforced and confirmed.

CONSTITUTIONALISM AS SPECTACLE

The hunger, curiosity, and passion of the densely networked conservative autodidacts in the postwar United States were fed by a far-flung archipelago of outlets that discussed and debated constitutional and political theory, and the symbiotic relationship between the former and the latter, eventually constituting a powerful political culture rich in arguments, symbols, signifiers, narratives, and meanings. The islands in this archipelago, which started to form at mid-century, included conservative book (Regnery) and magazine (*National Review, Human Events, Modern Age, Reader's Digest, Commentary, The Public Interest*) publishers, conservative radio shows (Fulton J. Sheen's *The Catholic Hour*, Clarence "Pat" Manion's *Manion Forum*, Paul Harvey, James Dobson's *Focus on the Family*, Rush Limbaugh), conservative television shows (Fulton J. Sheen's *Life Is Worth Living*, William F. Buckley Jr.'s *Firing Line*), conservative churches and, in more recent years, conservative TV networks and websites (Fox News, *National Review Online*), blogs, Twitter streams, and newsfeeds – to say nothing of the well-known think tanks (the American Enterprise Institute, The Heritage Foundation) and party, interest, and advocacy group politics. These crucibles and purveyors of conservative political thought helped construct an ideological world in which meanings, including constitutional meanings, were made, and a community – even a nation – was imagined. It is a world in which ordinary people were both entertained and instructed. Some graduated to new levels of sophistication as they advanced, as it were, from talk radio to Austrian economics. Those who partook were tutored in comprehensive understandings of the modern

[9] See, e.g., conservative best sellers like the books of the former Fox News host Bill O'Reilly.

predicament, the liberal threat, and the conservative solution. This involved much more than securing allegiances to a slate of policy preferences: it forged an identity – no less than a fundamental perspective on the world and movement members' place within it. Academic legalist pretensions notwithstanding, it is impossible to understand postwar conservative constitutionalism without a broader and deeper understanding of its embeddedness in broader philosophies, theologies, and historical narratives, as well as thoughts and emotions concerning nationalism, patriotism, and legitimacy.[10]

It is a mistake to limit the study of the taking and making of constitutional meaning to formal interpretations by judges of the constitutional text as part of the triadic resolution of legal disputes. To be sure, candidates, officeholders, intellectuals, social movement actors, ordinary people – and judges[11] – interpret the constitutional text. But as participants in a broader constitutional politics and culture, they also interpret the judicial interpretations such as *Brown* v. *Board of Education* (1954), *Engel* v. *Vitale* (1962), or *Roe* v. *Wade* (1973); political/constitutional spectacles such as Watergate; the leaking and publication of the Pentagon Papers; the Goodman/Cheney/Schwerner murders during Mississippi Freedom Summer; the Robert Bork Supreme Court confirmation hearings; the mobilization of social movements and social movement organizations like the NAACP and the National Organization of Women (NOW); the environmental and consumer movement litigation campaigns; key bureaucratic appointments; and historical watersheds like the Great Depression, the New Deal, the "loss" of China, the Hiss-Chambers spy case, the rise of Black Power, Jane Fonda's trip to North Vietnam, rising crime rates, urban disorder, and mass incarceration – to say nothing of the formal decisions made by other constitutional and quasi-constitutional actors like presidents, members of Congress, bureaucrats, and state and local

---

[10] Positivistic social science, like "attitudinal" studies of judicial "votes" on constitutional cases, cannot apprehend this core aspect of contemporary constitutional conservatism. Indeed, it rarely even tries, since the matter involves the messy process of the invention and assimilation of meaning, not simply tallies of votes or "positions." In this, it is the interpretation of facts and not the facts themselves that are critical. Facts do not come with "determinable meaning[s]." Edelman, *Constructing the Political Spectacle*, 1. See also Guy Debord, *La Societé du Spectacle* (Paris: Buchet/Chastel, 1967); Robert M. Cover, "The 1982 Supreme Court Term: Forward: *Nomos* and Narrative," *Harvard Law Review* 97 (1983): 4–68; Rogers M. Smith, "Political Jurisprudence, The 'New Institutionalism,' and the Future of Public Law," *American Political Science Review* 82 (March 1988): 89–108.

[11] See, e.g., Larry Kramer, *The People Themselves: Popular Constitutionalism and Judicial Review* (New York: Oxford University Press, 2005); Mitchell Pickerill, *Constitutional Deliberation in Congress: The Impact of Judicial Review* (Durham, NC: Duke University Press, 2004); Michael McCann, *Rights at Work: Pay Equity Reform and the Politics of Legal Mobilization* (Chicago: University of Chicago Press, 1994); George Lovell, *This Is Not Civil Rights: Discovering Rights Talk in 1939 America* (Chicago: University of Chicago Press, 2012); Ken I. Kersch, "Originalism's Curiously Triumphant Death: The Interpenetration of Aspirationalism and Historicism in U.S. Constitutional Development," *Constitutional Commentary* 31 (2016): 413–429.

government officials. Even events long past, like military victories or defeats (the Civil War), massacres, or foundings (the American Revolution), whatever their status as historical facts, are subject to remade meanings. "[P]olitical developments," Murray Edelman has rightly noted "are ambiguous entities that mean what concerned observers construe them to mean." The way that political events are presented "continuously constructs and reconstructs social problems, crises, enemies, and leaders and so creates a succession of threats and reassurances."[12]

Political meanings, like governing institutions and orders, might be relatively settled for long periods of time, whether within governing coalitions or in the populace more generally. But controversies over those meanings can be generated and stoked. In this sense, meanings are never permanently resolved: they are subject to being challenged and remade. Doing so provocatively is one way that political oppositions wrest control and win power.[13] The settlement and contestation of constitutional meaning in the United States have been a major part of this process. Explanations, interpretations, and arguments in politics and US constitutionalism have "careers." Part of the business of a political and ideological opposition is to end a career and find a new one to take its place. In this, the solution may precede the problem.[14]

The political-historical process of contestation and settlement does not merely involve efforts to destabilize and construct political coalitions (groups) but the very consciousness of political actors themselves (individuals) – their subjectivity, indeed, their identity. This process is inherently relational: the construction of a political self typically involves a positioning of that self vis-à-vis the political other, constructing identity through the cultivation of a sense of membership (belonging) and opposition.[15] In this, all manner of actions, events,

[12] Edelman, *Constructing the Political Spectacle*, 1–3, 10. See also Murray Edelman, *The Symbolic Uses of Politics* (Urbana: University of Illinois Press, 1964). For recent statements and elaborations, see David Blight, *Race and Reunion: The Civil War in American Memory* (Cambridge, MA: Harvard University Press, 2001); David Blight, *American Oracle: The Civil War in the Civil Rights Era* (Cambridge, MA: Harvard University Press, 2011); Rogers M. Smith, *Stories of Peoplehood: The Politics and Morals of Political Membership* (New York: Cambridge University Press, 2003); Rogers M. Smith, *Political Peoplehood: The Role of Values, Interests, and Identities* (Chicago: University of Chicago Press, 2015).
[13] Edelman, *Constructing the Political Spectacle*, 7–8, 10.
[14] Edelman, *Constructing the Political Spectacle*, 18–22. See also Victoria Hattam and Joseph Lowndes, "The Ground Beneath Our Feet: Language, Culture, and Political Change," in Stephen Skowronek and Matthew Glassman, editors, *Formative Acts: American Politics in the Making* (Philadelphia: University of Pennsylvania Press, 2007); Jack M. Balkin, "From Off the Wall to On the Wall: How the Mandate Challenge Went Mainstream," *The Atlantic* (June 4, 2012) (www.theatlantic.com/national/archive/2012/06/from-off-the-wall-to-on-the-wall-how-the-mandate-challenge-went-mainstream/258040/); Jack M. Balkin, "How Social Movements Change (Or Fail to Change) the Constitution: The Case of the New Departure," *Suffolk Law Review* 39 (2005): 27–65.
[15] Ziad Munson, *The Making of Pro-Life Activists: How Social Movement Mobilization Works* (Chicago: University of Chicago Press, 2009); Hochschild, *Strangers in Their Own Land*.

and people, past and present, are made to "stand for ideologies, values, or moral stances and they become role models, benchmarks, or symbols of threat and evil."[16] As such, for many politically involved and active people, political narratives – and for many movement conservatives, the constitutional narratives that helped constitute them – became important routes to a unified self. It is difficult to understand not only the policy preferences themselves but also the intensity of those preferences – the emotions – without some apprehension of this truth.

POLITICAL DISCOURSE AS POLITICAL REALITY

Political spectacles are made and mediated through language spoken in the public sphere. The language adduced in the public sphere evokes constructed and conditioned beliefs about "the causes of discontents and satisfactions, about policies that will bring about a future closer to the heart's desire," sensitizing political actors to "some political news, promises, and threats" and desensitizing them to others. Constructed meanings, chains of association, and stories about the past, present, and future are critical parts of this process, a process often of a character far from the rationalist "deliberative democratic" ideal so dear to our most hopeful political theorists. In political spectacles, the interested public is supplied with "stock texts," whether in general circulation or within more circumscribed scrums and subgroupings: "To maintain adequate support and acquiescence, aspirants for leadership and for social acceptance must choose from a circumscribed set of [these] texts."[17] The result is the establishment of a set of plural realities. In some periods, there are significant overlaps in these realities, even between ostensible opponents. In others, the divergent realities approach incompatibility, if not mutual incomprehensibility.

Movement conservatives in the postwar period enlisted constitutional arguments, appeals, and stories to frame their understandings of social problems: put otherwise, movement and, in turn, Republican Party leaders positioned themselves as interpreters and integrators of social experience in relation to constitutional norms and obligations. In an era of rapid social change, movement thinkers and political and intellectual entrepreneurs offered interpretations of these unsettling social changes that embedded constitutional arguments and stories in broader frames.[18]

While many still apply "classical" social movement theory to right-wing movements, treating their denizens as irrational, frustrated, excluded, and

---

[16] Edelman, *Constructing the Political Spectacle*, 2.

[17] Edelman, *Constructing the Political Spectacle*, 109–113; See also Hattam and Lowndes, "Ground Beneath Our Feet"; Smith, *Stories of Peoplehood*; Adam Sheingate, "The Terrain of the Political Entrepreneur," in Skowronek and Glassman, *Formative Acts*.

[18] Rory McVeigh, *The Rise of the Ku Klux Klan: Right-Wing Movements and National Politics* (Minneapolis: University of Minnesota Press, 2009), 5, 7.

marginalized, doing so could at most provide an incomplete account of the modern American conservative movement, which has always had a strong component of business and financial elites, as well as members of the established, mainstream middle class. Conversely, many – most recently Corey Robin[19] – present the conservative disposition as inherently one of powerful, and empowered, elites primarily concerned with the preservation of political, social, and economic hierarchies. Whatever the power of this understanding as a normative evaluation of conservative political thought and ultimate effects, it does not work descriptively for American conservatism, either in recent years or considered over the long term: many American conservatives, simply put, are not elites by any definition other than race privilege, while many liberals, including the Princeton- and Yale-educated New Yorker Robin (also white), indubitably are.[20] Postwar American conservatism involved an incipient, proto-constituency of segments of both the privileged and powerful and the dispossessed and powerless. As such, the interpretation of social, constitutional, and political relations offered by the movement had to be fashioned in a way that simultaneously, in complicated ways, promised to preserve, restore – and, indeed, remove – privileges.

Movement framings, which help construct both identities and presumed interests, built the movement itself by making collective action possible among the disparate groups and the members that ultimately comprised them. Fostering a sense of common cultural/political identity and defining and spotlighting the boundaries of the group – who is in and who is out – are ways to transcend status differences, bonding insiders and outsiders to each other as part of a newly imagined community. The frames that serve this function are, of necessity, made in time. Within the movement, the matter of which framing elements will be adopted and prevail is contested. Since the world changes, the process is, in its nature, ongoing: the frames are adjusted across time via informational feedback loops as part of the political program of expanding membership, with the aim of gaining and sustaining political power.[21]

[19] Corey Robin, *The Reactionary Mind: Conservatism from Edmund Burke to Sarah Palin* (New York: Oxford University Press, 2011).

[20] Hochschild, *Strangers in Their Own Land*; Thomas Frank, *What's the Matter With Kansas? How Conservatives Won the Heart of America* (New York: Henry Holt and Company, 2004); J. D. Vance, *Hillbilly Elegy: A Memoir of Family and Culture in Crisis* (New York: Harper, 2016).

[21] McVeigh, *Rise of the Ku Klux Klan*, 25, 36–39, 43, 45, 198. Social movement scholars refer to this temporal process as "frame alignment." David Snow, E. Burke Rochford Jr., Steven Worden, and Robert Benford, "Frame Alignment Processes, Micromoblization, and Movement Participation," *American Sociological Review* 51 (1986): 454–481. For concrete examples of frame adjustment on the Right, see Mary Ziegler, *Before Roe: The Lost History of the Abortion Debate* (Cambridge, MA: Harvard University Press, 2015) (abortion); Wayne Batchis, *The Right's First Amendment: The Politics of Free Speech and the Return of Conservative Libertarianism* (Stanford: Stanford University Press, 2016) (freedom of speech). On the wealthy and middle-class support for the

THE ARCHIPELAGO – THE DISSEMINATION AND DIFFUSION OF CONSERVATIVE IDEAS IN POSTWAR AMERICA

At mid-century, as the traditional story goes, movement conservatism was all but moribund. Beginning in 1933, the Old Right – Albert Jay Nock, Rose Wilder Lane, Isabel Paterson, John T. Flynn, Garet Garret, George Sokolsky, Fulton Lewis Jr., and others – had adamantly but unsuccessfully opposed Franklin Roosevelt's New Deal and then both the US entry into World War II and the country's ascendant leadership, and even involvement, in world affairs. In the 1930s and 1940s, the reactionary and isolationist Old Right's defeat on both fronts seemed total, amounting to complete repudiation. At mid-century, "consensus" intellectual elites casually but confidently explained from their perches in New York and Massachusetts that conservatism in America was finished once and for all: it had ceased to exist.[22] Some right-wing voices, to be sure, staggered on, well out of the political and cultural mainstream, like ideological dinosaurs from a Paleolithic political era. Old Right magazines like H. L. Mencken's curmudgeonly *American Mercury* continued to hawk curiosities – antique intellectual wares. Scattered fans remained of the Nashville Agrarians, who had taken a stand for aristocratic, chivalric, southern values that seemed ludicrously irrelevant to an urbanizing and suburbanizing polity transitioning into a new mass industrial, service, and consumer culture – the very conditions that had sparked their (last?) "stand" in the first place.[23] The libertarian magazine *The Freeman* nearly folded in 1954, leaving *Human Events* the last conservative magazine standing with any notable readership or influence. "Mr. Conservative," Ohio Senator Robert A. Taft, son of President and Chief Justice William Howard Taft, a promising contemporary if traditional voice on the rise since the late 1930s, died suddenly of cancer in 1953. The Republican Party was in the hands of the New York "kingmakers" who had selected Republican nominees for president from 1936 to 1960 (including then-President Dwight D. Eisenhower, who might have run in either party) and were positioned near the "vital center" of the American liberal consensus.[24]

---

modern conservative movement, see Lisa McGirr, *Suburban Warriors: The Origins of the New American Right* (Princeton: Princeton University Press, 2001); Kevin Kruse, *One Nation Under God: How Corporate America Invented Christian America* (New York: Basic Books, 2015); Donald Critchlow, *Phyllis Schlafly and Grassroots Conservatism: A Women's Crusade* (Princeton: Princeton University Press, 2005).

[22] See Lionel Trilling, *The Liberal Imagination: Essays on Literature and Society* (New York: Viking Press, 1950); Richard Hoftstadter, "Paranoid Style of American Politics," *Harper's Magazine* (November 1964).

[23] See Twelve Southerners, *I'll Take My Stand: The South and the Agrarian Tradition* (New York: Harper and Brothers, 1930); Peter Kolozi, *Conservatives Against Capitalism: From the Industrial Revolution to Globalization* (New York: Columbia University Press, 2017), 77–105.

[24] Michael D. Bowen, *The Roots of Modern Conservatism: Dewey, Taft, and the Battle for the Soul of the Republican Party* (Chapel Hill: University of North Carolina Press, 2011). See Arthur Schlesinger Jr., *The Vital Center: The Politics of Freedom* (Boston: Houghton Mifflin, 1949).

That said, it is well worth noting that whatever the state of the American conservative "movement" at the time, the nation's social status quo in the immediate postwar era remained quite conservative on several fronts, as measured by contemporary political standards. A hawkish anticommunism was one. While by the middle of 1954, having pushed his purges and attacks a bridge too far, the most strident anti-communist voice, Joseph McCarthy, was being roundly repudiated in the Army-McCarthy hearings (like Taft, McCarthy died young, in McCarthy's case, of acute liver failure brought on by a raging alcoholism), the anti-communist impulse remained strong. And, moreover, while the 1950s may not have been as unrelievedly staid as is typically assumed, and the cracks in the foundations may have been visible to the culture's structural engineers, especially *post hoc*, the era nevertheless remained one in which traditional authority and hierarchy (God, church, family, adults, law, business leaders, teachers, the police, and traditional norms concerning race, sex, and class and the public "presentation of self in everyday life") predominated.[25]

For those paying close attention, however, foundational, even radical, change was brewing in the culture and art of the Beats, the protest politics of the civil rights movement, the rise of the youth culture and anti-anticommunism, and with the Supreme Court's landmark desegregation decision in *Brown* v. *Board of Education* (1954) and resistance to police abuses, on a host of issues involving civil liberties and civil rights. Partisans of conservative ideas – or simply defenders of the status quo who did not yet identify as conservatives – increasingly felt an imperative to challenge liberals intellectually and politically, within both the then ideologically pluralistic Democratic and Republican Parties. By the early 1960s, it was clear that the Democrats were moving away from conservatism, and the Republicans were moving away from liberalism. Most dramatically, a call went out in the Republican Party for a candidate for president who would offer Americans a "choice, not an echo," a harbinger of the parties' impending ideological divide.[26]

One place to get a bead on the content of what conservatives would regard as a genuine choice is to look at the archipelago of postwar publications that were either expressly conservative or hospitable to conservative ideas – and there were many; it was not just the *National Review*.[27] For instance, promising

---

[25] See Risa L. Goluboff, *Vagrant Nation: Police Power, Constitutional Change, and the Making of the 1960s* (New York: Oxford University Press, 2016); Alan Petigny, *The Permissive Society: America, 1941–1965* (New York: Cambridge University Press, 2009).

[26] Nicole Hoplin and Ron Robinson, *Funding Fathers: The Unsung Heroes of the Conservative Movement* (Washington, DC: Regnery Publishing, Inc., 2008), 71; Phyllis Schlafly, *A Choice, Not an Echo* (Alton, IL: Pere Marquette Press, 1964). See also Philip M. Crane, *The Democrats' Dilemma: How the Liberal Left Captured the Democratic Party* (Whittier, CA: Constructive Action Inc., 1964); Paul Harvey, *Autumn of Liberty* (New York: Hanover House, 1954).

[27] Ken I. Kersch, "Ecumenicalism Through Constitutionalism: The Discursive Development of Constitutional Conservatism in *National Review*, 1955–1980," *Studies in American Political Development* 25 (Spring 2011): 86–116; Batchis, *The Right's First Amendment*.

"[a]n article a day of enduring significance, in condensed permanent booklet form," *Reader's Digest* magazine was a postwar bastion of digestible middlebrow takes on life, politics, and culture (it also published books offering condensed versions of classic works of literature). While it did not hew rigidly to a party line or focus chiefly on politics, *Reader's Digest* leaned right, in the guise of straight-shooting, morally centered, commonsense clarity. Lamenting in the wake of the John F. Kennedy assassination that "somehow in the years since World War II we seem to have lost clear sight of the ideals which have made this nation strong and great," the magazine declared itself in sympathy with "men of reason and goodwill" and denounced "extremists of many persuasions." Its values were traditional – proudly on the side of established authority and institutions. "We believe in the principles of Christianity," its editors frankly reiterated in 1964, declaring "It is time for parents to assert their authority once more. It is time for the churches and the schools to try harder than they are now trying to rebuild the moral fiber of this country. It is time for men of fair minds to speak out, with a great and persistent voice, against extremists of all flavors."[28] It was *Reader's Digest* that introduced many Americans to the libertarian Austrian economist Friedrich Hayek; the magazine serialized his soon-to-be-classic anti-socialist manifesto *The Road to Serfdom* (1944). It also published excerpts from Barry Goldwater's presidential campaign manifesto *The Conscience of a Conservative* (1960). It introduced middle-class suburbanites to the reflections of seminal neoconservative Irving Kristol. In 1968, Richard Nixon chose *Reader's Digest* as the outlet for re-launching his political career as a conservative law-and-order champion of the country's "silent majority."[29]

While general interest magazines like *Reader's Digest* looked at the world through a reflexively conservative lens, specialized professional periodicals like the *American Bar Association Journal* played a similar role on a more elite, specialized, and professionalized front. Prior to the mid-1960s, when it underwent a major shift in its political orientation that tracked the mainstream and professional politics of the era, the *ABA Journal* was generally quite conservative.[30] To many American lawyers, this orientation

---

[28] "'This Nation, Under God': A Statement by the Editors," *Reader's Digest* 84:501 (January 1964): 37–39.

[29] Richard M. Nixon, "What Has Happened to America?" *Reader's Digest* (October 1967): 49–54.

[30] By 1965, it was evident that the future Supreme Court Justice and then ABA President Lewis F. Powell Jr. had his back against the wall: he was forced to take what now seemed like a rearguard action arguing that the association strictly confine itself to questions regarding the administration of justice, and not take up controversial issues of social reform. Lewis F. Powell Jr., "The President's Page," *American Bar Association Journal* 51 (February 1965): 101, 120. Some members, to increasing effect, challenged this position. See, e.g., Alfred Connor Bowman, "What Price 'Effectiveness,'" *American Bar Association Journal* 55 (March 1969): 251–253. Ironically, Powell, in a private, behind-the-scenes memo to the leadership of the US Chamber of Commerce, was calling for a newly aggressive conservative defense of the free enterprise system

(as Tocqueville once insisted) seemed natural. "The entire training of a lawyer tends to develop conservative attitudes in his thinking," the profession's leading professional journal mused at mid-century: "His profession requires him to delve into the past. Precedents haunt him. Customs control his conclusions. Clients of the wealthy variety are not likely to be radical in their views or actions ... It is not surprising to find the successful lawyer taking a position a little to the right of center."[31]

Several hoary movement periodicals had long served the Right during its wilderness years. The by then defunct original version of *The Freeman* had been founded in the 1920s by the Old Right stalwart and elitist anarchist Albert Jay Nock; the magazine's new incarnation was run by a board of twenty businessmen, each with his own uncompromising views on contemporary politics.[32] At one point, the board members bitterly squared off over whether to endorse Dwight David Eisenhower or Robert A. Taft for president: Taft got the magazine's nod, and the Eisenhower supporters abruptly resigned, ending *The Freeman*'s latest incarnation. Its papers and effects were packed off to the libertarian Foundation for Economic Education (FEE) in Irvington-on-Hudson, New York. That scholarly center subsequently revived *The Freeman* but sharply reduced its political focus and introduced a new emphasis on free market economics – which the magazine's writers frequently associated with the limited government instituted by the Founders' Constitution.[33]

William and Henry Regnery's Foundation for Foreign Affairs (FFA) launched the traditionalist journal *Modern Age* in 1945, with subsequent financial infusions from Regnery's family foundation and the Marquette Charitable Organization.[34] Aspiring to "reach the minds of men who think of something

and business values. See Jefferson Decker, *The Other Rights Revolution: Conservative Lawyers and the Remaking of American Government* (New York: Oxford University Press, 2016), 39–50.

[31] "Are We 'Too Conservative'?" *American Bar Association Journal* 37 (1951): 40. See Alexis de Tocqueville, *Democracy in America* (Chicago: University of Chicago Press, 2000) (edited and translated by Harvey C. Mansfield Jr. and Delba Winthrop).

[32] Nock's original *Freeman* had lasted only four years (1920–1924). Michael Wreszin, *The Superfluous Anarchist: Albert Jay Nock* (Providence, RI: Brown University Press, 1971), ix, 53–71.

[33] Buckley, *Flying High*, 30; Murray N. Rothbard, "Life in the Old Right," *Chronicles: A Magazine of American Culture* (August 1994) (www.chroniclesmagazine.org/). The libertarian feminist Suzanne La Follette (1893–1983), who started as a protégé and assistant to Albert Jay Nock, was managing editor in the first two iterations of *The Freeman* (and a founder of the second, along with a short-lived predecessor, *The New Freeman*) before it was taken over by FEE, when she moved on to become managing editor of *National Review* (1955). See Jeff Riggenbach, "The Life and Work of Suzanne La Follette," *Mises Daily Articles* (June 24, 2011) (mises.org/library/life-and-work-suzanne-la-follette). FEE is still going strong today: https://fee.org/.

[34] When the FFA money dwindled in the mid-1970s, Henry Regnery approached the Intercollegiate Studies Institute about taking it over, which it did. *Modern Age* is still published by ISI today: https://home.isi.org/modern-age. Regnery had been closely associated with ISI since its inception

more than the appetites of the hour," *Modern Age* declared an intention "to pursue a conservative policy for the sake of a liberal understanding." To its editors, conservatism evinced a dedication "to conserving the best elements of our civilization [which] are in peril nowadays." "[A] preference for the wisdom of our ancestors" aside, they insisted that

[b]eyond this, we have no party line. Our purpose is to stimulate discussion of the great moral and social and political and economic and literary questions of the hour, and to search for means by which the legacy of our civilization may be kept safe. We are not ideologists ... With Burke, we take our stand against abstract doctrine and theoretic dogma. But, still with Burke, we are in favor of principle.[35]

Modern Age was resolutely high-minded, declaring that it intended "particularly to emphasize humane learning in the United States: religious and ethical matters, historical problems, and the foundations of politics." "Our object," the journal's editors pledged, "is not to pick quarrels, but to bring about a meeting of men's minds."[36]

The magazine *Human Events* was founded in Washington, DC, by Frank Hanighen and Felix Morley, inspired, Morley said, by a piece he had written for the *Saturday Evening Post* at the height of World War II entitled "For What Are We Fighting?" The answer, as the magazine's initial "Statement of Policy" declared, was to defend the foundational principles of the Declaration of Independence.[37] Initially published in newsletter broadsheet form because there was not enough money to print an actual magazine, at its inception *Human Events* served only a few hundred subscribers, almost all of whom, however, as we say today, were "influencers" or "opinion leaders."[38] During the magazine's first year, Henry Regnery stepped in with much-needed financial acumen and an infusion of cash and incorporated the magazine, installing Morley as its president, Hanighen as its vice president, and himself as treasurer. Each ponied up $1000 of his own money and got one-third of the magazine's stock. *Human Events*'s offices were soon moved out of Washington, DC to Chicago, Regnery's home base. *Human Events* initially published a supplementary pamphlet series to spotlight issues of current significance, which was soon spun off into a separate division. Over time, this spin-off acquired increasing significance for Henry Regnery, who became more and more preoccupied with the fact that while liberals and those on the Left had many forums for publishing their ideas in postwar America, conservatives had few. This soon led him to quit the textile business altogether and transition into book publishing. *Human Events* continued publishing as a magazine, with

---

and provided extensive funding for it through the Marquette Charitable Organization; he served as chairman of the ISI board in 1971. Hoplin and Robinson, *Funding Fathers*, 54. See https://home.isi.org/

[35] "Apology for a New Review," *Modern Age* 1:1 (Summer 1957), 2.

[36] "Apology for a New Review," 2.   [37] Hemmer, *Messengers of the Right*, 29, 31.

[38] Hoplin and Robinson, *Funding Fathers*, 39.

Morley and Hanighen, with Regnery's blessing, ultimately re-assuming complete control (they later decided to move the magazine back to its original home in Washington, DC). Regnery, in turn, newly devoted himself to launching Regnery [Book] Publishers in Chicago.[39]

Founded in 1947 with the expectation, long fulfilled, of sustaining economic loss for as long as it operated, Regnery joined a small stable of conservative publishers in the immediate postwar period that included Devin-Adair and Caxton Printers, and it soon grew into the leading publisher of conservative books, a position it retains to the present day.[40] The publishers' symbolic imprint was, and remains, the Porta Nigra gate at entrance to Trier, Germany, a symbol of the emergence and strength of Western civilization, and a nod to Regnery's German heritage.[41]

Early in the history of Regnery Publishers, in a bid to set the company's finances on a firmer foundation, Regnery entered into a partnership with Great Books Foundation to bring out classics like Aristotle's *Ethics*, Plato's *Republic*, and Adam Smith's *Wealth of Nations*, many of which were, remarkably, at the time, either untranslated or hard to find.[42] Founded in 1947 by University of

[39] Hoplin and Robinson, *Funding Fathers*, 40–41 (http://humanevents.com/). In 1961, *Human Events* launched the Human Events Political Action Conference, a subscriber-activist-political leader event held in Washington, DC. Leaders from Congress were selected for inclusion in this conference by their Americans for Constitutional Action (ACA) score scaling their commitment to conservatism. This conference was a precursor to the subsequent Conservative Political Action Conference (CPAC) (http://cpac.conservative.org/) (founded in 1973 by the American Conservative Union (ACU)). Hemmer, *Messengers of the Right*, 151, 190–192.

[40] Hoplin and Robinson, *Funding Fathers*, 35; Hemmer, *Messengers on the Right*, 36–38. See also Henry Regnery, *Memoirs of a Dissident Publisher* (New York: Harcourt, Brace Jovanovich, 1979). William Regnery told his son Henry that "If you ever begin to make any money in that business you are going into, you can be pretty sure that you are publishing the wrong kind of books" (quoted in Hoplin and Robinson, *Funding Fathers*, 42). The IRS nevertheless rejected Regnery Publishers application for nonprofit tax status.

[41] The Porta Nigra gate was transformed into a church in the Middle Ages. Napolean wanted to return it to its Roman form, but this was resisted and thwarted by the Godly citizens of Trier. Hoplin and Robinson, *Funding Fathers*, 42. Regnery was tied to the movement initially not only through his father but also by close association with the Mont Pelerin Society and the University of Chicago. Regnery's earliest publications were reprints from *Human Events* and responses in books like *In Darkest Germany* and *Our Threatened Values*, *Hitler in Our Selves* to the immediate post-WWII challenges to Western civilization. Hoplin and Robinson, *Funding Fathers*, 42–43. See also Hemmer, *Messengers of the Right*, 19–21.

[42] Hoplin and Robinson, *Funding Fathers*, 44; Alex Beam, *A Great Idea at the Time: The Rise, Fall, and Curious Afterlife of the Great Books* (New York: Public Affairs, 2008), 70–71; Hemmer, *Messengers of the Right*, 38. This role is assumed today by, among others, the Indianapolis-based Liberty Fund (www.libertyfund.org/), the Manhattan Institute's Veritas Fund, and the Jack Miller Center for Teaching America's Founding Principles and History (www .jackmillercenter.org/). In its early years, 10 percent of the books sold by Regnery publishers were Catholic school textbooks published for the Archdiocese of Chicago as a service to Catholic parents whose children were forced to attend (secular) government schools but, nevertheless, wanted their children to receive religious instruction. Regnery then moved in conjunction with Indianapolis businessman Pierre Goodrich (who founded the Liberty Fund in 1960) and Harold

Chicago President and Chancellor and former Dean of the Yale Law School Robert Maynard Hutchins and University of Chicago philosopher Mortimer Adler with money from the university and from Paul Mellon's Old Dominion Foundation, the Great Books Foundation had been created to provide reading material and support for the hunger (and vogue) at the end of World War II for reading groups centered on the classics of the Western canon.[43] Fueled by the moral clarity of the "Good War" and the intellectual curiosity and ambition of new "middlebrow" postwar middle class (including returning GIs), 2500 Great Books discussion groups flowered in private homes, public libraries, church basements, corporate conference rooms, army bases, chamber of commerce offices, and even prisons during its heyday from the late 1940s to the early 1960s.[44] While such groups did not exactly become the wave of the future, their

Luhnow of the Volker Fund, to establish a line of college textbooks on secular subjects like American history, Latin, and economics. Hoplin and Robinson, *Funding Fathers*, 49.

[43] Mortimer Adler was one of William F. Buckley's favorite guests on *Firing Line*, appearing many times. Beam, *Great Idea*, 64, 88, fn. 182. Adler converted to Roman Catholicism shortly before his death. Beam, *Great Idea*, 133. Mellon's Old Dominion Foundation also helped support St. John's College, Annapolis, Maryland – which, with its sister campus in Santa Fe, New Mexico, became Straussian "Great Books" redoubts (and where Leo Strauss ended his days, a Socrates *sans* hemlock, surrounded by a small coterie of acolytes) – and was a predecessor of the Andrew W. Mellon Foundation, named for Paul Mellon's father. See David Cannadine, *Paul Mellon: An American Life* (New York, Vintage, 2008), 617.

[44] These same trends led to the creation of Reader's Digest Condensed Books in 1950 and Britannica's Great Books. In this post-Nazi, early Cold War period, in many circles the realm of ideas, "moral relativist," "value free" scientific materialism was on the defensive, and humanism on the rise. Beam, *Great Idea*, 65–70; Edward Purcell, *Scientific Naturalism and the Problem of Value* (Lexington: University of Kentucky Press, 1973). See Dwight Macdonald, "Masscult and Midcult, I & II," *Partisan Review* 27 (Spring, Fall 1960): 203–33, 589–631; Joan Shelley Rubin, *The Making of Middlebrow Culture* (Chapel Hill: University of North Carolina Press, 1992). See also Herbert Storing, editor, *Essays on the Scientific Study of Politics* (New York: Holt, Rinehart, and Winston, 1962). While dean of Yale Law School (1927–1929), Hutchins had championed Legal Realism. But upon moving to the University of Chicago in 1930, he began to question the ability of empirical social science to solve important social problems and soon became an opponent of Legal Realism. As such, the turn to Great Books in this period should be considered in part as a reaction against Legal Realism. Hutchins eventually made his way all the way to Aristotelianism and Thomism. See Beam, *Great Idea*, 59 ("[Hutchins's] opponents [at the University of Chicago] spread rumors that Hutchins and Adler, who simply couldn't shut up about St. Thomas Aquinas, were plotting to convert the student body to Catholicism. Historian Tim Lacy writes that the Chicago faculty thought Hutchins 'was calling for the restoration of the medieval university.'"). Upon retiring from Chicago in 1952, Hutchins took up the cause of world government and universal justice. In 1959, he founded the Center for the Study of Democratic Institutions in Santa Barbara, California and joined the Committee to Frame a World Constitution (Beam, *Great Idea*, 94, 120–121). The official relationship between Regnery and the Great Books Foundation ended in 1951 after Regnery published William F. Buckley's vitriolic exposé *God and Man at Yale* (1951), upsetting the sensibilities of the heads of the high-minded foundation. Hoplin and Robinson, *Funding Fathers*, 47. Today, Regnery's Gateway Book series publishes new editions of (among others) Adam Smith's *Wealth of Nations* (1776), Orestes Brownson's *The American Republic: Its Constitution, Tendencies, and Destiny* (1866), John Locke's *The Reasonableness of*

approach did ensconce itself at least in the undergraduate curricula at both the University of Chicago and Columbia University, and at the twin "Great Books" colleges, St. Johns College (Annapolis, Maryland) and St. John's College (Santa Fe, New Mexico); the approach remains influential in Straussian political science departments, often housed at conservative Roman Catholic institutions. The origins of all of these, as such, were to be found in what the contemporary critic Mark Greif has called "the age of the crisis of man," a mid-century moment in which human values, and Western civilization, was understood to be in crisis, and under attack. Their express goal was to revive the serious study of the foundations of that civilization in its Great Books and to fervently defend that civilization and its principles against challenges – and what they took to be corruptions.[45]

As it happened, Regnery did not turn out to be dependent on its Great Books line for sales. The publisher's regular line succeeded right out of the gate with a stream of bestsellers: Freda Utley's *The China Story* (1951) on the "loss" of China to the communists; William F. Buckley Jr.'s *God and Man at Yale* (1951); and Russell Kirk's *The Conservative Mind* (1954), which was widely reviewed, including in Henry Luce's *Time* magazine, whose book review editor, Whittaker Chambers, devoted the entire July 4, 1954 section to Kirk's landmark compendium. After Kirk, Henry Regnery noted, the conservative movement – which had long shied away from the label "conservative," which for many years had been considered in bad odor – now had a proud name and calling card: Kirk had introduced them to a noble heritage, a sophisticated legacy that they could identify with in championing an alternative to the era's dominant liberalism.[46]

Christianity as Delivered in the Scripture (1695), *The Political Writings of St. Augustine*, St. Augustine's *Enchiridion on Faith, Hope, and Love* (circa 421), Romano Guardini's *The Lord* (1937) (with foreword by Joseph Cardinal Ratzinger [later, Pope Benedict XVI]), and St. Thomas Aquinas's *Treatise on Law* (circa 1265–1274). See also Harry S. Ashmore, *Unseasonable Truths: The Life of Robert Maynard Hutchins* (Boston: Little Brown, 1989).

[45] Mark Greif, *The Age of the Crisis of Man: Thought and Fiction in America, 1933–1973* (Princeton: Princeton University Press, 2015).

[46] Hoplin and Robinson, *Funding Fathers*, 44–48; Hemmer, *Messengers of the Right*, 38–40. See Bradley J. Birzer, *Russell Kirk: American Conservative* (Lexington: University Press of Kentucky, 2015). Favorably reviewed in the *New York Times*, Utley's *The China Story* caught the attention of Manhattan lawyer William Casey, later an intimate advisor to and CIA director for President Reagan, who, in private correspondence with Henry Regnery in 1953, told the publisher what a strong influence Utley's book had had on his thinking. In time, Regnery books were cited by many pivotal policy players in the Reagan administration as having had a major influence in shaping their thought. Regnery (www.regnery.com) remains a key player in contemporary conservatism, publishing, for example, Ann Coulter, *High Crimes and Misdemeanors: The Case Against Bill Clinton* (Washington, DC: Regnery, 1998); Ann Coulter, *Adios, America!* (Washington, DC: Regnery, 2015); Bernard Goldberg, *Bias: A CBS Insider Exposes How the Media Distort the News* (Washington, DC: Regnery, 2002); Bernard Goldberg, *A Slobbering Love Affair: The True (and Pathetic) Story of the Torrid Romance Between Barack Obama and the Mainstream Media* (Washington, DC: Regnery, 2009);

While Regnery began by advancing serious conservative ideas, promoting the foundational ideas of Western civilization, and downplaying market considerations, as its early spate of best sellers shows, it was always more than willing to stoke downmarket outrage. Its titles in this regard – some published as part of mid-century America's transformational new low-priced paperback market – presaged its later publication of the likes of Bernard Goldberg, Laura Ingraham, and Ann Coulter. Outside of Regnery, self-published books of considerable influence on the Right at about the same time – like Phyllis Schlafly's *A Choice Not an Echo* (1964), John Stormer's *None Dare Call It Treason* (1964), and J. Evetts Haley's *A Texan Looks at Lyndon: A Study of Illegitimate Power* (1964), which insisted that Johnson belonged not in the

Newt Gingrich, *To Save America* (Washington, DC: Regnery, 2010); Laura Ingraham, *Power to the People* (Washington, DC: Regnery, 2007); Mark Levin, *Men in Black: How the Supreme Court Is Destroying America* (Washington, DC: Regnery, 2005); Dinesh D'Souza, *The Big Lie: Exposing the Nazi Roots of the American Left* (Washington, DC: Regnery, 2017); Conrad Black, *Donald J. Trump: A Presidency Like No Other* (Washington, DC: Regnery, 2018); Phyllis Schlafly (with Ed Martin and Brett Decker), *The Conservative Case for Trump* (Washington, DC: Regnery, 2016); Philip Lawler, *Lost Shepherd: How Pope Francis Is Misleading His Flock* (Washington, DC: Regnery, 2018); Kevin R.C. Gutzman, *The Politically Incorrect Guide to the Constitution* (Washington, DC: Regnery, 2007), Edwin Meese III, Matthew Spalding, and David F. Forte, *The Heritage Guide to the Constitution* (Washington, DC: Regnery, 2005); Steven Calabresi, *Originalism: A Quarter Century of Debate* (Washington, DC: Regnery, 2007) (foreword by Antonin Scalia); Kevin A. Ring, *Scalia Dissents: Writings of the Supreme Court's Wittiest, Most Outspoken Justice* (Washington, DC: Regnery, 2004); and William Eaton's *Who Killed the Constitution? The Judges v. the Law* (Washington, DC: Regnery, 1988). Regnery's *The Heritage Guide to the Constitution* is advertised as follows: "'The Constitution,' pledged George Washington, 'is the guide which I will never abandon.' Can we say the same today? With the leadership of former Attorney General Edwin Meese III, and in conjunction with the nation's preeminent think tank – The Heritage Foundation – *The Heritage Guide to the Constitution* brings together more than one hundred of the nation's best legal experts to provide the first ever line-by-line examination of the complete Constitution and its contemporary meaning. Stressing the original intent of the Framers as the authoritative standard of constitutional interpretation, and never straying from the Constitution and the definitive writings of the Framers – especially the invaluable notes taken at the Constitutional Convention by James Madison, the widely recognized analysis in *The Federalist Papers*, and Supreme Court Justice Joseph Story's 1833 classic *Commentaries on the Constitution of the United States* – this volume is unique, comprehensive, and authoritative. Edited by David Forte and Matthew Spalding, *The Heritage Guide to the Constitution* is written not only to provide lawmakers and trained jurists with a reliable reference, but also to be explanatory, educational, and accessible to informed citizens and all students of the Constitution. No document is more central or more important to securing "the Blessing of Liberty to ourselves and our Posterity" than the United States Constitution, and no guide to the Constitution is more thorough, more enlightening, or more useful than *The Heritage Guide to the Constitution*." See Hoplin and Robinson, *Funding Fathers*, 52–53. In addition to these publishing ventures, Regnery gave generously to key movement incubators like the Young Americans for Freedom and the Philadelphia Society. Hoplin and Robinson, *Funding Fathers*, 55 (http://students.yaf.org/young-americans-for-freedom/; http://phillysoc.org/).

White House but in prison) – stuck a similar tone.[47] In postwar conservative publishing, serious instruction and downmarket outrage went hand in hand.

As is now well known, one of postwar conservatism's most visible and influential outlets was the magazine *National Review*, launched by the thirty-year-old William F. Buckley Jr. in 1955, with funding from his father, some of it by way of Henry Regnery.[48] Later remembered by the junior Mr. Buckley as "a conservative journal which took its place, very soon after its nativity, at the center of conservative political analysis in America," *National Review* endeavored from its inception to bring together "men and women of disparate inclinations" to forge an intellectual and political movement that could win public respect, ascend to prominence and preeminence, and assume the reins of government.[49]

A few years before founding *National Review*, Buckley, who, as an undergraduate had chaired the *Yale Daily News*, had made a splash by publishing *God and Man at Yale* (1951), an academic exposé of the sort that would later become a movement staple, attacking, long before the terms were invented and widely disseminated, "tenured radicals" and campus "political correctness."[50] Fueled in no small part by his traditionalist Roman Catholic faith, indignation on behalf of a Texas oilman father whose holdings were expropriated by (anticlerical) Mexican revolutionaries, and the mentoring of his gadfly Far Right Yale political science professor Willmoore Kendall, Buckley set upon his *alma mater* for its abandonment of its foundations in Western civilization – Christianity, patriotism, and free market capitalism – for the false gods of atheism and socialism. With the assistance of Kendall (and James Burnham and E. Howard Hunt), Buckley started his career immediately after graduation at the CIA and then moved on briefly to an associate editorship at

---

[47] Hemmer, *Messengers of the Right*, 166–176; See G. R. Schrieber, *The Bobby Baker Affair: How to Make Millions in Washington* (Chicago: Henry Regnery, 1964) (about an influence-peddling and call-girl scandal involving a top aide to Lyndon Johnson). Schlafly, *A Choice Not An Echo*; John Stormer, *None Dare Call It Treason* (Florissant, MO: Liberty Bell Press, 1964); J. Evetts Haley, *A Texan Looks at Lyndon: A Study in Illegitimate Power* (Canyon, TX: Palo Duro, 1964).

[48] Hoplin and Robinson, *Funding Fathers*, 55. Henry's grandfather Wilhelm Regnery, a Roman Catholic, had a strong political pedigree, having fled Germany to come to the United States in resistance to Bismarckian statism and, later, having lost friends to Nazism and Communism. His son William (Henry's father) got his start in textiles, working for William Volker and Company, and involved himself in politics by helping General Robert E. Wood establish the isolationist American First Committee (AFC) in September 1940 (the group was disbanded after Germany declared war on the United States). Henry got an engineering degree at MIT, and an MA in economics at Harvard, where he studied with Joseph Schumpeter and was turned off by socialist students at Harvard – a disposition sealed by his service in FDR's Resettlement Administration, with which he was initially sympathetic. Hoplin and Robinson, *Funding Fathers*, 36–38.

[49] William F. Buckley Jr., *Flying High: Remembering Barry Goldwater* (New York: Basic Books, 2008), ix–x.

[50] See, e.g., Roger Kimball, *Tenured Radicals: How Politics Has Corrupted Higher Education* (New York: Harper and Row, 1990).

the by then paleo-conservative and increasingly anti-Semitic *American Mercury*. With the assistance of his brother-in-law Brent Bozell, Buckley then published his second book, *McCarthy and His Enemies* (1954), a defense of the Wisconsin senator's crusading anticommunism.[51]

While he had attracted a national audience with his first two books, Buckley, who loved being in the mix of the political moment, had become increasingly frustrated with the time it had taken to produce them, inhibiting the rapid dissemination of his views in the public sphere. To solve this problem, Buckley determined to start a magazine instead. He first tried to purchase *Human Events* and *The Freeman*. Neither wanted to sell. He then sought start-up financing for his own magazine from both Regnery and Henry Luce, both of whom demurred. Finally, with a $100,000 investment from his father, who called in cash from Regnery, Buckley launched *National Review* in 1955.[52] He subsequently arranged for supplemental financing from investors who included California oil tycoon Henry Salvatori and South Carolina textile magnate Roger Milliken. But Buckley shrewdly made sure to structure the corporate stock to ensure that he maintained personal control.[53]

In the very first issue of *National Review*, Buckley published a "mission statement" announcing that the new magazine "stands athwart history, yelling Stop, at a time when no one is inclined to do so, or to have much patience with those who so urge it." "NATIONAL REVIEW is out of place," Buckley continued, "in the sense that the United Nations and the League of Women Voters and the *New York Times* and Henry Steele Commager are in place":

It is out of place because ... literate America rejected conservatism in favor of radical social experimentation. Instead of covetously consolidating its premises, the United States seems tormented by its tradition of fixed postulates having to do with the meaning of existence, with the relationship of the state to the individual, of the individual to his neighbor, so clearly enunciated in the enabling documents of our Republic.

---

[51] Hoplin and Robinson, *Funding Fathers*, 68–69; Hemmer, *Messengers of the Right*, 39–45. At the invitation of the conservative (albeit Democratic) Notre Dame Law School dean and talk radio host Clarence Manion, Bozell would later ghostwrite Barry Goldwater's *The Conscience of a Conservative* (1960).

[52] Hoplin and Robinson, *Funding Fathers*, 70.

[53] Hoplin and Robinson, *Funding Fathers*, 70–71, 127–128. An up-by-his-bootstraps businessman of modest origins, fervent anticommunist, and crusader against run-amok statism, the engineer Salvatori, an off-shore oil-drilling pioneer, was active in the 1964 Goldwater campaign and part of the group of influential businessmen who encouraged Ronald Reagan to run for governor of California in 1966. In 1969, Salvatori became the founding benefactor of the Henry Salvatori Center for the Study of Individual Freedom in the Modern World at Claremont McKenna College, today perhaps the leading fount of conservative – primarily Straussian – political thought (Leo Strauss himself moved to Claremont from the University of Chicago toward the end of his career, before moving to and dying at St. John's College, Annapolis). The Salvatori Center publishes the broadly influential *Claremont Review of Books*. The center devotes itself to "the study of political philosophy and freedom as it relates to American Constitutionalism and the American Founding" (www.claremontmckenna.edu/salvatori/) .

"I happen to prefer champagne to ditchwater," Buckley quoted that "benign old wrecker of the ordered society, [US Supreme Court Justice] Oliver Wendell Holmes" as once having declared, "but there is no reason to suppose that the cosmos does." *National Review* pronounced itself to "have come around to Mr. Holmes' view, so much so that we feel gentlemanly doubts when asserting the superiority of capitalism to socialism, of republicanism to centralism, of champagne to ditchwater – of anything to anything."

Apprehending the degree to which the country had abandoned foundational truths in favor of a fashionable relativism is not easy to see, Buckley conceded: "One must recently have lived on or close to a college campus to have a vivid intimation of what has happened. It is there that we see how a number of energetic social innovators, plugging their grand designs, succeeded over the years in capturing the liberal intellectual imagination. And since ideas rule the world, the ideologues, having won over the intellectual class, simply walked in and started to run things." Hoisting liberals by their own petard, Buckley condemned this appalling "age of conformity" they had wrought. "Conservatives in this country," he declared, "are non-licensed nonconformists." He expressed "the sincere desire to encourage a responsible dissent from the Liberal orthodoxy." "We offer," he attested:

besides ourselves, a position that has not grown old under the weight of a gigantic, parasitic bureaucracy, a position untempered by [a generation of] doctoral dissertations ... unattenuated by a thousand vulgar promises to a thousand different pressure groups, uncorroded by a cynical contempt for human freedom.

The Mission Statement was followed by a credenda setting out the magazine's core convictions. Among them were the convictions that

[1] It is the job of centralized government ... to protect its citizens' lives, liberty and property. All other activities of government tend to diminish freedom and hamper progress. The growth of government ... must be fought relentlessly ...

[2] The profound crisis of our era is ... the conflict between the Social Engineers, who seek to adjust mankind to conform with scientific utopias, and the disciples of Truth, who defend the organic moral order ...

[3] The century's most blatant force of satanic utopianism is communism. We consider "coexistence" with communism neither desirable nor possible, nor honorable ...

[4] The largest cultural menace in America is the conformity of the intellectual cliques which ... are out to impose upon the nation their modish fads and fallacies ...

[5] The most alarming single danger to the American political system lies in the fact that an identifiable team of Fabian operators is bent on controlling both our major political parties (under the sanction of such fatuous

and unreasoned slogans as "national unity," "middle-of-the-road," "progressivism," and "bipartisanship") ...

[6] The competitive price system is indispensable to liberty and material progress.

Besides commenting on topical events, *National Review* both cultivated conservative intellectual talent and regularly reviewed books published by Regnery.[54] Buckley's service to the movement extended outward. He midwifed the birth of the conservative youth group Young Americans for Freedom (YAF) on his Sharon, Connecticut, estate (September 9–11, 1960). YAF issued the landmark manifesto of conservative principles, *The Sharon Statement*,[55] groomed legions of (mostly) young men for conservative leadership, and served as the prototype for the efflorescence of conservative institutions that followed: The American Conservative Union (1964), The Fund for American Studies (1967), The Young America's Foundation (1969), and the Conservative Political Action Conference (CPAC) (1973).[56] Buckley's run for New York City mayor against liberal Republican John Lindsay (1965) also gave a major lift to the newly founded and influential New York State Conservative Party (1962) and led to the start of Buckley's long-running Emmy Award–winning (1968) PBS television political discussion show *Firing Line* (1966), which put serious conservative arguments and perspectives into direct dialogue with liberals and the Left on a broad array of topics in American

---

[54] Quoted in Hoplin and Robinson, *Funding Fathers*, 72, 74–75. Speaking at the thirtieth anniversary banquet for the magazine, President Ronald Reagan testified to *National Review*'s significance as follows: "If any of you doubt the impact of *National Review*'s verve and attractiveness, take a look around you this evening. The man standing before you was a Democrat when he picked up his first issue [of *National Review*] in a plain brown wrapper; and even now, as an occupant of public housing, he awaits as anxiously as ever his bi-weekly edition – without the wrapper. Over here is the Director of the Central Intelligence Agency [Bill Casey], who, besides running a successful presidential campaign in 1980, is the same New York lawyer who drew up the incorporation papers for *National Review*. Or ask any of the young leaders in the media, academia, or government here tonight to name the principal intellectual influence in their formative years. On this point, I can assure you: *National Review* is to the offices of the West Wing of the White House what *People* is to your dentist's waiting room ... I want to assure you tonight: you didn't just part the Red Sea – you rolled it back, dried it up, and left exposed, for all the world to see, the naked desert that is statism. And then, as if that weren't enough, you gave the world something different, something in its weariness it desperately needed, the sound of laughter and the sight of the rich, green uplands of freedom." Buckley himself celebrated in 1980: "With the election of Ronald Reagan, National Review assumes a new importance in American life. We become, as it were, an establishment organ; and we feel it only appropriate to alter our demeanor accordingly ... We have a nation to run" William F. Buckley Jr., "The Week," *National Review* (November 28, 1980), 1434, quoted in Hoplin and Robinson, *Funding Fathers*, 74.

[55] "The Sharon Statement," in Kramnick and Lowi, eds., *American Political Thought*, 1281.

[56] These organizations remain active and influential today. See http://conservative.org/; https://tfas .org/; http://students.yaf.org/young-americans-for-freedom/; http://www.yaf.org/; http://cpac .conservative.org/.

politics and culture. Buckley, moreover, served as the first president of Intercollegiate Studies Institute (ISI) (founded 1953), which nurtures young conservative talent on college and university campuses and, in recent years, has become in its own right a major publisher of conservative books.[57]

FINANCIAL SUPPORT FOR THE ARCHIPELAGO

The postwar conservative movement invested heavily in the incubation and dissemination of ideas.[58] Like the Progressive movement before it,[59] this conservative demarche was a transatlantic affair. The American Harold Luhnow had been inflamed and inspired by the Austrian economist Friedrich Hayek's *The Road to Serfdom* (1944) (Hayek was then living in England, teaching at the London School of Economics). Shortly after *The Road to Serfdom* was published, Luhnow assumed the presidency of the William Volker Fund, a Kansas City, Missouri–based charitable fund founded (1932) by Luhnow's businessman uncle and committed the fund, henceforth, to devoting the bulk of its resources to the development of conservative ideas.[60] The global influence of one of The Volker Fund's earliest gifts under Luhnow's direction was especially notable. In 1945, Hayek had written a letter from London to a key founding staffer at The Volker Fund, Loren Miller, expressing his profound worry about the rapid advance of socialism and the growing attacks upon Western civilization, and a desire to fight these developments through the marshaling of a countervailing phalanx of ideas.[61]

---

[57] Hoplin and Robinson, *Funding Fathers*, 80–83; Heather Hendershott, *Open to Debate: How William F. Buckley Put Liberal America on the Firing Line* (New York: Broadside Books, 2016) (https://home.isi.org/).

[58] See generally James Piereson, "Investing in Conservative Ideas," *Commentary* (May 1, 2005): 46–54.

[59] Daniel Rodgers, *Atlantic Crossings: Social Politics in a Progressive Age* (Cambridge, MA: Belknap Press of Harvard University Press, 1998).

[60] Hoplin and Robinson, *Funding Fathers*, 25–26. The fund was committed to the principle that once a grant was awarded, there would be no subsequent inference with the grantee or the free development of the grantee's ideas.

[61] In subsequent correspondence with the English chicken magnate Antony Fisher, whose reading of Hayek's *The Road to Serfdom* led him to establish the Institute for Economic Affairs (IEA) (1955), an influential English free market think tank that became the generative force behind Thatcherism, Fisher had told Hayek, whom he had first met in 1947, that he "thought you could sway mass opinion." "What I insisted," Hayek responded, "and what was strictly followed by the Institute was not to appeal to the large numbers, but to the intellectuals. My conviction [was] that, in the long run, political opinion is determined by the intellectuals, by which I mean ... the second-hand dealers in ideas – the journalists, school masters, and so on." Hoplin and Robinson, 159–160 (https://iea.org.uk/). The IEA subsequently sponsored the publication of many of Hayek's books, including *The Constitution of Liberty* (Chicago: University of Chicago Press, 1960). Although English, IEA's influence was felt in the United States. In the 1970s, Fisher encouraged Americans to establish something similar there, which led to the founding of the Manhattan Institute (1977) (www.manhattan-institute.org/), which, in turn, sponsored, among

Hayek wanted to convene a conclave of the world's leading scholars and advocates for classical liberal ideas for a discussion, to take place in Mont Pelerin, Switzerland. Although at the time Keynesianism was triumphant, even hegemonic, the success of *The Road to Serfdom* (1944) had encouraged Hayek in his belief there existed nevertheless an inchoate audience for classical liberal thought. In May 1945, The Volker Fund responded by writing Hayek a $2000 check, classified as "educational" philanthropy and earmarked to provide the travel expenses for scholars to make the trip to Mont Pelerin. Among those who attended the first meeting of what became known as the Mont Pelerin Society were University of Chicago economists Frank Knight, Aaron Director, Milton Friedman, and George Stigler (Stigler was then at Brown University), all founders of what became known as "Chicago School" economics.[62] Also in attendance were V. Orval Watts of the FEE (the publisher of *The Freeman*), John Davenport of Henry Luce's *Fortune* magazine, Henry Hazlitt of *Newsweek*, Felix Morley of *Human Events*, and Austrian School founder and New York University economics professor Ludwig von Mises. When, as dissenters from Keynesianism, they could not secure regular tenured faculty positions in the United States, The Volker Fund stepped up with the salary subventions that permitted Hayek to teach at the University of Chicago and von Mises at NYU. In time, Ronald Reagan himself, who was hardly alone, would frequently cite Hayek, von Mises, Friedman, and Hazlitt as among the small group of thinkers who set the course of his life toward conservatism.[63]

other things, the publication of Charles Murray's book *Losing Ground: American Social Policy, 1950–1980* (New York: Basic Books, 1984), the intellectual fount of welfare reform, and the influential neoconservative magazine *City Journal* (www.city-journal.org/). Similar views on the political value of the cultivation of ideas were later expressed by many on the Right such as Ben Wattenberg, who ventured that "A journalist, television personality, or think-tanker with some following probably has more influence on the way the world spins than do most of the 535 elected federal officeholders." Ben J. Wattenberg, *Fighting Words: A Tale of How Liberals Created Neo-Conservatism* (New York: Thomas Dunne Books, 2008), 107. It was John Maynard Keynes himself who had perhaps most famously made the point earlier, having once observed that "the ideas of economists and political philosophers, both when they are right and when they are wrong, are more powerful than is commonly understood. Indeed the world is ruled by little else. Practical men, who believe themselves to be exempt from any intellectual influences, are usually the slaves of some defunct economist. Madmen in authority, who hear voices in the air, are distilling their frenzy from some academic scribbler of a few years back." John Maynard Keynes, *The General Theory of Employment, Interest, and Money* (New York: Harcourt, Brace, 1936), 383–384.

[62] Director's sister Rose later married Milton Friedman and coauthored his widely read book making the case for free market capitalism, *Free to Choose: A Personal Statement* (New York: Avon Books, 1980), and assisted with the PBS series (1980) based on it. Friedman's landmark statement *Capitalism and Freedom* (Chicago: University of Chicago Press, 1962) was also prepared "with the assistance of Rose D. Friedman."

[63] Hoplin and Robinson, *Funding Fathers*, 26–30. See Angus Burgin, *The Great Persuasion: Reinventing Free Markets Since the Depression* (Cambridge, MA: Harvard University Press, 2012).

Nicole Hoplin and Ron Robinson have charted the dense web of influence spun by the Mont Pelerin Society in the second half of the twentieth century. Its attendees published prolifically: eight hundred articles by as early as 1954; eight members won Nobel Prizes in economics (Hayek, Friedman, Stigler, James Buchanan, Maurice Allais, Ronald Coase, Gary Becker, and Vernon Smith). Several rose to leadership positions in conservative governments around the world. Martin Anderson reported that twenty-two of the seventy-six economic policy advisors to Ronald Reagan's 1980 presidential campaign were Mont Pelerin Society members. Its members were central to the revival of classical liberalism in the second half of the twentieth century. Volker also funded the Intercollegiate Society of Individualists (later the Intercollegiate Studies Institute (ISI)), FEE, and the Institute for Humane Studies (IHS) and underwrote the publication of a host of landmark conservative books, including Frederic Bastiat's *The Law* (1850), Murray Rothbard's *Man, Economy, and State* (1962), Richard Weaver's *Visions of Order: The Cultural Crisis of Our Time* (1964), and the lectures that Milton Friedman later turned into *Capitalism and Freedom* (1962).[64]

Americans established their own conservative intellectual conclaves. Pierre Goodrich, for thirty-five years president of the Indiana Telephone Company, described himself not as an intellectual but as someone who was passionate about learning from intellectuals. Goodrich donated his fortune to establish the Indianapolis-based Liberty Fund, a leading publisher of classic and modern texts on traditional understandings of free markets and constitutional liberty. Goodrich also sponsored a series of academic tete-à-tetes (usually, in the form of reading groups) in which college and university professors, along with a smattering of independent scholars and think tank denizens, read from classic and modern works on politics, philosophy, and economics and discussed them in sessions and over meals – always outside of the (presumed corrupted) university setting. These conferences were aimed at nourishing enthusiasms and understandings that the academic participants might take back to their home campuses and, with no *quid pro quo* required, pursue in their teaching and scholarship.[65]

Colorado beer magnate Joseph Coors, a Cornell-educated engineer and enthusiast of David Hume, Adam Smith, and Mark Twain, was blown away by reading one of Regnery's early and most influential publications, Russell Kirk's *The Conservative Mind*.[66] Coors resolved afterward to create an influential institution in Washington, DC, "to provide timely policy information to members of Congress from a 'principled perspective.'" This became The Heritage Foundation (1973), the Reagan administration's most

[64] Hoplin and Robinson, *Funding Fathers*, 28–30; Burgin, *Great Persuasion*.
[65] Hoplin and Robinson, *Funding Fathers*, 148–166. See Dane Starbuck, *The Goodriches: An American Family* (Indianapolis: Liberty Fund Press, 2001).
[66] Hoplin and Robinson, 192. See also Decker, *The Other Rights Revolution*, 48, 73–76.

influential policy shop, a role it continued to play going forward –including, most recently, for Donald Trump.[67] Heritage has also been highly influential in formulating and disseminating the modern conservative movement's constitutional vision. In addition to its intellectual/scholarly work in the area, which has been extensive, the think tank has served as an entrepôt for conservative "cause lawyers": its semiannual "Legal Strategy Fora" hosts lawyers from approximately thirty conservative movement litigation organizations around the country, and convenes a monthly meeting for similar Washington, DC–based groups to inform participants about what the others are doing and about relevant new developments in government, and to help coordinate their work. It has also promoted collaboration where possible by convening seminars and filing amicus briefs in important constitutional cases.[68]

CONCLUSION

It is impossible to seriously discuss conservative constitutionalism in this formative era without studying its embeddedness in the broader currents of conservative political thought more generally – put otherwise, to situate conservative constitutional thinking and theory within "the deep story"[69] of the broader conservative movement. This deep story, as should go without saying, given what has previously been noted, was forged outside the law schools. Until relatively recently, as we will see in the next chapter, this was also true of the Right's explicitly *constitutional* thought. From its inception, political and constitutional thought on the postwar Right were inextricably intertwined in a way that simply was not the case on the modern liberal/Left where, as we shall also see in the next chapter, constitutional thought had been narrowed and professionalized into a rather one-dimensional academic discussion of the role of judges versus legislatures, and the professional judicial task of textual interpretation. On the postwar Right, journalists, economists, political theorists, and others all felt perfectly free – as the Rabbi Will Herberg did, and as William F. Buckley did in *National Review*'s mission

---

[67] Hoplin and Robinson, *Funding Fathers*, 196–197, 200–202, 209. See Jonathan Mahler, "All the Right People: How One Conservative Think Tank Stocked the Federal Government for the Trump Era," *New York Times Magazine* (June 24, 2018). In 1995, Heritage launched Townhall. com, an internet clearinghouse for conservative thought and opinion. Heritage also publishes *Policy Review*, one of the leading conservative public policy journals, and *The Heritage Guide to the Constitution*, which was at the side of Republican senators during recent Supreme Court confirmation hearings and serves as the bible of conservative originalist readings of the constitutional text. Coors was also active in mass politics, where he helped Phyllis Schlafly defeat the ERA and bankrolled Ward Connerly's American Civil Rights Coalition to promote California's antiracial preferences Prop 209.

[68] Ann Southworth, *Lawyers on the Right: Professionalizing the Conservative Coalition* (Chicago: University of Chicago Press, 2008), 127.

[69] Hochschild, *Strangers in Their Own Land*, 128, 135.

statement and credenda – to discuss constitutional issues, which, given who they were, the way they saw the world, and what they cared about, they did in ideologically embedded ways, with little reference to contemporary debates in the liberal legal academy. In this sense, there was little separation on the postwar Right between "popular" and professional constitutional discourse.

This fusion of the popular and the professional constitutional visions and the embeddedness of conservative understandings of the Constitution in broader political, theoretical, and ideological visions on the Right was made possible by the archipelago of conservative outlets where, during the Right's postwar wilderness years, serious thinkers spoke not only to one another but to wider audiences of conservatives and potential movement recruits who, these thinkers recognized, were indispensible to ultimately winning political power. Backed by true believers with fortunes, often possessed of a sense of existential threat and civilizational showdown natural enough to the era of World War II and the Cold War, a set of intellectual journals, magazines, and book publishers, supplemented by a host of mass media radio and television shows, created another ideational world to live in for the modern conservative movement that sought, in the heyday of American liberalism, to reset the nation's political and constitutional frames.

2

The Alternative Tradition of Conservative Constitutional Theory

The years between the end of World War II and the election of Ronald Reagan as president – conservatism's political wilderness years – were some of the richest in terms of conservative constitutional thought and theory. While hardly obscure to movement participants, and outsiders who know where to look, much – indeed, perhaps most – of this thought and theory has gone missing in accounts of American constitutionalism and constitutional theory. Given that conservatives were all but excluded from legal academia in this period – especially elite academia – this thinking hid in plain sight; the lawyers or legal academics who stole the constitutional theory limelight at mid-century were not conservatives. The unconsidered presumption of these lawyers and legal academics was that if they or their interlocutors were not doing it, it was not important constitutional theory. With a few exceptions, constitutional theory on the Right during the heyday of American liberalism was undertaken by journalist-intellectuals, independent scholars, and a small cohort of political philosophers typically working in political science departments. The work of these constitutional thinkers often followed very different lines from those engaged in by the era's well-known liberal academic constitutional theorists, even when, as sometimes happened, it was engaged with, and reacted against, that work. The questions it asked, and the framework within which it took up constitutional questions, were distinctive and often advanced theories that were disconnected from – albeit no less sophisticated than – the professionalized world of legal academia and professionalized constitutional theory.

One feature of this constitutional thought and theory that liberals might not suspect – and contemporary conservatives have chosen to forget – is not only that it was diverse but also that that diversity was structured by major theoretical disagreements – and, in some cases, battles. Although much of this work was "originalist" in a broad sense (it devoted considerable attention to its understanding of the nation's Founders, with an eye to the relevance of the Founding to contemporary political and constitutional questions), it was hardly consistently originalist in the narrow sense of insisting upon eighteenth-century understandings, or requiring either judicial deference to legislatures (judicial restraint) or, for that matter, in focusing on judges and their duties at all.

Another feature of conservative constitutional thought and theory in the heyday of American liberalism that might make many contemporary conservatives uncomfortable is that, considered over the long term, from a bird's eye perspective – that is, as I provide a scholarly account of it here – it was developmental: its emphases, arguments, and understandings changed across time in engagement with both world events and the altering interests, coalitions, and strategies within the conservative movement and the Republican Party. Put otherwise, postwar conservative constitutional thought "lived." As such, in practice, at least, "living constitutionalism" was prevalent on the postwar Right as well as the Liberal/Left, albeit perhaps less expressly.

While there were many debilities to being on the outside of political power looking in, one of the advantages of not holding responsibility for winning or losing elections or governing is the absence of goal-directed discipline from above, which allowed for the introduction and the relatively free play of ideas. And one of the advantages of being outside the academy is that one need not situate oneself within the delimiting lines of entrenched academic debates that, over time, can tend toward scholasticism, banality, and complacency (if not irrelevance).

The most prominent studies of "conservative legalism" in recent years have been accounts of conservative "legal mobilization" describing the ways in which, following the model set by liberal litigation groups like the NAACP and the ACLU, conservatives created institutions to undertake strategic litigation campaigns aimed at overturning liberal legal precedents that set the substructure of institutionalized liberalism and substituting a new set of conservative precedents in their stead.[1] While I do avail myself of this work on conservative legal mobilization at places along the way, the temporal center of gravity of this study is at a time when such campaigns, if dreamed of at all, were a mere glint in the eye of the modern conservative movement. After all, to even imagine that such strategic litigation campaigns might work requires that one have a hope of finding a receptive audience in the judges before whom one is arguing. Prior to the election of Richard Nixon as president in the late 1960s, but especially of Ronald Reagan in the early 1980s, conservatives had few realistic hopes in that regard. During their wilderness years, conservative constitutional thinkers and theorists were trafficking not in test cases but in political and constitutional visions. The cacophonous, multivocal discursive space in which they did so was strewn with immigrant Austrian economists, Fundamentalist and Evangelical Christians, classicist political philosophers, segregationists and white supremacists, sunburnt sagebrush libertarians, disillusioned and wavering New Deal and Great Society liberals, Ivy League

---

[1] For an earlier mobilization sometimes overlooked, see Daniel R. Ernst, *Lawyers Against Labor: From Individual Rights to Corporate Liberalism* (Urbana: University of Illinois Press, 1995).

social scientists, Neo-Thomists, pillars of the bar, Main Street Babbitts and business titans, Burkean traditionalists, and apostate ex-socialist and communist journalists, all of whom wrote about the Constitution in ways that were both serious and fundamentally different from the refined, professionalized discourse of the era's institutionalized academic liberal law professors.

These diverse political and constitutional visions preoccupied themselves with thought along certain lines – lines that, as the prospect of political success became real from the mid-1970s forward, narrowed into what became the legal academic theory of legal positivist originalism, as preached by conservative law professors Robert Bork (Yale) and Antonin Scalia (University of Virginia/University of Chicago), that emphasized a judge's duty of restraint in the exercise of his judicial review powers. This law school originalism actually represented a revival and appropriation by conservatives of the arguments for judicial restraint that had first been purveyed by Progressives in the early twentieth century when they had squared off against the activist *conservative* pre–New Deal Court. Conservatives like Bork and Scalia revived this old Progressive constitutional theory and hurled it back against the modern liberals whose progenitors had invented it, but in a new age of liberal (Warren/Burger Court) judicial activism. The charge was, in essence, hypocrisy.

There was little in this later, narrowed originalism that was necessarily conservative in any theoretical or ideological sense, although it was certainly conservative in its effects in its political and historical context, since it was aimed at kneecapping the development of recent liberal precedent and lines of constitutional development that had expanded, for instance, the regulatory powers of the federal government or the rights of criminal defendants. The earlier, more open conservative constitutional thought and theory undertaken outside of legal academia, however, had a deeper ideologically conservative substructure. Its preoccupations were, for instance, the underlying principles of government, often understood in terms of political theory (Aristotle, Machiavelli, Hobbes, Locke, Christianity, the rooted national community). Memory mattered in significant ways that went beyond the stories told about the Supreme Court's New Deal "switch-in-time": the early theory told stories about the rise (and decline) of Western civilization, the American Founding, Abraham Lincoln, and the Civil War. Those stories provided a deep context for contemporaneous legal developments that lent them resonance and meaning beyond justifying whether the application of a particular clause of the Constitution has been rightly applied in a contemporary constitutional case. In this way, the earlier period's constitutional thought and theory were much more closely tied to the identity-forging thrust of the modern conservative movement. Much of this work, either implicitly or explicitly, went well beyond asking whether the judge followed the law to much broader questions: Where have we been? Where are we now? What went wrong? How can we set things right?

CONSERVATIVE ORIGINALISMS

There were also quite a few proponents of originalism within postwar conservatism who pre-dated the legal academic originalism of the conservative law professors Robert Bork, Raoul Berger, and Antonin Scalia in the 1970s. One was the civil engineer and steel company executive Ben Moreell, who spearheaded Americans for Constitutional Action (ACA) (founded in 1958), which Moreell described as "a non-partisan, non-profit, nation-wide ... political action organization" devoted to the propositions, "first, that the Constitution of the United States, as originally conceived, provides a solid foundation upon which the structure of our free social order has been erected; and, second, that if we are to preserve that social order in America it is imperative that we protect its foundation against erosion or destruction." The focus of Moreell's ACA, however, was not the courts but Congress: it was initiated as a conservative answer to the liberal ADA (Americans for Democratic Action) to support constitutionally committed conservatives in congressional elections.[2]

As such, the ACA's focus was different from that of later originalist organizations like the Federalist Society. The ACA was not composed mainly of law students, law professors, and lawyers. In promoting its understanding of the Constitution, it did not target judges so much as the underlying sources of the liberal worldview. These included the Swedish sociologist Gunnar Myrdal's claim, prominently advanced in his landmark study *An American Dilemma: The Negro Problem and Modern Democracy* (1944), that the Constitution was unsuited to modern conditions. In doing so, the ACA took positions against broad interpretations of the general welfare clause, Congress's abdication of power to "an all-powerful Chief Executive," what it characterized as the bribery of the country's sovereign states through federal subsidies, and in favor of a constitutional amendment repealing the constitutionalization of the federal income tax through the adoption of the Sixteenth Amendment. Like the liberal ADA, the conservative ACA instituted a rating system for members of Congress, with the aim of "inform[ing] the people of the United States with respect to the probable effects of important legislative measures on the preservation of the basic values of our Constitution and, most importantly, the actual voting preferences of all Senators and Representatives."[3]

[2] See Hemmer, *Messengers of the Right*, 145–146; [ACA Advertisement], *Detroit Free Press* (May 31, 1963), 6. See also [ACA Advertisement], *The Palm Beach Post* (November 4, 1968), 21. The ADA had been founded in 1947 by, among others, Eleanor Roosevelt, John Kenneth Galbraith, Arthur Schlesinger Jr., Reinhold Niebuhr, and Walter Reuther.

[3] Admiral Ben Moreell, "Americans for Constitutional Action," *Human Events* 18:50 (December 15, 1961): 849–850, 849; Ben Moreell, "Americans for Constitutional Action: Principles and Purposes," address delivered to the Pensacola, Florida, Chapter of the ACA (September 27, 1966). See Andrew J. Glass, "Americans for Constitutional Action" in Judith G. Smith, editor, *Political Brokers: People, Organizations, Money, Power* (New York: Liveright/ National Journal, 1972), 35–68; Jonathan M. Schoenwald, *A Time For Choosing: The Rise of Modern American Conservatism* (New York: Oxford University Press, 2001), 222–227. *National*

Other conservatives in the early 1960s expressed similar originalist views. Some were apodictic about their originalism – although at the time this interpretive stance was simply asserted or assumed rather than argued for.[4] Writing for the *ABA Journal* in the early 1960s, the conservative Virginia lawyer S. Bruce Jones, for instance, cited Thomas Cooley's *Constitutional Limitations* (1868) as having laid down the foundational originalist rule of interpretation:

A cardinal rule in dealing with written instruments is that they are to receive an unvarying interpretation, and that their practical construction is to be uniform. A constitution is not to be made to mean one thing at one time and another at some subsequent time when the circumstances may have so changed as perhaps to make a different rule ... seem desirable. A principal share of the benefit expected from written constitutions would be lost if the rules they established were so flexible as to bend to circumstances or be modified by public opinion. It is with special reference to the varying moods of public opinion, and with a view to putting the fundamentals of government beyond their control that these instruments are framed, and there can be no such steady or imperceptible change in their rule as inherent in the principles of the common law.[5]

In 1962, American Bar Association President John C. Satterfield issued a stern assessment of current conditions, and a call to action to his membership. "[T]he government [now] emerging has little resemblance to that which was set up under the Constitution of the United States as adopted and amended by the several states," Satterfield warned, "The republic formed under the Constitution of the United States as adopted and amended by the several states is now being transformed into a ... centralized monolithic government with broad and sweeping control over the individual actions of citizens, extending to almost every phase of human relationship. These changes have resulted largely from judicial decisions rendered since the turn of the century." Satterfield called upon the nation's lawyers to awaken to the threat, and to speak out with "no hesitancy or timidity" on the Court's performance.[6]

Review's publisher William Rusher used the ACA ratings to determine which members of Congress would receive free copies of *National Review*. The ACA forged a close alliance with *Human Events*. Hemmer, *Messengers of the Right*, 146–148.

[4] See, e.g., Hamilton A. Long [Washington, D.C.], Letter to the Editor, *American Bar Association Journal* 49 (1963): 708, 712.

[5] S. Bruce Jones, "Heartbreaks for the Constitution," *American Bar Association Journal* 50 (August 1964): 758–761, 758, citing Thomas Cooley, *A Treatise on Constitutional Limitations Which Rest Upon the Legislative Power of the States of the American Union* 123 (8th ed., 1927). See also S. Bruce Jones, "A Warning: Was It Justified?" *American Bar Association Journal* 43 (January 1957): 55–58, 92–93; David Lawrence, "Does 'Might Make Right'?" *US News and World Report* (April 17, 1961), 110, 114–116; Howard Lydick, "The Supreme Court is Wrong," *Human Events* 24:19 (May 9, 1964): 11 (also citing Cooley for the proposition that "The meaning of the Constitution is fixed when it is adopted, and it is not different at any subsequent time when a court has occasion to pass upon it").

[6] John C. Satterfield, "President's Page," *American Bar Association Journal* 48 (July 1962): 595, 612, 662–663.

Many American lawyers took up Satterfield's call to reflect and speak out and did so in an originalist spirit. Dalton, Georgia's R. Carter Pittman recounted that "[i]n his *Discourses*, Machiavelli ... demonstrate[s] the integrity of the maxim that governments, to be long lived, must be frequently corrected and reduced to their first principles." "Why does not the American Bar Association compile into book form such documented articles dealing with the fundamental principles of our republican governments for use as reference material by students and others?" Pittman asked.[7] Los Angeles lawyer George W. Nilsson argued that a lack of knowledge of our Constitution and the founding principles of the Republic was making the United States a soft target, all too receptive to the communist propaganda then flooding the United States (he said) – Nilsson was alarmed by new evidence from US military psychiatrists that American GIs captured by the Red Chinese had been unable to resist brainwashing by their captors because of their ignorance of American history and the principles and structure of American constitutional government. Among the culprits in this horrifying state of affairs, Nilsson charged – "'Huns and Vandals' Within" – were the likes of Pennsylvania Senator Joseph Clark, Harvard Law Professor Arthur Miller, the liberal Harvard economist John Kenneth Galbraith, and Yale Law School Dean Eugene V. Rostow – who "advocate ideas that are diametrically opposed to the principles of The Declaration of Independence, the Constitution and the Bill of Rights."[8]

Writing in *Human Events* the following year, Jesse Helms – then a Raleigh, North Carolina, radio station executive and segregationist editorialist (and a future US senator (1973–2003) and Republican Party leader) – contended that "[d]uring the past generation, governmental processes have drifted so far from their original concept that our citizens no longer are being governed: they are being ruled."[9] Appealing (like S. Bruce Jones) to Thomas Cooley as an originalist authority, the Texas lawyer (and Prohibition Party activist) Howard Lydick attacked liberal Supreme Court Justice William O. Douglas's dismissiveness of the Article V amendment process as too slow by reminding readers that "[t]he meaning of the Constitution is fixed when it is adopted, and it is not different at any subsequent time when a court has occasion to pass upon it."[10] The dramatist, screenwriter, and former socialist-turned-conservative firebrand Morrie Ryskind (1895–1985) chimed in: "I do not maintain that the document the Fathers gave us came from Sinai, but surely few man-made tablets have come nearer perfection."[11]

---

[7] R. Carter Pittman [Dalton, Georgia], Letter to the Editor, *American Bar Association Journal* 47 (1961): 228.

[8] George W. Nilsson, "On the Battle Front: To Preserve, Protect and Defend the Constitution," *American Bar Association Journal* 48 (March 1962): 232–235, 232–234.

[9] Jesse Helms, "Curb the Supreme Court," *Human Events* 22:2 (July 13, 1963): 15.

[10] Howard Lydick, "The Supreme Court Is Wrong," *Human Events* 24:19 (May 9, 1964): 11.

[11] Morrie Ryskind, "They Were Giants Then," *Human Events* 32:1 (January 1, 1972): 6.

By the early 1970s, the traditionalist conservative political theorist George Carey (1933–2013), a Georgetown University government professor, was arguing in *Modern Age* that originalist understandings were the only legitimate approach to constitutional interpretation.[12] No Lockean liberal, Carey nevertheless reminded readers that the Constitution was a contract, binding until amended through constitutionally prescribed processes. Any other approach, he argued, led to "insurmountable difficulties that seem to defy rational resolution," though Carey insisted upon nuance by acknowledging that "the Constitution itself on many fundamental issues cannot be read independent of the prevailing morality of the time which, though not expressly articulated in the document, serves to give it a broader meaning, purpose, and moral framework."[13]

The Pulitzer Prize–winning *Washington Post* editor and former Haverford College president Felix Morley took a similarly nuanced contractualist view. "[C]onstitutional interpretation is more subtle than that of a will, or deed, or contract," he observed, "It must take cognizance of changing circumstance as well as of the collective purpose of the authors and of all amendments of their

[12] George W. Carey, "The Supreme Court, Judicial Review, and Federalist Seventy-Eight," *Modern Age* 18:4 (Fall 1974): 356–368. Carey was known within the movement for his insistence that the US Constitution was underwritten and undergirded by a "constitutional morality" – that is, by a virtuous, self-controlled, self-ruling, self-governing citizenry, and that self-government in one sphere was inextricably dependent upon self-government in the other. This morality, inherent from the Founding forward, derived from an understanding of foundational truths, as embodied in the country's Judeo-Christian heritage (the Puritans were especially significant for Carey), the English common law inheritance, and the traditional authority of Religion, Church, Parents – and free, constitutional government. Carey was critical of the corrosive effects that Enlightenment (liberal) thinking had had on this constitutional morality, as instantiated in the writings, e.g., of Thomas Jefferson (the Declaration of Independence), John Locke, and John Stuart Mill. In complicated ways, however, Carey rejected hermeneutical orthodoxy of the kind that frequently characterized law school originalism – and, indeed, other "schools" of political thought, liberal and conservative alike. Carey was collaborator and frequent coauthor in the 1960s with William F. Buckley Jr.'s Yale mentor Willmoore Kendall and maintained long-standing ties with Buckley himself. Among Carey's many books were *The Basic Symbols of the American Political Tradition* (Baton Rouge: Louisiana State University Press, 1970) (with Willmoore Kendall), *Liberalism Versus Conservatism: The Continuing Debate in American Government* (Princeton: D. Van Nostrand, 1966) (with Willmoore Kendall), *The Federalist: Design for a Constitutional Republic* (Urbana: University of Illinois Press, 1989), *In Defense of the Constitution* (Indianapolis, IN: Liberty Fund Press, 1995), *A Student's Guide to American Political Thought* (Wilmington, DE: ISI Books, 2004). Carey edited the Liberty Fund's edition of *The Federalist* (with James McClellan). In 1971, Carey also founded ISI's *The Political Science Reviewer*, which published "essay-length reviews of classic and contemporary studies in law and politics, as well as examinations of leading political science textbooks ... [with] [e]ach review provid[ing] in-depth evaluation without a narrow, over-specialized focus." (The journal is now based at the Center for the Study of Liberal Democracy at the University of Wisconsin, Madison) (https://politicalsciencereviewer.wisc.edu/index.php/psr). See Bruce Bartlett et al., "Farewell to a Constitutional Conservative," *The American Conservative* (June 27, 2013); Bruce Frohnen and Kenneth Grasso, editors, *Defending the Republic: Constitutional Morality in a Time of Crisis: Essays in Honor of George W. Carey*, 2nd ed. (Wilmington, DE: ISI Books, 2008).
[13] Carey, "The Supreme Court, Judicial Review, and Federalist Seventy-Eight," 358.

original work. Nevertheless, the interpretation must be in reasonable accord with the basic principles of the constitution. Otherwise, this 'organic law' is left without significance and the political form of the organism created is undermined."[14] For his part, writing in the early 1960s, *U.S. News and World Report* founder David Lawrence (1888–1973), who wrote extensively on constitutional issues over the course of his long and influential career, emphasized textualism, condemning the development (under FDR) of "a cult which believes that the 'spirit' of the Constitution is more important than the letter of the document." Lawrence called this "the doctrine of Machiavelli – that 'the end justifies the means.'"[15]

CONSERVATISM'S LIVING ORIGINALISMS

In this open and undisciplined period on the American Right, professions of originalism were supplemented by an array of what, by contemporary conservative standards, are rather flexible – one might even (following Jack Balkin) say "living" – originalisms.[16] A few, at least, writing in even the most traditionalist conservative journals like *Modern Age*, expressed outright hostility to originalist presumptions, occasioning little discernible backlash or controversy. One *Modern Age* writer, for instance, asked, "Who defends today the historic Constitution, now an archaic document, which in its historical form is dead" before moving on to more serious issues.[17] The linguist Mario Pei opined in the same forum that "[t]he American Constitution is probably the best document of its kind in existence. But history marches on. Issues and problems face us which the original framers could not even conceive of."[18] Pei criticized constitution worship, writing that "[t]he machinery of government itself is cumbersome, and far better suited to the eighteenth than to the twentieth century. Are we convinced that we have the best possible method of electing a President? Of apportioning representation? Of selecting Supreme Court justices and Cabinet members? Is no improvement possible in our system of multiple and multiplying taxation?" He complained that "it somehow has never seemed desirable to go over the Constitution as a whole, and bring it into line with present-day conditions and problems." Pei issued a call to put these issues back into the hands of the deliberative sovereign people

---

[14] Felix Morley, *Freedom and Federalism* (Chicago: Henry Regnery, 1959), 229.

[15] David Lawrence, "Downgrading the Constitution," *US News and World Report* (December 17, 1962): 104.

[16] Jack Balkin, *Living Originalism* (Cambridge, MA: Harvard University Press, 2014).

[17] Francis Wilson, "The Supreme Court's Civil Theology," *Modern Age* 13:3 (Summer 1969): 254.

[18] Mario Pei, "The Case for a Constitutional Convention," *Modern Age* 12:1 (Winter 1967/1968), 8–13. Pei, a Columbia University professor and renowned linguist, was the author of *The America We Lost: The Concerns of a Conservative* (New York: World Publishing Co., 1968). A staunch conservative, he was also, incongruously within contemporary conservatism, an internationalist who led the fight for the worldwide adoption of Esperanto.

once again in a new constitutional convention that would undertake a wholesale revision of the Constitution.[19] Pei had some specific revisions in mind. He thought it worthwhile for Americans to ask themselves in this new convention whether, in the modern world, the constitutional "right to life" might be properly understood to entail a right to "essential services in a modern mechanized world, such as light, heat, telephone, water, garbage disposal, the willful interruption of which endangers [their] life and health?" "It is high time," Pei insisted, "that the purely human rights of life, liberty, and property receive, along constitutional lines, the same careful scrutiny and definition that civil rights have been receiving in recent times."[20]

To the extent he was an originalist, perhaps the most widely published conservative commentator on constitutional issues of the period, James Jackson Kilpatrick (1920–2010), the *Richmond* [Virginia] *News Leader* editor who covered the Supreme Court and constitutional issues for *National Review*, evinced at least a healthy suspicion of some of the shibboleths later associated with the stance. Writing in the late 1960s, Kilpatrick – no moderate on the Warren Court or the Constitution – insisted that "[t]his seance theory, which treats Supreme Court Justices as table-knocking mediums, speaking in trance through the spirits of the founding fathers, is a theory of convenience. It is hokum." Alas, he concluded, "[c]onstitutionality is like beauty: it lies in the beholder's eye; and when the beholder sits in one of those nine great swivel chairs, the eye sees what it wants to see. The Constitution ... is what the judges say it is."

That said, Kilpatrick simultaneously held that the essence of a constitution as a *genus* is that it disciplines. He admiringly noted that "[t]o Judge Cooley, most famous of the professors of constitutional law, this rule of strict construction – to go first to the intention of the framers and ratifiers – was the very 'pole star' of constitutional adjudication." There was no opposition between this, however, in Kilpatrick's view, and at least the general idea of a living constitution:

Such an adherence to fixed meanings does not exclude the proposition that ours is a "living Constitution." Of course, the Constitution lives, in the enduring structure of government it created, in the separation of powers, in the spirit of human liberty that gives life to the Bill of Rights. But especially in questions of power, and in the meaning to be attached to particular words and phrases, the intention of the framers is critical. If this is scorned, judges become not interpreters, but amenders.[21]

[19] Pei believed, "Were one of our major political parties to sponsor a constitutional convention, it would mark itself in the eyes of the voters as the champion of true democracy and the will of the people." Pei, "Case for a Constitutional Convention," 9, 13. Today, similar calls tend to issue from the Left, most prominently, recently, from Sanford Levinson. Some contemporary conservatives have called in a more limited way for the passage of a set of restorative "liberty amendments." Mark Levin, *The Liberty Amendments: Restoring the American Republic* (New York: Simon and Schuster, 2013).
[20] Pei, "Case for a Constitutional Convention," 11.
[21] James Jackson Kilpatrick, "A Very Different Constitution," *National Review* (August 12, 1969): 794–800, 795–796.

Like Mario Pei, Kilpatrick was quite accepting of the idea that neither the 1787 Constitution nor the Founding more generally was either perfect or especially well adapted to modern conditions. If not insisting on a new constitutional convention, Kilpatrick at least asked that the Americans give serious consideration to Article V Amendments that could alter core provisions of both the original text and the crucial Civil War Amendments. He suggested, for instance, that "[t]he ambiguities of the welfare clause and the 14th Amendment ought to be tidied up," and that "we need a better procedure for electing Presidents."[22]

While not taking a position in favor of convening a new constitutional convention, no less a figure than Brent Bozell, William F. Buckley Jr.'s brother-in-law, orthodox-unto-ultramontane conservative Catholic, and the ghostwriter of Barry Goldwater's *The Conscience of a Conservative* (1960), adopted what might today be classed as a living constitutionalist approach – although Bozell disagreed with liberals about the results such an approach, properly applied, would and should yield in important constitutional cases.[23] Similarly, an article in the conservative *Reader's Digest* celebrating the career of Judge Learned Hand fondly alluded to Hand's view

that the law is a living, growing instrument which must keep pace with the developing needs of society. Judges, he believes, "must be aware of the changing social tensions in every society which will disrupt it, if rigidly confined." Thus a judge must continually decide how old law is to be applied to new problems – a process that *begins* by determining the original intent of the lawmakers.[24]

Other conservatives dismissed at least an overly doctrinaire originalism as simply unworkable. The *ABA Journal* in its conservative phase (on the cusp of its campaign for the adoption of the Bricker Amendment confirming the supremacy of the Constitution to international treaties and agreements) complained editorially as follows:

This reverence for the original architects of our Government assumes for them an infallibility that they would have been among the first to disclaim. Thought-stultifying clichés like "the wisdom of the Founding Fathers" can become dangerous because they are blind guides if slavishly followed ... Many of the problems of the present day will be more readily solved by a careful analysis of human nature than by antiquarian research into ancient history.[25]

---

[22] James Jackson Kilpatrick, "Tugwell's 'Model Constitution' Just Won't Do," *Human Events* 31:4 (January 23, 1971): 18.

[23] L. Brent Bozell Jr., *The Warren Revolution: Reflections on the Consensus Society* (New Rochelle, NY: Arlington House, 1966). See Brian Flanagan, "'New Ultramontanists': Why Do Some Catholics Fear Change?" *National Catholic Reporter* (August 13, 2018) (www .ncronline.org/news/opinion/new-ultramontanists-why-do-some-catholics-fear-change).

[24] Irwin Ross, "The Legend of Learned Hand," *Reader's Digest* 59:351 (July 1951): 105–109, 107 [emphasis added].

[25] "The Dead Hand," *American Bar Association Journal* 37 (1951): 440–441, 440.

NEOCONSERVATISM – LOOKING BEYOND IDEOLOGY TO WHAT WORKS

The group that came to be known as "neoconservatives" evinced a distinctive approach to constitutional questions that reflected their unique political predispositions as chastened social scientifically inclined liberals disillusioned by the direction liberalism was taking under the auspices of the Great Society and the gravitational pull of the New Left. Genus neoconservatives were public policy intellectuals. As such, they were more inclined to distill and critique the policy initiatives undertaken by those wielding liberal constitutional theory and court rulings inspired by it than to set out any unifying, ideal interpretive theory of how the Constitution should be read. When it came to public policy, neoconservatives were staunch critics of those who let good intentions blind them to the likely real-world consequences of their programs. In his critical assessment in *Commentary* of the state of the ACLU in the early 1970s, for instance, Joseph Bishop condemned the group for engaging in moral or "aspirational" readings of the Constitution – for taking the position that "the Constitution of the United States, read with the eyes of faith, hope, and sometimes charity, mandates Good and prohibits Evil," collapsing the distinction between quasi-religious moralizing and constitutional law. Implicitly appealing to the old Progressive/New Deal commitment to judicial restraint, which drew a sharp distinction between wise policy and good law, Bishop charged the ACLU with taking an approach that "differs very little from that which the National Association of Manufacturers used to advance against the National Labor Relations Act, the Securities Acts, and the rest of the seditious innovations of the New Deal." Bishop characterized the ACLU's constitutionalism as a motley set of "evangelistic sermons."[26]

Given neoconservatives' preoccupation with public policy rather than general and abstract constitutional theory, I will discuss constitutional arguments made by them not here, but rather in my two future books on postwar constitutional conservatism that emphasize more specific substantive issues. I make one partial exception by mentioning the Straussian Martin Diamond, discussed in detail later. Although not properly classed as a neoconservative himself, Diamond published important constitutional theory essays in *The Public Interest* which, along with *Commentary*, were the flagship neoconservative journals. If, as a political philosopher, he did not write in the typical neoconservative idiom, Diamond's conclusions, at least – as

---

[26] Joseph Bishop, "Politics and the ACLU," *Commentary* (1971): 51–52. See also Nathan Glazer, "Is Busing Necessary?" *Commentary* (1972): 44 (noting that, in ordering busing, the Court seemed to be unconsciously or unreflectively adopting specific substantive positions on public policy outside of its institutional competence); Elliot Abrams, "The Chains of the Constitution," *Commentary* 64:6 (December 1977): 84–85.

The Public Interest's editor Irving Kristol clearly recognized[27] – fit harmoniously with the core tendencies of the movement: a sense that the new departures in governance undertaken by the Progressives and New Dealers in the first third of the twentieth century were largely compelled by that era's massive political-economic changes. These new departures, they believed, were even admirable and worth not only accepting but also celebrating. That said, as Great Society liberalism and the New Left were reworking the New Deal, their concerns mounted. The group that came to be known as neoconservative grew increasingly preoccupied with the diverse ways in which regulatory, redistributive, and administrative liberalism occasioned its own problems, especially once it became marked by oversized ambitions, including a renegade new egalitarianism. Neoconservatives were proponents of thinking realistically in light of sober human truths about how a modern American state might work – its possibilities and its limits. On a parallel track, Martin Diamond wanted the same thing for the Constitution.

ORIGINALIST STRAUSSIANS, EAST AND WEST

Modern constitutional conservatism has come to be defined by its commitment to jurisprudence of "original intent" [28] or (as refined, to the eventual agreement of almost all conservative scholars active in these debates) to "original meaning."[29] Even the most careful historical account of the origins of originalism in contemporary American law, however, makes only passing reference to the intellectual movement that most originalist conservatives in politics and intellectual life, if not the law schools, were inspired by, weaned on, and today get their information from on the meaning of the Founders' achievement: the Straussians – the students of émigré University of Chicago philosopher Leo Strauss.[30] That this body of writing has gone unnoticed in

---

[27] Diamond and Kristol had been friends since their New York City childhoods. Like Kristol and other first-generation neoconservatives, Diamond had started on the Left, actively: in his youth he had been a leader in the New York City Socialist Party, had been personally close to Norman Thomas, and had cut a figure as a street corner socialist orator.

[28] Portions of the text to follow, in places somewhat revised, were first published in Ken I. Kersch, "Constitutional Conservatives Remember the Progressive Era," in Stephen Skowronek, Stephen Engel, and Bruce Ackerman, editors, *The Progressives' Century: Political Reform, Constitutional Government, and the Modern America State* (New Haven: Yale University Press, 2016), and are republished here by permission of Yale University Press.

[29] See Teles, *Rise of the Conservative Movement*. See Antonin Scalia, "Originalism: The Lesser Evil," *Cincinnati Law Review* 57 (1989): 849–865.

[30] Or the students of students of Strauss. Or the students of students of students of Strauss. Or the students of students of students of students of Strauss: the teaching is passed on in what are referred to internally as "generations" of Straussians. Strauss had been hired at the University of Chicago on the basis of a single interview with Robert Maynard Hutchins, who admired his devotion to the classic texts. Beam, *Great Idea at the Time*, 193. See Jacob Heilbrunn, *They Knew They Were Right: The Rise of the Neocons* (New York: Doubleday, 2008). See,

plain sight by those writing about originalism is an artifact of disciplinary boundaries: Straussians, especially in the postwar conservative movement's ascendency, rarely wrote for legal journals or directly engaged the legal literature on constitutional interpretation (though, today, second- and third-generation Straussians sometimes do). The Straussians were, nevertheless, the modern conservative movement's chief constitutional theorists and (ersatz) historians.[31]

Straussians have a strong sense of identity, both as individuals and collectively, as philosophers questing after Truth, on the model of the ancient Greeks. In practice, however, many Straussians write as centurions zealously guarding a Truth already discovered, possessed by the spirit of righteous mission as the defenders of a Faith. They are unrelenting in their commitment to preserving it from corruption, and successfully passing it on to the rising generations (what debates do take place are almost always internal – typically between clashing proponents of the East Coast versus West Coast Straussian paradigms, or over what to outsiders may seem like arcane scholastic disagreements concerning readings of a few touchstone thinkers).[32] Although

e.g., O'Neill, *Originalism in American Law and Politics*, 192–193. O'Neill does not mention Martin Diamond, the Straussian who devoted himself relentlessly to the significance and explication of the Founding. The Leo Strauss Center at the University of Chicago has posted a large number of reminiscences by Leo Strauss's students, along with recordings of some lectures by Strauss himself (transcripts of many of Strauss's lectures are also posted) (https://leostrausscenter .uchicago.edu/).

[31] The influence here was every bit as important – indeed, much more important – than the Straussian influence on foreign policy, a subject that, in the wake of the Iraq War, has received considerably more attention. See, e.g., Anne Norton, *Leo Strauss and the Politics of American Empire* (New Haven: Yale University Press, 2004); Heilbrunn, *They Knew They Were Right*. The literature on Strauss by Straussians is voluminous. See John A. Murley, editor, *Leo Strauss and His Legacy: A Bibliography* (Lanham, MD: Lexington Books, 2005); Kenneth L. Deutsch and John A. Murley, editors, *Leo Strauss, the Straussians, and the American Regime* (Lanham, MD: Rowman and Littlefield, 1999).

[32] See Gordon Wood, "The Fundamentalists and the Constitution," *New York Review of Books* (February 18, 1988); Michael L. Frazer, "Esotericism Ancient and Modern," *Political Theory* 34 (February 2006): 33–61. Of course, Straussians also hotly dispute the implications of the label, and some reject the East Coast–West Coast distinction. For a partial but significant overview by the late founder and leader of the West Coast camp, see Harry V. Jaffa, *Crisis of the Strauss Divided: Essays on Leo Strauss and Straussianism, East and West* (Lanham, MD: Rowman and Littlefield, 2012), and one from the East Coast camp by Michael and Catherine Zuckert, *The Truth About Leo Strauss: Political Philosophy and American Democracy* (Chicago: University of Chicago Press, 2006). The East Coast School is most often associated with Allan Bloom, Martin Diamond, Walter Berns, Thomas Pangle, and Harvey Mansfield, and the West Coast [Claremont] School with Jaffa and his disciple, Charles Kesler, and – more prominent lately, as West Coast Straussianism has expanded its influence – Thomas G. West. Steven Hayward recounts key aspects of the disagreements between Jaffa (West) and Berns (East). Steven F. Hayward, *Patriotism Is Not Enough: Harry Jaffa, Walter Berns, and the Arguments that Redefined American Conservatism* (New York: Encounter Books, 2017). The Zuckerts have also posited the category of "Midwest Straussians." For a critical but perceptive account of Strauss and his relationship to American politics from a different conservative perspective, see

some Straussians are temperamentally more relaxed and most vehemently deny
hewing to any orthodoxy, many are quick to sniff out heresy and to identify and
isolate the ostensibly mistaken philosophical move that has walked the
individual or nation – if not civilization itself – to the precipice of a chasm,
and cataclysm: they are trained on fixing the moment of corruption, of the fatal
philosophical error. Straussians are perpetually rallying for restoration of
founding principles – of Western civilization, of the US constitutional
republic, or if they hold the two compatible (as they as a group have tended to
do in more recent years) both. Their thought embodies and promotes the
conservative virtues of reverence, loyalty, piety, and restraint and takes the
American constitutional tradition – the American regime – rightly
understood, as the embodiment of these virtues.[33]

A core conviction of Straussians, which meshes nicely, albeit incompletely,
with orthodox, conservative Roman Catholicism and the natural moral order
traditionalism of the likes of Russell Kirk, is that a transcendent Truth is out
there, known, and accessible to the disciplined and well-trained mind, mostly in
classical works of ancient political thought ("Athens," in the Straussian
nomenclature) – but also, to a significant extent, in revealed religion
("Jerusalem") (the extent to which it resides in one or the other, or in what
proportion in each, and how, are perpetual subjects of Straussian debate, and
even bitter contention). Students are trained to love it, seek it, know it, and
promulgate it. As such, the school emphatically rejects and wars against Leo
Strauss's *bêtes noires*: historicism, relativism, and secularism, emphasizing
instead the eternal, unchanging "human nature," authority, sanctity, and
piety. Whether or not the movement's philosophers are theists (and rumor has
it that many are not), their outlook is, as William James would recognize,
essentially religious. The flip side of worshipping the wisdom of the ancients
was a fixation on heresy, corruption, decline, with a healthy dose of panic over
possibility of contamination.[34]

Paul Gottfried, *Leo Strauss and the Conservative Movement in America* (New York: Cambridge
University Press, 2012).

[33] See Jonathan Haidt, *The Righteous Mind: Why Good People Are Divided by Politics and
Religion* (New York: Pantheon, 2012). As Hayward put it, "Jaffa and Berns and their allied
camps that seem abstract or remote on the surface are connected to a serious question, perhaps
the most serious political question of this or any time: What kind of country is America?"
Hayward, *Patriotism Is Not Enough*, 3.

[34] William James, *The Varieties of Religious Experience: A Study in Human Nature* (New York:
Modern Library, 2002) [originally published 1902]. Hayward dedicates his recent book on Jaffa
and Berns to C. S. Lewis and introduces the book with an epigraph from a letter from Lewis to
a Catholic priest praising Saint Thomas More and William Tyndale for "the depth of their faith"
and humbly leaving their disagreements "to the judgment of God." Hayward, *Patriotism Is Not
Enough*, v. Although prominent and influential, Straussianism was far from the consensus
outlook within the broader conservative intellectual movement during the movement's ascendency. As will be explicated later in this chapter, it was for a long time sharply criticized by neo-
confederates (see, e.g., M. E. Bradford, "The Heresy of Equality: Bradford Replies to Jaffa,"

Leo Strauss himself did not write about the US Constitution: he was focused on the great texts of ancient and modern political philosophy. But one of his trademarks was the injunction that students read a text as the author intended it to be read – which, of course, is highly congenial to, if not consonant with, originalism as an interpretive method.[35] Strauss, moreover, was a strong defender of the value and importance of a "public orthodoxy," which, in the US context especially, is conducive to Constitution worship.[36]

The Strauss phenomenon arose in part out of the Great Books movement that Robert Maynard Hutchins had initiated at the University of Chicago, with the philosopher Mortimer Adler as perhaps the movement's most well-known public face, until the political philosopher Allan Bloom assumed the role following the publication of his exposé of American higher education's abandonment of the Great Books (and thus the pursuit of the highest moral and philosophical ideals) in *The Closing of the American Mind* (1987).[37]

Modern Age 20 (1976): 62; M. E. Bradford, "A Firebell in the Night: The Southern Conservative View," *Modern Age* 17 (Winter 1973): 9), positivistic social scientists later associated with neoconservatism (see, e.g., Stanley Rothman, "The Revival of Classical Political Philosophy: A Critique," *American Political Science Review* 56:2 (June 1962): 341–352), and libertarians (see, e.g., C. Bradley Thompson and Yaron Brook, *Neoconservatism: Obituary for An Idea* (London: Routledge, 2010)). On contamination and disgust, see Mary Douglas, *Purity and Danger: An Analysis of Concepts of Pollution and Taboo* (London: Penguin Books, 1966); William Ian Miller, *The Anatomy of Disgust* (Cambridge, MA: Harvard University Press, 1997); Barrington Moore Jr., *Moral Purity and Persecution in History* (Princeton: Princeton University Press, 2000); Martha Nussbaum, *Hiding From Humanity: Disgust, Shame, and the Law* (Princeton: Princeton University Press, 2006). On the focus on corruption and decline in republican thought, see Niccolo Machiavelli, "The Discourses" (c. 1517), in Niccolo Machiavelli, *The Prince and the Discourses* (New York: Modern Library, 1950), First Book, Chs. XVII–XVIII; Third Book, Ch. I ("To Insure a Long Existence to Religious Sects or Republics, It is Necessary Frequently to Bring Them Back to Their Original Principles"), Ch. VI; J. G. A. Pocock, *The Machiavellian Moment: Florentine Political Thought and the Atlantic Republican Tradition* (Princeton: Princeton University Press, 1975); Bernard Bailyn, *The Ideological Origins of the American Revolution* (Cambridge, MA: Harvard University Press, 1967). The turn to visceral social issues involving the body in US politics – the culture wars –joined the republican with the Victorian, and its attendant bodily revulsions.

[35] See Jeffrey Hart, *The Making of the American Conservative Mind: National Review and Its Times* (Wilmington, DE: ISI Books, 2005), 30.

[36] Hart, *Making of the American Conservative Mind*, 85. The key word here is "public." As philosophers and profound admirers of Socrates and the Athenian philosophic tradition, they are not supposed to submit to any orthodoxy in their philosophic investigations. As *political* philosophers, of course, they recognize the dangers to the polity of the public questioning of the Gods of the City. These matters, within Straussian thought, are complex, and related to Strauss's theory of "esoteric" writing by philosophers, who, it is said, are often pushed to conceal their (dangerous) thought between the lines of their texts. On Constitution worship, historically, on the Right, see Aziz Rana, "Progressivism and the Disenchanted Constitution," in Stephen Skowronek, Stephen Engel, and Bruce Ackerman, editors, *The Progressives' Century: Political Reform, Constitutional Government, and the Modern American State* (New Haven: Yale University Press, 2016).

[37] Allan Bloom, *The Closing of the American Mind* (New York: Simon and Schuster, 1987).

Adler's Great Books movement was part of the mid-century "masscult" (mass culture) phenomenon. But the Jewish-German exile Strauss's writings reflect the author's confrontation with the rise of Nazism in his own country, which he sought to diagnose and answer through philosophy – passionately searching for the philosophical equivalent of Chamberlain's capitulation at Munich. Strauss and his compatriots transformed this search and would-be diagnosis into a rarified, recondite elite movement of (usually) conservative political philosophers.[38] This entailed a certain irony, as neither of the initial great books champions Robert Maynard Hutchins nor Mortimer Adler was a conservative (Hutchins even ended his days as a champion of world federalism).[39] When a mischievous William F. Buckley Jr. goaded his *Firing Line* guest Adler in the 1980s by throwing the phenomenal sales figures at him for Bloom's *The Closing of the American Mind*, Adler punched back:

> [Bloom] and his master, Leo Strauss, teach the Great Books as if they were teaching the truth. But when I teach them, I want to understand the errors . . . They indoctrinate their students . . . Strauss reads Plato and Aristotle as if it was all true, i.e. women are inferior, and some men are destined to be slaves.[40]

When it comes the United States and its constitutional republic, much contemporary Straussian work is celebratory, if not hagiographic. In the postwar period, however, the Straussians worked their way toward patriotism. Straussianism's initial position was that the highest achievements in political philosophy were in the ancient world – Greece and (to a lesser extent) Rome. Modernity, including liberal modernity, was, in many important ways, a falling off. The United States, as such, far from amounting to an apotheosis, posed a problem. Drawing upon close readings of ancient political thought (mostly Greek) and of the moderns who had (problematically, in his view) set out in new directions, Strauss challenged the historicism, nihilism, relativism, and faith in progress rampant in the West and called for a return to the study of the eternal, transcendent truths of nature and natural right. Despite not writing about the Constitution – and reportedly voting for Adlai Stevenson (though some close to Strauss say that he also, later, expressed admiration for Barry Goldwater) – Strauss's writings became a foundation for new departures in conservative constitutional theory. In *Thoughts on Machiavelli* and *What Is Political Philosophy?* Strauss taught how important

---

[38] One would have only the barest inkling of the conservatism among Straussians from listening to the interviews with Straussians, and the lectures of Strauss himself, posted on the website of the University of Chicago's Leo Strauss Center, where the teaching(s) are presented as simple common sense: read important works of political philosophy, read closely and carefully, be skeptical, perpetually question, asking 'is this true'?, consider the political dangers surrounding the writers of the texts, and be open to the possibility that the writer was not able to openly say what was truly on his mind, and value serious discussion, debate, and friendship.

[39] Beam, *Great Idea at the Time*, 127, 192.

[40] Quoted in Beam, *Great Idea at the Time*, 128–129.

it was to have "a universal confrontation with the text." This approach proved adaptable to a consideration of the American political and constitutional system of government – or, as the Straussians would have it, the US political and constitutional "regime."[41]

No conservative scholar in the twentieth century was more influential in insisting upon the significance of the Founding for constitutional understanding than the socialist-turned-Straussian Martin Diamond. Diamond was the first of Strauss's students to focus not on traditional political philosophy but on American political thought – specifically, the Founding. Writing in the long shadow of, and in response to, the progressive critique of the Founding by Charles Beard and others, Diamond celebrated the Founders for their genius in arriving at an effective solution to the dilemmas of democratic government in the modern world.[42] By the 1950s, others besides Diamond had also begun to attack the Beardian account of the Founding. But Diamond uniquely insisted that that American Founding provided a "useable past ... available to us for the study of modern problems."[43]

In this project, Diamond joined a small cohort of early Cold War historians striving to unseat the then-dominant Progressive critique of the Founders' (allegedly) disfiguring elitism and mistrust of democracy.[44] Diamond insisted that the Founders remained "necessary," carrying "both the authority of the founding and a wisdom ... [un]surpassed within the American tradition." Catherine and Michael Zuckert – who have called Diamond's achievement the "rough equivalent to Strauss's rediscovery of the ancients" – praised Diamond's insistence that the Founding was "a beginning that must be re-won in the face of progressivist prejudices that steadfastly reject the beginning as superseded."[45]

---

[41] Leo Strauss, *Natural Right and History* (Chicago: University of Chicago Press, 1953). See also John Marini, "Progressivism, Modern Political Science, and the Transformation of American Constitutionalism," in John Marini and Ken Masugi, editors, *The Progressive Revolution in Politics and Political Science: Transforming the American Regime* (Lanham, MD: Rowman and Littlefield, 2005), 235–243. The one area in which Strauss's conservatism seemed most obvious to students – and it rarely did – was in his hostility to communism and the Soviet Union: Strauss was a staunch Cold Warrior. In context, however, this would not distinguish him from his era's Cold War liberals.

[42] Zuckert and Zuckert, *Truth About Leo Strauss*, 209–217. I draw on the Zuckerts' account in what follows, *Truth About Leo Strauss*, 214–215.

[43] Zuckert and Zuckert, *Truth About Leo Strauss*, 215.

[44] Douglass Adair, *Fame and the Founding Fathers* (New York: W. W. Norton, 1974) (Trevor Colbourn, editor)[essays from 1940s/1950s]; Robert E. Brown, *Charles Beard and the Constitution: A Critical Analysis of "An Economic Interpretation of the Constitution"* (Princeton: Princeton University Press, 1956); Forrest McDonald, *We the People: The Economic Origins of the Constitution* (Chicago: University of Chicago Press, 1958). See Charles A. Beard, *An Economic Interpretation of the Constitution of the United States* (New York: Macmillan, 1913).

[45] Zuckert and Zuckert, *Truth About Leo Strauss*, 209–221.

Diamond devoted his career to both explaining why Americans needed the Founders now, and how to get them right. He sympathized with Henry Cabot Lodge Sr.'s 1911 lament of the decline in what Diamond described as the once "universally held ... conviction ... by Americans of the original and continuing excellence of their Constitution." Like Lodge, Diamond held the Progressives responsible. "The conventional wisdom of those who give academic and intellectual opinion to the nation" had been formed by Charles Beard's contention that the Constitution was "the handiwork of a reactionary oligarchy" and by Populist and Progressive demands that the Constitution be democratized.[46] This fostered a fundamental misunderstanding of the relationship the Founders had struck between democracy and liberty and fomented a succession of misguided attempts at reform in democracy's name. Since the Progressive view of the Founding was "false in both history and political philosophy," Diamond called for a "renewed appreciation of our fundamental institutions and rededication to their perpetuation."[47]

The Progressives held that the Revolution's democratic spirit – as affirmed in the Declaration of Independence – had been snuffed out by the Founders in the Constitution, and in the rationalizations provided in *The Federalist*. Diamond, by contrast, treated the Declaration as a statement of Lockean contractualism, "neutral with regard to the democratic form," holding only that the people had the right to chose their own form of government. Diamond taught that "[s]ix writings tell nearly the whole story": "The Declaration of Independence, the Articles of Confederation, the proceedings of the Federal Convention, the Constitution, *The Federalist*, and the anti-Federalist essays." Diamond's understanding of American constitutionalism had a clear architecture. *The Federalist* he pronounced "the brilliant and authoritative exposition of the meaning and intention of the Constitution. The anti-Federalist essays are the thoughtful defense of the political tradition the Constitution was displacing." Diamond's description of the Founding put Founding Era disagreements at its center. "[T]he framers were not themselves unanimous regarding the actual character of the document they framed," he noted, "[f]urther, the Constitution was ratified on the basis of many understandings." He proudly noted, "there have been two centuries of amendment, interpretation, and the sheer working of great events and massive changes in our way of life. All these things," Diamond insisted, "must be taken into account in an understanding of what the Constitution was and is."[48]

In Diamond's systematic reading, the Constitution was designed to form a popular government that would sagely correct for democracy's well-known

---

[46] Martin Diamond, "The Declaration and the Constitution: Liberty, Democracy, and the Founders," *The Public Interest* 41 (Fall 1975): 39–55, 39, 40, 42–45.

[47] Diamond, "Declaration and the Constitution," 45.

[48] Martin Diamond, "What the Framers Meant by Federalism," in Robert Goldwin, editor, *A Nation of States* (Chicago: Rand McNally, 1963), 25–26, 42.

deficiencies (like the tyranny of the majority) by protecting the legitimate (low, modern) ends of government – security, "the pursuit of happiness," and the protection of rights. It was in this specific sense that the Founders were friends of democracy, an argument Diamond dilated on in a career-long exegesis of *The Federalist*.[49]

Unlike later Straussian constitutionalists (to say nothing of contemporary law school originalists), Diamond, who published in neoconservative outlets and was generally supportive of the New Deal and modern welfare state, threw a spotlight on Founding Era disagreements. Diamond venerated the Founders, but notably, he did not insist that we were strictly obliged to abide by their understandings. "With us the Founding Fathers have great authority," he explained in 1963:

> The Constitution they framed is our fundamental legal document. The worthiness of their work has rightly earned from us a profound respect for their political wisdom. [They thus] have for us the combined authority of law and wisdom ... But to pay our respect to that authority – *to know how to obey intelligently or, sometimes, when and how to differ intelligently* – we must know precisely what their Constitution meant and the political thought of which it is the legal expression. "What you have inherited from your fathers/You must first learn to make your own." Ours is such a patrimony that its possession requires constant recovery by careful study.[50]

Diamond lectured the liberals and conservatives alike of the time he was writing for, while professing Madisonianism, "fundamentally misconstru[ing]" the Constitution's nature by misreading a crucial portion of Federalist 51: "A *dependence on the people* is ... the primary control on the government; but experience has taught mankind the necessity of *auxiliary precautions*." The liberals of his time, he observed, favored the people over the precautions, and his era's conservatives "ambiguously accept[ed] the 'dependence' but ... vastly esteem[ed] 'auxiliary precautions.'"[51] Diamond believed they had both misunderstood Madison. Diamond argued that Madison had conceived of these two elements not as forcing a choice but rather as comprising a coherent whole entailing "the fundamental compatibility of the Constitution's restraining devices with a system of majority rule." While Diamond granted that the early twentieth-century Progressives were "understandably outraged by late-nineteenth century scholarship and statesmanship that tended to convert the Constitution into a fixed and immutable code enshrining liberty of contract," he argued nevertheless that they were mistaken in holding the Constitution to be fundamentally undemocratic, an error that was repeated by later liberals and conservatives alike. But this was little more than political

---

[49] Zuckert and Zuckert, *Truth About Leo Strauss*, 211–212.
[50] Diamond, "What the Framers Meant by Federalism," 25 [emphasis added].
[51] Diamond, "Liberals, Conservatives," 96–97 [emphasis in original].

gamesmanship. What liberals really objected to, Diamond observed, was "the character of the majorities that result from the constitutionally generated process of majority coalition." "The real complaint is that majorities simply do not act as Liberals want them to act" – in a way that would transform the human condition.[52] "The majorities generated by the constitutional system," that is, "reject or insufficiently accept the substantive politics and goals of Liberalism"; he held this to be the "Liberal's deepest ... [a]nd ... most accurate charge."[53]

Under the circumstances, liberals thus came to see programmatic political parties as their great hope: "To achieve this transformation, [the liberal] seeks the right kind of constitutional institutions to produce the right kind of party to produce the right kind of majority." Conservatives answered by anathematizing parties as constitutional corruptions. As such, Diamond concluded, "the Liberal dislikes the Constitution for what ... are correct reasons. The Conservative likes the Constitution for what ... are wrong reasons ... [making] the Liberal ... the intelligent foe of the Constitution and the Conservative its foolish partisan ... Given the dominance of either the Constitution would perish."[54]

Diamond found in Madison an altogether different and more congenial constitutional design.[55] "[F]or the founding generation," Diamond declared in another important *Public Interest* article, "it was liberty that was the comprehensive good, the end against which political things had to be measured; and democracy was only a form of government which, like any other form of government, had to prove itself adequately instrumental to the securing of liberty." The evidence for this reading was to be found, plainly, in both *The Federalist Papers* and in the Declaration of Independence's opening paragraph, which, Diamond declared, "does not mean by 'equal' anything at all like the general human equality which so many now make their political standard," but rather "equal political liberty."[56]

Progressives and liberals were certainly correct to say that the Framers were sharp critics of democracy. But these criticisms had to be contextualized: "The American Founders, like all sensible men before them, regarded *every* form of government as problematic, in the sense of having a peculiar liability to corruption, and they accepted the necessity to cope with the problematics peculiar to their *own* form of government." "*Of course*, the Founders criticized the defects and dangers of democracy," Diamond riposted, "and did not waste much breath on the defects and dangers of the other forms of government. For ... [t]hey were not founding any other kind of government;

---

[52] Diamond, "Liberals, Conservatives," 97–98, 106–108.
[53] Diamond, "Liberals, Conservatives," 97–98, 106–108.
[54] Diamond, "Liberals, Conservatives," 109.
[55] Diamond, "What the Framers Meant by Federalism," 47–49.
[56] Diamond, "Declaration and the Constitution," 47–49.

they were establishing a democratic form, and it was the dangers peculiar to it against which all their efforts had to be bent."[57]

Diamond criticized the early twentieth-century Progressives (and their liberal successors) for demanding "imprudent democratizing reforms" occasioning potentially serious threats to liberty. Making matters worse, in the 1960s and 1970s liberals launched yet another assault on the Founders' Constitution – "a vast inflation of the idea of equality, a conversion of the [Declaration's] idea of equal political liberty into an ideology." This "demand for equality in every aspect of human life ... [amounting to] a kind of absolutization of a single principle," when conjoined with the "absolutization of the democratic form of government understood as the vehicle for that complete equality" amounted to a systematic critique of the Founders' entire regime:[58] "This is a different posture toward democracy ... than that embodied in the American founding." Diamond wrote in opposition to those who would "[deny] democratic credentials to the traditional American posture toward democracy and thereby [tilt] the scales in favor of egalitarian claims against the present constitutional order." The country's bicentennial was a time for restoration.[59]

Instead of focusing on constitutional institutions and structures like the East Coast Straussian Martin Diamond, a different variety of Straussianism, most prominently conveyed in the "teaching" of Claremont McKenna College's Harry V. Jaffa, focused intently on rights: Jaffa held the commitment to the equality of natural rights as set out in the opening of the Declaration of Independence – and as reaffirmed by Abraham Lincoln's Gettysburg Address (1863) – to be the keystone of American constitutionalism.[60] Although a necessary compromise, the country's acceptance of the reality of chattel

---

[57] Diamond, "What the Framers Meant by Federalism," 51–52 [emphasis in original].

[58] Diamond, "What the Framers Meant by Federalism," 55.

[59] Diamond, "Declaration and the Constitution," 55. Diamond's originalism as outlined here, it is worth noting, was different from the legalist originalism being forged at about the same time by law professors Robert Bork and Raoul Berger. Preoccupied with matters of design, structure, and principle, Straussians said relatively little about judicial review and how it should be exercised. The law professors, by contrast, were focused primarily on remedying the "problem" of (Warren Court) judicial activism. Far from repudiating Progressivism, the law professors' strategy was to appropriate progressivism's majoritarianism – its conceptualization of judicial review as "countermajoritarian," its suspicion of a politicized judiciary, its call for judicial restraint, and its attack on "Lochnerism" – to indict Warren-era liberals for hypocrisy. See David E. Bernstein, "The Progressive Origins of Conservative Hostility to *Lochner v. New York*," in Johnathan O'Neill and Joseph Postell, editors, *Toward an American Conservatism: Constitutional Conservatism During the Progressive Era* (New York: Palgrave Macmillan, 2013).

[60] "We hold these truths to be self-evident, that all men are created equal, that they are endowed by their Creator with certain unalienable rights, that among these are life, liberty, and the pursuit of happiness." Declaration of Independence (July 4, 1776); "Fourscore and seven years ago our fathers brought forth on this continent, a new nation, conceived in Liberty, and dedicated to the proposition that all men are created equal." Abraham Lincoln, Gettysburg Address (1863), in Kramnick and Lowi, eds., *American Political Thought*, 683.

slavery at its Founding involved a terrible and tragic betrayal of the nation's foundational commitment to the equality of natural rights. In time, though, this commitment was redeemed by Lincoln's actions and thought, which redirected the nation to this constitutive proposition. As such, this variety of redemptive West Coast Straussianism is heavily focused on the Declaration and Lincoln – and the infinite number of ways in which their principles and teachings have been, and continue to be, ignored, flouted, or corrupted. In the annals of the Supreme Court, Exhibit A in this regard is Chief Justice Roger Taney's opinion in *Dred Scott v. Sandford* (1857).[61]

Devotees of this redemptive form of Straussianism have often moved promiscuously between claims to natural right and natural law (and a variety of understandings of each), preoccupied more with the alleged "relativism," positivism, rejection of God, denial of eternal Truths (including about human nature), and the teachings of revealed religion by their secular liberal antagonists (if not sworn enemies). Too much clarity about definitions on their own side of the great divide, the movement tacitly recognized, at least in its earlier stages, would have the unfortunate effect of spotlighting intellectual divisions within the conservative movement – such as by pitting classical liberal Lockeans (natural rights) against partisans of Roman Catholic theology (Thomistic natural law). In recent years, much of the intellectual work on the Right (including constitutional theory) has been aimed at tilling as much common ground here as possible, to underline that the Lockeans, Evangelicals, Fundamentalists, and right-wing Catholics and LDS/Mormons (and even a few, usually Orthodox, Jews) have much more in common with one another in fundamental ways than they do with (ostensibly) secular liberals ("progressives") – and that everything is at stake in the alliance of one side against the other.[62]

It should be noted that appeals to natural law on the Right were not confined to Straussians. They could come in the guise of appeals to Catholic natural law teaching, Enlightenment understandings of the "laws of nature," (Judeo-) Christian traditionalism, or some unspecified admixture of any or all of these. In a classic article in *The Public Interest* on the use of social science by the courts, the neoconservative Democratic New York Senator Daniel Patrick Moynihan defended such appeals in explaining the limitations of the understanding of law as a science propounded by the early twentieth-century

---

[61] See, e.g., Harry V. Jaffa, *Original Intent and the Framers of the Constitution: A Disputed Question* (Washington, DC: Regnery Gateway, 1994); Harry V. Jaffa, *Storm Over the Constitution* (Lanham, MD: Lexington Books, 1994).

[62] In recent years, as this alliance has solidified, West Coast Straussian scholarship has revisited the question of the relationship between natural right and natural law and, in an integrative spirit, sought to refine its understandings of the nature of the relationship. See, e.g., Thomas G. West, *The Political Theory of the American Founding: Natural Rights, Public Policy, and the Moral Conditions of Freedom* (New York: Cambridge University Press, 2017). See generally, Strauss, *Natural Right and History*.

"progressive realists." Moynihan "wonder[ed] at the legal realists' seeming perception of 'natural law' as pre-scientific." The idea of natural law, he explained, was perfectly consistent with science – as anyone who had studied the American Founding would recognize. Indeed, Moynihan attested, it was only through a commitment to natural law in some sense that Americans could arrive at a bedrock commitment to liberty. Moynihan praised Martin Diamond for reminding us that "the framers' respect for human rights, which constituted liberty as they understood it, was not an idiosyncratic 'value' of a remote culture but rather *the* primary political good, of whose goodness any intelligent man would convince himself if he knew enough history, philosophy, and science." Moynihan stood opposed to any suggestion that science, morals, and religion – and America's commitments to foundational freedoms – were antagonists.[63]

Joining Martin Diamond in the East Coast Straussian cohort writing about constitutional matters was Harry Jaffa's antagonist Walter Berns, another student of Strauss's from the University of Chicago. Where Diamond affirmatively set out his reading of how the Constitution was designed to work as a system and Jaffa insisted on professions of a redeeming Faith, Berns wrote extensively (and critically) on constitutional law as expounded by the contemporaneous Supreme Court: his first scholarly article was a critique of the Court's notorious eugenics decision *Buck* v. *Bell* (1927), and his first book, *Freedom, Virtue, and the First Amendment* (1957), was a critical survey of the Court's modern free speech jurisprudence.[64] While Berns's earlier work tended to advocate for jurisprudential statesmanship by virtuous judges who rightly understood the grounding of the US constitutional order as according with a substantive conception of the good, as the activist, egalitarian Warren Court took flight Berns pivoted. He increasingly downplayed his natural law/natural rights approach and became increasingly positivistic – if not in his political philosophy more generally, then at least as concerned the role of the judge.[65]

A MAJOR CONSTITUTIONAL THEORY DEBATE ON THE RIGHT: LOW BUT SOLID STRUCTURALISTS VERSUS REDEMPTIVE MORALISTS

One major axis of conservative movement constitutional debate between the 1950s and the mid-1970s publicly staged for an attentive, educated mass public through articles in conservative magazines like *National Review* was between

---

[63] Daniel Patrick Moynihan, "Social Science and the Courts," *The Public Interest* 54 (Winter 1979): 12–31, 13 [emphasis in original].

[64] Walter Berns, "*Buck v. Bell*: Due Process of Law?" *Western Political Quarterly* 6 (December 1953): 762–775; Walter Berns, *Freedom, Virtue, and the First Amendment* (Baton Rouge: Louisiana State University Press, 1957). See also Walter Berns, "Oliver Wendell Holmes, Jr.," in Morton Frisch and Richard Stevens, editors, *American Political Thought: The Philosophic Dimension of American Statesmanship* (New York: Charles Scribners Sons, 1971). See also Zuckert and Zuckert, *Truth About Leo Strauss*, 216.

[65] Hayward, *Patriotism Is Not Enough*, 154–158.

"deliberate sense" structuralists like Willmoore Kendall and Martin Diamond and redemptive (critics said "messianic") West Coast moralists like Harry Jaffa – and their various surrogates and partisans. None of these figures was a legal academic; all were political scientists primarily concerned not with giving normative advice to judges but with limning the nature of the American constitutional order writ large – that is, with American constitutionalism as a species of American political order and thought.

The maverick Yale political scientist Willmoore Kendall (1909–1967), one of the postwar Right's most brilliant political and constitutional theorists, was a man who enthralled, or appalled, nearly all who encountered him.[66] Like Harry Jaffa, Kendall referred to his own works as setting out not a "philosophy" or an "ideology," but rather simply as his "teaching."[67]

Like G. K. Chesterton, Kendall was a contrarian proponent of orthodoxy, which he defended not just in fact, but (in the *American Political Science Review* and elsewhere) theoretically as being of unique value in personal and political life.[68] Kendall's constitutional theory was derived from a close reading of the

---

[66] Kendall was once described by Dwight Macdonald as "a wild Yale don of extreme, eccentric, and very abstract views who can get a discussion into the shouting stage faster than anybody I have ever known." Dwight Macdonald, "On the Horizon: Scrambled Eggheads on the Right," *Commentary* (April 1, 1956). A more endearing portrait was drawn by Saul Bellow in "Mosby's Memoirs," where the title character Willis Mosby is based on Kendall. Saul Bellow, *Collected Stories* (New York: Viking, 2001), 355–373 [originally published in *The New Yorker* (July 20, 1968)]. See also George Nash, "The Place of Willmoore Kendall in American Conservatism," in *Reappraising the Right* (Wilmington, DE: ISI Books, 2009), 60–71. Kendall inspired Yale to take the rare, if not unprecedented, step of buying out his tenure contract to get rid of him (Kendall decamped to the rabidly orthodox Roman Catholic University of Dallas). While still at Yale, Kendall mesmerized William F. Buckley Jr. (Buckley and the Reagan, George H. W. Bush, and George W. Bush national security and intelligence official and diplomat John Negroponte were allegedly the only students ever to receive an "A" in a Kendall course). *National Review* editor and Dartmouth English professor Jeffrey Hart, another Kendall devotee, even reported that one can trace the origins of Buckley's famous enunciations and inflections (part Southern, part-Anglophilic) to the speaking style of the Oklahoma born-and-raised/Oxford-educated Kendall.

[67] Hoplin and Robinson, *Funding Fathers*, 64; Hart, *Making of the American Conservative Mind*, 163, 166 See also Jeffrey Hart, "Two Paths Home: Kendall and Oakeshott," *Triumph* 2:10 (October 1967): 28–34 (observing that "Both [Kendall] and [the conservative English political philosopher Michael] Oakeshott . . . are reflecting upon *constitutions*, getting at the roots of their respective political systems" [emphasis in original].

[68] Willmoore Kendall, "The 'Open Society' and its Fallacies," *American Political Science Review* 54:4 (December 1960): 972–979. G. K. Chesterton, *Orthodoxy* (New York: Dodd, Mead, and Co., 1908). Kendall was an outspoken defender of Wisconsin Senator Joseph McCarthy, and McCarthyism. See Willmoore Kendall, "McCarthyism: The Pons Asinorum of American Conservatism," in his *The Conservative Affirmation* (Chicago: Henry Regnery Co., 1963) (defining the central question as "are we or are we not going to permit the emergence, within our midst, of totalitarian movements?"). Kendall argued that "a vital democratic society has two functions, one is inclusive – *bring in the new ideas*, assimilate them. The other is exclusive, reject *unassimilable ideas*" [Italics in original]. Kendall defended only McCarthy's initiatives against *actual* communists and subversives, not unsubstantiated slanders and false prosecutions. See also Kendall student William F. Buckley Jr.'s *McCarthy and His Enemies: The Record and Its*

constitutional text, the American national experience (that is, US heritage and traditions), and (commonsense) political theory.[69] As Kendall understood it, the critical feature of the US Constitution was its foundation in popular sovereignty, as set out in the document's Preamble: the American constitutional order set out a framework of government designed to institute and implement as fundamental law the "deliberate sense" of the American people.[70]

Kendall wrote most extensively about the Constitution during the Warren Court's heyday and, as one would predict, he was no fan of its constitutional understandings. One thing the Court and the contemporaneous American liberals who supported it were getting wrong, in his view, was to overemphasize the role of both rights and (plebiscitary) direct democracy in the constitutional framework, thus seriously distorting the constitutional system.[71] Kendall took the Constitution's Preamble very seriously: he considered the rest of the text that followed a set of mechanisms for achieving the six co-equal goals it lists. But he recognized that the priority accorded to each of these six goals relative to the others would be different at different times. Which would take precedence at a particular time would depend on the deliberate sense of the people, as distilled through the appropriate constitutional forms, which were conducive to serious deliberation.[72] Kendall considered these goals to be the basic "symbols" of American politics (a label he adopted from the political theorist Eric Voegelin). They assumed the august status of symbols because they were "rooted in order of being, of permanent actuality," the portal through which we access and apprehend eternal Truth. For this reason, Kendall considered the American Constitution a sacred text, "perhaps touched by the divine." The high responsibility of subsequent generations of Americans was to preserve this legacy, and live well under it.[73]

Meaning (Chicago: Henry Regnery Co., 1954) (with L. Brent Bozell, Jr.) and Buckley's later novel *The Redhunter: A Novel Based on the Life of Joe McCarthy* (Boston: Little, Brown and Co., 1990), in which Kendall appears as a character.

[69] Hart, *Making of the American Conservative Mind*, 37.

[70] John A. Murley and John A. Alvis, editors, *Willmoore Kendall: Maverick of American Conservatives* (Lanham, MD: Lexington Books, 2002) (foreword by William F. Buckley Jr.). Kendall took the phrase from Federalists 71 and 63: "The republican principle demands that the deliberate sense of the community should govern the conduct of those to whom they intrust the management of their affairs; but it does not require an unqualified complaisance to every sudden breeze of passion, or every transient impulse which the people may receive from the arts of men, who flatter their prejudices to betray their interests." (Federalist 71 (Alexander Hamilton)); "Such an institution [the Senate] may be sometimes necessary as a defense to the people against their own temporary errors and delusions. As the cool and deliberate sense of the community ought, in all governments, and actually will, in all free governments, ultimately prevail." (Federalist 63 (Alexander Hamilton or James Madison)).

[71] Hart, *Making of the American Conservative Mind*, 38.

[72] Hart, *Making of the American Conservative Mind*, 167.

[73] Hart, *Making of the American Conservative Mind*, 168–169. Willmoore Kendall and George W. Carey, *The Basic Symbols of The American Political Tradition* (Baton Rouge: Louisiana

Although extensively published in his own right, Kendall's constitutional understandings gained a wider audience through the Dartmouth College English professor and *National Review* editor Jeffrey Hart (b. 1930), who adopted Kendall's understandings in his own journalistic writings on the Constitution and constitutional disputes in *National Review, Human Events*, and other popular movement outlets. Hart elaborated Kendall's theory, explaining that, in a Constitution designed structurally to implement the deliberate sense of the people, Congress was properly understood as the system's preeminent branch. There were two basic ways to frustrate this design: to overdevelop the powers of either of the other two rival branches, the (Article I) president or the (Article III) courts. Modern liberals achieved their policy objectives by doing precisely this, which amounted to imposing their views against the deliberate sense of the American people.

This led to predictable corruptions. "We thus have had the myth of the 'great' Presidents," Hart explained:

Washington, Jefferson, Lincoln, Roosevelt and Kennedy, perhaps Wilson. In the myth, such Presidents have unique vision into the national essence, and when the incumbent President is prepared to undertake wide liberal initiatives, he is assimilated to the "great men of the myth" ... When the man in the White House is not especially liberal, then the only way to short-circuit the deliberate sense structure is through the sacred court, whose priest-interpreters find new meaning in the familiar text of the Constitution.[74]

Across the 1970s, Hart explained the disagreements among conservatives over constitutional theory to *National Review*'s readers. In doing so, he distinguished two American constitutional traditions:

In the first ... the American system is conceived of as one based ultimately on the "deliberate sense" of the people. The Founders, consciously and with great ingenuity, designed a government in which "waves of popular enthusiasm" would find it exceedingly difficult ... to bring about rapid and fundamental change ... And the complex filter in the system of government they designed may be viewed as the functional equivalent of Burke's "custom" and of the unwritten restraints of the "British Constitution."

State University Press, 1970). See also Willmoore Kendall and George W. Carey, "What Is the American Myth?" *Triumph* 5:10 (December 1970): 11–19; Michael Lawrence, "Pro Multis: There Ought Be a Law," *Triumph* 6:1 (January 1971): 15. The seriousness with which Kendall and Voegelin take symbols echoes some prominent strains of the era's psychology and anthropology – e.g., the work of Carl Jung and Joseph Campbell, *The Hero With a Thousand Faces* (New York: Pantheon, 1949).

[74] Jeffrey Hart, "The Real Meaning Behind Nixon's Court Choices," *Human Events* 31:47 (November 20, 1970): 16. Will Herberg was somewhat critical of the outer reaches of the US civil religion, in which "Washington and Lincoln are ... raised to superhuman level, as true saints of America's civil religion. They are equipped with the qualities and virtues that, in traditional Christianity, are attributed to Jesus alone – freedom from sin, for example." Will Herberg, "America's Civil Religion: What It Is and Whence it Comes," *Modern Age* 17:3 (Summer 1973): 230.

Hart then explained,

[T]he other and rival American political tradition does not appeal to the "deliberate sense" of the people, but to a set of goals, posited as absolutes, which it claims to have discovered in certain key texts. The first is the "all men are created equal" clause of the Declaration of Independence, not in its original context, but as reinterpreted by the Gettyburg Address ... Other key texts are Amendments I thorough X, especially the First and, of course, the "equal protection" clause of the Fourteenth Amendment.[75]

While contemporary readers might be inclined to identify Hart's second tradition with contemporary liberalism, Hart was alluding to the constitutional philosophy of Harry V. Jaffa. In 1979, Charles Kesler, today a government professor at Claremont McKenna College, editor of the *Claremont Review of Books*, and a member of the board of governors of Claremont's Salvatori Center, but then a graduate student at Harvard, stumped for Jaffa in *National Review*. "A political movement cannot philosophize, but a decent one has need of a philosophy," Kesler insisted. He worried that "American conservatism sometimes resembles that false love of liberty, its self-examinations concluding in nothing more lasting or noble than ad hoc reactions to the New Deal, the Great Society, the New Frontier." Kesler warned that "this sort of poking around in the detritus of liberal social programs" was inadequate. Conservatism needed to define itself "less [by] a commitment to the past than [by] a commitment to certain truths applicable to past, present, and future." He added, "the scholar who, more than any other, has shown that the principles of that tradition, far from being 'mere rubbish – old wadding left to rot on the battlefield after the victory is won' – are in fact the living truths of just government and wise conservatism, is Harry V. Jaffa."[76]

Kesler's case for Jaffa was directed against the quite different constitutional visions propounded by other movement intellectuals who, although distinct from Kendall, nevertheless fell on his side of the structuralist/redemptive moralist divide.

---

[75] Jeffrey Hart, "Peter Berger's 'Paradox'," *National Review* (May 12, 1972): 511–516, 512. See also M. J. Sobran, "Saving the Declaration," *National Review* 30 (51) (December 22, 1978): 1601–1602, 1601. Hart published a history and memoir of his years at the magazine: Jeffrey Hart, *The Making of the American Conservative Mind: National Review and Its Times* (Wilmington, DE: ISI Books, 2006). See also Jeffrey Hart, *The American Dissent: A Decade of Modern Conservatism* (Garden City, NY: Doubleday, 1966).

[76] Charles Kesler, "A Special Meaning of the Declaration of Independence: A Tribute to Harry V. Jaffa," *National Review* (July 6, 1979): 850–859, 850. Jaffa had been a speechwriter for Barry Goldwater's 1964 presidential campaign and he became famous for penning the line in Goldwater's nomination acceptance speech asserting that "Extremism in the defense of liberty is no vice ... And ... moderation in the pursuit of justice is no virtue." For an account of the influence of the West Coast Straussian Claremont School on contemporary conservative politics – its denizens, among other things, were passionate supporters of both the Tea Party and Donald Trump – see Steven Teles, "How the Progressives Became the Tea Party's Mortal Enemy: Networks, Movements, and the Political Currency of Ideas," in Skowronek, Engel, and Ackerman, editors, *The Progressives' Century*. See also Hayward, *Patriotism Is Not Enough*.

The neoconservative editor of *The Public Interest*, Irving Kristol, for instance – reacting in significant part against the New Left and the counterculture of the 1960s – had been busy mounting a sustained defense of bourgeois values, a notable reversal from his days as a City College Trotskyist in the 1930s. That defense led him toward an interpretation of the American Revolution as a bourgeois revolution.[77] Kesler asserted, following Jaffa, that "it is hard to conceive that Americans would rise up to throw off British rule for reasons that could be embodied in a calm and legalistic document ... Of that abstract truth 'that all men are created equal,'" he noted, chagrined, "Kristol says nothing."[78]

Martin Diamond, like his friend Irving Kristol, characterized the Revolution in terms that were too bourgeois and prosaic for Kesler: Diamond, whose theory emphasized constitutional structure rather than the foundational truths of the Declaration, argued that the origins of the constitutional liberties of Americans arose in significant part from the regime's nature as a commercial republic.[79] Bowing respectfully to Diamond, Kesler conceded that "[t]he Declaration and the Constitution each embody, in some sense, the principle of the Revolution, but the relationship between them is unclear, which is the higher expression of those principles." To be sure, Diamond was properly esteemed as "the foremost expositor of the Constitution and The Federalist in our time, through his lucid, finely crafted essays on the Framers' views of democracy, liberty, and federalism." Kesler conceded that Diamond "[a]lmost single-handedly ... revived the study of The Federalist as a serious work of political philosophy."[80]

But Jaffa's constitutional philosophy, propounded in *Crisis of the House Divided* (1959), was of an entirely different order.[81] There, as Kessler reminded *National Review* readers, Jaffa recounted how "Lincoln led America through 'a new birth of freedom' – through a spiritual rebirth – because the first birth – the Founding – had been defective. Not merely because of the Constitution's compromises with slavery, but because of what those compromises

---

[77] See Irving Kristol, "The American Revolution as a Successful Revolution," in his *America's Continuing Revolution: An Act of Conservatism* (Washington, DC: American Enterprise Institute, 1975), reprinted in Irving Kristol, *Reflections of a Neoconservative: Looking Back, Looking Ahead* (New York: Basic Books, 1983), 78–94.

[78] Kesler, "A Special Meaning of the Declaration of Independence," 851.

[79] See Diamond, "Declaration and the Constitution," 39–55.

[80] Kesler, "A Special Meaning of the Declaration of Independence," 851. This was no small thing for Kesler, who assumed the editorship of one of the most widely sold versions of *The Federalist Papers* after the death of its initial editor, Clinton Rossiter, a suicide in the aftermath of the late 1960s student uprising at Cornell, where his middle-ground views and moderation left him despised by Left and Right alike – politically homeless. Alexander Hamilton, James Madison, and John Jay, *The Federalist Papers* (New York: Mentor, 1961) (Clinton Rossiter, editor). See Donald Downs, *Cornell '69: Liberalism on the Crisis of the American University* (Ithaca, NY: Cornell University Press, 1999).

[81] Harry V. Jaffa, *Crisis of the House Divided: An Interpretation of the Issues in the Lincoln–Douglas Debates* (Garden City, NY: Doubleday, 1959).

represented." Jaffa had placed the "equality of natural rights" at the core of American constitutionalism. In Kesler's assessment, "Jaffa's view of the character of our politics unfolds easily into an interpretation of the whole of U.S. history: which becomes the moral drama of conflict between self-government, as what the people will and self-government as what the people ought to will." "This," he insisted, "is history on the grand scale, similar to Charles A. Beard's or Louis Hartz's comprehensive interpretations, but truer to the moral character – one should say, truer to the facts – of American political life."[82]

---

[82] Kesler, "A Special Meaning of the Declaration of Independence," 854. Jaffa's understandings have served as the wellspring of the contemporary conservative constitutional vision some have called "Declarationism." With its intellectual core housed at Claremont McKenna College, in the *Claremont Review of Books*, and at Claremont's Henry Salvatori Center for the Study of Individual Freedom in the Modern World, Declarationism rests on the conviction that the Declaration of Independence is not only an inherent component of the US Constitution, but foundational. Declarationists understand the Declaration to be both philosophically and temporally prior to the Constitution. For, without a prior commitment to the (for many religious conservatives, purportedly Christian) proposition that all men are created equal, there is no basis for considering consent to the Constitution binding. That shared philosophical commitment created the American nation, which then composed and ratified the Constitution. Significantly, this understanding among many conservative intellectuals serves as a bridge between the Founders and conservative Catholics, Fundamentalist and Evangelical Protestants, and LDS/Mormons in a way that has underwritten what Seth Dowland has called their contemporary "co-belligerence." See Seth Dowland, *Family Values and the Rise of the Christian Right* (Philadelphia: University of Pennsylvania Press, 2015), 85. See, e.g., John Courtney Murray, SJ, *We Hold These Truths: Catholic Reflections on the American Proposition* (New York: Sheed and Ward, 1960); Francis A. Schaeffer, *A Christian Manifesto* (Wheaton, IL: Crossway Books, 2005); A. Scott Loveless, "The Forgotten Founding Document: The Overlooked Legal Contribution of the Declaration of Independence and California's Opportunity to Revive It Through Proposition 8," SSRN Working Paper (October 23, 2008). See also David D. Kirkpatrick, "The Right Hand of the Fathers," *The New York Times Magazine* (December 20, 2009), 24. Declarationism has the special virtue to many conservatives of putting them on the "right side" of civil rights: Lincoln is a hero to Declarationists – an affinity that had initially made them anathema to the movement's seemingly vanishing remnant of neo-confederates – who have reemerged in reaction, first, to the election of the nation's first black president Barack Obama, and then with the (liberal/progressive/apostate conservative) backlash against the racist Republican president Donald Trump. And, because of its appeal to natural law as the root of human equality, Martin Luther King Jr.'s "Letter from a Birmingham Jail" (1963) that quotes Thomas Aquinas – has been adopted as a core conservative Declarationist text. In recent years, Princeton's James Madison Program in American Ideals and Institutions, founded and directed Robert P. George, and his freestanding Princeton, New Jersey, think tank, The Witherspoon Institute, which is headed by an Opus Dei cleric, has assumed increasing leadership in the propagation of the Declarationist vision. Operating under a "teach the controversy" rubric, Witherspoon (which leveraged the sponsorship of the George W. Bush administration's National Endowment for the Humanities) launched a "Natural Law, Natural Rights and American Constitutionalism" web resource, with banner graphics (quotes and photos) juxtaposing the opening lines of the Declaration, Abraham Lincoln on the Declaration, and Martin Luther King Jr. (quoting Catholic natural law – here, St. Augustine) with the positivist counter-tradition, as represented by Oliver Wendell Holmes Jr. and Hugo Black. See www.nlnrac.org/ (for the initiative's announcement notice, see www.winst.org/ announcements/11_01_17_natural_law .php).

Jaffa himself battled intransigently across much of the postwar period against Diamond's structuralism and institutionalism, which Jaffa traced back to the malign errors made by Willmoore Kendall in *The Basic Symbols of the American Political Tradition* (1970). There, Kendall had claimed that "'[t]he Declaration itself gives no guidance on how or in what ways' American government should be structured, it anticipates merely that the people will shortly 'engage in some sort of deliberative process to establish that form of government.'" But, it is worth recalling that, at least prior to the achievements of the civil rights movement in the mid-1960s – the Civil Rights Act of 1964 and the Voting Rights Act of 1965 – perhaps Jaffa's greatest antagonists on the Right were agrarian or neo-confederate traditionalists like M. E. Bradford – discussed at length later – who had, after all, blamed Jaffa's hero Lincoln for having wrecked the Constitution. Arguing on Jaffa's behalf, Kesler noted, "[l]ike Kendall, Bradford sympathizes with the Confederacy, makes great sport of the freedom-loving–slave-holding Founding Fathers, and is scornfully critical of Lincoln, whom he anathematizes as a 'gnostic' force." Kesler disdainfully dismissed "the Taney-Kendall-Bradford interpretation."[83]

Kesler was convinced that the outcome of the debate over which constitutional vision should prevail within the movement would ultimately determine whether the nation, once restored to sound leadership, would flourish – or even, perhaps, survive. "The U.S. will become nothing if it suffers a great military defeat in the next war: but, more profoundly, the U.S. will become nothing if it becomes persuaded that it stands for nothing," Kesler warned.[84] "Conservatives who look to Jaffa's teaching, and to Lincoln's example," he wrote, "will see a kind of conservatism that lies between and above the extremes of libertarianism and traditionalism." He continued:

The danger of traditionalism's reverence for the past is that it is unreasonable, unprincipled ... no different from liberalism's unprincipled commitment to the future ... It does not acknowledge any objective standards ... [that] distinguish just from unjust, good from bad, true from false, and so provides us no guidance in choosing what elements of the past should be conserved as a matter of expedience, and what elements must be conserved as a matter of justice. Nor ... can it provide us with what the

---

[83] Kesler, "A Special Meaning of the Declaration of Independence," 855, 858. Kendall and Carey, *Basic Symbols of the American Political Tradition.* Bradford was the pick of Republican traditionalists to head the National Endowment for the Humanities in Ronald Reagan's first term; they were infuriated when he was spurned, largely at the behest of (mostly Jewish) neoconservatives, in favor of William Bennett. See George Hawley, *Right-Wing Critics of American Conservatism* (Lawrence: University Press of Kansas, 2016), 50–51, 56, 183. Taney wrote the majority opinion in *Dred Scott.* The "gnostic force" put-down is an enlistment of Voegelin.

[84] Kesler, "A Special Meaning of the Declaration of Independence," 859. The same spirit issuing from Claremont, it is worth noting, was behind the notorious "Flight 93 Election" article in the *Claremont Review of Books* (Fall 2016) advocating that defenders of the Constitution, in one last ditch move to try to save the republic, cast their votes for Donald Trump for president.

past does not furnish – living statesmanship and virtue ... Jaffa's interpretation of the American political tradition points toward a politics that prizes virtue more highly than does libertarianism, and reason more highly than does traditionalism.[85]

Jaffa himself lamented that the Declaration's insistence that "all men are created equal" was a "proposition that is anathema to American conservatives. It is hardly too much to say that they regard it with an aversion equal to that with which they regard 'all history is the history of class struggle.'" Moreover, American students had long been taught that

Jefferson departed from Locke in declaring that among man's unalienable rights were life, liberty, and the pursuit of happiness ... and not "property" or "estate." If man, in the state of nature, or by nature, pursues happiness, then by nature he pursues a *summum bonum* and does not merely flee a *summum malum*. This theoretical defect ... [in Hobbes and Locke is not a] defect of the Declaration.[86]

But do contemporary Americans have the faith to avail themselves of their rich heritage? Jaffa reminded readers that in *Natural Right and History* (1953), his teacher Leo Strauss asked one of the most momentous of questions: "'Does this nation in its maturity still cherish the faith in which it was conceived and raised? Does it still hold those 'truths to be self-evident?' ... Strauss believed those questions ought to have been answered in the affirmative. Until they could be so answered, he did not believe this nation, or the West, could recover its moral health or political vigor." It was the mission of conservative Americans to fight for the triumph of this faith.[87]

Responding to Kesler, M. J. Sobran and Jeffrey Hart answered Jaffa on Kendall's behalf. "Throughout his career," Sobran reported, "Kendall deplored the messianic pretensions ... of what we may ... call the Declaration Tradition, with its universalism and stress on individual rights." "Against this," Sobran explained, "he placed the Constitutional Tradition of government by consensus, which tended to mute sharp moral issues and scale down grandiose causes to politically assimilable dimensions."[88]

---

[85] Kesler, "A Special Meaning of the Declaration of Independence," 859.

[86] Harry V. Jaffa, "Another Look at the Declaration," *National Review* (July 11, 1980): 836–840, 836, 840. In the years before his death in 2015, Jaffa has been arguing for some time that Thomas Aquinas's thought was more important to the American Founding than John Locke's. See Harry V. Jaffa, "Natural Law and American Political Thought," Lecture in the America's Founding and Future Series, James Madison Program in American Ideals and Institutions, Princeton University, Princeton, NJ (September 29, 2003).

[87] Jaffa, "Another Look at the Declaration," 840. See Strauss, *Natural Right and History*.

[88] M. J. Sobran, "Saving the Declaration," *National Review* (December 22, 1978): 1601–1602, 1601. Hart's characterization of both Kendall and Strauss suggests that they are progenitors of originalism at least in the sense that both sought to read texts as their authors intended them to be read. Kendall sought to "define a constitutional orthodoxy based on common sense, American experience, and the founding texts, closely read." His approach was to start with the "'We the People' of the preamble filtered through the delaying and refining process of constitutional

Hart complained that "the interpretation of these key texts by the avatars of the rival [Declaration] tradition is ... completely unhistorical ... Does the Declaration tell us that it is the task of government to bring about equality of condition, or even equality of opportunity? ... The founders would have ridiculed either goal as preposterous." Plainly, the Declaration stood simply, if importantly, for the proposition that "Men are equal ... in their right to found and organize a government as they see fit."[89]

Hart was particularly troubled that Jaffa's theoretical tradition had "developed its own mythology, and, when not appealing to key sacred texts, invokes a series of quasi-messianic Great Presidents – Washington, Jefferson, Lincoln, Wilson, Roosevelt, Kennedy – each of whom, to quote Kendall again, 'sees more deeply into the specifically American problem, which is posed by the 'all men are created equal' clause of the Declaration of Independence.'" By these lights, "America will build a New Jerusalem which will be a commonwealth of free and equal men ... Through Him, through the Great President, we are to be reborn." Hart understood this political (and executive) messianism to be an affront to the Constitution – and politically dangerous as well.[90] For Hart, the debate about whether the "deliberate sense" or "abstract theory" would prevail within conservative constitutional thought framed the central constitutional issues of his time: "Busing, school prayer, pornography – the current litmus test issues," Hart insisted, "all seem to take their places within its parameters." If, as seemed to be the case, the Supreme Court and the federal bureaucracy were now careering out of control, it was because they had spurned Kendall's go-slow, consensus approach. Hart lamented that "[t]he greatest breaches in the defenses of the 'deliberate sense' conception of government have in fact most recently been made by the Supreme Court, and by the ukases handed down by executive agencies like HEW."[91]

The prominent libertarian Frank S. Meyer also came out swinging against Claremont's Harry Jaffa. Observing that both the deliberate sense and the abstract views had long pedigrees in American political thought, Meyer found it odd that Jaffa clung so tenaciously to the conviction that his understanding was the only legitimate interpretation of the American constitutional tradition. Jaffa's relentless high-mindedness, moreover, was a menace to free government.

forms, democratic instincts and experience combined with high political theory." See Hart, *Making of the American Conservative Mind*, 30, 36.

[89] Jeffrey Hart, "Peter Berger's 'Paradox,'" *National Review* (May 12, 1972), 512.

[90] Hart, "Peter Berger's 'Paradox.'" To the consternation of many conservatives, Jeffrey Hart endorsed Barack Obama for president in 2008. We might in part attribute this turn as a reaction against the influence of messianic Straussianism in the contemporary Republican Party. See Jeffrey Hart, "Obama is the Real Conservative," *The Daily Beast* (October 31, 2008) (www.thedailybeast.com/blogs-and-stories/2008-10-31/obama-is-the-true-conservative/).

[91] Hart, "Peter Berger's 'Paradox'," 512–513.

His "airy and cavalier lack of concern with how power is distributed," Meyer charged, "leaves him with no defenses, except hope, against the tendency of government to concentrate power and to ride roughshod over the individual. It fully explains his admiration of Jackson, Lincoln, et al."[92]

Frank Meyer placed liberty, not equality, at the core of the country's constitutional tradition – and Jaffa's hero, Lincoln, was no friend of liberty. "Professor Jaffa, since he regards the division of power as irrelevant to the 'principle of a free constitution,' [in favor of the view that what is crucial is the recognition that all men have rights which no government should infringe] does not begin to grasp the incalculable damage for which Lincoln is responsible," Meyer protested:

Jaffa ... chooses to base his critique of American slavery on the proposition that the American polity is in its essence dedicated to equality – and to center his vindication of Lincoln on Lincoln's role as the champion of equality. Nothing ... could be further from the truth ... The freedom of the individual person from government, not the equality of individual persons, is the central theme of our constitutional arrangements ... Freedom and equality are opposites.

Jaffa's Lincoln is the champion of equality, but Meyer's is "the creator of concentrated national power, the President who shattered the constitutional tension." These two Lincolns, Meyer insisted, are "one and the same man."[93]

CONSERVATIVE CONSTITUTIONAL THEORY DEBATES, TAKE TWO:
(SOUTHERN) POSITIVISM VERSUS (EQUALITY OF) NATURAL RIGHTS

In recent years, scholars have increasingly held the successes of the mid-twentieth-century's civil rights movement to have occasioned a "Second Reconstruction."[94] If apprehended as such, it is worth noting that some southerners who became modern "conservatives" reacted as badly to the Second Reconstruction as their predecessors had to the first. Through as late as the early 1980s (repudiating a long-standing strain of southern thought that had made its peace with the Civil War's outcome, and even with Lincoln),[95] the conservative movement continued to harbor a strong unreconstructed

---

[92] Frank S. Meyer, "Again on Lincoln," *National Review* (January 25, 1966): 71–72, 71. On Meyer, see Frank Meyer, *In Defense of Freedom: A Conservative Credo* (Chicago: Henry Regnery Co., 1962); Kevin J. Smant, *Principles and Heresies: Frank S. Meyer and the Shaping of the American Conservative Movement* (Wilmington DE: ISI Books, 2002).

[93] Meyer, "Again on Lincoln," 71, 72.

[94] See, e.g., Richard K. Vallely, *The Two Reconstructions: The Struggle for Black Enfranchisement* (Chicago: University of Chicago Press, 2004).

[95] See Merrill D. Peterson, *Lincoln in American Memory* (New York: Oxford University Press, 1994), 49, 252 (noting as evidence of the South's peace with Lincoln both a gentler view of Lincoln in the American South after Reconstruction faded into memory and the Virginia legislature's adoption in 1928 of a resolution in honor of Lincoln's birthday).

element of neo-confederatism on the one hand[96] and formalist, southern-based states' rights conservatism on the other.[97]

Contention over the true "meaning" of the Civil War, constitutionally and politically, began from the moment of Confederate General Robert E. Lee's surrender at Appomattox Court House.[98] Considered over the long term, the ideological valence of the meanings attributed to the war do not track the categories that contemporary political scientists use to distinguish "liberals" from "conservatives." But we can at least distinguish those who read the war narrowly from those who read it broadly and aspirationally. The former believed the war, and the three amendments it occasioned, ended slavery and perhaps guaranteed national enforcement of some basic rights. The latter believed the war effectuated a revolution in the constitutional order that transformed the relations between the national government and the states and provided national guarantees for the broad definition and aggressive enforcement of rights.[99]

"Conservatives," in the contemporary sense, were on both sides of this divide. Conservative, and often southern, defenders of states' rights and opponents of black social, civil, and political equality narrowly interpreted the implications of the war and the resulting constitutional changes. Those we would later recognize as libertarian conservatives, however – pro-market, pro-business, pro-property rights economic conservatives like Supreme Court

[96] See, e.g., M. E. Bradford, "Where We Were Born and Raised: The Southern Conservative Tradition," in *The Reactionary Imperative: Essays Literary and Political* (Peru, IL: Sherwood Sugden, 1990), 115, 115–134; Nancy MacLean, "Neo-Confederacy versus the New Deal: The Regional Utopia of the Modern American Right," in Joseph Crespino and Matthew D. Lassitter, editors, *The Myth of Southern Exceptionalism* (New York: Oxford University Press, 2010), 308, 308–312. It is important to note that, for much of the twentieth century, these conservatives could be found in both political parties; of course, in the first part of that century, most southern conservatives were Democrats.

[97] See, e.g., James Jackson Kilpatrick, *The Sovereign States: Notes of a Citizen of Virginia* (Chicago: Henry Regnery Co., 1957), 255–258.

[98] See, e.g., David W. Blight, *Race and Reunion: The Civil War in American Memory* (Cambridge, MA: Harvard University Press, 2001), 1 (opining that determining the lessons of the Civil War "has been the most contested question in American historical memory since 1863, when Robert E. Lee retreated back into Virginia, Abraham Lincoln went to Gettysburg to explain the meaning of the war, and Frederick Douglass announced 'nation regeneration' as the 'sacred significance' of the war").

[99] See Michael Vorenberg, "Bringing the Constitution Back In: Amendment, Innovation, and Popular Democracy During the Civil War Era," in Meg Jacobs et al., editors, *The Democratic Experiment: New Directions in American Political History* (Princeton: Princeton University Press, 2003); see also Jack M. Balkin, "The Reconstruction Power," *New York University Law Review* 85 (2010): 1801, 1806 ("When we strip away these doctrinal glosses and focus on the original meaning and structural purpose underlying the Reconstruction Amendments, we discover that the Reconstruction Power gives Congress all the authority it needs to pass modern civil rights laws, including the Civil Rights Act of 1964. That was the original point of these amendments, and that should be their proper construction today.").

Justice Stephen J. Field – read the Civil War as having worked a revolution in the constitutional order.[100]

MEL BRADFORD'S LINCOLN

As we move forward to the time in which modern ideological categories became political realities in the post–New Deal era, we can clearly discern a strain of the modern conservative movement that prominently adhered to the narrow understanding of the war's meaning, with all the attendant constitutional and political implications of that position. Melvin E. ("M. E." or "Mel") Bradford,[101] a proud native Texan and literature professor at the University of Dallas, was perhaps the most sophisticated and influential proponent of this neo-confederate current of thought in the second half of the twentieth century.[102] In constitutional matters, he was a strict

---

[100] See, e.g., *Slaughterhouse Cases*, 83 US (16 Wall.) 36, 94–95 (1873) (Field, J., dissenting) ("The [Fourteenth] amendment was adopted ... to place the common rights of American citizens under the protection of the National government ... A citizen of a State is now only a citizen of the United States residing in that State. The fundamental rights, privileges, and immunities which belong to him as a free man and a free citizen, now belong to him as a citizen of the United States, and are not dependent upon his citizenship of any State."). If the narrower reading of the Court's majority were to hold, the Fourteenth Amendment "was a vain and idle enactment, which accomplished nothing, and most unnecessarily excited Congress and the people on its passage ... [I]f the amendment refers to the natural and inalienable rights which belong to all citizens, the inhibition has a profound significance and consequence ... The privileges and immunities designated are those which of right belong to the citizens of all free governments." Ibid. at 96–97. See also *Munn v. Illinois*, 94 US 113, 140–44 (1877) (Field, J., dissenting) (arguing for a liberal construction of the Fourteenth Amendment to prohibit Illinois from regulating the amount a business could charge for use of a grain elevator). See, e.g., M. E. Bradford, *Original Intentions: On the Making and Ratification of the United States Constitution* (Athens: University of Georgia Press, 1993), 104 ("Despite the alteration that they made in the balance of American federalism, the Reconstruction amendments and early civil rights laws did not change the Constitution of the United States into a teleocratic instrument; a law with endlessly unfolding implications in the area of personal rights.").

[101] The account of Harry Jaffa and Mel Bradford, and the Jaffa-Bradford exchange, is drawn, somewhat revised, from Ken I. Kersch, "Beyond Originalism: Conservative Declarationism and Constitutional Redemption," *Maryland Law Review* 71 (2011): 229–282.

[102] James McClellan, "Walking the Levee with Mel Bradford," in Clyde N. Wilson, editor, *A Defender of Southern Conservatism: M.E. Bradford and His Achievements* (Columbia: University of Missouri Press, 1999), 35, 39. Trained by the poet Donald Davidson in the Fugitive and Agrarian literary circle in the Vanderbilt University English Department, Bradford was by trade a William Faulkner specialist. Thomas H. Landess, "The Education of Mel Bradford: The Vanderbilt Years," in Wilson, *Defender of Southern Conservatism*, 7, 8–9. See also McClellan, *Defender of Southern Conservatism*, 35, 39 (Bradford was "equally at home in philosophy, religion, classical studies, politics, and history" and took a special interest in literature of the South and American political rhetoric and thought). Davidson, Bradford's mentor at Vanderbilt, had once pronounced the Lincoln Memorial a brazen affront to southerners. Peterson, *Lincoln in American Memory*, 251.

constructionist, a position he advanced and defended from an expressly southern point of view.[103]

In the postwar period, many conservatives, such as Russell Kirk, left Lincoln off the maps they were drawing of the history of conservative thought.[104] By contrast, Lincoln was very much on Bradford's map as his frequent and perhaps predominant target.[105] Indeed, when President Ronald Reagan nominated Bradford to head the National Endowment for the Humanities, it was Bradford's long paper trail of attacks on Lincoln and Lincoln's constitutionalism that ultimately doomed the appointment.[106] Under a barrage of objections from within the conservative coalition by New York neoconservatives such as Irving Kristol, Norman Podhoretz, and others, Reagan was forced to withdraw the nomination, naming the Brooklyn-born, neoconservative Catholic moralist William J. Bennett in Bradford's place.[107]

Bradford proudly described himself as "an impenitent conservative Southerner."[108] In his many essays on the subject, Bradford described Lincoln as a moral zealot who, in the spirit of Oliver Cromwell, the French Revolutionary Jacobins, and the continental revolutionaries of 1848, sought to impose his moral vision on the United States through the power of an unconstitutionally unrestrained central state.[109] In an article taking its title from Thomas Jefferson's declared alarm at the Compromise of 1820, Bradford traced the history of the North's centralizing efforts, inflamed by "chiliastisic moral imperatives," to lay waste to the terms of the original constitutional compact.[110]

---

[103] Marshall I. DeRosa, "M. E. Bradford's Constitutional Theory: A Southern Reactionary's Affirmation of the Rule of Law," in Wilson, *Defender of Southern Conservatism*, 92–93 ("The Southernness of Bradford's scholarship was professionally problematical, as is evidenced by the academic ostracism imposed on him due to his Southern, states-rights brand of conservatism.").

[104] Russell Kirk, *The Conservative Mind, From Burke to Santayana* (Chicago: Henry Regnery Co., 1953).

[105] McClellan, *Defender of Southern Conservatism*, 35, 46–47.

[106] See David Gordon, "Southern Cross: The Meaning of the Mel Bradford Moment," *American Conservative* (April 2010): 34.

[107] Gordon, "Southern Cross." Bradford's support for George Wallace's 1972 Democratic presidential campaign was another problem for the nomination. See also Benjamin B. Alexander. "The Man of Letters and the Faithful Heart," in Wilson, editor, *Defender of Southern Conservatism*, 17, 31.

[108] M. E. Bradford, "A Fire Bell in the Night: The Southern Conservative View," *Modern Age* 17 (1973): 9.

[109] See, e.g., M. E. Bradford, "Dividing the House: The Gnosticism of Lincoln's Political Rhetoric," *Modern Age* 23 (1979): 10, 11 (interpreting Lincoln's 1838 Springfield Lyceum speech to reveal his true aim – "radical alterations in the basis and organization of American society").

[110] Bradford, "Fire Bell," 9–10. For an earlier articulation of the view of Lincoln as a centralizing despot who had flagrantly violated the terms of the constitutional compact, see Alexander Stephens, *A Constitutional View of the Late War Between the States: Its Causes, Character, Conduct and Results, Presented in a Series of Colloquies at Liberty Hall*, Volume 2, 34 (1868) (www.archive.oig/dctails/constitutionalview02steprich).

Bradford characterized Lincoln's touchstone, the Declaration of Independence, as the nation's "one serious flirtation with the millennial thing."[111] Its legacy was made all the more damaging, he explained, through the influence of those who would read it by the light of "Jacobin 'translations.'"[112] Abraham Lincoln was Exhibit A in this regard, by dint of his "misunderstanding of the Declaration as [conferring] a 'deferred promise' of equality," and the Civil War struggle as having culminated in what amounts to a "second founding." This understanding, Bradford explained, was "fraught with peril and carries with it the prospect of an endless series of turmoils and revolutions, all dedicated to the freshly discovered meanings of equality as a 'proposition' – a juggernaut ... powerful enough to arm and enthrone any self-made Caesar we might imagine." Bradford asserted that Lincoln, who was "very early, touched by a Bonapartist sense of destiny," imagined himself in precisely such a role.[113]

The danger of Lincoln's outsized sense of destiny was heightened by his religiosity, Bradford warned, since men who see themselves as "authorized from on High to reform the world into an imitation of themselves – and to lecture and dragoon all who might object" are frighteningly zealous: "[they] receive regular intimations of the Divine Will through prophets who arise from time to time to recall them to their holy mission."[114] The biblical element in Lincoln's rhetoric grew stronger as his political career progressed, Bradford observed.[115] Lincoln's characteristic and, in Bradford's view, disingenuous method as a moralizer was to demonize his enemies while only grudgingly deigning to recognize their constitutional rights. The political implications of this method over the long term were dire because "should slavery be gone, some new infamy was bound to be discovered by the stern examiners whose power depends upon a regularity in such 'crusades.'"[116]

Bradford contended that there was, in truth, "no worship of the law whatsoever" in Lincoln's political thought, "but instead devotion to perpetually exciting goals, always just beyond our reach." As such, Lincoln was "an enemy of the 'founding'" who became "a scripture in himself," committed to "the attribution of his own opinions to an antinomian revelation of divine will."[117] He regarded himself as a great man, the oracle of a political religion – most famously articulated in his Peoria Speech – and

---

[111] Bradford, "Fire Bell," 15.   [112] Bradford, "Fire Bell," 15.
[113] M. E. Bradford, "The Heresy of Equality: Bradford Replies to Jaffa," *Modern Age* 20 (1976): 62, 69.
[114] Bradford, "Heresy of Equality," 69.
[115] See, e.g., Bradford, "Heresy of Equality," 71. Lincoln's 1858 "House Divided" speech took its titular metaphor from Mark 3:25 [King James Version]: "And if a house be divided against itself, that house cannot stand."
[116] Bradford, "Heresy of Equality," 71.   [117] Bradford, "Heresy of Equality," 71–72.

the wellspring of a political theology that would eventually "replace Church with State."[118]

In Lincoln's "House Divided" speech, Bradford explained, the self-dramatizing Lincoln went so far as to cast himself in the role of Old Testament prophet. It was in this high-prophetic mode that he alluded to "the eternal struggle between these two principles – right and wrong – throughout the world." "All that remained of his evolution" at this point, Bradford observed, "was a claim to direct communication with the god of history, of which we hear a great deal once Lincoln got the crisis which he wanted."[119]

In his study of Lincoln's political rhetoric, commenced under the tutelage of Eric Voegelin's *The New Science of Politics,* Bradford limned Lincoln as a "backcountry *philosophe,* as 'secularist intellectual' and 'rational, progressivist superman,'" a politician combining a "gnostic formula [with] a special neo-Puritan twist":[120] "For the stage to come according to [Lincoln's] political eschatology [as set out in his address to the Springfield Young Men's Lyceum (1838)] may augur *either* a final perfection *or* an apocalypse, a complete inversion of the fortunate American unfolding already accomplished. That which comes soon may be either the kingdom or the beast.'" This Lincoln, Bradford argued, seeks "not preservation but change: radical alterations in the basis and organization of American society."[121]

Many, Bradford claimed, have misidentified Lincoln with the freedom of the southern Negro and have been misled by Lincoln's populist, Jacksonian posturing.[122] By temperament, however, the real Lincoln was a maniacal, tax-and-spend Whig, and an ideologist, "a promising young centralist" who saw government as the roaring engine for the advancement of his vision. Whigs like Lincoln, Bradford explained, "were uniformitarians to the core ... Local feeling and variety were [their] enemies ... They connected both with the passions; and passion forestalled the evolution of the Union which, in standard progressive

---

[118] Bradford, "Dividing The House," 13, 17, arguing that, in his Peoria address, Lincoln abandons the foundational political principle of compromise and, in a messianic religious turn, offers apocalypse as a genuine alternative.

[119] Bradford, "Dividing the House," 19–20.

[120] Bradford, "Dividing the House," 11 (internal citations omitted). Among those conversant in conservative political thought, this critique of rationalism in politics would resonate with students of Michael Oakeshott. See Michael Oakeshott, "Rationalism in Politics" [1962], in his *Rationalism in Politics and Other Essays* (Indianapolis, IN: Liberty Fund, 1991), and of the critique of the political philosophy behind the French Revolution as described by, among others, Gertrude Himmelfarb, *The Roads to Modernity: The British, French, and American Enlightenments* (New York: Knopf, 2004); Jaffa, *Crisis of the House Divided,* 228–229.

[121] Bradford, "Dividing the House," 11.

[122] Bradford, "Dividing the House," 16, noting that the trouble with Lincoln devotees "is that they identify his politics with freedom of the Southern Negro ... [a]nd that belief leads them to misconstrue what was his larger purpose, from the first."

fashion, they defined more by what it could be than by what it was or had been."
"[T]he final Lincoln ... [was] the worst ... For by him the real is defined in terms
of what is yet to come, and the meaning of the present lies only in its pointing
thither. This posture, when linked to one of the regnant abstractions of modern
politics," Bradford warned, "can have no other result than a totalitarian
order."[123] Bradford lamented that in the Civil War's aftermath, the nation
might have committed itself to a "second founding" that was "digestible –
suited under certain circumstances to accommodation with the first."
"Emancipation appeared to have changed nothing substantial in the basic
confederal framework," he concluded, "[n]either did it attempt any
multiracial miracles." Unfortunately, however, for some, "the connection
between blacks and American millennialism [only] intensified" in the
postbellum United States, when "Equality (capital 'E')" was placed at the
center of their political understandings. With the arrival of the Rights
Revolution in the mid-twentieth century, the Civil War moment at last
became "the Trojan Horse of our homegrown Jacobinism."[124]

Rights Revolution egalitarianism was founded upon an uncompromising
denial of localism, "a hatred of plenitude ... a denial of the variety of
Creation, 'abolishing the constitution of being, with its origin in divine,
transcendent being, and replacing it with a world-immanent order of being,
the perfection of which lies in the realm of human action [and proceeds from
a human dream]."[125] "Pure millennialism of the gnostic sort," Bradford
warned, "is ... ever restless, never satisfied ... [It] entails the fracturing of

---

[123] Bradford, "Dividing the House," 13, 16, 21. Furthering his point, Bradford borrows directly
from Eric Voegelin's *The New Science of Politics*: "Totalitarianism, defined as the existential
rule of Gnostic activists, is the end and form of progressive civilization." Bradford, "Dividing
the House," 24 fn. 84 (citing Eric Voegelin, *The New Science of Politics: An Introduction*
(Chicago: University of Chicago Press, 1952), 132. Bradford notes, additionally, "This entire
essay is in obvious debt to Professor Voegelin's discussion of Richard Hooker's critique of the
Puritan mind, *New Science of Politics*, 133–152." Bradford, "Dividing the House," 24, fn. 85.
For a similar understanding of Lincoln as a proto-authoritarian/totalitarian, on the model of
Bismarck or Lenin, see also Edmund Wilson, *Patriotic Gore: Studies in the Literature of the
American Civil War* (New York: Oxford University Press, 1962), xviii–xix ("Each of these men
[referring to Bismarck, Lenin, and Lincoln], through the pressure of the power he found himself
exercising, became an uncompromising dictator."). Lest one think Voegelin's ideas are of mere
antiquarian interest, the Eric Voegelin Society (EVS) regularly sponsors a large number
of panels – wildly disproportionate, one might think, to their numbers – at the annual meeting
of the American Political Science Association to this day. The EVS is a discursive community
that is highly critical of the menace of the sort of "progressivism" that Voegelin had limned in
The New Science of Politics. They are, that is, conservatives in the age of Barack Obama and
Donald Trump.
[124] Bradford, "Fire Bell," 10. See also Raoul Berger, *Government by Judiciary: The Transformation
of the Fourteenth Amendment* (Cambridge, MA: Harvard University Press, 1977), 14.
[125] Bradford, "Fire Bell," 11 (quoting Eric Voegelin, *Science, Politics, and Gnosticism: Two Essays*
(Wilmington, DE: ISI Books, 2004) [1968], 99–100 (insertion in original)).

hard won communal bonds in the implementation of someone's private version of the supernal good; and in a pluralistic society, implementation of such visions is usually perceived as moralistic aggression."[126]

"As the South has always recognized," Bradford explained, "patronizing, 'for-the-Negro' millennialism has had its primary meaning and ultimate promise exposed in those other species of Utopian hope for which it broke trail ... [I]t has been a stalking horse for objectives never able to command national assent – never *except* as they hid behind or within the ... one 'sacred' cause."' When these are achieved, diversity, culture, and ultimately freedom are lost.[127]

MEL BRADFORD'S JAFFA

Bradford's most immediate targets in setting out these understandings were not left-liberals (who almost certainly would not be listening to him), but fellow movement conservatives – and, specifically, Harry V. Jaffa.[128] Jaffa's insistence on the centrality to the American constitutional tradition of "Equality, with the capital 'E,'" Bradford thundered, "is the antonym of every legitimate conservative principle." "[T]here is no man equal to any other," he insisted, "except perhaps in the special, and politically untranslatable, understanding of the Deity. *Not intellectually or physically or economically or even morally* ... Such is, of course, the genuinely self-evident proposition."[129] The mistaken commitment to equality, Bradford warned, will lead ineluctably to a demand for the equality of condition, as advanced by an increasingly all-powerful Leviathan, a docile, manipulated populace under the control of an army of

---

[126] Bradford, "Fire Bell," 11. Although Bradford did not deny that a millennialist thread had run through all of American history, he insisted that history taught nevertheless that "the total nation has, characteristically, despised and rejected who or whatever aspired to dragoon its way to such beatitudes through the instruments of federal policy." Bradford, "Fire Bell," 11–12. Bradford goes on to point out that the only full exception to this rule is the "civil rights revolution," citing "reverse discrimination, racial quotas, assignment of teachers and workers by color, grading by court order, federal involvement with zoning practices or intervention in the relocation of business firms" as "positive millennialist injunctions."

[127] Bradford, "Fire Bell," 13.

[128] See Harry V. Jaffa, "Equality as a Conservative Principle," *Loyola of Los Angeles Law Review* 8 (1975) 471, 476 (reviewing Kendall and Carey, *The Basic Symbols of the American Political Tradition*), where Jaffa counterposes, as against Kendall and Carey, that "We believe that the Declaration of Independence is the central document of our political tradition."

[129] Bradford, "Heresy of Equality," 62 (emphasis in original). Jaffa was himself responding to Kendall and Carey's *Basic Symbols of the American Political Tradition*. Jaffa, "Equality," 476. Jaffa rejected the charge that he had any truck with modern utopian egalitarian understandings of equality, which go "far beyond the scope of law, and sometimes were in flat contradiction to the principles of the earlier demands for full equality under law." Jaffa, *Crisis of the House Divided*, 11. Jaffa noted that Lincoln himself had disapproved of the "temper and ... methods" of radical reformism. Jaffa, *Crisis of the House Divided*, 245.

elites. Far from being conservative, this is nothing more than "the Old Liberalism hidden under a Union battle flag."[130]

Lincoln's distorted understandings of the Declaration of Independence were bad enough. But Bradford believed that the West Coast Straussian Harry Jaffa had only compounded Lincoln's error through "his treatment of the second sentence of that document in abstraction from its whole: indeed, of the first part of that sentence in abstraction from its remainder, to say nothing of the larger text." Jaffa, Bradford observed, "filters the rest of the Declaration (and later expressions of the American political faith) back and forth through the measure of that sentence until he has (or so he imagines) achieved its baptism in the pure waters of higher law." In doing so, he "sets up a false dilemma: we must be ... 'committed' to Equality or we are 'open to the relativism and historicism that is the theoretical ground of modern totalitarian regimes." Only a firm commitment to that single phrase of the Declaration, Jaffa has oddly concluded, will save us from Hitler and Stalin.[131] "I agree with Professor Jaffa concerning the dangers of relativism," Bradford wrote, "[a] Christian must." But, all the same, "we must resist the tendency to thrust familiar contemporary pseudo-religious notions back into texts where they are unlikely to appear."[132]

As a Straussian, Jaffa had insisted upon treating the "all men are created equal" clause "as one of Lincoln's beloved Euclidian propositions." Jaffa and his ilk "have approached the task of explication as if the Declaration existed, *sui generis,* in a Platonic empyrean." They treat the Founding and the Constitution the same way. But "the Declaration is not implicit in the Constitution except as it made possible free ratification by the independent states. In truth, many rights are secured under the Constitution that are not present in the Declaration, however it be construed."[133]

The sort of unreconstructed neo-confederatism that some have argued serves as the grounding for postwar American conservatism is certainly evident – albeit in a distinctive guise – in the thought of M. E. Bradford. Bradford's rejection of the opening lines of the Declaration of Independence as constitutional touchstones, and of Lincoln as a constitutional vindicator and savior, along with his insistence on narrowly interpreting the meaning of the Civil War as having effectuated no sharp break with the "confederal" antebellum constitutional order, place him squarely within this old conservative tradition. Even so, Bradford's insistence on characterizing Lincoln as a slave to the

---

[130] Bradford, "Heresy of Equality," 64. The ludicrousness of this all-too-characteristic Straussian move, Bradford observed, demonstrated the problems arising "from the habit of reading legal, poetic, and rhetorical documents as if they were bits of revealed truth or statements of systematic thought." Bradford, "Heresy of Equality," 64.

[131] Bradford, "Heresy of Equality," 64.   [132] Bradford, "Heresy of Equality," 65.

[133] Bradford, "Heresy of Equality," 65, 68. See also Kendall and Carey, *Basic Symbols of the American Political Tradition,* 89–90, arguing that it was the Constitution and not the Declaration of Independence that started our nation, and that the Declaration instead had "establish[ed] a baker's dozen of new sovereignties."

Utopian, "uniformitarian," and, ultimately, totalitarian millennial abstractions allegedly characteristic of twentieth-century progressives, demonstrates his decidedly modern concerns. That said, at the time he wrote, Bradford's star was dimming on the postwar Right, and Jaffa's – who stands about as far from neo-confederatism as imaginable – was clearly rising.

HARRY JAFFA'S LINCOLN

Whatever its virtues as a species of political thought considered in the abstract, M. E. Bradford's truculently localist, pro-southern, neo-confederate conservatism was not likely to have much of a political future in the immediate post–civil rights era, when the states' rights position was tied so closely to the lost causes of racism and segregation. President Reagan's withdrawal of Bradford's nomination to head the National Endowment for the Humanities was a clear indication that whatever the standing of such views within the precincts of the out-of-power Old Guard, this vision would not serve within a Right that now controlled the national government and had realistic, long-term hopes of retaining that power. Harry Jaffa's influence, by contrast, was ascendant.[134]

By the 1980s, Jaffa was hardly a new figure on the intellectual Right. Credited with penning the most famous line of Barry Goldwater's speech accepting the Republican nomination for president in 1964,[135] Jaffa first propounded his constitutional theory back in the 1950s in his magisterial interpretation of the Lincoln-Douglas debates, *Crisis of the House Divided*, and subsequently reiterated and evangelized for in countless articles, lectures, and reviews. As law school constitutional theorists became more influential, and conservative academics found their foothold in this new world by hawking their own trademarked theory of textual interpretation – "originalism" – the political scientist Jaffa later recast his views in the prevailing originalist idiom.[136]

The earlier Jaffa was no uncritical worshipper of the American Founding. His writings emphasized its incompleteness, the sad failing arising out of the

---

[134] The most famous case of the public ascent of the Straussians is that of the University of Chicago political philosopher Allan Bloom, whose *The Closing of the American Mind: How Higher Education Has Failed Democracy and Impoverished the Souls of Today's Students* (New York: Simon and Schuster, 1987) became a conservative cause célèbre.

[135] "Extremism in the defense of liberty is no vice ... And ... moderation in the pursuit of justice is no virtue." Barry Goldwater, Speech Accepting the Republican Nomination for President (July 16, 1964). Jaffa was paraphrasing Cicero. See Karl Hess, *Mostly on the Edge: An Autobiography* (Amherst, NY: Prometheus Books, 1999), 168–170.

[136] See Jaffa, *Original Intent and the Framers of the Constitution*; Jaffa, "Equality as a Conservative Principle," 504 ("The principles of the Declaration ... are present in the very first words of the Constitution as those words were understood by those who drafted and adopted it"); Jaffa, *Crisis of the House Divided*.

compromises the Founders had made with chattel slavery.[137] These compromises, Jaffa argued, represented a more fundamental "inability" or unwillingness on the part of the Founders to commit themselves in the Constitution to the eternal, unchanging, God-given principles that grounded the nation's Declaration of Independence.[138] Jaffa contended that the capacity of the people to govern themselves, democracy, is "demonstrated" when the nation commits itself to living under submission to the natural law ("the Laws of Nature and of Nature's God" referenced in the Declaration), which embodies objective standards of right and wrong.[139] It was Abraham Lincoln who, belatedly, had completed the Constitution by placing the Declaration's commitment to natural rights at its core, redeeming America's (nearly) fatally flawed Founding with "a new birth of freedom."[140]

Like all Straussians, Jaffa read the American constitutional tradition through the lens of classical political philosophy. Tracing the term for "constitution" used in the ancient Greek texts – *politeia* – Jaffa noted that, for Aristotle, a *polis* was a partnership in *politeia,* where *politeia* "is not the laws, but rather the animating principle of the laws, by virtue of which the laws are laws of a certain kind." In finding the "life principle of the nation" in the Declaration, Jaffa explained, Lincoln understood American constitutionalism in precisely the same way. For Lincoln, Jaffa observed, "the relation of the famous proposition to the Constitution and Union corresponded to the relation of soul to body."[141]

This story of national redemption, pivoting on Lincoln, informed not only Jaffa's account of emancipation but also his reading of the entire arc and spirit of American history, as instantiated in its constitutional politics, from the Founding to the present. That politics is imagined as involving a perpetual, epic, and millennial conflict between the partisans of (unredeemed) legal positivism and a (saved) polity anchored in an uncompromising faith in natural law; a conflict between self-government understood as embodying what the people *will,* and self-government as embodying a struggle for the polity's adoption of what it *ought to will.* Jaffa believed that the nation's very survival depended upon a perpetually renewed national commitment to a redeemed Constitution – a Constitution that embodied (through the

---

[137] See, e.g., Jaffa, *Crisis of the House Divided,* 14, which discusses the Founders' acknowledgment that slavery was in conflict with the doctrine of the American Revolution, and their failure to end it despite this.

[138] Jaffa, *Crisis of the House Divided,* 315.   [139] Jaffa, *Crisis of the House Divided,* 314–315.

[140] Lincoln spoke of the nation's "new birth of freedom" in his Gettysburg Address. President Abraham Lincoln, Gettysburg Address (November 19, 1863).

[141] Jaffa, *Crisis of the House Divided,* 330–332. Like many Straussians, Jaffa was trained in ancient classical languages and believed that the wisest and deepest political philosophy had been articulated by the ancient Greeks.

principles of the Declaration, as vindicated by Lincoln) fixed, eternal standards of equality, justice, and truth.[142]

This epic conflict and choice had been publicly argued in its most dramatic and sophisticated form in the Lincoln-Douglas debates, which Jaffa pronounced the world's greatest political and philosophic text. There, Lincoln and Douglas did no less than debate "the universal meaning of the Declaration."[143] "No political contest in history was more exclusively or passionately concerned with the character of the beliefs in which the souls of men were to abide," Jaffa dramatically claimed.[144] He added:

> Neither the differences which divided the Moslem and Christian at the time of the Crusades, nor the differences which divided Protestant and Catholic in sixteenth-century Europe, nor those which arrayed the crowned heads of Europe against the regicides of Revolutionary France were believed by the warring advocates to be more important to their salvation, individually and collectively.[145]

Jaffa found a direct parallel between the position Abraham Lincoln took in those debates and the conception of classical natural right propounded by Jaffa's teacher Leo Strauss in *Natural Right and History* (1953).[146] Considered by Jaffa "the greatest political philosopher of the 20th century,"[147] Strauss had "proved" in *Natural Right and History* that by attempting to replace faith with reason, modern, as opposed to classical, philosophy had "laid the foundation of modern atheistic totalitarianism, the most terrible form of tyranny in human experience." While studying Plato's *Republic* under the tutelage of the master at The New School for Social Research (before Strauss moved to the University of Chicago), Jaffa had "discovered ... that the issue between Lincoln and Douglas was in substance, and very nearly in form, identical with the issue between Socrates and Thrasymachus." Stephen Douglas's defense of "the golden calf of popular

---

[142] See Kesler, "Special Meaning," 850, noting Jaffa's commitment to fixed standards of truth and liberty. The mission of the students of Leo Strauss is to commit their lives to the discovery, and propagation, of these truths, and to the idea of the centrality of Truth to politics, and to the American nation. Kersch, "Ecumenicalism Through Constitutionalism," 7. See generally Strauss, *Natural Right and History*. Jaffa wrote in significant part in opposition to the constitutional theory being advanced by other conservatives emphasizing the bourgeois, commercial, middle-class nature of the American Revolution, like Martin Diamond and Irving Kristol, and the structural nature of the constitutional order, as well as to the Burkean, consensus account of US constitutional development propounded by Willmoore Kendall, and, of course, as discussed, of the neo-confederatism of M. E. Bradford. Kesler, "Special Meaning," 851–852, 855, 857–858. See generally Kersch, "Ecumenicalism Through Constitutionalism."

[143] Jaffa, *Crisis of the House Divided*, 308. Jaffa titled the fourteenth chapter of *Crisis of the House Divided* "The Universal Meaning of the Declaration of Independence."

[144] Jaffa, *Crisis of the House Divided*, 308.   [145] Jaffa, *Crisis of the House Divided*, 308.

[146] Jaffa, *Crisis of the House Divided*, 1.

[147] Harry V. Jaffa, "Faith and Reason," *New York Times* (July 3, 2011), at BR 16, reviewing Robert C. Bartlett, *Aristotle's Nichomachean Ethics* (Chicago: University of Chicago Press, 2011) (with Susan D. Collins).

sovereignty" was in essence the position that might makes right – that the majority not only *does* rule but *should,* without any objective standard of wrong and right to serve as its compass. "Lincoln, however, insisted that the case for popular government depended upon a standard of right and wrong independent of mere opinion and one which was not justified merely by the counting of heads": "Hence," Jaffa concluded, "the Lincolnian case for government of the people and by the people always implied that being for the people meant being for a moral purpose that informs the people's being."[148]

Lincoln, for Jaffa, was the world-historical figure who stood fast when the great nation he led was most "tempted to abandon its 'ancient faith.'" Through close readings of a number of Lincoln's speeches presented in the form of "Teachings" concerning foundational principles of politics, Jaffa gave Stephen Douglas his due. Jaffa insisted that Douglas recognized and acknowledged that chattel slavery was morally wrong, notwithstanding his support for popular sovereignty. As a matter of politics, however, Douglas committed himself to value neutrality. He believed that the substantive issues involving slavery were constitutionally consigned to the state and territorial governments, and, as such, slavery was best apprehended constitutionally as "a jurisdictional question."[149] In his study of Lincoln's *Address before a Young Men's Lyceum* (1838), Jaffa explained Lincoln's very different approach. For Lincoln, the question of the capability of the people to govern themselves "was always twofold: it referred both to the viability of popular political institutions and to their moral basis in the individual men who must make those institutions work." Moral institutions could only be made and sustained by individually moral men.[150]

Here, Jefferson's decision in the Declaration of Independence to substitute "the pursuit of happiness" for John Locke's protection for "property" in his similarly worded *Second Treatise on Civil Government* (1689) loomed large for Jaffa. This substitution in phrasing proved to Jaffa that the United States was founded on the principle of the pursuit of moral virtue. While his contemporaneous fellow conservatives Irving Kristol and Martin Diamond were insisting that the American Revolution was essentially a bourgeois enterprise aimed at mitigating worldly evils and providing for the pursuit of worldly pleasures, Jaffa interpreted the philosophical import of the Declaration's opening to have launched a polity committed to the aspirational pursuit of the supreme Good – to "a transcendental affirmation of what it *ought* to be." By advisedly substituting the phrase "pursuit of happiness" for the word "property," in other words, Jefferson had remedied a core theoretical defect in the political philosophy of Hobbes and Locke and committed the new nation to the pursuit of moral perfection, understood by the lights of objective truth. For

---

[148] Jaffa, *Crisis of the House Divided,* 2–4.   [149] Jaffa, *Crisis of the House Divided,* 2, 44.
[150] Jaffa, *Crisis of the House Divided,* 185–186. Abraham Lincoln, Address before a Young Men's Lyceum (January 27, 1838).

Jaffa, this was what the Lincoln-Douglas debates, occasioned by the question of the constitutional status of chattel slavery, were all about.[151]

Jaffa made clear that the issues at stake in those debates are "still the fundamental issues in American politics."[152] He expressed (and long continued to express – until his death in 2015) profound concern about whether contemporary Americans had the faith to avail themselves of their rich constitutional heritage. It was the high responsibility of students of Leo Strauss to fight for this ancient faith, whose preservation would do no less than determine Western civilization's survival.[153]

ROMAN CATHOLIC NATURAL LAW AND ERIC VOEGELIN'S METAPHYSICAL MYSTICISM

Jaffa's reading of the Declaration of Independence as positing a unified supreme Good, with the nature of rights, as with all else, to be understood in light of this Good, harmonized with Thomist Roman Catholic theology. M. E. Bradford had critically observed, on this score, that Jaffa was attempting to understand America through the lenses of systematic philosophy – treating the country as standing for a philosophical "proposition" from which all else followed logically, philosophically, and theologically (which Bradford considered a fundamentally flawed approach to conceptualizing the history and politics of nations). Jaffa, who was Jewish, however, had himself made the connection between his understandings and Roman Catholic theology. Drawing a parallel between the American Founders and seminal Catholic thinkers, Jaffa noted early on that "whatever their differences," Thomas Aquinas and Thomas Jefferson "shared a belief concerning the relationship of political philosophy to political authority that neither shared with the last ten presidents of the American Political Science Association. It seemed to me that both believed it was the task of political philosophy to articulate the principles of political right, and therefore to teach the teachers of legislators, of citizens, and of statesmen the principles in virtue of which political power becomes political authority." Unlike modern social scientists and contemporary relativist, positivist progressive/liberals, both Jefferson and Aquinas were committed to the position that there are objective standards of right and wrong. Both believed, moreover, that democratic politics, properly understood, involved the advancement of the right and the Good: "the laws of nature mentioned in the Declaration."[154]

---

[151] Harry V. Jaffa, "Another Look at the Declaration," *National Review* 32 (1980): 836, 840. Kesler, "Special Meaning," 851–852. Jaffa, *Crisis of the House Divided*, 321 (emphasis in original).
[152] Jaffa, *Crisis of the House Divided*, 7.
[153] Jaffa, "Faith and Reason"; Jaffa, "Another Look at the Declaration," 836, 840.
[154] Jaffa, *Crisis of the House Divided*, 9, 11.

Catholic theologians took up the matter directly, without any necessary recourse to Leo Strauss. Not all of these were conservatives – but many were, and they published in conservative outlets.[155] The most prominent Catholic natural law theorist writing about the American constitutional order was John Courtney Murray, SJ,[156] a Jesuit theologian at the now defunct Woodstock College (which was absorbed into Georgetown University), and frequent contributor to the Jesuit magazine *America,* who, in his landmark statement of Catholic Declarationism, *We Hold These Truths: Catholic Reflections on the American Proposition* (1960), proposed a synthesis of Catholic natural law and American constitutional law that would place Roman Catholics at the heart of the American political and constitutional tradition.[157]

Murray was not easily classified politically in the early 1960s, just as he is not easily classified politically today. While Murray's thought has many attractions for contemporary conservatives, in his own time Murray's work was not aligned with conservatism: he challenged not only the Church hierarchy, which silenced him for a period, but also the core convictions of the nation's most conservative lay Catholics, who were convinced that American democratic liberalism was hopelessly incompatible with Catholic teaching. As the first major Catholic theologian to argue aggressively for the virtues of religious liberty, pluralism, the "distinction" between church and state, and the secular state, Murray was celebrated in his day by liberals and remains an important touchstone for Catholic liberals today. In time, despite earlier run-ins with the Church's reactionary hierarchy, Murray played a pivotal role in the Vatican II conclave that, in line with the views he had been advancing, modernized the Church's teachings. At the very moment when the United States was electing its first Catholic president, Murray, who was prominent enough to have his picture grace the cover of *Time* magazine, demonstrated through systematic philosophic argument starting with the principles articulated in the opening lines of the Declaration of Independence that good Catholics could be good Americans.[158]

The claim, indeed, went further, in a way that contemporary right-wing Catholics have picked up on aggressively. As the late Peter Augustine Lawler

---

[155] See, e.g., William J. Ellos, SJ, "Natural Law: A Phenomenological Essay in Defense of a Tradition," *Modern Age* 10:3 (Summer 1966): 261–268, 264. There were, however, a few clerical Straussians, the most prominent being the Boston College theologian Father Ernest L. Fortin (1923–2002).

[156] The discussion of John Courtney Murray, SJ, in this section is drawn, somewhat revised, from Ken I. Kersch, "Beyond Originalism: Conservative Declarationism and Constitutional Redemption," *Maryland Law Review* 71 (2011): 229–282.

[157] John Courtney Murray, SJ, *We Hold These Truths: Catholic Reflections on the American Proposition* (Lanham, MD: Rowman and Littlefield, 2005)[New York: Sheed and Ward, 1960].

[158] *Time* (December 12, 1960). See Peter Augustine Lawler, "John Courtney Murray as Catholic American Conservative," in Ethan Fishman and Kenneth L. Deutsch, editors, *The Dilemmas of American Conservatism* (Lexington: University Press of Kentucky, 2010).

(1951–2017), an influential contemporary Catholic conservative political theorist, noted, it was John Courtney Murray's conviction that *"only* the Catholic community," with its richer and deeper tradition and carefully cultivated systematic philosophy and theology, "could illuminate what was true and good about what our founders accomplished."[159] Who better than a Catholic theologian trained in natural law to explain to Americans the true meaning of the Declaration of Independence, as elaborated by its most profound and fervent proponent, Abraham Lincoln, "our most ambitious and philosophic president?" "If veneration for the true accomplishment of our political Fathers is the standard of citizenship," Lawler argued, "those within the Catholic natural-law community of thought are the least alienated of Americans today." "*Only* a Thomistic or natural-law understanding," Lawler claimed (following John Courtney Murray), "can make sense of our framers' accomplishment."[160]

Lawler argued, moreover, that far from being divisive, the Thomist philosophical method provides a common ground for discussions between Evangelical Protestants, with their emphasis on Revelation, and secular humanists, who prize Reason. Since its animating purpose is to synthesize Reason and Revelation (or, as Straussians put it in one of their animating tropes, "Athens and Jerusalem"), Thomism is the best available framework for appreciating, understanding, and explicating the implications of the American Founding and the US Constitution – or, indeed, of the meaning and creed of the American nation itself.[161]

In *We Hold These Truths,* Murray described the Declaration of Independence's statement that "all men are created equal" as a "theorem" or "proposition," "immortally asserted by Abraham Lincoln." The book is a Thomist exegesis of the nature and implications of this theorem or proposition, which Murray pronounced to be, indisputably, the rock upon which the American nation was built. Murray noted:

[159] Peter A. Lawler, "Critical Introduction," to Murray, *We Hold These Truths*, 2.
[160] Lawler, "Critical Introduction," 3, 4, 13 [emphasis added]. Similarly, the contemporary conservative intellectual historian Wilfred McClay defiantly, and rightly, concludes, "It would require a monumental misreading of Murray to attribute to him anything like a full-scale capitulation to contemporary American political and cultural life ... Murray's Catholicism came first. Rather than trim Catholicism's sails to fit American democratic sensibilities, he argued for the possibility that one could affirm American democratic institutions on a basis entirely faithful to the Catholic distinctives – one that might constitute a deeper and more satisfactory basis for that affirmation and aim not to destroy the founders' work but to fulfill it by addressing its inadequacies." Wilfred McClay, "The Catholic Moment in American Social Thought," in R. Scott Appleby and Kathleen Sprows Cummings, editors, *Catholics in the American Century: Casting Narratives of US History* (Ithaca, NY: Cornell University Press, 2012), 149–151. See Robert A. Orsi, "US Catholics between Memory and Modernity: How Catholics are American," in Appleby and Cummings, *Catholics in the American Century*, 15.
[161] Lawler, "Critical Introduction," 22.

Today, when the serene and often naive certainties of the eighteenth century have crumbled, the self-evidence of truths may legitimately be questioned. What ought not to be questioned, however, is that the American Proposition rests on the forthright assertion of a realist epistemology. The sense of the famous phrase is simply this: "There are truths, and we hold them, and we here lay them down as the basis and inspiration of the American project, this constitutional commonwealth." To our Fathers the political and social life of man did not rest upon such tentative empirical hypotheses as the postitivist might cast up ... The structure of the state was not ultimately defined in terms of a pragmatic calculus ... [T]hey thought the life of man in society under government is founded on ... a certain body of objective truth, universal in its import, accessible to the reason of man, definable, defensible. If this assertion is denied, the American Proposition is ... eviscerated at one stroke.[162]

While the American Proposition as stated in the Declaration and re-affirmed by Lincoln in his Gettysburg Address may have once truly been "self-evident," that was no longer clearly the case. Hard demonstrative intellectual, and perhaps political, work needed to be done.

The next natural question – especially in a vibrant democracy, where all power tends to be claimed by the *demos* – was "Do we hold these truths because they are true, or are these truths true because we hold them?" Murray answered the former: the truths are held because they are true, not simply because (in a democratic, majoritarian, consensus spirit) most people happened to believe them. That the American Proposition is true "is a truth that lies beyond politics; it imparts to politics a fundamental human meaning. I mean the sovereignty of God over nations as well as over individual men."[163]

As a nation firmly anchored in a commitment to God's sovereignty, the nation "was conceived [by its Founders] in the tradition of natural law." This was the case whatever the religion (or lack of religion) of those Founders: as Murray explained, they built better than they knew. This made Saint Thomas Aquinas truly "the first Whig," and natural law "the first structural rib of American constitutionalism." As a consequence, the American tradition of free government pivots on the "profound conviction that only a virtuous people can be free."[164]

It is a commitment to this principle, Murray continued, "that radically distinguishes the conservative Christian tradition of America from the Jacobin laicist tradition of Continental Europe," the latter of which worships the presumed autonomy of man, and his all-powerful individual reason. We know that people are virtuous only when they are "inwardly governed by the recognized imperatives of the universal moral law." This, of course, affects the way that rights are to be understood within the American constitutional tradition. It is a fact that "[t]he American Bill of Rights ... [is] the product of Christian history .... The 'man' whose rights are guaranteed in the face of law

---

[162] Murray, *We Hold These Truths*, viii–ix.   [163] Murray, *We Hold These Truths*, 28.
[164] Murray, *We Hold These Truths*, 28, 31–32, 36, 98, 106–107.

and government is, whether he knows it or not, the Christian man, who had learned to know his own personal dignity in the school of Christian faith."[165] As such, the content of those rights can only be defined and understood in light of the nature of the supreme Good, as set out in universal natural law. This places natural law philosophy at the center of the inquiry into the nature and proper application of the Bill of Rights.

While there is nothing inherently Catholic about natural law, Murray explained that the natural law tradition and, hence, the American constitutional tradition, finds its "intellectual home within the Catholic Church." "Catholic participation in the American consensus," Murray observed proudly, "has been full and free, unreserved and unembarrassed, because the contents of that consensus – the ethical and political principles drawn from the tradition of natural law – approve themselves to the Catholic intelligence and conscience." While mainline Protestantism may have moved away from the old English and American tradition in this regard, its foundations are "native" to Catholics. On the fundamentals, the "Fathers of the Church and the Fathers of the American Republic" were of one mind.[166]

Particularly in the modern context, Catholics had a special role to play as guardians of the foundations of the American Republic. No society without a substantive core can ever long survive, and, in the modern context of pluralism and democracy, the truths set out in the Declaration of Independence, according to Murray, articulate that core. Catholic natural law philosophy helps us understand and appreciate the nature of that core and its indispensability in the deepest possible way.[167]

These understandings have evinced a special attraction for the contemporary Catholic Right. As we have seen, they also harmonize extensively with Straussianism, which has a considerable influence in conservative intellectual and public policy circles, including magazine and book publishing, television (Fox News), and the internet. Drawing a sharp distinction between themselves and positivists, relativists, secular progressive liberals, and leftists, these conservatives emphasize their grounding in the timeless, unchanging, and transcendent Truths, as discerned through application of reason.

These conservatives emphasize that other nations – most notably, Hitler's Germany and Marxist totalitarian states like the Soviet Union – had no such grounding, with results that led to some of the worst catastrophes in human history. Straussians and the contemporary American Catholic Right suspect that secular progressives, in their denial of the natural law foundations of the American nation and its constitutional traditions, have more in common with America's greatest twentieth-century enemies than with its eighteenth-century Founders, whose principles were set out in the Declaration of Independence's

[165] Murray, We Hold These Truths, 39.　[166] Murray, We Hold These Truths, 39–41, 43.
[167] Murray, We Hold These Truths, 42–43, 74–75.

opening lines, or its Constitution, as redeemed by Lincoln through his rededication to the principles of the Declaration.[168]

To many on the Right, the situation is grave indeed, not just for America but also for the world. As the right-wing priest Father James Schall, SJ, a political philosopher at Georgetown University, warned in a review of one of Harry Jaffa's books:

> The American situation ... bears witness to a broader civilizational crisis ... [W]hen a universal civilization doubts that there are universal principles, the civilization built on them largely ceases to exist ... If America has now adopted relativist principles to replace those of its founding, then by retaining its universal sense of mission, it spreads profound disorder throughout the world wherever it may exercise its influence.[169]

On this, Father Schall observed admiringly, "Jaffa ... writes with the vigor and wrath of a prophet." For Schall, a conservative Thomist, it was Jaffa who taught us to see how contemporary liberals and progressives are the legatees of Stephen A. Douglas, while Catholic conservatives and their conservative evangelical and Fundamentalist Christian (and LDS/Mormon) allies were anchored firmly in the principles of unchanging natural law and stand proudly in the shoes of Lincoln.[170]

For his part, Eric Voegelin (1901–1985), a figure many conservatives have considered "a Columbus [of] the realms of the spirit,"[171] insisted similarly, as against the thrust of modern liberalism, that an ontological grounding was indispensible to political theory. Like Leo Strauss, Voegelin was a German émigré scholar, in Voegelin's case fleeing his position on the faculties of Law and Political Science at the University of Vienna one step ahead of the Nazis. A doctoral student of the eminent legal theorist Hans Kelsen, Voegelin's position in Vienna had become increasingly untenable because of his implacable opposition to Nazi racial theories. Voegelin taught for many years at Louisiana State University, returning for a short time to his native Germany

---

[168] See, e.g., Richard Sherlock, "The Secret of Straussianism," *Modern Age* 48 (2006): 208–211; Media Matters for America, quoting Bill O'Reilly, *The Radio Factor* (Fox News Radio, November 28, 2005) (http://mediamatters.org/mmtv/200511300007) (comparing the modern secular progressive movement to twentieth century totalitarian regimes, and claiming that "[i]n every secular progressive country, they've wiped out religion ... Joseph Stalin, Adolf Hitler, Mao Zedong, Fidel Castro, all of them. That's the first step. Get religion out of there, so that we can impose our big-government progressive agenda").

[169] James J. Schall, SJ, "Original Intent and the Framers of the Constitution: A Disputed Question," *Loyola Law Review* 41 (1995): 77–85, 79 (reviewing Harry V. Jaffa, *Original Intent and the Framers of the Constitution: A Disputed Question* (Washington, DC: Regnery Gateway, 1994)).

[170] Schall, "Original Intent," 81.

[171] Dante Germino, "Eric Voegelin's Contribution to Contemporary Political Theory," *The Review of Politics* 26:3 (July 1964): 378–402, 378. See Voegelin, *New Science of Politics*; Voegelin, *Science, Politics, and Gnosticism*; Eric Voegelin, *Order and History* (Baton Rouge: Louisiana University Press, 1956–1987) (Vols. I–IV).

as Max Weber Professor of Political Science at the University of Munich, before decamping once again for the United States, where he died during his tenure as the Henry Salvatori Distinguished Scholar at Stanford University's Hoover Institution. Like Strauss, Voegelin was preoccupied with what the twentieth-century European catastrophe they fled had revealed about the nature and trajectory of Western civilization and the "crisis of man."[172] And, like Strauss, Voegelin identified the rot at Western civilization's core as stemming from its abandonment of its moral foundations. Like the Straussians, Voegelin found those foundations in ancient political theory – Plato and Aristotle, in particular – but also, more than many Straussians (the issue is disputed), in the West's Christian heritage. As such, while there are many divergences and differences in counterposing Voegelinianism and Straussianism, the two schools have extensive affinities and share core intellectual and political preoccupations. Both are preoccupied with the crisis of the West (with Nazism, European fascism, and totalitarianism more generally as the clarifying, symptomatic evils), and both root that crisis in an abandonment of foundational moral Truths. In doing so, both Voegelinians and Straussians posit an opposition between a well-ordered ancient (and, to a lesser extent, medieval) world and a disordered modern one (the orienting Straussian opposition between "Ancients" and "Moderns") and devote sustained effort to calibrating the appropriate balance between (Human) Reason and (Transcendent) Revelation (for Straussians, "Athens and Jerusalem") in a well-ordered soul and polity. In doing so, moreover, both make a grudging decision to bear the burden of contemplating the ways in which a tragic but likely inevitable modernity can incorporate enough of the classical or Christian heritage in its sinews to instantiate, if not a good, then at least a good-enough society, conducive, to the extent possible, to human flourishing worthy of pride and allegiance.

Voegelin's theories are notoriously abstruse, with their intricacies debated within a redoubtable scholarly literature.[173] The essence of his complex, idiosyncratic, and esoteric theory of politics starts from a positivist empirical inquiry into the nature of "political reality."[174] Given the nature of that

---

[172] See Mark Greif, *The Age of the Crisis of Man: Thought and Fiction in America, 1933–1973* (Princeton: Princeton University Press, 2016); Lt. Colonel Montgomery C. Erfourth, "The Voegelin Enigma," *The American Interest* (December 10, 2014).

[173] See, e.g., Michael Federici, *Eric Voegelin: The Restoration of Order* (Wilmington, DE: ISI Press, 2002); Ted McAllister, *Revolt Against Modernity: Leo Strauss, Eric Voegelin, and the Search for a Post-Liberal Order* (Lawrence: University Press of Kansas, 1996); Mark Lilla, *The Shipwrecked Mind: On Political Reaction* (New York: New York Review Books, 2016); Gerhart Niemeyer, "Eric Voegelin's Philosophy and the Drama of Mankind," *Modern Age* 20 (Winter 1976); David Walsh, "Eric Voegelin and Our Disordered Spirit," *The Review of Politics* 57 (Winter 1995), 134.

[174] As Voegelin scholars have noted and discussed, the political philosopher's focus on lived reality seems to have been arrived at in part through the influence of the French philosopher Henri Bergson. On Bergson, particularly setting his views against that of the grand ambitions of

reality, the next question is how to live best within it. Voegelin's answer was that, given the nature of things, living well in political society required a core rootedness in "the ground of being" – the divine. In its classical and Christian phases, Western civilization was born and then built on this rock-solid ground of foundational Truths. This groundedness provided the basis for Western civilization's glories and achievements. Somewhere along the path, however, Western civilization had lost its way. A civilization that had once confidently adhered to and professed Truth had been enticed by the allure of "Gnosticism." Gnosticism promised that man could save himself and reach the highest realms of civilizational and personal accomplishment through his own knowledge and ambition (*gnosis* is Greek for "knowledge"). Western man turned from the ground of being and, through secular utopian visions of making a Heaven on Earth for himself, aspired to replace the "divine as the basis of order" by "man as the maker of order" (even conservatives who know little of the intricacies of the Voegelinian philosophy might be familiar with his most famous injunction against civilization-destroying utopian ambitions: "Don't immanetize the eschaton!").[175] Western civilization's emblematic catastrophes that had sought to do just that were Nazism and Communism (more recent Voegelinian writings identify progressivism, egalitarianism, Freudianism, [Millian] civil libertarianism, and feminism as ideological successors to Nazism and Communism).[176] A core, and related, error in the modern science of politics was to remain resolutely positivist, exiling questions of God's higher Truth, Higher Law, and the nature and requirements of the transcendent moral order, which provided indispensable aspirational goals and external constraints on the behavior and aspiration of man (unreliable but ostensible interpretations of the transcendent, Voegelin recognized, were also a problem).[177] And a core problem of a social order based on the modern science of politics is a denial of the truth that "a social order remains stable only to the extent that the bedrock moral and

a purely positivist science (as championed, e.g., by Albert Einstein), see Jimena Canales, *The Physicist and the Philosopher: Einstein, Bergson, and the Debate That Changed the Understanding of Time* (Princeton: Princeton University Press, 2016).

175 Erfourth, "Voegelin Enigma." This warning against the profound civilizational threat of the Icarian grasp at utopia is a theme that appears repeatedly in different strains of conservatism, whether in the anti-socialist polemics of Voegelin's Viennese compatriot Friedrich von Hayek's *The Road to Serfdom* (Chicago: University of Chicago Press, 1944), Whittaker Chambers's anti-communist testament *Witness* (New York: Random House, 1952), or thousands of statements in conservative public life – including, now, across the internet – that identify the modern American redistributive, administrative social welfare state as "the thin edge of the wedge" of one or the other form of totalitarian catastrophe. See Thomas Hoerber, *Hayek v. Keynes: A Battle of Ideas* (London: Reaktion Books, 2017), 3–11.

176 Glenn N. Schram, "The New Gnosticism: The Philosopher Eric Voegelin Finds an Old Christian Heresy to Be Very Much Alive," *Crisis Magazine* (November 1, 1990).

177 This was a major concern of Leo Strauss's as well. See Herbert J. Storing and Leo Strauss, *Essays on the Scientific Study of Politics* (New York: Holt, Rinehart and Winston, 1962).

legal-political traditions of western civilization remain intact."[178] One novel dimension of Voegelin's understanding which is not purely idealistic (in a philosophical sense) is that it takes extensive account of history: Voegelin held that the Truth is represented and conveyed not simply in esoteric texts accessible only to a philosophical elite (as for the Straussians),[179] but rather in a particular culture's political, cultural, and religious traditions. Thus, for Voegelin, "[t]he crisis of western civilization [is manifested in] the steady decay of truth in the symbols of order rooted in philosophic and spiritual traditions."[180] The truths of the "order of being" are represented symbolically in diverse societies in diverse ways, helping to constitute that society's unique consciousness. As such, understanding the science of politics required an acute awareness of existence spanning multiple dimensions of human experience, some of which, crucially, were transcendental, and thus knowable only through faith.[181]

In its insistence on the application of reason in conjunction with faith, in pursuit of the path to the well-ordered individual soul-in-community, Voegelin's project also shared the core preoccupations and approach of Roman Catholic theology. Voegelin's at times mystical work called upon individuals to order their souls according to reason, as discerned through this portal of multidimensional understanding, and for society – what Straussians call "the regime" – to be organized (governed/ruled) in a way that reflected and honored these imperatives.[182] As such, Straussians, conservative Catholics, and Voegelinians cohered into an intellectual community on the Right – debating and disagreeing, certainly – but nevertheless preoccupied with many of the same issues and sharing the same presuppositions.

Eric Voegelin himself, like Straussians and conservative Catholics, worried about the tendency of liberal democracies toward materialism and to relegating

---

[178] Erfourth, "Voegelin Enigma."
[179] Leo Strauss, *Persecution and the Art of Writing* (Glencoe, IL: The Free Press, 1952). See Arthur M. Meltzer, *Philosophy Between the Lines: The Lost History of Esoteric Writing* (Chicago: University of Chicago Press, 2014). For a highly critical account, notorious to Straussians, see S. B. Drury, "The Esoteric Philosophy of Leo Strauss," *Political Theory* 13 (August 1985): 315–337. See also Michael L. Frazer, "Esotericism Ancient and Modern," *Political Theory* 34 (February 2006): 33–61. See generally, Shadia B. Drury, *The Political Ideas of Leo Strauss* (London: MacMillan Press, 1988); Shadia B. Drury, *Leo Strauss and the American Right* (New York: St. Martin's Press, 1997).
[180] Erfourth, "Voegelin Enigma." This Voegelinian dimension is reflected in the title of Kendall and Carey's *The Basic Symbols of the American Political Tradition*. See generally "The Eric Voegelin-Willmoore Kendall Correspondence," *The Political Science Reviewer* 33 (2004).
[181] J. M. Porter, "Eric Voegelin: A Philosopher's Journey," *The University Bookman* 18 (Summer 1978).
[182] Germino, "Eric Voegelin's Contribution," 378, 379. Voegelin's views were heavily influenced by Bergson's emphasis on a mystical, experiential, intuitive, as opposed to purely analytic, understanding of the world. Far from being necessarily traditionalist in their implications, Bergson's theories helped inform the birth of modern art.

religion to the private sphere. But, nevertheless, like Leo Strauss himself, and most American Straussians, and like John Courtney Murray, SJ, and his followers on the Roman Catholic Right, Eric Voegelin and the Voegelinians decided to become confirmed, and even passionate, if unillusioned, defenders of US-style liberal constitutional democracy. All three groups did so despite the fact that, ultimately, they were not liberals. In fact, as Michael and Catherine Zuckert have detailed at length, the Straussians have become the leading defenders on the Right of US liberal constitutionalism. Most conservative Catholics today understand themselves to be passionate constitutional patriots. And, indeed, Voegelin's short-lived postwar return to Germany after living in the United States was in part motivated by a desire to spread US constitutional values to Germany and Western Europe. Of this too, now, they see themselves as centurions zealously guarding a Truth, in the spirit of righteous mission, aimed at civilizational and constitutional restoration and redemption.[183]

REACTING AGAINST THE WARREN COURT: THE POLITICAL INDETERMINACY OF METHODS AND PROCESS-BASED CONSTITUTIONAL THEORY

Given its focus on the relatively high-level conservative constitutional theory and political thought in the postwar period that, while prominent in movement outlets in both sophisticated and popularized form, has heretofore remained all but invisible to outsiders, this chapter, so far, has scanted on the more concrete, applied constitutional thought prompted by the era's Supreme Court rulings and political constitutional controversies. While the chapters that follow in this book are more concrete than this one, I will discuss more immediate constitutional thought more systematically in the two books that will follow the more abstracted overview of conservative thought, theory, and narrative (stories) presented here. The first of these, as noted, will canvas the conservative constitutionalism of government powers, structures, and institutions. The second will canvas the conservative constitutionalism of civil rights and civil liberties. In closing out this chapter, however, it will perhaps be useful to hover a bit closer to earth by looking at least at the way that some of the movement's big picture theorists reacted to contemporaneous events by invoking their broader constitutional understandings and visions.

The liberal decisions of the Warren Court, of course, hit conservatives – and those who did not then consider themselves conservatives but found themselves reacting in ways that were similar to conservatives – hard, provoking an intense reaction. Writing in *Modern Age*, for instance, the indubitably conservative Willmoore Kendall worried that the Right had been caught flat-footed:

---

[183] Erfourth, "Voegelin Enigma."

[T]he prayer decision [*Engel v. Vitale* (1962)] has caught the Conservatives intellectually unprepared – just as, in 1954, the school desegregation decision caught them unprepared intellectually; and just as, hard after the turn of the century, the Liberal attack on the American Political System ... caught them unprepared intellectually. American Conservatism ... seems to be in the *business* of being unprepared intellectually for the next thrust of the Liberal Revolution; the conservatives never do their homework until they have flunked the exam.[184]

Kendell lamented in 1964 that while "[l]iberal intellectuals ... have developed a theoretical base from which, carrying their rank and file with them, they can strike right to the heart of each issue as it presents itself," conservatives "are a movement ... rent not merely by divided counsels, but also by sharply conflicting views of political reality and, above all, of the American political system itself, and the proper role of Conservatives with respect to its proper functioning, its good health, and its preservation."[185]

Kendall especially lamented the state of intellectually serious conservative *constitutional* thought. While conservatives had long been adept at what had once been called "stand pattism" – stonewalling, "planting your feet in the mud and saying to the enemy 'You shall advance no further'" – they were hopeless at the sort of "elaboration and implementation of Conservative solutions ... through [the] skillful and realistic analysis only conservative intellectuals can provide ... if they are good at their job."[186] "We ... must stop frittering away our energies in *argument* with the Supreme Court – whether about the intention of the Framers of the Constitution and the First Amendment ... or about the 'clear meaning' of the words ... Concretely, we must withdraw from the great current debate on the so-called 'broad' interpretation versus the so-called 'narrow' interpretation," he thundered.[187] Conservatives must (in the recent parlance of Robert Post and Reva Siegel) develop a serious, comprehensive substantive vision.

From a contemporary vantage point, it is notable that in surveying the conservative movement's constitutional thought in the mid-1960s, Kendall saw no defining thought at all – just feckless *ad hoc* reaction. For Kendall, at least, originalism ("the intention of the Framers of the Constitution"), textualism ("clear meaning"), and strict constructionism ("the so-called 'narrow' interpretation") neither cohered as a program, nor were they intrinsically "conservative." This is because, as Kendall sagely recognized, pre-Bork, pre-Berger, and pre-Scalia, the prevailing state of constitutional theory was ideologically and intellectually inchoate: none of these postures, methods, and approaches at the time were uniquely claimed by conservatives or, relatedly,

---

[184] Willmoore Kendall, "American Conservatism and the 'Prayer' Decisions," *Modern Age* 8:3 (Summer 1964): 245–259, 250. *Engel* v. *Vitale*, 370 US 421 (1962).

[185] Kendall, "American Conservatism and the 'Prayer' Decisions," 250.

[186] Kendall, "American Conservatism and the 'Prayer' Decisions," 250.

[187] Kendall, "American Conservatism and the 'Prayer' Decisions," 250–251.

understood as necessarily leading to distinctively conservative results. While this is not the place to survey the era's contemporaneous liberal constitutional theory, given the beginning of its ascendency on the Right as *the* defining – and presumably effective – constitutional theory just a few years later, it is worth recalling that, at the time Kendall wrote, both originalism and textualism were equally claimed by at least some prominent constitutional theorists on the liberal-left. Neither, moreover, was understood to necessarily entail strict or "narrow" as opposed to "broad" constructionism.

As it happens, the first modern academic defense of originalism as an "ism"[188] – that is, as the only legitimate method for interpreting the constitutional text – in the guise of originalist textualism was by the University of Chicago Law School's Professor William Winslow Crosskey, who was not a conservative. Writing during the genesis and aftermath of the New Deal, Crosskey's chief goal was to place *broad* understandings of Congress's powers, particularly the commerce power, on a firm constitutional footing. As early as the 1930s, frustrated with the constitutional resistance being mounted against Franklin Delano Roosevelt's governing program, Crosskey had become convinced that the US Constitution was "the most misunderstood and misconstrued document ever written." A Chicago colleague later recalled, "Bill was quite sure that Congress had the constitutional power to do all the things the administration was backing in those days ... and he suddenly decided that he would write something to show them how they could do it."[189]

Appearing after an extended period of herculean scholarly labor, the result was the two-volume *Politics and the Constitution* (1953), which Crosskey dedicated "to the Congress of the United States, In the Hope that it May Be Led to Claim and Exercise for the Common Good of the Country the Powers Justly Belonging To It Under the Constitution." The book's opening stated the author's intention to "propound a unitary theory of the Constitution based, in part, upon the antecedent usage of the words in which the document is cast, and based, for the rest, upon certain legal and political ideas of the period in which the Constitution was written."[190]

Reviewing *Politics and the Constitution* the following year, Cornell Law School's William Tucker Dean was gobsmacked by Crosskey's originalist thesis, commenting with patent wonder at "[t]his simple plan, so simple that it is astounding no one pursued it before in the constitutional area."[191]

---

[188] James Fleming, *Fidelity to Our Imperfect Constitution: For Moral Readings and Against Originalisms* (New York: Oxford University Press, 2015), 3–4.

[189] Charles O. Gregory, "William Winslow Crosskey: As I Remember Him," *University of Chicago Law Review* 35 (Winter 1968): 243–247, 245.

[190] William W. Crosskey, *Politics and the Constitution in the History of the United States* (Chicago: University of Chicago Press, 1953) (2 vols.), 13–14.

[191] William Tucker Dean, "Review of Crosskey, Politics and the Constitution in the History of the United States," *American Bar Association Journal* 40 (1954): 314–316.

Crosskey's student Abe Krash also set out to describe this new animal invented by Crosskey, who "believed the Constitution could properly be understood only in the context of the actual events which preceded it and in light of the politics and economics, the law and the language of the age when it was written. [Crosskey] maintained that the Constitution should be interpreted as it was understood by an intelligent, well informed person in 1787."[192] "The problem he sets out to answer," Krash explained, "is this: How was the Constitution understood by an intelligent, well informed person when the document was drafted in 1787?" To answer this question, the professor "made an exhaustive survey of the eighteenth century American newspapers, pamphlets, public documents, correspondence, and the like ... With painstaking care, Crosskey ... reconstructed the locution of 1787. Applying the word-meanings of that period, he shows that the Constitution was an internally consistent, carefully constructed document."[193]

Krash later described Crosskey as having thrown "down the gauntlet to legal scholars on a number of fronts": "[Crosskey] dismissed the concept of an amorphous 'living' Constitution as a legal absurdity. He maintained that the historical, intended meaning of the Constitution could be demonstrated with a high degree of certainty, a point of view at odds with prevailing theories of documentary interpretation which stress ambiguity."[194] Crosskey, moreover, declared that any departure by judges from the application of original meaning amounted to little more than "politics" and should be considered an "illegitimate" exercise of judicial power (hence the book's title).[195] Over the course of its history, Crosskey lamented, the Court frequently engaged in politics, betraying the Constitution's true, original meaning.[196] While *Politics and the Constitution* was widely noticed, serious historians of the time regarded it as little more than hectoring and dogmatic law office history in which original

---

[192] Abe Krash, "William Winslow Crosskey," *University of Chicago Law Review* 35 (Winter 1968): 232–237, 234.

[193] Abe Krash, "A More Perfect Union: The Constitutional World of William Winslow Crosskey," *University of Chicago Law Review* 21 (Autumn 1953): 1–23, 2. See also Abe Krash, "The Legacy of William Crosskey," *Yale Law Journal* 93 (1984): 959–980, 962 (noting the relevance of Crosskey's originalist method to contemporary debates over originalism in the legal academy in the mid-1980s).

[194] Abe Krash, "The Legacy of William Crosskey," 978.

[195] See Clement Vose, "Crosskey on Shenanigans v. Science," *Journal of Politics* 17:3 (August 1955): 448–452. One reviewer of Crosskey's book noted that it was abundantly laced with "pejorative epithets" and remarked upon the author's "'no possible doubt' phraseology." R. K. Gooch, Review of *Politics and the Constitution in the History of the United States*, Two Volumes, *American Bar Association Journal* 40 (1954): 313–314.

[196] Crosskey was Robert Bork's constitutional law professor at the University of Chicago Law School. While this might suggest some direct influence on Bork's seminal conservative originalism, sources close to Bork have told me that Bork frequently skipped Crosskey's class and that Crosskey's pedagogical method, which involved hectoring his students incessantly with his fixed, strident point of view, made him anything but influential.

sources were put to willful use to advance what was clearly a contemporary political/ideological vision.[197]

Perhaps the best-known postwar liberal originalist was Hugo Black.[198] As a US senator from Alabama, Black was a vehement New Dealer and FDR supporter – vehement enough, when many other liberals blanched, to have backed FDR's "court packing" plan to ram the New Deal through in the face of the Court's constitutional objections. Black's clearest interpretive commitment as a Supreme Court justice, perhaps, was to textualism – that is, his emphasis on the duty of the judge to apply the plain meaning of the language of the Constitution's text in interpreting and applying the law. Many have conjectured that as a Southern Baptist this textualism came naturally to Black (Sanford Levinson had dubbed this interpretive stance "constitutional Protestantism"). As a judge, Black took the Constitution as his Bible: his job, as he saw it, was to read and apply its patent, literal meaning to the case at hand

---

[197] In a review in the *American Historical Review* of the posthumously published third volume of Crosskey's masterwork, the eminent historian Lance Banning described *Politics and the Constitution* as "[g]rounded ... on research that ranges widely, though selectively, through contemporary newspapers, legislative records, and superseded editions of collected writings but which systematically dismisses or neglects the most important secondary sources." Banning described the book as "a tour de force of scholarship subordinated to a point of view." "Countervailing evidence is repeatedly ignored or explained away. In passage after passage, contemporary language that might seem clear to any specialist in the history of the Confederation years is tortured into shapes that none will recognize. For all the claims to be recovering an eighteenth-century universe of discourse, the work shows little feeling for the period with which it deals. By ordinary standards of the discipline, it is outrageously bad history. By any test, it is a stunning feat of tendentious argumentation, a clever if exhausting brief for a position that Alexander Hamilton himself did not attempt to argue." Lance Banning, Review of William Crosskey and William Jeffrey, *Politics and the Constitution in the History of the United States*, Volume 3, *The Political Background of the Federal Convention. American Historical Review* 86:5 (December 1981): 1147–1148. In a review in the *American Political Science Review*, Charles A. Miller described *Politics and Constitution* as "a work of deliberate constitutional ideology in a historical mode, like that of Louis Boudin." Miller found Crosskey's take "explicitly political." Miller complained that "The Constitution, Crosskey holds, is a perfect document; that is, it describes a logically complete political system. Once its vocabulary is understood ... and once eighteenth century canons of legal construction are employed, the document becomes clear and unmistakable in its meaning." He added, that "Crosskey holds a remarkable view of the nature of history. In place of the complexity, uncertainty, compromise, or even luck, which normally make up political history, Crosskey had discovered a constitutional teleology, a single force that moves through American history in the years preceding the federal convention and knocks aside all other issues." Miller pronounced its originalist method highly idiosyncratic. Charles A. Miller, Review of William Crosskey and William Jeffrey, *Politics and the Constitution in the History of the United States*, Volume 3, *The Political Background of the Federal Convention, American Political Science Review* 75: 4 (December 1981): 1036–1038. *Plus ça change* – see Martin Flaherty, "History 'Lite' and Modern American Constitutionalism," *Columbia Law Review* 95 (1995): 523.

[198] See, e.g., Johnathan O'Neill, *Originalism in American Law and Politics: A Constitutional History* (Baltimore: Johns Hopkins University Press, 2005).

(Black was famous for carrying a copy of the Constitution in his breast pocket and pulling it out as necessary to expound upon its clear commands).[199]

Black added an originalist overlay to this textualism in the course of his extended advocacy on the Court for his position in favor of the total incorporation of the Bill of Rights via the due process clause of the Fourteenth Amendment. Section 1 of the Fourteenth Amendment (1868) – one of the Constitution's "Civil War" or "Reconstruction" amendments – provided that "No state shall make or enforce any law which shall abridge the privileges or immunities of citizens of the United States; nor shall any state deprive any person of life, liberty, or property, without due process of law; nor deny to any person within its jurisdiction the equal protection of the laws." This section of the amendment, arising as it did out of the firm conviction that the national government needed to assume a greater role in policing rights violations by the states (whose violation of fundamental rights, from one perspective, had caused the Civil War), enumerated the categories of violations in the three clauses that follow the "No state shall" language (borrowed from the short but significant list of proscriptions against the states of Article I, Section 10): (1) the privileges and immunities clause, (2) the due process clause, and (3) the equal protection clause. The implications of the first were quickly read out of the picture for most significant purposes by the Supreme Court in the very first case it heard interpreting that clause's meaning, The Slaughterhouse Cases (1873) (and the equal protection clause, which eventually proved immensely significant, is a separate subject).[200] As such, by default, the questions involving the new departure in the policing of rights violations by the states were all freighted onto the due process clause. Immediately, of course, a deluge of questions arose about how to interpret this new order. One of them involved the question of which rights were so fundamental that violations of them by states were newly proscribed, subject to the enforcement of the national government (whether by Congress – see Section 5 of the Fourteenth Amendment – or perhaps directly by the federal courts). Positions on this question were already being taken during the congressional debates in the Reconstruction Congress that ultimately drafted and proposed the amendment. Contending positions on this question were at the heart of Slaughterhouse (where the majority and dissenters disagreed about how narrowly or broadly to interpret this category of rights),

---

[199] Sanford Levinson, Constitutional Faith (Princeton: Princeton University Press, 1988). See also Mark Silverstein, Constitutional Faiths: Felix Frankfurter, Hugo Black, and the Process of Judicial Decision Making (Ithaca, NY: Cornell University Press, 1984).

[200] Recent scholarship – especially on the Right – has questioned the conventional story of Slaughterhouse as the turning point in this regard, arguing in favor of the Cruikshank case, which involves Second Amendment gun rights, instead. United States v. Cruikshank, 92 US 542 (1876). See Kurt Lash, The Fourteenth Amendment and the Privileges and Immunities of American Citizenship (New York: Cambridge University Press, 2014); Leslie Friedman Goldstein, "The Specter of the Second Amendment: Rereading Slaughterhouse and Cruikshank," Studies in American Political Development 21 (Fall 2007): 131–148.

and they reappeared periodically as the issue was raised in concrete cases across the late nineteenth and early twentieth centuries. Toward the very end of the nineteenth century, the Court held for the first time that one way to answer the question of "which rights" was by looking to the rights that had been protected in the Founding Era in the original Bill of Rights (1791) – an approach known as "incorporation" (early on, it was called "absorption," a term that fell out of use). This immediately presented another question: Did this mean that all of the provisions of the Bill of Rights were incorporated ("total incorporation"); only those provisions that were, in some sense, fundamental ("selective" or "partial incorporation"); all of the provisions of the Bills of Rights, plus any additional rights not set out there that the Court deemed fundamental ("incorporation plus"); or was the determining factor not the enumerated Bill of Rights but the determination that the right was fundamental, *tout court*. As the Rights Revolution in civil liberties and civil rights heated up post–New Deal, these questions became the subject of heated debate, on the Court and off. And given the ultimate textual ambiguity of the Fourteenth Amendment's due process clause, justices and prominent scholars soon moved to questions of what the framers of the Fourteenth Amendment had intended to do in the Reconstruction Congress.

This, of course, was originalism. The issue was vehemently disputed on the Court in a debate between Hugo Black and Felix Frankfurter initiated in the *Adamson* v. *California* (1947) decision.[201] Black's *Adamson* dissent arguing for total incorporation sparked a scholarly donnybrook on the question between William Crosskey and Charles Fairman of Stanford Law School. Without canvassing the details, it is enough to say that Black (and Crosskey) argued for total incorporation, with their argument adducing historical materials enlisted in an argument made on originalist grounds.[202] These debates were prominent both on the Court and in academia, and they had real consequences for the future path of the Court-led Rights Revolution concerning civil liberties. Originalist analysis of the Fourteenth Amendment became even more prominent at mid-century when it was enlisted in defense of, and in opposition to, the Court's landmark application of the equal protection clause to declare racial segregation in public schools unconstitutional in *Brown* v. *Board of Education* (1954).[203] While there were certainly liberals who spurned originalism on civil liberties and civil rights from the 1940s through the 1960s, liberal originalists like Hugo Black were certainly part of the debates, and prominently so.

In an essay on Justice Black in a then liberal (but transitioning) *Commentary* magazine in 1963, the pro–New Deal James Grossman defended the justice's

---

[201] *Adamson* v. *California*, 332 US 46 (1947).
[202] O'Neill, *Originalism in American Law and Politics*, 67–73.
[203] O'Neill, *Originalism in American Law and Politics*, 73–76. *Brown* v. *Board of Education*, 347 US 483 (1954).

originalist approach against those on the Right seeking to discredit him as "an outright New Dealer ... as if it were unseemly to uphold the New Deal on the basis of a conviction older and deeper than the newly converted majority's."[204] Noting crescendoing charges that when it came to civil rights, the Warren Court might "be imposing its own views of freedom, its very prejudices, on legislatures, as formerly its predecessors imposed theirs in the field of economics" – the charge of "judicial activism" or "Lochnerism" once hurled by Progressives and New Dealers at conservatives on the bench – Grossman observed that "Black's fundamental tactic has been to get us to accept as old what are really new views, he does not speak of the growth of the law and does not admit that he has any part in making it, as judges who have been teachers are so fond of doing." Rather, the justice holds himself out as "helping [to] restore the law to its original purpose." Of course, Grossman noted, Black was in fact doing no such thing. But, while "[m]ere reason may tell us that this is an absurd doctrinaire attitude," he observed, "it has been amazingly successful as a judicial method, and the vulgar test of success is not a bad one to apply in a field that has so few demonstrable rules as constitutional law."[205]

Not long after the truculently liberal Crosskey and Black began pioneering modern originalism and textualism, a prominent group of liberal, pro–New Deal academics began to recoil in horror at what they considered to be the activist, anti-democratic antics of the liberal Warren Court – and found themselves newly aligned along key dimensions with the era's rising constitutional conservatives like Willmoore Kendall. The most prominent were Philip Kurland of the University of Chicago Law School, Alexander Bickel of Yale Law School, and Raoul Berger of Harvard Law School.[206]

Like many of their colleagues in the postwar legal academy, this group did not want for liberal bona fides. Kurland, like Bickel, had been a law clerk to Supreme Court Justice Felix Frankfurter, who, although an A-list Progressive and New Deal insider (from his perch at Harvard Law School, he had played a major role in staffing the New Deal and had been appointed to the High Court by Franklin Roosevelt), retained his Progressive commitment to judicial deference to legislatures even as the mid-century Warren Court revolutionized

---

[204] James Grossman, "Justice Black and the Absolute," *Commentary* 36 (September 1963): 244–263, 244.

[205] Grossman, "Justice Black," 246, 248. See O'Neill, *Originalism in American Law and Politics*. Grossmann and O'Neill both give Hugo Black – and not Edwin Meese and, later, The Federalist Society – credit for launching contemporary discussions of originalism.

[206] The label "conservative" had lately been attached to Felix Frankfurter, which the Brandeis protégée, FDR intimate, and Supreme Court appointee – a man with clear progressive/liberal substantive commitments, but a consistent proponent of judicial restraint from the Progressive Era through the Warren years – chafed against strongly. See generally H. N. Hirsch, *The Enigma of Felix Frankfurter* (New York: Basic Books, 1981). On Frankfurter's role in staffing the New Deal more generally, see Peter Irons, *The New Deal Lawyers* (Princeton: Princeton University Press, 1993).

the relationship between progressive politics and an activist judiciary. Kurland joined Raoul Berger in writing and testifying on the constitutional ground rules that shored up the scholarly case for Richard Nixon's impeachment.[207] Although all three legal academics increasingly found themselves lauded by conservatives, they did not fit in with at least some strains of the modern conservative movement.

The cases of Kurland and Bickel were particularly complicated. The founder and editor of the mainstream scholarly *Supreme Court Review* (1960–1988), Kurland disdained dogmas, litmus tests, and ideologies and emphasized ambiguity and complexity. In memorializing Kurland, David Levi, a federal judge and the son of Kurland's former University of Chicago Law School colleague (and US Attorney General) Edward Levi, said that Kurland understood himself to stand "in a tradition of skeptical liberalism beginning with [Oliver Wendell] Holmes [Jr.]," "a tradition born in doubt rather than faith, and maintained by skepticism rather than belief." Kurland's heroes were Frankfurter, Justice Robert Jackson, and Judges Learned Hand and Jerome Frank (for whom he had also clerked).[208] Spotlighting Kurland's appreciation for complexity, and noting his good-natured pessimism, his University of Chicago colleague (constitutional law scholar, and later president of Stanford University) Gerhard Casper testified to Kurland's directness, impatience with cant, and skepticism of grand schemes, adding that Kurland insisted that the Constitution was "a complex system that cannot be reduced to one of its components." Kurland considered

[m]ajority rule, separation of power within the national government, the system of checks and balances, federalism, the Bill of Rights, and ... the independence of the judiciary ... [not] as separate topic[s] that can be treated in isolation, but as the Framers' interdependent devices for the restraint of brute power, however disguised, within American democracy.[209]

Like many who became neoconservatives, however, Kurland, a New York City (Brooklyn) native, in time became profoundly critical of the effects of the student movement of the late 1960s on the university.[210] He was a champion of

---

[207] Philip Kurland, *Watergate and the Constitution* (Chicago: University of Chicago Press, 1972); Raoul Berger, *Impeachment: The Constitutional Problems* (Cambridge, MA: Harvard University Press, 1972); Raoul Berger, *Executive Privilege: A Constitutional Myth* (Cambridge, MA: Harvard University Press, 1974). See also Raoul Berger, *Federalism: The Founders' Design* (Norman: University of Oklahoma Press, 1987).

[208] David Levi, "In Memoriam Philip B. Kurland," *University of Chicago Law Review* 64 (Winter 1997) 1, 4–5. Levi cited Kurland's article "Justice Robert H. Jackson – Impact on Civil Rights and Civil Liberties," 1977 *University of Illinois Law Forum* 551, 552" as illustrative of the core of Kurland's constitutional disposition.

[209] Gerhard Casper, "In Memoriam Philip B. Kurland," *University of Chicago Law Review* 64 (Winter 1997) 1: 10, 12

[210] See generally Joseph Dorman, *Arguing the World: The New York Intellectuals in Their Own Words* (Chicago: University of Chicago Press, 2001).

"the Founders' Constitution" (he and his colleague Ralph Lerner at Chicago's Committee on Social Thought assembled the important five-volume document compilation on the subject). Yet in 1987, Kurland spoke out against Robert Bork's appointment to the Supreme Court, condemning the federal judge – a pillar and pioneer of modern conservative originalism – as a dissembling opportunist.[211]

Kurland tended to address particular questions and issues on their own terms, as they arose. Despite the high esteem in which he held them, Kurland was never dogmatic about the Founders in a way that led him to deny the relevance of historical change, which he was perfectly comfortable discussing in constitutional terms, even when the change was informal (that is, not via the formal Article V amendment process). Long before the liberal Yale Law School scholars Bruce Ackerman and Akhil Amar became well known for their regime theories of US constitutional development, Kurland had set out the fundamentals of basically the same idea, positing, as Ackerman did later, an American constitutional order characterized by three regimes, the first from the Founding to (roughly) the Civil War, the second from the Civil War to the New Deal, and the third from the aftermath of the New Deal to the present.[212]

All the same, during the heyday of what scholars have called "history's Warren Court" in the mid-1960s, *Human Events* published a speech by Kurland expressing shock and uneasiness that "the justices have wrought more fundamental changes in the political and legal structure of the United States than during any period in our history since Chief Justice Marshall first wrote meanings into the abstractions of the Constitution's language."[213] Kurland set out a taxonomy of the Court's new departures and concluded, based on that assessment, that the Court was transforming the principle of equality into the overarching determinant of its constitutional decision making (a point that had also been made by Martin Diamond). This new departure, Kurland warned, both subordinated, if not destroyed, the federal system, and radically expanded the Article III judiciary's power vis-à-vis the other branches of the federal government.[214]

[211] Philip B. Kurland and Ralph Lerner, editors, *The Founders' Constitution* (Chicago: University of Chicago Press, 1987) (Vols. I–V)[subsequently republished by The Liberty Fund].

[212] Philip Kurland, "American Systems of Laws and Constitutions," in Daniel Boorstin, editor, *American Civilization* (London: Thames and Hudson, 1972). Not to say that this regime framework was not later critiqued by conservatives expressing concern for the integrity of the eighteenth-century Founding. See Lane V. Sunderland, "The Constitutional Analysis of Philip B. Kurland," *The Political Science Reviewer* 12 (Fall 1982): 167–206.

[213] Philip B. Kurland, "How the Supreme Court Is Remaking the United States," *Human Events* (January 23, 1965), 10.

[214] Kurland, "How the Supreme Court Is Remaking the United States." In 1957, in a discussion of the liberal bias of his fellow Supreme Court clerks, a young William Rehnquist (who clerked for Justice Robert Jackson) said, "Some of the tenets of the 'liberal' point of view which commanded the sympathy of a majority of the clerks I knew were: extreme solicitude for the claims of Communists and other criminal defendants, expansion of Federal power at the expense of

Like Kurland, Yale's Alexander Bickel and Harvard's Raoul Berger were similarly taken aback by the Warren Court's activism, the former from the perspective of someone preoccupied with questions of competence and prudence, and the latter from that of someone preoccupied with questions of fidelity. For his part, Bickel was closely associated with the "legal process" movement within legal academia – a movement whose origins were decidedly progressive/liberal but came to be seen as conservative (its members' protests notwithstanding) as the Warren Court Rights Revolution moved in a decidedly different direction (it is no accident that many of its denizens had, like Bickel, been clerks and protégés of Felix Frankfurter). Legal process scholars were liberal supporters of the New Deal, which they believed had instituted important changes in American government crucial for responsibly addressing modern conditions. Like many other New Deal liberals, however, they were concerned that the New Deal state lacked – or had not clearly or effectively articulated – its constitutional or rule of law foundations.[215] The problem in this regard was twofold. First, it presented a problem of justification, raising questions of legitimacy. Second, substantive constitutional values (and functional concerns) were at stake: issues concerning the concentration of power, popular participation, institutional competence, and so forth (the two dimensions, of course, were intertwined). Just as, at about the same time, the Cornell and Harvard political philosopher John Rawls began elaborating a theoretical liberal contractarian justification for the modern American state,[216] the Legal Process scholars proposed a process-oriented functionalism that endeavored to recommit modern liberals to institutional formalities and formal procedures that aimed to discipline the processes of government in service of traditional legal and constitutional ends. The movement rejected chaos, unpredictability, and will in favor of order, regularity, and principle.

Bickel's most influential book *The Least Dangerous Branch* (1962) remains a classic of American constitutional theory.[217] Its focus (as its titular allusion to Federalist 78 suggests) was the role of judges in the American constitutional order. In the book, Bickel defended a limited, albeit crucial, role for the courts in exercising the power of judicial review: he famously characterized the limiting conditions as "the passive virtues." As William Eskridge has emphasized, the

---

state power, great sympathy toward any government regulation of business – in short, the political philosophy now espoused by the Court under Chief Justice Earl Warren." William H. Rehnquist, "Who Writes Decisions of the Supreme Court?" *US News and World Report* (December 13, 1957).

[215] See Daniel Ernst, *Tocqueville's Nightmare: The Administrative State Emerges in America, 1900–1940* (New York: Oxford University Press, 2014); Anne M. Kornhauser, *Debating the American State: Liberal Anxieties and the New Leviathan* (Philadelphia: University of Pennsylvania Press, 2015); Orren and Skowronek, *The Policy State.*

[216] Kornhauser, *Debating the American State*, 175–220.

[217] Alexander M. Bickel, *The Least Dangerous Branch: The Supreme Court at the Bar of Politics* (Indianapolis, IN: Bobbs-Merrill Co., 1962).

institutions and process-oriented Legal Process project, whose concerns were generated by the rise of the New Deal order in the 1930s and 1940s, was thrown into chaos – or, perhaps more accurately, irrelevance – by the ascendant Rights Revolution of the mid-1950s forward. The reactions by Legal Process thinkers to the unanticipated chain of events launched by *Brown* v. *Board of Education* (1954) and the Montgomery Bus Boycott (1955) ran the gamut: (1) stunned silence (the pioneering Harvard Law School Legal Process scholars Henry Hart and Albert Sacks withheld the publication of their seminal text on the subject, *The Legal Process* (1958), and ultimately never published it);[218] (2) work with it by proposing theories that advocated restraint in judicial review in line with traditional Legal Process convictions, but that nevertheless left room for expanded judicial protection of rights, at least in some core cases (a path taken by Columbia Law School's Herbert Wechsler, Harvard/Stanford Law School's John Hart Ely, and the Alexander Bickel of *The Least Dangerous Branch*;[219] or (3) resist (the path taken, increasingly vehemently as history's 1960s exploded in the mid-to-late 1960s, by Kurland and the later Bickel of *The Supreme Court and the Idea of Progress* (1970)).[220] The legal historian Raoul Berger took a different route: full-throated outrage and opposition to what he characterized as a lawless, hell-bent, out-of-control, federal judiciary. Conservatives, it seemed, liked this reaction best.

A Ukrainian immigrant who settled in Cincinnati and had initially trained (and worked) as a classical violinist, Berger came from outside Legal Process circles – although, as a senior fellow in American Legal History at Harvard, he was certainly immersed in its generative milieu. Like the Legal Process scholars, Berger had been a supporter of the New Deal and had long understood himself as a liberal. His temperament and intellectual orientation, however, diverged sharply from those of the Legal Process practitioners. Berger's charge against the activist egalitarian Court – he fired his cannons against *Brown* – was of heresy and betrayal. The judges were out of control. And he had an answer: in interpreting the Constitution's text, the judges had to strap themselves to the mast of the intentions of the framers (Berger's focus in *Government by Judiciary* (1977) was on the framers of the Fourteenth Amendment, not the 1787 Constitutional Convention at Philadelphia). There was no issue of competence at stake for Berger: the heart of

---

[218] William M. Eskridge Jr., and Philip Frickey, "The Making of 'The Legal Process,'" *Harvard Law Review* 107 (June 1994): 2031–2055; Henry M. Hart Jr. and Albert M. Sacks, *The Legal Process: Basic Problems in the Making and Application of Law* (New York: Foundation Press, 1994 [1958]) (William M. Eskridge Jr. and Philip Frickey, editors).

[219] Herbert Wechsler, "Toward Neutral Principles of Constitutional Law," *Harvard Law Review* 73 (November 1959): 1–35 [critically reacting to *Brown* v. *Board of Education* (1954)]; John Hart Ely, "The Wages of Crying Wolf: A Comment on *Roe* v. *Wade*," *Yale Law Journal* 82 (1973): 920–949 [critically reacting to *Roe* v. *Wade* (1973)]; John Hart Ely, *Democracy and Distrust: A Theory of Judicial Review* (Cambridge, MA: Harvard University Press, 1980).

[220] Alexander M. Bickel, *The Supreme Court and the Idea of Progress* (New York: Harper and Row, 1970).

the issue was legitimacy – for a judge to do anything other than follow the framers' intent was illegitimate, a betrayal of a judge's duty. While conservatives certainly listened to, respected, and even admired Kurland, and often Bickel, it was Raoul Berger who ignited their passion. While other conservatives like Robert Bork – who was close to Bickel, and co-taught constitutional law with him at Yale Law School – had certainly argued essentially the same thing in a brief *Indiana Law Review* article published a decade earlier (1971), it was Berger's *Government by Judiciary* that launched a fighting faith.

NEOCONSERVATISM'S ERSTWHILE LIBERALS REACT TO THE BIRTH OF ORIGINALISM

Beginning in the late 1960s and early 1970s, what might have been seen as a pluralist discussion began to look more like a trajectory. There were some landmarks along the way. In his 1968 campaign for the presidency, Richard Nixon made a major point of pledging to appoint only "strict constructionists" to the bench.[221] An obscure but influential 1971 *Indiana Law Journal* article by Robert Bork had argued that a non-originalist approach to constitutional interpretation was not misguided or less than ideal, but illegitimate. Raoul Berger's *Government by Judiciary* (1977) appended a stream of exclamation points to that assertion, winning plaudits in the conservative press, which treated *Government by Judiciary* as a landmark manifesto.[222]

Berger's manifesto, however, did not win unanimous acclaim on the Right, at least as that political grouping was continuing to develop in the mid-to-late 1970s. Neoconservatives were perhaps *Government by Judiciary*'s most notable critics. Elliott Abrams – soon to be a controversial figure in the Reagan Era foreign policy establishment who was entangled in the Iran-Contra Affair, but also a Harvard Law School graduate – panned *Government by Judiciary* in *Commentary* magazine, siding in many respects with liberals.[223] Abrams reported incredulously that "[i]n Berger's view, the

[221] See Kevin J. McMahon, *Nixon's Court: His Challenge to Judicial Liberalism and Its Political Consequences* (Chicago: University of Chicago Press, 2011); Teles, *Rise of the Conservative Legal Movement*; Michael Graetz and Linda Greenhouse, *The Burger Court and the Rise of the Judicial Right* (New York: Simon and Schuster, 2016); Earl Maltz, *The Coming of the Nixon Court: The 1972 Term and the Transformation of Constitutional Law* (Lawrence: University Press of Kansas, 2016).

[222] Bork, "Neutral Principles and Some First Amendment Problems," 10. See Robert Post and Reva Siegel, "Originalism as a Political Practice: The Right's Living Constitution," *Fordham Law Review* 75 (2006–2007): 545–574, 547. "[F]or the first time," Post and Siegel note, "claims about fidelity to originalist interpretive methodology became a vehicle for widespread and sustained mobilization of conservatives," a powerful rallying cry "fus[ing] aroused citizens, government officials, and judges into a dynamic and broad-based political movement."

[223] Elliot Abrams, "The Chains of the Constitution," *Commentary* 64:6 (December 1977): 84–85. See O'Neill, *Originalism in American Law and Politics*, ch. 5 on Berger's role in the "restoration of originalism." Abrams later became better known nationally as undersecretary of state for Latin

sole sources of constitutional law are the historical record and the words of the Constitution itself ... Any attempt to break out of an ancient interpretation or definition is illicit. Our sole task is to discover the precise meaning the framers gave a passage, the 'original understanding,' and then to enforce it." Abrams was aghast at the implications. "With this view," he observed, "Berger cannot but oppose virtually every modern Court ruling on civil rights and civil liberties." For this reason, Abrams found Berger "as a constitutional theorist ... utterly inadequate."[224] "In his chronicle of American constitutional history," Abrams complained, Berger "gives us everything except that which is most important – an understanding of the role of the Constitution in our political system." According to Abrams,

As Robert McCloskey put it in The American Supreme Court, "Judicial review in its peculiar American form exists because America set up popular sovereignty and fundamental law as twin ideals and left the logical conflict between them unresolved." This conflict Berger overlooks entirely, or ... sees as being entirely resolved in the amendment process ... Yet had the framers had this in mind, one wonders why they made the process so difficult ... [O]ne is led to [conservative Yale Law professor and future Reagan appointee to the US Court of Appeals for the Second Circuit] Ralph Winter's conclusion ... "A written constitution with difficult amendment procedures strongly encourages the body politic to add to the document only general declarations on matters of great import, leaving room for growth and change in light of history and the perspective afforded by a deliberate elaboration as experience grows."[225]

If one wanted to find a predecessor for the sort of starched originalism propounded by Berger, Abrams argued, one need look no further than the crucial originalist provisions of Chief Justice Taney's opinion in Dred Scott. Abrams approvingly quoted Alexander Bickel's blistering critique of Taney's originalist stance stating, "such views, when they prevail, threaten disaster to government under a written constitution." Abrams concluded that originalism "sees the Constitution as a set of chains, and indeed ... would make it one."[226]

At about the same time, the emerging neoconservative William J. Bennett (then still a Democrat, but soon to be appointed head of the National Endowment for the Humanities and, subsequently, US Secretary of Education by Ronald Reagan) defended a jurisprudence of original intent in his review of the Straussian political scientist Walter Berns's The First Amendment and the Future of American Democracy (1976). Nevertheless, Bennett complained that "when [Berns] urges original understandings that push aside those of Jefferson and Madison, his own argument becomes strained." Originalism properly applied to the freedom of speech, Bennett said, vindicated the position of contemporary liberals, not traditionalist conservatives like Berns. On religion,

America in the Reagan administration, where he was a key figure, and lightning rod, in the Iran-Contra scandal.

[224] Abrams, "Chains of the Constitution," 84–85.

[225] Abrams, "Chains of the Constitution," 85.   [226] Abrams, "Chains of the Constitution," 85.

Bennett criticized Berns for downplaying the significance of Madison's *Memorial and Remonstrance on Religious Assessments* (1785). Bennett insisted on the centrality of "impolite and unwholesome speech" in the Founding Era, rejecting Berns's implication that the toleration of such speech – "license" – was a twentieth-century phenomenon. Furthermore, Bennett explained, not all the Founders were as comfortable as Berns was with the distinction between liberty and license. Bennett concluded, scathingly, "Berns himself, who, in his desire not to 'tolerate the intolerant,' moves uncomfortably close to the doctrine of 'repressive tolerance' enunciated by [New Left hero] Herbert Marcuse."[227]

For his part, the neoconservative Democrat Daniel Patrick Moynihan endorsed an originalism that set a high value on the wisdom of the Founders, and gave due regard to the duty of fidelity, but married both to a pragmatic, anti-dogmatic spirit. Determining the implications of the original meaning of the constitutional text to contemporary problems and questions, Moynihan recognized, was no easy task. After all, "Here was a common enough situation for the courts. They were asked to determine what it is the Constitution decrees with respect to matters that clearly were remote from the thoughts of those who drafted the document, including its various amendments ... Hence judges have had to interpret as best they could." That said, an interpretive nihilism could cut judges off, dangerously, from important, and relevant, constitutional meanings and commitments.[228]

The Founders' intent, Moynihan explained, was important because they thought hard and brilliantly about critical constitutional issues. When judges used history and got it woefully wrong, however, the consequences could be dire. A case in point for Moynihan was the Court's new "strict separationist" establishment clause jurisprudence. Moynihan favorably cited work by Walter Berns, Michael Malbin, Antonin Scalia, and Philip Kurland holding that jurisprudence to be detrimentally "nonhistorical." "[T]he establishment clause had been held to prevent legislatures from providing various forms of assistance to church-related schools, albeit that the establishment clause had the plain and unambiguous meaning – reflecting the Founders' intention – that Congress will not establish a national religion," Moynihan wrote. But, in time, "the Court's rulings on aid to private schools merely reflected a particular religious point of

---

[227] William J. Bennett, "The Role of the Court," *Commentary* 63:5 (May 1977): 79–84, 82–83; Walter Berns, *The First Amendment and the Future of American Democracy* (New York: Basic Books, 1976). See also David Lowenthal, *No Liberty for License: The Forgotten Logic of the First Amendment* (Dallas, TX: Spence Publishing 1997). Like Harry Jaffa, Lowenthal, a political scientist at Boston College, had been an early student of Leo Strauss's at the New School for Social Research. See Herbert Marcuse, "Repressive Tolerance," in Robert Paul Wolff, Barrington Moore Jr., and Herbert Marcuse, editors, *A Critique of Pure Tolerance* (Boston: Beacon Press, 1965).

[228] Daniel Patrick Moynihan, "Social Science and the Courts," *The Public Interest* 52 (Summer 1978): 69–84, 24.

view – i.e., that there is no public interest in the promotion of religion – which reached its peak of intellectual respectability in the 1920s and 1930s, the period in which most of the judges who made the decisions were educated." The resulting establishment clause decisions were "an intellectual scandal." Moynihan understood these as cases in which the justices were imposing their own historically constituted political views on the country, deserving of the same opprobrium that had been heaped by Justice Holmes upon his fellow justices in his famed *Lochner* dissent, where Holmes sharply retorted that "the Constitution does not enforce Mr. Herbert Spencer's *Social Statics*."[229]

These clear and direct reactions by significant figures notwithstanding, it is worth underlining that most neoconservatives who wrote about law and courts before the Reagan years engaged in relatively little theorizing about the proper way to interpret the constitutional text. They were, after all, liberal modernists who were chiefly scholars of public policy and administration: they accepted the New Deal "Constitutional Revolution" as both constitutionally correct and a *fait accompli* and reflected on the wisdom of particular policies of the modern administrative/social welfare state. Neoconservatives were preoccupied with the same broad policy imperatives that liberals were – urban renewal, the alleviation of poverty, civil rights – imperatives with which they repeatedly expressed sympathy. Their yardstick was not fidelity (law), but effectiveness (policy). As highly educated, urban, elite (and, often, Jewish, New York City) intellectuals who were self-conscious about their intellectualism and their status as an intellectual and public policy elite, the neoconservatives accepted the core of the legal pragmatist and realist argument that the best interpretation of the Constitution is one that solves problems and "works." Their primary challenge to liberal interpretations of the constitutional text, and to liberal judicial activism, was that the "living constitutionalism" that had been fashioned by liberals had systematically failed to achieve the functional objectives that it had imagined itself to be serving: constitutional liberalism had failed, not according to some yardstick of fidelity to eighteenth-century commitments, but on its own terms.

INTO THE 1980S: ORIGINALISM AS A DEMAND FOR JUDICIAL RESTRAINT

"A term that excites the imagination of large numbers of people and also helps to organize and discipline them," the political scientist Murray Edelman once observed in his reflections on the role of symbols in politics, "is a potent political instrument, though an uncertain one in its consequences."[230] Such was the case

---

[229] Moynihan, "Social Science and the Courts," 24–25, 30. See also Daniel Patrick Moynihan, "What Do You Do When the Supreme Court Is Wrong?" *The Public Interest* 57 (Fall 1979): 3–24.

[230] Murray Edelman, *Constructing the Political Spectacle*, 37.

with originalism, and its associated catch-phrase refinements – first, "original intent" and, subsequently, "original [public] meaning."[231]

Since the Progressive Era, first progressives and then, to a lesser extent, New Deal liberals had successfully framed the US Constitution as a flexible, organically developing "living" document, ultimately winning popular acceptance for – or at least acquiescence in – this vision.[232] Conservatives, of course, resisted. But only in the 1970s with the publication of the Raoul Berger's *Government by Judiciary* (1977) did a major public voice gain traction by truculently proposing "original intent" as a direct answer and counter – a polar opposite – to progressive/New Deal liberal living constitutionalism. If this was a voice in the wilderness, it was crying, and was heard, loud and clear.

Soon thereafter, with the election of Ronald Reagan as president, the voice was invited in from the wilderness to assume a place at the high table of political power. In 1982, conservative law students at Yale and the University of Chicago law schools – with the involvement of one of Ronald Reagan's closest advisors, Edwin Meese III, Robert Bork, and others – founded The Federalist Society for Law and Public Policy to build and disseminate originalist understandings in ways that, over time, forged legions of conservative originalist legal scholars, lawyers, and judges.[233] When, a few years later, Meese moved on from the White House to assume the duties of US attorney general (1985–1988), he aggressively marketed the use of the term (his predecessor, William French Smith, had been satisfied with a then more typical, amorphously traditionalist conservatism not anchored in any single, fighting-faith theory of constitutional interpretation). Meese also began using Federalist Society principles, and, in time, membership, to vet candidates for Republican appointments to the federal judiciary. When the powerhouse liberal Supreme Court Justice William Brennan, the preeminent doctrinal architect of the transformatively liberal Warren Court (1953–1969), rose to what he rightly took to be an ascending originalist challenge with a full-throated defense of the living constitution, the circle was complete: the terms of the debate were set, and the fight was

---

[231] See Sotirios Barber and James Fleming, *Constitutional Interpretation: The Basic Questions* (New York: Oxford University Press, 2007).

[232] See Kornhauser, *Debating the American State*, 33–36, 49–50, 222–223. Kornhauser recounts a range of progressive arguments that variously rejected the US Constitution in its entirety, as it then (unamended) structured US institutions, and even constitutionalism itself, to those that called for specific constitutional reforms, to conceptions of the Constitution as mutable and "living." Kornhauser argues that although their liberal successors abandoned their more extreme positions, they never arrived at a satisfactory theoretical position on the status of the Constitution with the establishment of the modern (New Deal) American state, a position that, for a long time, was adequate given the widespread public acquiescence in and acceptance of the operation of that state. See also Orren and Skowronek, *The Policy State*.

[233] Teles, *Rise of the Conservative Legal Movement*; Amanda Hollis-Brusky, *Ideas With Consequences: The Federalist Society and the Conservative Counter-Revolution* (New York: Oxford University Press, 2015).

joined.[234] In Murray Edelman's terms, "[t]he well-established, and therefore ritualistic reaffirmation of the differences institutionalize[d] both rhetorics."[235]

The originalist versus living constitutionalist debate orbited around the judge as its constitutional sun. The question at its core involved the method of interpretation to be employed by a judge in deciding a legal case, making this new version of conservative originalism "a matter of constitutional 'process' and 'role,' rather than constitutional substance."[236] The question was focused on the legitimacy of the judge's act of interpretation, and often presumed, for conservatives and liberals alike, that in a democratic polity, the appointed, life-tenured (federal) judge was in a highly problematic position when exercising the power (especially) of judicial review: that is, the judge was confronted with what Alexander Bickel had famously dubbed "the countermajoritarian difficulty." A judge exercising his power to declare unconstitutional legislation passed by the people's elected representatives in Congress (and signed by (for all intents and purposes) the popularly elected president) was performing an aberrant act: it needed to be justified. Constitutional theory – a theory of interpretation – provided that justification. And Bork, Berger, Meese, and The Federalist Society (1982) offered originalism as the *only* justification that worked. Put otherwise, only originalist judges had applied the law of the Constitution to the case at hand. Any other approach, and the

---

[234] Berger, *Government by Judiciary*; Edwin Meese III, Speech Before the American Bar Association, Washington, DC (July 9, 1985); and William J. Brennan, Speech at Georgetown University (October 12, 1985), in Jack Rakove, editor, *Interpreting the Constitution: The Debate Over Original Intent* (Boston: Northeastern University Press, 1990). Many take Robert Bork's 1971 *Indiana Law Journal* article setting out an originalist take on the First Amendment's protection for the freedom of speech to be the first significant articulation of modern originalism (as an "ism"). This may well be correct and is significant, although that article was tightly focused on one doctrinal area, highly professionalized and academic, and relatively without public profile. Robert H. Bork, "Neutral Principles and Some First Amendment Problems," *Indiana Law Journal* 47 (1971): 1–35. Later, of course, Bork would assume an outsized public profile as a partisan of originalism, and warrior in the battle between liberals and conservatives for the control of constitutional law and the Supreme Court. See Robert H. Bork, *The Tempting of America: The Political Seduction of the Law* (New York: Free Press, 1990). Interestingly, the highly restrictive "originalist" understanding of the freedom of speech advanced by Bork in this 1971 article – which limits the First Amendment's coverage to political speech – has been all but abandoned by the contemporary originalist Right. See Wayne Batchis, *The Right's First Amendment: The Politics of Free Speech and the Return of Conservative Libertarianism* (Stanford: Stanford University Press, 2016); Adam Liptak, "How Conservatives Weaponized the First Amendment," *New York Times* (June 30, 2018).

[235] Edelman, *Constructing the Political Spectacle*, 18–19. It was only a matter of time before liberals made the next move by appropriating originalism. See, e.g., Jack Balkin, *Liberal Originalism* (Cambridge, MA: Harvard University Press, 2014); Akhil Reed Amar, *America's Constitution: A Biography* (New York: Random House, 2005); Bruce Ackerman, *We the People*, Vol. 1: *Foundations* (Cambridge, MA: Belknap Press of Harvard University Press, 1991). Outside of intellectual circles, so far, however, the Left-Right framing and ritual seems quite sticky.

[236] Post and Siegel, "Originalism as a Political Practice," 552

living constitutionalist approach most obviously, was doing politics. And the judge had no business doing politics – "legislating from the bench," it was said. As such, originalism's focus as it took flight in the 1980s was on depoliticizing law to (allegedly) maintain the integrity of the democratic process.[237]

Not incidentally, this new world of constitutional theory, which structured debate on these matters from the 1980s until relatively recently, simultaneously professionalized and popularized the originalist stance. It professionalized it because, while certainly present in conservative movement constitutional thought since the mid-1950s, the narrowed focus on the judge and his allegedly "countermajoritarian" position in exercising his judicial review powers did not by any means define that thought, which was much more substantive and varied: it did not limit itself to questions involving judicial role and duty. By moving in this direction, of course, conservatives entered into direct engagement with the main lines of liberal/progressive constitutional theorists, who had been preoccupied with the same question of the relationship between judicial duty and role to interpretive theory since the late nineteenth century (it had been one of the central political issues of the Progressive Era). As theorists and thinkers who had now seriously joined the debate – that is, joined the debate as it had been long defined by legal academy Progressives – originalist conservative constitutional theorists started to be invited (in what it was hoped would be manageable numbers, to be sure) into the legal academy. The process was helped along by the realignment of the nation's party politics beginning in the 1980s toward a movement conservative Republican Party: conservative candidates for academic appointments now accumulated the experience and status markers especially important within the credential- and status-conscious legal academy – they were now both originalists *and* veterans of high-level executive branch appointments in the White House and Justice Department, and many of them had now clerked for the new cadre of conservative federal judges at the very highest levels, including the District of Columbia Circuit and the US Supreme Court. These conservative originalists were now credentialed and pedigreed and joined the constitutional theory debates in ways that liberal legal academics understood and rewarded. This new version of originalism was well on its way to professionalization and institutionalization.

But it was also on its way toward popularization. The call for a return to the Founders' Constitution and original understandings – for originalism – was broadly adopted by the movement as part of its call in the public sphere for the country's broader redemption from liberals and liberalism. The movement conservative Republican Party made the appointment of originalist judges a major part of its *political* campaigns: it became a major front in the cause of

---

[237] Barry Friedman, "The Birth of an Academic Obsession: The History of the Countermajoritarian Difficulty, Part Five," *Yale Law Journal* 112 (2002): 153. This involves the birth of what James Fleming has called originalism "as an ism." Fleming, *Fidelity to Our Imperfect Constitution*, 3–4.

"taking back the country," or, in the age of Trump, "Making America Great Again."

By the time the Republicans had come to appoint a critical mass, and perhaps even a majority, of federal judges, however, the originalist position was changing yet again to account for recent political developments: it was being reformulated to de-emphasize the "judicial restraint" that had been at the heart of its initial, modern, legal academic formulation – at least to the extent that "restraint" had been defined by a purported duty of judges to, in most cases, as a default rule, defer to democratically elected legislatures. Recognizing that many judges were now conservative, conservative constitutional theorists proved themselves newly ready to defend the aggressive exercise of countermajoritarian judicial review powers by conservative judges to advance substantively conservative ends. The political opportunity was simply too good to pass up. A "new" originalism serviceable to an activist conservative judiciary was born.[238]

CONCLUSION

In a sign of the relative success of conservative legal academics – including Robert Bork, Raoul Berger, Antonin Scalia – since the 1970s, and of the law student organization The Federalist Society (1982), people are perhaps to be forgiven for imagining that, in the postwar period, constitutional theory was constituted all but exclusively by a commitment to originalism, understood as we, and conservative law professors, understand it today. This chapter has made clear, however, that modern conservative originalism, rather than amounting to a static commitment at long last achieved, was actually a developmental phenomenon: it emerged across time in its modern form as a consensus position within a conceptually, and sometimes politically, fractured movement that across events and in reaction to their liberal/progressive counterparts, was working, during its postwar wilderness years, to forge a functional political unity.

The modern conservative movement can certainly be characterized as having been originalist all along, in the sense that following classical understandings of history's shape, it posited a Founding, a growth and flourishing, followed by a hubristic and decadent decline and fall, and a summons to redemption and renewal. But, during its wilderness years, that originalism was much more capacious than its current legal academic version, which focuses largely on the role and duties of judges in interpreting legal texts, at times to the point of (ultra-professionalized) scholasticism. This more capacious constitutional theorizing and thought on the pre–Reagan Right was hardly arcane: it was everywhere on the postwar Right. But because of the liberal regime's dominance in the media,

---

[238] Keith E. Whittington, "The New Originalism," *Georgetown Journal of Law and Public Policy* 22 (2004): 599–613.

press, and academia, it has remained, to most, hidden in plain sight: serious conservatives have known about it, and ordinary conservatives, perhaps not even consciously, have been influenced by it, but it has been all but invisible to most Americans, including the most serious (liberal) constitutional scholars, and even historians.

During modern conservatism's postwar wilderness years, conservatives engaged in relatively open and, at times, bitter debate about serious matters of constitutional theory, as understood within a broader framework of political theory and philosophy, American political thought, and American history – that is, not as a simple matter of hermeneutics concerning the proper way to read legal texts. One major axis of these debates was between theorists who emphasized the modern foundations of the American polity and modern understandings of human nature as largely self-interested, and, in light of those understandings, held the polity to have been foundationally committed to the "low but solid" objectives of peace, good order, and prosperity and the protection of rights, and those theorists who, by contrast, looked to the American regime as aspiring to classical virtues of justice, virtue, and human flourishing, as enshrined in the American tradition through a redemptive understanding of the Declaration of Independence's professed commitment to the equality of natural rights. Others joined this debate from their own angles. Neo-confederates like Mel Bradford, for instance, took an aggressively legal positivist position against any imputation of natural rights theory to American constitutional law.

These debates were clearly joined in their time on the Right. But they were not static. Things happened, including the ascendency of the civil rights movement and Warren Court liberal judicial activism (the Rights Revolution). Race played a crucial role. Far from remaining a simple redoubt of intransigent racism and neo-confederatism, the Right – in some cases, difficultly and painfully, to be sure – evolved, or changed. Particularly after the passage of the Civil Rights Acts of 1964 and the Voting Rights Act of 1965, Mel Bradford's neo-confederate star fell as Harry Jaffa's redemptive constitutionalism centered on the natural rights language of the Declaration of Independence, the Lincoln-Douglas debates, the fight against chattel slavery, and the Civil War rose. A Murrayist Roman Catholicism closely associated with the Church's Vatican II reforms (1962–1965) posited an assimilationist vision that positioned Roman Catholics as good and full Americans, in significant part because of their commitment to the principle of the equality of natural rights, as set out in the Declaration of Independence (as a group, Roman Catholic conservatives were always more likely to be avowedly antiracist than (white, southern) Fundamentalist and even Evangelical Christians). This Murrayist vision fit well, of course, with the redemptive constitutionalism of the West Coast Straussians. The neoconservatives, a group that originated in the mid-1960s, had been the most liberal on race of all on the ascending Right: more than a few liberals who became neoconservatives had, indeed, personally participated in the civil rights movement, including Freedom Summer (1964) and the Selma to Montgomery voting rights marches (1965). They could ally with a redemptive constitutionalism in ways that they could never do with Mel Bradford's neo-confederatism (as noted, they were largely responsible for blocking President Reagan's appointment of Bradford to head the National Endowment for the Humanities).

As will be detailed at greater length in the chapters that follow, even southern religious conservatism was changing. Segregationist Fundamentalism began to decline – largely in response to a succession of legislative and judicial defeats – and the relatively more racially progressive (or at least indifferent) Evangelicalism was ascendant. By the mid-1970s, a rising generation of Fundamentalists shifted to new issues – what came to be known as the "culture wars." A new civilizational frame within which to situate constitutional theory on the Right emerged. In the legal academy, a group of liberal legal process scholars like Alexander Bickel and Philip Kurland became increasingly critical of the role that an activist Warren and Burger Courts were playing in crowding out politics in the formulation of public policy. Borrowing from the progressive frame of the courts versus democracy, moreover, an emergent cohort of law school originalists like Robert Bork, Raoul Berger, and Antonin Scalia found themselves making common cause with these anti-judicial activist Legal Process scholars to formulate the philosophy we now know as democracy and judicial restraint promoting conservative originalism. And, given the context at the time, this was a position that, whatever their actually broader and more nuanced views, many conservatives were willing to sign onto – especially with the prospect of political power in their sights. Once the Reagan administration took power, the process of institutionalization began, and we arrive at where I began this concluding section: with the restraintist, legal academy version of originalism understood as the alpha and omega of conservative constitutional theory itself.

In recent years, of course, with many conservative judges on the bench, and a conservative movement that is advancing itself now in significant part through popular, as opposed to legal academic, constitutional theory, the restraintist version of originalism has lost much of its cachet, and an aggressive "new" originalism that licenses the active assertion of judicial review power by conservative judges, guided by substantive understandings of constitutional meaning (as opposed to a general imperative of deference by judges to democratically elected legislatures), is ascendant. In this context, I believe, it was only a matter of time before the conservative movement began to return to the substantive constitutional theory of the postwar period, which took place outside of the law schools, and was not (overly) preoccupied with the judicial role and the duty of restraint, and was more focused on the nature and what they took to be the broader legitimate – and illegitimate – purposes of American constitutional government itself. It is here that, in the years to come, we will find the future of conservative constitutional theory.

3

Stories About Markets

In the heyday of the US liberal social welfare state as built by the Progressives and New Deal, Fair Deal, New Frontier, and Great Society liberals, the postwar conservative movement worked its way toward a vigorous defense of diverse visions of anti-regulatory free market capitalism. In doing so, conservatives advanced arguments and stories about how these visions were either consistent with or compelled by the strictures and principles of the US Constitution, rightly understood.

On this score, it is perhaps not vividly enough remembered, the modern movement was beginning from a position of total rout: it was in the realm of economics that Albert Jay Nock's notion of conservatives as constituting "the Remnant" was perhaps most apt.[1] Herbert Hoover's "rugged individualism" and "fifth freedom" – the right to private property – bore the brunt of the blame for the most devastating economic collapse in American history. Credited with leading the country out of the Great Depression into an era of almost unimaginable mid-twentieth-century prosperity, the nation's leaders adopted interventionist Keynesianism as the country's official macroeconomic theory.

In a paradigmatic instance of the political scientist Elmer Schattschneider's dictum "policy creates politics," the New Deal liberal regime, built in significant part on the pillar of state protection of labor unions through the National Labor Relations ("Wagner") Act, the new state sponsored and empowered its own most sustaining constituency. Broad understandings of private property rights and sharp limits on the powers of government to regulate economic markets and on government's taxing and spending powers had, it seemed, been thoroughly discredited. To stubbornly continue to see the world through this

---

[1] Albert Jay Nock, "Isaiah's Job," *The Freeman* 6 (December 1956): 31–37 (excerpted from Albert Jay Nock, *Free Speech and Plain Language* (New York: William Morrow, 1937)). Nock borrowed the notion of the remnant from the English poet and critic Matthew Arnold, one of his heroes. Michael Wreszin, *The Superfluous Anarchist* (Providence, RI: Brown University Press, 1971), 74–75, *et seq.*

framework marked one as a curmudgeon, if not a crank. Believers in free markets were up against it, facing stupendous odds.

Starting out in the 1930s, the first wave of champions of unregulated capitalist markets saw themselves as a dispossessed class – dispossessed first by Left-Wing Populism, Progressivism, and, the last straw, Franklin Delano Roosevelt's *dirigiste* New Deal that had, in effect, locked in a new – conservatives would say, an outlaw – regime for the foreseeable future. The Old Right of the 1930s–1950s, championed by Robert McCormick, John T. Flynn, Isabel Paterson, and Rose Wilder Lane, sustained a fringe but perfervid opposition to the new order.[2]

In the mid-1950s, conservatives in Congress were already moving to expose the ways in which, in their view, the nation's richest and most powerful were throwing their weight around behind the scenes to steer the country leftward. In his report as counsel to the congressional committee commissioned to investigate the great tax-exempt foundations ("The Reece Committee") – a committee formed, it was said, despite staunch opposition from the media and the financial elite – René Wormser, a New York City estate lawyer, unearthed and detailed the ways in which the Rockefeller, Ford, and Carnegie Foundations were working within the nation's educational, government, and the media establishments to convert America to socialism.[3] As these investigations were launched, the former Eisenhower administration official,

[2] See Maxwell Bloomfield, *Peaceful Revolution: Constitutional Change and American Culture from Progressivism to the New Deal* (Cambridge, MA: Harvard University Press, 2000). The writer and *New York Herald Tribune* columnist Isabel Paterson's *The God of the Machine* (New York: G. P. Putnam's Sons, 1943) contrasted the dynamism of the free market with the stifling effects of statist do-goodism. Rose Wilder Lane's *The Discovery of Freedom: Man's Struggle Against Authority* (New York: The John Day Company, 1943) celebrated the dynamism of individuals and the ways in which it is liberated by markets and stifled by centralized states. Both appeared the same year as the better-known Ayn Rand novel *The Fountainhead* (Indianapolis, IN: Bobbs-Merrill Co., 1943). This group of three women was dubbed the "Libertarians of '43." See David Beito and Linda Royster Beito, "Selling Laissez Faire Antiracism to the Black Masses: Rose Wilder Lane and the Pittsburgh Courier," *The Independent Review* 15:2 (Fall 2010): 279–294, 281; Stephen D. Cox, *The Woman and the Dynamo: Isabel Paterson and the Idea of America* (London: Routledge, 2004). Both Paterson and Lane were raised on farms in pioneer families on the western prairies (Paterson in Alberta, Canada). Lane's mother, Laura Ingalls Wilder, wrote about her own prairie upbringing (in close conjunction with Lane) in the Little House children's book series that later inspired a popular television series starring Michael Landon and Melissa Gilbert. See Caroline Fraser, *Prairie Fires: The American Dreams of Laura Ingalls Wilder* (New York: Metropolitan Books, 2017). See also Jennifer Burns, "The Three 'Furies' of Libertarianism: Rose Wilder Lane, Isabel Paterson, and Ayn Rand," *Journal of American History* 102 (3) (December 2015): 746–774.
[3] René Wormser, *Foundations: Their Power and Influence* (New York: Devin-Adair, 1958). See Alice O'Connor, "The Politics of Rich and Rich: Postwar Investigations of Foundations and the Rise of the Philanthropic Right," in Nelson Lichtenstein, editor, *American Capitalism: Social Thought and Political Economy in the Twentieth Century* (Philadelphia: University of Pennsylvania Press, 2006), 228. Out of print for many years, Wormser's report has now been

Duke Law School professor, and author of *The Republican Looks at His Party* (1956), Arthur Larson, for one, was hopeful. In the 1930s and 1940s, he recalled, "it was assumed that the world was moving toward statism." By the end of the Eisenhower years, however, Larson saw the United States moving in the direction of "enterprise democracy." This was a critical shift, because Larson explained, "full-blown state ownership of the economy has never existed side by side with personal freedom." For this reason, the fight for economic liberty was always about more than mere economic liberty: the task for Republican defenders of free markets involved no less than "hastening the good life for all men."[4]

In postwar conservatism's early years, especially, there was some ambiguity about how all this related to the US Constitution. While the influential, albeit idiosyncratic, Old Right "individualist" libertarian Albert Jay Nock, author of, among other works, *Our Enemy, The State* (discussed later), had dated the beginning of the US "post-constitutional [that is, post-freedom] period" to 1789,[5] his young admirer, the recent Yale University graduate William F. Buckley Jr. – whose father was a close friend of Nock's and frequently hosted the individualist at his Connecticut estate – laid the blame not on the nation's Founders but on the socialists of the sort who had lately infiltrated its universities, including his *alma mater*, Yale. As Buckley cheerily explained in *God and Man at Yale* (1951), he had entered Yale with the firm belief "that free enterprise and limited government had served this country well and would probably continue to do so in the future" – if the nation's robust religiosity and individualism were not subverted by indoctrination by "atheistic socialists."[6]

Most in the modern movement on this score followed Buckley rather than Nock. Conservative arguments concerning free markets were often inextricably tied to arguments about constitutional design and constitutional fidelity in what came to be viewed as some of the modern conservative movement's most canonical statements. The founding document of the Young Americans for Freedom, *The Sharon Statement* (1960), midwifed by Buckley on his Sharon, Connecticut, estate not long after the publication of *God and Man at Yale*, would declare that "WE, as young conservatives believe ... THAT the

republished. René Wormser, *Foundations: Their Power and Influence* (San Pedro, CA: Covenant House Books, 1993).

[4] Arthur Larson, "The World is Learning the Impact of Economic Freedom," *Reader's Digest* 74:444 (April 1959): 105–110, 106, 110 [reprinted, condensed, from Arthur Larson, *What We Are For* (New York: Harper and Bros, 1959)]; Arthur Larson, *A Republican Looks at His Party* (New York: Harper, 1956). Larson became known as a key spokesman for the era's moderate Republicanism. His views, it was said, reflected the views of Eisenhower himself, with whom he worked closely and directly. See David Stebenne, *Modern Republican: Arthur Larson and the Eisenhower Years* (Bloomington: Indiana University Press, 2006).

[5] Nock, *Our Enemy, The State*, chap. 5.

[6] William F. Buckley Jr., *God and Man at Yale* (Chicago: H. Regnery, 1951).

Constitution of the United States is the best arrangement yet devised for empowering government to fulfill its proper role, while restraining it from the concentration and abuse of power."[7] The worshipful view of the Constitution as a great charter of freedom was similarly articulated in Barry Goldwater's *The Conscience of a Conservative* (1960), published that same year, a book commissioned by Notre Dame constitutional law professor and dean Clarence Manion and written by Yale Law School graduate L. Brent Bozell, Jr., (Barry Goldwater later jocularly attested that, indeed, he had read it). That book, taken by many to be the most sophisticated, succinct statement of the movement's postwar political vision, began with a broadside against the political understandings of the contemporaneous Republican Party. Goldwater, the book's putative author, targeted Arthur Larson's *The Republican Looks at His Party* for what he – that is, also, Manion and Bozell – held to be a critical omission that exemplified the Eisenhower Era Republican Party's "unqualified repudiation of the principle of limited government": Larson's book had made no reference to the Constitution, nor did it make "any attempt to define the legitimate functions of Government." If this is where the Republican Party was, it was appalling. On this, in the long run, Manion and Bozell, and not Larson, would have the last word.[8]

THE LIBERTARIANS – ALBERT JAY NOCK AND THE AUSTRIAN ECONOMISTS

Not long after the publication of William Graham Sumner's bracingly brutal anti-government manifesto *What Social Classes Owe to Each Other* (1883), Elbert Hubbard published *A Message to Garcia* (1899), an inspirational essay implicitly emphasizing some similar themes in an entirely different register. Hubbard's tract was a celebration of the can-do spirit of the true American who does not look to others for help but rolls up his sleeves, takes the bull by the horns, and, on his own initiative, wrestles problems to the ground all by himself.[9] The Garcia of the essay's title was a potential US ally, an insurgent whose whereabouts in the mountains of Cuba were unknown at the outbreak of the Spanish-American War. Eager for Garcia's help, President William McKinley needed to get a message to him at once. One enterprising volunteer, Rowan, stepped up to the task, and – without asking a single question about

---

[7] Buckley, *God and Man at Yale*; Young Americans for Freedom, *The Sharon Statement* (1960), in Kramnick and Lowi, eds., *American Political Thought*, 1281.

[8] Barry Goldwater, *The Conscience of a Conservative* (New York: McFadden, 1960), 15. When Goldwater won the Republican Party nomination for president in 1964, Larson actively campaigned for Lyndon B. Johnson.

[9] Elbert Hubbard, *A Message to Garcia: Being a Preachment* (E. Aurora, NY: The Roycrofters, 1914)[1899]. Hubbard and his wife were killed in 1915 when the ocean liner on which they were traveling to England, the RMS *Lusitania*, was torpedoed by a German U-boat.

where, why, and how – took McKinley's letter in hand and accomplished the difficult deed.

Hubbard heaped on the praise:

By the Eternal! there is a man whose form should be cast in deathless bronze and the statue placed in every college of the land. It is not book-learning young men need ... but a stiffening of the vertebrae which will cause them to be loyal to a trust, to act promptly, concentrate their energies: do the thing – "Carry a message to Garcia."[10]

Pronouncing himself "well-nigh appalled at times by the imbecility of the average man – the inability or unwillingness to concentrate on a thing and do it," at his "incapacity for independent action, this moral stupidity, this infirmity of the will, this unwillingness to cheerfully catch hold and lift," Hubbard not only told the story but sold it, to fabulous acclaim, as a message for his times. Speaking to the then live question of the possibility of instituting socialism, Hubbard wondered, "If men will not act for themselves, what will they do when the benefit of their effort is for all?"[11]

As the twentieth century approached, Hubbard was disconcerted by "much maudlin sympathy expressed for the 'downtrodden denizens of the sweat-shop' and the 'homeless wanderer searching for honest employment,' and with it all often go many hard words for the men in power." Alas, he complained, "[n]othing is said about the employer who grows old before his time in a vain attempt to get frowsy ne'er-do-wells to do intelligent work; and his long patient striving with 'help' that does nothing but loaf when his back is turned." Hubbard empathized with the employer's constant struggle, as he saw it, to weed out – fire – the disloyal, lazy, and incompetent and hire the loyal, industrious, and skilled: "It is the survival of the fittest," he explained. "[S]elf-interest prompts every employer to keep the best – those who can carry a message to Garcia." Employees who carry with them "the insane suspicion that his employer is oppressing, or intending to oppress, him" are among the worst.[12]

"[W]hen all the world has gone a-slumming," Hubbard raised his voice in dissent, "I wish to speak a word of sympathy for the man who succeeds – the man who, against great odds, has directed the efforts of others." "There is no excellence, per se, in poverty," he reminded, "rags are no recommendation; and all employers are not rapacious and high-handed, any more than all poor men are virtuous."[13] To the extent we attack or burden those who reach for success, who display what Sumner had called the "industrial virtues," civilization will decline. To the extent we value and esteem them, by contrast, it will advance and progress. Hubbard explained that it was entirely natural that in a well-governed society, the shiftless will end in poverty. And, in salubrious contrast, the hardworking and industrious will always find their services in high demand:

[10] Hubbard, *Message to Garcia*, 19–20.   [11] Hubbard, *Message to Garcia*, 20–21, 24–25.
[12] Hubbard, *Message to Garcia*, 27–29.   [13] Hubbard, *Message to Garcia*, 32–33.

they will succeed by dint of their own virtues and efforts, as someone is always willing to sign on a man willing to Take a Message to Garcia.

While certainly not a sophisticated exposition of a theory of government, what Elbert Hubbard's *Message to Garcia* offered instead was an inspirational brief, and exhortation to a mass readership, for the species of virtue he deemed of surpassing value to a vibrant commercial society like the modern United States – for industrial virtue as a civic or republican virtue. Indeed, *A Message to Garcia* welded industrial and civil/republican virtues: Hubbard moved back and forth between the call from the president of the United States to drop all and assume great risks for the country at the moment that it first heard the shattering thunderclap of war to a parallel call by a private employer, perhaps an industrialist, to his employees to get his job done and not trouble the boss over petty problems that, if he were plucky and resourceful, the employee would take the initiative to solve himself (the busy producer boss, one of society's builders, presumably had better things to do). As such, Hubbard imagines the soldier/runner and the uncomplaining, loyal, and industrious employee as kindred American heroes.

Not long after, in *Our Enemy, The State* (1935), Albert Jay Nock offered a *cri de coeur* on behalf of a country where, as Hubbard had apparently sensed, these virtues were increasingly being devalued, and lost. Hubbard did not fix the moment the downward slide had begun. But Nock did: his culprits were the authors of the country's Constitution – the Founders – the very men whom his conservative movement progeny would later come to worship.[14] The American constitution that had truly served to protect the widest scope for liberty, Nock's highest value, had been the Articles of Confederation, he explained, a document that the greedy, scheming, self-serving Founders, out to feather their own nests by first creating and then appropriating central state power, had illegitimately and mendaciously conspired to replace: the progressive historian Charles Beard, a frequent target of contemporary conservative constitutionalists as a betrayer of "The Founder's Constitution," could hardly be said to have been harsher in his judgment of the Framers than Nock, the conservative hero – who cites Beard repeatedly and favorably throughout his book. In *Our Enemy, The State*, Nock called the 1789 constitutional Founding an "unscrupulous" and "dishonourable" "*coup d'état.*"[15] The Founding's disastrous and unconscionable "conversion of social power into State power," Nock further explained, had been only reinforced by the development of the "party system," which continued the criminal looting and hollowing out of society by the ongoing transfer of power to the state through a rolling *coup d'état*, with government

---

[14] Nock, it should be said, like Friedrich von Hayek and Milton Friedman, did not identify himself as a conservative: he called himself an individualist. All the same, his writings became a touchstone for many key thinkers in the modern conservative movement. For a subtle intellectual portrait, see Wreszin, *Superfluous Anarchist*.

[15] Nock, *Our Enemy, The State*, chap. 5.

power perpetually aggrandized through the redistribution of coercively extracted largesse – aided and abetted by the substantive and institutional (Federalist) constitutional vision forged by John Marshall's Supreme Court (1801–1835). By the time he published *Our Enemy, The State* in the 1930s aghast at the latest drive toward statism by Franklin Delano Roosevelt, Nock lamented, most Americans no longer knew what true (constitutional) liberty was. The few who did amounted to what was implicitly a sort of secret society – whom Nock famously dubbed "The Remnant."

While Nock blamed the American Founders for the decline of constitutional liberty in the United States, a major school of economic thought being forged in Europe, responding to the situation on the ground there, instead fingered socialism as liberty's chief antagonist. The "Austrian" economics of Ludwig von Mises, Friedrich Hayek, and Wilhelm Röpke, foreign scholars based in Vienna, London, and Geneva, in time came to have a seminal effect on the economic and political understandings of postwar American conservatives, after writings by the Austrians – like both von Mises and Hayek themselves, personally – were imported into America.[16] As such, of course, in its genesis and first half-century of development, Austrian economics had nothing to do with, or say about, the US Constitution.[17]

Austrian economics is a distinctive form of economic thought that, while striking many of the same themes as other strains of libertarianism and neoclassical economics, is rooted in its own unique theories and convictions. Founded, most say, by Carl Menger (1840–1921) and extended through the work of his students Friedrich von Wieser and Eugen Böhm von Bawert, Austrian economic thinking began with Menger's subjective theory of value, which denies that goods have any objective value and holds that the value of any good is determined by the subjective value an individual places on it. The approach's second foundational assumption is that of the purposive individual. Studies in Austrian economics are forged by logical deduction from these *a priori* assumptions and principles. As such, unlike much of modern mainstream economics, studies in Austrian economic science are, not just in fact but by theoretical conviction, qualitative rather than quantitative,

---

[16] Outside conservative circles, von Mises and Hayek remained square pegs in round holes: both Mises and Hayek remained academic outsiders who owed their university positions (at New York University and the University of Chicago, respectively) not to ordinary appointments and salaries, but to outside funding by conservative activists and foundations.

[17] It could be argued that the transatlantic currents of postwar conservatism were almost as swift as those of an earlier generation of American progressives. See Daniel T. Rodgers, *Atlantic Crossings: Social Politics in a Progressive Age* (Cambridge, MA: Belknap Press of Harvard University Press, 1998). See also Angus Burgin, *The Great Persuasion: Reinventing Free Markets Since the Depression* (Cambridge, MA: Harvard University Press, 2012); Daniel Stedman Jones, *Masters of the Universe: Hayek, Friedman, and the Birth of NeoLiberal Politics* (Princeton: Princeton University Press, 2012). Austrian economics also influenced the economic policy directions taken by Charles de Gaulle in France, Luigi Einaudi in Italy, and, later, Margaret Thatcher in England.

expressly rejecting empiricism and, along with it, mathematical and statistical economics. In the sense that it involves rigorous deduction from core assumptions and principles, it is determinedly philosophical.[18]

The most senior Austrian economist to attain influence on the American Right was Ludwig von Mises (1881–1973), a relentless opponent of government coercion of human behavior broadly understood, but first and foremost in economic markets.[19] In *The Theory of Money and Credit* (1912), von Mises sought to integrate macro- and microeconomic theory by demonstrating the micro/individual choice foundations of broader, economy-wide phenomena. This laid the groundwork for the core argument of von Mises's book, which argued for the superiority of the gold standard as the basis for sound monetary policy. In *Socialism* (1922), von Mises trained a spotlight on what he considered to be socialism's moral smugness in claiming foundationally that, unlike its purportedly morally obtuse opponents, it made human equality its foremost concern. Von Mises invited his readers to interrogate this presumptuous claim more rigorously. Von Mises argued that, its self-serving claims notwithstanding, socialism's true commitment was not to equality of opportunity but rather equality of result. Given that people were not equal in their talents, intelligence, initiative, or anything else, the commitment to equality of result ran counter to human nature and human experience. Hence, when government sought to use its coercive powers to enforce the equality of result through the redistribution of wealth, the results, in the nature of things, were disastrous. Redistribution to bring about equality of result thwarted economic and other forms of social progress. Worse, the government's commitment to this utopian project was dependent on the perpetual expansion of the coercive powers of the state, as manifested by what von Mises took to be the ceaseless expansion of the coercive powers of government bureaucracies. Socialists, moreover, had demonized the agents and engines of wealth creation, capitalists and entrepreneurs, and through (redistributive) taxation stifled their productive initiatives. Socialism was unnatural. For societies it was disastrous. Nevertheless, von Mises lamented, its core assumptions were evident everywhere at the time he wrote in the redistributionists' goals and policies of the world's modern, ostensibly capitalist or "mixed capitalist," bureaucratic and social welfare states.

---

[18] Hawley, *Right-Wing Critics of American Conservatism*, 155–156.

[19] Ludwig von Mises, *The Theory of Money and Credit* (Indianapolis, IN: Liberty Classics, 1980) [1912]; Ludwig von Mises, "Economic Calculation in the Socialist Commonwealth" (1920), in Friedrich Hayek, editor, *Collectivist Economic Planning* (London: Routledge, 1935); Ludwig von Mises, *Socialism: An Economic and Sociological Analysis* (1922) [translated into English by J. Kahane, and published in the United States by Macmillan in 1936]; Ludwig von Mises, *Bureaucracy* (New Haven: Yale University Press, 1944); Ludwig von Mises, *The Anti-Capitalist Mentality* (Princeton, NJ: Van Nostrand, 1956); Ludwig von Mises, *Human Action: A Treatise on Economics* (New Haven: Yale University Press, 1949); Ludwig von Mises, *Liberalismus* [Liberalism] (United States: Important Books, 1927). All of von Mises's major works are available in stylish contemporary editions, sold at subsidized low prices, by The Liberty Fund.

Austrian economists like von Mises are sometimes casually classed as thoroughgoing materialists and apologists for selfishness and greed. But the Austrians did not disregard moral concerns or, like Ayn Rand (discussed later), hold selfishness to be the preeminent virtue. Von Mises argued that free market capitalist economics set the baseline conditions for a morally grounded society. As he explained at length in *Human Action* (1949), free markets worked through human relationships. The choices made by individuals in the economic sphere involved efforts by the whole person, in both material and nonmaterial senses acting as a moral free agent, to remove "uneasiness" from his experience and to better his life and situation. Since each person is different in what he values economically and non-economically and in what makes him uneasy, the freedom to make choices without interference or coercion from government is the cornerstone of human freedom, understood in the deepest moral sense.

Government coercion of an individual in making these choices – social engineering – von Mises argued, is ultimately tyrannical. People define themselves and their lives through these foundational choices – that is, through action that is "human" in its fullest sense. It is, in this sense, that there is no such thing as "society": indeed, it was from von Mises that conservative British Prime Minister Margaret Thatcher was drawing when she provocatively asserted, in a much-noted comment, flummoxing her antagonists, that "there is no such thing as society." In the beginning, and in the end, von Mises argued, there are only individuals, making choices and interacting, striving to live and better their lives.[20]

Von Mises's student and associate, the German economist Wilhelm Röpke further developed the argument for the moral foundations – and moral superiority – of the free market capitalist system. A veteran of the German trenches in World War I, an experience that shocked and scarred him, and, later, an opponent of the Nazis, which led him into exile, first in Istanbul, then in Geneva, Röpke was, like von Mises, a Mont Pelerin Society founder. Before he was driven into exile, the Nazis banned Röpke's book *Economics of a Free Society* (1937), whose theme was the interrelationship between economic and political freedom.[21] *Economics of a Free Society* devoted significant attention to the baneful effects of the taxation of wealth which, Röpke argued, discouraged not only innovation and wealth creation but, even worse, placed that wealth in the hands of government bureaucrats, who were themselves a political class with their own private interests and agendas. These self-interested bureaucrats – politicians,

---

[20] While he wrote primarily about economics, von Mises was opposed to efforts by governments to enforce personal morality. He believed, however, that market choices and interactions were suffused by it.

[21] Wilhelm Röpke, *Economics of a Free Society* (Chicago: H. Regnery Co., 1963) (Die Hehre von der Wirtschaft, translator).

really, rather than public servants – were less effective at solving social problems than were free capitalist markets themselves.

Much of Röpke's postwar work, including his influential *A Humane Economy* (1957), arose out of his reflections on the contrast in the Cold War division of his native Germany between a market-oriented West Germany and an ostensibly egalitarian, but tyrannical, socialist East Germany – put otherwise, between an open society and its enemies.[22] Reared in a traditionalist Protestant home, Röpke also emphasized the centrality to a market economy of the concept of "free will," which lent a deep moral foundation to the concept of "market choice." It was the freedom to make choices, including choices about what to do with one's property and earnings, that gave man the freedom to be truly human, lending dignity to man in his engagement with others. Far from being hyper-individualistic, Röpke argued, free market dynamics were interactive and relational. To the extent that government, with its laws and bureaucratic oversight, constrained an individual's choices – including an individual's choices involving the extension of charity to the less fortunate – it was complicit, in a moral sense, in circumscribing an individual's full humanity. Man, Röpke recognized, was far from perfect. But to the extent that government sought to compensate for and correct his imperfections, it would, in the end, end up crushing not only his economic but his moral potential.

To the extent that governments – sometimes driven by a mistaken understanding of Christian teaching concerning charity – sought to eliminate life's natural inequities, Röpke explained, the end result would be a dictatorial or totalitarian government that brutally prevents the individual from living as a moral being through the exercise of his God-given free will. In a truly humane economy, Röpke argued, charity will be a private affair, and no business of government. To the extent that the charitable function is assumed by the (social welfare) state, the government is forced to appropriate more and more of its people's property through taxation, in the process undercutting their ability and undermining their habit of charitable giving of their own free will.[23] The spiral of the effort of the social welfare state to right the world's inequalities, Röpke warned, was ever downward from individualism into collectivism, since, in the nature of things, the number of inequalities in the world is infinite. The result would inevitably be ever more government and ever less freedom. Free choice would be whittled down to a nub by schemes of social improvement instituted by government for ostensibly noble purposes.

Government involvement in the economy intolerably constricted the scope of an individual's free will not only by directly coercing his choices through laws and regulations and by appropriating his money and property, about and through which he can exercise his choices, through taxation, but also by

[22] See Karl Popper, *The Open Society and Its Enemies* (London: Routledge, 1945).
[23] See also Bertrand de Jouvenel, *The Ethics of Redistribution* (Cambridge: Cambridge University Press, 1952).

sapping the initiative and will of those who come to rely upon its largesse. The ostensible beneficiaries of the social welfare state would soon become its wards. As individuals, Röpke argued, these beneficiaries became dependent men: they were systematically drained of the habit of self-reliance, initiative, moral choice and ultimately of human dignity. The most productive and the least productive alike would lose the spirit of enterprise, and the will to innovate, advance, and create. Not least of all, sapping the initiative of society's capitalist entrepreneurs would stifle economic growth – the source, of course, of the largesse that the welfare state was depending on to run its redistributive project. As national income diminished, the state, increasingly starved of cash, was forced to crack down more and more to get the money it needed, instituting a spiral of ever more laws, ever more regulation, and ever higher taxes, which can only end in economic ruin and political tyranny. As such, welfarism was the enemy of human, and humane, values, of individual liberty and morals – and, ultimately, of society's sustaining moral and economic health.[24] Fortunately, for Americans, at least, Röpke explained by the late 1950s, the nation's Founders instituted a constitutional system and order in which the chief objective had been the protection of the free choice of individuals. Röpke devoted particular attention to the Founders' commitment to federalism and localism, which served to break the impulses toward large central government where, he argued, the drive to socialism was most likely to originate and thrive.

Certainly the most widely read book penned by an Austrian economist was Friedrich Hayek's *The Road to Serfdom* (1944), which, addressing a free world on the verge of an epochal victory over the Nazis, far from celebrating the impending triumph, sounded the alarm for Western civilization's looming next war. The West's inhabitants, Hayek at full throttle cried, their imminent victory notwithstanding, were in mortal danger of becoming, if not Nazis, then just like the Germans who had cleared the path for National Socialism. The profoundly disturbed Hayek discerned in the ostensibly free West "the same determination that the organization of the nation ... achieved for purposes of defense ... be retained for purposes of creation ... [dangerously informed by] the same contempt for nineteenth-century liberalism, the same ... fatalistic acceptance of 'inevitable trends.'" We have "been progressively moving away from the basic ideas on which Western civilization had been built," chiefly "that freedom in economic affairs without which personal and political freedom has never existed in the past," he warned.[25]

Recounting the movement from feudalism to liberal modernity, Hayek argued in *The Road to Serfdom* that "[t]he gradual transformation of a rigidly organized hierarchic system into one where men could at least attempt to shape their own lives ... is closely associated with the growth of commerce." Under a liberal, market society, "[t]he fundamental principle [is] that in the

[24] See also de Jouvenel, *Ethics of Redistribution.*
[25] Hayek, *Road to Serfdom*, 2–3, 12–13, 68–71.

ordering of our affairs we should make as much use as possible of the spontaneous forces of society, and resort as little as possible to coercion." Ironically, however, it was liberalism's monumental success that tempted men in liberal societies to move on to what they misunderstood to be the natural next step of engineering top-down solutions to liberal modernity's remaining social problems such as (as they saw it) the inequality of wealth. Hayek considered the temptation of central economic planning an existential threat to the very conditions that had made modern liberty possible. This, squarely set out by Hayek in his manifesto, was the threat that socialism posed to freedom, that collectivism posed to individualism.

Hayek, in line with the understandings of the Austrians as a group, did not argue on behalf of the individual on the grounds that "man is egoistic, or selfish, or ought to be." Perhaps his most distinctive contribution to economic thought, for which he was later awarded the Nobel Prize in Economics, was that the most significant feature of free markets was their role in registering and communicating knowledge and information: put otherwise, markets were uniquely successful as foundations for social ordering because individuals knew best what they needed and wanted. Central planners lacked this information. For planners to make decisions for the society as a whole in the absence of knowledge of where it was that the individuals who comprised society wanted to go would be "as if a group of people were to commit themselves to take a journey together without agreeing where they want to go: with the result that they may all have to make a journey which most of them do not want at all." Under such systems, planners are "given power to make with the force of law what to all intents and purposes are arbitrary decisions."[26]

One of the abiding virtues of liberalism for Hayek, as for other liberals like John Locke, was that it worked to constrain the exercise of arbitrary power through a rigorous adherence to the rule of law. Liberal legalism (in its classical form, at least) accomplishes this task by the promulgation of laws oriented not

---

[26] Hayek, *Road to Serfdom*, 14, 17, 19–23, 26–27, 32–42, 59–62, 66; William F. Buckley Jr. adopted Hayek's collectivism versus individualism frame in *God and Man at Yale* and took it a step beyond Hayek in marrying it to his Christian conservative (in his case, right-wing Catholic) religious vision ("I myself believe that the duel between Christianity and atheism is the most important in the world. I further believe that the struggle between individualism and collectivism is the same struggle reproduced on another level."). In his blockbuster book *Witness* (1952) published the following year, Buckley's hero Whittaker Chambers transposed the individualism versus collectivism opposition into one pitting freedom against communism, which, in turn, Chambers announced, "has posed in practical form the most revolutionary question in history: God or Man?" One might say that, as Chamber's framed it, for a society to take the decision to commit to economic planning was to succumb to the temptation "whispered in the first days of the Creation under the Tree of the Knowledge of Good and Evil: 'Ye shall be as gods' ... The Communist vision is the vision of Man without God. It is the vision of man's mind displacing God as the creative intelligence of the world. It is the vision of man's liberated mind, by the sole force of its rational intelligence, redirecting man's destiny and reorganizing man's life and the world." Whittaker Chambers, *Witness* (New York: Random House, 1952).

toward substantive ends, which it leaves to individuals to determine, but by "laying down a Rule of the Road." "The state should confine itself to establishing rules applying to general types of situations and should allow the individuals freedom in everything which depends on the circumstances of time and place," Hayek argued. As such, the legislative power is not, as some modern, progressive, welfare state liberals would have it, simply the handmaiden of what the democratic majority might want, or a government official to whom legislative power is delegated, often with wide discretion, draws upon to formulate and promulgate regulations in the ostensible public interest. In a free, liberal society, Hayek argued, the legislative power will be limited by an implied "recognition of the inalienable right of the individual, inviolable rights of man." It was for this reason that economic liberty – the rule of law limitations placed on governments in the economic sphere – was not less important than other forms of freedom, like so-called personal rights including the freedom of speech and religion, but paramount. Economic liberties were paramount, that is, not because Hayek was a materialist and valued money and wealth accumulation above all other values, but because they were the *sine qua non* of every other sort of liberal freedom. Nowhere was this fact about freedom more clearly illustrated than in communist societies like Soviet Russia, where, following Marx, economic liberties were the first to go, and the loss of every other freedom followed.[27]

In the wake of the widely disseminated *Road to Serfdom* – which was serialized in abridged form in *Reader's Digest* in 1945[28] – high-end popularizers like the journalist John Chamberlain carried and sustained the influence of Austrian economic thought both within the US conservative movement and in attentive precincts of the mass public. Chamberlain himself made a case for economic liberty in his book *The Roots of Capitalism* (1959).[29] Like von Mises, Röpke, and Hayek before him, Chamberlain began by tracing the moral roots of a free society to its commitment to free will. Free will, Chamberlain argued, presumed a genuine freedom of choice. This necessarily entailed the option of making bad choices as well as good ones. Among the choices made by free, self-directed individuals were choices concerning labor

[27] Hayek, *Road to Serfdom*, 72–75, 78, 84, 102–109; John Locke, *Second Treatise on Civil Government* (1689).

[28] See Juliet Williams, "The Road Less Traveled: Reconsidering the Political Writings of Friedrich von Hayek, in Lichtenstein, editor, *American Capitalism*, 213.

[29] John Chamberlain, *The Roots of Capitalism* (Princeton: Van Nostrand, 1959). See also John Chamberlain, *The Enterprising Americans: A Business History of the United States* (New York: Harper and Row, 1963). The Yale-educated Chamberlain was an editor and writer for *Fortune* and *Life* magazines, the first editor (with Suzanne LaFollette and Henry Hazlitt) of *The Freeman*, a frequent book reviewer for the *New York Times*, and author of the forewords to the first American edition of both Hayek's *The Road to Serfdom* (1944) and Buckley's *God and Man at Yale* (1959). For Chamberlain's intellectual trajectory, in his own words, see John Chamberlain, *A Life With the Printed Word* (Chicago: Regnery Gateway, 1982). See also Edmund A. Opitz, "A Reviewer Remembered: John Chamberlain, 1903–1995," *The Freeman* 45 (6) (June 1995).

and the acquisition and alienation of property. Any system challenging the commitment to free, including (although certainly not limited to) choices in the economic sphere, Chamberlain argued, whether it realized it or not, had set itself on the road to collectivism. In setting out down that dangerous road, Chamberlain argued that economic freedoms would be the first to be downgraded in status and jettisoned. But, as day followed night, so-called personal freedoms would naturally follow as an implication of the rejection of the value of choice in favor of ostensibly collective social goals. Given the nature of this progression, Chamberlain argued, property rights must be considered the first freedom: for a society that does not protect them, in the end, all is lost.

In his argument explicating the moral foundations of capitalism, Chamberlain offered a case study in the spurning of economic liberty, the case of regulation gone wild in eighteenth-century France. Chamberlain explained that the context had been set by France's subscription to Enlightenment rationalism, which harbored a dangerous obsession with finding rational solutions to every posited social problem. The siren-song belief in the world perfected through reason had led to an endless upward trajectory in regulation. Unfortunately, however, the world as it actually existed was not amenable to these would-be solutions: people were irrational, and planners, besides being self-interested and power hungry, were ignorant.

America's constitutional Founders, Chamberlain explained – adding a dimension that some of the Austrians like Röpke, perhaps tutored by their US compatriots, had started to touch upon in the late 1950s – had known better and avoided these snares. The constitutional system they designed forswore any grand ambitions concerning the control of economic interactions: The Founders' Constitution had given a wide berth to free choice, providing breathing room for a diversity of economic approaches and solutions. Recently, however, Chamberlain warned, things had begun moving in very different, and disturbing, directions. Here, he singled out the case of the explosion of federal regulation pursuant to Congress's (purported) powers under the Article I, Section 8 Commerce Clause, which the courts, unfortunately, had ultimately rubber-stamped.[30]

Chamberlain next advanced his case through the classic (Adam) Smithian framework. He explained how under a capitalist economic system, the pursuit of private interest benefits not only the individual but also the whole society. No one better exemplified the virtues of this dynamic, Chamberlain attested, than the American businessman, who, thanks to the genius of capitalism, did both well and good. The American businessman had brought world-class knowledge and acumen to the table. Alas, he was all too often thwarted by government, which had little understanding of the on-the-ground realities of competitive markets and business landscapes or, because businesses needed to plan, the

---

[30] See *National Labor Relations Board v. Jones and Laughlin Steel*, 301 US 1 (1937); *Wickard v. Filburn*, 317 US 111 (1942).

problems created for businesses when the regulatory environment they were operating within was wracked by uncertainty.

In the twentieth century United States, government power had been unleashed. But it had often grown incrementally – and, hence, obscurely. Many of these incremental expansions of government power were undertaken with justifications that might have at the time seemed reasonable and helpful. But over time, whether apparently or stealthily, the powers of government had accumulated. At this point, all told, Americans needed to ask whether constitutional liberty in America had been lost. Government was out of control; it was borderline omnipotent. The regulations ran so thick, and the regulatory environment was so caked with inconsistencies, that no one now could tell whether or not they were in compliance– or whether compliance was even possible. The byzantine US tax code was a case in point.

While drawing upon the Austrian economics of von Mises, Röpke, and Hayek, Henry Hazlitt's early *Economics in One Lesson* (1946) (like Milton Friedman's later *Capitalism and Freedom* (1962), to be discussed later) considered implications of these ideas for specific areas of public policy. *Economics in One Lesson* focused on the unintended consequences and system effects of key policies of the modern American regulatory/social welfare state.[31] Such meliorist public policies, Hazlitt – dubbed "The People's Austrian"[32] – observed, were typically designed with a particular problem, target, or objective in mind. But he observed that such policies often had broader and, as it unexpectedly turned out, undesirable spillover effects to which the policy makers, with their optimism and zeal for solving problems through government action, were characteristically and tragically oblivious. Keynesian government spending aimed at priming the GDP during macroeconomic downturns, Hazlitt explained, had played a major role in inducing the self-reinforcing expansion of government bureaucracies, which, in turn, put a damper on economic growth through the attendant high and increasing levels of taxation necessary to support them. This, of course, tamped down growth, growth that, given the policy logic of the modern social welfare state, required even more Keynesian spending. The cycle continued *ad infinitum*.

Hazlitt taught that one of bureaucracy's chief dynamics is the search for more and more clients for itself. Thus, once it is created and empowered, it tends toward ceaseless expansion, fueled by either deficit spending or higher taxation, which, in time, kills the growth on which it depends. This leads, ultimately, to the cascading corruption of the entire political system, and to the crippling of

---

[31] In the depths of the Great Depression, Hazlitt had influentially reviewed the English language publication of Ludwig von Mises's *Socialism* (1936) in the *New York Times* (January 9, 1938).

[32] Randall G. Holcombe, editor, *15 Great Austrian Economists* (Auburn, AL: Ludwig von Mises Institute, 1999); Randall G. Holcombe, *Advanced Introduction to the Austrian School of Economics* (Northampton, MA: Edward Elgar, 2014).

the economy. We would do well to remember, Hazlitt urged his readers, that all the money spent by the government comes from the people. The more the government spends, the more it crowds out private spending. He explained that to a significant extent, politicians take up the business of selling government services – which they frame as fixing problems – with the primary aim of getting reelected. Votes are thus effectively bought through the unending expansion of government entitlements. As such, the major task of government is to serve itself.[33] To make matters worse, these dynamics sparked inflation. In the long run, the cascade of bad consequences from government expansion vitiated the very purpose for which the spending had been undertaken in the first place. In this tragic spiral, all were losers – everyone except the government itself and the (current and would-be) bureaucrats who staffed it.

Fortunately, Hazlitt observed, the architect of the US Constitution, James Madison, had known better: he had designed a constitutional system that would keep these dynamics to a minimum. Hazlitt ended by applying these understandings in thumbnail critiques of government subsidies, price supports, minimum wage laws, and rent control.

William Henry Chamberlin underlined the constitutional point in the *Wall Street Journal* in the early 1950s. "In reading through the American Constitution it is remarkable how often those 'negative' words, 'no' and 'not' recur," Chamberlin observed: "[O]ut of these and many other limiting and prohibiting clauses in the Constitution merged the edifice of our civil political liberties ... Where the state is kept within bounds by a long series of 'Thou Shalt Nots' by strict legal limitations on its power the individual enjoys the best prospect of a free and happy and prosperous life."[34] For its part, *Reader's Digest* warned that an activist central government raised serious civil liberties issues. "It is not enough to laugh off the question of cost, or the infringement on personal freedom which the injection of Government intervention into [a wide array of] spheres entails, as simply 'the propagation of the reactionaries,'" it insisted.[35]

From the 1960s into the 1970s, the banner of an Austrian-inflected libertarianism was carried forward perhaps most prominently by Murray Rothbard, a Bronx-born, Columbia University–educated libertarian-anarchist of at times ambiguous political identity on the Left-Right spectrum, about which he cared not a fig. Much of Rothbard's succession of odd alliances – at different points he had been a compatriot of right-wing populists like Joseph McCarthy, the 1960s New Left, the Black Panthers, conservative libertarians like Frank Meyer, paleo/traditionalist conservatives like Patrick Buchanan, and the Ku Klux Klansman David Duke, and had written both for *Ramparts* and

[33] Henry Hazlitt, *Economics in One Lesson* (New York: Harper and Bros., 1946).
[34] William Henry Chamberlin, "Case for 'Thou Shalt Not,'" *Wall Street Journal* (March 16, 1950), 8.
[35] "That 'Mandate' Again," *Reader's Digest* 56:334 (February 1950), 108 [reprinted from *New York Herald Tribune* (November 5, 1949)].

National Review – arose, Rothbard insisted, not out of changing views (he vehemently denied any such changes) but rather to altered contexts: Rothbard was willing to sign on with whoever at any moment was dropping the most explosive bombs on state power and taking the biggest risks to bring it to its knees. Rothbard wrote many, many articles, but only one book – *For a New Liberty* (1973), in which he offered an overview, from an early 1970s vantage point, of his views.[36]

THE PROBLEM OF FEDERAL SPENDING

What, then, was to be done? One of the dividing lines within the postwar Republican Party was between those committed to the rollback of federal spending and the New Deal social welfare state and those who, while inclined to hold the line or cut some of its programs, took it to be the new baseline for American government. Those in the former group dubbed those in the latter, including New York governor and Republican presidential candidate Thomas E. Dewey and President Eisenhower, "me-too" politicians. The *Wall Street Journal* and other conservative outlets campaigned against "me-tooism" and the notion that "the source of all welfare and security is the State and that men can have it from the State but not without the State."[37]

Warnings about the ominous growth of the federal budget and budget deficit were common on the Right, which never accepted the new baseline. This spending was commonly understood as undertaken not for the general interest but to spread spoils to special interests. Designing men and self-serving interests were leveraging government handouts – that is, appropriating and redistributing the hard-earned dollars of American taxpayers – to get themselves elected to public office.[38] As such, under post–New Deal conditions, the political process

---

[36] Murray N. Rothbard, *For a New Liberty: A Libertarian Manifesto* (Auburn, AL: Ludwig von Mises Institute, 1973). See Doherty, *Radicals for Capitalism*, 378–384. The institutional center of Austrian economics in the United States today is the Ludwig von Mises Institute in Auburn, Alabama, which, among many other things, publishes the *Quarterly Review of Austrian Economics* (https://mises.org/). See Hawley, *Right-Wing Critics of American Conservatism*, 170–171.

[37] "The 20th Century," *Wall Street Journal* (February 13, 1950), 4. See also "No Curse After All," *Wall Street Journal* (May 5, 1950), 6; "174 Years Later," *Wall Street Journal* (July 3, 1950), 4; Letter to the Editor, "A Lifelong Republican" [Montclair, NJ] to the *Wall Street Journal* (November 15, 1950), 8. See Michael D. Bowen, *The Roots of Modern Conservatism: Dewey, Taft, and the Battle for the Soul of the Republican Party* (Chapel Hill: University of North Carolina Press, 2011); Jefferson Cowie, *The Great Exception: The New Deal and the Limits of American Politics* (Princeton: Princeton University Press, 2016), 162–163.

[38] "Is There Room in the Poorhouse for 149 Million People?" *Reader's Digest* 56:333 (January 1950), 99 [reprinted from an advertisement in *Automotive News* (n.d.)]. Stanley High, "The Time to Stop the Spenders Is *Now*," *Reader's Digest* 56:336 (April 1950): 130–134. At the end, the article offers readers a list of "four positive things you can do *now* to help stop spenders, cut Government costs and end the trend toward the All-Powerful State."

ran by "buying people with their own money."³⁹ Farm subsidies were a case in point – "a fair illustration of what happens when the Government helps a special group maintain or increase its share of the national income regardless of the group's contribution to that income."⁴⁰ Many "farmers realize that there is need for some kind of farm program," John Strohm acknowledged in *Reader's Digest* in the early 1950s, "but they want it kept simple. They don't like to see Big Government get bigger, and controls get more rigid."⁴¹ One *ABA Journal* correspondent thought that Harry Hopkins's formulation had captured the dynamic perfectly: "[T]ax and tax, spend and spend and spend, elect and elect and elect."⁴² Viewed from this perspective, liberals got no credit for meaning well (even if their efforts were naïve or misguided): their piety was little more than a cover for self-advancement, self-aggrandizement, and self-interest.

Had any constitutional authority licensed this new departure? In a long "originalist" expose for the *ABA Journal* in the early 1960s, George Nilsson explained that the federal government was seizing more and more power pursuant to "the alleged general welfare clause," which, starting in the 1930s, had became a liberal lodestar for novel interpretations seeking to legitimize a turn in unauthorized directions.⁴³ To be sure, Nilsson acknowledged, Alexander Hamilton had promoted expansive understandings of the national government's constitutional powers. But the Constitutional Convention as a whole had repudiated Hamilton's views: "[C]an anyone for a minute think that the colonists generally, and the members of the convention specifically, would have adopted a constitution which granted general welfare powers to the Federal Government?" The answer, to Nilsson, was obvious.⁴⁴

In the mid-1950s, another *ABA Journal* writer, George Morton, argued that the Constitution was being fatally "undermined by 'public welfare' laws such as 'social security', wage, price, public housing and rent controls, and by the administrative agencies of government." "[I]n carrying out the various

³⁹ Frank R. Kent, "Salute to Byrd," *Wall Street Journal* (March 13, 1950), 4.
⁴⁰ John Strohm, "Let's Stop Trying to Legislate Farm Income!" *Reader's Digest* 74:445 (May 1959): 101–104; "What You Can Do About the Incredible Farm Scandal," *Reader's Digest* 75:447 (July 1959): 21–22 [reprinted, condensed, from *Life* (April 20, 1959)]; "Farm Politics vs. the People," *Reader's Digest* 56:336 (April 1950): 1–4, 1–2 [reprinted, condensed, from *Fortune* (January 1950)].
⁴¹ John Strohm, "Big Government is in Your Country, Too," *Reader's Digest* 56:338 (June 1950): 51–53 [excerpts reprinted from *Country Gentleman* (March 1950)].
⁴² John F. Schmidt [Peoria, Illinois], Letter to the Editor, *American Bar Association Journal* 47 (1961): 332, 336. See also George W. Nilsson, "There Is No 'General Welfare Power' in the Constitution of the United States," *American Bar Association Journal* 47 (January 1961): 43–47, 43.
⁴³ See, e.g., *Steward Machine Co. v. Davis*, 301 US 548 (1937); *Helvering v. Davis*, 301 US 619 (1937).
⁴⁴ Nilsson, "There Is No 'General Welfare Power' in the Constitution of the United States," 43, 44, 47. But see Robert B. McKay, "Taxing and Spending for the General Welfare: A Reply to Mr. Nilsson," *American Bar Association Journal* 48 (January 1962): 38–42.

welfare laws, government agents and agencies, though believing themselves to be loyal citizens, are acting like the Greek enemies of ancient Troy in the Trojan War, who concealed themselves within a great wooden horse, " Morton charged. Unfortunately, these enemies within our walls have continued to pass unrecognized because they have heretofore successfully passed themselves off as loyal, law-abiding, and public-spirited friends:

And for nearly twenty years, these ... unrecognized enemies of our Constitution, concealed within the Public Welfare Trojan Horse, have been coming out and proclaiming themselves to be the only loyal friends of the common man ... [T]hey have been aided in their seizure of power and its growth, by the United States Supreme Court, whose interpretations of the Constitution, especially in interstate commerce, labor and social security welfare cases, have helped to undermine and destroy much of its original plain meaning.[45]

This "has served to undermine and destroy the morale and courage of the individual citizen to provide for his own future, and that of his family, by his own efforts, earnings, savings and resources, traditional in American history – the American way." In a peroration, Morton warned that

[e]ither this nation ... must return to the fundamental principles on which free government was founded in 1787, or our liberties, guaranteed by our Constitution, will disappear, just as they did in France in the French Revolution, in Germany under Hitler, in Italy under Mussolini, and in Russia under Lenin and Stalin. With them "public welfare" was the road to tyranny.[46]

Others also tied constitutional economics to individual character. In the late 1940s, Frank Holman struck this theme in his American Bar Association Presidential Address:

Now we have before us the phenomenon by which through government fiat and legislative policy it is sought to level out *all* inequalities so that the thrifty and the improvident, the industrious and the shiftless, shall be *made* equal ... [W]e have almost a cult claiming not mere equality of opportunity but "superior rights" where time-worn ideas of self-reliance, self-support and self-discipline are no longer encouraged. Pressure groups now expect and demand to be taken care of by the government upon an equal basis with and at the expense of citizens who do strive and work.[47]

"The easiest way to sell each new step toward statism," Holman warned, "has been to work on the emotions of the people through some catch phrase like 'social justice', or 'economic equality' or 'racial equality'. We follow these banners emblazoned with catch phrases without thinking what they mean or how they affect the basic principles of our form of government." When these

---

[45] George E. Morton, "Social Security: The Trojan Horse Inside Our Walls," *American Bar Association Journal* 40 (February 1954): 135–139, 136.

[46] Morton, "Social Security: The Trojan Horse Inside Our Walls," 137–138.

[47] Frank E. Holman, "The President's Annual Address: Must America Succumb to Statism?" *American Bar Association Journal* 35 (October 1949): 801–879, 803.

banners are unfurled in public debate, a considerable dose of *caveat emptor* is in order, Holman warned.[48] Brooks Harman of Odessa, Texas, went so far as to declare Social Security an affront to his moral and religious convictions. "I have always been taught and read from my Bible that we are to honor our parents," Harman began. But "[t]he whole Social Security fabric presupposes that we will cease honoring our parents and that now we want the Government or some social organization to honor our parents ... Social Security is nothing ... but a purchase of votes by those people who have no faith in the teachings of Jesus Christ."[49]

Writing as the newly appointed chair of the US President's Commission on National Goals in 1960, the political scientist, Brown University president, and Eisenhower advisor Henry M. Wriston complained in *Reader's Digest* that "[i]n far-off days we were not ashamed to speak about rugged individualism. But somewhere in the 1930s, rugged individualism became associated with industrial piracy, with exploitation of one's fellow men. So we denounced it." Looking back from 1960, Wriston now believed that, in all that, "[w]e went too far." He pronounced himself opposed to any thoroughgoing materialism – which, after all, was one of communism's cardinal sins. Wriston was also opposed to steering the nation's youth away from art, poetry, music, and into subjects that would prepare them to defend national security. "Among all the tragic consequences of depression and war, this suppression of personal self-expression through one's life work is among the most poignant," he observed. That said, Wriston was against the "sentimental and superficial idea that people should somehow be made equal."[50]

These moral and philosophical concerns were translated into positions on public policy. In the mid-1960s, for instance, they were drafted into service in the fight against Great Society legislation that sought to leverage the federal government's largesse to coerce states, through tax penalties on employers, into providing more generous unemployment compensation. Writers in *Reader's Digest* and elsewhere complained that such legislation "would ... put pressure on the states to surrender their traditional rights to determine who should get jobless pay, how long the payments should last and how much they should be" and "This is nothing less than total revolution in our system for giving benefits to the unemployed ... one more giant step toward domination of the states by a monolithic government in Washington." The unemployment compensation legislation, moreover, might very well lead to a "benefit bonanza," spurring welfare cheats and "further encourage[ing] a growing class in America – the

[48] Holman, "Must America Succumb to Statism?" 804.
[49] Brooks L. Harman [Odessa, Texas], Letter to the Editor, *American Bar Association Journal* 40 (1954): 186.
[50] Henry M. Wriston, "What's Wrong with Rugged Individualism?" *Reader's Digest* 77:460 (August 1960): 25–28, 26–27 [reprinted, condensed, from the *Wall Street Journal* (June 1, 1960)].

voluntarily unemployed."[51] The journalists Earl and Anne Selby characterized the Watts riots (1965) in Los Angeles as an example of "the disastrous effects of public welfare." In a 1966 article for *Reader's Digest*, the Selbys quoted a black Los Angeles minister complaining that "[p]eople get *on* welfare, but they don't get *off*. The result is that welfare trains whole families to live on the handouts of relief." The Selbys warned that we "must not let joblessness descend into a perpetual cycle of relief." Ultimately, "*the price of public assistance is loss of human dignity.*"[52] Such views flowed like tributaries into the Right's old, deep, and wide river of free market thought. While some of this thought certainly had racial overtones,[53] black conservatives like Theodore Roosevelt Mason ("T.R.M.") Howard, George Schuyler, Zora Neale Hurston, and, later, Thomas Sowell and Walter Williams were on board. These African Americans drew liberally on themes of self-help, individual initiative, and free enterprise that had found its most influential early expression in the work and career of Booker T. Washington.[54]

What then was to be done? By the 1970s, many conservatives were campaigning hard for a balanced budget amendment to the US Constitution. An article by Eugene Methvin in *Reader's Digest* drew attention to the campaign and championed its significance. "Never before in the nation's history," Methvin cheered, "has so widespread a movement for constitutional change developed over such fundamental issues as the proper size of government and the way our elected representatives wield the powers to tax

---

[51] Earl and Anne Selby, "New Grab for Federal Power: Unemployment Benefits," *Reader's Digest* 88:526 (February 1966): 56–59, 56, 57, 59. See also "One More Federal Intrusion," *Wall Street Journal* (April 24, 1958), 10. Later, the Roberts Court struck down this sort of coercion as unconstitutional. *National Federation of Independent Businesses* v. *Sebelius*, 567 US 519 (2012). A Chicago native and graduate of the journalism school at Northwestern, Earl Selby was a legendary, hard-bitten Philadelphia columnist and editor.

[52] Earl and Anne Selby, "Watts: Where Welfare Bred Violence," *Reader's Digest* 88:529 (May 1966): 67–71, 67–68, 70–71 [emphases in original]. Far from just popping off on these matters, Earl Selby's interest in race was heartfelt and sustained. See Earl and Miriam Selby, *Odyssey: Journey Through Black America* (New York: G.P. Putnam's Sons, 1971).

[53] See Cowie, *The Great Exception*, 181. See also Ira Katznelson, *Fear Itself: The New Deal and the Origins of Our Time* (New York: Liveright Publishing Co., 2013); Ira Katznelson, *When Affirmative Action Was White: An Untold History of Racial Inequality in Twentieth Century America* (New York: W.W. Norton, 2005).

[54] David Beito and Linda Beito, *Black Maverick: T.R.M. Howard's Fight for Civil Rights and Economic Power* (Urbana: University of Illinois Press, 2009); David Beito and Linda Royster Beito, "Isabel Paterson, Rose Wilder Lane, and Zora Neale Hurston on War, Race, the State, and Liberty," *The Independent Review* 12:4 (Spring 2008): 553–573; George S. Schuyler, *Black and Conservative: The Autobiography of George S. Schuyler* (New Rochelle, NY: Arlington House, 1966); Jeffrey B. Leak, editor, *Rac[e]ing to the Right: Selected Essays of George Schuyler* (Knoxville: University of Tennessee Press, 2001). See Robert J. Norrell, *Up From History: The Life of Booker T. Washington* (Cambridge, MA: Belknap Press of Harvard University Press, 2009). For later developments, from the Reagan administration on, see Michael L. Ondaatje, *Black Conservative Intellectuals in Modern America* (Philadelphia: University of Pennsylvania Press, 2009).

and spend." "This contentious scene would not faze the men who wrote the Constitution," Methvin explained, "[F]or the debate has focused public attention once again on some eternal verities about public power, its exercise, abuse and safeguards. What healthier way for Americans to celebrate the approaching 200th birthday of their Constitution?"[55]

Some on the right nevertheless had reservations. Marvin Stone, the editor of *US News and World Report* (1976–1985), opposed a balanced budget amendment. While agreeing that wasteful spending was a serious problem, and that, under normal conditions, the federal budget should be balanced, to put such an amendment in the Constitution would be inappropriate, and a threat to the economy.[56]

THE HEROIC AMERICAN BUSINESSMAN: AYN RAND AND BEYOND

In the heyday of American liberalism, the situation, many conservatives believed, was dire. In the late 1940s, the former head of the Alabama State Bar, state attorney general, state judge, and president and chair of the Alabama Power Company William Logan Martin, for instance, warned his fellow lawyers in the *ABA Journal* that the nation was witnessing "a never-ending attack on private capital through the imposition of burdensome taxes so that private enterprise may stagger – all these point the way to a socialistic state in which the citizen, once architect of his own welfare and his own fortune, becomes merely a pawn."[57] The journalist William Henry Chamberlin observed that "[a] century ago individualism was so deeply rooted in Britain that there was no recognized obligation to provide free schools or pure water by public authority." "Today," however, "the excesses are all on the collectivist side." Especially in the past two decades, we were witnessing "a long process of erosion of economic liberty and self-reliance" involving a "tremendous stock of stilts, props, pillows, cushions and straitjackets for what was once a system that walked confidently on its own feet." We were creating nothing less than "the

---

[55] Eugene H. Methvin, "A Constitutional Amendment to Balance the Budget?" *Reader's Digest* 115:687 (July 1979): 95–98, 96–98.

[56] Marvin Stone, "A Constitutional Convention?" *US News and World Report* (March 12, 1979), 96. See also "ABC's of a Constitutional Convention," *US News and World Report* (February 12, 1979), 67. Stone later served as deputy director of the US Information Agency in the Reagan administration.

[57] William Logan Martin, "New York and National Health Insurance: Foundations of a Welfare State?" *American Bar Association Journal* 35 (September 1949): 735–739, 739. See also "How Far Has 'Creeping Socialism' Crept?" *Reader's Digest* 63:378 (October 1953): 127–128. Martin wrote extensively on constitutional matters. He was active in the ABA, where, among other things, he proposed the organization support a constitutional amendment allowing the states to amend the Constitution without the participation of Congress. See "Jurisprudence and Law Reform," Report of the ABA House of Delegates, *American Bar Association Journal* 42 (April 1956): 386. On Martin, see Carl B. Rix, "William Logan Martin – 1883–1959," *American Bar Association Journal* 45 (April 1959): 371.

handout state."[58] In an article from the *Harvard Business Review* condensed for publication in the *Reader's Digest* in the early 1960s, Paul Mazur, a senior partner at Lehman Brothers, proclaimed Cold War Americans to be "at war with a dictatorship in which the individual is subservient to the state." Yet we seemed to be moving in the same direction here at home. Mazur noted, "the late Robert Taft believed that a government whose economy exceeded 25 percent for public expenditures was in fact a socialist state." With one of the highest tax burdens in the world, he warned, the United States was indeed on the road to socialism. Something had to be done.[59] Washington, DC, lawyer O. R. McGuire absolved his fellow attorneys of the charge of having undermined "the traditional American individual enterprise system of government." "[I]t would be doing the lawyers in the Congress an injustice," McGuire insisted, "to assume that they willingly fastened statism, bureaucracy, and the welfare state around their own necks and the necks of their fellow-Americans." Citing John T. Flynn's Old Right *The Road Ahead* (1949), McGuire explained, the true culprits in the precipitous descent of the United States into socialism were the metastasizing number of "selfish" "pressure groups" systematically leveraging government to advance their private interests and those of their own at the expense of the American people: "The correct answer as to why this has occurred is found in the number and power of pressure groups."[60]

Such views were perhaps no more stridently, and effectively, expressed than in the writings of the Russian Jewish émigré Ayn Rand. A controversial figure both within the movement and beyond it, Rand arrived on the American cultural scene in the 1940s and 1950s with her didactic philosophical novels *The Fountainhead* (1943) and *Atlas Shrugged* (1957) (the former was made into a Warner Brothers film (1949) directed by King Vidor and starring, among others, Gary Cooper, Patricia Neal, and Raymond Massey). In *Capitalism: The Unknown Ideal* (1966), a collection of essays, most of which had been previously published in the Randian journals *The Objectivist Newsletter* and

[58] William Henry Chamberlin, "Over the Falls," *Wall Street Journal* (April 7, 1950), 4. See also William Henry Chamberlin, "A Formula for G.O.P." *Wall Street Journal* (April 10, 1950), 6.

[59] Paul Mazur, "Big Danger in Big Government," *Reader's Digest* 79 (July 1961): 125–127, 125–127. [condensed from the *Harvard Business Review* (September/October 1960)].

[60] O. R. McGuire (Washington, DC), Letter to the Editor, *American Bar Association Journal* 36:3 (March 1950): 245–246. For a collection of McGuire's speeches condemning the growth of administrative/executive absolutism in the United States, see Colonel O. R. McGuire, *Americans On Guard* (Washington, DC: American Good Government Society, 1942). The anti-militarist Flynn, a graduate of Georgetown Law School and Old Right stalwart, was a famed isolationist (he was a founder of the America First Committee), anti–New Dealer (he likened it to Mussolini's fascism), and McCarthyite. John T. Flynn, *The Road Ahead: America's Creeping Revolution* (New York: Devin-Adair, 1949) (which was widely distributed by the New York–based Committee for Constitutional Government). See also John T. Flynn, *The Decline of the American Republic and How to Rebuild It* (New York: Devin-Adair, 1955); John T. Flynn, *The Roosevelt Myth* (New York: Devin-Adair, 1948). The Ludwig Von Mises Institute of Auburn, Alabama, currently has made a number of Flynn's books available online in their entirety.

The Objectivist, Rand and her compatriots (including a young Alan Greenspan – the future Reagan-appointed chairman of the Federal Reserve Board (1987– 2006)) mounted a moral defense of capitalism, in part by systematically explicating Rand's understanding of its philosophy.[61] The collection's title is significant: by the time Rand was writing in the mid-1960s, she argued that capitalism had become "unknown" to Americans. It had once flourished in the United States, in the late nineteenth century. But it had been abandoned under the auspices of progressivism and (modern) liberalism, which had erected the interventionist modern welfare/regulatory/administrative state on its ruins.[62]

[61] Ayn Rand, *Capitalism: The Unknown Ideal* (New York: New American Library, 1966). See also
      Ayn Rand, *The Virtue of Selfishness: A New Concept of Egoism* (New York: Signet Books,
      1964).

[62] Rand praised the American Founders for having set the basic conditions for the full flowering of a
      truly free capitalist society, perhaps for the first time in human history. But, at the same time, she
      noted that the Constitution they created left considerable room for statist development. Only in
      the late nineteenth century did the latent capitalist promise of the Constitution become fully
      realized – before being brutally strangled in its budding youth by statist progressives and New
      Dealers. See Rand, *Virtue of Selfishness*, 33, 93, 95, 113, 114 ("A pure system of capitalism has
      never yet existed, not even in America; various degrees of government control had been under-
      cutting and distorting it from the start. Capitalism is not the system of the past; it is the system of
      the future – if mankind is to have a future"; "All previous systems had regarded man as a
      sacrificial means to the ends of others, and society as an end in itself. The United States regarded
      man as an end in himself, and society as a means to the peaceful, orderly, *voluntary* coexistence
      of individuals. All previous systems had held man's life to belong to society ... The United States
      held that man's life is his by *right*, that a right is the property of an individual, that society as such
      has no rights, and that the only moral purpose of government is the protection of individual
      rights"; "This was the essential meaning and intent of America's political philosophy, implicit in
      the concept of individual rights. But it was not formulated explicitly, nor fully accepted nor
      consistently practiced. America's inner contradiction was the altruist-collectivist ethics. Altruism
      is incompatible with freedom, with capitalism and with individual rights. One cannot combine
      the pursuit of happiness with the moral status of a sacrificial animal"; "[T]he Founding Fathers
      of the American Revolution ... identif[ied] the nature and the needs of a free society ... [and]
      devised the means to translate it into practice"; "[A]lthough certain contradictions in the
      Constitution did leave a loophole for the growth of statism, the incomparable achievement
      was the concept of a constitution as a means of limiting and restricting the power of the
      government.") [Emphases in original]. See also Ayn Rand, *For the New Intellectual* (New
      York: Signet Books, 1961), 25, 53–54 ("The unprecedented social system whose fundamentals
      were established by the Founding Fathers, the system which set the terms, the example, and the
      pattern for the nineteenth century – spreading to all the countries of the civilized world – was
      capitalism. To be exact, it was not a full, perfect, totally unregulated *laissez-faire* capitalism.
      Various degrees of government interference and control still remained, even in America, as
      deadly cracks in the system's foundations. But during the nineteenth century, the world came
      close to economic freedom, for the first and only time in history. The degree of any given
      country's economic freedom was the exact degree of its progress. America, the freest, achieved
      the most"; "The New Intellectuals must remind the world that the basic premise of the Founding
      Fathers was a man's right to exist for his own sake, neither sacrificing himself to others nor
      sacrificing others to himself; and that the political implementation of this right is a society where
      men deal with one another as *traders*, by voluntary exchange to mutual benefit. The moral
      premises *implicit* in the political philosophy of the Founding Fathers, in the social system they

While Rand, a Russian exile and expatriate who had fled the Bolsheviks, had no truck with socialism or communism, both of which she loathed, she was especially troubled by what she saw as the fiction – fantasy, even – that the postwar United States was living under a pragmatic "mixed system" that had fashioned a humane middle way harmonizing the interests of individual and community.

American defenders of this middle way justified it in significant part as, during the Great Depression most prominently, having "saved capitalism." Rand would have none of it. This, for her, was a cover story that had hoodwinked millions of Americans who failed to see that rather than saving capitalism, the early twentieth century and the ongoing, statist onslaught had utterly destroyed it. By this point, many Americans felt comfortable insisting that they were basically in favor of capitalism, but supported the more humane mixed system that took the edge off it in the interest of the common good. But Rand insisted that by now they were utterly ignorant of actual capitalism – "the unknown ideal" of her title.

Rand's core argument – which replicates that made in the late nineteenth century by William Graham Sumner in *What Social Classes Owe to Each Other* (1883) – was that the sole legitimate purpose of government was to ensure "peace, order, and the guarantees of rights." Those rights, for Rand, were first and foremost the classic Lockean (and Jeffersonian) liberal rights to life, liberty, property, and the pursuit of happiness – although, as a militant atheist, there was no suggestion in Rand that such rights were, in any sense, "God given."[63] This understanding required that government jettison entirely the more recent tasks assigned to it, which involved setting collective purposes, solving social problems, and achieving collective goals – what had come to be known, inaccurately, she insisted, as advancing the public or collective interest, or the interests of the community as whole. Government's sole legitimate function was to act (as Sumner had explicated at length) as a neutral arbiter of disputes, preventing physical violence, and adjudicating disputes over rights pursuant to the rule of law as it left individuals unencumbered in pursuing their own purposes and interests, including their economic interests, as underwritten by

---

established and in the economics of capitalism, must now be recognized and accepted in the form of an *explicit* moral philosophy"; "It was the morality of altruism that undercut America and is now destroying her. From her start, America was torn by the clash of her political system with the altruist morality. Capitalism and altruism are incompatible; they are philosophical opposites; they cannot co-exist in the same man or in the same society. Today, the conflict has reached its ultimate climax: the choice is clear-cut: either a new morality of rational self-interest, with its consequences of freedom, justice, progress and man's happiness on earth – or the primordial morality of altruism, with its consequences of slavery, brute force, stagnant terror, and sacrificial furnaces.") [Emphases in original].

[63] Hawley, *Right-Wing Critics of American Conservatism*, 104–105. Like her fellow secular, materialist, Russian, Jewish, exile anarchist Emma Goldman, Rand considered religion (and religious belief) a form of slavery.

their own property, time, and earnings. The government was to forswear any goal-directed, purposive, *dirigiste*, or corrective involvement in the economy. So far as economics was concerned, its sole purposes were to guarantee rights to private property and adjudicate disputes over property rights.

It infuriated Rand that capitalism had come to have such a bad name in the modern United States – was sneered at with the epithet *laissez-faire* (let be-let do), as if the mere statement that one was committed to doing one's own thing and leaving others free to do theirs was a self-evident abomination, a moral failing. Rand and her followers saw it entirely the other way round. Far from being a moral failing, letting be and letting do, and (as William Graham Sumner had put it) minding one's own business,[64] was actually a moral ideal and evinced not only a defensible but also a superior ethics.

To understand this, one needed to understand the philosophy of capitalism. Rand held capitalism's foundational premise to be radical individualism. She held it to be an ethical and moral ideal that the individual came first, a position that critics might be more likely to forgive (putting aside, for the moment, Rand's congenital Manicheanism and cult of virility)[65] if they recall Rand's horror – indeed, trauma – at the total erasure of the individual she had witnessed as the daughter of a well-to-do St. Petersburg family whose property had been seized by the Bolsheviks during the Russian Revolution. Inevitably, given her nature, Rand responded by elaborating and championing a framework in which individual freedom was everything. Capitalism was an ideal, Rand held, because, under capitalism, the individual was free to live his life uncoerced. All of his social, political, and economic interactions were self-directed, voluntary, and freely chosen, according to his own reasoned judgments, tastes, interests, and best lights. Some sneeringly called this selfishness and amorality. Rand called it freedom and argued that an individual's rational pursuit of his self-interest, egoism, far from being a moral failing, was the highest ethical ideal.[66]

It enraged Rand to no end that those who had lived most successfully by these ideals, who had truly authored their own lives, who created and built, since the establishment of the modern social welfare/administrative/regulatory state, had been censured – indeed, sneered at – as mere businessmen (for Marxists, "bourgeois materialists"), if not demonized as cruel, heartless, predatory,

---

[64] Sumner had said that "[e]very man and woman in society has one big duty. That is, to take care of his or her own self," adding that "A free man in a free democracy has no duty whatever toward other men of the same rank and standing, except respect, courtesy, and goodwill ... [H]e should be left free to do the most for himself that he can, and should be guaranteed the exclusive enjoyment of all that he does." William Graham Sumner, *What Social Classes Owe to Each Other* (New York: Harper and Brothers, 1883).

[65] Rand had denounced "the cult of moral grayness." Ayn Rand, "The Cult of Moral Grayness," *The Objectivist Newsletter* (June 1964), republished in Rand, *Virtue of Selfishness*, chap. 9.

[66] See Rand, *Virtue of Selfishness*, 13–35.

tooth-and-claw "robber barons."[67] In recent years, in the United States, of all places, Rand's adopted home and refuge from the Bolsheviks, these capitalists had been anathematized, mocked, and scapegoated. To Rand, they were heroes. Indeed, she literally made them the heroes of *The Fountainhead* and *Atlas Shrugged*. For Rand, businessmen were creators, and creators were businessmen. They were, in a sense, freedom's greatest artists, and the capitalist system provided the canvas. Hectoring, harassing, and hemming in these great men with rules and regulations and antitrust laws and draining away their capital through taxation was more than small-minded: it was execrable. What's more, it was immoral. Free exchange in economic markets was inherently ethical: it involved the meeting of moral equals, uncoerced, entering into a voluntary relationship, under conditions of freedom. It was high time for the United States, that traditional incubator, protector, and champion of independence, individualism, and individuality – as guaranteed, Rand taught, by its founding constitutional order[68] – to return to the now unknown ideal that it had once rightly and proudly cherished.[69]

One need not be up to the übermensch standard set by Howard Roark in *The Fountainhead* to have basked in the praise mid-century conservatives lavished on the American businessman.[70] Some Old Right champions of capitalism, like Rose Wilder Lane, at least evinced ambivalence: while hewing to an uncompromising anti-statism, they did not feel a corresponding compulsion

---

[67] This has become a major, by now widely disseminated, theme of contemporary movement conservative historians. See, e.g., Burton Folsom, *The Myth of the Robber Barons: A New Look at the Rise of Big Business in America*, 6th edition (Herndon, VA: Young America's Foundation, 2010 [1987]). For an earlier study in the same vein, see John T. Flynn, *Men of Wealth: The Story of Twelve Significant Fortunes from the Renaissance to the Present Day* (New York: Simon and Schuster, 1941).

[68] Rand, *Virtue of Selfishness*.

[69] In addition to Greenspan, Republican corporate and governmental leaders like ExxonMobil CEO and former Donald Trump Secretary of State Rex Tillerson and Speaker of the House Paul Ryan counted themselves among those for whom Rand had been formative. Rand's Objectivist philosophy has relatively few home bases in the precincts of contemporary conservative academia, though it is championed by the Clemson Institute for the Study of Capitalism (https:// capitalism.sites.clemson.edu/) and in the somewhat domesticated readings of Rand by the University of Texas Objectivist philosopher Tara Smith (whose PhD is from Johns Hopkins). See Tara Smith, *Ayn Rand's Normative Ethics: The Virtuous Egotist* (New York: Cambridge University Press, 2006); Tara Smith, *Moral Rights and Political Freedom* (Lanham, MD: Rowman and Littlefield, 1995). Leonard Peikoff's independent Ayn Rand Institute (www .aynrand.org) also champions the cause. See also Leonard Peikoff, *The Ominous Parallels: The End of Freedom in America* (New York: Stein and Day, 1982) (introduction by Ayn Rand) (comparing the intellectual culture of the United States to that of Weimar Germany, and suggesting that, as in that case, that culture is setting the stage for a Fascist/Nazi takeover). Peikoff is a New York University–trained (BA., MA., PhD) philosopher.

[70] Rand, *The Fountainhead* . Jennifer Ratner-Rosenhagan oddly omits any mention of Rand in her otherwise superb study of the influence of Nietzsche on American political thought. Jennifer Ratner-Rosenhagan, *American Nietzsche: A History of an Icon and His Ideas* (Chicago: University of Chicago Press, 2012).

to celebrate entrepreneurs and business executives as folk heroes.[71] Most conservative admirers of businessmen at mid-century probably fell somewhere between Ayn Rand's Nietzschean worship of the capitalist übermensch and Lane's casual indifference. They understood businessmen as dutiful citizens, working hard to fulfill their (important and indispensible) social responsibilities – admirable, in their own way.

As the Cold War dawned in the late 1940s, many conservatives felt increasingly acutely that capitalism had been the scapegoat in the country's domestic politics for far too long, and were convinced that, after four terms of Franklin Delano Roosevelt, it was overdue for an uncompromising defense of its superiority. Some still spoke the language of the Old Right. The World War II Pacific theater hero General Douglas MacArthur, recently fired by President Harry Truman for his insistence on moving on from Korea to attack Mao and liberate Communist China, was a major public voice in this register. "Our economic stature built under the incentives of free enterprise is imperiled by our drift through the back door of confiscatory taxation toward State Socialism," MacArthur warned. Following the *Message to Garcia* script, MacArthur complained that "[t]here has resulted an inevitable suppression of the incentive to maximize human energy, to encourage creative initiative, and to transform capital in one form to produce capital more needed in another." "This process is sapping the initiative and energies of the people," the general remonstrated, "and leaves little incentive for the assumption of those risks which are inherent and unescapable in the forging of progress under the system of free enterprise." "More and more we work not for ourselves but for the State," he complained, "Expenditure upon expenditure, extravagance upon extravagance have so burdened our people with taxation and fed the forces of inflation that our traditionally high standard of life has become largely fictitious and illusory." "Our remaining tax potential has been so depleted," MacArthur predicted, "that, if the reckless policies of government continue unchecked, the direct confiscation of capital to meet the ensuing obligations is almost inevitable" and "Therein lies the blueprint to a Socialist State. Therein lies the great issue now before our people – shall we preserve our freedom, or yield it to a centralized government under the concept of Socialism."[72]

[71] David Beito and Linda Royster Beito "Selling Laissez Faire Antiracism to the Black Masses: Rose Wilder Lane and the *Pittsburgh Courier*," *The Independent Review* 15:2 (Fall 2010): 279–294, 285. In more recent years, conservatives have moved very much in a Randian direction in this regard. See, e.g., Folsom, *Myth of the Robber Barons*. It seems to me that this Randian turn played a major role in the embrace of Donald Trump for president of the United States by Republican Party voters.

[72] Douglas MacArthur, *Revitalizing a Nation: A Statement of Beliefs, Opinions, and Policies Embodied in the Public Pronouncements of General of the Army Douglas MacArthur* (Chicago: Heritage Foundation, 1952) (correlations and captions by John M. Pratt), 69–72. M. T. Phelps additionally argued that whenever the federal government is engaged in business, it is in competition with private enterprise. M. T. Phelps, "A Critical Look at Trends in Today's Government," *US News and World Report* (December 28, 1959), 83–85, 84.

Others, though, were striking a somewhat different tone. In *Reader's Digest*, John Hay "Jock" Whitney, publisher of the *New York Herald Tribune*, complained in the early 1950s, "People who can swallow all the four letter words in *From Here to Eternity* without a gulp, blush when anyone mentions that horrid word, *capitalism*."[73] "[W]e have confused what capitalism *was* with what capitalism *is*," Whitney contended:

We still conceive of the capitalist as a man with icy eyes and an enormous belly, who wears a high silk hat to bed. We envisage him as the owner of corporate empires in which tens of thousands of economic serfs bow to his whims. In this picture, human rights are regularly sacrificed on the altar of greed, and the capitalist is the personification of all evil. The only thing wrong with this picture is that it bears not the slightest resemblance to modern capitalism.[74]

These days, Whitney explained,

A moral base has been built into our industrial fabric and the result has been a people's revolution that surpasses in speed and social impact anything the world has ever known. The ingredient of this revolution has not been violence but freedom: the voluntary cooperation of free men to shape a free economic system along lines that would provide the greatest productivity and the greatest security for all Americans.

The distance between what was and what is when it comes to economics in a free society was thus great and could not be ignored. In postwar America, capitalism was "the most misunderstood system in the world." To be sure, Whitney acknowledged, things were not perfect: many improvements were still necessary. Business had a "moral responsibility of the highest order." But "[i]t is the kind of responsibility that can be developed only where men are free – where no little clique of supermen makes all the decisions and issues all the orders."[75] Similarly, writing a little later in *Reader's Digest*, the Catholic priest, chaplain general of the French Resistance, and author of *Images of America* (1959), R. L. Bruckberger praised the American businessman for his role in reorienting capitalism away from its traditional boom-and-bust cycles and tendencies toward cut-throat competition, citing Henry Ford in particular for socially responsible leadership in instituting the eight-hour day and doubling his workers' wages. Bruckberger praised Ford's commitment to the view that "business and industry [are] first and foremost ... a public service." "[B]usiness" Bruckberger explained to his readers, "itself exists to serve mankind," just as does medicine.[76]

---

[73] John Hay Whitney, "Freedom Is Our Business," *Reader's Digest* 60:361 (May 1952): 79–82, 79.

[74] Whitney, "Freedom Is Our Business," 79–80.

[75] Whitney, "Freedom Is Our Business," 79–82, 80–81.

[76] R. L. Bruckberger, "The Great 20th-Century Revolution," *Reader's Digest* 75: -450 (October 1959): 37–40, 38, 39 [reprinted, condensed, from *Life* (July 13, 1959)]. Bruckberger's *Image of America* (New York: Viking, 1959) has recently been republished by the conservative Catholic Assumption College political theorist Daniel Mahoney. R. L. Bruckberger's *Images of America:*

The Reverend Norman Vincent Peale reported in *Reader's Digest* in 1950 that troubled businessmen had been approaching him, unhappy about being judged by their fellow parishioners on Sunday mornings. They wondered aloud to Peale whether there was "'any place for me, a businessman, in a church which promotes the idea that our American business system is inherently unchristian?'" They asked Peale more pointedly, "'Does it make sense that I should continue to contribute from my earnings from capitalism to those who use my gifts to undermine it?' 'What am I to think of the honesty of church leaders who, believing that capitalism is unchristian, solicit my capitalist-produced contribution?'"[77] The problem was not Christian teaching itself, Peale said he explained to them, but liberal ministers purporting to speak in its name: "They are not the church," but a "pink minority"; "[T]hey use the church as a means through which, in the name of religion, they misrepresent and discredit America and the American economic system." Certainly, Peale argued, capitalism could and should be made more Christian. But it hardly followed that Christian ideals would be better served by any other economic system. The capitalist economic system offered the best hope for "our Christian ideal of man and our hope for his progress." American businessmen should, as Christians, be proud.[78] A year later, William F. Buckley Jr.'s famously attacked his *alma mater* Yale University in *God and Man at Yale* (1951) along the very same lines. Like the businessmen whose experiences Peale had recounted in *Reader's Digest*, Buckley emphasized that Yale's wealth and eminence were based on the philanthropic largesse of successful capitalists who were employing a faculty that was, in turn, teaching hostility to capitalism. It was time for defenders of the American capitalist way to step up, speak out, and retake control.[79]

Perhaps the most dramatic episode in the push for capitalist restoration was Vice President Richard Nixon's televised July 1959 confrontation with Soviet premier Nikita Khrushchev in a model kitchen at the American National Exhibition in Moscow (part of a recently launched series of cultural exchanges between the rival countries and economic systems). In what became one of the emblematic incidents of the Cold War, the "kitchen debate" proudly showcased American consumer goods and the postwar suburban American lifestyle. Pointing to the dishwasher, Nixon told Khrushchev that the kitchen resembled those all over his native suburban Southern California, where the houses were stuffed with modern conveniences that eased life's burdens and were affordable

---

A Political, Industrial, and Social Portrait (New Brunswick, NJ: Transaction Publishers, 2009) (introduction by Daniel J. Mahoney). Bruckberger was a critic of classical economics and opposed the view that profit should be the sole motive of business.

[77] Norman Vincent Peale, "Let the Church Speak Up for Capitalism," *Reader's Digest* 57:341 (September 1950): 126–130, 127.

[78] Peale, "Let the Church Speak Up for Capitalism," 126–130, 128, 130.

[79] William F. Buckley Jr., *God and Man at Yale: The Superstitions of Academic Freedom* (Chicago: Regnery, 1951) (Introduction by John Chamberlain). See also Young Americans for Freedom, "The Sharon Statement" (1960).

and available to broad swathes of the American working class (like steelworkers, Nixon said, although he admitted that at that moment they happened to be on strike). Khrushchev parried that one need not work to have a roof over one's head in the Soviet Union: in the USSR, housing was a fundamental human right. The consumer backdrop triggered a contentious argument between the two about the respective desirability of the opposed economic and political systems.[80]

The nation's CEOs themselves put pen to paper to make their own case, explaining their virtues to their countrymen and tallying their contributions to the age of a more mild and benign post-Dickensian administrative and consumer capitalist world – a capitalism with its sharp edges sanded down which they (and their companies) often took credit for forging with an eye to the common good.[81] From the 1950s forward, corporate executives and attorneys who understood themselves as practitioners of learned professions seemed to relish the opportunity to play the historian or the legal or political theorist teaching professional and popular audiences who might not otherwise give the matter due consideration. In the *ABA Journal*, for instance, the counsel for the Mutual Benefit Life Insurance Company, Charles W. Kappes Jr., observed with dismay, "[w]hile it is no longer tabu to discuss politics or religion on social occasions, it is still prudent to avoid mentioning the role of government in business lest one call down upon himself the seven deadly offspring of such discussions: prejudice, intolerance, recrimination, a profound ignorance and disregard of facts, dyspepsia, the jaundiced eye, and, all too often, broken friendships." Kappes sought to buoy his fellow lawyers with the knowledge that the nation's Founding Fathers had been partisans of a free enterprise capitalism in which private management, not the state, made the key business decisions. In so doing, Kappes was careful to explain that while the American Founders had *not* been proponents of "tooth-and-claw" *laissez-faire*, "free enterprise has been the accepted relationship between government and business since the founding of the Republic." The fact that "it was never written as such into either the Constitution or the Bill of Rights" notwithstanding, it was "an integral *part* of the American way of life": "[T]he American of colonial days, no less than his descendent and successor today, tended to consider government a friendly enemy, a necessary evil, something one must keep his eye on." After getting up a good head of steam, Kappes could not resist adding somewhat incongruously that, although "it may be justified"

[80] See Lizabeth Cohen, *A Consumer Republic: The Politics of Mass Consumption in Postwar America* (New York: Vintage Press, 2003).
[81] Roger M. Blough (CEO, US Steel), *Free Man and the Corporation* (New York: McGraw-Hill, 1959); Ralph J. Cordiner (CEO, General Electric), *New Frontiers for Professional Managers* (New York: McGraw-Hill, 1956); Crawford H. Greenewalt (President, DuPont), *The Uncommon Man: The Individual in the Organization* (New York: McGraw-Hill, 1959); Crawford H. Greenewalt, "Big Business Is Essential to Our Economy," *Reader's Digest* 56:338 (June 1950): 127–129; Theodore V. Houser (CEO, Sears, Roebuck), *Big Business and Human Values* (New York: McGraw-Hill, 1957).

substantively, "[t]he concept of government's having a potential for good is a modern heresy."[82]

While many conservative businessmen were proud to credit the modern business corporation with underwriting the nation's wildly successful growth and geographic expansion, they were also eager to acknowledge that the rise of the corporate economy had not taken place without ill-effects. "Its bitter by-products," many conceded, "included the depletion of our national resources, the erosion of the land and the people – yearly industrial deaths in the tens of thousands and accidents in the hundreds of thousands; child labor and sweat-shops; filth and brutality." Of course, the corporate economy's rise occasioned "dissatisfaction for those who were the losers in the competitive struggle, such as the farmer and the laborer; and for those whose skin was not thick enough – the humanitarians of varying stripe, shape, and color." Kappes declared himself opposed to the tooth-and-claw ethics of the Social Darwinists. Morality and nonmaterial values and principles extending beyond the profit motive were important:

[B]y raising the beguiling image of a Xanadu which never existed in space and dating it back to a golden age which never existed in time, the classical economists ... produced the rationale by which in certain areas the beneficent American system of free enterprise was contorted into the doctrine of *laissez-faire* – the anarchic view that business is above the law and beyond the reach of government; that government may not and must not "meddle" in economic matters; that politics and economics are separate and distinct and that a curtain as of magic fire impenetrably insulates one from the other.[83]

Kappes explained to those who argued that *laissez-faire* had been central to the nation's heritage from the American Revolution forward that, in fact, "government has been inextricably engaged in a joint venture with business from the beginning" in a way that was pro–free enterprise, but not pro–*laissez-faire* (which Kappes described variously as "a theoretician's dream," an "extremist position," and "dead"): "Finally, and tardily ... Congress did take some faltering steps toward correcting some of the more blatant abuses with respect to child labor, adulterated foods, unsanitary working conditions and the like."[84]

One of the defenses of the values of free enterprise and businessmen that has recently become most widely known was that undertaken in the early 1970s by

---

[82] Charles W. Kappes Jr., "The Second American Revolution: Free Enterprise Under the Bill of Rights," *American Bar Association Journal* 46 (June 1960): 597–602, 597–598, citing Bruckberger's *The Image of America*, 256. Kappes notes that "although economic free enterprise is not guaranteed by the terms of the Constitution, either explicitly or even implicitly, a number of property rights are protected by it" (he cites the Article I Contract Clause, the Third and Fourth Amendment privacy protections, and the Fifth Amendment's Takings and Due Process clauses).

[83] Kappes, "The Second American Revolution," 598, 600.

[84] Kappes, "The Second American Revolution," 597, citing Bruckberger's, *The Image of America*, 256.

Richmond, Virginia attorney, American Bar Association president, and future Supreme Court Justice Lewis Powell Jr. In a confidential strategy memo prepared for the US Chamber of Commerce entitled "Attack on the American Free Enterprise System," Powell struck a set of themes that had been familiar on the Right, and within the American bar – and a preoccupation of earlier ABA presidents – at least since the early 1950s. In his memo, however, Powell ran the ball a few yards down the field by setting out an agenda for a powerful organization of American businessmen that involved defending what Powell took to be their rightful, and valuable, prerogatives.[85] "No thoughtful person can question that the American economic system is under broad attack," Powell reported to the Chamber. What they were witnessing in the early 1970s, he declared, was "quite new in the history of America": "We are not dealing with sporadic or isolated attacks from a relatively few extremists or even from the minority socialist cadre." Instead, "the assault on the enterprise system is broadly based and consistently pursued. It is gaining momentum and converts." Disturbingly, the attack had gone mainstream, Powell emphasized, in particular, at colleges and universities ("the single most dynamic source" of the attack) and in the media – all, he pointed out, as had Norman Vincent Peale and William F. Buckley Jr. before him, funded and sustained by American business.[86]

Powell answered a number of specific charges, such as the fusillade of incoming mortars aimed at selective tax incentives for American businesses – which the media had pejoratively dubbed "tax breaks," "loop holes," or "tax benefits" – alleged sops for the wealthy and big corporations, as if, Lewis Powell angrily riposted, these "tax breaks" would not benefit society as a whole. "This setting of the 'rich' against the 'poor,' of business against the people," Powell charged, "is the cheapest and most dangerous kind of politics." Unfortunately, up until now, "the painfully sad truth is that business, including the boards of directors and the top executives of corporations great and small and business organizations at all levels, often have responded – if at all – by appeasement, ineptitude and ignoring the problem." While there have been exceptions, Powell lamented that businessmen "have shown little stomach for hard-nose contest

---

[85] Confidential Memorandum, "Attack on the American Free Enterprise System," Lewis Powell Jr. to Mr. Eugene B. Sydnor Jr., Chairman, Education Committee, US Chamber of Commerce (August 23, 1971). Jefferson Decker, *The Other Rights Revolution: Conservative Lawyers and the Remaking of American Government* (New York: Oxford University Press, 2016), 39–50. The memo was later leaked to the syndicated columnist Jack Anderson, who cited it in criticizing Powell's objectivity as a Supreme Court Justice. See Kim Phillips-Fein, *Invisible Hands: The Making of the Conservative Movement from the New Deal to Reagan* (New York: W. W. Norton, 2009), 161–162; Mark Schmitt, "The Legend of the Powell Memo," *American Prospect* (April 25, 2005).

[86] Powell followed Buckley in continuing to allude to the presumably dire situation at Yale (as described this time by Stewart Alsop). Powell singled out Ralph Nader and Yale Law Professor Charles Reich (author of the counterculture classic *The Greening of America* (New York: Random House, 1970)) as especially destructive forces.

with their critics, and little skill in effective intellectual and philosophical debate," a complaint that Buckley had made earlier in *God and Man at Yale*. That, Powell told the Chamber, needed to change.[87] For "the ultimate issue may be survival – survival of what we call the free enterprise system, and all that this means for the strength and prosperity of America and the freedom of our people." A coordinated effort on that score was essential: "Strength lies in organization, in careful long-range planning and implementation, in consistency of action over an indefinite period of years, in the scale of financing available only through joint effort, and in the political power available only through united action and national organizations." Powell saw the Chamber as uniquely situated to lead that organized campaign. He then provided a roadmap for the group on how it might proceed over the long term – in academia, the media, and law – in strategically advancing their objectives.[88]

Powell's organizational path was followed, not just by the US Chamber of Commerce but also by the conservative movement more generally. The Powell Memorandum provided much of the foundation for the prospectus that the former California Governor Ronald Reagan aide Ronald Zumbrun and California businessman J. Simon Fluor subsequently used to establish the property rights litigation group the Pacific Legal Foundation (1973), a pioneer of the conservative public interest law movement.[89] On the eve of Reagan's election as president, M. Bruce Johnson published a multifaceted defense of corporate America against the critiques of liberals and the left, who had complained variously about the corporate world's mistreatment of labor, its price fixing, lack of social responsibility, and opposition to regulation, and other failings. Johnson's book, *The Attack on Corporate America* (1978), provided the movement with a list of compelling talking points in advancing its broader case within institutions (it became an article of faith of the Reagan Era conservative movement that institutions and ideas went hand-in-hand).[90] At this opportune moment, a slew of new conservative think tanks that spent considerable time addressing economic and constitutional questions and issues were launched, including The Heritage Foundation (1973), The Cato Institute (1977), and The Manhattan Institute (1977). Somewhat later, programs in American constitutionalism, constitutional democracy, American ideals and institutions, the American Founding, civic education, and American political thought – all with a substantive tilt toward conservative understandings – were

---

[87] Buckley made the same criticism of conservatives more generally. Buckley, *God and Man at Yale*.

[88] Powell ventured that "Under our constitutional system, especially with an activist-minded Supreme Court, the judiciary may be the most important instrument for social, economic and political change."

[89] Decker, *The Other Rights Revolution*, 56–58.

[90] See Steven M. Teles, *The Rise of the Conservative Legal Movement: The Battle for Control of the Law* (Princeton: Princeton University Press, 2008); E. Bruce Johnson, editor, *The Attack on Corporate America: The Corporate Issues Sourcebook* (Coral Gables, FL: Law and Economics Center, University of Miami Law School, 1978).

founded either as academic grant-giving philanthropies or as college and university programs and centers to advance the conservative movement's substantive constitutional vision.[91] Complementing this were a broad array of conservative legal organizations, which advanced their cases in the nation's courts, including to an increasingly conservative federal judiciary, trained by organizations like The Federalist Society, to understand and be receptive to these arguments.[92]

CONSERVATIVE CRITICS STEP BACK: AGAINST THE CAPITALIST ÜBERMENSCH AND TOWARD A HUMANE CAPITALIST NATION

While Murray Rothbard may have blanched at Ayn Rand's grandiose claims to originality and the cultishness of her following, he nevertheless remained a deep admirer of her thought. By contrast, while Whittaker Chambers may have loathed economic collectivism, her economic philosophy appalled him. Chambers – the most famous ex-communist apostate in American history and a hero of the postwar Right, found Rand's worshipful attitude toward capitalism – and capitalists – repugnant. In a contemporaneous review of Rand's *Atlas Shrugged* (1957) in *National Review*, Chambers eviscerated Rand's novel, and her economics.[93] While it seemed to be finding a passionate readership, "[t]he news about this book," in Chambers's view, "seems to me to be that any ordinarily sensible head could not possibly take it seriously, and that, apparently, a good many do." Chambers found *Atlas Shrugged* "preposterous" and "remarkably silly." Rand's dystopian novel was framed as a bulletin from the future United States at the moment of the final showdown between the champions of free enterprise and the collectivist "looters." While the book is presented as fiction, Chambers observed that Rand "is saying in effect, [this] 'is how things really are. These are the real issues, the real sides. Only your blindness keeps you from seeing it, which, happily, I have come to rescue you from.'" Of course, Chambers underlined that he and his fellow conservatives harbored many of the same complaints as Rand did about the modern collectivist state and its oppositional relationship to capitalism and capitalists. That said, Chambers insisted that any realistic assessment of the situation required that one deal with realities, not cartoons. Rand, Chambers complained, "deals wholly in the blackest blacks and the whitest whites. In this fiction everything, everybody, is either all good or all bad, without any of those

---

[91] See Amy J. Binder and Kate Wood, *Becoming Right: How Campuses Shape Young Conservatives* (Princeton: Princeton University Press, 2013).

[92] See Teles, *Rise of the Conservative Legal Movement*; Southworth, *Lawyers on the Right*; Amanda Hollis-Brusky, *Ideas with Consequences: The Federalist Society and the Conservative Counterrevolution* (New York: Oxford University Press, 2015); Decker, *The Other Rights Revolution*.

[93] Whittaker Chambers, "Big Sister Is Watching You," *National Review* (December 28, 1957) (www.nationalreview.com/2005/01/big-sister-watching-you-whittaker-chambers/).

intermediate shades which, in life, complicate reality and perplex the eye that seeks to probe it truly."[94]

Altas Shrugged, the erstwhile Columbia University literature student[95] observed, was a Manichean story of no-holds-barred class warfare. The businessman at the center of Rand's story, he noted, was not typical of American businessmen, save "the occasional curmudgeon millionaire" (Chambers noted the heavily erotic overtones to Rand's characterizations of businessmen who, for her, are not only rich but also "breathtakingly beautiful"). In Rand's world, the collectivist "looters" – "ogreish," archetypical "Left-Liberals, New Dealers, Welfare Statists, One Worlders" –

loot because they believe in Robin Hood, and have got a lot of other people believing in him, too. Robin Hood is the author's image of absolute evil – robbing the strong (and hence good) to give to the weak (and hence no good). All "looters" are base, envious, twisted, malignant minds, motivated wholly by greed for power, combined with the lust of the weak to tear down the strong, out of a deepseated hatred of life and secret longing for destruction and death.[96]

Chambers was one of the first to note that Rand's "operatic businessmen are, in fact, Nietzschean supermen." By contrast, "her ulcerous leftists are Nietzsche's 'last men.'" The businessmen ultimately win in *Atlas Shrugged*

by declaring a general strike of brains, of which they have a monopoly, letting the world go, literally, to smash. In the end, they troop out of their Rocky Mountain hideaway to repossess the ruins ... It is then, in the book's last line, that a character traces in the dirt, over the desolate earth, the Sign of the Dollar, in lieu of the Sign of the Cross, and in token that a suitably prostrate mankind is at last ready, for its sins, to be redeemed from the related evils of religion and social reform.[97]

It is this abject "philosophical materialism" – shared, Chambers observed, by Karl Marx – that in the end appalled him most: the former atheist and communist Chambers was by this time a committed Christian. In Rand's belligerently godless world, however, "in the degree to which problems of complexity and instability are most bewildering to masses of men, a temptation sets in to let some species of Big Brother solve and supervise them." "One Big Brother is, of course," Chambers conceded, "a socializing elite." But "Miss Rand, as the enemy of any socializing force, calls in a Big Brother of her own contriving to do battle with the other. In the name of free enterprise ... she plumps for a technocratic elite (I find no more inclusive word than technocratic to bracket the industrial-financial-engineering caste she seems to have in mind)." "When she calls 'productive achievement' man's noblest

---

[94] Chambers, "Big Sister Is Watching You."
[95] Gifford Maxim, a major character in the celebrated Columbia University English professor Lionel Trilling's novel *The Middle of the Journey* (New York: Viking Press, 1947) was based on Chambers, whom Trilling had known since their undergraduate days at Columbia.
[96] Chambers, "Big Sister Is Watching You."   [97] Chambers, "Big Sister Is Watching You."

activity,' she means, almost exclusively, technological achievement, supervised by such a managerial political bureau." Rand understood herself to be calling for "an aristocracy of talents." The reality was that what she was demanding would end ineluctably in dictatorship, because "in the modern world, the pre-conditions for aristocracy, an organic growth, no longer exist, so that the impulse toward aristocracy always emerges now in the form of dictatorship." Indeed, Chambers observed, "something of this implication is fixed in the book's dictatorial tone, which is much its most striking feature." He forcefully concluded that "[o]ut of a lifetime of reading, I can recall no other book in which a tone of overriding arrogance was so implacably sustained. Its shrillness is without reprieve. Its dogmatism is without appeal" and "Dissent from revelation so final (because, the author would say, so reasonable) can only be willfully wicked."[98]

At about the same time, in the early 1950s, the University of California, Berkeley, sociologist Robert Nisbet thought it was important to remind people that whatever the virtues of capitalism, it alone was not enough.[99] Nisbet put in a word for the role of intermediate groups and for nonmaterial values and principles in an economy committed to free enterprise. Nisbet reminded conservatives (and others) that "there has never been a time when a successful

---

[98] Chambers, "Big Sister Is Watching You." Interestingly, although staunchly anti-socialist, anti-progressive, and anti–New Deal, no less a figure than Friedrich Hayek was quick to insist – in two major works spanning his career – that he was not a proponent of *laissez-faire*, or a worshipper of unregulated markets. It "is important not to confuse opposition against this kind of planning with a dogmatic laissez-faire attitude," Hayek insisted, "It does not deny but even emphasizes, that, in order that competition should work beneficially, a carefully thought-out legal framework is required and that neither the existing nor the past legal rules are free from grave defects." Hayek, *Road to Serfdom*, 36. See also Williams, "The Road Less Traveled," in Lichtenstein, editor, *American Capitalism*, 213–227. Hayek denied that *homo economicus* constituted an indigenous part of his much-admired British common law evolutionary tradition. Indeed, he considered *laissez-faire* doctrine to be a paradigmatic example of rationalism, a foreign element introduced into the tradition by such figures as John Stuart Mill. Hayek favored, rather, a respect – but never a blind respect – for traditions and customs. Friedrich A. Hayek, *The Constitution of Liberty* (Chicago: University of Chicago Press, 1960), 60–61, 67.

[99] Nisbet's work transcended political categories, serving as a touchstone for both conservatives and, in time, the 1960s counterculture/New Left. A California native and student of Frederick J. Teggart at the University of California, Berkeley, Nisbet taught sociology at Berkeley, the University of California, Riverside (where he was also dean and vice-chancellor), the University of Arizona (briefly), and at Columbia University, where he held the Albert Schweitzer Chair. After retiring from Columbia, Nisbet moved to the American Enterprise Institute in Washington. In 1988, President Ronald Reagan chose Nisbet to deliver the National Endowment for the Humanities' prestigious Jefferson Lecture. See Robert A. Nisbet, *The Quest for Community* (New York: Oxford University Press, 1953). For general discussions of Nisbet's life, career, and thought, see Robert G. Perrin, "Robert Alexander Nisbet," *Proceedings of the American Philosophical Society* 143:4 (December 1999): 693–710; Robert G. Perrin, "Nisbet and the Modern State," *Modern Age* 39 (1997): 39–47; Brad Lowell Stone, "A True Sociologist: Robert Nisbet," *The Intercollegiate Review* (Spring 1998): 38–42; Susan McWilliams, "Hometown Hero," *The American Conservative* (February 1, 2010).

economic system has rested upon purely individualistic drives or upon the impersonal relationships so prized by the rationalists. There are always ... associations and incentives nourished by the non-economic processes of kinship, religion, and various other forms of social relationships."[100] "[O]ne may write persuasively about creeping totalitarianism and ... about the felicities of the free market as Hayek and others have recently done," Nisbet affirmed. "No one can seriously question the abstract superiority of a society in which freedom of economic choice exists compared with a society in which it does not," he attested. Moreover, he agreed that there was also a very real "danger to economic freedom created by increasingly political controls at the present time." That said, however, Nisbet warned that "[n]ot all the asserted advantages of mass production and corporate bigness will save capitalism if its purposes become impersonal and remote, separated from the symbols and relationships that have meaning in human lives":

Economic freedom cannot rest upon moral atomism or upon large-scale impersonalities. It never has. Economic freedom has prospered, and continues to prosper, only in areas and spheres where it has been joined to a flourishing associational life. Economic freedom cannot be separated from the non-individualistic contexts of association and community of moral purpose.[101]

Henry Luce's *Time* magazine was one of the culture's chief mid-century avatars of the heroic vision of American capitalism that had so inspired Douglas MacArthur and his admirers. Luce's *Time* – Whittaker Chambers's home base, after all – may have been anti–New Deal, but Luce – who, after all, coined his vision of an impending "American Century" – was not looking backward but forward. Luce's commitment to American capitalism anticipated – and, perhaps, informed – the sunnier "morning in America" optimism of Ronald Reagan and the New Right by celebrating the American success story premised on "a traditional social arrangement of home, family, and religion." This vision helped orient national understandings not simply through policy positions or even constitutional resistance, but through a politicization of traditionalist visions of the core institutions of civil society as symbols of true Americanism. Whereas much of the earlier *laissez-faire* anti– New Deal resistance was anchored in Victorian culture and the worldview of privileged individualist Protestant elites, Luce, who golfed with and was a close friend of John Courtney Murray, SJ, a frequent contributor to Luce's *Life* magazine, and whose wife, Clare Boothe Luce, was a celebrated Catholic

---

[100] Robert Nisbet, *Quest for Community*, 238. See also Daniel Bell, *The Cultural Contradictions of Capitalism* (New York: Basic Books, 1976). Nisbet was nevertheless critical of modern social welfare states to the degree that they undermined these intermediate institutions. The *Wall Street Journal*, though, editorialized against the constitutionality of blue laws (in defense of "the old argument that the one to determine what is in the public good is the public and not the state"). "It's Good for You," *Wall Street Journal* (December 19, 1956), 10.

[101] Nisbet, *Quest for Community*, 239–240.

convert, took what can be characterized as a more Catholic-friendly vision of American conservatism rooted less in an intransigent anti-statism than in moral traditionalism and an unapologetic and, at times, lachrymose patriotism.[102]

Writing in *Modern Age* later in the early 1970s, the University of Illinois philosopher Frederick Will, father of the conservative columnist George F. Will, distanced himself from the blow-it-up attitude some on the Right had toward the modern administrative/regulatory and social welfare state, choosing instead to expound upon the institutional foundations of a successful capitalist economy. "[T]he kind of healthy competition we wish to promote between commodities, producers, or vendors," the elder Will explained, "is not realized by simply letting the contest between the competitors severely alone ... It is not the kind of condition that is realized automatically, if we leave the competition alone. Rather, it is a delicate condition that requires careful promotion; it is a garden that must be cultivated lest it degenerate into a patch of weeds."[103] "Misunderstanding of this aspect of our freedom," Will argued,

can and does lead to a disastrous failure of nerve where action is needed to protect it ... It is a form of disciplined social practice, which, no less than football, basketball, or any moderately complex game, requires to be carried on in accordance with certain rules, if there is to be successful performance ... And, as in the case of commerce, too, there is a real difference between fair and unfair competition; and there is such a thing as the destruction of the market.[104]

In the end, there is no such thing as an unregulated, *laissez-faire* market – because "freedom is a product of institutions."[105]

THE TRANSLATION TO MATHEMATICS – FREE MARKET ECONOMICS
IN THE POSTWAR ACADEMY

Both the professional and public cultures of the postwar United States placed a surpassing value on the possibilities of the hard sciences to reshape knowledge and the world for the better. This extended to the social sciences, where, viewed by the lights of this ethos, economics was the exemplar. In this context, the urge toward systematization and scientific modeling of core ideas was highly prized, setting new academic research agendas, often supported by government grants,

---

[102] Luce played a significant role in the process on the Right of placing conservative Catholics at the center of the national (and constitutional) project. See Anthony Burke Smith, *The Look of Catholics: Portrayals in Popular Culture from the Great Depression to the Cold War* (Lawrence: University Press of Kansas, 2010), 92, 103.

[103] Frederick L. Will, "Philosophy, Institutions, and Law," *Modern Age* 16:4 (Fall 1972): 379–386, 383. Frederick Will received his PhD in philosophy at Cornell in 1938 and taught at the University of Illinois for his entire career. The recipient of a Guggenheim Fellowship and a Fulbright to Oxford University, he spent much of his career as an analytic philosopher, but late in life repudiated analytic philosophy.

[104] Will, "Philosophy, Institutions, and Law," 384.

[105] Will, "Philosophy, Institutions, and Law," 385.

leading to successful academic careers and recognition by prestigious prizes and awards. However influential it was on the postwar Right in its commitment to deductive reasoning from *a priori* principles, Austrian economics was out of step with this postwar scientific ethos and rank ordering of value. This made Austrian economists like Mises and Hayek seem to many within the period's academic and professional elite figures out of time, fusty throwbacks to the Old World intellectual culture of prewar Vienna. This, as much, if not more than their political conservatism (or, as they would have it, classical liberalism), prevented either Mises or Hayek from securing permanent academic positions in the postwar United States. By contrast, it is worth recalling that John Maynard Keynes, while certainly a brilliant conceptual thinker and prose stylist, was also fluent in high-level mathematics: his economic theories, set out most expansively in his *General Theory of Employment, Interest, and Money* (1936) launched thousands of mathematically sophisticated research agendas in economics – and indeed, the entire academic field of modern macroeconomics. While there was no shortage of conservatives who were proud to stand out of time and face the disdain of those they derided as the "fashionable" in the interest of Truth, whose time, they were convinced, would slowly come round again, other conservatives had different ambitions: they wanted to challenge the new mathematically sophisticated demand-side Keynesian economics on its own modern terms. And they did.

This challenge to the dominant administrative, regulatory, welfare state liberalism was mounted *within* the precincts of postwar professional economics, as opposed to, as with the Austrians, from outside it. The battle was initiated on the two major fronts of economics as a contemporary social science, macroeconomics and microeconomics – the former concerned with the functioning of the big picture economy, such as issues of growth, employment, productivity, money, and trade, and the latter with the science of individual choice and decision making in markets. The University of Chicago economist Milton Friedman, who was trained in the discipline's mainstream at Columbia University, was seminal on both the macro- and microeconomics fronts: Friedman's mathematically sophisticated *A Monetary History of the United States* (1963), written with Anna J. Schwartz, challenged conventional demand side/Keynesian understandings of the relationship between Franklin Roosevelt's New Deal and the trajectory of the Great Depression, and became a touchstone of modern macroeconomics.[106] At about the same time, Friedman's *Capitalism and Freedom* (1962), although not itself mathematical, explained in a sophisticated but accessible way the value and virtues – economic, political, and moral alike – of capitalist markets. It became an agenda-setting classic of neoclassical and, in time, movement conservative microeconomics.[107]

---

[106] Milton Friedman and Anna J. Schwartz, *A Monetary History of the United States* (Princeton: Princeton University Press, 1963).

[107] Milton Friedman, *Capitalism and Freedom* (Chicago: University of Chicago Press, 1962).

In *Capitalism and Freedom* (1962), Friedman picked up the ball where the Austrians and (especially) Henry Hazlitt had left it and ran it farther down the field, to the cheers of an even larger crowd.[108] In the book, Friedman reflected at length upon the relationship between familiar and seemingly broadly accepted public policies of the modern American social welfare state and the nation's purported commitment to individual freedom, and he concluded that the former had proved deeply problematic for the latter. As a public service, *Capitalism and Freedom* offered concrete, market/freedom-friendly public policy alternatives.

Friedman's overarching argument in *Capitalism and Freedom* was that, in contradistinction to an economic order committed to free market capitalism, the modern welfare state undermined individual self-esteem, self-sufficiency, sense of control, character, and initiative – all of which, by contrast, capitalism felicitously cultivated. As with the Austrians, including Hayek in *The Road to Serfdom*, one of Friedman's major themes was the interrelation between economic and personal freedoms (the garrulous New York City/New Jersey native especially emphasized the First Amendment's freedom of speech).

After laying out his broad theoretical vision about markets and freedom in two opening chapters entitled "The Relation Between Economic Freedom and Political Freedom" and "The Role of Government in a Free Society," Friedman devoted each of the book's subsequent chapters to a specific contemporary public policy question, many of which had not been considered open questions until the questing and irrepressible Friedman made them so. *Capitalism and Freedom* marched down the line: monetary policy, international trade policy, fiscal policy, public education, civil rights, labor, occupational licensing, income distribution, social welfare policy, antipoverty policy. For each, Friedman made a focused, lucid, and intellectually sharp argument for market solutions over state-directed approaches.

In its own succinct and accessible brief opposing liberal individualist to planned societies, opposing capitalism to socialism, Hayek's *Road to Serfdom* had operated at a higher, more abstract – one might say "principled" – level. While there was no daylight between Friedman and Hayek regarding principles, Friedman now provided conservatives with what Hayek had not yet attempted (and on which some passages of *The Road to Serfdom* concerning government intervention in the economy were, for many, too mealymouthed): a public

---

[108] Friedman's *Capitalism and Freedom* is an accessible – especially by the standards of economics – but still a relatively dense book. During the Reagan years, Milton and Rose Friedman penned a popular introductory overview of free market economics *Free to Choose: A Personal Statement By Milton and Rose Friedman* (New York: Harcourt, Brace, Jovanovich, 1980), which served as an even more accessible companion to a multi-part PBS television series on the topic, a guided tour narrated by the puckishly appealing Friedman himself, who had recently been awarded the Nobel Prize in Economics (1976).

policy road map for conservatives in power.[109] The arguments in *Capitalism and Freedom* sparked new thinking on the Right that in the 1970s began to inform the movement's growing network of think tanks and publishing venues. In time, the menu of market-oriented public policies that Milton Friedman had introduced in *Capitalism and Freedom* would reach the pinnacle of political power with the election of Ronald Reagan as president. Within the policy-making precincts of that administration, Friedman's influence was pervasive.

At about the same time that Friedman was formulating and disseminating his views, a rigorously mathematical (and, hence, professionalized) new "public choice" approach to microeconomics was being forged by scholars of diverse or, perhaps more accurately, ambiguous political incidences, although, over time, the archconservative University of Virginia, Virginia Tech, and George Mason University economist James Buchanan became perhaps the field's most influential figure. As the influence of the Austrians continued to grow, especially outside the precincts of the academic, professional social sciences, scholars working all three veins of postwar conservative economic thought began meeting and talking under the auspices of the Mont Pelerin Society, whose proceedings reached a wider audience through coverage by the *Wall Street Journal*.[110] Soon, these three economists – all Mont Pelerin Society members – would receive the highest honor their profession bestows, the Nobel Prize in Economics: Friedrich von Hayek (Austrian, 1974), Milton Friedman (macro/micro, 1976), and James Buchanan (micro, 1986).[111]

The theme that government spending ostensibly undertaken for the public good instead advanced private (special) interests aimed at private ends, a process whose essence William Graham Sumner had limned in *What Social Classes Owe to Each Other* (1883), was scientized and systematized during the Cold War.[112] Back in the late nineteenth century, Sumner had called it

---

[109] Hayek, who was more a theoretician, did address a spate of broad public policy arenas in Part III of his soup-to-nuts masterwork – of which Margaret Thatcher purportedly declaimed "This is what we believe" – *The Constitution of Liberty* (Chicago: University of Chicago Press, 1960), where Part I was devoted to Principles, Part II to Law, and Part III to Policy. The book, dedicated "To the unknown civilization that is growing in America," was published just a few years before Friedman's *Capitalism and Freedom*. Hayek and Friedman, of course, were both at the University of Chicago at the time, with Friedman in the economics department and Hayek on the Committee on Social Thought, where his salary was paid by the William Volker Fund. Hayek subsequently set out an intricate and abstract theory of law and its relation to liberty – and free constitutional government – in his three-volume *Law, Legislation and Liberty* (Chicago: University of Chicago Press, 1973/1976/1979) (Volume I: *Rules and Order*; Volume II: *The Mirage of Social Justice*; Volume III: *The Political Order of a Free People*).

[110] William Henry Chamberlin, "Whig Revival?" *Wall Street Journal* (September 20, 1957), 6.

[111] Angus Burgin, *The Great Persuasion: Reinventing Free Markets Since the Depression* (Cambridge, MA: Harvard University Press, 2012).

[112] On science as a major new departure in this era, see David A. Hollinger, *Science, Jews, and Secular Culture: Studies in Mid-Twentieth Century American Intellectual History* (Princeton: Princeton University Press, 1996).

"jobbery." In the mid-twentieth century, the new public choice economics called it "rent seeking." Both argued that it was so extensive and severe, so much at the core of what governments did, that the only sensible approach was to cauterize it by sharply limiting the powers of governments to tax, spend, and regulate.[113]

S. M. Amadae has situated the rise of the new public choice/rational choice economics within the distinctive political economy of the Cold War United States.[114] In *Rationalizing Capitalist Democracy*, Amadae chronicled the ways in which "the self-interested, strategic, rational actor became the central figure around which the reexamination of traditional Enlightenment themes and problems of government was based." This new approach was immensely influential in shifting prevailing academic and, in time, popular theories of democratic politics away from the concepts and conceptions that had long undergirded them – "the public," "the public interest," "the public good," or, to use the language of the US Constitution itself, "the general welfare."[115] The core argument of the new rational choice/public choice economics was that concepts like "the public," "the public good," or "for the good of society" were, if examined dispassionately, incoherent. Public choice/rational choice scholars argued, moreover, they could demonstrate or prove this through deductive logic, as systematized – modeled – through mathematics. It was not the values or personal moral convictions of conservatives but science itself that proved that, in the end, there was only the self-interested, self-seeking actor choosing – in politics as in economics. One implication of this understanding was that the study of political science as a science was ultimately reducible to the study of economics. Indeed, the argument was that political decision making could not be properly understood other than as a form of economic decision making by rational actors in "political markets": in the end, it was economics all the way down. These understandings helped incubate modern "game theory," which before long would rival Keynes's achievement in its professional fecundity: game theory could be adopted by highly trained, mathematically sophisticated social scientists as part of career-building academic research agendas branded and accepted as cutting-edge academic social science. In its initial Cold War context, this new science of capitalist democracy served as an ostensibly rationally demonstrabe scientific answer to the organicist understandings of state and society being advanced by the Marxist/Communist world. Public choice models emphasized individualism and pluralism and explained how

---

[113] S. M. Amadae, *Rationalizing Capitalist Democracy: The Cold War Origins of Rational Choice Liberalism* (Chicago: University of Chicago Press, 2003).
[114] Amadae, *Rationalizing Capitalist Democracy*.
[115] The Preamble to the Constitution states, "We the People of the United States, in Order to ... promote the general Welfare ... do ordain and establish this Constitution for the United States of America." Article I, Section 8, provides that "The Congress shall have Power [to] ... provide for the common Defence and general Welfare of the United States."

societies rooted in such understandings promised not only growth and wealth but also political freedom.[116]

While a recent mass-market history by Duke historian Nancy MacLean has attributed these new economic models to the efforts of postwar movement conservatives,[117] the truth is more complicated. Seminal figures in rational choice/public choice economics like John von Neumann and Oskar Morgenstern, Kenneth Arrow, John Nash, Anthony Downs, and other prominent game theorists were not in any sense movement conservatives; while one might, of course, characterize the implications of their work as ultimately "conservative," they understood themselves as rigorously neutral, dispassionate scientists, associated, for example, with J. Robert Oppenheimer's Institute for Advanced Study in Princeton, New Jersey, or the Santa Monica-based national security/nuclear strategy think tank the Rand Corporation. In its origins, at least, this was the mainstream social science of a rationalist, university, foundation, think tank and government-based Cold War–era policy elite – of what David Halberstam famously called "the best and the brightest." When the Rand Corporation's outspokenly right-wing Albert Wohlsetter set aside the intricate mathematics of his fellow Rand social scientists to issue a series of relatively simplified (or simplistic) warnings about what he took to be US military unpreparedness based on qualitative assessments that the country was dangerously vulnerable to Soviet missile strikes, Wohlsetter was ostracized at Rand and then pushed out: he moved on to the political science department at the University of Chicago, where he became a Straussian fellow traveler. While the cohort of Rand scholars from period included conservatives like Wohlsetter, James Buchanan, and William Niskanen, they also included liberal but mathematical professional economists like Mancur Olson, Paul Samuelson, and Robert Solow. In short, the rational choice/public choice/game theoretic model first arrived at to solve Cold War strategic, military problems in service of the national security state became the basis for consensus, mainstream economics. As such, the boundary between goal-directed policy science and the more removed "pure" science did not exist.[118]

[116] Amadae, *Rationalizing Capitalist Democracy*, 3–4, 15–23. Amadae demonstrates the emergence of this scientific program directly out of the calls launched in the mid-1940s by Joseph A. Schumpeter's *Capitalism, Socialism, and Democracy* (New York: Harper, 1942), Friedrich Hayek's *The Road to Serfdom* (Chicago: University of Chicago Press, 1944) (foreword by John Chamberlain), and Karl Popper's *The Open Society and Its Enemies* (Princeton: Princeton University Press, 1945).

[117] Nancy MacLean, *Democracy in Chains: The Deep History of the Radical Right's Stealth Plan for America* (New York: Viking Press, 2017).

[118] Amadae, *Rationalizing Capitalist Democracy*, 27–45, 76–77. See John von Neumann and Oskar Morgenstern, *Theory of Games and Economic Behavior* (Princeton: Princeton University Press, 1944); Kenneth Arrow, *Social Choice and Individual Values* (New York: Wiley, 1951); Anthony Downs, *An Economic Theory of Democracy* (New York: Harper, 1957); James Buchanan and Gordon Tullock, *The Calculus of Consent: Logical Foundations*

Drawing and building upon the work of Anthony Downs, Kenneth Arrow, the conservative economists Buchanan and Gordon Tullock and other theorists of "social choice," contemporary "public choice" theorists developed highly sophisticated mathematical models of politics and public policy rooted in their understanding of politics and policy as reducible to individualistic sciences concerned with the study of self-interested individuals pursuing private, personal objectives. Much of the previous work of mainstream economists had been directed at questions of *market failure* – that is, cases like those involving externalities, where free markets did not work to efficiently allocate resources, requiring, most believed, government intervention. Much of this new work, however, focused instead on *government failure*, or, more precisely, on conditions under which voting and other forms of collective decision making either failed to yield agreement at all (the collective action problem) or yielded agreements that were nonrepresentative, suboptimum, inefficient, or even (viewed normatively) illegitimate. And, in line with its origins in the rise of the rational, individualistic, professional social science in the 1940s and 1950s, this work offered itself as apolitical, positivistic, and scientific.[119]

The seminal public choice work that set out expressly constitutional understandings was James Buchanan and Gordon Tullock's *The Calculus of Consent: Logical Foundations of Constitutional Democracy* (1962), a work that MacLean rightly identifies as written by conservatives.[120] In *The Calculus of Consent*, Buchanan and Tullock launched a major assault on the theory or, they might say, the assumption, that the enactment of laws by popularly elected legislatures – legislation – represented the apotheosis of democracy and, as such, was a good thing. That now common (but increasingly challenged) understanding of the democratic *bona fides* of legislation had served as a legitimating foundation for much of the early twentieth-century Progressive Movement, and, subsequently, of the active, activist social welfare state committed to passing laws ostensibly aimed at advancing the collective public interest; it also served as the basis for modern progressive (and, later, conservative) theories of judicial review – that is, of modern constitutional theory – which called for judicial restraint based on a default principle of deference to ostensibly democratic legislatures. Buchanan and Tullock argued

of *Constitutional Democracy* (Ann Arbor: University of Michigan Press, 1962); Mancur Olson, *The Logic of Collective Action: Public Goods and the Theories of Groups* (Cambridge, MA: Harvard University Press, 1965).

[119] Downs, *Economic Theory of Democracy*; Arrow, *Social Choice and Individual Values*. See MacLean, *Democracy in Chains*, 41–42.

[120] Buchanan and Tullock, *Calculus of Consent*. See also James M. Buchanan, *The Limits of Liberty: Between Anarchy and Leviathan* (Chicago: University of Chicago Press, 1975); James M. Buchanan, *Constitutional Economics* (Oxford: Blackwell, 1991); James M. Buchanan, *The Logical Foundations of Constitutional Liberty* (Indianapolis, IN: Liberty Fund, 1999); James M. Buchanan, *Politics as Public Choice* (Indianapolis, IN: Liberty Fund, 2000).

in aggressive opposition that rather than being legitimately democratic and public-spirited, legislation – whether or not passed in the name of the public good – is, typically, little more than legalized theft.[121]

Buchanan, who had received his PhD in economics from the University of Chicago in 1948, where he was a student of Frank Knight's, animadverted against an "organismic" understanding of the "state" as a unified body or entity, acting with any discernible "purpose." Buchanan, moreover, condemned "the normative delusion, stemming from Hegelian idealism ... [that] the state was ... a benevolent entity and those who made decisions on behalf of the state were guided by consideration of the general or the public interest."[122] Buchanan's work makes clear why the term "public interest" became a *bête noire* of public choice theorists: the concept, along with the related concepts of "social welfare" and the "general welfare," was not only chimerical but founded upon dangerous assumptions. "The public" or "society" is not "organismic." It is not a unified entity, with a readily identifiable "interest."[123] When they hear such terms bandied about, piously, in public debate, Buchanan and Tullock were telling people, in effect, that they had better watch their wallets. The public choice economists insisted that, moving forward, an "individualistic" rather than an "organismic" perspective must be the starting point for all future considerations of constitutions and the state.[124]

---

[121] As described in *The Calculus of Consent*, this was modeled as the problem of "the external costs that the individual expects will be imposed on him if *any* single individual in the group is authorized to undertake action *for the collectivity* ... [U]nder such a rule the individual must anticipate that many actions taken by others which are unfavorable to him will take place, and the costs of these actions will be external costs in the same sense that the costs expected from private activities might be external ... The private operation of the neighborhood plant with the smoking chimney may impose external costs on the individual by soiling his laundry, but this cost is no more external to the individual's own private calculus than the tax cost imposed on him unwillingly in order to finance the provision of public services to his fellow citizen in another area ... Under the extreme decision-making rule which allows any individual in the whole group to order collective action, the expected external cost will be much greater than under any private organization of activity." In an understated announcement of their agenda, Buchanan and Tullock argue, "The fact that collective action, under most decision-making rules, involves external costs of this nature has not been adequately recognized." Buchanan and Tullock, *Calculus of Consent*, 65–66.

[122] James M. Buchanan, "Socialism Is Dead But Leviathan Lives On," in his *Post-Socialist Political Economy* (Lyme, CT: Edward Elgar, 1997), 85, quoted in Amadae, *Rationalizing Capitalist Democracy*. I draw extensively on Amadae's book in the overview that follows.

[123] This is what Margaret Thatcher meant when she famously declared that "There is no such thing as society" ("Margaret Thatcher in Quotes," *The Spectator* (April 8, 2013)), although perhaps she was simply quoting from Ayn Rand, who had said so directly ("Since there is no such entity as 'society,' since society is only a number of individual men...."). Rand, *The Virtue of Selfishness*, 92.

[124] Amadae, *Rationalizing Capitalist Democracy*, x, 143. On the role of the economic think tank in informing Thatcher's conservative thought and policy, see Kersch, "Ecumenicalism Through Constitutionalism."

As they understood it and modeled it mathematically as economists, the state – worst of all a centralized state – or legislature, or bureaucracy licensed by the legislature, could be demonstrated, through *a priori* deduction, to amount to no more than a readily accessible, free-flowing tap before which self-seekers (in the economics jargon, rent seekers) could position themselves to draw down the resources provided by others through taxation. By doing so, the individual actors who, in reality, constituted what has been mystically called "the state" were advancing their private, personal interests, and not any broader "public good." Indeed, they were parasites, using the cover of the state and disingenuous appeals to the common good to advance their own personal interests. Critical to this understanding was Buchanan and Tullock's decision to model state actors, whether legislators or bureaucrats, not as public servants, whether as agents or trustees of the voters who elected them (for legislators) or as dispassionate experts or public servants (for bureaucrats) but rather as self-interested, self-seekers who happened to be working – grifting – in governments, where they were well positioned to trade the government benefits and largesse they controlled, marshaled coercively through taxation, to augment their power and advance their interests. The system was one of "[t]ax, tax, spend, spend, elect, elect."[125] As such, government was a thoroughgoing racket.

Under these conditions, as Nancy MacLean has emphasized, democracy itself – that is, majority rule – was hardly going to provide a solution. Majority rule, after all, was also the means by which the have-nots, always more numerous, could take from the haves, using their larger numbers to coercively and systematically redistribute income and other wealth, including private property, from the few to the many. This is why Buchanan and Tullock emphasized the importance of constitutionalism – systems that limit the powers of government pursuant to a rule of fundamental law – over democratic majoritarianism: the latter, after all, was a significant part of the problem. And it is why Buchanan and Tullock preferred the constitutional rules as enforced by the stiff-spined, "activist," "countermajoritarian" justices of the pre–New Deal Lochner Era – later dubbed by some on the Right "the Constitution in Exile" – than they did to those that had followed the "Constitutional Revolution of 1937," which had sharply limited the viability of any claims of "economic rights," subjecting business and economic regulation to the all-but-unchecked powers of the nation's democratically elected officials, and purportedly public-spirited regulators, bureaucrats, and administrators.[126]

---

[125] The formulation was apparently invented by the head of Franklin Roosevelt's New Deal Works Progress Administration (WPA) Harry Hopkins, as quoted from a 1938 interview by conservative *New York Times* columnist Arthur Krock. Hopkins was, of course, embarrassed by the quotation, and the two feuded a bit afterward about whether he had actually said it.

[126] MacLean, *Democracy in Chains*, 71–72, 77–81, 98, 149–153, 185–186. MacLean, however, does not give due attention to the fact that pure majoritarian democracy had always been considered a problem by mainstream (and conservative) American constitutional thinkers from

Positioning themselves squarely in the liberal contractarian tradition, Buchanan and Tullock proceeded from the position that individuals construct constitutions to advance their individual interests. They insisted, moreover, that this understanding was inherent in the theory of the American Founding advanced, for instance, in the Constitution itself, *The Federalist Papers*, and other key Founding texts.[127] As such, later developments in the trajectory of the American constitutional tradition – like the nationalization of politics, policy, and rights occasioned by the Civil War Amendments, and the subsequent construction of the modern administrative state (whether properly authorized or not) – had corrupted the nation's original constitutional design and moved it away from its foundational individualism toward socialism. *The Calculus of Consent*, as such, was "an unprecedented contribution to political theory that reinvents the logical foundations of constitutional theory so that it resembles the logic of the marketplace."[128]

Notably, even, or perhaps especially, the most conservative rational choice and public choice theorists did not see themselves as especially pro-business. They were preoccupied, rather, with the perils of regulatory capture, a preoccupation that underwrote interesting affinities with leftist critiques of the modern liberal administrative state.[129] In any case, the logical and mathematical sophistication of this work has made it into one of the major paradigms driving contemporary social science, especially economics and political science. Accordingly, its practitioners have ascended to the heights of their professions, with all the status, influence, and capacity to teach, reproduce, influence, and set professional "boundary conditions" concerning who gets tenure, where, what gets published, where, and what wins prizes that that accomplishment implies.

In this, as S. M. Amadae has rightly and importantly emphasized, the public choice/rational choice/game theoretic framework has been highly successful. While, as she notes, the theory behind such paradigms is "so recondite as to require the likes of ... John Nash [the Princeton University mathematician, and

the Founding forward, from James Madison, to Stephen J. Field, to William Graham Sumner, to Martin Diamond. To be sure, majoritarianism has had its proponents, including Jacksonians and key progressives – which is why many of them called for either eliminating or sharply restricting the powers of judicial review. In short, the potential dangers that majoritarian democracy posed to rights were hardly the invention of James Buchanan and public choice theory.

[127] Amadae, *Rationalizing Capitalist Democracy*, 137–138.
[128] Amadae, *Rationalizing Capitalist Democracy*, 139.
[129] See Peter Bachrach and Morton S. Baratz, *Power and Poverty: Theory and Practice* (New York: Oxford University Press, 1970); Theodore J. Lowi, *The End of Liberalism: The Second Republic of the United States* (New York: W. W. Norton, 1969); Grant McConnell, *Private Power and American Democracy* (New York: Vintage Books, 1970). See generally Richard M. Merelman, *Pluralism at Yale: The Culture of Political Science in America* (Madison: University of Wisconsin Press, 2003); Ronald Kahn, *The Supreme Court and Democratic Theory: 1953–1993* (Lawrence: University Press of Kansas, 1994).

economics Nobel laureate who was the hero of Ron Howard's Oscar-winning "Best Picture" film *A Beautiful Mind* (2001)] to fully understand its mathematical intricacies, the degree to which it has come to pervade the popular discourse by the early years of the twenty-first century cannot be overestimated." From the 1970s onward, in particular, the theory's tenets have spread "into leading financial, policy, educational, and legal institutions, which have adopted its language and approaches to decisionmaking problems."[130]

THE DEVELOPMENT OF LAW AND ECONOMICS

James Buchanan and Gordon Tullock's *Calculus of Consent* focused on foundational themes of constitutional structure. But the rational choice literature in economics developed an extensive, ground-level influence under the auspices of the "law and economics" movement in legal academia which, beginning in the 1970s, imported this framework into the study and, subsequently, the quotidian life and practice of American law. The history of the origins and trajectory of the law and economics movement within the legal academy constitutes a significant part of Steven Teles's widely noted book *The Rise of the Conservative Legal Movement: The Battle for Control of the Law* (2008). There, in setting out the long pre-1970s backstory, Teles roots the movement in the accidents of faculty hiring at the University of Chicago Law School in the early 1930s, when the economist Henry Simons, in part for personal reasons, moved from Chicago's economics department to its law school. At the time, the social sciences were being rapidly and aggressively integrated into academic approaches to the study of law by the Legal Realists, who were closely associated with, first, the Progressive Movement, and then New Deal Liberalism. So the migration of Simons from Chicago's economics department to its law school would seem to be a move in tune with its times.

In truth, the case was quite otherwise. The Realist application of social science to law was undertaken in the spirit of the founding of the modern social sciences in the United States – that is, as part of an effort to help inform the policies of the activist, problem-focused, meliorist, and expert "new" American social welfare, regulatory, and administrative state. From this perspective, law was understood as a form of goal-directed policy making. And, as policy making, it was thought, it should fully avail itself of the findings of the modern social sciences. When law itself was a subject of study, the Legal Realists held, it was best approached and understood through social science's analytic prisms.

In this regard, Henry Simons was actually an anomaly, a throwback, a man out of time: his economics, classical economics, shared by some fellow members of the University of Chicago economics department at the time like Frank

---

[130] Amadae, *Rationalizing Capitalist Democracy*, 5. See also MacLean, *Democracy in Chains*.

Knight and Jacob Viner, was the very paradigm that the new social sciences entering the legal academy through Legal Realist circles had sought to displace (the University of Chicago trio of Frank Knight, Jacob Viner, and Henry Simons trained both Milton Friedman and James Buchanan, and Knight had teamed up with the Austrian economists Ludwig von Mises and Friedrich Hayek to found the elite, transnational neoclassical economics revivalist group the Mont Pelerin Society). By the late 1930s, Simons had becoming increasingly troubled by the expansion of the New Deal state, and the restrictions it was placing not only on the free market but also on freedom more generally. Fired by his reading of Hayek's *The Road to Serfdom* (1944), which warned of a rapid turn toward socialism and, by implication, onward to totalitarianism in the formerly free West, Simons had played a key role in arranging for *The Road to Serfdom*'s publication in the United States by the University of Chicago Press.

Teles reports that an ideologically sympathetic University of Chicago colleague of Simons, Aaron Director, explained Simons's general mood at that time by reporting that Simons "thought doomsday was upon us." Simons imported this spirit, rapidly gaining momentum as a fighting faith, into the University of Chicago Law School, where he worked aggressively to create an academic beachhead – soon a fortress – for the study and propagation of classical economics, taking care all the while to fortify it against interference from his colleagues and university administrators. Simons arranged for conservative foundation funding from the Volker Fund to establish an institute for law and economics at Chicago's law school. He proposed Aaron Director as its leader. The law school's dean agreed, on the condition that Director teach one law school class. While the institute never got off the ground, Director had nevertheless been successfully hired as a member of the law school's faculty. And as such he set to teaching his single class: Economic Analysis and Public Policy.

What proved in time to be a remarkable trajectory had been launched. Director, it turned out, was a whirlwind academic entrepreneur: he hired like-minded scholars to the University of Chicago faculty, founded the *Journal of Law and Economics* (1958), which Director co-edited with the future Economics Nobel laureate (1991) Ronald Coase (a related law and economics journal, the *Journal of Legal Studies*, was launched at Chicago in 1972). This vortex came to influence countless students, many of whom went on to become noted lawyers, scholars, and judges, including major players in law and economics like Coase, Robert Bork, and Richard Posner, all of whose writing became touchstones of the new law and economics field. Here, the University of Chicago law professor Posner's *Economic Analysis of Law* (1973), a math-free text that offered law students with no prior training in economics an accessible *prêt-à-porter* framework for analyzing law became seminal.[131]

---

[131] Teles, *Rise of the Conservative Legal Movement*, 90–95; Burgin, *Great Persuasion*; MacLean, *Democracy in Chains*, 121–126. While an undergraduate at Yale, Aaron Director had been a

More important than the particular policy positions they arrived at, Posner and Coase set out a template for analyzing legal problems – whatever the subject – that proved immensely influential. Like pure economics, the economic analysis of law began from the assumption that the basic unit of analysis should be the self-interested, goal-directed, individual pursuing his objectives under conditions of scarcity. The laws and the institutions of legal systems set the rules of the game in which these goal-directed actors operated. Since markets were understood by economists to, under most conditions, provide for the most efficient allocation of resources possible, through a cost-benefit analysis of laws and rules, economic analysis of the law typically arrived at the conclusion that the best laws were those that came closest to replicating the conditions of the market – that is, of non-coerced, consensual exchange. Given the almost unimaginably thick tangle of laws and rules that had been instituted from the top down by governments since the early decades of the twentieth century United States – and which had exploded with the New Deal and Great Society especially – it was foreordained that law and economics scholars would find that much of the legal and policy landscape of the contemporary regulatory and administrative state made no sense at all: it was rife with inefficiencies and redistribution. Law and economics scholars argued that regulation through legislation was less efficient than regulation through traditional (pre-1900) common law rules, that administrative agencies allocated resources according to political rather than efficiency criteria, and that litigation was often costly and dysfunctional. The prescription in many cases, as viewed from this framework, was fairly simple: make sure the property rights of private actors are clearly defined and enforced, roll back top-down rules and regulations, and set economic actors free to pursue their goals within unencumbered markets. Under such reformed conditions, private bargaining would lead to mutually beneficial agreements entailing efficient outcomes. This would provide the conditions for not just economic but also political freedom.

This framework became particularly influential during the Reagan administration, when it helped form much of the foundation for President Reagan's program for administration, regulation, and the courts. As it did so, Teles has explained, its reach and prestige expanded, in the face of considerable

---

leftist/socialist gadfly in cahoots with his friend Mark Rothko, who became a major abstract expressionist painter. After college, following stints as a coal miner and fruit picker, Director worked as a teacher of labor history at a radical labor union school in Oregon. Douglas Martin, "Aaron Director, Economist, Dies at 102," *New York Times* (September 16, 2004). See Ronald Coase, "The Problem of Social Cost," *Journal of Law and Economics* (October 1960): 1–44; Richard Posner, *Economic Analysis of Law* (New York: Little, Brown and Co., 1973); Robert Bork, *The Anti-Trust Paradox: A Policy at War With Itself* (New York: Basic Books, 1978). The topics subjected to economic analysis in Posner's relatively short book included property, contracts, torts, crime, civil and criminal procedure (that is, the standard first-year curriculum in law schools), regulation, taxation, and antitrust and anti-discrimination law. Neither Posner nor Bork had any advanced training in economics – only law degrees.

liberal resistance, in the legal academy (at the outset, through the aggressive entrepreneurship of Henry Manne), in the bar, and on the bench, where, today, if still a minority, the law and economics framework remains firmly established and respected, including at the nation's leading law schools like Harvard and Yale.[132]

CHRISTIAN CAPITALIST CONSTITUTIONALISM

Given the Roman Catholic Church's historic anti-liberalism, which included opposition to the very concept of individual rights, it required a considerable amount of ideological/theological work before right-wing Catholics became aggressive proponents of free market capitalism.[133] Protestants were there long before. One need not wholly subscribe to the sociologist Max Weber's *The Protestant Ethic and the Spirit of Capitalism* (1905) to observe that Protestantism was one major conduit in the United States, if not always of the ideology of the free market, than at least of its close kin, business values and the gospel of success. In one of the early touchstones of the prosperity gospel, the businessman Bruce Barton's *The Man Nobody Knows* (1925), for instance, introduced Christian Americans to a Jesus of whom, he believed, they were ignorant, a Jesus who was goal directed and upwardly mobile and possessed all the attributes of worldly success. This is someone whom they should emulate, Barton was suggesting. Many responded by enlisting Jesus's teaching as a justification for the economic status quo – by, cynics might say, justifying the ways of man to God. The cause was subsequently championed by a motley assortment of motivational speakers, salesmen, and Christian (often Pentecostal) ministers, including Oral Roberts, Gordon Lindsay, Zig Ziglar, and Joel Osteen.[134]

The movement gained momentum in the mid-twentieth century, perhaps not coincidentally during the time of a waxing Cold War anticommunism. Indeed, on the eve of the Cold War, the influential Michigan-born Fundamentalist Carl

---

[132] Teles, *Rise of the Conservative Legal Movement*, 181–219.

[133] See, e.g., Michael Novak, *The Catholic Ethic and the Spirit of Capitalism* (New York: Free Press, 1993).

[134] Stephen Prothero, *American Jesus: How the Son of God Became a National Icon* (New York: Farrar, Straus, and Giroux, 2003), 106; Max Weber, *The Protestant Ethic and the Spirit of Capitalism* (London: Routledge, 2001) [1905] (Talcott Parsons, translator; Introduction by Anthony Giddens); Gordon Lindsay, *God's Master Key to Prosperity* (Dallas, TX: Christ For the Nations, 1960); Oral Roberts and G. H. Montgomery, *God's Formula for Success and Prosperity* (Tulsa, OK: Abundant Life Press, 1966); Zig Ziglar, *See You at the Top* (Gretna, LA: Pelican Publishing, 1975); Zig Ziglar, *Confessions of a Happy Christian* (Gretna, LA: Pelican Publishing, 1978). Joel Osteen, a Houston, Texas, televangelist, satellite radio star, and Oral Roberts University dropout, has written several best-selling books, including *Your Best Life Now: 7 Steps to Living at Your Full Potential* (New York: Warner Faith Publishers, 2004). It is worth noting that, in emphasizing human potential, the prosperity gospel downplays sermonizing about sin and God's wrath: as a strain of "conservatism," it is forward looking and optimistic.

McIntire issued his battle cry *The Rise of the Tyrant: Controlled Economy versus Private Enterprise* (1945), which, presaging later pronouncements by the Reverend Jerry Falwell and others on the Reagan-era Religious Right, expressly declared the social welfare state in America to be communism's Trojan horse. God was on the side of capitalism: Carl McIntire held it to be no less than a divine command – the Almighty's own economic theory. The mainline Protestant denominations, which supported the social welfare state, the fire and brimstone McIntire charged, were not simply misguided: they were heretics. They had not simply adopted a bad economic theory: they had repudiated Christian teaching, pridefully spurning God's Holy Word. If atheism and hostility to private property and capitalism were the pillars of America's enemies, right-wing Christians seemed to reason, then the love of God, private property, and free markets must be the fighting faiths of its friends. If any doubts remained, to underline the point, it was decided at this time to chisel the motto "In God We Trust" onto the nation's money itself – an emblematic Cold War statement.

Deep-pocketed Christian businessmen invested prodigiously in disseminating their understandings of the relationship between free market capitalism and God's command. Among the most prominent was the Sun Oil Company (Sunoco) Chairman J. Howard Pew, who, with a like-minded coterie, underwrote the founding of the Christian Freedom Foundation (CFF). CFF launched a newsletter called *Christian Economics*, which it distributed widely among the nation's Protestant clergy: its masthead read "We stand for free enterprise – the economic system with the least amount of government and the greatest amount of Christianity."[135]

The purported theoretical opposition between libertarians and religious traditionalists within the modern conservative movement is based on

---

[135] Williams, *God's Own Party*, 38–39, 45; T. Jeremy Gunn, *Spiritual Weapons: The Cold War and the Forging of an American National Religion* (Westport, CT: Greenwood Publishing, 2009), 120–130; Kevin Kruse, *One Nation Under God: How Corporate American Invented Christian America* (New York: Basic Books, 2015); Eckard V. Toy, "Christian Economics, 1950–1972," in Ronald Lora and William Henry Longton, editors, *The Conservative Press in Twentieth Century America* (Westport, CT: Greenwood Press, 1999), 163–169. Pew was also one of the main sponsors of *Christianity Today*. See Mary Sennholz, *Faith and Freedom: The Journal of a Great American, J. Howard Pew* (Grove City, PA: Grove City College, 1975); J. Howard Pew, "Governed by God," *The Freeman* (July 1957): 9–11. See Carl McIntire, *The Rise of the Tyrant: Controlled Economy vs. Private Enterprise* (Collingswood, NJ: Christian Beacon Press, 1945); Carl McIntire, *How Red is the National Council of Churches?* [pamphlet, 1950]; Carl McIntire, *Author of Liberty* (Collingswood, NJ: Christian Beacon Press, 1946); Gary North, "The Moral Dimensions of FEE," *The Freeman: Ideas on Liberty* 46:5 (May 1996). North was president of the Institute for Christian Economics (Tyler, Texas), and a trustee of the libertarian Foundation for Economic Education (FEE), *The Freeman*'s publisher. This discussion draws extensively from the very useful Lee Haddigan, "The Importance of Christian Thought for the American Libertarian Movement: Christian Libertarianism, 1950–71," *Libertarian Papers* 2, 14 (2010) (libertarianpapers.org).

misunderstandings of libertarianism, on the one hand, and religious traditionalism, on the other, at least as they actually existed in the postwar United States. While certain intransigent enemies of the state on the postwar Right were militant atheists – the Russian-born Ayn Rand being the most prominent case-in-point – others rooted their libertarianism, proximately, in "the laws of nature, and Nature's God" (as Jefferson articulated it in the Declaration of Independence (1776)), John Locke's natural rights to "life, liberty, and property" (Locke's *Second Treatise on Civil Government* (1689)), or, as with the Austrian economists, in moral theories emphasizing free will and human dignity. Many of these libertarians traced these rights back to an understanding of an unchanging "human nature," which, for those so inclined, it was easy enough to describe as "man, as God has created him."

Fundamentalist, evangelical, and other leading conservative Christian voices started not with the Declaration of Independence, Locke's *Second Treatise* or assumptions consonant with them, or Ludwig von Mises, but with a professed commitment to the life of Jesus, and the literal Word of God. God had given man free will. As such, it was the heavy responsibility of Christians to live according to the teachings of the Bible in making choices in all areas of their lives, including economic choices. In the economic sphere, an individual exercised his free will most prominently in his choice as to what to do with his property. For these Christians, the foundational understanding of free will, the rights of conscience, and private property rights were each bound up inextricably with the others. As they saw it, many of the commitments, policies, programs, and initiatives that defined the modern redistributionist, regulatory, social welfare state – taxation, wealth redistribution, inflationary monetary policy (encouraged by movement away from "sound" money – the gold standard) – all trenched upon the American's ability to live his life as a Bible-believing Christian, since such a life entailed a man's freedom to make unimpeded choices about what to do with his property, in consultation with his conscience, as informed by the word of God. The modern social welfare state was thus an attack not simply on his material interests, property rights, or economic liberty but also on his *religious* freedom. For the believing Christian, the unimpeded earning of profit was Biblically sanctioned, stewardship was a responsibility, and freedom was a moral obligation.[136] This meant that most – or, indeed, for those at the extremes, any – government involvement in the economy other than to vigorously enforce property rights must be strictly limited. Put otherwise, the Bible had not only sanctioned but also commanded free market capitalism.

Outlets like the CFF's *Christian Economics* seamlessly married Bible-based Christian teaching with the championing of free market capitalism and the scourging of government regulation. The newsletter's staff economists, George

---

[136] Haddigan, "The Importance of Christian Thought for the American Libertarian Movement," 6, 23. See H. Edward Rowe, "The Christian Scriptures and Freedom," *Christian Economics* (September 6, 1966).

Koether and Percy L. Greaves Jr., had studied with Ludwig von Mises. Von Mises himself, Friedrich von Hayek, and William Röpke, none of whom is typically associated with the Religious Right, were all *Christian Economics* contributors.

Christian Economics did not celebrate selfishness and materialism. Those who ran and sponsored the newsletter, including the oil company executive J. Howard Pew, firmly believed that Christians had a duty to help others in economic need, including the poor. They believed, however, that charity and philanthropy lost all their meaning in the Christian sense if they were not undertaken by the individual, motivated by Christian teaching, acting of his own volition without command or compulsion, in the private sphere. To the extent that the state interfered with the ability of individuals to exercise these choices concerning their property through taxation, or displaced their role in doing so through social welfare and social services programs that, to make matters worse, undercut the initiative of those they purported to help, sapping their own free will, it was the enemy both of Christian charity and the poor.

The concept of "social justice," Christian conservatives argued, had been corrupted when it was enlisted in justifying the establishment and in defense of the modern welfare state. Real social justice meant that each individual would get a fair recompense for his efforts and initiatives when those efforts and initiatives were properly and productively directed. When mainline denominations and Catholics before the inception of the market-oriented contemporary US Catholic Right enlisted the term to champion the extension of state power to ostensibly help the poor, they were taking an objectively anti-Christian stance that they had mislabeled and cynically marketed as "Christian." The "Social Gospel" and liberal/progressive understandings of the pursuit of social justice were travesties of Church and state alike.

Crucially, Christian conservatives were also being tutored at this time by movement thinkers, many from within their own ranks, in a deep story holding that the relationship between the state, private property, and markets they were advancing was a – the – genuine *American* understandings, and it had been the political philosophy of the nation's Founders and the Constitution's Framers. These deep stories held that it was the nation's Constitution and its Bill of Rights, as read through the lens of Christian free market capitalism, that had made the US Founding exceptional: unique, uniquely good, and supremely successful. It was the Founders who had first "[drawn] the line near the end of the spectrum which gave minimum scope to Caesar and maximum scope to God."[137]

---

[137] Haddigan, "The Importance of Christian Thought for the American Libertarian Movement," 7, 10, 12, 14. In his contribution to a similarly themed journal, *Faith and Freedom*, Herbert Hoover – consistent with his widely lauded practice in his life – emphasized the importance of private charity and, especially, society's intermediate, voluntary associations, in relieving the suffering of the poor and others facing misfortune. Herbert Hoover, "Should Government Be Our Brother's Keeper?" *Faith and Freedom*, 10:2 (1959–1960). See also Rev. Edward W. Greenfield, "Cavalcade of Concerns," *Faith and Freedom*, 10:2 (1959–1960), 16; George

By the 1970s, high-level movement intellectuals like Edmund A. Opitz were setting themselves to the task of merging free market capitalism with Christian theology in works like *Religion and Capitalism: Allies, Not Enemies* (1970).[138] Opitz (1914–2006), a Congregationalist minister, had a long and deep background in Christian free market libertarianism: he had begun his career in 1951 as a leader of his fellow Congregationalist The Reverend James Fifield Jr.'s Southern California–based Spiritual Mobilization.[139]

Opitz's libertarianism was heavily influenced, first, by his reading of Albert Jay Nock and, then, of Austrian economics: he was a committed enough Nockian to found a fellowship of conservative and libertarian ministers that, following Nock, he called "The Remnant" (1957), and, a few years later, the Nockean Society (1963). During these same years, Opitz began his long tenure (1955–1992) as a senior staff member at the Foundation for Economic Education (FEE) in Irvington-on-Hudson, New York, where he was also the long-serving book review editor of FEE's flagship publication *The Freeman.*

After opening *Religion and Capitalism: Allies, Not Enemies* with the pronouncement that "[t]his book deals with the problem of the proper ordering of our economic affairs within the framework supplied by Christian values," Opitz immediately turned to Ludwig von Mises's *Human Action* and Wilhelm Röpke's *Economics of a Free Society* (and, later, Hayek) to provide the argument's foundation. Opitz framed the book as an extended, and often intricate, argument against the concept of "Christian socialism," which he condemned as "a contradiction in terms" and "rank folly."[140] Opitz lamented that, in contrast to Christian Socialism:

There has never been an organized Christian Capitalist movement, and no slogan has ever appeared saying that Christianity is the religion of which capitalism is the practice. The argument has been advanced, however, that acceptance of the main features of the Christian philosophy implies a free society and a limited government, with economic affairs organized in terms of the market; and this book spells out that argument at some length.[141]

While fully acknowledging that in the long history of the West, the Church had frequently stood in opposition to political liberty, Opitz argued, nevertheless, that the very idea of individual liberty had been premised on Christian

Sokolsky, "Freedom – A Struggle," *The Freeman* (October 2, 1950), 14 [cited in Haddigan, 14, 19].

[138] Edmund A. Opitz, *Religion and Capitalism: Allies, Not Enemies* (New Rochelle, NY: Arlington House, 1970). See also Edmund A. Opitz, *The Powers that Be: Case Studies of the Church in Politics* (Los Angeles: Foundation for Social Research, 1956); Edmund A. Opitz, *Religion: Foundation of a Free Society* (Irvington-on-Hudson, NY: Foundation for Economic Education, 1996); Edmund A. Opitz, *The Libertarian Theology of Freedom* (Tampa, FL: Hallberg Publishing, 1999) (with blurbs from Ron Paul, M. Stanton Evans, and Michael Novak).

[139] Opitz opened the group's East Coast office. On Fifield's Spiritual Mobilization, see Kruse, *One Nation Under God, passim.*

[140] Opitz, *Religion and Capitalism*, 5–6, 81–82, 102.   [141] Opitz, *Religion and Capitalism*, 7.

foundations – that is "His creatures . . . [in time, demanded] conditions of outer freedom to match the inner liberty stressed in the Gospels."[142] These demands, Opitz emphasized, were at the heart of the American founding:

The framers of our basic political documents and the people for whom they spoke were end products of the long religious and cultural heritage of Christendom. They willed religious, political, and social liberty as a necessary corollary of their religious commitment, and our relatively free society was, in part, a projection of the teaching of the colonial churches . . . The original American equation had a built-in religious dimension; our premises about the nature and destiny of man, our understanding of right and wrong, the code governing our manners and customs all came as part of our religious heritage.[143]

Immediately after this, Opitz thundered that "[t]he free society is now under alternating siege and attack from several quarters . . . communism, fascism, welfarism, and others . . . The tide that once flowed in the direction of human emancipation has turned, and now moves in the opposite direction, toward a collectivized existence in which individual lives are submerged for the greater glory of the state." It was bad enough that secular forces were pushing the United States in this direction. But that America's mainline Christian denominations had joined them, in part through unleashing the government through their faithless constitutional understandings, was inexcusable.[144]

Opitz forswore market fundamentalism: markets did not magically get everything right. Nor were market and moral virtues synonymous: "The God of religion transcends human affairs," Opitz affirmed.[145] But market and moral virtues were closely related. "Political theory in our tradition," Opitz explained:

is based on the assumption that men must be free in society because each person has a destiny beyond society which he can work out only under conditions of liberty. In other words, the inner and spiritual liberty of man proclaimed in the Gospels implies the outer and social freedom needed for its completion. Loyal to these premises, the peoples of the West began their long and painful ascent toward the ideal of political liberty.[146]

Citing the Declaration of Independence, Opitz underlined that we derive not only our rights but also our very natures from God. Our entire political – and constitutional – tradition is premised, Opitz insisted, on ethical monotheism, natural law (understood in relation to a permanent, transcendent moral order), and "the Christian kingdom of Heaven." Citing Hayek's *Road to Serfdom* and Mises's *Socialism*, Opitz argued that since the means individuals choose to achieve their ends were inherent in economic liberty, that liberty was inextricably tied to every other form of freedom. Restrictions on economic

---

[142] Opitz, *Religion and Capitalism*, 16.

[143] Opitz, *Religion and Capitalism*, 16–17. Here, as elsewhere in the book, Opitz frequently references Tocqueville.

[144] Opitz, *Religion and Capitalism*, 16–17.   [145] Opitz, *Religion and Capitalism*, 79–80, 89, 92.

[146] Opitz, *Religion and Capitalism*, 93.

freedom prevented men from living as free, self-determining agents according to their natures, ethics, consciences, and values. Accordingly, "the most appropriate way of organizing economic life, granted a Biblical outlook, is the free market way. Christianity is geared to human nature and the free economy accords with the nature of things, so this is a natural pairing off."[147] From all this, Opitz concluded, as had the sociologist and Episcopal minister William Graham Sumner before him, "[t]he true prototype of government is the constable" or night watchman: that is, the neutral, non-purposive arbiter of disputes; purposes are to be determined not by the state, but by individuals.[148]

As the conservative movement assumed government power in the Reagan administration with the help of a newly Republican-voting cohort of religious Roman Catholics (a significant component of the "Reagan Democrats"), Catholic thinkers followed in the footsteps of Opitz's *Religion and Capitalism* by offering their own densely argued ideological/theological tomes. In this, Michael Novak's *The Spirit of Democratic Capitalism* (1982) led the way (*Commentary*'s reviewer described Novak's book as "a stunning achievement" and, neglecting Opitz, as "perhaps the first serious attempt to construct a theology of capitalism").[149] Novak was himself an ex-liberal Democrat who had worked as a speechwriter and policy advisor for Robert F. Kennedy, Eugene McCarthy, and George McGovern; anti–Vietnam War activist; and champion of the Church's Vatican II reforms of the early 1960s in which the Church moved to reconcile itself with modern liberalism. In this bellwether book, he began by claiming that the communal life that the Church had always valued had been promoted by the constitutional protections for pluralist liberty, including religious liberty and the freedom of association, afforded by democratic capitalism. After first addressing the issue of whether capitalism was good for the Church, Novak moved on to his more universal claims. Capitalism, he argued at length, provided the best context – certainly

---

[147] Opitz, *Religion and Capitalism*, 95, 102, 106, 112, 201. On the Constitution specifically, Opitz emphasizes, "the authors of our Constitution . . . believed that a higher law was written into the nature of the cosmos, which right reason could discover, and to which the statutes of men should conform. Legislation is just if it accords with natural law; unjust if it does not." He offers an extended critique of then current liberal theories of constitutional majoritarianism (e.g., by James MacGregor Burns), which echoed the arguments of many earlier progressives, in favor of a defense of countermajoritarian natural and constitutional rights, federalism, and the separation of powers. Opitz, *Religion and Capitalism*, 201, 216–217, 220–229, 248–251. Needless to say, Opitz's argument here does not posit a duty of judicial deference to majoritarian legislatures.

[148] Opitz, *Libertarian Theology of Freedom*, 31–35, 47–48. See also Opitz, *Religion and Capitalism*, 17–19, echoing William Graham Sumner's concerns regarding jobbery and plutocracy.

[149] Michael Novak, *The Spirit of Democratic Capitalism* (New York: Simon and Schuster, 1982). Samuel McCracken, "Michael Novak, The Spirit of Democratic Capitalism," *Commentary* (July 1, 1982) [Book Review]; William Grimes, "Michael Novak, Catholic Scholar Who Championed Capitalism, Dies at 83," *New York Times* (February 19, 2017).

better than the supposedly morally superior, and indubitably more self-righteous, socialism – within which free individuals could husband their creativity and cultivate their virtues. Market capitalism provided the social conditions most conducive to the promotion of the virtues and habits most consistent with Judeo-Christian values. Novak's argument, as such, was premised not (in the first instance, at least) on claims about efficiency or productivity but rather on humanistic, moral claims concerning capitalism based not on its productivity but on its purportedly peerless capacity for promoting a healthy sociability, personal growth and development, and virtue. Like many on the Old Right before him, Novak, furthermore, was careful to stipulate that he found the cliché of the grasping and self-seeking businessman less relevant in his own time than to the brutal tooth-and-claw days of yore, when capitalism had been truly cut-throat and Dickensian.

Novak made his case in part through a sustained comparison of the respective developmental trajectories of the United States and Latin America, arguing that the latter region's political and economic underdevelopment had been in part a consequence of the Latin American Catholic Church's hostility to capitalism. In doing so, the bridge-building Novak praised the contrasting Protestant work ethic, with its attendant commitment to individual initiative, which had underwritten the US's considerably more successful developmental trajectory. The traditional Catholic approach to these matters, Novak explained, had been forged in a medieval context in which the chief concern was the equitable distribution of a static wealth base. He considered that medieval teaching less relevant in a modern capitalist context characterized by dynamic wealth creation. Novak declared himself at one with the Church in caring about poverty and social justice. But he argued that Catholic theology, properly understood, treated both concerns as commanding the personal commitment of the faithful for which a society organized around free markets provided ample room: the alleviation of poverty and social justice were no business of the state.[150]

For a number of conservative thinkers, the case against the modern statutory, regulatory, and policy-making state was underwritten not just by stipulations concerning powers and limits of government as set out in the

---

[150] See also Michael Novak, *Free Persons and the Common Good* (Lanham, MD: Madison Books, 1989); Novak, *Catholic Ethic and the Spirit of Capitalism*; Michael Novak, *Business as a Calling: Work and the Examined Life* (New York: The Free Press, 1996); Michael Novak and Edward Wayne Younkins, *Three in One: Essays in Democratic Capitalism, 1976–2000* (Lanham, MD: Rowman and Littlefield, 2001). Novak also founded the militantly right-wing Catholic *Crisis* magazine (with Ralph McInerny), which bills itself as "a voice for the faithful Catholic laity" (www.crisismagazine.com/). In recent years, until his death in 2017, Novak was a scholar at the American Enterprise Institute, and a visiting professor at Far Right Roman Catholic Ave Maria University. See www.michaelnovak.net/ See also Edward W. Younkins, *Flourishing and Happiness in a Free Society: Toward a Synthesis of Aristotelianism, Austrian Economics, and Ayn Rand's Objectivism* (Lanham, MD: University Press of America, 2011).

Constitution but also by understandings of where the residual appropriate powers of government would lie should a faithful constitutional order ever be restored. These conservatives argued that in the case of constitutional restoration, Anglo-American common law would do much, if not all, of the necessary legal governing. This prospect appealed to many Christian conservatives in part because they were taught that unlike the Constitution itself – which never mentions God and, to all appearances, at least, is relatively secular – (Anglo)American common law was inherently, and foundationally, Christian.[151]

In 1982 – the same year Michael Novak published *The Spirit of Democratic Capitalism*, John W. Whitehead, a leading Evangelical Christian conservative author, activist, and litigator, founded The Rutherford Institute, a pioneering Evangelical Christian litigation group designed to counteract the influence of liberal legal groups like the ACLU. That same year, Whitehead published *The Second American Revolution* (1982), which has sold more than 100,000 copies and was also made into a documentary film. Along with Francis Schaeffer's *A Christian Manifesto*, *The Second American Revolution* played a significant role in igniting the constitutional activism of contemporary Evangelical Christian conservatives. Under the manifest influence of R. J. Rushdoony's Christian Reconstructionism, Whitehead's book, which I contextualize and discuss at length in Chapter 5 on "Evangelical and Fundamentalist Christian Stories," was an attack on the role that American courts have played in creating and advancing "the pagan state." Interestingly, Whitehead was a critic of the Supreme Court's so-called Lochner (economic substantive due process) jurisprudence of the late nineteenth and early twentieth centuries, which placed many progressive efforts aimed at policing the American workplace beyond the constitutional pale. Nevertheless, by implication – or through interpretation – Whitehead's elevation of the status of the traditional common law helped underwrite broader efforts on much of the Right to cut back sharply on federal (and state-level) regulation that left only the relatively limited

---

[151] See Isaac Kramnick and R. Laurence Moore, *The Godless Constitution: A Moral Defense of the Secular State* (New York: W.W. Norton, 2005). Some conservatives nevertheless cite the notation in Article VII that the document was "done in Convention by the Unanimous Consent of the States present the Seventeenth Day of September *in the Year of our Lord* one thousand seven hundred and Eighty seven" as evidence that the Constitution patently presupposed Christianity. US Constitution, Article VII [emphasis added]. See, for example, Felix Morley, *Freedom and Federalism* (Indianapolis, IN: Liberty Fund, 1981 [1959]), 302. Others hold the Constitution's godlessness – the upshot of which was the tolerance of the nation's original sin of slavery – to have been corrected by Abraham Lincoln, whose reading of the Constitution incorporated the Declaration of Independence, which expressly mentioned both "the Laws of Nature and Nature's God" and that "all Men are created equal" and "endowed by their Creator with certain unalienable Rights." See Ken I. Kersch, "Beyond Originalism: Conservative Declarationism and Constitutional Redemption," *Maryland Law Review* 71 (2011): 229–282.

strictures and remedies of the common law, such as, in environmental law, the traditional common law tort of nuisance, in place.[152]

PRIVATE PROPERTY RIGHTS

Many postwar conservatives were alarmed by what they took to be an assault on rights of property "that would have been unthinkable to the Founding Fathers." "If the State can take a man's property," the *Wall Street Journal* warned in the late 1950s, "it can and will take his freedom."[153]

The southern traditionalist Richard Weaver discussed the matter at length in *Ideas Have Consequences* (1948), where he had pronounced the right to property "the last metaphysical right remaining" – "metaphysical . . . because it does not depend on any test of social usefulness." Property was "a self-justifying right," a "sanctuary"; property owner and property were fused into a single being – as in marriage, the two became one. Like other conservatives, Weaver reminded readers that property rights underwrote other rights, including rights of conscience and free expression: the English professor contrasted Henry David Thoreau's freedom of "noble preference" and "unorthodox utterance" as ultimately dependent upon his plot of land at Walden Pond, contrasting Thoreau's circumstances to Walt Whitman's vulnerability as a federal government employee in Washington, DC.[154] The "individual centers of control" instituted by private property, moreover, had made genuine pluralism

---

[152] See R. J. Rushdoony's *This Independent Republic: Studies in the Nature and Meaning of American History* (Nutley, NJ: Craig Press, 1964); *The Nature of the American System* (Nutley, NJ: Craig Press, 1965); *The Roots of Reconstruction, Law and Liberty* (Portland, OR: Ross House Books, 1971); and *Institutes of Biblical Law*, Vols. 1–3 (Nutley, NJ: Craig Press, 1973). In 1965, Rushdoony founded the Chalcedon Institute, which is committed to the advancement of Reconstructionist Christianity. See http://chalcedon.edu/ . "Post-Millennial" Reconstruction calls for the rule here and now, on earth, by the literal word of God, as set out in the Bible – particularly in the Old Testament. See generally Walter Olson, "Invitation to a Stoning: Getting Cozy with Theocrats," *Reason* (November 1, 1998). See also Frances Fitzgerald, *The Evangelicals: The Struggle to Shape America* (New York: Simon and Schuster, 2017), 340–347. In a particularly well-known example, Justice Antonin Scalia, appealed to the still available common law nuisance remedy for environmental damage in voiding a state environmental regulation. *Lucas* v. *Carolina Coastal Commission*, 505 US 1003 (1992). Portions of the text here were previously published in Ken I. Kersch, "Constitutive Stories About the Common Law in Modern American Conservatism," in Sanford V. Levinson, Joel Parker, and Melissa S. Williams, editors, *Nomos LVI: American Conservatism* (New York: New York University Press, 2016), and are reprinted here by permission.

[153] "An Assault on Property," *Wall Street Journal* (August 20, 1957), 10.

[154] This theme was foundational on the postwar right: it was a core argument of, among other major works, Wilhelm Röpke's *The Economics of a Free Society* (1937), Hayek's *The Road to Serfdom* (1944), and Milton Friedman's *Capitalism and Freedom* (1962). See also, e.g., M. T. Phelps, "A Critical Look at Trends in Today's Government," *US News and World Report* (December 28, 1959), 83–85, 84 (Fourth Amendment Search and Seizure/privacy rights). See James W. Ely Jr., *The Guardian of Every Other Right* (New York: Oxford University Press, 1992).

possible. The modern state was the sworn enemy of such pluralism: it simply "does not comprehend how anyone can be guided by something other than itself. In its eyes pluralism is treason." Fortunately, Weaver noted, the Constitution's protection for private property rights were "unequivocal."[155]

The passionate defense of private property rights did not imply a condemnable materialism. Far from being merely of material value, property ownership was "a benevolent institution" conducive to the cultivation of virtue. While "tread[ing] gingerly" to avoid penning a paean to bourgeois virtues – in Weaver's view, a Yankee excrescence – Weaver argued that private property should be understood as "providential." It counteracted provincial man's tendency toward presentism by metaphysically merging past, present, and future. Moreover, because private property embodied past and future, it elicited from its owners "the exercise of reason and imagination." "That I reap now the reward of my past industry or sloth, that what I do today will be felt in that future now potential – these require a play of mind," he explained. Conjuring Aesop's ant and the grasshopper, Weaver argued additionally that modern social welfare states (through, e.g., their provision for the indigent elderly) were a "demoralizing" force: they systematically stripped individuals of the virtues they might cultivate to address the march of time in all its existential fullness. While conceding that "the dislocations of capitalism" might justify some limited poor relief, Weaver nevertheless affirmed, "no society is healthful which tells its members to take no thought of the morrow because the state underwrites their future. The ability to cultivate providence, which I would interpret literally as foresight, is an opportunity to develop personal worth."[156]

One of the most significant early pushbacks against the new activist state in the name of property rights during the heyday of American liberalism was the tax resistance movement of the early 1950s. Of course, as the recent "Tea Party" movement aggressively reminded, such resistance was hardly new in American history. Moreover, many of the most prominent of these postwar anti-tax activists like Rose Wilder Lane and Isabel Paterson were denizens (vestiges, even) of the prewar Old Right.[157] Nevertheless, the issue was taken

[155] Weaver, *Ideas Have Consequences*, 131–132, 136–137. Weaver was no friend of (Yankee) corporate or finance capitalism. In *Ideas Have Consequences*, he animadverted against monopoly power, big business, and the "abstract property of stocks and bonds, the legal ownership of enterprises never seen ... [which] destroy[s] the connection between man and his substance without which metaphysical right becomes meaningless." Weaver praised a [Jeffersonian] distribution in small ownerships, and independent small farms and businesses. Weaver, *Ideas Have Consequences*, 132–133.

[156] Weaver, *Ideas Have Consequences*, 138.

[157] There had been an extensive anti-tax thread to the conservative opposition to the New Deal, and beginning in 1939, conservatives launched an extended campaign for a constitutional convention to cap the rates of federal taxation on incomes, gifts, and inheritances. David T. Beito, *Taxpayers in Revolt: Tax Resistance during the Great Depression* (Chapel Hill: University of North Carolina Press, 1989); Fred P. Graham, "The Role of the States in

up anew during the Truman and Eisenhower years. In 1952, for instance, the noted tax lawyer Roswell Magill complained in *The Saturday Evening Post* (as reprinted in *Reader's Digest*) that one way to appreciate the severity of the problem – as Americans certainly should – was to observe that for the average commuter, "[f]rom the alarm clock which wakes him up to the toast that he chews as he dashes for his train, practically everything he touches has been taxed in one form or another."[158] It went without saying that, for Magill, this was self-evidently appalling.

On this issue, three estimable women led the charge: Vivien Kellems, Rose Wilder Lane, and Isabel Paterson. Kellems (1896–1975) was a wealthy industrialist (she was founder and president of the Kellems Cable Grip company, whose grips were used in the construction of the Chrysler Building, the George Washington Bridge, and other structures), feminist (she was a strong proponent of the Equal Rights Amendment), and an outspoken opponent of taxes in general, and the federal income tax in particular. In 1948, adamant that the federal requirement that she withhold taxes from the paychecks of her employees at Kellems Cable Grip was unconstitutional; spoiling for a test case, Kellems brazenly defied the law mandating federal withholding.

Kellems's defiance was a sensation. In defending her actions, she was one of the first women to appear on NBC's newly launched news program *Meet the Press* (September 26, 1948), and on Eleanor Roosevelt's Sunday television show *Today with Mrs. Roosevelt* (March 3, 1950), where the subject was "Is the tax system of the US unfair?" Kellems subsequently set out her position and story at greater length in her book *Toil, Taxes and Trouble* (1952).[159] There, Kellems argued that the federal tax system inaugurated by the Sixteenth Amendment (1913) had laid waste to the provision for taxation that had been "so carefully designed and perfected by the brilliant men who wrote our Constitution." "When we adopted this income tax amendment," Kellems contended, "we departed from our constitutional method of taxation":

For one hundred and twenty-five years, the Federal Government had levied taxes and they were always apportioned among the several States. Why do you suppose the Constitution is so specific and so explicit that Federal taxes shall be uniform and apportioned among the States? For one reason only. Our forefathers were determined to build a republic with equal opportunity and equal responsibility for each and every one of us. They knew that the power to tax is the power to destroy, and they did not wish

---

Proposing Constitutional Amendments," *American Bar Association Journal* 49 (December 1963): 1175–1183, 1176, fn. 8 (providing list of congressional hearings on the subject).

[158] Roswell Magill, "How High Can Taxes Go?" *Reader's Digest* 60:357 (January 1952): 63–66, 63 [reprinted, condensed, from *The Saturday Evening Post* (September 1, 1951)]. Magill was Treasury Secretary Andrew Mellon's chief lawyer during the Harding administration in the 1920s and went on to serve in Franklin Roosevelt's administration under Treasury Secretary Henry Morganthau. He subsequently taught federal taxation at Columbia Law School.

[159] Vivien Kellems, *Toil, Taxes and Trouble* (New York: E.P. Dutton, 1952) (book available on Hein Online database: https://home.heinonline.org/).

to have one group of citizens, or one part of the country penalized for the unfair advantage of another.[160]

It was the tax system as originally designed by the Founders that had helped make the United States "the richest, most powerful nation in the world." Then "[w]e chucked our proven system of taxation out the window, and we passed the income tax. Gone was our uniformity, gone was our apportionment among the States. And with uniformity and apportionment went a great deal more – our fundamental American rights." The income tax started its career at the relatively painless level of 2 percent, Kellems explained. But it had been moving upward ever since, at present to exorbitant, even confiscatory, rates. Once the barn door had been opened, the rest of the horses ran out too: Congress had enacted a capital gains tax "which slapped business right in the face and sent it reeling into the corner." This was followed by a capital stock tax, and also a tax on dividends. Before long, New Dealers were enacting a new tax "every day or two! They rained upon us as the gentle dew from Heaven. 'Tax and tax, spend and spend, elect and elect,' quoth the delighted Harry Hopkins." The dynamic had been set in motion, it seemed, perpetually. "Soak the rich ... The formula worked like magic for political purposes but it threw our country into the deepest and most tragic depression of our history. The depression of the 1930's was a tax depression. Business simply could not function," Kellems insisted.[161]

While certainly critical of the consequences of the nation's tax system, a significant part of her argument rested on constitutional rights claims. Kellems argued at length that the federal income tax and other federal taxation schemes trenched on the Fourth Amendment's protection against unreasonable searches and seizures and the Fifth Amendment's protection of the right against self-incrimination and deprived persons of property without due process of law. These Fourth and Fifth Amendment violations seriously implicated what Kellems called "the right of privacy." She pronounced the income tax "the strongest weapon ever placed in the hands of an unscrupulous government." "As long as that Amendment is a part of our Constitution," Kellems concluded, "our freedom is in jeopardy."[162]

Kellems's own resistance was to the then new legal requirement that, as an employer, she withhold federal taxes from her employees' paychecks. What she objected to specifically, she said, was that the federal government had, in effect, conscripted her as its tax collector, a class of people who had long been "feared and hated." Under a "crafty" Roosevelt administration that relished stoking class hatreds and antagonism, it was "not accidental that this job was placed

---

[160] Kellems, *Toil, Taxes and Trouble*, 17–18. See also William G. Halby, "Is the Income Tax Unconstitutionally Discriminatory?" *American Bar Association Journal* 58 (December 1972): 1291–1293, 1292; Frank Chodorov, *The Income Tax: Root of All Evil* (New York: Devin-Adair, 1954).
[161] Kellems, *Toil, Taxes and Trouble*, 18–19.   [162] Kellems, *Toil, Taxes and Trouble*, 20.

upon the employer." The federal government was driving yet another wedge between the employer and the employee, deliberately instigating "misunderstanding and dissension" among the American people.[163]

Long after the adoption of the Sixteenth Amendment, others continued to attack the income tax. Conservatives reminded Americans that back in the late nineteenth century, the Supreme Court had firmly, and rightly, voided the federal income tax as unconstitutional.[164] That decision had been outrageously overridden by the Sixteenth Amendment – "a grave political blunder" that did permanent damage to the logic and functioning of the American constitutional order. A letter to the *Wall Street Journal* reminded *Journal* readers in 1951 that "[v]ery few of the members of Congress and of the state legislatures, who voted for the Sixteenth Amendment to the Constitution, realized that, in sanctioning a progressive income tax, they were implementing one of Karl Marx's schemes for the destruction of the system of free enterprise." Like other conservatives, the correspondent explained that the "[t]he huge sums of money raised by this means tend to maintain in power whatever party is in control of its distribution and to develop a monolithic or one party state." As such, the amendment was "a sinister menace to our institutions."[165]

A more comprehensive defense of free enterprise that included a frontal assault on the income tax was launched in the mid-1940s by Willis E. Stone, a Colorado-born, Los Angeles–based engineer, in the campaign for a proposed "Liberty Amendment" to the Constitution which, as *Human Events* described it, "requires that the US government get out of competition with any kind of private enterprise ... that no laws or treaties shall weaken the amendment ... and that three years after the change's ratification the 16th Federal income tax Amendment shall stand repealed and the government shall cease to levy taxes on personal incomes, estates and/or gifts."[166] The National Committee for

---

[163] Kellems, *Toil, Taxes and Trouble*, 21. Kellems's war on federal taxation continued for the rest of her long life. See *Kellems v. Commissioner of Internal Revenue*, 58 T.C. 556 (1972); *Kellems v. Commissioner of Internal Revenue*, 474 F.2d 1399 (2nd Cir., 1973). See Westbrook Pegler, "Vivien Kellems Is Most Republican Republican of All," *The Evening Independent* (February 6, 1960); Andy Logan, "Grips and Taxes," *The New Yorker* (February 3, 1951), 36; Gloria Swanson, "Unforgettable Vivien Kellems," *Reader's Digest* (July 1975), 143; Bill Kaufman, "The Woman Who Didn't Withhold," *The American Enterprise* (September 1, 2000). David M. Gross, editor, *We Won't Pay! A Tax Resistance Reader* (CreateSpace 2008), 419–428; James L. Potts, "The Relation of the Income Tax to Democracy in the United States," *Western Political Quarterly* 10:4 (December 1957): 911–925; Carolyn C. Jones, "Vivien Kellems and the Folkways of Taxation," in Daniel Ernst and Victor Jew, editors, *Total War and the Law: The American Home Front in World War II* (Westport, CT: Praeger, 2002).

[164] *Pollack v. Farmers' Loan and Trust Company*, 157 US 429 (1895).

[165] Clarence B. Hewes [Washington, DC], Letter to the Editor, *Wall Street Journal* (November 28, 1951), 10. The author called for the repeal of the Sixteenth Amendment and its replacement by a sales tax (with those with the lowest incomes exempted), and a return to the gold standard. See also Betsey Newton [Salisbury, MO], Letter to the Editor, *Wall Street Journal* (January 2, 1952), 8.

[166] "The 24th Amendment," *Human Events* 19:29 (July 21, 1962), 460; "Liberty Amendment Committee Continues Drive in 44 States," *Human Events* 23:7 (February 15, 1964), 8. The

Economic Freedom (succeeded from 1959 on by the Liberty Amendment Committee) launched *Freedom* magazine to advance its cause and spearhead the amendment's adoption. The committee remains active to this day.[167] The campaign against the income tax, and taxes generally, was joined by other prominent figures as well, some of whom, like the World War I flying ace, FDR nemesis, and retired chairman of the board of Eastern Airlines, Captain Eddie Rickenbacker, took a star turn on the conservative lecture circuit with a stump speech campaigning for two positions: get the United States out of the United Nations and abolish the income tax.[168] Many warned that industrial growth, the foundation of American economic and military strength, was imperiled by the nation's modern tax policies. In a 1953 article in *Reader's Digest*, for instance, the chairman of US Steel Benjamin F. Fairless explained

article noted that this would not affect the corporate income tax. "The Liberty Amendment," *Human Events* 24:20 (May 16, 1964) [reprinted from *Indianapolis Star*]. The Liberty Amendment's text provided: "Sec. 1. The Government of the United States shall not engage in any business, professional, commercial, financial or industrial enterprise except as specified in the Constitution. Sec. 2. The constitution or law of any State, or the laws of the United States shall not be subject to the terms of any foreign or domestic Agreement which would abrogate this amendment. Sec. 3. The activities of the United States Government which violate the Intent and purposes of this amendment shall, within a period of three years From the date of the ratification of this amendment be liquidated and the Properties and facilities affected shall be sold. Sec. 4. Three years after the ratification of this amendment the sixteenth article of amendment to the Constitution of the United States shall stand repealed and thereafter Congress shall not levy taxes on personal incomes, estates, and/or gifts."

[167] See Willis E. Stone, "How to Stop Paying Taxes," *The American Mercury* (June 1958), 41–44; Willis E. Stone, *Where the Money Went* (Los Angeles: Fact Sheet, 1971); Stone, *Instead of Taxes*; Stone, *Ten Lessons on the Constitution* (1974). Stone also founded and edited *American Progress* magazine. Howard Jarvis, who led the tax revolt that enacted Proposition 13 in California, had served on the national board of the Liberty Amendment Committee. Donald T. Critchlow, *The Conservative Ascendency: How the GOP Right Made Political History* (Cambridge, MA: Harvard University Press, 2007), 165; Sara Diamond, *Roads to Dominion*, 51–52. See Isaac William Martin, *Rich People's Movements: Grassroots Campaigns to Untax the One Percent* (New York: Oxford University Press, 2013). The campaign for this amendment continues on the Right, with former Texas congressman Ron Paul as its most prominent backer. See http://libertyamendment.org/.

[168] See Fred G. Clark, *The Socialist Sixteenth – A National Cancer* (California Committee for Economic Freedom, 1961) (Address by Fred G. Clark at the Annual Staff Meeting Banquet, Advisory and Field Board, Eastern Airlines, Inc., Deauville Hotel, Miami Beach, FL) (Introduction by Captain E.V. Rickenbacker). Fred G. Clark (1890–1973) was an Ohio-born oil-refining and insurance entrepreneur and businessman, close friend of Herbert Hoover, and staunch free market advocate. An opponent of Franklin Roosevelt and the New Deal, Clark publicized his views through the American Economic Foundation (which he founded, and which, along with the Intercollegiate Society of Individualists, the Foundation for Economic Education, and the Christian Freedom Foundation, sponsored "The Hall of Free Enterprise" at the 1964 World's Fair), a radio program on the NBC Blue Network (*Wake Up, America!* (1940–1946)), several books, and many editorials for newspapers and magazines. *Hall of Enterprise: Groundbreaking at the New York World's Fair 1964–1965* (New York World's Fair 1964–1965 Corporation, May 8, 1963) [pamphlet].

that "[w]hen we permit anything to impair it, either in old established industries or in small, new enterprises, we are destroying our future ability to survive as an independent people." Fairless complained that "in recent years the fiscal policies of the federal government have placed an almost intolerable burden on businesses of every size" and "[P]rofits are the food which supports the life and growth of our business population, just as wages provide the food which nourishes our human population. If too much of that economic food is taxed away, these populations will wither from malnutrition." Taxes, moreover, destroy incentives to produce. Since they are passed on to purchasers, corporate taxes were actually little more than hidden sales taxes. Quoting John Marshall's opinion in *McCulloch* v. *Maryland* (1819), as had Vivien Kellems before him, Fairless rousingly emphasized that "[t]ruly, the power to tax is the power to destroy."[169]

In a defense of the Reed-Dirksen Amendment that would have imposed a ceiling on federal tax rates published in the *ABA Journal* the following year, Raymond Rice noted that "the income tax now accounts for more than 80 percent of all federal tax collections – a figure that conforms exactly to the pattern of 'heavy progressive income tax' proposed by the Marx-Engels Communist Manifesto as the most effective device for the destruction of private enterprise." Grants-in-aid were destroying state sovereignty. "Far easier it is to become enmeshed in a Washington-woven web of grants and contributions, with their attendant conditions, regulations, restrictions and directives, than to find a way to escape." This, in turn, "stimulate[s] reckless spending and breeds ever-increasing centralization of power." It was time to return to a more sensible, and legitimate, system.[170]

Reams were written in defense of business and management. Many of these defenses conceptualized the business corporation as the property of the

---

[169] Benjamin F. Fairless, "Taxation: The Power to Destroy America's Future," *Reader's Digest* 62:370 (February 1953): 113–116, 113–115. *McCulloch* v. *Maryland*, 17 US 316 (1819). For a recent foray, see, e.g., Amity Schlaes, *The Greedy Hand: How Taxes Drive Americans Crazy and What to Do About It* (New York: Random House, 1999).

[170] Raymond F. Rice, "The Income Tax: Fiscal Frankenstein Monster," *American Bar Association Journal* 40 (June 1954): 506–509, 507–508. See Theodore R. Meyer, "The Reed-Dirksen Amendment: A Re-Examination of Our Income Tax Theory," *American Bar Association Journal* 42:1 (January 1956): 42–45, 93–95; Robert B. Dresser, "The Reed-Dirksen Amendment: Developments in the 83d Congress," *American Bar Association Journal* 39 (March 1953): 206–208; Robert B. Dresser, "The Reed-Dirksen Amendment: Further Developments," *American Bar Association Journal* 40 (December 1954): 1051–1053; Robert B. Dresser, "The Case for Tax Relief," *The Freeman* 5:3 (September 1954): 86–88; Robert B. Dresser, "The Case for the Income Tax Amendment: A Reply to Dean Griswold," *American Bar Association Journal* 39 (January 1953): 25–28, 84–87; Erwin N. Griswold, "Can We Limit Taxes to 25 Percent?" *Atlantic Monthly* (August 1952). The amendment had been endorsed by the ABA House of Delegates (February 1952). Dresser, a graduate of Yale and Harvard Law School, was a prominent conservative Rhode Island attorney. "Robert B. Dresser, Lawyer and Conservative Spokesman," *New York Times* (September 27, 1976).

owners, operating under the stewardship of its managers. Regulation, taxation, and other government-imposed restraints and obligations were taken as akin to government appropriation, denying what Richard Weaver had characterized as the "metaphysical" (or, put otherwise, the deontological) status of property rights: they remade the rights into the tools of the activist state, protected when useful to advancing that state's policies and disregarded when not. As C. P. Ives later recounted in *Modern Age*, the New Deal labor system initiated by the Wagner Act extensively regulating employer-employee relations had "effectively 'sterilized' property's managerial discipline of cost and cash-flow," damaging productivity, and, hence, the rate of capital formation, which put the United States at a strong disadvantage vis-à-vis the rest of the industrialized world.[171] The expansion of government, fueled by ever-higher tax rates (the appropriation of the hard-won earnings of industrious individuals), thinned the ranks of private businesses and prevented the entrepreneurial establishment of new ones. This governmental assault had been licensed by a series of constitutional transgressions. The broad interpretation of the Article I Commerce Clause – imposed, *US News*'s David Lawrence insisted in the early 1960s, by a "judicial oligarchy" enthroned during the New Deal – conferred expansive new powers on the federal government to control private business, with a blithe disregard for rights.[172]

Modern liberal understandings of Article II executive powers, significantly furthered by Franklin Roosevelt and Harry Truman, were also proving highly detrimental to constitutional property rights. Robert Nisbet, for example, took President Truman's seizure of the nation's steel mills during the Korean War as a signal manifestation of this danger, which, by extension, had troubling implications for the future of other constitutional rights. "[U]nder the doctrine of 'inherent powers' on which the steel seizure was based," Nisbet wrote, "there could be no guarantee of the rights of property and with the disappearance of those rights there would also go the rights of persons." Fortunately, the *Wall Street Journal* editorialized, the Vinson Court had stood up to the president. Without that line of defense, rights of all sorts were only as secure as the whims of a president's declaring "necessity."[173]

Many conservatives, including many outside the South, were profoundly troubled by what they took to be the burgeoning civil rights movement's brazen attacks on constitutionally protected private property rights. The agitation for laws barring racial discrimination by private businesses menaced

---

[171] C. P. Ives, "Judges Under Judgment," *Modern Age* 20:1 (Winter 1976), 106–109, 107.

[172] David Lawrence, "Our Vanishing Constitution," *US News and World Report* (July 20, 1964), 104.

[173] "The Steel Decision," *Wall Street Journal* (June 3, 1952), 10. *Youngstown Sheet and Tube* v. *Sawyer*, 343 US 579 (1952).

the freedom of association, they said.[174] Some, like the former Special Deputy Attorney General of New York Alfred Avins, additionally argued that laws compelling business owners to serve black customers also violated the Thirteenth Amendment.[175] Alluding to *Truax* v. *Raich*'s (1915) defense of the right of every person to freely practice any lawful occupation, Avins insisted that an onslaught of civil rights laws was making the American businessman into a slave of the government, forcing him, literally, into involuntary servitude. "It is one of the most compelling ironies of history," Avins observed, "to find that, in 1964, Negroes are demanding laws to compel whites to serve them in the very same occupations which they themselves were freed from serving whites in 1864, and demanding this under the name of 'freedom.'"[176]

The systematic legal defense of conservative understandings of property rights in a more hopeful, forward-looking vein began in California in the early 1970s when veterans of Governor Reagan's staff, frustrated by the flurry of "public interest" lawsuits that they saw as persistently delaying if not thwarting the governor's policies, decided to form their own public interest law firm, the Pacific Legal Foundation (PLF), to intervene on behalf of the powers of state governments in the name of democratically elected majorities. They soon realized, however, that, just as often, the forces with which they were doing battle were as likely to be found inside the government making public policies as outside the government frustrating them. Soon, the PLF pivoted, and began waging war on the regulatory state. Instead of

[174] David Lawrence, "The Era of Anarchy," *Reader's Digest* 89:535 (November 1966): 127–128, 128, reprinted, condensed, from *US News and World Report* (August 29, 1966). See also David Lawrence, "The Only Hope," *US News and World Report* (June 10, 1963), 112.

[175] The Thirteenth Amendment to the US Constitution provides that "Neither slavery nor involuntary servitude, except as a punishment for crime whereof the party shall have been duly convicted, shall exist within the United States, or any place subject to their jurisdiction."

[176] Alfred Avins, "Maybe it's Time to Look at the Antislavery Amendment," *US News and World Report* (May 11, 1964): 82–84, 83. *Traux* v. *Raich*, 239 US 33 (1915) (voiding Arizona law requiring businesses employing over five people to maintain a workforce that is at least 80 percent "qualified electors or native-born citizens" of the United States). See *Heart of Atlanta Motel, Inc.* v. *United States*, 379 US 241 (1964); Linda McClain, "Involuntary Servitude, Public Accommodations Laws, and the Legacy of *Heart of Atlanta Motel, Inc. v. United States*," *Maryland Law Review* 71 (2011): 83–162. The New Yorker Avins had served as staff counsel to the US Senate Judiciary Committee under the chairmanship of South Carolina segregationist Senator Strom Thurmond, and as special advisor to Virginia's segregationist Commission on Constitutional Government. Avins had prepared the nearly 800-page tome *The Reconstruction Amendments' Debates: The Legislative History and Contemporary Debates in Congress on the 13th, 14th, and 15th Amendments* (Richmond, VA: Virginia Commission on Constitutional Government, 1967), a compendium of the original debates and documents, for the Virginia Commission on Constitutional Government, which it used to argue that the commission, which spearheaded massive resistance to *Brown* v. *Board of Education* in the state, was acting in accordance with the original intent and understanding of those, who had written and adopted those amendments. Avins went on to help found the white supremacist Liberty Lobby. William P. Hustwit, *James J. Kilpatrick: Salesman for Segregation* (Chapel Hill: University of North Carolina Press, 2013), 98–99.

lamenting the aggressive assertion of individual rights and due process claims, as many conservatives had been doing across the Warren Court Rights Revolution, however, they decided to champion such claims, on behalf of economic rights. Among their most passionate causes were property rights.[177]

Jefferson Decker had argued that given its historical context, this was not a simple resurrection of pre–New Deal, Old Right understandings of constitutional property rights. This was not because the substantive understandings of the rights was different, but because the context had changed: the newly pervasive social regulation of the late 1960s and early 1970s had "changed how many Americans experienced the federal government." Since the 1930s, a series of social movements – the civil rights movement, second-wave feminism, the consumer protection movement (e.g., Ralph Nader's Public Citizen), and the environmental movement – had cascaded across the political landscape. Over time the denizens of these

---

[177] Decker, *Other Rights Revolution*, 1–11, 57–63; Teles, *Rise of the Conservative Legal Movement*, 60–62. The decision to support economic substantive due process was not new on the postwar Right. In the late 1950s, for example, Richard Carpenter, a professor at Loyola Law School in Chicago, wrote articles in the *ABA Journal* (as did others) arguing that the New Deal's repudiation of the doctrine of economic substantive due process – the basis for, among other things, the Court's notorious *Lochner* v. *New York*, 198 US 45 (1905) decision – had been mistaken. While the *laissez-faire* model had gone too far in one direction, Carpenter argued, the total repudiation of the idea that economic liberties were protected by the due process clause(s) – e.g., such as by Justices Hugo Black and William O. Douglas in their opinions in the *Williamson* v. *Lee Optical*, 348 US 483 (1955) case – amounted to unjustified extremism in the opposite direction. Carpenter praised instead the middle-way opinions on the matter that chose instead to balance the police powers claims of the states with appeals to constitutional rights. Among these praiseworthy middle-way approaches, as Carpenter saw it, were the views set out by Supreme Court Justices John Marshall Harlan, Edward White, and William Day in their *Lochner* dissents; by William Howard Taft in his dissent in *Adkins* v. *Children's Hospital*, 261 US 525 (1923); and by Charles Evans Hughes in his opinion for the Court in *West Coast Hotel* v. *Parrish*, 300 US 379 (1937). These justices, Carpenter explained, "did not lock the scale upon which they weighed the competing interests of freedom and authority, but ... at most [made] a makeweight on the side of legislative authority." Carpenter criticized Justice William O. Douglas for referring to economic liberty as little more than a "school of thought." If it is that, Carpenter underlined, "it is the school of thought in whose context our revolution was fought and our Constitution framed." Like later scholars, Carpenter wrote that many of the laws that had been struck down in the late nineteenth and early twentieth centuries amounted to little more than what contemporary public choice scholars call rent seeking: they "were designed to hamper particular commercial groups or industries in the interest of their politically more powerful competitors." Richard V. Carpenter, "Our Constitutional Heritage: Economic Due Process and the State Courts," *American Bar Association Journal* 45 (October 1959): 1027–1029, 1027–1029. *Williamson* v. *Lee Optical*, 348 US 483 (1955). See also Richard V. Carpenter, "Substantive Due Process at Issue: A Resume," *U.C.L.A. Law Review* 5 (January 1958): 47. See David E. Bernstein, "*Lochner* Era Revisionism, Revised: *Lochner* and the Origins of Fundamental Rights Constitutionalism," *Georgetown Law Journal* 82 (2003): 1; David E. Bernstein, *Rehabilitating Lochner: Defending Individual Rights Against Progressive Reform* (Chicago: University of Chicago Press, 2011); Richard A. Epstein, *How Progressives Rewrote the Constitution* (Washington, DC: Cato Institute, 2007).

movements had graduated from being government outsiders to government insiders: they were now staffing federal agencies. By the 1970s, when Americans interacted with government officials, they were no longer interacting with colorless, apparently apolitical bureaucrats but with activists self-evidently steeped in liberal/left movement politics. When it came to property and land management issues – and, in the West, given the extensive government ownership of Western lands, Americans interacted regularly with national government officials – they were increasingly dealing with liberal environmentalists, many with few if any roots or experience in the region, and they resented it.[178]

The PLF was the first conservative litigation group to receive tax-exempt status as a nonprofit, public interest organization. After several false starts, the organization succeeded in challenging the new California Coastal Commission's decision to take the low-cost route (to government) of imposing stringent land-use regulations for aesthetic and environmental protection purposes on coastal property, as opposed to the high-cost route of "taking" the land by purchasing it, either through voluntary market exchange or the coercive exercise of the government's eminent domain powers.[179]

These successes led the group toward an increasing specialty in land-use issues. The PLF soon found itself part of "the sagebrush rebellion," a property rights movement sweeping the American West and spreading nationally, across the 1970s and 1980s. At this time, conservatives across the country established a succession of regionally based property rights groups on the PLF model, including the Mountain States Legal Foundation (MSLF), the Gulf and Great Plains Legal Foundation, and others.[180] And, beginning in the 1970s, a new conservative strain of property rights scholarship pioneered by the University of San Diego Law School's Bernard Siegan (discussed later), subsequently joined,

---

[178] Decker, *Other Rights Revolution*, 20–25, 79. Decker reminds us, "The federal government owns approximately 85 percent of Nevada, two-thirds of Utah, and nearly half of Arizona, Colorado, and California."

[179] The California Coastal Commission imposed the new regulations that had been advocated – and defended as constitutional – by the new "public trust" theory of land regulation that had been recently advanced by University of Michigan Law Professor Joseph Sax. Joseph P. Sax, "The Public Trust Doctrine in Natural Resource Law: Effective Judicial Intervention," *Michigan Law Review* 68 (1970): 471–566; Joseph P. Sax, "Takings, Private Property, and Public Rights," *Yale Law Journal* 81(2) (December 1971): 149. Decker, *Other Rights Revolution*, 65–66. See Carol M. Rose, "Joseph Sax and the Idea of The Public Trust," *Ecology Law Quarterly* 25 (1998): 351–362. Sax later joined the Bill Clinton administration as an aide to US Interior Secretary and former Arizona Governor Bruce Babbitt.

[180] The Mountain States Legal Foundation was bankrolled by the conservative Colorado beer magnate Joseph Coors, and headed by James Watt – later President Reagan's secretary of the interior. Utah's Rex Lee, a Mountain States Legal Foundation board member and litigator, later served as President Reagan's solicitor general. Decker, *Other Rights Revolution*, 64–94; Teles, *Rise of the Conservative Legal Movement*, 62–66. The Gulf and Great Plains Legal Foundation was later renamed the Landmark Legal Foundation.

most prominently, in the 1980s by the University of Chicago Law School's Richard Epstein, lent the cause intellectually sophisticated, and citable, academic support.[181]

THE THREAT OF LABOR UNIONS TO "THE RIGHT TO WORK"

Many conservatives vigorously opposed the protections the New Deal state had newly afforded to organized labor by underwriting labor union power. While it also incorporated traditional common law understandings, much of this resistance was waged on constitutional grounds.[182]

This opposition, however, was not new to the postwar Right. In its modern incarnation, it had developed coincident with the American labor movement in the late nineteenth and early twentieth centuries, when "the labor question" was perhaps the era's defining political question ("the Sphinx's Riddle," Edward Bellamy had dubbed it in _Looking Backward_ (1888)). Employers, backed by the courts wielding traditional common law doctrines concerning the law of master and servant and conspiracy, along with a robust constitutional liberties doctrine involving Fifth and Fourteenth Amendment due process property and other individual rights, organized to fight back by challenging labor power.[183]

Chad Pearson has recently chronicled the early twentieth-century rise of "defense associations" fighting for "open shop" legislation in opposition to "labor trusts," what Pearson calls "the first-wave open shop movement."[184] While this movement proved "especially successful in the South," it was a national movement with a strong presence as well in the Midwest and urban Northeast. It had close ties, even then, to the Republican Party, drawing in part on that party's commitment to free labor, enterprise, and liberal individualism that had been originally forged in conjunction with the opposition to chattel

---

[181] Richard A. Epstein, _Takings: Private Property and the Power of Eminent Domain_ (Cambridge, MA: Harvard University Press, 1985). Supreme Court Justice Antonin Scalia's land-use opinions on the High Court drew heavily on the arguments advanced in this work. See, e.g., _Lucas v. Carolina Coastal Commission_, 505 US 1003 (1992).

[182] See Sophia Z. Lee, "Whose Rights? Litigating the Right-to-Work, 1950–1980," in Nelson Lichtenstein and Elizabeth Tandy Shermer, editors. _The American Right and U.S. Labor: Politics, Ideology, and Imagination_ (Philadelphia: University of Pennsylvania Press, 2012).

[183] Karen Orren, _Belated Feudalism: Labor, the Law, and Liberal Development in the United States_ (New York: Cambridge University Press, 1991); Victoria Hattam, _Labor Visions and State Power: The Origins of Business Unionism in the United States_ (Princeton: Princeton University Press, 1993); Daniel Ernst, _Lawyers Against Labor: From Individual Rights to Corporate Liberalism_ (Champaign-Urbana: University of Illinois Press, 1995); George Lovell, _Legislative Deferrals: Statutory Ambiguity, Judicial Power, and American Democracy_ (New York: Cambridge University Press, 2003); Chad Pearson, _Reform or Repression: Organizing America's Anti-Union Movement_ (Philadelphia: University of Pennsylvania Press, 2016).

[184] Pearson, _Reform or Repression_, 2–3, 25.

slavery.[185] This ideological bedrock within the party emphasized the "right to work" of each American individual – that is, the right of an individual to earn a living in an honest trade, by choice and without coercion. This right was understood to apply equally to employees and employers alike. Viewed from this perspective, to force an employee to join a labor union as a condition of his employment (the closed shop – one of the major goals of the early twentieth-century labor movement) entailed a major restriction on an individual's basic freedom. It also meant that requiring that an employer recognize a union trenched on his freedom and flexibility to run his businesses – which he was held to own as his own private property, a constitutionally protected fundamental right – as he saw fit. This was not simply a matter of autonomy, without regard to the broader public good. As many employers and their defenders saw it, unions operating in closed shops tended to impose across-the-board rules, without regard to employee productivity and merit. They tended to reinforce the status quo, hamstringing operations in constantly changing markets and industries. And they generated unrest and instability in industry through their often unjustified work stoppages. Successful businesses in dynamic markets provided jobs. To the extent they prospered, it was argued – which the employer had every incentive to make sure that they did – successful businesses provided the basis for a working and middle-class prosperity for millions of Americans, an unambiguous public good. In this way, during the first-wave open shop movement, the opposition to the closed shop under the guise of the right to work was forged under an ethos not of selfishness, but of stewardship. As Pearson summarized it, these employers often "identified themselves as enlightened visionaries partially responsible for the welfare of 'the common people,' repeatedly show[ing] a willingness to protect individual nonunion workers against challenges from a 'monopoly-imposing,' often hostile, and sometimes lawless labor movement." They were practical, honest, fair-minded, and public spirited. These employers, by contrast, understood labor organizers campaigning for the closed shop as selfishly grasping, unscrupulous, and lawless troublemakers causing an array of problems for employers and employees alike, of which they seemed only dimly aware, if they cared at all. Topping it all off was the galling self-righteousness of the partisans of organized labor. Crusaders for the open shop took themselves to be tutoring the average worker in his own best interests, with a blithe disregard for the fact that the self-interest of employers (actual or potential) and employees was not adversarial, but mutual. As such, union organizers were problem makers, while employers were problem solvers.[186]

---

[185] See Kersch, *Constructing Civil Liberties*, 137–143; Eric Foner, *Free Soil, Free Labor, Free Men: The Ideology of the Republican Party Before the Civil War* (New York: Oxford University Press, 1970).

[186] Pearson, *Reform or Repression*, 4–5, 8–11, 23–24. Pearson's *Reform or Repression* treats the first wave of the southern wing of the right to work movement at 182–215. Although it would

Pearson emphasizes that the first-wave open shop movement was of ambiguous ideological/political incidence: it was not necessarily, and certainly not exclusively, "conservative," as would make sense given the movement's (proximate) ideological roots in antislavery liberalism. To be sure, some of the most significant business leadership of the movement was provided by peak employers groups like the National Association of Manufacturers (NAM), and the American Anti-Boycott Association (AABA), along with a vast array of industry-specific organizations like the American Foundrymen's Association (AFA) and the National Metal Trades Association (NMTA), all of which would, in almost all contexts, be properly classified as "conservative" under (American) understandings of the term. Nevertheless, some of the era's most prominent reformers also, at various times and to various degrees, lent their support for the open shop. These included the social gospel leader Washington Gladden, the "muckraking" journalist Ray Stannard Baker, the crusading progressive Theodore Roosevelt, the progressive philosopher and activist John Dewey, the "people's lawyer" Louis D. Brandeis, and progressive groups like the National Civic Federation (NCF).[187] In this, reformist partisans of the open shop emphasized individual freedom, antimonopoly, peace, and fairness. Race further complicated the political incidence of the issue, as most of the unions pursuing the closed shop were at the time racially discriminatory. This meant that a closed shop was, in practice, a white-only shop. In this context, one could advocate for the open shop as a means of advancing civil rights.[188]

In what (building upon Pearson) it seems proper to call the "second wave" of the American right to work movement, the issue broke much more cleanly along the conservative-liberal divide. What had intervened was, of course, the labor regime forged by the New Deal: the National Labor Relations ("Wagner") Act had instituted a state-mandated closed-shop collective bargaining regime under the stewardship of the newly created National Labor Relations Board – what Sophia Lee has described as a new "Workplace Constitution." Liberals considered the new order a permanent form of "progress" implemented by the one-way ratchet of state development.

---

be interesting to carefully compare the perhaps divergent political philosophies of the southern and northern wings of the movements, which Pearson does in passing, only briefly, by implication, one imagines that the southern version was not rooted in "free labor" Republican Party ideology, as Pearson's discussion of Ku Klux Klan founder Nathan Bedford Forrest's involvement in it suggests. Doing so, however, is beyond the scope of this brief overview.

[187] Pearson, *Reform or Repression*, 11–15, 24–55, 56–87, 92, 96; Ernst, *Lawyers Against Labor*.

[188] See Kersch, *Constructing Civil Liberties*, 188–195; Ken I. Kersch, "The New Deal Triumph as the End of History? The Judicial Negotiation of Labor Rights and Civil Rights," in Ronald Kahn and Ken I. Kersch, editors, *The Supreme Court and American Political Development* (Lawrence: University Press of Kansas, 2006), 169–226; Paul Frymer, *Black and Blue*; Reuel Schiller, *Forging Rivals: Race, Class, and the Collapse of Postwar Liberalism* (New York: Cambridge University Press, 2015); Pearson, *Reform or Repression*, 198–206, 216–225; Sophia Z. Lee, *The Workplace Constitution: From the New Deal to the New Right* (New York: Cambridge University Press, 2014), 1–3, 5–6, 15–55.

Conservatives regrouped as an outsider movement seeking retrenchment or repeal. In the second wave, the right to work became an unambiguously conservative cause.[189]

The process of charting conservative opposition to this new regime over time is complicated by the intercession of race and civil rights: the Democratic Party coalition had risen to power and established the new governing regime in large part driven by its commitment to solving the labor problem. This initial reform imperative, however, was sequentially followed at mid-century by a new reform imperative involving civil rights. When racially discriminatory labor unions were afforded monopoly status and, at the same time, African Americans joined the New Deal liberal Democratic coalition, the stage was set for innumerable developmental conflicts, compromises, and settlements. These took place across time, often subtly and *sub rosa*, in shifting doctrines, interpretations, and practices of administrative boards and agencies, in courts within the newly empowered national administrative state, and at the state level as well. Sophia Lee has expertly charted this often arcane series of legal and administrative shifts and adjustments. The ascendant second-wave right to work movement strategically forged its program in response to this now moving target. As such, the positions taken by the postwar second-wave right to work movement were both continuous and discontinuous with the positions conservatives had taken during the struggle's first wave.

One of the most notable discontinuities was that second-wave right to work conservatives joined African American civil rights activists in promoting an expansive understanding of the Fourteenth Amendment's state action doctrine. That doctrine, which had been read narrowly by the Supreme Court in the *Civil Rights Cases* (1883), emphasized the "No State Shall" language of the Fourteenth Amendment provision proscribing the "mak[ing] or enforce[ing] [of] any law which shall ... deprive any person of life, liberty, or property, without due process of law ... [or] deny to any person within its jurisdiction the equal protection of the laws." A broad reading of the Amendment's "No State shall" language would allow Congress and the courts to proscribe racially discriminatory conduct by private actors like privately owned purveyors of transportation, places of public accommodation and amusement by finding a hook – typically an indirect or limited link between the private actor's business and some form of government support. As the civil rights cause was taken up by the liberal Warren Court (1953–1969), the Court began to hold that even extremely tenuous links between private actors and the state constituted "state action," thus unleashing national supervisory and regulatory power.[190] By contrast, a narrow reading of the Fourteenth Amendment's "No State shall" language

---

[189] Lee, *The Workplace Constitution*.
[190] See *Shelley v. Kraemer*, 334 US 1 (1948)(Vinson Court); *Burton v. Wilmington Parking Authority*, 365 US 715 (1961).

had insulated racially discriminatory conduct by private actors from government interference and supervision, confining that conduct to the autonomous private sphere, an understanding that, incidentally, could also be characterized involving a protection of rights: the right of a private individual, for instance, to own and do as he would with his constitutionally protected private property.

Like bus lines, taxi services, hotels, restaurants, and theaters, labor unions were private organizations. But, in this context at least, partisans of the open shop wanted to hold them to have sufficient involvement with the government to subject them to constitutional standards (in time, the issue became moot with the passage of the Civil Rights Act of 1964, which regulated private institutions via expansive New Deal understandings of the Commerce Clause – and specifically included labor unions among its targets of potentially discriminatory private institutions).[191]

What Lee calls "the industrial pluralist" model of the workplace Constitution – that is, the immediate product of the New Deal's first reform imperative of empowering autonomous labor unions via the National Labor Relations Act as government-protected counterweights to the concentrated power of corporate employers – rendered the internal operations of labor unions impenetrable to government regulation. That impenetrability blocked the government from opposing racial discrimination within unions, something that was not a major concern for most at the time but soon became one as the New Deal regime moved forward through time. As liberalism changed with the advent of civil rights, the nature of the workplace constitution was altered as well.

Under the auspices of the new government-sponsored industrial pluralist labor regime, closed shops and union membership soared. The influence of the institutions that had led the first-wave right to work movement and had mounted a failed resistance to Franklin Roosevelt, such as the National Association of Manufacturers and the American Liberty League, withered. But as soon as the early 1940s, the second wave was already forming under the auspices of the NAM and the newspaper columnist Westbrook Pegler, who challenged what they saw as government support for the coercive powers of organized labor that was arrayed against the choices and liberties of free individuals. On Labor Day 1941, the *Dallas Morning News*'s William Ruggles issued a "Right to Work Magna Carta" and proposed a constitutional amendment to institute its provisions.[192]

One of the most visible individual leaders of the rising second-wave movement was the conservative film director Cecil B. DeMille, who produced

---

[191] Lee, *Workplace Constitution*. The Article I, Section 8, Commerce Clause reads: "The Congress shall have Power ... To regulate Commerce with foreign Nations, and among the several States, and with the Indian tribes."

[192] Lee, *Workplace Constitution*, 58–60.

and directed many of the era's great Biblical epics, including *The King of Kings* (1927), *The Sign of the Cross* (1932), *Samson and Delilah* (1949), and *The Ten Commandments* (1956) (starring the later gun-rights stalwart Charlton Heston). Years before *National Review* founder William F. Buckley Jr. would undergo the same experience while working on his *Firing Line* television program for PBS in the 1960s, DeMille blanched when he was told in 1944 that as a radio broadcaster, he was required to join the American Federation of Radio Artists union and to pay one dollar in union dues. DeMille refused, insisting that the requirement amounted to coerced political speech. A founding member of the Motion Picture Alliance for the Preservation of American Ideals (1944), DeMille forged connections between the right to work and the anti-communist causes. He joined with a group of anti-union businessmen to form the DeMille Foundation for Political Freedom, which emphasized the Constitution and constitutional rights. Across the 1940s, DeMille and his compatriots pushed courts to issue injunctions against labor unions on the grounds that their actions had impinged upon individuals' natural, constitutional, and common law rights to work; to practice a lawful vocation; and to earn a livelihood free from the outside coercion of others – a right for which there was considerable pre–New Deal precedent (claims that, in their time, made the NAACP sit up and take notice).[193]

An opportunity opened up with the public anger over the strike wave occasioned by the end of World War II. As tens of thousands of demobilized soldiers were seeking work, the strikes sparked fears among Americans not only that they would be unable to find work in the new peacetime economy but also that the nation would slip back into depression. Republicans capitalized on this opportunity, seizing sweeping control of both houses of Congress in 1946. One of the Republicans' first items of business was to land a major counterpunch against the industrial pluralist New Deal labor regime by passing a law over President Harry S Truman's veto that Cecil B. DeMille and others had prominently championed, the Taft-Hartley Act (1947). In addition to implementing new protections for employer free speech rights (typically to criticize unions and verbally advocate against them to their employees), requiring anti-communist affidavits for union leaders, and imposing new restrictions on strikes and boycotts, Taft-Hartley banned the closed shop and licensed states to pass open shop laws. At the behest of conservatives, but with the support of civil rights advocates, moreover, the act gave the NLRB the power to police unfair labor practices not just by employers, as had been the case under the Wagner Act,

---

[193] Lee, *Workplace Constitution*, 56–57, 62–68. See Amy Wallhermfechtel, "Shaping the Right to Work: The Cecil B. DeMille Foundation's Role in State and National Right to Work Campaigns," PhD Thesis, St. Louis University (2014). Conservatives, now in power on the Supreme Court in the early twenty-first century, have pointedly revisited – and remade – the constitutional law on these issues. See, e.g., *Janus* v. *AFSCME*, 585 US – (2018).

but by labor unions as well. This was a potentially significant breach to industrial pluralist union impermeability.[194]

Although it had taken a hit, and the situation was now more mixed, the New Deal regime still largely predominated. So far as constitutional opposition was concerned, the second-wave right to work movement's next steps reflected its distinctive temporal/developmental context. While the movement's early twentieth-century first wave had availed itself of then prevailing Lochner Era economic liberty arguments, the movement's second wave confronted a postwar new regime that placed a special value on minority rights claims under government-managed political pluralism. Accordingly, second-wave advocates strategically pivoted, emphasizing what they characterized as post–New Deal organized labor's status as a powerful economic monopoly. In part under DeMille's ongoing leadership, appealing to the natural rights set out in the Declaration of Independence and the Bill of Rights – the First (free speech, religious liberty), Fifth (due process liberty), and Ninth Amendments, as supplemented by the Fourteenth Amendment (due process liberty) – the second wave emphasized the claims of the powerless, the little guy, the outsider facing the controlling, crushing giant of postwar organized labor.

There were analogies to slavery, and invocations of *Dred Scott*. In addition to making these arguments in courts, the second-wave movement seized the opportunities it had won in Taft-Hartley to take the campaign to the states, where it pushed, with considerable success, for the passage of a raft of state-level right to work laws.[195] The 1950s brought new initiatives, including the founding of anti-union organizations like the United Railroad Operating Committee (which took advantage of key 1951 amendments to the Railway Labor Act), the National Labor-Management Foundation, William T. Harrison's Committee for Union Shop Abolition, and the ongoing DeMille Foundation efforts. As time went on, these groups increasingly availed themselves of civil rights movement victories in the Supreme Court that were newly construing the Fourteenth Amendment's state action requirement broadly, to more effectively target racially discriminatory private organizations. State right to work committees spread and, in 1954, the National Right to Work Committee was formed.[196]

Conservative movement thinkers reinforced the second wave's on-the-ground activism. Some considered the issue from rather lofty heights. The

[194] Lee, *Workplace Constitution*, 52–55, 75.   [195] Lee, *Workplace Constitution*, 70–78.
[196] Lee, *Workplace Constitution*, 116–125. These new state action cases included *Smith v. Allwright*, 321 US 649 (1944) (applying Fourteenth Amendment rights protections against political parties); *Shelley v. Kraemer*, 334 US 1 (applying Fourteenth Amendment rights protections to racially restrictive real estate covenants); *Burton v. Wilmington Parking Authority*, 365 US 715 (1961) (applying Fourteenth Amendment rights protections to a privately owned coffee shop that rented space in a public building); *Public Utilities Commission v. Pollack*, 343 US 451 (1952); *American Communications Association v. Douds*, 339 US 382 (1950).

French political economist and philosopher Bertrand de Jouvenel, who had – and has – a conservative readership in the United States, argued that the dignity of labor had been degraded by the establishment of the wealth redistributing modern social welfare state itself, which refused to recognize the unique talents and abilities of each individual: it treated them not as individuals but simply as members of economic classes. Such views nestled neatly into the argument, advanced by Friedrich Hayek and others, that contrary to the myths perpetuated by (liberal/progressive) historians, the nineteenth and early twentieth centuries had hardly been periods marked by widespread labor exploitation. The implication of this view, of course, was that the state support for organized labor that followed had been a solution in search of a problem.[197] For his part, Richard Weaver praised the South's hostility to labor unions, which he rooted in the southern character, in the laudable predisposition of southerners to defend the status quo. Southerners were graced by "the comparative absence of that modern spirit of envy which has so unsettled things in other parts of the world," Weaver sang.[198] As such, in the South, "[t]rade unionism runs up against both the distrust of analysis and this hesitancy about tampering with a prevailing dispensation." "Whereas modern social doctrine encourages a man to question the whole order of society if he does not have as much as somebody else," Weaver explained, "the typical Southern farmer or millhand tends to regard fortune, like nature, as providential. From his point of view there is nothing written in the original bill of things which says that the substance of the world must be distributed equally. Nor was there anything ... to tell him that he is entitled to the best of everything."[199] Some, of course, refused to accept the label "anti-labor," or argued that it was liberals and progressives who were truly hostile to labor.

Others, however, married principle to the more concrete concerns of public policy and constitutional law. In *Economics in One Lesson* (1946), Henry Hazlitt challenged the shibboleths of a demand-side Keynesian economics that argued that state policies that instituted an ever-rising minimum wage and artificially boosted workers' wages by empowering labor unions would help the economy and its workers to prosper. Later, following Hazlitt, Arizona Senator Barry Goldwater set himself in staunch opposition to the New Deal constitutional and legislative victories of the American labor movement. The minimum wage instituted by the Fair Labor Standards Act (FSLA) had raised prices and increased unemployment, Goldwater argued, striking blows against

---

[197] De Jouvenel, *Ethics of Redistribution*; Friedrich Hayek, editor, *Capitalism and the Historians* (Chicago: University of Chicago Press, 1954). De Jouvenel's writings have been published and republished in the United States and are respectfully read within the serious precincts of the US postwar Right.

[198] Richard M. Weaver, "Aspects of the Southern Philosophy," *The Hopkins Review* 5:4 (Summer 1952), 2–21, reprinted in George M. Curtis III and James J. Thompson Jr., editors, *The Southern Essays of Richard M. Weaver* (Indianapolis, IN: Liberty Press, 1987), 198.

[199] Weaver, "Aspects of the Southern Philosophy," 200.

the very people the law had ostensibly been designed to help. The Constitution, when properly interpreted, had once served as a barrier to such unfortunate enactments, Goldwater explained: "The founding fathers, in writing our Constitution, were careful to limit the powers of the federal government to those specifically enumerated, and to leave all other powers to the states." Goldwater added, "Up to 1933, this power was limited to regulation of commerce in its actual movement across state lines. But since then a mass of legislation has been enacted, which extends federal control over local business." Among this mass was the minimum wage law that initially, Goldwater claimed, had been enacted as a Great Depression emergency measure and not intended to apply to local retail businesses. Because "it permit[ed] the hand of federal bureaucracy to reach down into the states and fumble with the economic structure," the FSLA violated the Tenth Amendment, the place where the Constitution enshrined "states' rights, the keystone of our republic." The result was a constitutional excrescence that also happened to be bad policy that hurt the poor. The Founders had known better.[200]

Many conservatives regarded labor union power as a form of illegitimate monopoly power. The Wagner Act "extended certain remarkable privileges – or indulgences – to officials and members of labor unions not available to other segments of our population," a correspondent complained in the *ABA Journal*.[201] The New Deal had instituted government "protection of giant monopolies of labor where the top man takes his cue from his government and imposes his taxes on helpless employees in the form of dues which he uses to extend and strengthen his own power."[202] Labor laws afforded unions (indefensible) special privileges, which permitted them to trench with impunity upon the rights of business owners and their fellow workers alike, such as by legally sanctioned picketing.[203]

In *Freedom and Federalism* (1959), Felix Morley explained that labor unions were a form of monopoly power of the sort that "[t]he men who wrote the Constitution were personally familiar with." As such, Morley placed the Taft-Hartley Act (1947) in the direct line of the late nineteenth- and early twentieth-century Sherman (1890) and Clayton (1914) antitrust acts. The sponsors of all three acts had understood that monopoly power led to corruption, and, indeed,

[200] Barry Goldwater, "Let's Talk Sense About Minimum-Wage Laws," *Reader's Digest* 78 (March 1961): 81–85, 82–85. The Tenth Amendment to the US Constitution holds that "The powers not delegated to the United States by the Constitution, nor prohibited by it to the States, are reserved to the states respectively, or to the people."

[201] Burt Drummond [Buffalo, New York], Letter to the Editor, *American Bar Association Journal* 44 (1958): 4, 10.

[202] William Logan Martin, "New York and National Health Insurance: Foundations of a Welfare State?" *American Bar Association Journal* 35 (September 1949): 735–739, 739.

[203] "The Newspaper Strike," *Wall Street Journal* (December 11, 1953), 8; "Labor and the Monopoly Laws," *Wall Street Journal* (March 10, 1954), 10; "In Whose Hands?" *Wall Street Journal* (November 23, 1956), 6.

an "appalling corruption ... has affected the leadership of a large portion of trade unionism in the United States." To make matters worse, the threat was more general and radiated outward: "[T]he greater the degree of governmental intervention in the affairs of society [as to underwrite the power of organized labor], the greater will be the internal corruption of society, justifying – or being used to justify – ever more intervention and thereby an even closer approach to totalitarianism."[204]

The radical augmentation of federal executive power during the New Deal – of which Morley was an inveterate critic – had drained power away from almost all other government and economic agencies. "The one notable exception," he observed, however, "was in the case of labor unions, which were strengthened by governmental action without being subjected, in any significant manner, to governmental control." Morley disagreed with those alleging "that this exception was made to guarantee the support of organized labor for the Democratic Party." Morley's own view was that, in the end, "the trade unions also would have been brought to heel if Mr. Roosevelt had continued much longer in office."[205]

By the mid-1960s, *US News and World Report's* David Lawrence was complaining that "[t]he economic life of the country is threatened with disruption by labor groups with unrestricted power, which are interfering with a sound functioning of the private-enterprise system." Lawrence added, "The use of campaign funds by labor groups to buy a majority of the votes of Congress is well-known."[206] The *Wall Street Journal* told its readers that "[t]he major purpose [of labor unions] no longer is the betterment of the members – through collective demands for higher wages, more leisure and all that unions seek in the way of higher living standards; the purpose of unions now is to serve as a quasi-political form of power as a counterweight to management's power."[207] Donald Richberg, formerly one of FDR's closest advisors and a principal architect of his National Recovery Administration (1933), joined Lawrence in opposing labor unions, as did the former progressive legal luminary Roscoe Pound, a founder of "sociological jurisprudence."[208] The National Right to Work Committee (founded in

[204] Morley, *Freedom and Federalism*, 11–12, 40–41. See also Robert F. Kennedy, *The Enemy Within* (New York: Popular Library, 1960) (foreword by Arthur Krock). Morley similarly attributed the rise of juvenile delinquency – a flashpoint issue of the times – to the rise of (monopolistic) compulsory education.

[205] Morley, *Freedom and Federalism*, 105, 151–152, 183.

[206] David Lawrence, "The Era of Anarchy," *Reader's Digest* 89:535 (November 1966): 127–128, 127, reprinted, condensed, from *US News and World Report* (August 29, 1966).

[207] "'Right to Work' Laws," *Wall Street Journal* (February 12, 1957), 6. See also "Union Immunities," *Wall Street Journal* (April 11, 1958), 6 (discussing approvingly Roscoe Pound's anti-union tract *Legal Immunities of Labor Unions* (Washington, DC: American Enterprise Association, 1957)).

[208] See, e.g., Donald R. Richberg, *Labor Union Monopoly: A Clear and Present Danger* (Chicago: H. Regnery, 1957); Roscoe Pound, "Legal Immunities of Labor Unions," in Philip Bradley,

1955) provided an institutional base for the second-wave right to work movement. It was soon joined by the National Right to Work Legal Defense Fund (1968), whose name bears the imprint of the (mostly liberal/left) Public Interest Law Movement that was on the rise at the time it was established in the mid-to-late 1960s. The *Wall Street Journal*, among other outlets, lent the movement editorial support.[209]

As the campaign moved forward through the 1960s and 1970s, right to work advocates regularly struck constitutional themes. "The liberal of yesteryear," a conservative lamented in the early 1960s, "believed that the Constitution guaranteed man the right to work where he pleased, when he pleased, and for whom he pleased so long as he could secure employment." By contrast, "[t]he liberal of today believes the right of the person to work when, where, and for whom he pleases is a union-granted privilege – not a God-given right."[210] Alas, it now fell to conservative proponents of the right to work to defend the erstwhile liberal position of aggressively protecting the beleaguered individual's God-given constitutional rights. James Jackson Kilpatrick argued that the right to work without being forced to join a labor union was a fundamental (unenumerated) Ninth Amendment right. "If a man's right to work is not a 'fundamental right,'" Kilpatrick ventured, "it may be asked, what is?"[211] Carrying forward into the 1960s the constitutional arguments he had first made in the early 1940s, the

Edward Chamberlin, Roscoe Pound, and Gerard D. Reilly, *Labor Unions and Public Policy* (Washington, DC: American Enterprise Association, 1957); Murray N. Rothbard, *Man, Economy, and State, with Power and Market* (Auburn, AL: Ludwig von Mises Institute, 2009), 898. See John Fabian Witt, *Patriots and Cosmopolitans: Hidden Histories of American Law* (Cambridge, MA: Harvard University Press, 2007), chap. 4.

[209] "Main Line Issue," *The Wall Street Journal* (December 7, 1955), 14. See also Thomas S. Schrock, "The Liberal Court, the Conservative Court, and Constitutional Jurisprudence," in Robert A. Goldwin, editor, *Left, Right and Center: Essays on Liberalism and Conservatism in the United States* (Chicago: Rand McNally & Co., 1965), 103–104, 120 (suggesting a more conservative Court start with "occupational freedom," rather than with contractual liberties). See also Walter Gellhorn, *Individual Freedom and Governmental Restraint* (Baton Rouge: Louisiana State University Press, 1956). Both the National Right to Work Committee (www .nrtwc.org/) and the National Right to Work Legal Defense Fund (www.nrtw.org/) remain active today. Anti-union activism by business interests and others, of course, goes back much further, but that is beyond the scope of this study. See Daniel Ernst, *Lawyers Against Labor*; George Lovell, *Legislative Deferrals*; William E. Forbath, *Law and the Shaping of the American Labor Movement* (Cambridge, MA: Harvard University Press, 1991).

[210] N. M. Mason, "Modern Liberals Shame Ancestors," *Human Events* 17:31 (August 4, 1960), 327.

[211] James Jackson Kilpatrick, "Will Court Hold 'Right to Work' as a Constitutional Right?" *Human Events* 27:40 (October 7, 1967), 14. See also Sanford T. Wiener [Los Angeles, California], Letter to the Editor, *Wall Street Journal* (January 18, 1955), 12 (arguing that the right to work is a Ninth Amendment constitutional right). The Constitution's Ninth Amendment reads "The enumeration in the Constitution, of certain rights, shall not be construed to deny or disparage others retained by the people." See also James J. Kilpatrick, "Will Courts Order Disclosure of Right-to-Work Contributors?" *Human Events* 35:22 (May 31, 1975), 11, citing *NAACP v. Alabama*, 357 US 449 (1958).

Dallas Morning News editorialist William Ruggles declared that the compulsory payment of union dues violated the First, Fifth, and Ninth Amendments. It was coerced speech. It precluded the individual from making fundamental choices about his life. It was an assault on liberty.[212]

Some found it necessary to push back against the enlistment of modern economic theory in the service of the restriction of vouchsafed constitutional rights. The former Harvard economics professor (1938–1948) Philip Bradley wrote to refute the argument advanced in Congress and endorsed by the Supreme Court that compulsory unionism was appropriate because workers who chose to not join a union nevertheless benefited as "free riders" from the nonexclusive benefits that unionization brought to the union shop as a whole. Bradley argued that unions could survive even in the absence of closed shop laws. Regardless, those laws were assaults upon an individual worker's basic freedoms.[213] New York University (and, later, Wake Forest) Law School professor and Austrian economist Sylvester Petro argued that labor unions were hostile to the freedom of association and the freedom of contract. They, moreover, trenched upon constitutional protections for private property.[214]

Repeating a parallel that had been made several years earlier by Felix Morley, Milton Friedman had devoted a chapter of *Capitalism and Freedom* (1962) to

---

[212] William B. Ruggles, "Will Constitutionality of Forced Unionism Finally Be Decided?" *Human Events* 27:46 (November 18, 1967), 10. [reprinted from *Dallas Morning News*]. Ruggles used the phrase in an editorial calling for a twenty-second amendment to the US Constitution guaranteeing the right to work with or without union membership. *Dallas Morning News* (September 1, 1941 [Labor Day]). As Ruggles proposed it in 1941, the amendment would read: "No person shall be denied employment because of membership in or affiliation with a labor union; nor shall any corporation or individual sign a contract to exclude from employment members of a labor union or persons who refuse to join a union; nor shall any person against his will be compelled to pay dues to any labor organization" (available on the website of the National Institute for Labor Relations Research at www.nilrr.org/2006/05/16/william-ruggles-labor-day-editorial-right-work/).

[213] Philip Bradley, "Involuntary Participation in Unionism," in Chamberlin, Bradley, Pound, and Reilly, *Labor Unions and Public Policy*. See also Philip D. Bradley, *Involuntary Participation in Unionism* (Washington, DC: American Enterprise Institute, 1956); Philip D. Bradley, editor, *The Public Stake in Union Power* (Charlottesville: University of Virginia Press, 1959); Philip D. Bradley, *Constitutional Limits to Union Power* (Washington, DC: Council on American Affairs, 1976). On Bradley's chapter on "Freedom of the Individual Under Collectivized Labor Arrangements" (in his book *The Public Stake in Union Power*), the estimable Mancur Olson, whose classic book includes a chapter on "The Labor Union and Economic Freedom," writes: "Bradley's curious, polemical essay shows such an unthinking bias against the closed shop, and such confused arguments, that there is no reason to give his conclusion any weight." Mancur Olson, *The Logic of Collective Action: Public Goods and the Theory of Groups* (Cambridge, MA: Harvard University Press, 1965) 69, fn. 10.

[214] Sylvester Petro, *The Labor Policy of the Free Society* (New York: The Ronald Press Company, 1957); Sylvester Petro, *The Kohler Strike: Union Violence and Administrative Law* (Chicago: Regnery, 1961); Sylvester Petro, *The Kingsport Strike* (New Rochelle, NY: Arlington House, 1967). Petro, a member of the Mont Pelerin Society and a founder of the New York State Conservative Party, was active in the National Right to Work Committee.

criticizing, side-by-side, both monopolies in industry and monopolies in labor, the latter of which he noted had, since the New Deal, been aided and abetted by the federal government. In a lecture he delivered in the late 1970s entitled "Who Protects the Worker?" Friedman this time followed up on arguments that had been made to a wider conservative readership in the 1940s by Henry Hazlitt. In that lecture, Friedman outlined the case against unions from the perspective of a free market economist.[215] If you were to ask most people to what they attribute the tremendous rise of workers' standard of living over the course of the past century, most people would credit labor unions, Friedman observed. He then challenged this familiar account. Most of the credit, Friedman insisted, should go to capitalism itself – that is, to the robust economic development and growth that create new industries and jobs. Unionization may have raised the wages for certain categories of workers, particularly the highly skilled workers whose abilities were relatively rare and in high demand. These workers, after all, essentially held, at least temporarily, a monopoly on much-needed skills in a market that required them. For other workers, unionization's effects were much more dubious: unionization may have raised wages for some workers, but it likely lowered them for others, including for non-union workers. To the extent that unions advocated for more rules and regulations for businesses, unions increased American business's production costs. By doing so, they either kept businesses from expanding as much as they otherwise would have – not incidentally, Friedman noted, creating demand for the hiring of additional workers – or passed on their higher costs to consumers in the form of higher prices. This inflation had the effect of both lowering aggregate demand and reducing the purchasing power of consumers. Among the most damaging regulatory demands of organized labor was, first, for the establishment of a minimum wage, and then for its perpetual increase. The result was less hiring, particularly of the young, the unskilled – and, Friedman noted, significantly, and especially problematically – young African American men.

It should be noted that while arguments like these came to define the "conservative" position during the heyday of American liberalism, there were, nevertheless, some important voices on the postwar Right that supported a strong labor movement. Chief among these were conservatives like Robert Nisbet and Wilson Carey McWilliams who attributed special value to civil society's intermediate institutions and private associations. Such conservatives – or, as they later came to be known to some, "communitarians" – placed labor unions in the same category as churches, families, and localities as bulwarks of a robust, self-governing free society. As residual New Deal Democrats, many

---

[215] Milton Friedman, Lecture delivered at WQLN TV, Erie, Penn., 1978. See Henry Hazlitt, *Economics in One Lesson* (New York: Harper and Bros., 1946), chaps. 18, 19 – "Minimum Wage Laws" and "Do Unions Really Raise Wages?" See also Henry Hazlitt, *The Conquest of Poverty* (1973), chap. 13 ("How Unions Reduce Real Wages" – initially delivered as a lecture to the Mont Pelerin Society, Munich, West Germany (1970)).

neoconservatives also held fast to their support for organized labor. Some Evangelical Christians were pro-labor as well. The influential Fundamentalist minister Carl McIntire likened the right to join a union to the liberty of religious conscience – though, consistent with his belief in individual choice, he nevertheless opposed the closed shop.[216]

Others writing from a business perspective sought to enroll organized labor, provided it did not go off the rails, in the nation's broad pro-capitalist coalition. These conservative writers gave labor unions credit for their work in moving the nation above and beyond the tooth-and-claw Darwinian capitalism of the industrial revolution's heyday, and for humanizing industrial conditions. Thanks "to intelligent reform, a new kind of capitalism has come about in which 'employe[e]s are part of the enterprise, not enemies.' Organized labor's policy has been to correct the defects of free enterprise but not to destroy free enterprise."[217] Like many businessmen, the president of Grand Union supermarkets worried, nevertheless, that the nation was fast approaching the point where "[m]any segments of labor now believe that work is something to be avoided even if it wrecks our economic system." He called for the inclusion of the worker's voice directly in company policy making and management, and making the worker a fully enrolled part of the management team.[218]

Over time, however, whatever position this group of conservatives who supported organized labor may have harbored in the past – or continued to harbor – became increasingly muted within the conservative movement as a whole. Some changed their minds. Others, increasingly, spoke on the issue only *sotto voce*, if they raised it at all, especially in movement fora. As union membership dwindled, or as the remaining redoubts of unionism clustered in disfavored areas (public school teacher unions, public employee unions), these theoretically pro-union conservatives concentrated on more immediate issues; they moved on to other things.

LIBERTY, EQUALITY, AND POVERTY

While some conservatives celebrated all but unfettered capitalism on the ground that liberty was the supreme American political value,[219] others argued that free

---

[216] Nisbet, *Quest for Community*, 31–32, 240–241; Carl McIntire, *Author of Liberty* (Collingswood, NJ: Christian Beacon Press, 1946), 83–85, 103.

[217] "A Fresh View of Capitalism," *Reader's Digest* 69:411 (July 1956): 137–138, 138 [reprinted, condensed, from *Life* (April 9, 1956)].

[218] Lansing Shield [President, Grand Union Company], "What's Wrong with Work?" *Reader's Digest* 60:358 (February 1952): 100–102, 101–102.

[219] See, e.g., Young Americans for Freedom, *The Sharon Statement* (1960) ("THAT the market economy, allocating resources by the free play of supply and demand, is the single economic system compatible with the requirements of personal freedom and constitutional government, and that it is at the same time the most productive supplier of human needs; THAT when government interferes with the work of the market economy, it tends to reduce the moral and

market capitalism simultaneously advanced equality, which was also important. Communism, which supposedly put equality first, "may have talked the talk, but it did not walk the walk." Fred G. Clark and Richard Stanton Rimanoczy explained in *Reader's Digest* in the late 1950s that with the protections it afforded for private property rights, no economic system was more conducive to the fair distribution of income that Karl Marx had demanded than capitalism.[220] Another writer pointed out at about the same time the (supposed) irony: "[O]f all the greatest industrial nations, the one that clings most tenaciously to private capitalism has come closest to providing abundance for all in a classless society."[221]

The theme was repeated in the pages of *Reader's Digest* throughout liberalism's heyday. One article explicated the dynamics in a celebration of what the political theorist Antonio Gramsci had called "Fordism."[222] The

physical strength of the nation, that when it takes from one to bestow on another, it diminishes the incentive of the first, the integrity of the second, and the moral autonomy of both; ... THAT the forces of international Communism are, at present, the greatest single threat to these liberties."), which heavily emphasized liberty and addressed equality only by implication, from the claim that the market economy was "the most productive supplier of human needs."

[220] Fred G. Clark and Richard Stanton Rimanoczy, "What Marxism Promises, US Capitalism Delivers," *Reader's Digest* 70:418 (February 1957): 173–174 [reprinted, condensed from Fred G. Clark and Richard Stanton Rimanoczy, *The Economic Facts of Life* (New York: The American Economic Foundation: November, 1956) (pamphlet)]. See also Fred G. Clark, *Magnificent Delusion* (New York: Whittlesey House/McGraw-Hill, 1940); Fred G. Clark and Richard Stanton Rimanoczy, *How We Live – A Simple Dissection of the Economic Body* (New York: D. Van Nostrand, 1944); Fred G. Clark and Richard Stanton Rimanoczy, *Money* (Princeton: D. Van Nostrand Co., 1947); Fred G. Clark and Richard Stanton Rimanoczy, *How to Be Popular Though Conservative* (Princeton: D. Van Nostrand Co., 1948); Fred G. Clark and Richard Stanton Rimanoczy, *How to Think About Economics* (Princeton: D. Van Nostrand Co., 1952). Clark was a Cleveland and New York businessman (chiefly oil refining and insurance). He founded the prohibition/Eighteenth Amendment repeal group The Crusaders, and had his own radio show in the 1930s, *The Voice of the Crusaders*, which broadcast sustained opposition to the New Deal. Clark, a proponent of free markets, founded and chaired the American Economic Foundation (1939–1973) to explain economics to a mass audience. Clark moderated a radio program on the NBC Blue network called *Wake Up, America!* (1940–1946), which consisted of a diverse complement of experts debating political and economics issues (Clark's guests included Herbert Hoover (with whom he was especially close), Robert Taft, Norman Thomas, Max Lerner, Henry Hazlitt, Arthur Garfield Hays, and others). The conservatively hosted, but diverse and respectful engagement of those with different views prefigured the approach William F. Buckley Jr. took in his later PBS television show *Firing Line*. Clark created "The Hall of Free Enterprise" at the 1964–1965 World's Fair in New York, which included plaques setting out "The Ten Pillars of Economic Wisdom." His papers are housed at the Herbert Hoover Presidential Library and Museum https://hoover.archives.gov/research/collections/manuscriptfindingaids/clark.html).

[221] "The Continuing American Revolution," *Reader's Digest* 67:400 (August 1955): 72 [reprinted, condensed, from *Life* (May 16, 1955)]. See generally Cohen, *Consumer's Republic*.

[222] See Antonio Gramsci, *Prison Notebooks* (New York: Columbia University Press, 1992) [1929–1935]. The Fordist dynamic (re: low-cost, mass-produced housing) underwrote Richard Nixon's defense of capitalism in his Kitchen Debate with Nikita Khrushchev.

banker, man-of-letters, and champion of Franco-American friendship Lewis Galantière explained in the magazine that to sell mass-produced goods, a society's people needed the broad wherewithal to purchase them. For this reason, in capitalist societies there was a strong incentive for businesses to both lower production costs and raise wages. Capitalism in its European form – the satanic industrial capitalism of yore[223] – Galantière explained, had ignited class warfare. Capitalism in its American form, by contrast, had been characterized by harmony between the capitalists and the workers, in both their economic interests and ways of life. "American workers," Galantière observed:

> don't strike to obtain relief from misery but to get a bigger share of the economies that result from higher efficiency and lower production costs. In our country both management and workers have motorcars, bathrooms, laborsaving kitchen equipment, telephones, adequate leisure. Both are nourished by much the same diet and tended by doctors and dentists from the same professional schools. The children of both have access to university education and the professions.

Unlike their European counterparts, American businessmen were "enlightened." Much was lost, Galantière concluded, when discussion of these issues evinced a "failure to distinguish between a capitalism which works for the few and a capitalism which works for the many."[224]

The editor of the syndicated Sunday supplement magazine *This Week*, William I. Nichols, complained in the early 1950s that "[t]o many people, the word Capitalism carries negative overtones of old errors and old abuses. In no way does it imply the dynamic, expanding system of today, constantly changing, but always moving toward one goal – *to create more goods and greater well-being for more people.*" Nichols noted that the word "capitalism" had been coined under the harsh conditions of the industrial revolution. But those conditions were a thing of the past. Under the "New Capitalism," "more and more people [were getting] an increasing share of production, whether in the form of higher wages, lower prices or better goods." Nichols suggested that "[w]e need a new word to describe our system – imperfect, but always improving – where men move forward freely together, working together, building together, producing always more and more, and sharing together the rewards of their increased production. If we find the right term, it could be a decisive factor in the global battle for the minds of men."[225]

---

[223] See, e.g., Friedrich Engels, *The Condition of the Working Class in England* (1845).

[224] Lewis Galantière, "The Second American Revolution," *Reader's Digest* 58:347 (March 1951): 48–50, 48, 50. Galantière was perhaps best known in the United States for his translations of the work of his friend Antoine de Saint-Exupéry.

[225] William I. Nichols, "Wanted: A New Name for 'Capitalism.'" *Reader's Digest* 58:349 (May 1951): 3–4 [reprinted, condensed, from *This Week Magazine* (March 4, 1951)] [emphasis in original].

Henry Hazlitt elaborated on the theme in *The Conquest of Poverty* (1973).[226] Writing in the wake of President Lyndon Johnson's "War on Poverty," Hazlitt addressed the contention that unlike liberals (or socialists), conservative proponents of free market capitalism did not care about the poor. In a sweeping consideration of the matter, assessed against a long historical backdrop, Hazlitt affirmed that it was right to care about the economic well-being – and, indeed, human flourishing more broadly understood – of all, including those living in poverty. Traditional social welfare state thinking about poverty, however, had largely misunderstood the phenomenon. The greatest boon for the poor in the history of the modern West had been the introduction of market capitalism, which had dramatically lowered the rate of infant mortality, broadly improved health and longevity, increased levels of literacy and education, raised workers' standard of living, and provided employment and broader life possibilities for the poor unparalled in all previous human history. If only government were to get out of the way with its ostensibly well-intentioned efforts to help the poor through ever-expanding government entitlements and regulations, funded by higher and higher taxes, and let markets do their work, considerably more might be done: there was no poor relief like a dynamic and flourishing free market capitalism. Hazlitt ended the book with the claim that the expectations that socialists and their fellow travelers had entertained about eliminating poverty through aggressive government intervention had actually been generated by the miraculous successes of capitalism itself, which, for the first time in human history, had put these possibilities within reach. Expectations born of the impatience generated by the successes of free market capitalism itself, Hazlitt worried, were currently running too hot – they were on overdrive. Impatience was now threatening the goose laying the golden eggs. Hazlitt made a plea for patience. Things were getting better – let capitalism work its magic.

INTO THE 1970S AND 1980S: SUSTAINED REFLECTION ON THE CONSTITUTION AND CAPITALISM

Many conservatives posited a close, and, for some, seamless, relationship between market capitalism and the Constitution. As early as the mid-1960s, the University of California, Santa Barbara, Straussian Thomas Schrock was arguing that the conservative pre–New Deal Supreme Court had been the keeper of the flame of the original "Madisonian" understanding of the Constitution, notwithstanding his understanding that the Old Court had been a proponent of *laissez-faire*, whereas James Madison had not. Both the Old Court and Madison, Schrock explained, believed strongly in both popular government and natural rights, in marked contrast to the radically different

---

[226] Hazlitt, *Conquest of Poverty*.

understandings of the progressive/liberal hero Oliver Wendell Holmes Jr. Schrock conceded that Madison had placed a greater emphasis on distinguishing the respective constitutional powers of the states and the national government than had the pre–New Deal Court. The Commerce Clause had clearly had a "nationalizing purpose" and embodied "[t]he Framers' double standard – trust of the Congress and distrust for the states" (on the latter, he cited the Article I, Section 10, Contract Clause), which reflected their understanding that the legislator with the larger constituency was more likely to aim at justice rather than narrower, more partial interests.[227] The post-1937 liberal Supreme Court, Schrock observed, might have "restored to Congress its proper regulatory powers," but, at the same time, it had also "halted meaningful review of state economic regulation."[228]

In the end, Schrock was ambivalent, critical of both the Old (pre–) and New (post–New Deal) Supreme Courts, neither of which, in his view, had gotten the Constitution right. "As the conservative Court was blind to the political setting of economic activity, so the liberal Court has been less considerate than it might have been of the economic setting within which popular free expression is likely to thrive," Schrock contended. He acknowledged, however, that "[t]he triumph of the corporate means of acquiring and holding property was unquestionably a major determinant of the liberal Court's decision to release the state and national governments from the fetters with which the conservative Court had bound them."[229]

At various times, Martin Diamond, one the most influential Straussian constitutional theorists, whom I discussed at length in Chapter 2, "The Alternative Tradition of Conservative Constitutional Theory," expressed a similar ambivalence about the advent of the modern regulatory/administrative state. Nevertheless, Diamond's classic book *The Democratic Republic* (1970) was perfectly clear on at least one point: that the Constitution had been

[227] Thomas S. Schrock, "The Liberal Court, the Conservative Court, and Constitutional Jurisprudence," in Robert A. Goldwin, editor, *Left, Right and Center: Essays on Liberalism and Conservatism in the United States* (Chicago: Rand McNally & Co., 1965), 87–120, 90–94, 98. Schrock was also a lawyer who, before studying with Strauss at the University of Chicago, had graduated from New York University Law School. The Article I, Section 10, Contract Clause requires that "No State shall ... pass any ... Law impairing the Obligation of Contracts."

[228] Schrock, "The Liberal Court, the Conservative Court," 96, 99, 101, 107. Schrock also argued that the conservative pre–New Deal justices were convinced that a sentinel judiciary could single-handedly guarantee rights. Madison, by contrast, believed that "the security of rights depends upon the regulation of interests." Schrock, moreover, argued against drawing sharp distinctions between economic and personal or "expressive" rights. He was, furthermore, skeptical that the doctrine of incorporation (which applied the protections of the Bill of Rights to the states via the Due Process Clause of the Fourteenth Amendment) had any constitutional basis.

[229] Schrock, "The Liberal Court, the Conservative Court," 108, 112.

specifically designed to serve as the foundation for a commercial republic.[230] Early in the Reagan administration, the American Enterprise Institute's Constitutional Studies Program convened a conference, and offered a rounded, scholarly consideration of the matter by conservatives. The diverse views from within the movement were published in Robert Goldwin and William Schambra's collection *How Capitalistic Is the Constitution?* (1982).[231] There, Marc Plattner, who was trained as a Straussian political philosopher by Walter Berns, Allan Bloom, and others at Cornell, followed Martin Diamond in arguing that there was a deep, "intrinsic connection" between the constitutional system designed by the American Founders and capitalism.[232] In saying as much, however, Plattner was careful to note that he did not mean *laissez-faire* capitalism, but simply "an economic system that allows all citizens freely to acquire, possess, and dispose of private property and encourages them to devote themselves to the pursuit and enjoyment of wealth." This understanding, Plattner emphasized, was compatible with the modern social welfare state, although he did note that he found frankly redistributionist policies aimed at economic equality problematic.[233]

Plattner acknowledged that his understandings on the consonance between the Constitution and capitalism had been heavily influenced by Diamond. Like Diamond, Plattner argued from *The Federalist*,[234] beginning with Publius's theory[235] of the extended republic. In Federalist 10, the argument began,

[230] Martin Diamond et al., *The Democratic Republic* (2nd ed.) (Chicago: Rand McNally & Co., 1970), chap. 4. See also Harry M. Clor, "American Democracy and Radical Democracy," in Robert A. Goldwin, editor, *How Democratic Is America? Responses to the New Left Challenge* (Chicago: Rand McNally & Co., 1969): 70–108, 87. The argument was made largely from Federalists 10, 51, and 56. One student of Diamond's characterized his contemporaneous politics to me as "[Gerald] Ford Administration Republican."

[231] Robert A. Goldwin and William A. Schambra, editors, *How Capitalistic Is the Constitution?* (Washington, DC: American Enterprise Institute, 1982). Goldwin had been a student of Leo Strauss's at the University of Chicago. Schambra had studied with Martin Diamond. Among many other influential posts on the Right during the Reagan years, and beyond, Schambra (like Gary L. McDowell) served as a close advisor to President Reagan's Chief of Staff and Attorney General – and originalist impresario – Edwin Meese III.

[232] Marc F. Plattner, "American Democracy and the Acquisitive Spirit," in Goldwin and Schambra, editors, *How Capitalistic Is the Constitution?* 1–21, 2, 19, 22. In the same volume, a contributor from the Marxian left agreed that "the Constitution is fundamentally and inescapably capitalistic." Edward S. Greenberg, "Class Rule Under the Constitution," in Goldwin and Schambra, eds., *How Capitalistic Is the Constitution?* 22–48.

[233] See also Marc F. Plattner, "The Welfare State vs. the Redistributive State," *The Public Interest* 55 (Spring 1979): 28–48.

[234] Plattner, "American Democracy and the Acquisitive Spirit," 2–9. See 2, fn. 3.

[235] Straussians typically characterize the arguments made in The Federalist as having been made by a single purported author, the pseudonomyous "Publius," rather than, as we know, the actual individual authors of the various Federalist essays James Madison, Alexander Hamilton, and John Jay (or, alternatively, as representing the Constitutional Convention as largely involving a series of compromises among disparate interests). The decision to present the essays as written by the single (fictive) author, Publius, as the Straussians conceive it, is both is faithful to the

Publius had placed a foundational emphasis on the diverse faculties of men, and, hence, their diverse propensities for acquiring property. Classical republicanism presumed a high level of moral austerity, public spiritedness, and homogeneity of manners and opinion among the populace. But this did not comport with the Founders' understandings of human nature, which held that men could be counted on to be self-seeking, and not overly virtuous. It thus followed, Plattner argued, that Publius had adjudged the small republics associated with civil republicanism inappropriate for the new country. In this, Montesquieu (1689–1755) served: the French political thinker had highly esteemed England's commercial society and praised its constitutional separation of powers as one of the means best constituted to advance the broader public interest under such conditions. Under these circumstances, it is not surprising that Montesquieu's thought had significantly influenced America's Founders.[236]

The large US republic was characterized by complexity and was composed of a wide spectrum of interests, including economic ones. Its constitutional order provided a salutary institutional framework for the robust clash of countervailing interests, through checking and checked powers: its foundational premises assumed both capitalism and a diversity of interests. Publius had deepened this understanding in Federalist 44 with recognition that avarice – a vice – was nevertheless conducive to habits of prudence, sobriety, and the regulation of morals – virtues. These virtues arising out of a vice were conducive, it fortuitously turned out, to freedom: given their prevalence in a robust commercial society, government had the luxury of leaving individuals alone on these matters, which was conducive to widespread personal liberty.[237]

For this to work, *The Federalist* had recognized that property rights had to be assiduously protected. One of the foremost problems in the Founders' minds, however, was that political power in a republic resided with the majority, but the wealthy were always in the minority. Plattner explained that thus, in a republic, Publius had held that "the greatest danger to property rights is that the poorer members of society may unite to defraud or despoil the wealthy." The Founders had done what they could to mitigate this problem, by, for example, establishing large electoral districts across a geographically extended

authors' intent and emphasizes the (fictive?) coherence of their constitutional vision. See also Herbert Storing, "The Federal Constitution of 1787: Politics, Principles, and Statesmanship," in Ralph A. Rossum and Gary L. McDowell, editors, *The American Founding: Politics, Statesmanship, and the Constitution* (Port Washington, NY: Kennikat Press, 1981); Herbert Storing, "The Constitutional Convention: Toward a More Perfect Union," in Morton J. Frisch and Richard G. Stevens, editors, *American Political Thought: The Philosophic Dimensions of American Statesmanship* (Itasca, IL: F. E. Peacock Publishers, Inc., 1983), reprinted in Joseph Bessette, ed. *Toward a More Perfect Union: Writings of Herbert J. Storing* (Washington, DC: AEI Press, 1995).

[236] Plattner, "American Democracy and the Acquisitive Spirit," 4–6.
[237] Plattner, "American Democracy and the Acquisitive Spirit," 6–7, 9.

space, which would be conducive to the election of the society's "better" men – who were often wealthier, and thus more likely to be sympathetic to property rights, and, in a less precarious position, to take a long-term view – as representatives. On this, at least, the nation's Founders were of one mind: "The inviolability of the rights of property appears to have been accepted by the full range of American political thinkers of the constitutional era – anti-Federalists as well as supporters of the Constitution, agrarians as well as proponents of commerce and manufacturing."[238]

The conservative University of Alabama historian Forrest McDonald (1927–2016) took a different view. McDonald argued that there had been no precise conceptual connection at the time of the Founding between the protection of private property rights, in which the American Founders were staunch believers, and a capitalist economic system, at least as we have come over time to understand the nature and operation of such systems.[239] The point was conceptual. McDonald explained that "[f]or property to be capital it must be employed as capital, which is to say used for the purpose of creating more property." The Founding era marked the beginning of the "transformation from ancient zero-sum conceptions of economic activity to modern growth-oriented conceptions." The Founders were living and writing at a time in which pre-capitalistic and anti-capitalistic ideas were still in robust circulation, including in Bolingbroke's sharp distinction between society's producers and nonproducing members (the latter, speculators who idly profited through interest on notes and other forms of financial opportunism and manipulation); the physiocrats' understanding of land as the only source of wealth; and mercantilism, which envisaged an active and aggressive role for the state in promoting economic development aimed at the augmentation of the state's power and prestige in the international system. Americans of the Founding era, McDonald argued, had been biased against capitalism in two significant ways. First, they had considered personal property inferior to real property – land. Second, their laws had not fully recognized the negotiability of personal (monetary) notes. Economic growth, they noted with alarm, raised the threats of luxury and economic inequality that were, in many respects, affronts to republican liberty. Accordingly, the rates and prices of many services at the time of the Founding had been set by law, often according to common law understandings of "fair value" and "just price," and marketing practices were heavily regulated. State and local governments were given a wide scope to exercise their police powers in the economic sphere, and these powers were "traditionally ... exercised in ways inimical to entrepreneurship and a free market." On all this, the historian McDonald observed against the apodictic philosopher Plattner, the Founders were decidedly not of one mind. Alexander

---

[238] Plattner, "American Democracy and the Acquisitive Spirit," 14–16.
[239] Forrest McDonald, "The Constitution and Hamiltonian Capitalism," in Goldwin and Schambra, editors, *How Capitalistic Is the Constitution?* 49–74.

Hamilton, McDonald argued, was clearly a force for change. He played no small part in fighting against the intense mistrust of fiscal and financial systems that were pervasive at the time. The Constitution set the framework for the new country's political order. Hamilton's fiscal program laid the basis for a capitalist economy. In time, the two became intertwined.[240]

The classical liberal Bernard Siegan (1924–2006), a University of Chicago Law School graduate and longtime professor at the University of San Diego Law School, where he directed the law school's law and economics program, boldly (and baldly) opened his contribution to the American Enterprise Institute volume with the following assertion:

> In my opinion, the U.S. Constitution provides for and secures a capitalist economy. The existence of capitalism requires that private enterprise and private markets be legally safeguarded and allowed to function freely. Government intervention in the economy is permissible, but only when very special circumstances demand it. Were it correctly interpreted our present Constitution would accord sufficient protection for the commercial liberties … to enable our economic system to function in a manner largely consistent with this description of capitalism.[241]

---

[240] McDonald, "The Constitution and Hamiltonian Capitalism," 50, 51–53, 55–57, 60, 67, 72–74. See also Forrest McDonald, *Novus Ordo Seclorum: The Intellectual Origins of the Constitution* (Lawrence: University Press of Kansas, 1985); Forrest McDonald, *Alexander Hamilton: A Biography* (New York: W.W. Norton, 1979). The pervasiveness of state and local economic (and morals) regulation from the founding forward (on into much of the nineteenth century) in the way that McDonald describes has been reemphasized in William Novak, *The People's Welfare: Law and Regulation in Nineteenth Century America* (Chapel Hill: University of North Carolina Press, 1996). The republican concern for problems of luxury and economic inequality discussed by McDonald has recently been treated at length by Clement Fatovic, *America's Founding and the Struggle Over Economic Inequality* (Lawrence: University Press of Kansas, 2015). See also Ganesh Sitaraman, *The Crisis of the Middle Class Constitution* (New York: Alfred A. Knopf, 2017).

[241] Bernard Siegan, "The Constitution and the Protection of Capitalism," in Goldwin and Schambra, editors, *How Capitalistic Is the Constitution?* 106–126, 106. See also Bernard Siegan, *Economic Liberties and the Constitution* (Chicago: University of Chicago Press, 1980); Bernard Siegan, *Other People's Property* (Lexington, MA: Lexington Books, 1976); Bernard Siegan, editor, *Government, Regulation, and the Economy* (Lexington, MA: Lexington Books, 1980); Bernard Siegan, *The Supreme Court's Constitution: An Inquiry into Judicial Review and Its Impact on Society* (New Brunswick, NJ: Transaction Publishers, 1987). Siegan was nominated by President Reagan for the US Court of Appeals for the Ninth Circuit but, after a bitter fight, was rejected by the Senate Judiciary Committee. Conservative legalists who were concerned with judicial activism were nearly as critical of Siegan as were liberals, in much the same way this variety of legal conservatives criticize the activist tendencies of contemporary constitutional libertarians Randy Barnett and Richard Epstein (the latter is very much a successor to Siegan – taking up, for instance, many of the same issues like property rights and law and economics, particularly land-use (including zoning) laws, and the Fifth Amendment's takings clause). Seigan was one of the earliest of modern conservative legalists to defend the concept of substantive due process and the Court's use of that doctrine in *Lochner* v. *New York* (1905) – that is, of the "New Originalism." See Keith Whittington, "The New Originalism," which argued against judicial quiescence in the face of rights violations, conceived of in conservative originalist terms. See also Decker, *The Other Rights Revolution*, 66.

Siegan argued that the body of the original Constitution protected these commercial liberties, but that the Fifth and Fourteenth Amendments soon augmented the protections. Siegan's argument here is expressly originalist in its contemporary sense:[242]

Underlying this analysis is the assumption that a consensus exists among jurists and constitutional scholars that the intentions of constitutional framing bodies should be strictly observed when to do so would be advantageous or not harmful for modern society ... In the absence of cause necessitating a different interpretation, there is no reason to depart from the terms and meanings of the fundamental law.[243]

The Supreme Court, Siegan argued, had taken this view from roughly 1897 to 1937, when it had held that both state and federal regulation of economic activity be starkly limited – a position, he complained, the liberal court had since abandoned.

The Supreme Court's wisdom during this limited period in the late nineteenth/early twentieth century (the Lochner Era), Siegan explained, had been vindicated by new, cutting-edge scholarship in law and economics and public choice economics, which had demonstrated the high costs that attend economic regulation, including those entailed in the market for regulation by the adoption of rent-seeking legislation, which benefits the few at the expense of the many. Alas, Siegan explained, the prospects for the passage of such legislation are always good, given that it entails concentrated benefits and diffused costs.[244] The sheer volume of rent-seeking legislation of this sort is enormous – with much of it flying under the deceptive banner of laws ostensibly designed to advance the public interest championed by so-called advocates for the public interest. Most of this, Siegan explained, is actually special interest legislation, whose costs outweigh its benefits. To make matters worse, the higher prices caused by this mountain of special interest legislation are akin to a regressive tax that disproportionately hurts the less well-off.[245]

"The first question that needs to be asked," American Enterprise Institute scholar Stephen Miller began his contribution to the institute's volume, is "What did the framers intend?"[246] The intellectual historian Miller situated

---

[242] Siegan, "The Constitution and the Protection of Capitalism," 106. Siegan's academic home, the University of San Diego Law School, where he started teaching in 1973, became a center of originalist thought and discussion, a legacy that continues to the present day. It is home to the Center for the Study of Constitutional Originalism (www.sandiego.edu/law/centers/csco/).

[243] Siegan, "The Constitution and the Protection of Capitalism," 106–107.

[244] Siegan, "The Constitution and the Protection of Capitalism," 119, citing Richard Posner, *Economic Analysis of Law*, 2nd ed. (Boston: Little, Brown and Co., 1977). See James Q. Wilson, *Bureaucracy: What Government Agencies Do and Why They Do It* (New York: Basic Books, 1989).

[245] Siegan, "The Constitution and the Protection of Capitalism," 107, 118, 122–123.

[246] Stephen Miller, "The Constitution and the Spirit of Commerce," in Goldwin and Schambra, editors, *How Capitalistic Is the Constitution?*, 148–169, 149. See also Stephen Miller, *Special Interest Groups and American Politics* (New Brunswick, NJ: Transaction Publishers, 1983).

the American Founding between Thomas Hobbes's view that if liberty is allowed to flourish, the result will be "violent factional discord" and Viscount Bolingbroke's view that commerce sapped the health of the nation. Miller argued that the American Founders' understanding had been that commerce made liberty and tranquility possible because, as "parties from interest," in contradistinction from "parties from principle," economic factions were unlikely to become violent, or, put otherwise, and following Adam Smith and David Hume, that commerce bred nonviolent faction (Miller underlined that "[t]he road from Hume and Smith to the authors of *The Federalist* is direct."). The primary objective of the Founders, Miller argued, had been political stability. Given that, they would have questioned the pursuit of either economic liberty or economic equality if they came to believe that either was impeding political stability. In light of this, Miller argued, "It is misguided to assume ... that the boundaries of the public sector can remain fixed; they will always change with changing circumstances" and "The essential subject of debate ... should be ways of fostering commercial growth while both ensuring the safety of the nation and providing for those who – for whatever reason – have not been able to provide for themselves."[247]

Miller challenged a reading of Federalist 10 that implied that Madison thought discord would result from "property-based factions." Miller answered that Federalist 10 had actually held that this is not likely to happen in "civilized" – read "commercial" – societies. Citing Federalists 12 and 34, Miller argued that the Founders further believed that the mere fact that a society was commercial was insufficient to preserve its domestic tranquility: commerce needed to be continually expanding. The Founders believed, moreover, that a strong national government was essential to achieving that economic objective.[248]

In this sense, Miller argued, nineteenth-century *laissez-faire* dogma, the very period that Siegan had praised and justified in light of the Founders' understandings, in fact had done violence to the Framers' original understandings: the views of E. L. Godkin, William Graham Sumner, Milton Friedman, and other "doctrinaire libertarians" were not consistent with views of the Framers on these matters. "The relationship between economic freedom and political freedom ... is more complex than most contemporary conservatives allow," Miller insisted. "[T]he dire predictions of Hayek, Friedman, and other proponents of laissez faire that the growth of government interference in the economy would undermine political freedom have not been borne out," Miller observed, "There has been no road to serfdom."[249]

---

[247] Miller, "The Constitution and the Spirit of Commerce," 153–154, 156, 167.
[248] Miller, "The Constitution and the Spirit of Commerce," 158, 160, 164.
[249] Miller, "The Constitution and the Spirit of Commerce," 161–163.

"The authors of *The Federalist*," Miller contended, "would not have refrained from supporting government policies that restricted the operations of the market in order to preserve liberty. It cannot be said that they would have approved of unions or the vast increase in government regulation of the 1960s and 1970s, but it can be said that they would not have disapproved of these changes in principle." As such, Miller argued that the broad categories adduced in these debates like "capitalist" and "socialist" were not especially helpful. The Founders had been "moderately hopeful about the future of predominately commercial societies": "Madison, Hamilton, and Jay were obviously not socialists, but neither were they capitalists; they were men who hoped that their political economy would make it more likely that Americans would be orderly, temperate, and moderate – and thus make it more likely that the new American republic would survive."[250]

CONCLUSION

Supporters of the modern liberal constitutional regime told themselves still familiar stories about the genesis and trajectory of modern liberalism. These emphasized the horrors of the rise of late nineteenth-century tooth-and-claw industrial capitalism; the bold spotlighting of these horrors by truth-seeking "muckraking" journalists; the heroism of a succession of brave, uncompromising reformers and reform movements; the waxing influence of these movements as progressives sought and won influence in office; the temporary retrenchment of the 1920s; and, finally, when the path was at last cleared by the devastation of the Great Depression, the sweeping establishment, institutionalization, and constitutionalization of the modern administrative/social welfare state that, far from destroying capitalism, saved it.

Postwar conservatives told a very different story about this historical trajectory and had been doing so since at least the 1950s – straight through the heyday of American liberalism. This chapter has shown that their accounts were diverse. Albeit critical of what they took to be some of its excesses and antibusiness values and policies, mainstream conservative Republicans in the period joined their party's moderates and liberals in basically accepting the New Deal revolution and its constitutionalization. The "movement conservatives" who supported Robert Taft, Barry Goldwater, and Ronald Reagan, however, rejected not only modern New Deal policies but also the story about the nation's political and economic trajectory that underwrote them. While, again, as we have seen, understandings, even within movement conservatism, varied, the

---

[250] Miller, "The Constitution and the Spirit of Commerce," 163, 169. See also Walter Berns and Stephen Miller, *Prosperity and the Constitution: The Founding Fathers, Commerce, and the Corporation* (Washington, DC: American Enterprise Institute, 1981).

stories told were clearly distinguishable from those of liberals. Rather than being a shop of horrors, many held the freewheeling late nineteenth- and early twentieth-century capitalist "take off" to have been a golden age of opportunity, invention, building, productivity, prosperity ... and liberty. When not foreign socialist plants, muckrakers and reformers were resentful, snobbish, and ignorant elitists who little understood the economic requirements and conditions that would, if left to their natural workings, elevate the conditions not only of the wealthy but of ordinary Americans to heights previously unimagined in all of human history. Harassed and increasingly hemmed in by counterproductive or pointless rules and regulations issued from distant government offices with only the haziest understandings of on-the-ground conditions, the nation's producers were able to manage a "return to normalcy" in the 1920s, once Progressivism had exhausted itself and foundered after World War I. The desperation unleashed by the cataclysm of the Great Depression – itself perhaps caused and certainly prolonged by the federal government's disastrous interventionist response – gave the reformers now in charge the opportunity to enact an unprecedented and unconstitutional slate of emergency measures from their well-stuffed grab bag of reforms dating back at least to the Progressive Era. This time, however, a second return to normalcy echoing that of the 1920s was not in the cards. The liberals had learned their lesson the first time. This time, they were ruthless. Franklin Delano Roosevelt threatened to pack, and ultimately cowed, the Supreme Court. State policies were instituted and implemented in ways that were not only self-reinforcing and self-maintaining, but self-expanding: the people were bought off with government "entitlements" promising "security," as opposed to freedom; labor unions were afforded legally enforceable monopoly power; and wealth was systematically channeled and redistributed through government tax and regulatory policies from a small minority (wealthy producers) to the overwhelming majority (the poor, the relatively poor – read, often, as lazy, unsuccessful, and parasitic), in a perpetual motion dynamic that the close political advisor to FDR, Harry Hopkins, in a rare moment of candor, had described as "tax, tax, spend, spend, elect, and elect."

The policy positions of postwar movement conservatism – often, given the movement's position in the wilderness in the heyday of American liberalism, framed as opposition to or critique of some newly proposed or instituted liberal policy measure – were clear enough to many. The larger stories that conservatives were telling about the great arc of twentieth-century US economic history, however, have been relatively submerged and underappreciated. And these were immensely significant, as they provided the framework within which the isolated positions on discrete public policy issues assumed deeper meanings and were assimilated into a larger political cause. Those stories made it possible for the movement's denizens, and potential denizens, to not simply take positions on particular issues but to imagine an identity and motivate them to enlist in a campaign and a cause calling for the restoration of free market capitalism and constitutional freedom in a way that would reanchor the country in its Founding commitment to economic prosperity and constitutional freedom.[251]

[251] For both a more theoretical statement of these dynamics as a form of constitutional development, and recent developments on the Right in this regard, see Ken I. Kersch, "Constitutional Conservatives Remember The Progressive Era," in Stephen Skowronek, Stephen Engel, and Bruce Ackerman, editors, *The Progressives' Century: Democratic Reform and Constitutional Government in the United States* (New Haven: Yale University Press, 2016).

4

Stories About Communism

While, as many have noted, a staunch anticommunism was a defining feature of postwar American conservatism, prior to the 1960s, fervent anticommunism, as such, was hardly the sole province of conservatives. It set the foundational commitment of one of the era's leading liberal organizations, Americans for Democratic Action (ADA), branded the leadership of mainstream labor unions like the American Federation of Labor (AFL), and the convictions of much of their rank-and-file. A fervent anticommunism was the consistent position, in word and deed, of leading liberal politicians like Harry S Truman, John F. Kennedy, Robert F. Kennedy, Hubert Humphrey, and Lyndon Baines Johnson – all classic "Cold War liberal" anticommunists. There were probably some important differences between conservative and liberal anticommunists in this period – less when it came to foreign policy, more when it came to a countervailing concern for domestic civil liberties. But, that said, between the 1940s and the 1970s, anticommunism was the consensus position for the mainstream of both major political parties, and, within them, of liberals and conservatives alike.[1]

The Vietnam War shattered this consensus, with many liberals not only coming to oppose the war, but also blaming it on an ill-judged anticommunist zeal. In the crucible of the antiwar movement, an anti-anticommunist alliance was forged between newly disillusioned liberals, remnants of the Old Left, and an ascendant New Left. Worlds collided at the 1968 Democratic National Convention where, after unprecedented and nationally televised violence, the party's core constituencies, as represented by Chicago's Democratic Irish

---

[1] See Jennifer Luff, *Commonsense Anti-communism: Labor and Civil Liberties Between the World Wars* (Chapel Hill: University of North Carolina Press, 2012); Manfred Berg, "Black Civil Rights and Liberal Anticommunism: The NAACP in the Early Cold War," *Journal of American History* 94:1 (June 2007): 75–96. There were also many liberals who believed that the threats posed by domestic communism were at least exaggerated – a position most prominent toward the Left end of the (non-communist) liberal-Left spectrum.

Catholic Mayor Richard J. Daley and the city's working-class police force, did open battle with the New Left. The Democrats in Chicago nominated the liberal Cold Warrior and LBJ Vice-President Hubert Humphrey for president, tearing the party asunder.[2] Meeting in Miami, the Republicans nominated the Alger Hiss nemesis and House Un-American Activities Committee (HUAC) stalwart Richard Nixon.[3] The bottom fell out from under the Democrats, many of whom detested their party's nominee as a pro-war candidate: the Democrats would be entirely remade before they assembled to choose their next nominee, South Dakota Senator George McGovern.[4] The Republican Richard Nixon won in a landslide that, many have recognized in retrospect, set the nation on the path to a new conservative era.

In many respects, the conservative bill of particulars against the enemy ideology had a hoary lineage: it traced at least as far back as the (pre–Bolshevik Revolution) late nineteenth century. Communism was radical, statist, alien, anti-individual, and anti–free market. Moreover, and worst of all, as was increasingly emphasized in later years by the likes of the American Legion and battalions of devout Christians, it was atheistic. In a freshly coined moniker that had legs, University of Notre Dame law professor and right-wing impresario Clarence "Pat" Manion dubbed it "Godless communism."[5] It was as such that communism became, for many on the Right, the enemy above all others – the existential threat to the very survival of John Winthrop's "City on a Hill," of God's chosen nation.

For many on the Right, communism was not simply a fact of a dangerous, competitive, and even existentially fraught interstate system, but a heuristic for understanding domestic politics – and, in particular, recent developments in the trajectory of the American regulatory and administrative state. Marxist doctrine held that concerted action by the working class would lead to the revolutionary overthrow of capitalism. But, at least since Lenin's articulation of his theory that the proletarian revolution would be midwifed by a centralized, disciplined communist party vanguard, the belief in elite leadership became a core tenet of the communist idea.[6] Late nineteenth-/early twentieth-century

[2] Several prominent neoconservatives and, subsequently, Reagan administration foreign policy officials like UN Ambassador Jeanne Kirkpatrick had been Humphrey Democrats and insisted that between the 1960s and the 1980s, their politics had not changed at all.
[3] See Frank Kusch, *Battleground Chicago: The Police and the 1968 Democratic National Convention* (Chicago: University of Chicago Press, 2004); Norman Mailer, *Miami and The Siege of Chicago: An Informal History of the Republican and Democratic Conventions of 1968* (New York: Signet Books, 1968).
[4] Bruce Miroff, *The Liberals' Moment: The McGovern Insurgency and the Identity Crisis of the Democratic Party* (Lawrence: University Press of Kansas, 2007).
[5] William Pencak, *For God & Country: The American Legion, 1919–1941* (Boston: Northeastern University Press, 1989). See also the erstwhile New Dealer Raymond Moley Jr.'s sympathetic account *The American Legion Story* (New York: Duell, Sloan and Pearce, 1966).
[6] Vladimir Lenin, *What Is to Be Done?* (1902).

libertarian constitutionalists like Joseph Choate, James Beck, William D. Guthrie, and Supreme Court Justice Stephen J. Field had condemned socialism as a threat to property rights and bedrock constitutional liberties, and many of their successors on the Old Right continued their critiques of Progressivism and the New Deal along these more formalist, constitutionalist lines. A new strain of Cold War conservatives, however, looked back less to the constitutional surrender of 1937[7] and turned more toward the perils of international communism's Leninist turn, which they enlisted as a heuristic for understanding, tarring, and damning the liberal thought-leaders and policy intellectuals now building out the modern American state: these administrative and regulatory thought-leaders and policy intellectuals, as seen through this heuristic's prism, were the domestic analogues to Soviet communism's vanguard Leninist cadres. To take just one example, the conservative Washington journalist Stewart Alsop insisted that "Communism is not the invention of the masses, hungry or otherwise":

It is the invention of intellectuals and for more than fifty years the intellectuals have been trying to sell Communism to the masses ... Just as in the case of Hitler and the men who surrounded him, these men were unable to adjust to the society in which they found themselves and when that society refused them the leadership they thought they deserved, they determined to overthrow the society and seize the leadership. That is exactly what a few people were up to in Washington in the 1930s. They made no bones about it.[8]

Alsop drew a direct analogy between the new governing cadres in Washington that emerged out of Franklin Roosevelt's New Deal and the "new class" intellectuals and bureaucrats who had seized control in communist countries.[9] Through motivated, "entrepreneurial" political framing, this strain of anticommunism married a reading of the trajectory of the Russian Revolution and a critique of Lenin's vanguard theory to an attack on the modern American state's administrators and policy intellectuals. The framing dovetailed extremely effectively, for good measure, with the traditional suspicion of a distant centralized governing elite that had long constituted a major theme

---

[7] *NLRB* v. *Jones and Laughlin Steel*, 301 US 1 (1937); *West Coast Hotel* v. *Parrish*, 300 US 379 (1937).

[8] "Who Communists Are," *Wall Street Journal* (September 22, 1950), 4. See Herman Wouk's bestseller *The Caine Mutiny* (New York: Doubleday, 1951), which was awarded a Pulitzer Prize in 1952 and made into both a movie starring Humphrey Bogart, and a highly successful play, *The Caine Mutiny Court-Martial*. See Richard Hofstadter, *Anti-Intellectualism in American Life* (New York: Alfred A. Knopf, 1963).

[9] Stewart Alsop, "What I Saw in Khrushchev's Uneasy Empire," *Reader's Digest* 76:457 (May 1960): 53–59, 58 [reprinted, condensed, from *The Saturday Evening Post* (January 30, February 6 and 13, 1960)]. Referencing Milovan Djilas, *The New Class: An Analysis of the Communist System* (London: Thames and Hudson, 1957). See Karl Marx, *The Communist Manifesto* (1848); Lenin, *What Is to Be Done?* (1902).

in American political thought, from the antifederalists, to the Jacksonian Democrats, to the Populists.[10]

There were conservatives, however, who, in some ways, inverted this critique – prominent libertarians Felix Morley and Murray Rothbard had no love for vanguard, power-hungry statist elites. But alert to (Progressive) Randolph Bourne's cautionary dictum that "war is the health of the state," they also recognized that any state that is militarized and on a national security warpath is also itself, potentially, an invasive, power-hungry state: the proposed remedy could be as lethal as the disease. As fervent anti-statists concerned first and foremost with immediate protections for individual liberty at home, Morley and Rothbard both took aggressive stands against Cold War–era militarism.[11]

Others of a libertarian bent expressed concerns about the threats that an overzealous anticommunism posed to civil liberties. The *Wall Street Journal*, for instance, rallied to the Fifth Amendment as a crucial constitutional stay across the 1950s and early 1960s. Attesting that "[w]e don't like government by bureaucratic whim," the *Journal* cheered the Supreme Court's decision forbidding the State Department from refusing to grant passports to Americans who would not answer questions about communist affiliations. If Congress truly believed there was a national emergency requiring such passport denials, the *Journal* suggested, Congress should make an official declaration to that effect: in the absence of a genuine, officially declared emergency, Americans should be free to travel abroad.[12] Key movement conservatives of a libertarian bent, including the staunchly anticommunist Arizona Senator Barry Goldwater, opposed the 1950 Internal Security Act's requirement that Communist Party members register with the federal government on the ground that it violated the Fifth Amendment's

---

[10] See Hofstadter, *Anti-Intellectualism in American Life*. Since Arthur Schlesinger Jr. had tried to claim the Jacksonian Democrats for the late President Franklin Roosevelt, this represented a direct challenge to the would-be liberal framing. See Arthur Schlesinger Jr., *The Age of Jackson* (Boston: Little, Brown, and Co., 1945), which was awarded the Pulitzer Prize in History in 1946.

[11] See Murray Rothbard, *The Betrayal of the American Right* (Auburn, AL: Ludwig von Mises Institute, 2007)[c. 1970s]; Felix Morley, *Federalism and American Freedom* (Chicago: Regnery, 1959). Others on the right were also worried about militarism. See, e.g., Robert Nisbet, *The Quest for Community: A Study in the Ethics of Order and Freedom* (New York: Oxford University Press, 1953). For a later scholarly study of the tensions from an international relations perspective, see Aaron Friedberg, *In the Shadow of The Garrison State: American Anti-Statism and Its Cold War Grand Strategy* (Princeton: Princeton University Press, 2000).

[12] " Liberty's Greater Loss," *Wall Street Journal* (August 27, 1953), 6; "The Abuse Is Everywhere," *Wall Street Journal* (September 9, 1953), 10; "The Passport Decision," *Wall Street Journal* (June 18, 1958), 12; "Mr. Robeson Takes a Trip," *Wall Street Journal* (July 14, 1958), 8. See also *Kent v. Dulles*, 357 US 116 (1958); *Aptheker v. Secretary of State*, 378 US 500 (1964). See Alan Rogers, "Passports and Politics: The Courts and the Cold War," *The Historian* 47 (August 1985): 497–511; Daniel A. Farber, "National Security, the Right to Travel, and the Court," *The Supreme Court Review* (1981): 263–290.

constitutional guarantee against self-incrimination: they cheered when the Supreme Court ultimately voided the law.[13]

When it came to Senator Joe McCarthy himself, the Right was not of a piece either. While William F. Buckley Jr. and Brent Bozell were more than willing to acknowledge McCarthy's faults and excesses, they nevertheless were willing to stand behind him on the ground that, while those who were against him had their heads in the sand, McCarthy had at least gotten the essentials right. They, like many other conservatives, were willing to count McCarthy a hero.[14] The conservative movement's libertarians, however, scorned the crusading Wisconsin Republican senator. Others who in time would be classed as neoconservatives either took more nuanced positions (like Irving Kristol) or were highly critical of McCarthy (like Democratic Washington Senator Henry "Scoop" Jackson).[15]

Time's passage altered the conservative movement's understanding of communism's chief threats. These layered over earlier attacks rooted in the ideology's war on God and private property and its empowerment of a ruthlessly interventionist intellectual policy vanguard. At times, the movement's anticommunism seemed to arise from oblique, now largely forgotten, angles. Some conservative Cold Warriors, for example, passionately advocated for birth control on the grounds that an overpopulated, and, hence, impoverished, third world would prove all the more susceptible to communist subversion. Many, including the ragingly drunk and recklessly dishonest Roman Catholic McCarthy himself, considered communism a plot designed to weaken the moral fiber of the United States, softening it up in preparation for the country's ultimate moral subversion: this understanding underwrote the Right's enlistment of anticommunism in a wide range of domestic moral crusades. Allegations of communist influence and direction were consistently launched against the civil

[13] Barry Goldwater, "Court Decision Doesn't Prevent Government Registration of Reds," *Human Events* 25:50 (December 11, 1965), 11. On the trajectory of the Supreme Court in the communist cases, see Lucas A. Powe Jr., *The Warren Court and American Politics* (Cambridge, MA: Harvard University Press, 2000), chaps. 4,6. Other libertarians let into ostensibly civil libertarian Democrats for failing to adequately appreciate and protect civil liberties and civil rights more generally. Douglas Caddy and M. Stanton Evans, for instance, scored Supreme Court Justice Hugo Black for his vote and opinion in the *Korematsu* Japanese internment decision [*Korematsu* v. *United States*, 323 US 214 (1944)], writing that "Black's indifference to the liberty of citizens who had done nothing to suggest disloyalty to America – except to be born members of a certain race – contrasts glaringly with his hot defense of the 'rights' of men and women sworn to destroy his country." Douglas Caddy and M. Stanton Evans, "Hugo Black: A Study of Conflict: The Story of the Ku Klux Klan's Favorite 'Liberal,'" *Human Events* 16:50 (December 16, 1950), 2.

[14] William F. Buckley Jr. and L. Brent Bozell Jr., *McCarthy and His Enemies: The Record and Its Meaning* (Chicago: H. Regnery Co., 1954).

[15] Ben J. Wattenberg, *Fighting Words: A Tale of How Liberals Created Neo-Conservatism* (New York: Thomas Dunne Books, 2008), 105.

rights movement, including by Evangelical and Fundamentalist Christians, based on the suspicion that its willingness to challenge authority and aggressively criticize US laws and policies could only be part of a broader plot to hand the country over to its enemies.[16]

THE PROBLEM WITH COMMUNISM: PRINCIPLES

Liberals have long alleged that the postwar Right's outsized anticommunism arose out of conservative fears of an ideology and force that they neither knew nor understood.[17] Whatever truth this might have had for the rank-and-file, including the "Populist" Right, the charge was patently false as concerned the movement's most outspoken anticommunist intellectuals. Huge swathes of the intellectual leadership of the postwar conservative movement – including James Burnham, Max Eastman, Will Herberg, Richard Weaver, John Dos Passos, William Henry Chamberlin, Whittaker Chambers, Irving Kristol, and innumerable others – had begun as communist or socialist intellectuals steeped in radical political thought. While William F. Buckley Jr., the faithful son of devoutly Catholic Texas oil baron, had been a conservative from the cradle, the editorial board of the early *National Review* was stuffed with ex-communist intellectuals.[18] While their temperament and judgment are certainly open to question, to hold that the Right's chief failing as intransigent anticommunists to be a "fear" arising out of "ignorance" is facile unto false.

The pre-conversion political allegiances of these conservatives, and other liberals and leftists, should be understood in context. From the late nineteenth century forward, there was always a strong strain on the Right, and in the mainstream of the (Lockean/Hartzian) liberal individualist United States, critical of "socialism" and (in time) "bolshevism." Prior to the Moscow Trials (1936–1938), part of Stalin's brutal purges against the Bolshevik old guard, and the Hitler-Stalin Pact (1939), the Soviet Union was not especially unpopular in the United States: indeed, in context many looked more favorably upon it then than they ever had before. During the Popular Front period of the 1930s, the Communist Party USA (CPUSA) moved toward the mainstream by reversing course and supporting the New Deal. And many Americans increasingly valued the USSR as an ally, standing with the United States against an expansionist Nazi Germany. If one squinted in the 1930s – and many had strong incentives to do so – communism could appear to have been humanized and Americanized. At a time when much of the Right was staunchly isolationist – and, in some

---

[16] Elaine Tyler May, *America and the Pill: A History of Promise, Peril, and Liberation* (New York: Basic Books, 2010), 37, 42.

[17] See Corey Robin, *Fear: The History of a Political Idea* (New York: Oxford University Press, 2004); Hoftstater, *Anti-Intellectualism*.

[18] John Patrick Diggins, *Up From Communism: Conservative Odysseys in American Intellectual Development* (New York: Columbia University Press, 1994).

cases, in condign alliance with Adolph Hitler – the Popular Front liberal-left was a natural home for patriotic, internationalist anti-fascism.[19]

To the extent that ex-communist anticommunist conservative intellectuals were bedeviling to so many, it was less because of fear arising out of ignorance than because, as the scales fell from their eyes, while shedding their old (Leftist) ideas and adopting new (Rightist) ones, their temperaments had changed not a whit. Many seemed to have simply transferred their radical faith, zeal, militancy, and Manicheanism from communism to anticommunism: many of these men (and a few women) simply did not have a moderate bone in their bodies. And their Manichean arguments from the Right, in contrast to their earlier Manichean arguments from the Left, found much more fertile popular and populist grounds in the still largely white, Christian, liberal individualist United States.[20]

Anticommunist extremism came in both populist and intellectual versions, the latter largely issuing from New York City, where *National Review*'s James Burnham had once cavorted with Leon Trotsky.[21] It was not always easy to tell one from the other, nor, in the end, might those differences have mattered much politically: the two had basically the same objectives. On the extreme populist anticommunist Right were The John Birch Society and groups like nationalist leader Harry T. Everingham's We the People![22] They flocked to books like *Red Channels: The Report of Communist Influence in Radio and Television* (1950) (published by *Counterattack: The Newsletter of Facts to Combat Communism*) and John Stormer's *None Dare Call it Treason* (1964). The intellectual version

---

[19] Susan Jacoby, *Alger Hiss and the Battle for History* (New Haven: Yale University Press, 2009), 38, 41, 68–75, 78, 89–90. See Benjamin Alpers, *Dictators, Democracy, and American Public Culture: Envisioning the Totalitarian Enemy 1920s-1950s* (Chapel Hill-: University of North Carolina Press, 2003). In his detailed survey of articles in the Old Right magazine *American Review* from the 1930s and 1940s, Jonathan Skaggs has unearthed extensive, if not clearly predominant, sympathy for Hitler and the Nazis on the Right in this period. Skaggs, "The Old Right and Its Influence on the Development of Modern Conservatism" (PhD Dissertation, Oklahoma State University, 2014). The poster-boy for this conservative isolationism in alignment with Hitler was the aviation hero Charles Lindbergh.

[20] The case is similar today for former New Left firebrands turned Rightists like the former *Ramparts* editor – and Donald Trump champion – David Horowitz. See David Horowitz, *Big Agenda: President Trump's Plan to Save America* (West Palm Beach, FL: Humanix Books, 2017).

[21] See, e.g., Letter, Leon Trotsky to James Burnham (January 7, 1940), published as "An Open Letter to Comrade Burnham," in Leon Trotsky, *In Defense of Marxism* (New York: Pioneer Publishers, 1942). See Alan Wald, "From Trotsky to Buckley," *Jacobin* (September 15, 2017).

[22] See Harry Everingham, *U.S.A. Beyond the Crossroads: Documented Proof of the Plot to Socialize America* (Chicago: We the People! 1952); Harry Everingham, *Action for Patriots to Save Self-Government for America* (Tulsa, OK: US Day Committee, 1958); Harry Everingham, *The Truth About the Supreme Court: Why Do They Free Convicted Communists?* (Chicago: Fact Finder, 1962); Harry Everingham, *How Can Your Church Fight Communism?* (Phoenix, AZ: We the People! 1968). On the John Birch Society's relations with other organizations on the Right, see Hemmer, *Messengers of the Right*.

stated its case in books like Burnham's *The Coming Defeat of Communism* (1950), and the University of Notre Dame political scientist Gerhart Niemeyer's congressionally commissioned *The Communist Ideology (1959–1960)* and *An Inquiry into Soviet Mentality* (1956) (Niemeyer was credited by Barry Goldwater as a critical influence on his thinking).

Conservative southerners, Richard Weaver argued, were instinctively anticommunist. "With its individualism, its belief in personality, its dislike of centralized government, and its religiosity," Weaver explained, "the South sees in the communist philosophy a combination of all it detests. If that issue comes to a showdown, there will never be any doubt as to where the South stands":[23] "It will stand in the forefront of those who oppose the degrading of man to a purely material being, and it will continue to fight those who presume to direct the individual 'for his own good' from some central seat of authority."[24]

Southerners like Weaver were all too aware that many Americans thought of the South as the country's most fascistic region. Weaver emphatically denied it. Citing the region's vehement anticommunism, that aspersion, he said, got it exactly backward: against conventional wisdom, the South was the nation's chief bulwark *against* fascism. After all, "the South was the first section of the United States to sense an enemy in [European] fascism." This "was indicated not only by polls of opinion, but also by its ardor in preparing for the fight." On the surface, at least, Weaver conceded that this might seem anomalous since, in many respects, "the tenets of its own faith, sealed with Confederate blood and affirmed in many a post-bellum oration," resembled those of Europe's New Order. "That the Southern whites considered themselves *Herrenvolk* in relation to the Negro," he accepted, "is one of the obvious features of our sociological landscape, and belief in the influence of blood and soil is powerful with them, as with any agrarian people." "Why then the deep, instinctive hostility of the South to Hitler and his allies?" Weaver asked.[25]

The key was the French Revolution, "with its emphasis upon individual liberty and its belief in self-operating laws." Simply put, the South never accepted its principles. As the South surveyed European fascism, "the world before the French Revolution look[ed] at the world after the French Revolution and [found] it hateful." "The Fascist regimes of Europe," Weaver explained:

[23] Richard M. Weaver, "The Southern Tradition," *New Individualist Review* 3:3 (1964), 7–17, reprinted in George M. Curtis III and James J. Thompson Jr., editors, *The Southern Essays of Richard M. Weaver* (Indianapolis, IN: Liberty Press, 1987), 228.

[24] Richard M. Weaver, "The South and the American Union," in Louis Rubin and James Jackson Kilpatrick, *The Lasting South: Fourteen Southerners Look at Their Home* (Chicago: H. Regnery, 1957), reprinted in Curtis and Thompson, *The Southern Essays of Richard M. Weaver*, 255.

[25] Richard M. Weaver, "The South and the Revolution of Nihilism," *The South Atlantic Quarterly* 43:2 (April 1944), 194–198, reprinted in Curtis and Thompson, *Southern Essays*, 183.

mark[ed] ... an end to that great epoch of society. From 1789 to 1914 the ideas released by this great transformation made irresistible headway until they had destroyed in every center of influence the ancient system of feudalism. Society was changed from a hierarchy, from a state with a corporate form, held together by traditions, bonds of sentiment, and a vision of the whole, into the undifferentiated democratic mass, with free competition regarded as the sole means of measuring position and power. This meant change from a more or less articulated order into an unlimited number of groups and individuals engaged in self-promotion. It was supposed by liberal thinkers that this change represented a permanent rectification of society, in which all injustices, both those inherited from the past and those proceeding from ignorance and malice, would be removed.[26]

Civil rights were not a preoccupation of Weaver or others of his general bent, to say the least – including the Nashville Agrarians, an eminent group of reactionary writers and literary and cultural critics associated with Vanderbilt University in the 1930s who mounted a sustained critique of industrial capitalism, arguing instead for the virtues of rural and small-town life (though, famously, civil rights became a preoccupation of Robert Penn Warren's).[27] But some other conservatives at least ventured the view that anticommunism (and, conversely, support for capitalism) were consistent with an antislavery, pro–civil rights stance. One *Reader's Digest* writer, for instance, reminded readers that chattel slavery long antedated capitalism. It was, moreover, capitalist countries that had ultimately eliminated it. Slavery, however, still existed in communist countries "on a wider scale than ever before in history."[28]

The black intellectual George Schuyler (1895–1977), associate editor and chief editorialist of the *Pittsburgh Courier*, now typically classed as an influential early black conservative, criticized American communists, whom he blamed for proffering a false picture of the state of the American Negro that misleadingly stressed a supposed "hatred between whites and blacks." Books like Richard Wright's *Native Son* (1940), Lillian Smith's *Strange Fruit* (1944), and Howard Fast's *Freedom Road* (1944), and a string of films, like *Home of the Brave* (1949), and Sidney Poitier's debut feature *No Way Out* (1950), Schuyler insisted, were the spawn of this communist propaganda. "Actually," Schuyler argued, "the progressive improvement of race relations

---

[26] Weaver, "South and the Revolution of Nihilism," 194–198.
[27] See Robert Penn Warren, *Segregation: The Inner Conflict in the South* (New York: Modern Library, 1956).
[28] William I. Nichols, "Wanted: A New Name for 'Capitalism'" *Reader's Digest* 58:349 (May 1951): 3–4, 3 [reprinted, condensed, from *This Week Magazine* (March 4, 1951)] [emphasis in original]. An important line of recent scholarship, rejecting the traditional characterization of Louis Hartz and others of the Old South as a precapitalist, "feudal" region, holds chattel slavery to have been heavily implicated in southern (and global) capitalism. See Sven Beckert, *Empire of Cotton: A Global History* (New York: Vintage, 2014); Edward Baptist, *The Half Has Never Been Told: Slavery and the Making of Modern American Capitalism* (New York: Basic Books, 2014).

and the economic rise of the Negro in the United States is a flattering example of democracy in action." "The most 'exploited' Negroes in Mississippi," he emphasized, "are better off than the citizens of Russia or her satellites." "[I]nstead of being apologetic," Schuyler complained, "Americans should be proud that their free system has been capable of such elasticity."[29]

COMMUNISM AND THE FOUNDATIONS OF FREE GOVERNMENT: WHITTAKER CHAMBERS AND DOUGLAS MACARTHUR

The postwar Right's most indelible anticommunist statement was Whittaker Chambers's *Witness* (1952), a riveting memoir by an ex-communist (and, purportedly, "ex-homosexual") who at last found God and repented his sins.[30] *Witness*'s impact was especially powerful because, at the time it was published during the heyday of the McCarthy Era in the early 1950s, Chambers had already become famous: the book was published in the wake of Chambers's headline-grabbing testimony fingering a paragon of the eastern Ivy League policy elite, Alger Hiss, as a Soviet spy operating at the pinnacles of Washington power. Chambers had publicly alleged that during his time as a New Deal insider in the 1930s (and FDR aide at Yalta), Hiss, the golden-boy, Harvard-educated WASP and Felix Frankfurter protégé, had also been both an active member of Chambers's communist cell and a spy for the Soviet Union. *Witness* was published in the aftermath of the media circus surrounding, first, Chambers's testimony before the House Un-American Activities Committee unmasking Hiss as a spy – the first publicly televised congressional hearing – and, then, Hiss's subsequent trial for perjury in federal court in New York City after his ill-considered lawsuit against Chambers for defamation.[31]

Important in its own right as a high-profile spy case, the Hiss-Chambers phenomenon took on immense ideological significance as a cynosure for contention over the future of American constitutional government. Susan Jacoby described its import in this regard: "If Hiss was a lying Communist Party member taking orders from the Kremlin as well as a State Department

[29] George S. Schuyler, "The Phantom American Negro," *Reader's Digest* 59:351 (July 1951): 61–63 [reprinted, condensed, from *The Freeman* (April 23, 1951)]. See generally George Schuyler, *Black and Conservative: The Autobiography of George S. Schuyler* (New Rochelle, NY: Arlington House, 1966); Oscar R. Williams, *George S. Schuyler: Portrait of a Black Conservative* (Knoxville: University of Tennessee Press, 2007). See also Zora Neale Hurston, "Why the Negro Won't Buy Communism," *American Legion Magazine* 50 (June 1951): 14–15, 55–60.

[30] Besides selling widely in its own right, Chambers's testimony was summarized and recounted in the pages of *Look* and *Reader's Digest*. Whittaker Chambers, "What Is a Communist?" *Reader's Digest* 63:378 (October 1953): 19–22 [reprinted, condensed, from *Look* (July 28, 1953)]. In the late 1960s, moreover, Regnery acquired the paperback rights to the book and distributed it to college students. Hoplin and Robinson, *Funding Fathers*, 49–50.

[31] Jacoby, *Alger Hiss*, 97.

aide at the Yalta Conference, he could be and was used as Exhibit A in support of the long-held right-wing contention that if you scratched a New Deal liberal, you might just as easily find a socialist or a communist." For liberals, on the other hand, including many vehemently anticommunist liberals, Hiss represented and symbolized the liberal devotion to FDR's New Deal for the American people that had built out the nation's modern regulatory and social welfare state, and the country's emerging commitment to civil liberties – two of the three pillars (the third being the commitment to civil rights) of modern liberal constitutionalism in the heyday of American liberalism.[32] For conservatives, Alger Hiss's treachery served as an illustration that any effort to effectively separate communism and socialism from modern liberalism was ultimately hopeless: they were all in it together – variations on a dangerous, perhaps diabolical, theme.[33]

Witness was a conversion story, the testimony of a former communist who had found God, renounced evil, and was redeemed. The implication was that by telling his tale, the patriot Chambers was offering his country the opportunity to effect its own redemption.[34] A sick-souled Christian Scientist with a pervading sense of a world permeated by sin and evil, Whittaker Chambers's sensibility was profoundly religious, both when he believed in God and when he did not.[35] In *Witness*, Chambers placed the blame for communism squarely on atheism's serpent-like lure. Like right-wing Evangelicals and others on the 1970s and 1980s Religious Right, Chambers pronounced man a deifying animal: he declared it the first principle of man's nature to worship a higher power. If man did not worship God, he would end by worshiping man – and the consequences would be catastrophic.[36]

---

[32] See *US* v. *Carolene Products*, 304 US 144 (1938), fn. 4.

[33] Jacoby, *Alger Hiss*, 13–15, 26, 166–167. Chambers was a seminal figure for both William F. Buckley Jr. and Ronald Reagan. Jacoby observes, "[T]he guilt or innocence of Alger Hiss remains today what it was in the fifties – a symbolic and real indicator of which side you were, and are, on." In this way, it resembled the similar controversy concerning the guilt of the accused – and convicted and executed – Soviet spy Julius Rosenberg, and his wife Ethel. See also Allen Weinstein, *Perjury: The Hiss-Chambers Case* (New York: Alfred A. Knopf, 1978).

[34] Chambers claimed that with the help of God he was ultimately able to effectively suppress his homosexual impulses. Although he did not mention it in *Witness*, Chambers was regularly having anonymous sex with men while wrestling with his commitment to communism. Jacoby, *Alger Hiss*, 83, 124. If, as Jack Balkin, argues, redemption is a major theme of US constitutional politics, Chambers's story must count as one of the tradition's most significant redemption narratives. See Balkin, *Constitutional Redemption: Political Faith in an Unjust World* (Cambridge, MA: Harvard University Press, 2011). See also Jason Frank, *Constituent Moments: Enacting the People in Postrevolutionary America* (Durham, NC: Duke University Press, 2010), chap. 7.

[35] James, *Varieties of Religious Experience*. James contrasted the sick-souled religious with their more optimistic brethren who hewed to a "religion of healthy-mindedness."

[36] In his *New York Times* review of *Witness*, Sidney Hook – second to none in his anticommunism – spotted the problem: "The view that man must worship either God or Stalin faces many formidable theoretical difficulties and has the most mischievous practical consequences ... It is

In a 1953 interview for *Reader's Digest*, Chambers explained communism's special allure for members of the intellectual and progressive liberal elite. There were many highly educated people in the Communist Party, he had observed – "doctors, scientists, engineers, artists, economists, teachers – a surprising number from top American universities." The twentieth century's crisis of faith, "a failure of belief in and respect for the traditional forms of authority," had made such men ripe for the devil's picking. "Men crave authority," Chambers insisted, "which is a regulating and ordering principle in thought and life. Communism claims it offers a new, practical faith. It is an aggressive faith that rejects God and calls upon man to stand alone, to use resources of his own, especially technology and science, to create his own heaven on earth."[37]

At about the same time as the Hiss-Chambers episode and the publication of Chambers's memoir and *cri de coeur*, General Douglas MacArthur, the victorious commander of US forces in the Southwest Pacific during World War II – of late dismissed by President Truman as commander of the American-led United Nations forces in the Korean War for an excessive anticommunist zeal-unto-subordination by pushing for a military attack on Communist China – advanced similar themes and enjoined his country to act, reinforcing his status as a conservative hero. The oracular MacArthur warned his fellow Americans that "[h]istory fails to record a single precedent in which nations subject to moral decay have not passed into political and economic decline. There has been either a spiritual reawakening to overcome the moral lapse, or a progressive deterioration leading to ultimate national disaster." The greatest strength of the United States, MacArthur declared, resided in those of its citizens who loved God and country more than themselves. It was these Christian patriots who would lead us "toward a restoration to public and private relationships of our age-old standards of morality and ethics – a return to the religious fervor which animated our leadership of former years to chart a course

---

unfortunate that Chambers could not have given a wiser and more generous expression to his faith. The logic by which he now classifies liberals and humanists with the Communists is not unlike the logic by which, when a Communist, he classified them with Fascists ... I should hope that Chambers himself would recoil from the implications of his present view that there is no loyal political opposition outside the Faith. When heresy is identified with the enemy, we shall have seen the end of democracy." Sidney Hook, "The Faiths of Whittaker Chambers; His Many-Faceted Autobiography Sheds Light on Our Complex and Tragic Times," *New York Times* (May 25, 1952).

37 Chambers, "What Is a Communist?" On the West's "crisis of faith" as a defining moment, see Mark Greif, *The Age of the Crisis of Man: Though and Fiction in America, 1933-1973* (Princeton: Princeton University Press, 2015). Rather than seeing man's craving of authority as an aberration, or personality flaw – *pace* Adorno – Chambers saw it as part and parcel of his existential condition. See Theodor Adorno, *The Authoritarian Personality* (New York: Harper Bros., 1950). For Chambers, only faith in God prevented authority-craving man from inclining toward evil: it naturally set him toward the Good.

of humility and integrity as best to serve the public interest" – if only we would let them.[38]

The objective of "the evil forces of Communism," however, was to overthrow religion, because religion stood "as the most formidable barrier to their advance." One of the chief tools of the communists in pursuing their objective was to "undermine public and private morals as a means of weakening and rendering indefensible areas of intended absorption." Given that, the rise of the world's communist nations served "to warn all free men of the depravity which has inevitably replaced spirituality where their dominion over peoples and races has become complete." "[O]ur greatest hope rests upon two mighty symbols," MacArthur declared, "the Cross and the Flag." Our objective must be "to preserve inviolate that mighty bulwark of all freedom, our Christian faith."[39]

MacArthur's understanding of the United States as a Christian nation, anchored in a belief in God – and, more precisely, Our Lord Jesus Christ – fit into a broader push on the Right in the 1950s for a significant expansion in "ceremonial deism" (Eugene Rostow) that, among other things, ultimately led to the addition of "In God We Trust" to the currency and the "One Nation Under God" language to the Pledge of Allegiance – which had been adopted as the country's official pledge to the flag only as recently as World War II (1945). From the standpoint of contemporary constitutional originalism, this push for an expanded ceremonial deism in the 1950s has somewhat embarrassing origins: it is traceable to efforts by northern ministers in 1861 who attributed the cataclysm of the Civil War to the wholesale absence of God from the country's Constitution, which seemed plain enough to them, at least. These ministers launched a campaign to rectify that founding error by adding a "Christian Amendment" to the Constitution (which Abraham Lincoln – sainted by the contemporary Religious Right – apparently did not support).[40]

That proposed amendment has reared its head in various guises ever since, most notably perhaps in the mid-twentieth century, when the industrialist-turned-Republican senator from (then conservative) Vermont Ralph Flanders, a Senate Prayer Breakfast stalwart, sought to revive it. Again acknowledging that the Constitution, alas, made no reference to Our Lord Jesus Christ, the

---

[38] Douglas MacArthur, *Revitalizing a Nation: A Statement of Beliefs, Opinions, and Policies Embodied in the Public Pronouncements of General of the Army Douglas MacArthur* (Chicago: Heritage Foundation, 1952) (Correlations and captions by John M. Pratt), 14–15.

[39] MacArthur, *Revitalizing a Nation*, 17, 20, 21.

[40] Kruse, *One Nation Under God*, 96–97, 100, 102. Scrambling contemporary ideological categories, at least until recently, the push for the amendment at this time had been led by northern abolitionists, including Massachusetts Senator Charles Sumner (1811–1874), who was on the Radical Republican left of his time. Similarly, the author of the Pledge of Allegiance (1892) – *sans* any reference to God – the Reverend Francis Bellamy (1855–1931), a Baptist firmly committed to the strict separation of church and state, was also a northerner from upstate New York, and a (Christian) socialist.

senators pushing to rectify the error argued that great men like George Washington and Abraham Lincoln had lent their support for a corrective Christian Amendment and asked that the Library of Congress assemble the evidence of Washington's and Lincoln's commitment (the evidence did not exist, and thus it was never assembled). Others put a different spin on the absence of references to God and Jesus in the Constitution by arguing that while such references might not be part of the document's written text itself, they *were* part of its indispensible, foundational background presumptions and understandings, without which the Constitution made no sense (an argument, incidentally, that is increasingly pervasive on the contemporary Evangelical and Fundamentalist Christian and Roman Catholic Right). The order went out to return to historical documents of the colonial era and the early Republic to find statements and quotations that affirmed that the nation had been founded on a rock-solid foundation of an unwavering Christian faith. Within this framework, the Christian Amendment was not understood as adding something that was not already there, but confirming in writing something that indubitably was, and always had been. Yet again, however, even at the peak of the Cold War against "Godless Communism" and the period's palpable religious revivalism (reflected on the Supreme Court in a classic statement by the (very) liberal Justice William O. Douglas, no less), the proposed Christian Amendment failed. This time, however, there were some next-best substitutes waiting in the wings.[41]

Leadership on getting the country to adopt what Kevin Kruse has called its "twin mottos" of ceremonial deism was enthusiastically assumed – perhaps surprisingly, given this history (but actually not at all, given the account provided in the "Right Wing Roman Catholic Stories" in Chapter 6 in this book) – by the nation's Catholics who, of course, were steeped in a Thomist theological framework that emphasized reasoning from first principles. As Clarence Manion, Fulton J. Sheen, John Courtney Murray, and others who wrote about the Constitution never tired of propounding, the nation and the Constitution had been founded upon the Rock of Faith. And, why, after all, shouldn't the nation, in such trying times, officially acknowledge at least *that*, to inspire and sustain us? While Catholic civic organizations, clerics, and individuals led the fight, those of other faiths (including even Jews) in both political parties and of diverse political ideologies and, ultimately, and crucially, President Eisenhower, signed on to the simple statement of ceremonial deism in the words "In God We Trust" and "One Nation Under God." Even civil liberties groups like the American Civil Liberties Union, busy in the McCarthy Era frying other fish, did not lodge any, or any serious, objections. As Kruse summarized it, the phrase "One Nation Under God" especially "quickly claimed a central position in American political culture," becoming "an

---

[41] Kruse, *One Nation Under God*, 96–98. See *Zorach v. Clauson*, 343 US 306 (1952) ("We are a religious people whose institutions presuppose a Supreme Being.").

informal motto for the country, demonstrating the widespread belief that the United States had been founded on religious belief and was sustained by religious practice."[42]

A CRIMINAL CONSPIRACY POSING A "CLEAR AND PRESENT DANGER"?

Although acknowledging that "a number of authoritative minds think otherwise," when *Reader's Digest* asked Whittaker Chambers whether he believed the Communist Party should be outlawed in the United States, Chambers answered "I do." "[I]f it is to work and grow," he emphasized, it "must have live contacts with the world around it, must be able to send its poisonous filaments through the social body it is seeking to destroy." Chambers drew a sharp distinction between radical political beliefs and criminal conspiracy. Communism fell into the latter category. Government had the power – indeed, the duty – to fight for self-preservation. In *Heresy Yes – Conspiracy No* (1952), the Deweyian pragmatist and erstwhile Marxist New York University philosopher Sidney Hook explicated the same distinction at greater length and explained why, while the belief in and advocacy of Marxism constituted a heresy, membership in the Communist Party involved a conspiracy.[43] And, in an article supporting the Supreme Court's decision in *Dennis v. United States* (1951), in which the Court put its constitutional imprimatur on the government's treatment of the CPUSA as a criminal conspiracy, the Cornell University Straussian Walter Berns reminded readers that freedom of opinion was hardly the highest value in politics. Berns argued, moreover, that, so far as communism was concerned, it was well-nigh impossible as a practical matter to separate beliefs from action.[44] The liberal anticommunist justices of the Supreme Court like Robert Jackson

---

[42] Kruse, *One Nation Under God*, 99–100, 102–104, 110–111. The leading figure in pushing for the addition of the "One Nation Under God" language to the Pledge, Louis Rabaut, was a liberal Catholic Democratic congressman from Detroit.

[43] Chambers, "What Is a Communist?" 21, 22. See *Dennis v. US*, 341 US 494 (1951). Hook's Marxism was always unique, emphasizing the outlook, in a Deweyian pragmatic vein, as entailing non-dogmatic scientific experimentation: it never entailed any sort of obedience to the Communist Party or belief in irrefutable iron laws of history. See David Sidorsky, "Sidney Hook," *Stanford Encyclopedia of Philosophy* (Winter 2015).

[44] Walter Berns, "Freedom and Loyalty," *The Journal of Politics* 18:1 (1956): 17–27, 20. See also "The Refusal to Answer," *Wall Street Journal* (June 18, 1953), 6 ("We believe that the rightness or wrongness of a refusal to answer inquiries concerning Communist affiliation hangs on the question whether a valid distinction can be drawn between Communism and other varieties of political thought ... [S]imon-pure Communism preaches world revolution by violence whereas political sects which the state may safely tolerate do not. This newspaper regards the distinction here indicated as good and valid." The paper nevertheless acknowledged that "there is some degree of risk involved in singling out any color of political thought as being dangerous to our concept of political freedom" and called for the prudent exercise of the investigatory power.).

(a Franklin Roosevelt appointee), advanced similar views in both *Dennis* and other subversion cases of the 1950s.[45]

"Nothing is more important than that America should preserve her own civil liberties while frustrating the agents of Communist tyranny," Max Eastman, the former John Dewey student, Greenwich Village radical, *The Masses* editor, and brother of ACLU Founder Crystal Eastman, wrote in *Reader's Digest*. Like Chambers, Hook, and Berns, Eastman emphasized that "[w]e cannot accomplish this without keeping clear the distinction between the rights of free speech, press and assemblage and the right of organizing to overthrow the government that guarantees these rights." Eastman insisted that he took civil liberties guarantees seriously. If the party were to be outlawed, he worried, it was certainly possible that "bigoted standpatters will abuse the law to silence all agitation and stop all change. They certainly will if they can." Still, the notion that in outlawing and suppressing the party, the United States was abandoning its traditional democratic freedoms was, in Eastman's estimation, a canard with "no basis whatever except in Communist propaganda." "A government which fails to suppress a conspiracy to overthrow it," he declaimed, "is not democratic but weak."[46] "The right of revolution proclaimed by Jefferson, reiterated by Abraham Lincoln, and recalled also in milder terms by Woodrow Wilson," Eastman explained, "was a right of the people to overthrow a government which had become tyrannical. It was not a right of open advocates of tyranny to overthrow the government of the people."[47] The communists were taking advantage of the Supreme Court's clear and present danger test,[48] which they understood "opens a free field to their ultra-modern technique for overthrowing governments by gradual infiltration, long-term demoralization and patiently hammered-in lies and false poses of democracy." The author of the Court's test,

---

[45] Powe, *Warren Court and American Politics*, chaps. 4, 6.

[46] Max Eastman, "Why We Must Outlaw the Communist Party!" *Reader's Digest* 57: 341 (September 1950): 42–44,. See Christoph Irmscher, *Max Eastman: A Life* (New Haven: Yale University Press, 2017). Max Eastman himself had been one of the criminal defendants charged under the World War I Era Espionage Act prosecution of the radical journal he edited, *The Masses*, as a threat to national security. The landmark decision of the US District Court for the Southern District of New York, written by Judge Learned Hand, vindicated Eastman and *The Masses* on First Amendment grounds – one of the earliest decisions in a doctrinal trend that would come to require proof of a close connection between the speech in question and actual conduct to remove the speech from First Amendment protection. *Masses Publishing Co.* v. *Patten*, 234 F. 535 (1917). Given his extensive experiences as a radical writer and publisher during World War I and the Red Scare, this is an area of constitutional law that Eastman knew extremely well – indeed, helped midwife into existence.

[47] See also "A Threat to Our Judicial System," Editorial, *American Bar Association Journal* 39 (1952): 932–933, 933 (insisting that "the lawyers of the nation must rouse themselves to continuing aggressive defense against this sinister threat to the very existence of our judicial system and the administration of justice under the law ['the very foundation of our liberties'] as we have known it.").

[48] *Schenck* v. *United States*, 249 US 47 (1919); *Abrams* v. *United States*, 250 US 616 (1919) (Justices Holmes and Brandeis, dissenting).

Justice Oliver Wendell Holmes Jr., Eastman adjudged, likely never understood the implications it would have for the mid-twentieth-century communist conspiracy. "The doctrine of 'clear and present danger,'" he noted, "belongs to the age before world revolution against democracy became an elaborately worked-out technically scientific enterprise."[49]

"The people," Eastman announced, "are not deceived by the effete notion that a free country, in order to continue free, must sanction conspiracies against freedom." Certainly, "[i]t will be painful to all liberal Americans to suppress an organization calling itself a political party." But, like Hook, Eastman held that "[i]ts pretense to be a 'party' is a political trick. We must devise legislation that will defeat this trick, and yet *not* outlaw freedom of opinion. It is the only way, in this unprecedented crisis of democratic history, that such freedom of opinion can be preserved."[50]

There were other issues beyond whether or not the party should be outlawed. These included requirements that communists register with the federal government, that would-be public employees (including public school and public university teachers) sign loyalty oaths, and bans on party members from serving as officers of labor unions and working in defense plants.[51] Many found the Supreme Court's voiding of the law banning communists from working in defense plants emblematic of the corruptions wrought by the High Court's liberalism. "By the same reasoning," one conservative editorialist

---

[49] Eastman, "Why We Must Outlaw the Communist Party!" 43. See *Gitlow* v. *New York*, 268 NY 652 (1925) (involving the prosecution of Communist Party member Benjamin Gitlow – who himself later migrated from Left to Right (see Benjamin Gitlow, *I Confess: The Truth About American Communism* (New York: E. P. Dutton and Co., 1940) (Introduction by Max Eastman); Benjamin Gitlow, *The Whole of Their Lives: Communism in America* (New York: Charles Scribner's Sons, 1948)) – for the distribution of the "Left Wing Manifesto" calling for revolution under New York State's Criminal Anarchy Law). Justice Holmes's dissent in *Gitlow* ventured that "If, in the long run, the beliefs expressed in proletarian dictatorship are destined to be accepted by the dominant forces of the community, the only meaning of free speech is that they should be given their chance and have their way."

[50] Eastman, "Why We Must Outlaw the Communist Party!" 44. See also Eugene Lyons, "The Men the Reds Hate Most," *Reader's Digest* 57:343 (November 1950): 109–113, 111–112, reprinted, condensed, from *The American Legion Magazine* (October 1950). (Asserting that "[t]heir so-called Party has finally been identified as a branch office of a world-wide plot to overthrow democratic governments, our own included, by force and violence," and noting that "the people who bemoan our lost liberties when Communists are investigated apparently saw no violation of civil rights, no vile political motivation, when witnesses were asked whether they ever belonged to the Bund, the Klan, the Silver Shirts.")

[51] See generally Ellen Schrecker, *Many Are the Crimes: McCarthyism in America* (Boston: Little, Brown and Co., 1998); Powe, *Warren Court and American Politics*, chaps. 4, 6; "The Supreme Sophistry of the Warren Court," *Human Events* 25:26 (June 26, 1965), 12 [reprinted from *Richmond News Leader*], criticizing the Court's decision in *United States* v. *Brown*, 381 US 437 (1965) essentially overruling *Douds*. In instituting this regulation, the anticommunist Congress had availed itself of the broad understanding of Congress's Article I, Section 8, commerce powers as applied to the regulation of the workplace as sanctioned by liberal New Deal constitutional precedents. See, e.g., *NLRB* v. *Jones and Laughlin Steel Co.*, 301 US 1 (1937).

argued in the late 1960s, "a cell in the United States composed of the Viet Cong and Communist North Viet Nam would have a 'protected' right to employment in American defense facilities and perhaps within the Pentagon itself, notwithstanding the fact that we are at war."[52] In the aftermath of the Court's decision, Illinois Republican Senator Everett Dirksen went so far as to call for a constitutional convention that would curtail the Supreme Court's jurisdiction in this area.[53]

Before the Warren Court, "the sovereign right of any nation to exclude or deport undesirable aliens" had been clear and beyond question, conservatives observed. The current Supreme Court, however, was unjustifiably enlisting the Fifth Amendment's due process clause to protect aliens, and resident aliens especially. The Court had expressed special concern with the government's use of confidential information in making deportation decisions. But when internal subversion posed a serious threat to national security, one writer in the *ABA Journal* argued, "[t]he Constitution ... should be construed in accordance with its purpose ... without such preoccupation with civil rights as to endanger national survival."[54]

"PLEADING THE FIFTH"

The invocation of the Fifth Amendment by both criminal defendants and those called to testify in legislative hearings in communist subversion cases erupted into a major constitutional dispute in the 1950s. Under a banner heading in 1954 declaring that "[p]erhaps not since the early thirties has a constitutional amendment been as much a topic of conversation among all our citizens," the *ABA Journal* sponsored a roundtable debate on the Fifth Amendment. In opening the debate, the Harvard Law School dean, the moderate conservative Republican Erwin Griswold, reviewed the history of the Fifth Amendment's privilege against self-incrimination, stressing its links with the Anglo-American legal tradition's abolition of torture.[55] While praising the Fifth Amendment generally, however, the published responses to Griswold alluded to dissatisfaction with "what seems to them a judicial

52 "Supreme Court OK's Employment of Communists in Defense Plants," *Human Events* 27:51 (December 23, 1967), 6 [reprinted from the *Chicago Tribune*].
53 Paul Scott, "In the Works: Major Congressional Move to Curb the Supreme Court," *Human Events* 28:3 (January 20, 1968), 8. See Powe, *Warren Court and American Politics*, chaps. 4, 6.
54 Frank B. Ober, "Communism and the Court: An Examination of Recent Developments," *American Bar Association Journal* 44 (January 1958): 35–89, 84, 85, 89. See *Fong Yue Ting* v. *United States*, 149 US 698 (1893). Deidre Moloney, *National Securities: Immigrants and Deportation Policies Since 1882* (Chapel Hill: University of North Carolina Press, 2012).
55 Erwin N. Griswold, "The Fifth Amendment: An Old and Good Friend," *American Bar Association Journal* 40 (June 1954): 502–536, 502–503. The Fifth Amendment to the US Constitution, in relevant part, reads that "No person ... shall be compelled in any criminal case to be a witness against himself."

extension of its principles and aims never contemplated by its authors."
Citing the invocation of the Fifth by public school teachers, Austin Wyman,
for instance, complained that the teachers were claiming "a constitutional
[self-incrimination] privilege which does not exist ... for reasons of personal
loyalty to friends, or because of a sense of unfairness in harming them by
disclosing their identity ... lending the personal shield [provided by the
Amendment] to another." "It goes without saying that no responsible
educational institution in this country will retain on its teaching staff
a known Communist," Wyman added, emphasizing, "the right to its use is
not lawfully transferrable." The witness asserting the Fifth, moreover, and
importantly, "has no way of knowing what other evidence might be coupled
with his to make a complete chain; he cannot possible know whether in fact
his evidence, however trivial he may consider it, might even be the missing
link needed for the punishment of one or a group who have betrayed their
country."[56] Following these debates, Erwin Griswold decided to defend
invocations of the Fifth Amendment at length, and answer his critics, in
a book entitled The Fifth Amendment Today (1955). That statement too,
however, met with a set of vehement responses and rejoinders, not least by
Sidney Hook in Common Sense and the Fifth Amendment (1957).[57]

While many liberals came to see a refusal to testify in these investigations into
possible communist subversion as the epitome of civil libertarian heroism, and
the willingness to testify in the hearings as a repudiation of core American
values of individual liberty,[58] conservatives took the invocation of the Fifth
Amendment by those called to testify about subversion before Congress as
cowardly and ignoble – if not borderline treasonous. "This frequent running
for shelter to the Fifth Amendment suggests the mentality of a conspirator, not
of a forthright advocate of an unpopular idea," William Henry Chamberlin –
like Whittaker Chambers, himself a former communist – countered:
"Communists and Communist sympathizers may be within their legal rights if
they choose to plead fear of self-incrimination. But they cannot have their cake

---

[56] Austin L. Wyman, "The Fifth Amendment: The Case of the Three Professors," American Bar
Association Journal 41 (September 1955): 801–805, 802–803.

[57] Erwin Griswold, The Fifth Amendment Today: Three Speeches (Cambridge, MA: Harvard
University Press, 1955); Sidney Hook, Common Sense and the Fifth Amendment (Chicago:
Regnery, 1957).

[58] See, e.g., Lillian Hellman, Scoundrel Time (Boston: Little, Brown and Co., 1976);
Victor Navasky, Naming Names: The Social Costs of McCarthyism (New York: Viking,
1980). Howard Fast, "Why the Fifth Amendment?" Masses & Mainstream, 7 (February
1954): 44–50. Perhaps the most famous case on the American cultural scene was that of the
film director Elia Kazan, who did "name names," and was ever after anathematized by liberal
Hollywood. Kazan soon thereafter directed the classic film On the Waterfront (1954), which
positioned as heroic its lead character Terry Malloy's (Marlon Brando) willingness to name
names in an investigation ferreting out corruption on the mob-dominated – as a stand-in for
communist infiltrated – Brooklyn docks.

and eat it too. They cannot expect the same esteem they would deserve if they showed more candor." Far from heroes, these people were "artful dodgers, rather than rebel prophets."[59] Editors of Right-leaning newspapers wondered "[i]f the Constitution is in fact as flexible as it is proclaimed to be on those infrequent occasions when the Liberals rejoice in it, then oughtn't it to be flexible enough to permit the government to take effective action against political subversion and loyalty risks?"[60]

A battle over the scope of Congress's investigation powers in this era – most prominently in the House Un-American Activities Committee (HUAC) – pitted countervailing claims of legislative authority, responsibilities, and power and Fifth Amendment rights. When viewed from this perspective, it is worth noting that the respective positions taken by liberals and conservatives in the domestic subversion/national security battles of the 1950s inverted the constitutional positions that the opposed political camps had earlier taken from the Progressive Era through the New Deal. During the earlier period, progressives and their liberal successors, while promoting new forms of economic and social regulation, had pioneered the view that the Constitution afforded broad fact-gathering powers to Congress to collect information to advance the broader public interest. Conservatives in the earlier period, by contrast, had mounted staunch constitutional resistance rooted in individual rights claims under the Fourth and Fifth Amendments.[61] Although by the mid-twentieth century, both sides had jettisoned the stances of their progenitors with nary a glance backward, it was the conservatives who gleefully skewered contemporary liberals for their hypocrisy.

Leading conservative outlets like the *Wall Street Journal* and *National Review* vigorously argued that Congress had broad powers to counter subversion through broad-ranging investigations.[62] *National Review*'s first constitutional law/Supreme Court columnist, C. Dickerman Williams (1900–1998), a former law clerk to Chief Justice William Howard Taft (and the father of future US Court of Appeals for the District of Columbia Circuit Judge Stephen F. Williams, a Ronald Reagan appointee), discussed these issues extensively for years. Dickerman Williams began by suggesting – at first, naïvely, then devilishly – that on the question of the government's power at both the state and federal levels to gather information from individuals in the broader public interest, there was remarkably little

---

[59] William Henry Chamberlin, "Artful Dodgers," *Wall Street Journal* (May 6, 1953), 12. See also "Fishing and the Fifth Amendment," *Wall Street Journal* (March 29, 1957), 12 ("We need the Fifth Amendment. We also need fishing expeditions.").

[60] [Syndicated] Editorial, *The Salt Lake City Tribune* (June 29, 1964); *The Cincinnati Enquirer* (July 1, 1964); [untitled editorial] (July 7, 1964) 16:1.

[61] See Kersch, *Constructing Civil Liberties*, 29–66. Ken I. Kersch, "The Reconstruction of Constitutional Privacy Rights and the New American State," *Studies in American Political Development* 16 (Spring 2002): 61–87.

[62] "The Threat to Civil Liberties," *Wall Street Journal* (February 23, 1956), 12.

partisanship.[63] Recounting a series of debates on the matter Williams had engaged in with Erwin Griswold at Harvard and Marquette, Dickerman Williams noted that "as often happens ... [t]he principal agreements between us were ... not so much about the history and fundamental principles of the Fifth Amendment as about the policy and propriety of their application."[64] Williams, however, took Griswold to task for praising a recent Florida Supreme Court decision that had reversed the state's disbarment of a lawyer for pleading the Fifth Amendment in response to questions about his Communist Party membership.[65] Williams asked whether, if $10,000 were missing from the till of a bank, and a clerk had refused to answer their questions about it, they would be justified in firing him, to which Griswold replied in the affirmative. Williams responded: "I fail to see the distinction. We all know that the Soviet Union has enlisted many Americans in a conspiracy to overthrow the government." Griswold, he said, had thus implicitly agreed with him that "if a witness is silent at a hearing or trial when his conduct is questioned, the trier of facts should draw an adverse inference against the witness."[66]

Williams made much of what he took to be the inversion of the position Griswold and his Harvard Law School colleagues had taken on the issue in the early twentieth century, when the law school's faculty had heavily involved itself in building the modern administrative state:

[A]s he is dean of the Harvard Law School, it is not unfair to contrast what he is saying now with what members of the faculty of the Harvard Law School were saying in the 1920s. Justice Felix Frankfurter, then a prominent professor there, wrote "Hands Off the Investigations" in 1924, a work sufficiently described by stating its title. Dean Landis, predecessor of Dean Griswold, wrote a masterly legal essay entitled "Constitutional Limitations on the Congressional Power of Investigation" in 1926, an essay that remains

---

[63] C. Dickerman Williams, "Reflections on the Fifth Amendment," *National Review* (December 21, 1955): 1:15, 15. See also C. Dickerman Williams, "Problems of the Fifth Amendment," *Fordham Law Review* 24:19 (1955): 26–30; Griswold, *Fifth Amendment Today*. Griswold was an establishment Republican from the party's liberal, Rockefeller wing. Williams, also a Republican, was a lawyer in private practice in New York City. He specialized in civil liberties, including free speech, and served as both a board member and head of the American Civil Liberties Union. Williams represented William F. Buckley Jr. and *National Review* in a libel suit brought by the Nobel Prize–winning chemist and peace activist Linus Pauling and in Buckley's efforts – discussed in Chapter 3 on "Stories About Markets" – to avoid compulsory enrollment in the American Federation of Television and Radio Artists union as a condition for the production and broadcast of his television show *Firing Line*. See Wolfgang Saxon, "C. Dickerman Williams, 97, Free Speech Lawyer, Is Dead," *New York Times* (August 30, 1998).

[64] Williams, "Reflections on the Fifth Amendment," 15.

[65] *Sheiner* v. *State*, 82 So.2d 657 (Florida, 1955).

[66] Williams, "Reflections on the Fifth Amendment," 15. The *Wall Street Journal* borrowed this banker example in its editorial defending the dismissal of allegedly communist teachers who had invoked the Fifth Amendment. "The Law and Ethics and Mr. Beck," *Wall Street Journal* (May 22, 1957), 12.

to this day the ablest presentation of the theory that the congressional power of investigation is substantially unlimited.[67]

Dickerman Williams concluded:

[I]t is unfortunate, if not tragic, that the Harvard Law School – with its energy, intelligence and prestige, and its militant stand on the side of disclosure during the investigations of monopoly in the 1890s and 1900s, of corruption in the 1920s and of questionable business practices in the 1930s – should be identified with the cause of concealment today, when the country is confronted with the far more serious danger of Soviet penetration.[68]

Reacting to the *Watkins* v. *United States* (1957) case involving a labor union activist called to testify before HUAC who agreed to discuss his connection to the Communist Party and the party's current but not its past members, Williams complained that "[t]hese issues had been thought to be put to rest by the Supreme Court decisions in the law suits resulting from the Teapot Dome and Daugherty investigations, but have now been reopened." Williams compared *Watkins* with the Supreme Court decisions arising out of those two earlier Harding administration scandals: *McGrain* v. *Daugherty* (1927) and *Sinclair* v. *United States* (1929).[69] In both cases, Dickerman Williams noted, the Court

[67] Williams, "Reflections on the Fifth Amendment," 25. See Felix Frankfurter, "Hands Off the Investigations," *New Republic* 38 (1924): 329; James M. Landis, "Constitutional Limitations on the Congressional Power of Investigation," *Harvard Law Review* 40 (1926): 153. Douglas Caddy and M. Stanton Evans made the same point about Alabama Senator and future Supreme Court Justice (and, like Felix Frankfurter, FDR appointee) Hugo Black, who, as they saw it, had been pro-investigations in the 1930s and, hypocritically, anti-investigations in the 1950s. Douglas Caddy and M. Stanton Evans, "Hugo Black: A Study of Conflict: The Story of the Ku Klux Klan's Favorite 'Liberal,'" *Human Events* 16:50 (December 16, 1950), 1. A conservative lawyer, Caddy would become the national director for the Young Americans for Freedom (YAF), and, while working for Richard Nixon's Committee to Re-Elect the President (CREEP), played a small but dramatic part in the Watergate Scandal as, briefly, the lawyer for the Watergate burglars, and for the burglary's planner E. Howard Hunt.
[68] Williams, "Reflections on the Fifth Amendment," 25.
[69] C. Dickerman Williams, "The Watkins Case," *National Review* (March 21, 1956): 1, 23. The Daugherty case arose out of Senate efforts to question the brother of US Attorney General Harry Daugherty in an investigation of the AGs conduct of his office. The brother refused to testify and was subsequently arrested by resolution of the Senate. The Supreme Court upheld the arrest and the obligation of the brother to testify on the grounds that the "powers and duties of the Attorney General ... are subject to regulation by congressional legislation." The *Sinclair* case involved the refusal of the head of Sinclair Oil, Harry F. Sinclair, to testify before a Senate committee investigating the Teapot Dome lease on the grounds that the government had brought suit to cancel the lease and was seeking his testimony to get information to advance their interest in those lawsuits. The Supreme Court upheld the Senate's right to Sinclair's testimony pursuant to its investigation of that lease and held that it was "not abridged because the information sought to be elicited may also be of use in such suits." *McGrain* v. *Daugherty*, 273 US 135 (1927); *Sinclair* v. *United States*, 279 US 263 (1929); *Watkins* v. *United States*, 98 US App. D.C. 190, 233 F. 2d 681 (1956), reversed and remanded in *Watkins* v. *United States*, 354 US 178 (1957).

had applied a single test: "[D]id the question relate to a subject which Congress had the power to legislate? If so, the question was proper and the fact that the information might have importance in other connections was irrelevant to the witness's duty to answer."[70]

Williams remarked upon the liberal federal appellate judge who wrote the *Watkins* opinion's own inversion of his earlier position on the question. As a law professor prior to his 1937 appointment to the DC Circuit by President Franklin Roosevelt, Judge Henry White Edgerton had published an "outstanding work of legal scholarship" in which

he condemned judicial interference with Congress; his primary ground was that the beneficiaries of such interferences were unworthy people, viz., "smugglers," and "exploiter of prostitutes," "activities which cannot be carried on without money," "illicit liquor dealers," "office-holders and lawyers," "receivers of stolen goods," "business" ... That he should be the author of an opinion such as that in the Watkins case sharply illustrates the reversal in the Liberal attitude towards public information via congressional investigation that has taken place since the 1930s.[71]

Williams could only count this as evidence of "the cult of concealment now sweeping the Liberal community."[72] Later, when the Supreme Court affirmed the appellate decision in Watkins, *National Review* complained, "Congress's power was never questioned before Watkins, nor was the right of Congress itself to decide whether and how investigations were related to the legislative process."[73]

Conservatives expressed the same views in other fora. In an article for *The American Legion Magazine* (reprinted in *Reader's Digest*), Eugene Lyons (1898–1985), yet another socialist/communist fellow traveler who later migrated right, scored the "reckless, ferocious attack by Communists and self-styled 'liberals'" on the House Un-American Activities Committee since its 1938 inception. "Ordinary folk fear to speak out for the committee," Lyons

[70] Williams, "The Watkins Case," 23. "In the Watkins case, there was no doubt that the question related to a subject within the congressional power of regulation, viz, Communist infiltration of labor unions. The bill upon which the hearing was held subsequently was enacted into law. [But] [a]ccording to Judge Edgerton's opinion, Congress had no power of exposure because it has no 'powers of law enforcement' ... This is a most remarkable and sweeping conclusion. Judge Edgerton reached it without explanation and without citation of authority. It disregards the view of such eminent political scientists as John Stuart Mill, Woodrow Wilson and others that publicity is an essential element of the legislative process. Legislation cannot be enacted without the support of public opinion, and lacking information, public opinion is without the basis to provide support."
[71] Williams, "The Watkins Case," 30, citing Henry White Edgerton, "The Incidence of Judicial Control of Congress," *Cornell Law Quarterly* (May 1937).
[72] Williams, "The Watkins Case," 30.
[73] "New York Times Debates an Issue," 344. The magazine also criticized the Court for its subsequent decision in *Sacher* v. *United States* applying the *Watkins* rule to the Senate Internal Security Subcommittee. *National Review* 5 (May 31, 1958), 507. *Watkins* v. *United States*, 354 US 178 (1957); *Sacher* v. *United States*, 356 US 576 (1958).

complained, "know[ing] that epithets like 'reactionary' and 'Fascist' will be their reward for candor," typically hurled by elites like teachers, writers, artists, scientists, and clergy, who were seemingly indefatigable in running down the committee. Lyons declared himself a partisan, insisting that "[t]he right of Congress to investigate any area of the nation's life is of the essence of democratic government."[74]

The Princeton and Balliol College, Oxford–educated James Burnham, the author of *The Web of Subversion* (which *Reader's Digest* serialized in May and June 1954), analogized the congressional committees investigating domestic communism to the Roman Tribunes, which had served as a model to the nation's Founders as they created Congress's first investigatory committees. "Congressional investigators can reflect the ignorance and the passions of the people as well as the people's traditional wisdom, loyalty and strength," Burnham conceded. All the same "they are irreplaceable champions of our liberty."[75]

Like his compatriots, Burnham relished quoting both Felix Frankfurter's and Hugo Black's earlier defenses of a broad understanding of Congress's investigations powers.[76] Burnham rehearsed the long history of such committees, including their successes in ferreting out corruption in the Teapot Dome and Crédit Mobilier scandals. "Only Congressional investigation could have produced such results," Burnham noted. "Individual citizens were helpless. The courts were powerless to initiate action. The executive agencies were either unaware of what was happening or conniving at it. Tribunes of the People, armed with sufficient power, were required to expose the wrong-doing, arouse public opinion and force remedial action." That they were able to perform this function effectively was a tribute to the Constitution's design in conferring upon Congress the powers and responsibilities for making and changing laws and monitoring them after they were passed. Congressional committees with broad investigatory powers were essential to its fulfillment of those duties.[77]

---

[74] Eugene Lyons, "The Men the Reds Hate Most," *Reader's Digest* 57:343 (November 1950): 109-113, 109-110, reprinted, condensed, from *The American Legion Magazine* (October 1950). Like Dickerman Williams, Lyons wielded Felix Frankfurter's influential earlier defense of such inquiries "Hands Off the Investigations" (published in *The New Republic* in 1924) as damning evidence of liberal hypocrisy.

[75] James Burnham, "Tribunes of the People," *Reader's Digest* 66:394 (February 1955): 59–64, 59 (reprinted, condensed, from *The Freeman* (February 1955)). The article announces that Burnham's "Tribunes of the People" will be the subject of discussion on Theodore Granik's educational program "Youth Wants to Know" on NBC (Sunday, February 13, 1955).

[76] He noted that in 1936 Black had said: "Public investigating committees exist always in countries where the people rule. They have always been opposed by groups that seek or have special privileges." Burnham, "Tribunes of the People," 60. See also Irwin Ross, "What Good Are Congressional Investigations?" *Reader's Digest* 71:426 (October 1957): 60–64, 60, 64; "The Right of Exposure," *Wall Street Journal* (March 13, 1957), 12.

[77] Burnham, "Tribunes of the People," 60–63.

Burnham argued that the Fifth Amendment was being inappropriately deployed as a smokescreen to thwart the Congress in its legitimate and important work: hundreds of witnesses were hiding behind it.[78] In assessing whether they had any legitimate grounds, Burnham recurred to the Fifth Amendment's history. "What is this Fifth Amendment?" he asked. "Has it anything to do with freedom of thought or civil liberties, as those who have been invoking it pretend?" The rights and privileges vouchsafed by the amendment, Burnham noted, were not a part of England's ancient common law liberties; they were not protected by Magna Carta, or in the English Bill of Rights. In the United States, its application to legislative hearings – as opposed to testimony in courts with the power of criminal conviction – was novel, and recent. If someone pleads the Fifth, Burnham emphasized, *"it is not a principle of any procedure under Heaven that we should overlook such replies in forming our judgment about what a man has been and has done."*[79]

Burnham complained:

Some liberals, taken in by this [civil libertarian] propaganda, are afraid that it is a "threat to civil liberties" to suggest there is something improper in Fifth Amendment silence ... They pretend that we should make no distinction between a man who replies frankly and readily to significant questions put to him by authorized investigating bodies and another who remains silent on the plea of self-incrimination. This is, of course, ridiculous.

If someone had not committed a crime, then their answer would not tend to incriminate them. "The Fifth Amendment," Burnham insisted, "was never interpreted to permit a man to refuse at his own choosing to testify against others, or to matters of fact that are of proper interest to a court, jury or authorized investigating body." Burnham argued that "[a]ll public employees should be required to waive immunity with respect to testifying about their official acts," and that any who refused to do so should be fired. "There is nothing tyrannical in this," Burnham held (borrowing from the Dickerman Williams–Erwin Griswold exchange): "Would a bank president hire as a cashier a man who refused to answer questions concerning theft and his acquaintance with robbers?"[80]

---

[78] James Burnham, "Fog Around the Fifth Amendment," *Reader's Digest* 64:384 (April 1954): 21–25, 21. See James Burnham, *The Web of Subversion: Underground Networks in the U.S. Government* (New York: The John Day Company, 1954).

[79] Burnham, "Fog Around the Fifth Amendment," 22 [italics in original]. See also Richard C. Baker, "Self-Incrimination: Is the Privilege an Anachronism?" *American Bar Association Journal* 42 (July 1956): 633–689, 634.

[80] Burnham, "Fog Around the Fifth Amendment," 23–24. See also H.S.J. Sickel (Philadelphia, Pennsylvania), Letter to the Editor, *American Bar Association Journal* 43 (1957): 196–202, 200, 202 (arguing that the language of the Fifth Amendment plainly applies to criminal proceedings, not congressional investigations, and that "certain 'intellectuals', with pro-Russian natures, thoughts, and ideas conceived the use (misuse) of the Fifth Amendment for the purpose of defeating our governmental efforts").

When a raft of Supreme Court decisions limiting the government's investigatory powers was handed down on June 17, 1957 (including *Watkins*), Forrest Davis, a former FDR supporter and chief Washington correspondent for *Newsweek* during World War II who had moved rightward as a *Saturday Evening Post* writer, insisted that what J. Edgar Hoover had dubbed "Red Monday" "may well mark the date in the future as our 18th Brumaire" – the *coup d'état* that brought Napoleon Bonaparte to power. "[T]he Warren Court," Davis claimed, had "precipitated a constitutional crisis long in the making which, should Congress defend its prerogatives, will give rise to a struggle for power reminiscent of the quarrels between King and Commons in Stuart and Hanoverian England."[81] Such judicial "absolutism," simply would not stand:

What the Court did in Watkins was to ride down the congressional right to investigate, to press it within narrow limits of legislative intent, to surround witnesses with a wall of immunity, and specifically to deny the Congress's right "to expose for the sake of exposure," which was the Chief Justice's belittling term for the right of "informing," a right which Woodrow Wilson, in his Congressional Government, placed above even the Congress's legislative function![82]

Davis additionally complained that "by adding the First Amendment's guarantee of free speech and the common-law right of privacy to the Fifth Amendment as a screen between Congress and the witness," *Watkins* had made "future inquiries dependent on the leave of those under investigation."[83] For his part, the conservative Georgia lawyer R. Carter Pittman complained, "the words 'in any criminal case' have been completely and effectively deleted from the privilege." "Like the jury system, and like the presumption of innocence," he insisted, "it was designed to shield patriots from arbitrary power – not criminals from all power."[84]

---

[81] Forrest Davis, "The Court Reaches for Total Power," *National Review* 4 (July 6, 1957) 33, 33. See Arthur J. Sabin, *In Calmer Times: The Supreme Court and Red Monday* (Philadelphia: University of Pennsylvania Press, 1999); Powe, *Warren Court and American Politics*, chaps. 4, 6.

[82] Forrest Davis, "Court Reaches for Total Power," 33.

[83] Forrest Davis, "Court Reaches for Total Power," 33–34. Like Dickerman Williams, Davis, also citing Felix Frankfurter and Hugo Black, was quick to note Red Monday's inverted constitutional politics. Davis canvassed the outrage with which progressives had greeted the Supreme Court's decision in *Kilbourn* v. *Thompson*, 103 US 168 (1881), which had sharply limited Congress's investigatory powers, and cited as a case in point James M. Landis's "Constitutional Limitations on the Congressional Power of Investigations," which asserted that "no standard of judgment can be developed from Kilbourn v. Thompson. Its result contradicts an unbroken congressional practice, continuing even after the decision, with the increasing realization that committees of inquiry are necessary in order to make government effectively responsible to the electorate." Davis, "Court Reaches for Total Power," 34. See generally Kersch, *Constructing Civil Liberties*, 45–49, for a discussion of *Kilbourn* in developmental context.

[84] R. Carter Pittman, "The Fifth Amendment: Yesterday, Today and Tomorrow," *American Bar Association Journal* 42 (June 1956): 509–594, 509–510. Pittman was at the same time a prominent constitutional opponent of the civil rights movement. See R. Carter Pittman, *Equality v. Liberty: The Eternal Conflict* (Richmond: Virginia Commission on Constitutional Government, 1960).

In the *ABA Journal*, Robert C. Baker also emphasized the self-incrimination privilege's recent origins, dating no further back than the relatively recent, and atypical, "era when our Revolutionary fathers had acquired a hypersensitivity about governmental tyranny." "During most of the nineteenth and the earlier part of the twentieth centuries," Baker observed, "the concern over civil liberties abated considerably ... The American people had learned to take these liberties in their stride and demand only that they be given a sensible and rational application. They were satisfied if a reasonable balance was struck between personal freedom, on the one hand, and the public security, peace and good order, on the other." When conflicts arose, they were usually resolved in favor of concerns about peace, security, and good order. Contemporary civil libertarians were now seeking to make "civil rights" preeminent among society's concerns – a distortion of the American constitutional and political tradition. For these civil libertarians, "such rights have assumed almost the proportions of a fetish, an obsession, a mania; they have become an overwhelming, an all-consuming passion. These people are as disquieted about invasions of personal freedom as some of our ultra-conservative brethren are regarding the dissemination of Communistic propaganda." While those like "the Harvard savant" Erwin Griswold "would make the privilege available virtually to everyone and under almost any set of circumstances," Baker's view was that the rights of the criminal defendant must be understood in light of his duties not only to the innocent, but also in light of the peace and good order of the larger society which has served and protected him.[85]

After his own historical survey, Eugene Methvin, a senior editor at *Reader's Digest* who wrote frequently about the Supreme Court, constitutional law, and civil liberties, argued that "judicial elaboration has stretched the 5th Amendment and created new hurdles in criminal investigations." On this score, the innovation wrought by the Supreme Court in *Counselman* v. *Hitchcock* (1892) extending the self-incrimination privilege to witnesses, as opposed to criminal defendants, had been misguided. The error had been compounded by the innovation of allowing it to be invoked by those testifying in legislative hearings, as opposed to in criminal court. Methvin noted that, in fact, the Constitution had been so clear about this that he could not find a single instance in the nation's first 159 years in which a witness before Congress had ever invoked it.[86]

[85] Richard C. Baker, "Self-Incrimination: Is the Privilege an Anachronism?" *American Bar Association Journal* 42 (July 1956): 633–689, 634–635, 686–687.
[86] Eugene H. Methvin, "Let's Restore the Fifth Amendment," *Human Events* 30:9 (February 28, 1970), 8. *Counselman* v. *Hitchcock,* 142 US 547 (1892). See Kersch, *Constructing Civil Liberties,* 45–52. Methvin later published *The Rise of Radicalism* (New Rochelle, NY: Arlington House, 1973), an early entry in the intellectually ambitious, if not necessarily reliable, books on the Right that traced the New Left and Black Power movements back to Rousseau and – ludicrously – the Marxist-Leninism of Hitler and Mussolini (neither Hitler nor Mussolini were Marxist-Leninists). For a later examples of the ilk, see Jonah Goldberg, *Liberal Fascism:*

"Most thoughtful people probably would not care to see any part of the Fifth Amendment abolished. Still less do they care to see it abused," ventured John F. O'Conor of the legal department of the American Smelting and Refining Company, writing in the *ABA Journal*.[87] But no one has ever abused it as much (he said) as those refusing to answer questions about their communist loyalties before legislative investigating committees. Their testimony was not being coerced: the sole issue involved the legal implications of the witness's silence. In the end, O'Conor concluded, "It seems obvious enough ... that the witness who refuses to state whether or not he is a member of the Communist Party is either a Communist or a perjurer. If, as he asserts under oath, the answer would actually incriminate him, he must be a Communist. If he is not a Communist, the answer would not incriminate him, and he has perjured himself."[88] For his part, President Eisenhower's Attorney General Herbert Brownell saw a way around the problem: he advocated a law that would grant immunity from prosecution based on the witness's testimony.[89]

"No American uncontaminated by Communism has lost his good name because of congressional hearings on un-American activities," observed New York's aggressively anticommunist Francis Cardinal Spellman. Anyone who refused to answer questions before Congress, he told Catholics and others, "deserves to be held in suspicion because he constitutes a threat to our country's freedom, which has been won at too great a cost to be lightly lost." The government, after all, "has the right to know the kind of men it employs. It has a right to expect that its citizens will not have a divided loyalty." The cardinal warned that "[t]he anguished protests against 'McCarthyism' are not going to dissuade Americans from their desire to see Communists exposed and removed from positions where they can carry out their nefarious plans." As to the foreign opprobrium that supposedly would rain down on the United States for daring to protect itself, Cardinal Spellman was defiant: "If American prestige is going to suffer in Europe because of our understandable desire to keep our free society immune from Communist subversion, then it seems more a reflection upon European standards of honor and patriotism than on ours."[90]

The Secret History of the American Left from Mussolini to the Politics of Meaning (New York: Doubleday, 2008); Dinesh D'Souza, *The Big Lie: Exposing the Nazi Roots of the American Left* (Washington, DC: Regnery, 2017). See generally Ken I. Kersch, "Constitutional Conservatives Remember the Progressive Era," in Stephen Skowronek, Stephen Engel, and Bruce Ackerman, editors, *The Progressives' Century: Political Reform, Constitutional Government, and the Modern American State* (New Haven: Yale University Press, 2016).

[87] John F. O'Conor, "The Fifth Amendment: Should a Good Friend Be Abused?" *American Bar Association Journal* 41 (April 1955): 307–370, 307.

[88] O'Conor, "The Fifth Amendment," 307–370, 307–308.

[89] Herbert Brownell Jr., "The Bill of Rights: Liberty and Law Are Inseparable," *American Bar Association Journal* 41 (June 1955): 517–521, 520.

[90] Francis Cardinal Spellman, "In Answer to Our European Critics," *Reader's Digest* 64:384 (April 1954): 26–27.

Congressional investigating committees have a long history, and that history has, inevitably, been dotted with abuses, Irwin Ross noted, before pressing on to his conclusion that "[o]ver the long haul the good done by these inquiries has far outweighed the damage." Ross praised the Supreme Court's *Watkins* decision for holding these committees – what the Court called "the eyes and ears of Congress" – to their proper sphere, appropriately, given the value we properly place on civil liberties: "Obviously it is not the purpose of a Congressional committee to depose a union president or send a criminal to jail. Committees may not usurp the function of a grand jury or court. But if in the course of its proper business a committee spotlights a band of thieves or subversive conspirators the country is well served." The committees, moreover, helpfully roused public concern over the critical issue of domestic subversion.[91]

There were conservatives who also criticized HUAC even as they ultimately lent it their support. Max Eastman complained about "the loose acts of the House Committee on Un-American Activities," whose name he did not like: "No committee, Congressional or other," Eastman complained, "can decide what activities are American. Their business is with *seditious* and *treasonable* activities." "The committee has done many admirable and indispensible things," he noted. But "it has also done many foolish and damaging things." Still, in the end, the problem it was grappling with remained: liberty of opinion must be preserved, and revolutionary conspiracy must be stopped.[92] Eugene Lyons similarly adjudged that "[w]hile its career has naturally been marked by errors, false starts and indiscretions, [HUAC] will stand comparison with any Congressional undertaking of that scope." His ultimate assessment was that "[t]he committee is far from perfect – what Government body is flawless? – but it has been for 12 years and remains today the one successful enterprise in exposing Stalin's agents, spies and dupes in our midst."[93]

Rather than opposing HUAC for trenching on civil liberties and constitutional rights, some libertarians praised it on separation of powers grounds as a hopeful instance of increased congressional assertiveness at a time when the modern administrative state had distorted the constitutional system by too broadly limiting Congress's powers while radically augmenting those of the executive. In a lengthy article surveying the rise of executive power in conjunction with the "emasculat[tion]" of Congress, Frank Meyer called for a strengthening of Congress's investigatory powers as a possible means of bringing the executive branch to heel: "Far from being restrained, as the

[91] Irwin Ross, "What Good Are Congressional Investigations?" *Reader's Digest* 71:426 (October 1957): 60–64, 60, 62, 64; "The Right of Exposure," *Wall Street Journal* (March 13, 1957), 12.
[92] Max Eastman, "Why We Must Outlaw the Communist Party!" *Reader's Digest* 57:341 (September 1950): 42–44, 44.
[93] Eugene Lyons, "The Men the Reds Hate Most," *Reader's Digest* 57:343 (November 1950): 109–113, 111–113, reprinted, condensed, from *The American Legion Magazine* (October 1950). See also Ross, "What Good Are Congressional Investigations?" 60–64, 60, 64; "The Right of Exposure," *Wall Street Journal*.

current hue and cry demands, the investigatory powers will have to be much expanded, if the fundamental constitutional concept of checks and balances is to survive."[94]

FEDERALISM, EXECUTIVE POWER, AND ANTICOMMUNISM

It is important to recall, as the previous discussion has suggested, that while anti-anticommunist liberals of the era often saw anti-subversion measures as implicating civil liberties pure and simple, conservative constitutionalists focused on countervailing concerns involving the affirmative powers of government, considered those measures in a much broader context with implications for many other issues – and, indeed, for the rightful understanding of federalism and the separation of powers.

Questions of the rightful constitutional powers of the states, typically remembered as largely raising civil rights issues at mid-century, were apprehended by conservatives as pertaining to an array of contemporaneous policy areas being debated at the same time, including federalism and executive power.[95] The Supreme Court's decision in *Pennsylvania* v. *Nelson* (1956), for instance, ignited a major constitutional contretemps. Conservatives were outraged when in *Nelson* the Court "by sheer assertion" held that it is inherently the prerogative of the *federal* government to police subversives, with the corollary implication that *state* anti-subversion statutes were categorically unconstitutional because they interfered with the Smith Act's federal regulatory scheme.[96] A *National Review* editorial pleaded angrily that even the Justice Department's brief in the case had resisted arguing for this

---

[94] Frank S. Meyer, "The Revolt Against Congress," *National Review* (May 30, 1956) 2: 9, 10. See also "Power and Privilege," *Wall Street Journal* (April 3, 1958), 8 ("The Constitution is pretty plain, we think, as to who has the power in any ultimate showdown between the executive and the legislative branch. It is Congress."). *National Review*, of course, subsequently praised the Supreme Court's about-face on these issues in *Barenblatt* and *Uphaus*, which, on the cusp of the 1960s "Rights Revolution," turned out to be short lived. "The Court in Retreat," *National Review* (June 20, 1959), 7: 136, 136. ("By the Barenblatt and Uphaus opinions the Court implicitly admits that the investigatory power is a corollary of the legislative function.") *Barenblatt* v. *United States*, 360 US 109 (1959) (upholding the conviction of a professor for contempt of Congress against a First Amendment challenge arising out of his failure to testify about his communist associations before the House Un-American Activities Committee); *Uphaus* v. *Wyman*, 360 US 72 (1959) (upholding the conviction of the director of a New Hampshire summer camp for contempt for refusing to cooperate with the New Hampshire state legislature's investigation into subversive activities).

[95] See "Return to States Rights," *National Review* 1 (April 18, 1956): 4. See generally Ken I. Kersch, "Beyond Segregationist Subterfuge: Stories About Federalism in Postwar Conservative Constitutionalism," Paper presented at the American Studies Program Workshop, Princeton University, Princeton, New Jersey (October 2012).

[96] The constitutional question, it is worth noting, is the same as that involved in recent disputes over the respective powers of the states and the national government to police illegal immigration. See *Arizona* v. *United States*, 567 US 387 (2012).

position.[97] The shocked editors observed, "the states *have always been in the anti-sedition business.*"[98]

The states' rights issue was also raised in *Slochower* v. *Board of Education* (1956), which *National Review* dubbed the case of the "Fifth Amendment Professors."[99] There, the Court ruled that it was unconstitutional for municipalities to summarily dismiss employees who had invoked the Fifth Amendment when questioned about matters pertaining to their official conduct. "Once again," C. Dickerman Williams declared, "we find the Court guilty of irresponsible interference with local authority."[100] "The merit of such a statute may be debatable," Williams conceded, "but it is difficult to understand how it can take property without due process of law."[101]

Many conservatives also focused on the constitutional prerogatives of the executive in a constitutional separation of powers regime. Conservatives expressed consternation at what they took to be an increasingly common notion among liberals – which "until the last few years ... had never been suggested" – that federal employees had a constitutional right to their jobs, and that, when facing dismissal, they were entitled to full-scale trials, at which they had a right to confront the witnesses against them under the Sixth Amendment's Confrontation Clause.[102] C. Dickerman Williams wondered when this had become the liberal party line. In an article in *National Review*, Williams needled liberal grandee Arthur Schlesinger Jr., author of *The Age of Jackson* (1945) who, Williams noted, had once been such a swooning celebrant of Old Hickory's claims of sweeping executive powers to remove any and all from government employment unchecked, at will. Williams found more recent antecedents for at-will removal from federal employment in a McKinley administration executive order (July 27, 1897), which, at the time, the *New York Times* had supported as "a notable stride" and "an important bulwark of the merit system." No less a figure than the Progressive paladin Wisconsin Senator "Fighting Bob" LaFollette had, in fact, codified McKinley's action into federal law in August 1912. "Indeed," Williams explained to *National Review* readers, "it was Senator La Follette who made explicit that 'no examination of witnesses nor any trial or hearing shall be required except in the

---

[97] "The Court's Pleasure," *National Review* (April 25, 1956), 5. See also Henry Hazlitt, "Court or Constitution?" *National Review* (September 1, 1956) 2: 14, 14. *Pennsylvania* v. *Nelson*, 350 US 497 (1956).

[98] "The New York Times Debates an Issue," *National Review* (April 12, 1958) 5: 342, 343 [emphasis in original]. See Bozell, *The Warren Revolution*, 58–59.

[99] C. Dickerman Williams, "The Case of the Fifth Amendment Professors," *National Review* (March 23, 1957) 3: 285. *Slochower* v. *Board of Education*, 350 US 551 (1956).

[100] "The Court's Pleasure," *National Review* (April 25, 1956), 5.

[101] C. Dickerman Williams, "Fourteenth Amendment Legislation," *National Review* (May 16, 1956): 1: 17.

[102] US Constitution, Amendment Six, provides that "in all criminal prosecutions, the accused shall enjoy the right ... to be confronted with the witnesses against him."

discretion of the officer making the removal.'" Interestingly, Dickerman Williams observed, "Complaints against this procedure, if any, did not gain public attention until after President Truman's executive order of March 21, 1947 providing for a loyalty program and the Security Risk Act of August 26, 1950." But, under the circumstances, Truman's order was manifestly reasonable:

The evidence establishes beyond peradventure that the Soviet Union recruits secret agents through the Communist Party and Communist fronts, who are instructed to, and frequently do, transmit information to the Soviet apparatus and influence policy on behalf of the Soviet Union: that the Soviet Union has developed the Fifth Column technique to an extent unprecedented in the history of great powers.[103]

In a subsequent take, Williams reminded readers that the government employer-employee relationship was not, as many claim, inherently republican, but feudal. There was no requirement, he insisted, that someone be convicted of a crime to remove them from employment: it is enough that they had lost the confidence of their superiors. But "[t]oday we see on every hand a ... tendency to treat employment as a matter of status."[104] Our republican Founders understood better: "James Madison, 'the Father of the Constitution,' himself had declared an unqualified removal power to be solely 'an executive power.'"[105]

None of this, Williams – who was in many respects a civil libertarian – made clear, was a defense of the government's dismissal policies as they had actually been practiced. Indeed, Williams regretted that "the present security program would appear to be working somewhat less than perfectly." He was troubled that "the government appears to be making no attempt to defend the program or to explain the instances of apparent maladministration of which the public continually hears."[106]

After vigorously praising the Bill of Rights as "a precious heritage," "a ringing and eternal challenge to the totalitarian philosophy that would make of man a helpless robot in the hands of an all-powerful state," William Henry Chamberlin, the Haverford- educated former Greenwich Village radical and Bolshevik sympathizer turned relentless anticommunist,[107] drew a sharp

---

[103] C. Dickerman Williams, "The Problem of Security," *National Review* (February 22, 1956) 1: 19, 19.
[104] C. Dickerman Williams, "Republican or Feudal?" *National Review* (February 16, 1957) 3: 159.
[105] "New York Times Debates an Issue," 343. See also "A Little Disloyalty," *Wall Street Journal* (June 14, 1956), 14.
[106] C. Dickerman Williams, "Removal of Federal Employees: Sound Discretion and Constitutional Rights," *National Review* (January 18, 1956), 1: 22. He added, "Security officers are not infallible; neighbors and associates are quite likely to confuse Communism with interest in anti-Communism, doctrinaire Socialism, world government, race relations, etc. ... To continue to rely on associations in respect of security has its dangers." Williams, "The Problem of Security," 20.
[107] See William Henry Chamberlin, *Soviet Russia: A Living Record and History* (Boston: Little, Brown & Co., 1930); William Henry Chamberlin, *The Confessions of an Individualist* (New York: Macmillan Co., 1940); William Henry Chamberlin, *Blueprint for World*

distinction between the use of a man's unwillingness to testify in a criminal prosecution against him and its enlistment in an assessment of his fitness to hold "a position of public or private trust and confidence." "[E]mployment," Chamberlin emphasized, "is not a right, but a privilege."[108]

Conservatives warned in the late 1950s that the Warren Court seemed to be returning to "its pre-Korean [War] policy of putting such a strong emphasis on civil rights that the executive and legislative branches (federal and state) may be hampered in their efforts to defend the country from subversives." A writer for the *ABA Journal* defended the Hatch Act extensions (1955) that reaffirmed the federal government's power to require employee loyalty oaths and to fire and refuse to hire communists. Any executive, including one in the government, had an inherent power to hire and fire at will. Admittedly, "in this comparatively new and delicate field injustices have arisen from faulty administration of the loyalty program." But "[t]hese instances have been exaggerated in the public mind by ignorance of the *nature* of the proceedings and the tremendous publicity given to a few *causes célèbres.*"[109]

CONSERVATIVES, LIBERALS, AND CIVIL LIBERTIES: THE CHALLENGE OF COMMUNISM

In 1952, under the subheading "Do We Defend our Rights by Protecting Communists?" the former City College Trotskyist and future neoconservative eminence Irving Kristol (father of the future "East Coast" Straussian, *Weekly*

Conquest (Chicago: Human Events, 1946); William Henry Chamberlin, *America's Second Crusade* (Chicago: Regnery, 1950); William Henry Chamberlin, *The Evolution of a Conservative* (Chicago: Regnery, 1959).

[108] William Henry Chamberlin, "Constitutional Confusion," *Wall Street Journal* (September 29, 1953), 10. Chamberlin also applied this thinking to state-level actions against public university and school teachers. For teachers, he argued, "[c]haracter, as well as scholarship, is a reasonable qualification." And "membership in or affiliation with a movement implacably hostile to American ideals and institutions, blindly devoted to an alien dictatorship and opposed to any semblance of freedom of thought and inquiry is certainly a formidable disqualification for honest and effective teaching." See also "Pensions and the Fifth Amendment," *Wall Street Journal* (August 20, 1954), 6 (approving of government denial of pensions to employees who invoke the Fifth Amendment in inquiries into subversion); "Obvious Cause," *Wall Street Journal* (January 3, 1955), 10 (approving of General Electric's firing of employees who invoke the Fifth Amendment in inquiries into subversion).

[109] Frank B. Ober, "Communism and the Court: An Examination of Recent Developments," *American Bar Association Journal* 44 (January 1958): 35–89, 35, 38. See also " Loyalty and Public Office," *Wall Street Journal* (March 5, 1952), 8 (supporting the Supreme Court's decision in *Adler v. Board of Education* (1952)); Garet Garrett, "Court and Classroom," *Wall Street Journal* (March 14, 1952), 4. ("Why should an art teacher impart ideas about socialism? Why should a teacher of history in the public schools be openly hostile to Franco's Spain? Why should the English teacher wish to measure with praise or criticism, revolutionary overtones in novels or plays? Is the subject literature or politics? Is the wisdom or unwisdom of the Korean war a proper school room subject for 'teaching' children?")

Standard founder, former Fox News commentator, and Never Trumper Bill Kristol) published "'Civil Liberties,' 1952 – A Study in Confusion" in *Commentary* magazine. While dismissing Joe McCarthy himself as "a vulgar demagogue" dripping with "irresponsible rhetoric," Kristol's main interest and target were the Wisconsin senator's liberal critics – "the Alan Barths, the Henry Steele Commagers, the Zechariah Chafees, the Howard Mumford Jones's, the Ralph Barton Perry's, [and] the William O. Douglases."[110] Kristol found in the attacks of these professional anti-anticommunists on "McCarthyism" evidence of an all-too-typical academic sensibility. They were fatuously quixotic, and the wooly stories they told themselves were fairy tales. "On the one side," as liberals in academia saw it, "are the men of intellect and sensibility, fair-minded and generous-hearted ... On the other are the mindless men, the kind who get elected to office when the spirit of the age reverts to primitivism." Of course, their "ready quotations from Jefferson about the trees of liberty and the blood of tyrants, the sonorous repetition of Justice Holmes's dissenting opinions, the schoolmaster's measured accents alternating with prophetic indignation – the whole battery has failed significantly to make an impression on the dominant American mood." Nevertheless, "in proportion as they fail in strength, they gain in their sense of petulant righteousness." Kristol wondered: "Is it conceivable that the line was incorrectly drawn in the first place?" He continued, "For there is one thing that the American people know about Senator McCarthy; he, like them, is unequivocally anti-Communist. About the spokesmen for American liberalism, they feel they know no such thing. And with some justification."[111]

Typical of the anti-anticommunist genre, Kristol reported, was a 1947 *Harper's* magazine article by the Columbia University historian Henry Steele Commager, prominently reprinted in Howard Mumford Jones's *Primer on Intellectual Freedom* (1949) ("Evil won a transient victory in the seats of power and Good won a permanent niche in the anthologies – a familiar tale," Kristol snidely observed). In that article, Commager had written critically of the McCarthyite reaction to an educational presentation about Russia by a Russian schoolgirl at a Washington, DC, public school. While Commager had indignantly described that speech as containing "nothing that any normal person could find objectionable," Kristol had tracked down the text of the girl's speech, which, it turned out, was an unremitting paean to the freedoms of Soviet society. Commager's report had been profoundly misleading: "Professor Commager can argue that it will not harm American school children to encounter an occasional Communist apologist in the flesh; one may even go further to say it would do them good." But to have introduced the girl as an informed reporter rather than a communist apologist had been deceitful:

---

[110] Irving Kristol, "'Civil Liberties,' 1952 – A Study in Confusion," *Commentary* (1952), 229, 231.
[111] Kristol, "'Civil Liberties,' 1952," 228–229.

[E]verything she said should have been objectionable to every normal person, and especially to a historian like Professor Commager – for the good and sufficient reason that it was a tissue of lies. For Professor Commager to defend the rights of Communists to free speech is one thing, for him to assert that there is nothing objectionable in mendacious pleading in support of Communism is quite another. The conclusion "any normal person" will draw from such behavior is that, for whatever reason, his critical faculties are less alert when he looks out of the left corner of his eye.

The problem was the lens of ideology through which Commager had viewed the encounter. Commager, Kristol observed, "seems to be seduced by the insidious myth according to which Communism is a political trend continuous with liberalism and democratic socialism," a myth, Kristol acidly noted, shared by McCarthy himself, and one that Kristol – who was, at the time, still a liberal – found reprehensible when lodged by conservatives against the New Deal. All too many liberals were allowing idealistic motives to trump any charges of communist taint.[112]

Kristol demanded intellectual honesty from (his fellow) liberals in their defenses of civil liberties: "[I]f one wishes to defend the civil liberties of Communists (as the Senator [McCarthy] does not), one must do so on the same grounds that one defends the civil liberties of Nazis and fascists – no more, no less." "[I]f a Nazi had, in 1938, addressed a high-school audience in this country, extolling the accomplishments of Hitler's regime, presenting a thoroughly fictitious account of life in Nazi Germany, never once mentioning the existence of concentration camps," Kristol asked, "would Professor Commager find in such a speech 'nothing that any normal person could find objectionable'?":

Unfortunately, it is quite as impossible to tell the citizens of Oshkosh, some of whom have suffered personal loss as a result of the war in Korea, that there is no harm in having their children taught the three R's by a Communist, as it would have been to persuade the citizens of Flatbush in 1939 that there was no cause for excitement in their children being taught by a Nazi, or to convince a businessman that it is a smart practice for him to pay a handsome salary to someone pledged to his "liquidation."[113]

Immense distortions, Kristol contended, were being wrought by "the gross metaphysic of the liberal Manichee, apportioning the universe to 'forward-looking' and 'backward-looking' demiurges." Strangest of all, perhaps, was the moralizing penchant of civil libertarians for defending staunch party-line communist fellow travelers, apparently in "all sincerity," as nonconformists and free thinkers. This was "a refusal to see communism for what it is: a movement guided by conspiracy and aiming at totalitarianism, rather than merely another form of 'dissent' or 'nonconformity.'"[114]

[112] Kristol, "'Civil Liberties,' 1952," 229–234.
[113] Kristol, "'Civil Liberties,' 1952," 230, 236.
[114] Kristol, "'Civil Liberties,' 1952," 230–232, 235.

Kristol's article provoked a vigorous response from *Commentary* readers, including the magazine's own Alan Westin, an influential Columbia University civil liberties scholar, whose views, the editors said, spoke for "many others who felt that Mr. Kristol's treatment of the subject showed insufficient concern for the preservation of civil liberties." Westin noted that Kristol's charge that the liberal civil libertarians were soft on communism ignored anticommunist work by liberal anticommunist groups (like the Americans for Democratic Action), in the process "adroitly strip[ing] [them] of their anti-communist beliefs." This amounted to "a smear" through "fine phrase-making." "A smear is still a smear," Westin riposted, "even when done in onomatopoeia."[115]

Westin also homed in on an undercurrent in Kristol's article, evincing "serenity" about denying civil liberties protections to communists. Kristol, Westin argued, had cagily "redefined the term 'civil liberties'" in a way that absolved himself from having to take a stand on the day's most vexing civil liberties controversies. As such, in his article, Kristol had "so effectively side-stepped the problem of civil liberties that he is standing forty yards to the rear, throwing rocks at the foibles of the participants." In troubled times, it was essential, Westin said, "to restate the bedrock principle upon which our constitutional freedoms rest."[116]

Sidney Hook's response focused on the Smith Act, which he criticized while offering suggestions about how needful legislation aimed at communist subversion might have been more sensitively drafted. In the end, however, Hook emphasized,

> However doubtful the wisdom of enacting the Smith law [in its current form], the wisdom of now repealing it is even more doubtful. Such repeal would give new life to an illusion whose widespread and pernicious character was partly responsible for the original enactment of the Act: namely, that the Communist party is a political party like any other on the American scene and therefore entitled to the same rights and privileges as all other American political parties.

Hook joined Kristol in scoring the fatuousness of the liberal academic mind, and lamenting its grip on college and university faculties. Of course, civil liberties, rightly understood, were important; they should be protected through "continuing the process of reasonable amendment" of the laws appropriately enacted to protect the country from domestic subversion.[117]

The future UC-Berkeley and Harvard University sociologist Nathan Glazer, then an editor at *Commentary* (and, subsequently, in conjunction with Irving Kristol and Daniel Bell, a co-founder of the pioneering neoconservative policy journal *The Public Interest* (1965)) emphasized the need for forthright and

---

[115] Alan F. Westin, "Our Freedom – and the Rights of Communists: A Reply to Irving Kristol," *Commentary* 14 (July 1952): 33–40, 33, 35.
[116] Westin, "Our Freedom," 35–36.
[117] Sidney Hook, "Does the Smith Act Threaten Our Liberties?" *Commentary* 15 (January 1953): 63–73.

honest discussion. "A generation raised on campaigns for the defense of the civil liberties of socialists, pacifists, anarchists, and an outspoken or queer teacher here or there," Glazer wrote, "encountered no perplexities to trouble and confuse its mind about defending dissidents ... But now the matter has become more difficult and complex." Glazer set out the unstated ideological assumptions of postwar liberal social science that, in his view, had, unfortunately, deformed the debate. Assessing Samuel A. Stouffer's *Communism, Conformity, and Civil Liberties: A Cross-Section of the Nation* (1955), a public opinion survey sponsored by the Ford Foundation's Fund for the Republic (which was committed to the defense of civil liberties), Glazer homed in on the class dimensions of the public opinion data on the civil liberties issue. "The general finding that the community leaders are more tolerant than the ordinary run of people," Glazer observed,

> will come as no surprise to readers of public opinion polls, who have long known that the educated take civil liberties more seriously than the rest of the country does. The fact, however, that even commanders of the American Legion posts and regents of the Daughters of the American Revolution are far more liberal than the American people in general, is a surprise .... [T]he American populace is ... woefully indifferent to the ordinary requirements of democracy.

Then again, the Ford Foundation survey found, "Most people just don't seem to be terribly concerned about domestic Communism – or any political issue." "The concentrations of the 'less tolerant,'" the study had found, "are to be found among the old, the poorly educated, Southerners, and small-town dwellers and farmers." Labor union leaders, presumed liberals, though, were no more tolerant than presidents of chambers of commerce.[118]

Glazer observed that "Professor Stouffer does not study the problem of Communism directly, but treats it as part of the larger problem of 'conformism.'" Stouffer also blithely placed those worried about a communist threat into the "intolerant" category. "[W]hat has been forgotten," the sociologist Glazer complained, "is that as a matter of fact there are people who perceive the Communist threat and yet are tolerant." Glazer suggested that "we may ... decide that the best policy is to try to increase their number. And this can be done not only by teaching tolerance to those who perceive the Communist threat, but teaching the tolerant about Communism."[119]

---

[118] Nathan Glazer, "Civil Liberties and the American People: Tolerance and Anti-Communism," *Commentary* 20 (August 1955): 169–176, 169–172. Samuel A. Stouffer, *Communism, Conformity, and Civil Liberties: A Cross-Section of the Nation* (Garden City, NY: Doubleday, 1955). See also Luff, *Commonsense Anticommunism*.

[119] Kristol made a similar point in commenting on the romanticization of nonconformism. Irving Kristol, "The Adversary Culture of the Intellectuals," *Encounter* 53 (October 1979). See also Norman Podhoretz, "The Know-Nothing Bohemians," *Partisan Review* 25 (Spring 1958): 305–311; Norman Podhoretz, "The Beat Generation," *Partisan Review* 25 (Summer 1958): 476–479; Glazer, "Civil Liberties and the American People," 173–174.

In light of these social scientific slights of hand, Glazer went on to explain the perils of an ideologized – though apparently neutral and value-free – social science, and to set out the types of errors to which it is prone: "We are all familiar with the kind of thinking that Dr. Stouffer has, I think, inadvertently fallen into: the position that says, if we want people to be more tolerant of Negroes, it is possibly best that they should not believe there are a disproportionately large number of Negro criminals and paupers – even though there are." The flaw here is in "slavishly accept[ing] whatever cluster of attitudes fall together at any given moment as organically and necessarily related." "In any case," Glazer insisted,

it would seem crucial to determine whether internal Communism represents a threat or not: if it does not, there is no conflict between the values of truth and tolerance. If it does, then there is a conflict ... But on this crucial *if*, Dr. Stouffer does not commit himself. Dr. Stouffer, I think, would like to take the position that the threat is exaggerated; but hampered by a crippling notion of scientific objectivity, he never quite decides to take the leap.

"Because there is no way of deciding the extent of the Communist threat with the methods of public opinion research," Glazer observed, "Dr. Stouffer finds it impossible to take a stand on this question. And yet if social science is to make a contribution to a problem it must try to encompass it in all its reality – and not limit itself to that part of it which falls within the purview of its favorite methods." Alas, "Dr. Stouffer works with one major value – tolerance. Everything else is secondary. And what is associated (statistically speaking) with tolerance should flourish like the green bay tree, and what is associated with intolerance should wither away and die, if we are to have a good society." "It is possible," Glazer summed up, "to be intolerant out of sadistic and brutal inquisitiveness about other people. It is also possible to be 'intolerant,' at least to some extent, out of a love of one's country and a rational and strong belief that it is so seriously threatened that certain measures, unnecessary in other times and in the face of other enemies, may be necessary."[120]

CHRISTIAN ANTICOMMUNISM

The New York City Jews who started out as Left-Wing anticommunists who would either migrate toward or soon be classed as part of the conservative coalition, like Irving Kristol, Sidney Hook, and Nathan Glazer, shared their staunch anticommunism with born-to-the-breed Rightists of the sort many of them would have never otherwise encountered in Brooklyn or the Bronx. Their

---

[120] Glazer, "Civil Liberties and the American People," 174–175. When a law was passed mandating that communist affiliated organizations register all the printing or publishing equipment they had access to, the *Wall Street Journal*'s editorial writers criticized it on free press grounds, arguing that "[s]uch laws could conceivably more endanger [the] Constitution than thwart the evil." "Chipping Away?" *Wall Street Journal* (August 10, 1954), 8.

new compatriots harbored different understandings of, and attitudes toward, communism's dangers.

It is hard to imagine Kristol, Hook, or Glazer emphasizing – at least prior to the 1980s – as did John F. O'Conor of the American Smelting and Refining Company, that the red-hot core of the problem was that communists are "atheistic." The communist, O'Conor elaborated, places "his own belief of what is good above compliance with Divine and human laws."[121] For Christians like O'Conor, the problem was not so much the communist's absence of faith, but his allegiance to an alternative faith, a counter-religion, hell-bent on "ferreting out and crushing doubters and infidels," bent on conquering the Christian West.[122] Its gods were Man, and Man's handmaiden, the secular State.[123] As revolutionaries bent on societal transformation, atheistic communists had done no less than declare war on Christianity and Christians: Conservative Christians understood themselves and theirs as standing ready to fight the Holy War for God and country – and the future of the Free World. Leadership in sounding the alarm was assumed by figures such as "the quintessential Cold War revivalist" the Reverend Billy Graham, who linked the redemption of individual souls to the success of the nation in its existential standoff with communism. The Holy War pitted the forces of communism, led by Satan himself, against Christ's legions, garrisoned in the godly United States.[124]

Reader's Digest had an outsized attraction to human interest stories involving Christian soldiers in this war. Stanley High, the former *Christian Herald* editor, FDR speechwriter, and *Reader's Digest* senior editor, insisted

---

[121] John F. O'Conor, "The Fifth Amendment: Should a Good Friend Be Abused?" *American Bar Association Journal* 41 (April 1955): 307–370, 309. It is worth noting that the American Smelting and Refining Company, a mining concern operating chiefly in the US West and Mexico, and today known as ASARCO, was actually founded (in 1899) by Jewish New Yorkers – the Guggenheims – and headquartered in New York.

[122] Eugene Lyons, "Khrushchev: The Killer in the Kremlin," *Reader's Digest* 71:425 (September 1957): 102–109, 103, 105; Stanley High, "Do Billy Graham's 'Crusades' Have Lasting Effect?" *Reader's Digest* (September 1955): 77–82, 79.

[123] See, e.g., Norman Vincent Peale, "Let the Church Speak Up for Capitalism," *Reader's Digest* 57:341 (September 1950): 126–130, 128.

[124] Steven P. Miller, *Billy Graham and the Rise of the Republican South* (Philadelphia: University of Pennsylvania Press, 2009), 22–23. Graham counted among his many influential supporters and interlocutors the founder and publisher of Time-Life, Henry Luce, and FBI Director J. Edgar Hoover. The Rev. Billy James Hargis was another prominent evangelical Cold War revivalist. See, e.g., Billy James Hargis, *Communist America: Must It Be?* (Tulsa, OK: Christian Crusade, 1960); Billy James Hargis, *The Facts About Communism and Our Churches?* (Tulsa, OK: Christian Crusade, 1962); Billy James Hargis,, *Communism: The Total Lie* (Tulsa, OK: Christian Crusade, 1963); Billy James Hargis,, *A Satanic Conspiracy Undermines the USA* (Tulsa, OK: Christian Crusade, 1972); Billy James Hargis,, *Why I Fight for a Christian America* (Nashville, TN: Thomas Nelson, 1974). See also Kruse, *One Nation Under God*; Timothy H. Sherwood, *The Rhetorical Leadership of Fulton J. Sheen, Norman Vincent Peale, and Billy Graham in the Age of Extremes* (Lanham, MD: Lexington Books, 2013).

in the mid-1950s that a lasting peace could only be achieved through the "reviving among free peoples of a dynamic religious faith." "Western democracy," High argued, "must base its appeal on more than freedom, more than prosperity, it must base its appeal on *religion*." Freedom could triumph only if fortified by "multitudes of ordinary men and women stirred and exalted by religious faith": "The goal should be nothing short of inviting every single person in every single country who believes in a Supreme Being to join in this mighty, intense act of faith." Americans, with a heritage that included Benjamin Franklin's appeal for daily prayers at the Constitutional Convention as "the threat of failure loomed" and Abraham Lincoln's appeals to God when "the fate of the Union [was] at stake," were truly a light unto the world in this twilight civilizational struggle.[125]

Testimonies from Red China, where the world was witnessing "the most frightful regimentation in history," abounded in *Readers' Digest*.[126] The magazine, for instance, recounted the good works of the Rev. Waltston Hayes, a Pennsylvania minister who "sent the first well-trained native Christian ministers throughout ... [China] to preach not only the Gospel but Western civilization and its benefits." The communists, however, were ruthless in their treatment of Hayes's son, who had determined to carry on his father's mission, harassing, arresting, imprisoning, and ultimately brainwashing him – all in a fanatical effort to turn the younger Hayes "against God, Christianity, the United States, everything he believed in." He was up against it, and how. But "John Hayes' faith had always been very real, and he had long felt close to his God." After "pray[ing] as he had never prayed before," *Reader's Digest* recounted, Hayes was delivered from the brainwashing of the Reds and held fast to his love of God, country, and Jesus Christ.[127]

Madame Chiang Kai-shek shared the centrality of Christian prayer to her life in *Readers' Digest*'s pages. There, she recounted how, just before her mother's death, her mother had succeeded in converting Madame Chiang's husband, the Chinese Nationalist leader Chiang Kai-shek, to Christianity and got him, on the eve of their marriage, to promise her daughter that he would diligently study the Holy Bible. Now, Madame Chiang, the First Lady of Formosa (Taiwan), reported, "Every morning at 6:30 we pray together and share devotional reading and discussions. Every night before retiring, we also pray together." Madame Chiang recounted how she had founded, and leads, a prayer group in

---

[125] Stanley High, "Our Prayers Could Change the World," *Reader's Digest* 66:394 (February 1955): 56–58, 56–57 [emphasis in original]. See Jean Edward Smith, *FDR* (New York: Random House, 2007), 364.

[126] James Bell, "The Nightmare of Life in China's Communes," *Reader's Digest* 74:443 (March 1959): 37–41, 37–38. The description of "regimentation" was the same lodged against FDR by opponents of the New Deal. See, e.g., Herbert Hoover, *The Challenge to Liberty* (New York: Charles Scribner's Son's, 1934).

[127] Frederic Sondern Jr., "The Brainwashing of John Hayes," *Reader's Digest* 67:399 (July 1955): 27–32, 28, 30.

Formosa, which has met "every Wednesday afternoon ... without fail for five years." "It has been part of the Communist technique to rob us of our faith," she reported. Christians needed to reassert themselves, to evince "the spiritual fire to *insist* on a better world." "'[T]he family that prays together, stays together,'" she taught. "Would it not also," she asked, "be true of nations?"[128]

Like Madame Chiang, Harold R. Medina, a New York City US district judge appointed to the bench by Harry Truman who presided over the 1949 trial of eleven leaders of the Communist Party USA (CPUSA) under the Smith Act, also testified in *Reader's Digest* of the centrality of prayer to his life and, indeed, his public function as a judge. Describing himself as "a more or less typical American," Medina explained that "[f]rom boyhood I have had an implicit and unquestioning faith." The judge noted "that humility and prayer are as important in my daily work as a knowledge of the law." Over time, Medina became "more and more aware that I am a servant not only of the people but of Someone else." He came to appreciate that, as a federal judge, "my work was a part of a universal fabric, part and parcel of the moral law, divine in origin": "The mysterious presence makes itself felt in every trial in my courtroom. It is as if Someone is always watching me, urging me to make sure that my rulings are conscientious and merciful. More and more I come to realize that my acts will be futile unless each one fits into the moral law which governs all." Medina recounted the immense difficulties he faced in trying the leaders of the CPUSA, and how God had seen him through: "It took me a long time to realize what the Communists were trying to do to me – to wear me down until I lost my self-control and occasioned a mistrial. But as I felt myself getting weaker and weaker, and found the burden more and more difficult to bear, I sought strength where I have sought it all my life, from the one Source that never fails ... Someone else was with me, all the way."[129]

Communism's ultimate goal was to subvert God by subverting his hearth and home, the place where he was more honored than any other nation on earth: the United States of America. Viewed in this framework, moves by the Supreme Court to take God out of the nation's public schools were seen as part and parcel of the communist master plan. The effort was succeeding in Europe, once a secure base of Christian civilization. In Germany, "[t]he Communists moved first to choke the church by getting at the children," Stanley High reported, "The long-established German system of religious instruction in the public schools was abolished; religious instructors were fired." Laymen there tried to organize outside religion classes but – recounting events undoubtedly

[128] Madame Chiang Kai-shek, "The Power of Prayer," *Reader's Digest* 67:400 (August 1955): 52–58, 53, 55, 57–58 [emphasis in original].
[129] Judge Harold R. Medina, "Someone Else on the Bench," *Reader's Digest* 59:352 (August 1951): 16–18. The article is bannered above the title with the words "A famous jurist tells of the help he has received through prayer." The convictions obtained in Medina's courtroom were subsequently upheld by the US Supreme Court in *Dennis* v. *United States*, 341 US 494 (1951).

aimed at reminding readers of the US Supreme Court's recent release-time decision in *McCollum* v. *Board of Education* (1948) – "[t]o discourage attendance, the Communists forbade them to hold classes until two hours after the end of the school day. Classes were then moved into private homes." In Germany's state schools, High reported, "an intensive course indoctrinated them in the 'scientific basis of our new, progressive society.'" In a book given to every German schoolchild, the Christian faith was labeled "superstition," and organized Christianity was described as a means by which "reactionary forces suppress the people."[130] One wondered: could it happen here? All signs indicated that the process had already begun.[131]

CONCLUSION

The developmental trajectory of the stories conservatives told about communism in the postwar era was distinctive. Those stories were most intense – seared into the minds of not only conservatives but also the country as a whole – during the first four years of the 1950s, just as the modern conservative movement was being launched. The timing was not coincidental. While the Old Right had been shaped in reaction to Franklin Roosevelt's New Deal and the US rise to world leadership, the modern movement was galvanized by the outbreak of the Cold War and the civil rights movement. While the Cold War had begun a few years earlier (1947), the emotional impact of conservative anticommunism was ramped up by the McCarthy Era's (1950–1954) intensity. It was in this crucible that the modern movement's anticommunist frame was forged. As such, its development involved not so much an evolution of the frame's contents over time – the evolutionary pattern followed by liberals from the 1930s onward – but, rather, variations in the degree to which movement participants held fast to an essentially fixed frame, in both its substance and intensity, as new incidents arose and circumstances changed. Not unrelatedly, it also involved variations in the extent to which movement participants chose to apprehend unfolding incidents and events through this frame's prism. For many movement participants, it was always the early 1950s, a moment of existential choice, with the future of Western civilization imminently at stake. The question

---

[130] Stanley High, "Red Germany's Losing War Against the Church," *Reader's Digest* 71:426 (October 1957): 198–201, 199, 200. *McCollum* v. *Board of Education*, 333 US 203 (1948). In the *McCollum* case, which was brought by an atheist, the Supreme Court declared release time from classes specifically for religious instruction to violate the First Amendment's Establishment Clause. High's account implicitly places the Supreme Court in a position analogous to the East German communist leadership.

[131] High warned his readers that liberals – particularly the "militant minority" of liberal Protestant clergy who claimed to be Christians – could be just as dangerous in this regard as out-and-out atheists. Stanley High, "How Radical Are the Clergy?" *Reader's Digest* 58:348 (April 1951): 118–120, 118, 120.

"which side are you on?" for them always went to the heart of the issue. And they were adamant that not only in their views on foreign policy but also on issues like domestic regulation and administration, civil liberties, and civil rights, liberals and the liberal-left were, at base, on the side of the enemy.

The trajectory of right-wing anticommunism was shaped by the intensity of the perceived danger. As William James has observed, "where the character, as ... distinguished from the intellect, is concerned, the causes of human diversity lie chiefly in our *differing susceptibilities of emotional excitement*, and in the *different impulses and inhibitions* which these bring in their train."[132] For most on the postwar Right, anticommunism was more than an intellectual or a policy position: it was a profoundly resonant emotional universe, a world in which they lived.

The tenor and register of conservative anticommunism differed from that of liberal anticommunism of even the most uncompromising sort. While anticommunist liberals tended to apprehend communism as chiefly a threat to modern liberal democracy, conservatives tended to be obsessed with it as evil *per se* – a subtle but significant difference. Many on the Right considered communism first and foremost as a repudiation of God, and, indeed, a challenge and threat to their personal faith and salvation.[133] As such, their anticommunism triggered a religious zealotry itching to go toe-to-toe with the anti-Christian foe.

This was apparent in some of the postwar Right's most prominent conversion stories. In these, Hard Left, atheistic communist zealots like Whittaker Chambers became Hard-Right believing Christian zealots, undergoing conversion experiences in which they publicly repudiated evil, were washed in the waters, and born again.[134] A single powerful idea moved to the center of the convert's being: everything else "re-chystallize[d] about it." For those like Chambers, a man with "an inborn genius for certain emotions," it was not enough to no longer practice communism: it had to be repudiated so as to work a total, galvanizing transformation of his being. For these converts, a renewed commitment to their country and its governing principles was not simply a change of political views, but a path to no less than a unified self, in which "a period of storm and stress and inconsistency" was supplanted by "a firmness, stability, and equilibrium." As such, the conversion brought a state of Grace, by which "the soul arrives ... at a certain fixed and invincible state ... which is

---

[132] William James, *The Varieties of Religious Experience: A Study in Human Nature* (New York: Modern Library, 2002 [1902]), 287 [emphasis in original].
[133] William James noted that while evil is undoubtedly a disease, "worry over disease is itself an additional form of disease, which only adds to the original complaint." Such worry can paradoxically end as "a way of maximizing evil ... based on the persuasion that the evil aspects of our life are of its very essence, and that the world's meaning most comes home to us when we lay them most to heart." James, *Varieties of Religious Experience*, 144, 148.
[134] John 3:3.

genuinely heroic, and from out of which the greatest deeds which it ever performs are executed."[135]

The tenor and register of conservative anticommunism also differed from that of liberal anticommunism in that conservatives found the existential threat lurking in the country's modern New Deal administrative, regulatory, and social welfare programs, and in new statutory and constitutional initiatives promoting civil liberties and civil rights, all of which, of course, liberal anticommunists strongly supported. Anticommunist Cold War liberals like Arthur Schlesinger Jr., Reinhold Niebuhr, and (pre–Reagan administration) Jeanne Kirkpatrick, Scoop Jackson, and Richard Perle (who were later classed as neoconservatives) drew few if any analogies between the trajectory of domestic liberalism involving the modern American regulatory and social welfare state, civil liberties, and civil rights and either support for, or a dangerous complacency about, communism and the communist threat. There was, to be sure, a real conflict and opposition between Marxist communism and market capitalism. But many on the Right were adamant that there could be no grey areas, compromises, or middle grounds. Along these lines, as noted, some ex-communist Rightists in particular seemed to have simply substituted an absolutist stance on free markets for their erstwhile communist faith. Indeed, they often took liberal denials of communist affinities and professions of their moderation to be either dissembling or fatuous. John Chamberlain and others frequently attributed the mainstream media's bias against them, their ilk, and their cause to "journalists who had grown up in the depression era [and] distrusted the whole free enterprise position." "Being half-heartedly socialists themselves," Chamberlain ventured, "they couldn't really see they had a mission to oppose the Communists." Although liberals might not be communists by conviction, they were nevertheless, at least, fellow travelers. In an era in which the future of the free world was at stake – including the survival of the United States as a free country – support for administrative and social welfare state liberalism came perilously close to treason. Liberals could facilely conclude that communism was not a realistic threat in the United States, and that Americans needed new constitutional understandings to grapple pragmatically with modern conditions. But, for conservatives, such shallowness posed immense, and perhaps fatal, dangers. Of this, they were certain, and understood.[136]

---

[135] James, *Varieties of Religious Experience*, 185–186, 196, 218, 252, 286, 291.

[136] John Chamberlain, "Freedom of the Press and National Security," *Modern Age* 17:3 (Summer 1973), 242. See Stormer, *None Dare Call it Treason*. See also Hemmer, *Messengers of the Right*. Liberals, of course, saw this broad-brush tarring of New Deal liberalism as intellectually crude and politically cynical, involving witch hunting and "guilt by association." Conservatives, by contrast, saw it as a deepening of understanding, the product of an intellectual odyssey in which, through intellectual investigation, they had gotten down to first principles through philosophy and intellectual (and political) history. It was the product not of alarmism, crudeness, and recklessness, but as progression toward depth, connection, and insight.

It is worth noting that many liberals themselves became emotionally inflamed by the communist issue – from the opposite direction, leading to an intense and elaborated anticommunist versus anti-anticommunist dynamic. The political culture of the early postwar period especially featured dramatic pitched battles that pitted a zealous anticommunism against an equally zealous anti-anticommunism, the latter exemplified, for instance, by Arthur Miller's play *The Crucible* (1953), which implicitly likened the emotional excitements of zealous anticommunism to the Salem [Essex County, Massachusetts] Witch Hunts (the play became a public school staple). The specter of actual nuclear war with the USSR, moreover, fed the dynamic as it weighed increasingly heavily, with many beginning to worry that an unhinged obsession with communism might tip the United States into a nuclear war, a threat nearly realized in the Cuban Missile Crisis (1962) – a theme that was the basis of some of the most culturally resonant films of the early 1960s including *On the Beach* (1961), *Fail-Safe* (1964), and *Dr. Strangelove* (1964). President Lyndon Johnson's infamous, though quickly withdrawn, "daisy ad," tying Republican presidential candidate Barry Goldwater's unrelenting anticommunist fervor to the outbreak of a nuclear holocaust is one of the most infamous cases-in-point.[137] Many liberals asked, "Was mutual co-existence really all that bad?"

As the sense of threat perceived by liberals (and moderate conservative Republicans) declined after Stalin's death (1953) and Khrushchev's Secret Speech (1956) to a closed session of the 20th Congress of the Communist Party of the Soviet Union denouncing Stalin and his crimes, movement conservatives sensed softness, if not treachery, and doubled down: demanding, as they always had, rollback rather than co-existence. In time, the Vietnam War opened up a chasm between anticommunist liberals and anticommunist conservatives. As the war intensified, and the antiwar movement grew, pro-war liberal anticommunists found themselves increasingly classed as "neo" conservatives. Some worked their way toward joining the conservative movement and even served in its foreign policy establishment – while largely muting their still liberal views on domestic policy, including civil liberties and civil rights.[138]

As is well known, conservative views on communism – many of which, as noted, were shared in the period by anticommunist liberals – did, of course, affect constitutional law directly as a matter of doctrine concerning the freedom of speech, "academic freedom," the freedom of association, due process, and other civil liberties. But, here, after the period of initial toughness, the broader trend was all in the liberalizing direction, to the point where some wondered whether in fact some of the earlier precedents like *Dennis v. United States*

---

[137] Jacoby, *Alger Hiss*, 129–133.
[138] Lucas Powe charts this waxing and waning pattern in the communism-related jurisprudence of the liberal (anticommunist) Supreme Court in relation to ebbs and flows in the perceived danger. Powe, *Warren Court and American Politics*, chaps. 4, 6.

(1951) had been *de facto*, if not explicitly, overruled. More importantly, for purposes of this study, was that the anticommunist frame was so resonant on the Right that it could not help but shape the emotional tenor of all sorts of constitutional stances taken by conservatives in seemingly far-flung areas – really, almost any area open to the framing of friends v. enemies, patriots v. traitors, Americans v. foreigners, state v. the individual, and the faithful v. the Godless. Anticommunism provided an almost Jungian template for the thoughts and feelings of the postwar movement Right. It is in this regard that it was immensely, and pervasively, significant.

In the late twentieth century, of course, the Cold War ended. But even with the collapse of the Soviet Union, the divergent stories told about communism on the Left and Right still signified: conservatives and liberals told different stories about what had happened, and how. Who ultimately brought down the Soviet Union? Many liberals held that it collapsed of its own accord, with an assist from the reform-minded Mikhail Gorbachev. Conservatives did not buy this blasé and, ultimately, passive theory: they believed it not only scanted the role of a succession of un-illusioned, iron-willed, and heroic Western anticommunists (for many on the Right, Winston Churchill was the model) but implied that they had exaggerated the communist threat all along. After the collapse of the Soviet Union, *National Review*'s John O'Sullivan spoke for many on the Right by giving the chief credit to the unrelenting, uncompromising leadership of President Ronald Reagan, Pope John Paul II, and British Prime Minister Margaret Thatcher – and the American military – which, as liberals whined and complained, mocked and satirized, and begged for disarmament and "peace," took on the most powerful and aggressive foe that liberty has ever known – and won. Against persistent opposition, indifference, and even mockery by liberals, one of the greatest victories for freedom and the good in all of human history had been achieved, in partnership with the like-minded and like-willed abroad, by the American conservative movement. They, and the victorious West, were poised for the next steps in forging the path of freedom.[139]

---

[139] John O'Sullivan, *The President, the Pope, and the Prime Minister* (Washington, DC: Regnery 2008).

5

Evangelical and Fundamentalist Christian Stories

Conservative Evangelical and Fundamentalist Christians became a core part of the modern conservative movement, and of the Republican Party electoral "base," beginning in the late 1970s and early 1980s, when, coalescing as the "Religious Right," they became a pillar of the Reagan coalition. From its early twentieth-century inception, Fundamentalist Christianity has been resolutely anti-modern and reactionary. By contrast, the political valence and partisan allegiances of Evangelical Christianity, a major force in American life and politics since the First (circa 1740) and Second (circa 1790) Great Awakenings, have been fluid, reflecting changes in both the center of gravity among believers themselves and the orienting political context. As much a force for progressive and even radical causes before 1900, it inspired both abolitionism and the socialist-inflected, progressive Social Gospel.[1]

Evangelical Christians believe the Bible is the literal word of God, and the final authority in matters of faith and practice. Unlike Catholics, who afford a considerable role for human reason in discerning God's order and commands, Evangelicals emphasize the conversion experience, through which one is "born again." Preaching God's "good news" or Gospel to a fallen world, Evangelicals hold that one of a person's surpassing purposes in life is to bring others to the same crossroads of conversion and rebirth, where they too will acknowledge the authority of Scripture, and confront the promise of salvation and eternal life.

The Evangelical adherence to Biblical literalism and belief in the significance of being born again have many, often subtle and indirect, political implications.

---

[1] See Michael Kazin, *A Godly Hero: The Life of William Jennings Bryan* (New York: Alfred A. Knopf, 2006); John Compton, *The Evangelical Origins of the Living Constitution* (Cambridge, MA: Harvard University Press, 2014). On the Social Gospel, see Eldon J. Eisenach, editor, *The Social and Political Thought of American Progressivism* (Indianapolis: Hackett Publishing Company, Inc., 2006), chap. 7.

Evangelicals, for instance, have tended to mistrust the character, or at least its groundedness, of those who have not had these experiences or reject the Bible as the literal word of God. This feeds a suspicion of nonreligious institutions and of secularism and religious and political liberalism that are not anchored in Biblical truths.[2]

The Evangelical Christian disposition so important in the nineteenth-century United States was reborn in an increasingly conservative guise in a post–World War II resurgence, when it became aggressively anticommunist and insistent upon (re)instating traditional understandings of the (Protestant) moral order. At this time, however, the center of gravity of the emergent postwar Evangelical conservatism did not fall clearly into either of the nation's major parties since, for most of the postwar period, both the Democratic and Republican Parties had conservative and liberal wings. Only from the late 1960s onward, as "culture war" issues loomed larger, and the parties became more ideologically uniform – in significant part through Evangelical influence – did the "New Evangelicals" move decisively toward the Republicans and became a lynchpin of the contemporary Religious Right.[3]

Several organizations and outlets served as home bases and crossroads for mid-twentieth-century American Evangelicals. Harold Ockenga, pastor of Boston's Congregationalist Park Street Church, created an institutional home for postwar Evangelicals by founding the National Association of Evangelicals (NAE) in 1942. They got a mainstream public voice in 1956 when Ockenga, in conjunction with the theologian Carl C. F. Henry, launched the magazine *Christianity Today*. Under Henry's leadership as *Christianity Today*'s founding editor, the magazine established itself as a conservative answer to the liberal *Christian Century*.[4] Evangelicalism's prominence was soon raised exponentially with the ascendency to the public and political stage of "America's chaplain" (and co-founder of *Christianity Today*), the Reverend Billy Graham. Graham was especially significant in lending the movement a friendlier face (and faith) than had been presented by some of its more apocalyptic, fire-breathing, old school preachers. As such, Graham made

[2] Ronald H. Nash, *Evangelicals in America: Who They Are, What They Believe* (Nashville, TN: Abingdon Press, 1987), 15, 21, 22; Stephen P. Miller, *Billy Graham and the Rise of the Republican South* (Philadelphia: University of Pennsylvania Press, 2009), 8. See also Sanford Levinson, *Constitutional Faith* (Princeton: Princeton University Press, 1988); James Davison Hunter, *Culture Wars: The Struggle to Define America* (New York: Basic Books, 1991).
[3] Daniel K. Williams, *God's Own Party: The Making of the Christian Right* (New York: Oxford University Press, 2010), 2–3.
[4] See Joel A. Carpenter, editor, *Two Reformers of Fundamentalism: Harold John Ockenga and Carl F. H. Henry* (New York: Garland Publishing, 1988); Harold Lindsell, *Park Street Prophet: A Life of Harold John Ockenga* (Wheaton, IL: Van Kampen Press, 1951); James DeForest Murch, *Cooperation without Compromise: A History of the National Association of Evangelicals* (Grand Rapids, MI: William B. Eerdmans, 1956). Stephen J. Nichols, editor, *J. Gresham Machen's the Gospel and the Modern World and Other Short Writings* (Phillipsburg, NJ: Presbyterian and Reformed Publishing, 2005).

important contributions in positioning Evangelical Christianity to win friends and influence people in the postwar United States.[5]

Anticommunism was a high priority for what came to be known as the "New Evangelicals." This anticommunism figured prominently in the stories the New Evangelicals told about the United States and its Constitution. Both the NAE and the Reverend Billy Graham were aggressively – indeed, foundationally – anticommunist.[6] Graham preached that the United States was indubitably God's chosen nation. It had nevertheless, he said, suffered an egregious moral lapse: it had been weakened by widespread immorality and sin. This weakening had made it vulnerable to communist takeover. To survive, and prevail, in the fight against its Godless mortal enemy, America need to come to Jesus – to experience a regenerating spiritual revival that would give it new life, and save it. Once saved, America would be positioned (once again) to serve as a beacon to the wider world.[7] In his Christian Crusade, the Reverend Billy James Hargis, Graham's more fire-and-brimstone fellow preacher, warned his flock that communism – which he described, in the end, as "simply Atheism" – was Satan's tool to destroy America: Hargis called for the outlawing of the Communist Party USA (CPUSA). Hargis specifically reminded Americans of their legacy as inheritors of the country's original settlers, who "[w]ith a Bible under one arm, and a musket under the other ... were willing to fight for their faith and their freedom."[8] Prodded by their perception of the communist threat, both Hargis and Graham rejected the view that Christianity was simply a matter of personal faith, confined to the (constitutionally protected)[9] private sphere: it was one of their core convictions that Christianity, traditional Christian morals, and American ideals and institutions, were providentially conjoined.

Graham's Americanism, mass following, and congenial personality made him catnip for ambitious Cold War–era politicians, further expanding his influence, and that of his fellow Evangelicals. In 1953, under his tutelage, President Dwight David Eisenhower, an ecumenical Kansan whose parents had named him after the famed nineteenth-century evangelist Dwight Moody, launched the National Prayer Breakfast. In 1954, the words "Under God" were added to the Pledge of Allegiance. In 1955, the words "In God We Trust" were placed on all American currency. The historian Daniel K. Williams has described this period as "a time of unprecedented cooperation between the federal government and the nation's religious leaders," and argued that "by the end of the 1950s, Evangelicals had ... begun to think of the United States as

---

[5] Nash, *Evangelicals in America*, 89; Williams, *God's Own Party*, 28. Dale Carnegie, *How to Win Friends and Influence People* (New York: Simon and Schuster, 1936).

[6] Williams, *God's Own Party*, 4, 19.   [7] Williams, *God's Own Party*, 23–24.

[8] Williams, *God's Own Party*, 40–42.

[9] Protected by, among other inherent guarantees (like natural rights), the First Amendment's Religious Liberty and Establishment Clauses ("Congress shall make no law respecting an establishment of religion, or prohibiting the free exercise thereof.").

a Christian nation and the Republican White House as an ally in a righteous cause."[10]

It is important to note that while anticommunism was their driving political frame at the time, Evangelicals were more favorably disposed than their fundamentalist Christian brethren to the new rising political frame of the era's liberals: civil rights.[11] Although cautious and measured in his actions, and an outspoken critic of law breaking and civil disobedience, Billy Graham, a native North Carolinian, was, by the era's standards, a racial moderate. From the moment it was decided, Graham praised the Supreme Court's *Brown v. Board of Education* (1954) decision and lent his verbal support to southern blacks fighting racial segregation (Graham invited the Reverend Martin Luther King Jr. to lead a prayer at one of his prayer rallies). That said, although Graham supported civil rights for moral/religious reasons, he viewed the civil rights cause through the lenses of a Cold Warrior: Graham believed the denial of equal rights to blacks disadvantaged the United States in winning hearts and minds throughout the world in the global fight against communism, in which he believed US leadership was indispensible. Getting right with the issue of legal equality under law was important to the exercise of that leadership.[12] It is worth noting as well that Graham was largely absent from the late-developing Evangelical opposition to abortion rights. After being burned by his association with the corrupt President Nixon, whom he had trusted, Graham decided to become largely apolitical: given the timing, this meant that he did not take a public stand on the issue.[13]

While mid-twentieth-century Evangelical Christianity had much in common with the Fundamentalist Christianity – discussed later – with which it is often confused and conflated, it is important to note that it emerged in its

[10] Williams, *God's Own Party*, 24, 26–28, 31. See also Jonathan Herzog, *The Spiritual-Industrial Complex: America's Religious Battle Against Communism in the Early Cold War* (New York: Oxford University Press, 2011) (emphasizing the close connections and common sense of mission among religious leaders and business, political, media, and military elites in the late 1940s and early 1950s). As Steven K. Green has demonstrated, Evangelicals considered the United States "a Christian nation" long before this as well. Steven K. Green, *The Second Disestablishment: Church and State in Nineteenth Century America* (New York: Oxford University Press, 2010).

[11] For my understanding of modern liberalism as shaped by sequential frames set first by the labor problem and then by civil rights, see Ken I. Kersch, "The New Deal Triumph as the End of History? The Judicial Negotiation of Labor Rights and Civil Rights," in Ronald Kahn and Ken I. Kersch, editors, *The Supreme Court and American Political Development* (Lawrence: University Press of Kansas, 2006): 169–226. See Kersch, *Constructing Civil Liberties*, 134–234.

[12] Williams, *God's Own Party*, 28–29, 46–48. See also Mary Dudziak, *Cold War Civil Rights: Race and the Image of American Democracy* (Princeton: Princeton University Press, 2000); Azza Salama Layton, *International Politics and Civil Rights, 1941–1960* (New York: Cambridge University Press, 2000); Thomas Borstelmann, *The Cold War and the Color Line: American Race Relations in the Global Arena* (Cambridge, MA: Harvard University Press, 2001).

[13] Frank Schaeffer, *Crazy for God: How I Grew Up as One of the Elect, Helped Found the Religious Right, and Lived to Take All (or Almost All) of It Back* (Cambridge, MA: Da Capo Press, 2007), 290.

contemporary form in the 1940s in direct and self-conscious opposition to Fundamentalist Christianity's theological rigidities. As such, the religious disposition of American Evangelicals was self-consciously distinctive from Fundamentalism: the movement had deliberately adopted the more optimistic label "Evangelical" in part to distinguish it from Fundamentalism's anger, pessimism, and fatalism.[14]

FUNDAMENTALIST CHRISTIANS

While Evangelical Christianity in America traces its origins back to the colonial era, Christian Fundamentalism's origins are relatively recent: it is a reactive, defensive disposition forged in the early twentieth century in response to an emergent set of challenges posed by Darwinism, and modernity more generally, to traditional Christian understandings. Christian Fundamentalism was forged with the express aim of preserving – defending – America's (presumably) traditional Christian moral order against what Fundamentalists took to be its rapidly rising opponents and their influence. Fundamentalist Christians are declinists: at mid-century, and before, they saw the world around them descending headlong into Godlessness and decadence. The decline and fall of the Roman Empire was a frequently referenced precedent. They read contemporary events, including public policy initiatives and, later, Supreme Court decisions, as portents of the coming collapse of Christian civilization – what some called "end times." Salvation – redemption – was to be found in faith, and its incubator, the traditional American family.[15]

Fundamentalism had many fronts, and fringes. "Premillennial dispensationalists" believed that, in time, perhaps very soon, Jesus Christ would deliver the United States from sin, dramatically swooping in to at long last save the nation. Fundamentalists devoted themselves to getting the word out about this imminent great event. In this momentous task, radio and later television proved critical: indeed, Fundamentalists successfully lobbied the Federal Communications Commission to classify religious broadcasts as public service programming.[16] Christian Reconstructionists – "postmillennial dispensationalists" – believed that the Christian Church had been commanded to be actively involved in this world, here and now, in fighting apostasy and

---

[14] Williams, *God's Own Party*, 4.

[15] Williams, *God's Own Party*, 12–14; Seth Dowland, *Family Values and the Rise of the Christian Right* (Philadelphia: University of Pennsylvania Press, 2015). Needless to say, this is the "traditional American family" as they understood it – not the family described by the historian Stephanie Coontz. Stephanie Coontz, *The Way We Never Were: American Families and the Nostalgia Trap* (New York: Basic Books, 1992).

[16] See Heather Hendershot, *What's Fair on the Air: Cold War Right-Wing Broadcasting and the Public Interest* (Chicago: University of Chicago Press, 2011); Heather Hendershot, *Shaking the World for Jesus: Media and Conservative Evangelical Culture* (Chicago: University of Chicago Press, 2004); Hemmer, *Messengers of the Right*.

Godlessness by reestablishing Biblical law on earth. Only after this task was accomplished would Jesus return in his Second Coming.[17] Despite their radicalism, both pre- and postmillennial beliefs in time came to influence important political actors within an increasingly radicalized Republican Party, helping to set the frames through which they, and the broader Republican Party establishment, came to understand the Constitution and the Supreme Court.

While Evangelical Christianity had been prominent and a powerful influence on the nation's public life across the nineteenth century, Fundamentalism's relationship to the public sphere has been more irregular and contested: it remains the subject of considerable debate among historians. A key event in the history of the Fundamentalist engagement in the public sphere – and American constitutionalism – was the public relations fiasco of the Scopes Trial in Dayton, Tennessee, in the 1920s, in which Fundamentalists were widely portrayed as rubes and buffoons who clownishly had sought to deny the plain teachings of science in not only denying Charles Darwin's theory of natural selection but also persecuting and prosecuting those who sought to teach otherwise.[18] Some historians have argued that this debacle led to their total retreat from politics, a claim that other historians dispute. Nevertheless, it is fair to say at least that both before and after Scopes, many Fundamentalists believed that participation in ordinary politics was pointless: their attention should be focused not on the trivialities of this world, but on readying themselves and theirs for the world to come. In time, however, provoked by various developments in the increasingly secular postwar culture around them, especially over the course of the 1960s and 1970s – including the Supreme Court's outlawing of government sponsored prayer and Bible reading in the public schools in *Engel* v. *Vitale* (1962) and *Abington* v. *Schempp* (1962) under the presumed auspices of the First Amendment's Establishment Clause, and then, subsequently, by the Court's holding that a woman had an individual constitutional right to terminate her pregnancy in *Roe* v. *Wade* (1973) – an increasing number of Fundamentalist Christians began to argue that an unwillingness to involve themselves in politics was contrary to God's plan and God's role for them in advancing it. Through diverse theological routes, an increasing number of Fundamentalist Christian leaders, among them the Reverend Francis Schaeffer and, subsequently, following Schaeffer's leadership, the Reverend Jerry Falwell, the founder of the leading Religious Right group The Moral Majority (1979), repudiated separatism, and called for

---

[17] Nash, *Evangelicals in America*, 71. See Rousas J. Rushdoony, *The Foundations of Social Order* (Nutley, NJ: Presbyterian and Reformed Publishers, 1972). Rushdoony wrote frequently about law and American constitutionalism and was an early influence on John Whitehead, the founder of the conservative litigation group the Rutherford Institute (discussed later in this chapter). See Dowland, *Family Values*, 15, 99–100.

[18] See Edward Larson, *Summer for the Gods: The Scopes Trial and America's Continuing Debate Over Science and Religion* (New York: Basic Books, 1997).

the involvement of their brethren in pursing cultural renovation. Under this new path, instead of withdrawing, they were to involve themselves in the nation's intellectual and cultural debates by actively applying the Gospel to social, economic, and political problems.[19]

OVERCOMING DIVISION: CONFRONTING CATHOLICISM AND CIVIL RIGHTS

Since today Evangelicalism and Fundamentalism are both core constituencies of the Religious Right – and, by extension, the movement conservative Republican Party – it is perhaps too easy not only to confuse and conflate these two right-wing dispositions, but to assume that they were natural theological and political allies. This, in fact, was not the case. For them to join together as allies on the "Christian Right," which also, eventually, and even more anomalously, came to include right-wing Roman Catholics, the movement needed to undertake considerable "culture work" – to theorize its way toward cooperation.[20]

Evangelicals and Fundamentalists were distinguishable groups; the former had drawn clear lines of identification separating themselves from the latter, who were relative newcomers. The suspicion was mutual. Fundamentalists, for example, were suspicious of Billy Graham's willingness to cooperate with mainline Protestants who, after all, did not accept Biblical inerrancy. Many Fundamentalists, including the pastor of Lynchburg, Virginia's Thomas Road Baptist Church and Liberty University founder the Reverend Jerry Falwell – founder of the Moral Majority and a key backer of Ronald Reagan – diverged from the positions taken by Graham and other Evangelicals in actively opposing civil rights. Falwell was a staunch segregationist: he saw the civil rights movement as a stalking-horse for an all-powerful central government, if not the work of the Devil and a Soviet plot (if the two were not one and the same) and opposed it at every turn. For Jerry Falwell, the civil rights movement was Marxist, pure and simple: it represented no less than a full-court press to embarrass the United States and thwart it in its global war against communism. Falwell, moreover, like many devoutly Christian racists and segregationists, argued that God had sanctioned segregation. Many Fundamentalists, moreover, believed not only that a literal reading of the Bible permitted racial segregation but also that it *commanded* it. As such, racial separation was a religious duty, and a matter of conscience and religious liberty.[21] As they saw it, in opposing civil rights, Fundamentalist Christians were contributing at once to the nation's fight against socialism, communism,

---

[19] George Marsden, *Reforming Fundamentalism: Fuller Seminary and the New Evangelicalism* (Grand Rapids, MI: William B. Eerdmans, 1987); Dowland, *Family Values.*
[20] Hattam and Lowndes, "The Ground Beneath Our Feet."
[21] See Linda McClain, *The Rhetoric of Bigotry: Controversies Over Marriage and Civil Rights* (New York: Oxford University Press, forthcoming).

and centralized big government, and to the advancement of God's inerrant word. In doing so, they increasingly cast themselves as the last line of defense of the nation's venerated traditions and Founding constitutional order, with which they tightly identified their vision.[22]

In the 1950s and 1960s, Fundamentalists were profoundly suspicious of the distant central government, which they viewed simultaneously as a threat and portent. They had been alarmed in the 1920s when a Roman Catholic, Al Smith, captured the political party to which most of them were a part, the Democrats, and became its nominee for president, threatening to subvert the country by subsuming it to papal – that is, foreign sovereign – control. No sooner had the threat of a Roman Catholic conquest been averted than the metastasizing federal government was being stocked with sympathizers, if not agents, of Godless communism. Most southern (Fundamentalist) ministers had initially been supporters of Franklin Delano Roosevelt's New Deal, whose programs served their relatively poor and lower-middle-class constituencies. But they were becoming increasingly suspicious of the Democrats, and of the burgeoning centralized bureaucracy its leaders seemed to be cultivating.[23]

Whatever their differences and disagreements, both Evangelical and Fundamentalist Christians had long agreed that, far from being neutral toward religion – the understanding that the Supreme Court was moving toward at mid-century[24] – the Constitution, and, hence, the nation, was anchored by a foundational Christianity. By the late 1940s, even the more moderate NAE had joined with the Fundamentalists in campaigning for a "Christian Amendment" to the Constitution which would specifically acknowledge Jesus Christ as Lord in the document's text.[25] While tension between Fundamentalists and Evangelicals remained high in the 1940s and 1950s, both groups were beginning to prefer an affirmative patriotism over (pessimistic) declinist prophecy: the hope was, increasingly, that if the country were to confess and repudiate its sins and recommit itself to its foundational teachings, the nation itself could be born again. Put otherwise, it could be saved – redeemed – by constitution patriotism.[26] This made constitutionalism about more than a theory about the proper reading of the text: it was, in William James's terms, a religious "experience," suffused with emotional resonance. And it was, moreover, evangelical: it involved the preaching of

---

[22] Nash, *Evangelicals in America*, 68; Miller, *Billy Graham*, 7; Williams, *God's Own Party*, 4–5, 33–35, 46–48.

[23] Williams, *God's Own Party*, 34–39. See also Joseph Lowndes, *From the New Deal to the New Right: Race and the Southern Origins of Modern Conservatism* (New Haven: Yale University Press, 2008); Darren Dochuk, *From Bible Belt to Sunbelt: Plain-Folk Religion, Grassroots Politics, and the Rise of Evangelical Conservatism* (New York: W.W. Norton, 2011).

[24] *Everson v. Board of Education*, 330 US 1 (1947).   [25] Williams, *God's Own Party*, 15–17.

[26] See Jack M. Balkin, *Constitutional Redemption* (Cambridge, MA: Harvard University Press, 2011).

the "Good News" of the American Founding, and a baptism in the nation's Constitutional Faith.

Evangelicals and Fundamentalists found sustained common cause once again in the early 1960s in their shared opposition to the presidential candidacy of the Roman Catholic John Fitzgerald Kennedy. Because both insisted that by character and heritage the United States was an inherently Protestant nation, both harbored deep fears that, in line with its history, traditions, and (pre–Vatican II) doctrines and dogmas, the Catholic Church sought to obliterate America's constitutionally enshrined separation of church and state. The Protestant denomination most committed to that separation, the Southern Baptists, launched an all-out campaign to thwart Kennedy's bid for the White House on precisely those grounds.[27]

The Kennedy victory was a blow. But during the campaign, in a noted speech to an assembly of Protestant ministers in Houston, Texas, Kennedy had declared himself a strong supporter of church-state separation, a position he made good on during his time in the White House.[28] Indeed, many of his former Protestant opponents would come to believe that Kennedy's convictions on that point were proving all too strong for their tastes. When, during his administration, the Supreme Court handed down its landmark decisions declaring government sponsored prayer and Bible reading in the public schools to violate the First Amendment's Establishment Clause,[29] Evangelicals and Fundamentalists began to suspect that the greater threat to the country might be less each other – or even Roman Catholics – than atheists and secularists bent, as they saw it, on removing God from American public life, which, they increasingly worried, could speed the nation into a downward spiral of moral decline. As the revolutionary social changes and the chaos of the 1960s and 1970s followed close on the heels of these landmark Establishment Clause rulings, many conservative Christians found their worst fears of a secularist turn confirmed.

When the *Brown* v. *Board of Education* (1954) decision outlawing racial segregation in public institutions – a decision that, for many years, Fundamentalists, especially, refused to accept – was powerfully reinforced by the passage of the 1964 Civil Rights Act banning racial discrimination in most private institutions and the 1965 Voting Rights Act that forbade the most blatant racial discrimination in voting, a key chapter in the history of the relationship between conservative Evangelicals and Fundamentalist Christians drew to a close: one of the chief barriers to cooperation between the groups, some marginal figures excepted, had been removed. The two groups, later to be

---

[27] Williams, *God's Own Party*, 19, 49–52.
[28] See John F. Kennedy, Speech to the Greater Houston Ministerial Association, Rice Hotel, Houston, Texas (September 12, 1960) (www.jfklibrary.org/learn/about-jfk/historic-speeches/address-to-the-greater-houston-ministerial-association).
[29] *Engel* v. *Vitale*, 370 US 421 (1962) (prayer); *Abington* v. *Schemmp*, 374 US 203 (1963) (Bible reading).

joined by conservative Catholics, began to unite as "social conservatives," or just "conservatives," finding common cause in the fight against abortion, gay rights, and liberalism and secularism and progressivism more broadly, forming the shock brigades of the New Right or Religious Right of what would soon become known as the "culture wars."[30]

CONSERVATIVE CHRISTIAN CONVERGENCE: THE DEVELOPMENT OF CULTURE WAR CO-BELLIGERENCE

A crucial figure in forging this increasingly sustained unified front – a new "co-belligerence"[31] that brought conservative Evangelicals, Fundamentalists, and Roman Catholics together in the fight against the (purportedly) secularist liberalism that was allegedly undermining American religion, the American family, and American morals – was the Pennsylvania-born, Presbyterian minister and theologian Francis Schaeffer (1912–1984) who, across the 1970s and into the early Reagan administration, convinced many conservative Christians that it was time to launch an aggressive political campaign to reclaim America for God: Schaeffer was the seminal theorist and intellectual strategist responsible for the establishment of the Religious Right, and of its integration as a core constituency of the modern Republican Party.

The charismatic founder of the L'Abri religious community in Switzerland, Schaeffer did not start out favorably inclined towards sunny Evangelicals like the Reverend Billy Graham, Papists, or bridging theological divides. As his son Frankie, a filmmaker and novelist who later repudiated the Christian Right and chronicled his upbringing in *Crazy for God* (2007),[32] recalled, "During my childhood, I was very aware of who had compromised and who hadn't. [John Gresham] Machen [a leader of the Fundamentalist Christian revolt at the Princeton Theological Seminary in the early twentieth century] had *not* compromised. Billy Graham *had*, when he invited liberal theologians, even a Roman Catholic, to participate in his New York 1957 crusades." His parents, Frankie reported, "were very critical of the fund-raising methods of the Billy Grahams ... and other high-powered evangelicals who didn't really 'live by faith' but who used 'slick worldly methods' ... 'Those American Christians' were all just too commercial, too worldly.'" The senior Schaeffer had long considered Graham "a very weird man indeed who lived an oddly

[30] Williams, *God's Own Party*, 5–6, 58–59; Nash, *Evangelicals in America*, 92; Dowland, *Family Values*. *Engel* v. *Vitale* (1962); *Abington* v. *Schempp* (1963).

[31] I adopt the term from Dowland, *Family Values*, 85.

[32] Schaeffer, *Crazy for God*, 4, 341, 358. Frankie Schaeffer reports that the publication of his memoir detailing his disillusionment with Evangelical Christianity and departure from the Republican Party led to a flood of emails that "seemed to boil down to 'Do what we say Jesus says – and if you don't, we'll kick your head in!'" Schaeffer, *Crazy for God*, 4.

sheltered life in a celebrity/ministry cocoon." But, in the late 1960s, the senior Schaeffer's views had started to shift.[33]

The chaos of the 1960s and a rising secularism were increasingly unsettling Schaeffer. But it was the Supreme Court's decision in effect declaring abortion a constitutional right that galvanized him into a new chapter in his professional and political life. The Court's ruling in *Roe* v. *Wade* (1973) did not itself directly occasion any strong reaction in Schaeffer, who had long dismissed the simmering abortion controversy as primarily a Catholic issue: it took sustained arguments from his son Frankie, who had just had his first child, to finally bring him around. But, belatedly, at least, Schaeffer brought to the cause all the zeal of a convert: he came to see the abortion question as not only a matter of abortion itself but also as a symbol of the decline of a nation – and, indeed, a civilization – that had disastrously chosen to abandon the Christian Faith on which all of its achievements and belief in moral limits had been premised.

Turning in earnest to pro-life politics in the 1970s, Schaeffer teamed up with his exceptionally talented filmmaker son (who later became a Hollywood director) first to make the film series *How Should We Then Live?* that chronicled the long trajectory, as the Schaeffers understood it, of Western (Christian) civilization, and subsequently, in conjunction with the celebrated professor of pediatric surgery at the University of Pennsylvania and surgeon-in-chief at the Children's Hospital of Philadelphia C. Everett Koop, the follow-up series *Whatever Happened to the Human Race?* that focused more intently on abortion, presenting it as a symbol of the West's repudiation of its Christian heritage and impending descent into barbarism. Laden with prodigious and seemingly sophisticated layers of history, philosophy, and art, the films – catnip for autodidacts – signaled intense study, depth, and learning.[34] Both film series, which were brimming with searing, unforgettably vivid visual imagery, were widely screened on the Right, including for Republican members of Congress; soon after the latter series' release, President Ronald Reagan appointed Koop surgeon general of the United States (1982–1989). If he had only made these two seminal series of films, Schaeffer's status as a major figure in American politics (if all but completely ignored by the secular liberal mainstream) would have been confirmed. But Schaeffer, and those in his circle, became actively involved in the formation of a broader pro-life movement. The popular acclaim for the *How Should We Then Live?* and *Whatever Happened to the Human Race?* on the Christian and Republican Party Right led to both films being written up as books by Crossway, a small religious publisher that, largely by

[33] Schaeffer, *Crazy for God*, 116–117, 257, 315.
[34] Schaeffer, *Crazy for God*, 255–256. Frankie Schaeffer later observed, "[t]he evangelicals ... loved the fact that Dad, somewhat like the author C.S. Lewis, was a kind of proof that we evangelicals weren't as dumb as the secularists said we were." Frankie added "The irony was that Lewis and my father were not 'evangelicals' in the American sense of the word. Lewis was an Anglo-Catholic; and Dad liked art better than theology and people better than rules and was most comfortable in a room full of hippies."

dint of Schaeffer's bestsellers, grew into an Evangelical publishing powerhouse.[35] Schaeffer made appearances on the Christian Right *Focus on the Family* radio show, and his books were given away free by the tens of thousands by Focus's founder (1977), Dr. James Dobson.[36] Koop teamed up with the influential Reverend Harold O. J. Brown, a professor at Trinity Evangelical Divinity School in Deerfield, Illinois, and the Reformed Theological Seminary in Charlotte, North Carolina, to found the pro-life legal and political advocacy group Christian Action Network (today known as "Care Net").[37] Brown, a longtime religion editor of the right-wing *Chronicles: A Magazine of American Culture*,[38] a publication of the right-wing Rockford Institute,[39] subsequently played a critical role in forging the founding statement of Christian Right co-belligerence "Evangelicals and Catholics Together."[40]

[35] Schaeffer, *Crazy for God*, 257. The 2005 publisher's foreword to a new edition of the book version of Schaeffer's *How Should We Then Live?* explained to new readers that "few Christians have had greater impact during the last half of the twentieth century then Dr. Francis A. Schaeffer."

[36] Schaeffer, *Crazy for God*, 294.   [37] www.care-net.org/   [38] www.chroniclesmagazine.org

[39] www.rockfordinstitute.org

[40] www.firstthings.com/article/1994/05/evangelicals-catholics-together-the-christian-mission-in-the-third-millennium. Among the signatories were Charles Colson, Father Avery Dulles, SJ, Richard Land of the Southern Baptist Convention, Bill Bright of the Campus Crusade for Christ, Father Richard John Neuhaus, George Weigel of Washington DC's Ethics and Public Policy Center, the attorney William Bentley Ball, Harvard Law School's Mary Ann Glendon, Wheaton College's Mark Noll (now at the University of Notre Dame), Boston College theologian Peter Kreeft, Cardinal John O'Connor of New York, the American Enterprise Institute's Michael Novak, and the Reverend Pat Robertson. Given his extensive direct involvement with constitutional law, it is worth saying a bit more about William Bentley Ball (1916–1999). A prominent Catholic constitutional lawyer in private practice in Harrisburg, Pennsylvania, Ball had earned his law degree from Notre Dame in 1948 and taught constitutional law at the Villanova University School of Law from 1955 to 1960, where he was a founding member of the faculty. He went on to serve as general counsel to the Pennsylvania Catholic Conference for the next eight years and as vice-chairman of the National Committee for Amish Religious Freedom. Ball argued *Lemon* v. *Kurtzman*, 403 US 602 (1971) and *Wisconsin* v. *Yoder*, 406 US 205 (1972) and eight others landmark Establishment Clause cases in the Supreme Court and participated in other significant ways in twenty-five such cases (including *Zobrest* v. *Catalina Foothills*, 509 US 1 (1993)). He was in the forefront of the Catholic Church's efforts to block the Kennedy and Johnson administrations from denying federal money to parochial schools. Ball also testified before Congress against federal policy on the dissemination upon request and coordination of birth-control information to individuals and public agencies. At the time, he also appeared as general counsel to the Pennsylvania Catholic Conference of Bishops. A close friend of Russell Kirk, Ball was active in the Pennsylvania Equal Rights Council, the Christian Legal Society, and the Catholic League for Religion and Civil Rights. He was one of the leaders of the effort to forge alliances between Catholics and Evangelical Christians and, as noted, a signatory of *Evangelicals & Catholics Together: The Christian Mission in the Third Millennium*. See William Bentley Ball, editor, *In Search of a National Morality: A Manifesto for Evangelicals and Catholics* (Grand Rapids, MI: Ignatius, 1992); William Bentley Ball, *Mere Creatures of the State? Education, Religion, and the Courts* (Notre Dame, IN: Crisis Books, 1994) (Preface by Richard John Neuhaus). See Steven M. Krason [president, Society of Catholic Social Scientists], "In Memorium: William Bentley Ball," *Catholic Social Science Review* (1999):

The troika of Schaeffer, Koop, and Brown was the driving intellectual force behind the pro-life movement, emphasizing that movement's grounding, as they saw it, in a deep moral and philosophical commitment to the significance of human life. *How Should We Then Live?* offered a sweeping historical and philosophical narration of the rise and fall of the Christian West from a Christian Right perspective, with the decline attributed to a rising secularism that had led, first, to Nazism and then to *Roe* v. *Wade*.[41] This analysis of Western culture, Lane Dennis of Crossway Books has attested, "has deeply influenced a generation of Christian leaders," adding that "[m]any of Schaeffer's insights carry the prophetic ring of truth concerning the moral, spiritual, and intellectual upheaval of our day." To this day, these two films, and the books that were drawn from them, remain "standard works ... in thousands of evangelical high schools, colleges, and seminaries around the world." For many Evangelicals in the 1970s and afterward, Francis Schaeffer was "their first, and perhaps only, introduction to what 'we' think about art, history, and culture, and politics – not to mention the 'life issues' ... the book companions to the films are ... a mainstay of every evangelical library, having sold several million copies."[42]

FRANCIS SCHAEFFER AS LEGAL AND CONSTITUTIONAL THINKER

While one can spend considerable time in Francis Schaeffer's corpus without encountering explicit legal and constitutional thought, that thought is the consistent subtext of Schaeffer's broader political-theological vision: it is fused to or embedded within his discussions of history, philosophy, theology, political theory, art, and culture. As such, Schaeffer's thought has been one of the major intellectual tributaries informing modern conservative thinking about the Constitution, and the more general legal understandings of the modern conservative movement, and the contemporary Republican Party.[43]

The best place to get a relatively succinct statement of Schaeffer's legal and constitutional understandings as embedded in his broader theological framework is in a book he published at the beginning of the Reagan

---

329–331; William Bentley Ball, "Religious Liberty: The Constitutional Frontier" [unpublished paper, n.d.], cited in Steve Hallman, *Christianity and Humanism: A Study in Contrasts* (Tupelo, MS: American Family Association, 1984).

[41] Lane Dennis of Crossway Books observed that "Schaeffer's basic analysis of Western culture has deeply influenced a generation of Christian leaders," adding that "Many of Schaeffer's insights carry the prophetic ring of truth concerning the moral, spiritual, and intellectual upheaval of our day."

[42] Schaeffer, *Crazy for God*, 260.

[43] See Daniel Schlozman, *When Movements Anchor Parties* (Princeton: Princeton University Press, 2016). See also David Karol, *Party Position Change in American Politics: Coalition Management* (New York: Cambridge University Press, 2009); Christopher Baylor, *First to the Party: The Group Origins of Political Transformation* (Philadelphia: University of Pennsylvania Press, 2017).

administration, relatively late in his life and career, *A Christian Manifesto* (1981),[44] which Schaeffer offered as a Christian response to Marx and Engels's *The Communist Manifesto* (1848), and the American Humanist Association's first (1933) and second (1973) Humanist Manifestos.[45] Schaeffer began with diagnosis: around the turn of the twentieth century, a barely noted "shift in world view [had taken place] ... a fundamental change in the overall way people think and view the world and life as a whole." Over time, "Christianity and spirituality were shut up to a small, isolated part of life," relegated to the (ostensibly) private sphere, fundamentally distorting our apprehension of reality, since "nothing concerning reality ... philosophy, theology and the church, art, music, literature, films, and culture in general ... is not" created, underwritten, and anchored by the Christian God.[46]

"[S]ociety, government, and law" are part of that single reality. One could understand them either secularly or as Christians. It was an either/or proposition: the two were "separate entities that cannot be synthesized." A "liberal theology" corrupted by the Enlightenment nevertheless tried to concoct a mixture.[47] And, when hard judgments were required regarding which elements of this adulterated mixture should be applied to serious moral questions, "in each case ... liberal theologians have always come down ... on the side of the nonreligious humanist." Liberal theology was thus little more than "humanism expressed in theological terms." Exhibit A was Christian clergy and churches that supported abortion rights.[48]

"*Humanism*," Schaeffer explained, stemmed from Christian heresy: it placed "[m]an at the center of all things and [made] him the measure of all things,"

[44] Francis A. Schaeffer, *A Christian Manifesto* (Wheaton, IL: Crossway Books, 1981). The idea for the book had a legal and constitutional provenance: it arose from a talk Schaeffer had given at plenary session of the Christian Legal Society Conference in South Bend, Indiana, in April 1981. "The discussion period following the lecture with the attending lawyers stirred my thinking further," Schaeffer reported, "Since the talk I have read many legal briefs and records of specific cases." *A Christian Manifesto* was a revised and extended version of the talk. Schaeffer, *A Christian Manifesto*, 11.

[45] Schaeffer, *Christian Manifesto*, 13. See *Humanist Manifesto I* (American Humanist Association, 1933) (https://americanhumanist.org/what-is-humanism/manifesto1/) and *Humanist Manifesto II* (American Humanist Association, 1973) (https://americanhumanist.org/what-is-humanism/manifesto2/).

[46] Schaeffer, *Christian Manifesto*, 9, 17, 19–20. For a later iteration by a legal scholar who helped forge the co-belligerent Christian Right and is a leader in its campaign to import its precepts into constitutional law, see Robert P. George, *The Clash of Orthodoxies: Law, Religion, and Morality in Crisis* (Wilmington, DE: Intercollegiate Studies Institute, 2002). See also Richard John Neuhaus, *The Naked Public Square: Religion and Democracy in America* (Grand Rapids, MI: William B. Eerdmans Publishing Co., 1984).

[47] Whatever his role in forging Christian Right co-belligerence, Schaeffer repeatedly reaffirmed his objections to Catholic theology, which, like Enlightenment thought, he thought gave too prominent a role to human reason – that is, to the reasoning of hopelessly flawed and fallen human beings, as against the Holy Scripture's literal word of God.

[48] Schaeffer, *Christian Manifesto*, 21–22.

recognizing "no standards outside of himself." It was arrogant, prideful, selfish, and egotistical. Alas, humanism "today controls the consensus in society, much of the media, much of what is taught in our schools, and much of the arbitrary law being produced by various departments of government." And "[n]owhere have the divergent results of the two total concepts of reality, the Judeo-Christian and the humanist ... been more open to observation than in government and law."[49]

The foundation of any and all law was "God's written Law." In "content and authority ... neither church nor state were equal to, let alone above, the Law ... [N]o one has the right to place anything, including king, state or church, above the content of God's Law."[50] In applying this understanding to the United States, Schaeffer trained his attention on the Scottish theologian and political thinker Samuel Rutherford (1600–1661), whose *Lex Rex* (1644) Schaeffer idiosyncratically pronounced foundational to American political, legal, and constitutional thought.[51]

Schaeffer traced a direct lineage from Rutherford to the Scottish-born College of New Jersey (today, Princeton University) clergyman, professor, and president John Witherspoon, to Witherspoon's undergraduate (and postgraduate) student James Madison, to the Constitution of the United States, which, in Schaeffer's simplistic account, James Madison wrote. Schaeffer's argument was that if only people knew this forgotten lineage, they would see that Rutherford's Christian understandings had formed the beating heart of the US Constitution. *Lex rex*, Schaeffer explained, means law is king, a revolutionary reversal of the then prevailing Latin maxim *rex lex* – the king is law. This meant, Schaeffer explained, that "the heads of government are under the law, not a law unto themselves."[52]

---

[49] Schaeffer, *Christian Manifesto*, 23–24. [50] Schaeffer, *Christian Manifesto*, 29.
[51] Schaeffer, *Christian Manifesto*, 5.
[52] Schaeffer, *Christian Manifesto*, 32. Today, as previously noted, the Witherspoon Institute in Princeton, New Jersey (www.winst.org), a conservative think tank devoted to promotion of Christian Right understandings of natural law constitutionalism, serves as an institutional home base for the cultivation, inculcation, and promotion of these understandings, both as set out here and as subsequently refined and developed with an eye to bridging sectarian and other religious divides within the movement. Witherspoon's founder Robert P. George is also the founder of the American Principles Project (https://appfdc.org/) (the APP's original website and statements (www.americanprinciplesproject.org) have been taken down and replaced by this newer website of the group's related foundation; the original materials can be found via some web archival sleuthing). Witherspoon is led by the Opus Dei lay-cleric (numerary) Luis Tellez. Its program on Religion and the Constitution was spearheaded by the right-wing Catholic University of Notre Dame law professor Gerard V. Bradley and was run by the right-wing Catholic Matthew Franck until fall 2018, when Franck moved up the street to become the associate director of George's James Madison Program at Princeton University.

Robert George's APP aggressively promoted the appointment of former Notre Dame law professor Amy Coney Barrett to the Supreme Court by Donald Trump, emphasizing that the liberal Democratic California Senator Dianne Feinstein had "mocked" Barrett by declaring in her 7th Circuit confirmation hearing that "The dogma lives loudly within you." Feinstein's

This was the core idea that had formed the basis for the American Founding. The American Founders "knew they were building on the Supreme Being who was the Creator, the final reality. And they knew that without that foundation everything in the Declaration of Independence and all that followed would be sheer unadulterated nonsense." This was especially important as "many of those who came to America from Europe came for religious purposes. As they arrived, most of them established their own individual civil governments based on the Bible."[53]

This had implications for contemporary constitutional doctrine and Supreme Court decision making. Given this history, heritage, and lineage, Schaeffer declared it "totally foreign to the basic nature of America at the time of the writing of the Constitution to argue a separation doctrine that implies a secular state." "Today," Schaeffer complained, "the separation of church and state in America is used to silence the church ... [to effect] a total separation of religion from the state. The consequence ... leads to the removal of religion as an influence in civil government."[54] This was an abomination:

To have suggested the state separated from religion and religious influence would have amazed the Founding Fathers. The French Revolution that took place shortly afterwards, with its continuing excesses and final failure leading quickly to Napoleon and an authoritative rule, only emphasized the difference between the base upon which the United States was founded and the base upon which the French Revolution was founded.

On this, "History is clear and the men of that day understood it."[55]

In a chapter entitled "The Destruction of Faith and Freedom," Schaeffer directly addressed the corruptions wrought by humanist-derived contemporary legal thought and law school teaching, complaining that, in part through the purported exile of William Blackstone from the core curriculum, the Christian

attack has been enlisted as a Christian Right rallying cry – yet more evidence of the liberal/ progressive war on Christians – in the ongoing campaign to redeem and reclaim the Supreme Court. See Adam Liptak, "Two Judges Exemplify the Choices Trump Faces in a Supreme Court Pick," *New York Times* (July 3, 2018) (www.nytimes.com/2018/07/03/us/politics/trump-supreme-court-judges-kavanaugh-barrett.html). Given Francis Schaeffer's hostility to Catholicism, it is interesting to note the formative role that right-wing Catholic leadership has played in forging a co-belligerent Christian Right and seeking to import that co-belligerence into American constitutional law.

In the early 2000s, Professor George initiated a successful effort to have a large statue of John Witherspoon erected and placed in a central location on the Princeton University campus. See also Jeffry H. Morrison, *John Witherspoon and the Founding of the American Republic* (South Bend, IN: University of Notre Dame Press, 2005). Morrison holds advanced degrees from Boston College and Georgetown University and teaches at Pat Robertson's Regent University, which was founded in 1977 as the Christian Broadcasting Network University.

[53] Schaeffer, *Christian Manifesto*, 33–34.   [54] Schaeffer, *Christian Manifesto*, 34, 36.
[55] Schaeffer, *Christian Manifesto*, 37, alluding to, among others, William Blackstone, John Adams, and Joseph Story. For a contemporary analysis by a prominent conservative historian, see Gertrude Himmelfarb, *The Roads to Modernity: The British, French, and American Enlightenments* (New York: Alfred A. Knopf, 2004).

foundations of US law had been erased, and American law students were trained instead in "secularized, sociological law" – "law that has no fixed base but law in which a group of people decides what is sociologically good for society at any given moment; and what they arbitrarily decide becomes law." Schaeffer cited the thought of Oliver Wendell Holmes Jr. as the paradigmatic example.[56]

This argument, set out succinctly in *A Christian Manifesto*, had underwritten Schaeffer's two earlier and more historically, philosophically, theologically, and visually elaborated film series *How Should We Then Live?* and *Whatever Happened to the Human Race?* that Schaeffer had released to a broad (Christian, conservative, Republican) audience a few years earlier in the late 1970s.[57] While rarely discussed as key statements of legal or constitutional theory – if discussed at all – outside the movement, both film series presented memorable critiques of the modern Court and, indeed, of modern "progressive" jurisprudence, which, drawing from the nomenclature of the early (progressive) Legal Realists like Roscoe Pound, Schaeffer dubbed "sociological law."

How Should We Then Live? was a multi-episode documentary history of Western art and culture. *Whatever Happened to the Human Race?* was a multi-episode documentary on the brave new world of bioethics, emphasizing abortion. In both, *Roe v. Wade* was taken not only as a bad, or even evil, decision but as a signifier and symbol for nothing less than society's abandonment of God and, consequently, the decline of Western civilization itself. *Roe* had sounded the claxon announcing an existential choice: will Christians stand by silently as evil triumphs and Western civilization dies, or will they stand up and fight for Christ? An epic battle had begun.

While such a call might be made crudely and simplistically, the films did not take that route: they presented a subtle and apparently learned critique of modernity, while memorably situating the Supreme Court's jurisprudence within that modernity. The ostensible subject of the ten-part documentary film *How Should We Then Live?* is the history of art in the context of the development of Western civilization. The viewer is led, guided, and instructed throughout by the sure voice of an omniscient narrator – in this case the Reverend Francis Schaeffer. Schaeffer strolls confidently – the picture of learned man thinking – through historical sites, ruins, costumed reenactments, galleries, and great buildings, observing, commenting, and teaching.[58] But *How*

---

[56] Schaeffer, *Christian Manifesto*, 41.

[57] These first appeared as films but were so popular that Schaeffer (and Koop) subsequently published book versions. Francis A. Schaeffer, *How Should We Then Live?* (Wheaton, IL: Crossway Books, 1976); C. Everett Koop, MD, and Francis A. Schaeffer, *Whatever Happened to the Human Race?* (Wheaton, IL: Crossway Books, 1979).

[58] Given the drift of university campuses in recent years, one of the more remarkable developments in the self-conception of Evangelical and Fundamentalist Christians is that they are among the West's last remaining defenders of intellectual freedom. This has at long last allowed them to move beyond the characterization of them – in their own minds at least, and in the stories they

Should We Then Live? is palpably political from the outset. The film is didactic: each episode is structured around a repeatedly reiterated theme and leads to a powerful, concluding lesson.

Schaeffer begins with the present, situating contemporary political struggles as the latest chapter in an ongoing battle between good and evil as old as Western civilization itself. The series begins by warning viewers that the West is on the precipice of another societal collapse, a descent into barbarism and a Dark Age. The only hope is that by learning this history, Americans might triumph over error and live in the light given us by God through salvation by his Lord, Jesus Christ.

The first episode starts not with the pagan democracies of ancient Greece – before God's Truth was revealed to the world – but with Rome, when man had a choice to accept God's Truth or reject it. It opens solemnly and reverently: we gaze upon a triptych stained-glass window, intimating meaning and eternity. The mood is suddenly shattered by a cut to chaotic images of the urban American unrest of the 1960s and 1970s, including bombings and buildings ablaze, to the sound of gunshots and sirens. A man is handcuffed; another, clutching a rifle, is dead. The police are barely holding up against the enveloping chaos. They beat demonstrators. A domestic war has erupted. "There is a flow to history and culture," Schaeffer speaks calmly but firmly, more in sorrow than in anger: "This flow is related to what people think. What they think will determine how they act." In a world teetering between chaos and authoritarianism, what are we to do? How should we be? To answer, we must delve into history. Only by beginning at the beginning can we gain the necessary perspective on modern man's predicament.

Rome was great in many ways, Schaeffer explains. But it "had no real answers to the basic problems that all humanity faces." The Romans had no basis for knowing right from wrong. They mistakenly built society upon the quicksand of their "opinions." When that did not avail, they turned to finite and limited gods modeled on ordinary men and women. When their society collapsed, Rome turned toward authoritarianism; its emperors ruled as gods. The early Christians stood against this and were martyred: their faith threatened

tell themselves – as anti-reason and antiscience, a characterization fixed in the broader culture since the 1920s Scopes "Monkey Trial," which they have long resented. Schaeffer and his ilk – and the new framings advanced by a proliferation of scholarly Western Civilization and Constitutional Democracy Programs on university campuses that have thrived with conservative financial support – have made it possible for these Christian conservatives to shake the Scopes albatross. The Religious Right had been significantly aided in this reframing by the postmodernist, poststructuralist, anti-colonialist, and identity-based movements of the campus Left, which turned ordinary off-campus liberals and progressives, who knew little of these things, into sitting ducks for the charge that they were anti-Truth, anti-American, and anti–Western Civilization – not to mention intolerant and anti-intellectual. See generally Amy Binder and Kate Wood, *Becoming Right: How Campuses Shape Young Conservatives* (Princeton: Princeton University Press, 2013).

the unity of the "totalitarian" state, and its culture.[59] If they had worshipped both Jesus and Caesar, Schaeffer ventures, they would have been tolerated. But, like the early Christians, who brooked no false gods, the Romans eschewed syncretism. This clash between the Christian Truth and "the flux of the relativistic Roman world," we learn, closely resembled the current clash between Bible-believing Christians and the Godless state. So too did the clashing cultures. The decadent, Godless Romans were violent and obsessed with sensual gratification; they engaged in "rampant sexuality." Recalling and portending Divine Retribution, ancient paintings depicting lesbianism and phallus worship flash across the screen, followed by scenes of Pompeii in ruins. Before long, Rome collapsed.

In time, Christianity became Rome's official religion. But its populace slid into apathy: its art became decadent, its music bombastic, and its elites sybaritic. To counteract this "inward rottenness," the state assumed more and more power, and freedom was circumscribed. Burdened by the cost of an ever-expanding government, Rome's economy collapsed. The prospect of rescue by a new authoritarianism became more and more appealing.

In contrast to the simple and spare Christian Church of the first century A.D., where the Bible, and the Bible alone, was preached as "the absolute, infallible word of God," the medieval Christian society that followed drifted toward a lavishness that, as reflected in medieval art, moved away from the representation of "real people" to an affinity for "symbols" and the "otherworldly" mysticism of the Roman Catholic Church, which was all too comfortable mixing Church and state, the latter of which the Church consecrated, and whose machinery it enlisted to enforce compulsory tithes.

To be sure, the Middle Ages were in many respects a period of cultural advance laying the basis for the Renaissance and Reformation. But the Bible's teachings were being supplemented – corrupted – by the all-too-human teachings of the Church. Saint Thomas Aquinas "opened the floodgates," elevating the worldly Church above Holy Scripture and nourishing an overconfidence in man's reason and intellect. Thomas mixed the Christian and the classical, downplaying the significance of the Fall. Philosophy, fed by man's swelling pride, grew increasingly autonomous, raising the once unthinkable question among Christians: Is the Bible really necessary?[60] The perversion of Christianity by the medieval

---

[59] Here, Schaeffer anachronistically and inaccurately calls ancient Rome "totalitarian." This suggests a parallel between the Rome of the Caesars and the contemporaneous USSR, and positions Christians in heroic and parallel resistance to both.

[60] Princeton's Robert P. George, who has devoted a significant amount of his time to uniting Catholics and Protestants for conservative political action and is active in Christian Right efforts to capture the Supreme Court, has diplomatically ventured that the objection lodged by Protestants that Catholic thought places too much confidence in man's reason is the objection to his own work that most seriously concerns him, intellectually and theologically. Notably, the problem of reconciling "Athens" and "Jerusalem" – Reason and Faith – is perhaps the chief conundrum of Straussian political thought. In this way, while Evangelical and Fundamentalist

Catholic Church led Western man to an impasse: should he follow the path of "absolute truth" or turn down the alluring roads of humanism or relativism?

As Western civilization stood at a crossroads, the Renaissance brought a new humanism. Its admittedly glorious art placed man at the center of a realistically depicted space, formulated mathematically by man's mind.[61] As the period's autobiographies and portrait paintings demonstrated, the individual artist assumed a new importance. Renaissance humanism sought nothing less than man's autonomy. "[T]he die was cast" for a "rebirth" of the golden age of pagan Greece and Rome. Saint Thomas Aquinas's decision to base his theology on the teachings of the pagan Aristotle set Western philosophy on a new course, evident in the era's masterpieces like Raphael's *The School of Athens*[62] and Michelangelo's *David* – not the Biblical David, after all, but a hymn to the greatness and beauty of man. Leonardo's drawings of the human anatomy – blood vessels, muscles, and bones – "failed" by not situating man within God's meaningful unity. Humanism's natural conclusion was pessimism: it would all end in despair.[63]

But then came the Reformation, which "turn[ed] away from the humanistic elements that had entered into the Church in the Middle Ages." The Bible was translated into vernacular languages. Johann Sebastian Bach musically celebrated God's unification of the particular and the universal. Reformed Christian congregations approached God directly by lifting their voices in peerless Christian hymns. Reformed Christianity recognized the innate dignity of individuals and their vocations, so manifest in the Dutch paintings of the time depicting individuals going about their daily lives and the wonders of God's creation.

The "age of revolutions" episode of the film series opens with a judge passing in front of a painting in a Swiss courthouse that reminds all who see it that the "Bible gives a basis, not only for morals but for law." In the painting, justice is not depicted blindfolded but as seeing; her sword is pointing not up, but down – to the written law of God. These set the foundations of northern Europe in the wake of the Reformation, which freed citizens from arbitrary government power, foundations committed to writing, we learn, by Samuel Rutherford, who had a profound influence on the US Constitution. It was faithful Christians and the Christian consensus that provided the basis for our nation's unique

---

(Protestant) conservatives, Roman Catholic conservatives, and Straussians may disagree on many things, they are all focused on the same basic questions and problems in a way that sharply distinguishes them from progressive/liberals, most of whom are probably not even aware that this is the central puzzle and problem preoccupying the most important conservative political and constitutional theorists.

[61] This is perhaps an allusion to the revolution in the visual depiction of perspective inaugurated by the Florentine artist Brunelleschi.

[62] This turn to philosophy, the argument suggests, implicates the sin of pride.

[63] But see Joshua Foa Dienstag, *Pessimism: Philosophy, Ethic, Spirit* (Princeton: Princeton University Press, 2006).

commitments to inalienable rights, government by consent, and the right of revolution. The documentary then cuts to images of Philadelphia's Independence Hall, where the US Constitution was framed.

Schaeffer then turns to the French Revolution and distinguishes it sharply from the American. The French had tried to replicate the achievements of the English "without the Reformation base, which gave freedom without chaos." Starting only with "Voltaire's humanist Enlightenment base, the result was a bloodbath and a rapid breakdown in the authoritarian rule of Napoleon." The French Declaration of the Rights of Man was a desperate stab at genuine constitutionalism. But it had "nothing to rest upon." Within two years, it was a dead letter. Events spun out of control. Christianity was shunted aside, and the French bowed down before the Goddess of Reason (the film's visuals swell with scenes of slaughter and the sound of blood-curdling screams). The Terror, Schaeffer explains, was "the product of the humanist, enlightenment base" emphasizing the perfectibility of man and society – the same commitments that animated the Russian Revolution, culminating in a dictatorship of a secular elite.

To be sure, Schaeffer acknowledges, Christians too have done some terrible things. There are two areas where a recommitment to Christian principles was especially needed: first, race discrimination, and second, the stewardship of accumulated wealth. Chattel slavery was based on a race prejudice holding blacks to be less than human. Its sordid story, Schaeffer explains, involved Arabs capturing Africans and selling them to slave traders, who treated them with untold cruelty. Against all of this, Christians did not speak out sufficiently. For its part, the industrial revolution affronted the dignity of the individual and neglected the compassionate use of accumulated wealth. Men and women were forced to work long hours, and children were abused, all of which the Bible forbids. Again, most Christians did not speak out sufficiently, against either this behavior or the utilitarianism philosophy that justified it.[64]

Schaeffer's account of "the scientific age" defends Galileo and Copernicus and laments understandings holding scientific truth and God's revealed truth to be antagonistic. It was not always thus: founders of modern science like Pascal believed that "man was special, because Christ had died upon the cross for him"; Pascal distinguished "how?" from "why?" Newton began with a personal Creator God, and Francis Bacon believed in the Bible and the Fall. God gave man benevolent dominion over nature and charged him with investigating His marvelous creation. Western scientists lived "in the thought forms brought forth by Christianity." "[W]ithout this base," Schaeffer intones, "modern western science would have never been born" (the film cuts to an image of a Boeing 747 taking off).

---

[64] In both of these cases Schaeffer (slyly) condemns Christians for their passivity in not challenging these evils, rather than for actively engaging in them. As such, the damage is done not by Christians doing wrong, but by Christians remaining silent.

Schaeffer then explains why Einstein's theory of relativity was not really relativistic: it did not undercut the idea of eternal Truth at the heart of the Christian tradition. Darwin, however, was a different matter: he posited an unbroken line from the molecule to man, "merely on the basis of time and chance," without any how or why: "Tragically, after one has accepted the concept of survival of the fittest, all restraints are removed." While strolling through the Olympic Stadium built by the Nazis to host the 1936 Berlin Olympics, interspersed with archival footage of Nazi rallies and parades, Schaeffer explains that Darwin laid the groundwork for twentieth-century racism. The film cuts to images of concentration camps.

Today, Schaeffer adds sorrowfully, proponents of genetic engineering were using "exactly the same arguments." "When the Christian consensus died, it left a vacuum" that "will tend to be filled by an elite, to form an authoritarian state" operating according to "sociological law." Christians believe man is unique and has unique dignity; they do not start from "what is sociologically accepted at the moment." "As a Christian," Schaeffer explains, "I have a reference point in the Bible." I have "something by which to judge things by" – "cubby holes ... as it were ... to fit the thoughts that are being thrown at me." Otherwise, "I am just left naked." Facts simply cannot be understood independent of (Christian) values. To attempt to do so leads not only to arbitrariness but also to arbitrary absolutes.[65] The film cuts to the Soviet Union where we learn political prisoners were subjected to mental reconditioning in penal colonies. But the process need not be so crude: ideas can recondition as well. The film then cuts to a simulation of the government surreptitiously putting drugs in the public water supply.

We see a man drawing a circle, representing unified knowledge. A different man crosses it out. Another comes along and draws a circle. And yet another crosses *that* out. And so goes the metaphor: man has sought to make his way by reason alone. Finally, humanistic man "gave up his hope of a unified answer," and a dark side of humanity came to the fore. In an affront to both civilization and reason, the political philosopher Jean-Jacques Rousseau sought no less than absolute freedom by placing the individual rather than God at the center of the universe, making Rousseau a hero to bohemians, libertines, and primitivists ever since, who thrilled to his revolt against all values and restraints.[66] Social action was grounded in no more than "the general will" – the will of society – the wellspring of Robespierre's bloodthirsty and tyrannical French Revolutionary Terror.

[65] The rejection of Max Weber's Fact-Value distinction is also a major theme of the Straussians. Herbert Storing, editor, *Essays in the Scientific Study of Politics* (New York: Holt, Rinehart, and Winston, 1962) (epilogue by Leo Strauss); Nasser Behnegar, *Leo Strauss, Max Weber, and the Scientific Study of Politics* (Chicago: University of Chicago Press, 2003).

[66] See Norman Podhoretz, "The Know-Nothing Bohemians" *Partisan Review* 25 (Spring 1958): 305–311; Norman Podhoretz, "The Beat Generation," *Partisan Review* 25 (Summer 1958): 476–479; Norman Podhoretz, "The Adversary Culture and the New Class," in B. Bruce-Briggs, editor, *The New Class?* (New Brunswick, NJ: Transaction Books, 1979); Irving Kristol, "The Adversary Culture of the Intellectuals," *Encounter* (October 1979).

At this point, it seemed, no basis for morals or law remained. Kant, Hegel, and Kierkegaard sought unity and meaning in the universe without recourse to God, to no avail. Existentialists fashioned an entire philosophy on the conviction that life is absurd and meaningless, and positing that one can validate one's self and achieve meaning through an act of will. Schaeffer illustrates the absurdity of this by showing a frail old woman crossing the street and explaining that, from an existentialist point of view, an individual could achieve meaning equally by either assisting her or running her down. In real life, we must choose between right and wrong.

What is the solution for modern man's predicament? Aldous Huxley believed that the answer could be found inside one's own head anytime through the ingestion of mind-altering drugs, a hope that animated the 1960s counterculture, including its turn to Eastern religions and even demons (the occult).[67] The church itself, Schaeffer charged, bore some responsibility: its modern liberal theology helped create the vacuum into which these horrors rushed. Schaeffer underlined his contrasting approach to the Bible: "I read it exactly the way it was written ... I read it as a straightforward statement of what was meant ... [I read it to answer] the questions that humanistic philosophy could not, when I asked 'Is this truth?'" The episode ends with images of a burned-out city block, an abandoned car, a Hindu deity, and announcements of the death of God.

Citing Kandinsky's observation that modern art was born in the movement from unity to fragmentation, Schaeffer begins the documentary's next episode with a lesson on the French Impressionist painters, who, he explains, depicted reality as a dream, leaving their successors, the post-Impressionists, with the problem of the loss of meaning. Cézanne reduced nature to its basic geometric forms, evident in the broken, fragmented appearance of his work, carried forward first into Picasso's cubism and then more generally into Dadaism, which championed the idea of "the ultimate absurdity of everything." Finally, the human disappeared completely: we were left with the drip paintings of Jackson Pollack, where all is chance.

Schaeffer's parallel account of the trajectory of classical music arraigns Claude Debussy with opening the door to fragmentation by turning to perpetual variation that never resolved, and we soon arrived at the atonality and dissonance of Schoenberg and Stockhausen, and then ultimately to John Cage, who believed that the universe was characterized fundamentally by change, leading to either "sheer noise," Dadaist absurdity (*Music for Marcel Duchamp*), or silence (*4½ minutes of Silence*). This was not art but anti-art: it

---

[67] Aldous Huxley, *The Doors of Perception* (New York: Harper, 1954). The 1960s rock group The Doors took their name from Huxley. Here, Schaeffer positions Christianity as entailing a belief in reason rather than a turn to non-reason. But Schaeffer defines "reason" in a specific way – as involving the successful search for a unified meaning to life that can only be found in (Protestant) Christianity's direct engagement with Holy Scripture.

was bald intellectual statement. Modern art, music, and dance did not fit the universe that actually existed, since the universe is not random. Nor did they reflect man's true nature. Schaeffer contrasted this trajectory with the beauty of Bach's *Goldberg Variations*. The film's soundtrack then goes silent, and we hear the lonely howl of a wolf.

In literature, modern man's despair was reflected in T.S. Eliot's *The Wasteland*, the novels and plays of Sartre and Camus, and depicted in the post-human, hero-less films of Ingmar Bergman, Frederico Fellini, Luis Buñuel, and Michelangelo Antonioni, whose subject was life's emptiness in the age of non-reason. Adrift, modern man turned in on himself, proclaiming, "I want to be left alone, and I don't care what happens to the man across the street, or across the world," and "I want my own lifestyle undisturbed," and craved fame and material consumption.

In the 1960s, professors were teaching their students that life had no fixed values or meaning, although the professors themselves did not seem to be living that conviction. Students saw this inconsistency and, understandably, Schaeffer ventures, revolted. A drug and Hippie scene blossomed. Tragically, however, the rebellious students alighted upon the wrong solutions.[68] The cult of drug taking crystallized into an ideology; fiascos marred the rock festivals at Altamont (1969) and the Isle of Wight (1970). The New Left collapsed into violence. A crushing apathy followed.

Outside of the United States, the young turned instead to the materialist philosophies of Marxism, Leninism, and Maoism, and their attendant tyrannies, so sadly reinforced by the crushing of the Hungarian revolt in 1956 and the Prague Spring (1968), and so ably chronicled by Aleksandr Solzhenitsyn. Communism was "a Christian heresy": it used phrases like the "dignity of man" borrowed from Christianity while separating them from their source. Against the backdrop of the radical feminist, antiwar and civil rights activist, and communist American professor Bettina Aptheker speaking, Schaeffer explained that communism had two streams: the idealistic utopian and the orthodox hard core. Communist ideology was perhaps most evident in the United States today in the creation of "arbitrary law."[69]

In the documentary's climax, Schaeffer contends that the culmination of all modernity, communism included, was the belief that the law could be autonomous from God: "The man who opened the door for this perhaps

---

[68] The Straussian political philosopher Allan Bloom offers the same diagnosis and opinion about these events in *The Closing of the American Mind: How Higher Education Has Failed Democracy and Impoverished the Souls of Today's Students* (New York: Simon and Schuster, 1987).

[69] See Bettina F. Aptheker, *Intimate Politics: How I Grew Up Red, Fought for Free Speech, and Became a Feminist Rebel* (Emeryville, CA: Seal Press, 2006); Bettina Aptheker, "Red Feminism: A Personal and Historical Reflection," *Science and Society* 66 (Winter 2002/2003): 519–526. Aptheker is currently a Distinguished Professor in the Feminist Studies program at the University of California, Santa Cruz.

more than anyone else, was Oliver Wendell Holmes." As a result, "The Constitution of the United States today can be made to say almost anything on the basis of sociological, variable law." The nation's courts were making law by the lights of the same relativistic, humanistic premises that had underwritten communism. Astonishingly, many did not realize that "arbitrary law has swept over the western world as well."

There was no better illustration of this than the Supreme Court's 1973 decision in *Roe* v. *Wade*, in which the Court "passed the abortion law." Here, the film shows Francis Schaeffer walking down the steps of the Supreme Court, with a sharp cut to pictures of a developing fetus, emphasizing the baby's eyes, heart, fingers, and toes. As the High Court's white marble pillars and façade loom, Schaeffer quotes from Justice Byron White's dissent in *Roe* denouncing the Court's decision as an exercise of "raw judicial power." Schaeffer laments that most people accepted the ruling because they assumed it to be "sociologically helpful": "What we are left with is sociological law. And that is all. And nobody knows where it will end." He then compares the Court's declaration of a constitutional right to an abortion to a slave being arbitrarily declared a nonperson by a declaration of positive law. We hear the cry of a baby being born.

If this is what the American Constitution is held to mean, Schaeffer asks, what will become of the aged, the ill, and society's other vulnerable members? Can we accept as constitutionally legitimate, and right, whatever policy happens to garner 51 percent of the vote? This is the dilemma a society faces when the Christian consensus undergirding it has disappeared. Schaeffer then types out a sentence, which he asks viewers to memorize: "If there is no absolute by which to judge society, society is absolute." If that is so, anything is possible.

In the absence of a Christian consensus, society can head in only one direction: to rule by a technocratic elite all too ready to set arbitrary absolutes. The situation was dire: this new, manipulative authoritarian elite tells us "please do not think of the model of Hitler and Stalin," that "what we are facing is something, much, much more subtle." But Schaeffer insists that the analogy is apt. The situation will be made even worse by the unprecedented powers of the modern media to manipulate public opinion.

One of the terrible political dilemmas of our time, he continues, in the documentary's final episode, is that many people who purport to care about civil liberties are simultaneously "totally committed to the fact that the government has the responsibility to solve every problem," raising the specter of authoritarianism, which will emerge from the executive, from Congress, and from a "manipulative, authoritarian ... Imperial Judiciary." It is time, Schaeffer concludes, to move away from the familiar political polarities of "Left" and "Right." The real threat to our society comes from a rising elite that fills the vacuum left by the loss of the Christian consensus. That elite imposes a government of its own devising upon society to prevent it from descending into chaos. If this happens to deliver the personal peace and affluence the people seem to crave, Schaeffer worries, then who will stand up to this tyranny?

This terrible predicament allows for only two alternatives: (1) an arbitrary order imposed by an elite or (2) a return to Biblical revelation. The latter is the right road to take. Christianity's superiority resides in the fact that it "cannot be accepted merely as a means to an end sociologically." Christians possess "a truth that gives us a unity of all knowledge, and of all of life" – here, the film cuts first to images of a humble early Christian community in the Roman Empire, sharing wine and song, and then to the Roman coliseum, with intimations of martyrdom. It is the high obligation that "the people who have this base to strive to influence the surrounding consensus, regardless of the cost," Schaeffer intones as the documentary reaches its rousing conclusion: "People act upon the basis of what they think ... The problem is having the right world view, acting upon it, the world view that gives men and women the truth of what is."

Schaeffer followed up *How Should We Then Live?* with *Whatever Happened to the Human Race?* focused on abortion and bioethics. Following mysterious imagery of a mother and children in white traversing a field, this series also opens with sirens – this time ambulances. At stake is a child's life: the film cuts to a hospital, where a premature newborn is saved through the heroic efforts of committed doctors and nurses.[70] The music shifts from alarming to uplifting, and Francis Schaeffer poses a fundamental question: Why is a human life worth saving? Because man is made in the image of God. Until recently, we learn, with some infamous exceptions, human beings were regarded as special. Today, however, a utilitarian philosophy predominates: "What is declared to be legal is [the] only standard as to what is morally right." The societal consensus has shifted from Christianity to humanism.

As apocalyptic music plays, we confront an apparently endless succession of caged lab rabbits and rats. As we move down the line, we suddenly and shockingly come upon a baby in the cage, wailing. A new post-Christian understanding has been spread by the media and taught in our schools, we learn; by now it is blindly accepted. The film cuts to a junkyard, where junked automobiles are being hoisted and rearranged by cranes. As Christian ethics have been abandoned, Schaeffer explains, many have come to believe that life unfolds mechanically, by chance, and without regard to values. Once confined to the laboratories, these theories have made their way to the streets. The film cuts incredibly quickly – subliminally – to the façade of the US Supreme Court. God, we are told, has been excluded from the picture.

Francis Schaeffer appears and sits on a dusty, smoking junk heap. Even a few years ago, he tells us, this would have been unthinkable, as would have been complacency toward abortion, infanticide, and euthanasia. We see a baby carriage sitting incongruously in the junkyard, then a young girl walking with her parents. They pass in front of the Supreme Court. Schaeffer appears. They are changing our view of law, he explains. Today, we are governed by arbitrary

---

[70] This time, the opening scenario is of Christians saving life, as in the previous film it was of Christians saving civilization.

sociological law "which a small group . . . in some branch of government thinks is good for the sociological, economic good of that moment," even on matters of life and death. This group wields its power through courts, the handmaidens of humanism. We are told, again, that the Supreme Court in *Roe* "passed the abortion decision." Justice White's dissent attacking *Roe* as an assertion of raw judicial power is quoted.

A second narrator appears, Dr. C. Everett Koop, who explains that his objections to abortion are based not only on morals but also logic.[71] The film offers vivid images of developing fetuses, whose developmental milestones Koop explicates, before graphically describing an array of brutal abortion techniques. The film cuts to an image of thousands of dolls strewn across a desolate white landscape, as far as the eye can see. Wind howls across the barren land. Snow? Salt. Koop surveys the scene from a pedestal. This is the site of the Biblical Sodom, he explains, "a place of evil and death." In our own time, we have witnessed "the death of moral law." And people scoff at Christian ethics! There have been 6 million abortions since 1973 – 6 million dead – sanctioned by the Supreme Court.[72] Another doctor testifies that the Court "gave to my profession an almost unlimited license to kill," "relinquish[ing] the role of the healer to become the social executioner." On these matters, we are told, there are no religious disagreements: God-given life is sacred, and abortion on demand is a euphemism for man playing God.

The second episode opens with ominous music as baby-dolls roll off a conveyer belt. A man leans over doing "quality control" – pulling defective babies off and tossing them in the "reject bin." Today, doctors are routinely practicing infanticide, we learn. Koop convenes a discussion of people with severe disabilities who, we see, in their own ways, are leading meaningful lives and flourishing. We are reminded that totalitarian governments dispose of the disabled; societies built on a Christian base do not. Physicians are pledged to save lives and alleviate suffering. Abortion, once extraordinary, is now used casually, as a form of birth control: "What ever happened to notions of right and wrong?"

The film then cites a recent article from the *New England Journal of Medicine* on death by the deliberate withholding of medical treatment, followed by a montage of a couple strolling down a supermarket aisle, causally picking products off the shelves. They come upon a shelf stocked with live children,

---

[71] This is the primary posture of Robert P. George, who insists that his views on these matters are not (only) religious but a matter of strict logic and reason. The two are consistent: put otherwise, his religious views are demonstrably logical and represent the only rational position on these matters. David D. Kirkpatrick, "The Right Hand of the Fathers," *New York Times Magazine* (December 20, 2009), 24.

[72] The number, of course, is meant to signify. The film also alludes here to the Supreme Court's decision in *Tennessee Valley Authority* v. *Hill*, 437 US 153 (1978), noting, by contrast, the extreme measures the Court had taken to protect the life of the endangered Little Tennessee River fish, the snail darter.

packaged in Bubble Wrap™ – for sale. The wife picks up one, matter-of-factly considers it, and returns it to the shelf. She then picks up a different one and considers whether to add it to her cart.

The film cut to images of enslaved African American people walking slowly across the façade of the Lincoln Memorial, and then, in a single long column, trudging wearily up its steps. Slavery was the arbitrary classification of blacks as nonhuman for economic convenience. Today, it is economically expedient to abort unwanted fetuses and eliminate imperfect babies. In every age, we are told, some group is branded as subhuman, be it the black, the Jew, or the unborn child. The Supreme Court's *Dred Scott* (1857) decision is mentioned, and we learn that the Supreme Court has been wrong more than once on crucial moral issues. Churches tolerated and even justified slavery, and these have their counterparts today. The episode ends with Francis Schaeffer ascending the steps of the US Capitol and cuts to the American flag flying high above its dome.

This next episode opens with a folksong-rag:

When I was in my mother's womb, you nearly put me in the tomb, yes you did . . . [to the animated image of crawling baby gradually progressing to walking]

> Well I know you didn't think it a sin,
> But you surely tried to sucker me in
> By the time I was seven,
> You told me there's no heaven
> Yes you did.
> You said we just got here by chance
> . . .
> When I got to 70
> You said I had to go . . .
> So you wheeled me off down the hall
> And you said this is better for us all.

"Life is a continuum, from conception until death," Francis Schaeffer intones, as a family wheels grandma off to her death, handing her off to a coldblooded nurse. The film goes dark. The elderly are the next category to be classed as nonhuman, we are warned: the Supreme Court "could be a death warrant for you and me in a few years." Demographic pressures are creating ever-stronger incentives: "[T]he thin edge of the wedge of the euthanasia movement is the so-called 'living will.'" It will be a short step to 'active euthanasia' – killing. Far-fetched? Think of how far-fetched *Roe* would have seemed just ten years earlier: "Once the Judeo-Christian base is gone, almost any inhumanity is possible." The documentary cuts to Bergen-Belsen, followed by Dachau, Auschwitz, and Buchenwald. We are ushered into the Room of the Eternal Flame of Yad Vashem.

Francis Schaeffer is solemnly studying and turns to face us. "Euthanasia was an integral part of the Nazi program," he explains. Terms like "rights" and "compassion" are "stolen from a more compassionate age and then used for manipulation." They lend "barbarous ideas ... emotional respectability."

We must stand against "situation ethics" and human meddling in God's affairs. The film cuts to images of Hitler: the cooperation of ordinary Germans laid the groundwork for the Nazi genocide.[73] A psychiatrist who testified at Nuremberg explains that the Holocaust had originated with the idea that "there is such a thing as life not worthy to be lived." Jews were killed first, then the frail, the infirm, and the mentally challenged. Physicians helped plan it, and most churches acquiesced. A series of phrases in white calligraphy on a black background flash in succession:

> "Termination of Pregnancy"
> "Death with Dignity"
> "Final Solution"

Schaeffer wanders forlornly through ruins of gas chambers and crematoria. "I challenge you to be a real person in this impersonal age ... come to your senses: you are people, made in the image of the personal God, who created all people in his image," he pleads. Schaeffer tells the story of Moloch – the God whose devotees worshipped him by offering up their own children as sacrifices. The churches must fight the anti-humanist trends in dark times: they should offer day care for parishioners and aid the handicapped. Christians must get personally involved. They cannot and should not slough off to the (secular humanist) state these basic responsibilities.

We see a monument on a beach inscribed:

> To those who were robbed of life, the unborn, the weak, the sick, the old, during the dark ages of madness, selfishness, lust, and greed for which the last decades of the twentieth century are remembered.

The inscription is on a pedestal supporting a sculpture of a mother holding a baby, backlit by the sun. The episode closes with Schaeffer's declaiming, "This is the great moral test of our age which I am laying before you. The choice is yours to make."

The next episode also opens with a folksong-rag:

> Two hundred years ago, we helped the African
> We brought him to a land of great opportunity.
> And though at first he didn't find it easy
> Wasn't it wonderful that he could be free?

---

[73] The film cites Richard L. Rubenstein's *The Cunning of History: Mass Death and the American Future* (New York: Harper and Row, 1975), described in a *Kirkus Review* précis "that the 'final solution' represented the triumph of bureaucratic organization applied to the problem of surplus or redundant populations; [Rubenstein's] fear is that overpopulation and shrinking world resources are likely to make 'administrative massacre' a commonplace in the years to come. The first step toward death, he contends, comes when a group of people is bureaucratically 'redefined' to exclude it from citizenship – as the Germans did with the Jews." Schaeffer and Koop are situating abortion rights, euthanasia, and other "life" issues – not to mention the modern US "administrative state" – in this context and frame.

Forty years ago we helped the Jew man.
We kept him out of trouble on a lowly German farm
And now we'd like to help you
We want to make sure you come to no harm.

We see a reenactment of the Pilgrims arriving on America's shores, followed by an abrupt cut to an animated song-and-dance number to the tune of Cole Porter's "Anything Goes": high-spirited doctors on a stage are gleefully vacuuming up fetuses. The pillars of the Supreme Court descend, and we see the inscription carved above them: "Equal Justice Under Law." In the animated sequence, dancing, black-robed Supreme Court justices wield their gavels to crush men in wheelchairs desperately trying to flee. There is applause, and a curtain call. Doctors, nurses, and Supreme Court justices join hands in a chorus line interspersed with Nazi officers. An uncompromising adherence to the much-mocked Christian view, we are told, is the only way to resist evil.

An animated sequence features a barbershop quartet trying to sing without a pitch pipe: "What confusion! What disaster!" This is a foolish stab at "Truth without a capital 'T.'" "It is not only the iron curtain countries that operate on the basis of a relativistic morality," Schaeffer explains. The West is also dominated by a materialistic worldview that has no basis for distinguishing cruelty from compassion, injustice from justice. With their theories of endless cycles, Eastern religions provide no answers. "One would have imagined at this point that Western man would be glad for a solution to the various dilemmas facing him," Schaeffer wonders, "and would welcome an answer that does answer the big questions." A series of words, in all capital letters, flash in succession across the screen: "SOLUTION," "TRUTH." The film presents yet another animated sequence, this time of a villain tying a helpless woman to train tracks. We know the hero is on the way. But Schaeffer suggests that we imagine for a moment that there is no hero, and that the woman's situation is hopeless. How would she react? She might be courageous; she might pitifully concoct a chimerical hope against actual knowledge of her impending doom, which would lead most people to despair (Schaeffer cites the Existentialists). "People are hungry for something that will give them a meaning in life." "And people are afraid." "Society can have no stability when based on a world view that has no absolute roots in truth."

Yet another animation – this time of three (orchestral) conductors: the first launches into a piece by Debussy; the second, Beethoven's Ninth Symphony; and the third, a Sousa march. They squabble. "One world view," Francis Schaeffer lectures, "can explain the existence of the universe and its form, and the uniqueness of people. That is the world view given us in the Bible." The Bible is "objectively true ... it does give the answers." "It is God who gives the answers. Man's reason does not create the answers. It only recognizes the answers." "Man must choose to accept God's truth."

The final episode opens with a naked infant on his back in a chain-link cage. "In our own time," abortion "has become ... a selfish, absolute right, sanctioned by the state." "The life of one group in society has been arbitrarily reclassified as nonhuman ... purely for sociological considerations" to "a strange silence by the legal and medical professions." The film cuts to images of caged, enslaved African American people, then caged Jews and the elderly. A bell tolls. The sound of a beating heart. Society, we are reminded, "has scoffed at and rejected Christian morality." "The real problem is a false view of truth." The film cuts to an image of a windswept desert, then to images of the Holy Land, where God revealed himself to man. Francis Schaeffer stands atop Mount Sinai. Then, as he walks along the shore of the Sea of Galilee, he recounts the story of doubting Thomas and quotes Jesus: "Blessed are those who have not seen, and believe."

The documentary ends.

THE POLITICAL IMPACT OF FRANCIS SCHAEFFER'S FILMS

The younger Frankie Schaeffer took the lead in extensively marketing *Whatever Happened to the Human Race?* and *How Should We Then Live?* to (Christian) popular audiences and Republican elected officials and operatives alike. Considered together, the films culminated in an aggressive assault on abortion and the contemporary Supreme Court.

As the previous summaries make clear, however, the film series did not start out this way – at least in a focused way. As the elder Schaeffer initially imagined the films, the core thesis of *How Should We Then Live?* "was that the best of Western culture, art, freedom, and democracy could be traced to a Christian foundation. And that foundation was under attack from humanist and secular ideas and elites. In consequence, we were losing our freedoms because there were no longer absolutes that we could all agree on to guarantee them."[74] When Francis and Frankie Schaeffer began their work on this series, the elder Schaeffer did not want to even mention abortion: the film was already in production when the Supreme Court handed down the *Roe* v. *Wade* decision in 1973, and, as noted, abortion was not one of the elder Schaeffer's chief concerns. It was a major concern, however, of his son, who later explained that "[m]y antiabortion fervor was strictly personal. It had a name, Jessica, my little girl, proof that conception is good, even an unexpected teen conception." Frankie later regretted that he had "goaded my father into taking political positions far more extreme than came naturally to him." Indeed, the son and the father had heated arguments over abortion, with the elder Schaeffer insisting that the issue was off the table:

"How can you say you believe in the uniqueness of every human being if you won't stand up on this?" I yelled. "I don't want to be identified with some Catholic issue. I'm not putting my reputation on the line for them!" Dad shouted back. "So you won't speak out

---

[74] Schaeffer, *Crazy for God*, 260–261.

because it's a Catholic issue?" "What does abortion have to do with art and culture? I'm known as an intellectual, not for this sort of *political thing!*" shouted Dad. "That's what you always say about the Lutherans in Germany!" I yelled. "You say they're responsible for the Holocaust because they wouldn't speak up, and now you're doing the same thing!"[75]

Frankie reported that afterward his parents prayed extensively about the matter and ultimately arrived at the conclusion that their son's view was "prophetic." Francis decided to rewrite the last two episodes of *How Should We Then Live?* to focus on abortion and to enlist the new *Roe* decision in the film as an illustration of "the prime example of the erosion of the values that once made the West great," placing the *Roe* decision within a wider civilizational frame that made it not just about women and babies but also a symbol of the corruption of Western civilization itself.[76] As Frankie later characterized it, "The impact of our two film series, as well as their companion books, was to give the evangelical community a frame of reference through which to understand the secularization of American culture, and to point to the 'human life issue' as the watershed between a 'Christian society' and a utilitarian relativistic 'post-Christian' future stripped of compassion and beauty."[77]

The joining of the abortion issue and the civilizational framing were critical to the subsequent selling of the film to powerful conservatives on the incipient New Right. Frankie had been responsible for raising the funds necessary to make the film in the first place, work that took place pre-*Roe*. The natural source of funding for Schaeffer's message about the rise of secular humanism and the secular humanist war on Bible-believing Christians was, naturally enough, wealthy Evangelicals. "At first I was nervous" in meeting and facing these bigwigs, he reported. "But I soon got used to telling wealthy evangelicals that it was time to 'take our country back,' to 'answer the humanists,' to 'defend our young people,'" he later recounted.[78]

Strategies were formulated, and donor idiosyncrasies were canvassed. The Grand Rapids, Michigan, Evangelical Christian media figure and communications specialist Billy Zeoli, a key advisor to the Schaeffers (and to local politician Gerald R. Ford), informed them, for instance that "'Mary Crowley [the founder of Home Interiors and Gifts] doesn't like to be asked,' ... 'You have to get her to take you to her private chapel and pray about the project with her. Make *sure* you kneel down next to her *and hold her hand!* Then let *her* ask you how to help.'" With Rich DeVos (also a Grand Rapids native, and graduate of the local Calvin College), the founder and president of Amway – and the father-in-law of Donald Trump's Secretary of Education Betsy DeVos, who married Richard DeVos Jr.– the tactic was different. "'Talk to Rich about saving capitalism!' Billy would say. 'Tell him your Dad is standing up to the socialists! Do *not* talk about art!' With the 'Hunt

[75] Schaeffer, *Crazy for God*, 266–267.   [76] Schaeffer, *Crazy for God*, 261, 265–267.
[77] Schaeffer, *Crazy for God*, 273.   [78] Schaeffer, *Crazy for God*, 261–262.

boys' [the Texas oil and silver tycoons] as Billy called them, he advised 'Don't talk too fast! Do *not* mention the word 'intellectual.' Stick to the simple Gospel. We're doing this for Jesus! Got it?'"[79]

When the film was eventually released, it got a royal rollout and was taken on a fifteen-city grand tour for Christian audiences that included an event at New York City's Madison Square Garden. Frankie estimated that they spoke to more than forty thousand people at events in which the participants spent a full day first watching each of the film series episodes in succession and then joined in discussions led by Frank (and, later in the tour, Frankie) Schaeffer. Crowds of this size, Frankie Schaeffer later observed, may have been par for the course for Evangelical crusades and Pentecostal revivals. But this was different. "[E]vangelicals were coming to us to watch movies about art history and to head Dad talk about philosophy!" And, as the tour progressed, the crowds grew. "By the end ... Dad was one of the most sought-after and best-known evangelical leaders in the United States."[80]

Dallas Cowboy's quarterback Roger Staubach introduced the film to an audience of six thousand members of the general public, and half of his Dallas Cowboys teammates.[81] The Schaeffers were encouraged, including by C. Everett Koop who had seen *How Should We Then Live?*, to make another documentary film series, one that would focus specifically from its inception on the abortion issue.[82] Prominent Catholic conservatives soon got wind of these developments. "After Bishop Fulton J. Sheen saw the abortion-related episode of *How Should We Then Live?* and then heard from Dr. Koop that we were working on a pro-life series," Frankie later recounted, "he invited (the conservative producer and publisher) Jim Buchfuehrer and me to meet him in his Park Avenue apartment. Sheen wanted to strategize on ways to advance the pro-life cause ... 'The problem is,' Sheen said, 'that abortion is perceived as a Catholic issue. I want you to help me change that. The unborn need more friends.'" In his meeting with Sheen, Frankie kept mum about one obstacle that he knew he would have to overcome back home: his father despised the Catholic Church. "I grew up on Dad's stories about the extreme cruelty of the Spanish Roman Catholic Church and how the bishops were in league with Franco and the fascists," Frankie recalled.[83] "Before I left," Frankie remembered, "Sheen blessed me by making the sign of the cross over me. From that time on, we had the full cooperation of the Roman Catholic Church in America." This soon led, in turn, to an influx of money from Catholic civic organizations like the Knights of Columbus.[84]

---

[79] Schaeffer, *Crazy for God*, 262. [Emphases in original]   [80] Schaeffer, *Crazy for God*, 269.

[81] President Donald Trump recently conferred the Presidential Medal of Freedom on Staubach. Michael Tackett, "Trump Awards Medals of Freedom to Elvis, Babe Ruth, and Miriam Edelson," *New York Times* (November 16, 2018) (www.nytimes.com/2018/11/16/us/politics/presidential-medal-freedom-adelson.html).

[82] Schaeffer, *Crazy for God*, 270.   [83] Schaeffer, *Crazy for God*, 283–284.

[84] Schaeffer, *Crazy for God*, 284. Evangelical elites and leaders were initially quite wary of *Whatever Happened to the Human Race?* Frankie reported. But grassroots Evangelicals were

Once *Whatever Happened to the Human Race?* was completed, it became part of an ascending "Schaeffer juggernaut" on the American Right.[85] A major cultural and Republican Party phenomenon was in full swing, albeit completely under the radar of the largely liberal mainstream media. Although rarely reported on, both films were widely screened, and innumerable discussion groups formed. To meet the seemingly unslakable demand, book versions of the film series were drafted and published by Crossway. Although they never appeared on the *New York Times* best-seller list, which ignored Christian bookstores, both books were actually massive best sellers, outstripping in sales many of the (non-Christian) books that the *Times* had deemed eligible for its coveted "best-seller" status.[86]

Jack Kemp, a Republican congressman and former professional football player from Buffalo, New York famous as an evangelist for "supply side economics" (later Ronald Reagan's secretary of housing and urban development and a Republican vice-presidential nominee), stepped in as a conduit for the Schaeffers to the Republican Party, just as Fulton Sheen had served as the Schaeffer's conduit to the Catholic Church. Frankie Schaeffer later recalled how he had been introduced to Jack and his wife Joanne after Joanne had started a book club composed of approximately twenty wives of senators and congressmen who had met to read and discuss Francis Schaeffer's books (at one point what they had dubbed the "Schaeffer Group" hosted Francis Schaeffer himself to lead the discussion).[87]

When *Whatever Happened to the Human Race?* was released, Frankie and Jim Buchfuehrer "set up the 16-mm projector in Jack's living room, and we gave Jack and Joanne a private five-hour screening of [the film]." Frankie said, "Jack liked the movies and was ... genuinely moved. He also immediately saw the possibilities for the Republican Party." "By the end of that evening (actually, it was nearer dawn)," Frankie reported, "the pro-life cause had a new champion. From then on, Jack would give Koop, Dad, and myself, access to everyone in the Republican Party." Not long after this private screening, Kemp arranged for a special screening of three specially prepared episodes (cut to 90 minutes) of *Whatever Happened to the Human Race?* at the Republican Club in Washington, DC, that was attended by more than fifty US congressmen and twenty US senators. Francis Schaeffer himself introduced the film and took questions from the audience. Frankie reported that the session lasted more than four hours and that the party faithful were riveted: no one left early. Soon afterward, the National Right to Life Committee purchased airtime on the ABC affiliate television station in Washington to broadcast the same ninety-

---

enthralled and, gradually, aided by the nastiness and condescension of pro-choice forces at the time that helped alienate them, the full Evangelical community came on board. Schaeffer, *Crazy for God*, 291.

[85] Schaeffer, *Crazy for God*, 275.   [86] Schaeffer, *Crazy for God*, 286–287.
[87] Schaeffer, *Crazy for God*, 284–285.

minute version of the film.[88] Frankie Schaeffer accurately reported,[89] "it was my father and I who were amongst the first to start telling American evangelicals that God wanted them involved in the political process. And it was the *Roe v. Wade* decision that gave Dad, Koop, and me our platform."[90]

These films made abortion "*the* Evangelical issue," placed abortion at the heart of the culture wars, and forged the new co-belligerence among formerly antagonistic elements of Christian conservatism – Evangelicals, Fundamentalists, and Roman Catholics – in which they united against what they now saw as a "secular left" well on the way to destroying America and Western civilization. They, moreover, successfully worked to have this version championed to increasing effect by the contemporary Republican Party.[91] Frankie Schaeffer toured the country to screen his films and present his argument. "I must have done The Speech over a hundred times in the year or two after *Whatever Happened to the Human Race?* came out," he recalled, "Shorthand version: Abortion is murder; secular humanism is destroying us; turn back to our Christian foundation; vote Republican."[92] Schaeffer and his growing legion of followers were not alone in conveying this message or a message similar in its essential framing: it fit synergistically with other conservative visions of civilizational and constitutional decline, as championed by both Straussians and libertarians (whether or not they were Christian believers), despite their many disagreements. All nevertheless came to understand themselves as part of a common community allied against a common enemy – secularists, liberals, and, increasingly, progressives.[93]

"By the end of the *Whatever Happened to the Human Race?* tour," Frankie Schaeffer recounted, "we were calling for civil disobedience, the takeover of the Republican Party, and even hinting at overthrowing our 'unjust pro-abortion government.'" "Inspired by my father's call for civil disobedience in his best-selling *A Christian Manifesto* [1982] (and also urged to action by [Schaeffer's other book published that same year] *A Time for Anger* [1982]), the picketing of abortion clinics by evangelicals started on a large scale. Formerly passive evangelicals began talking about shutting the abortion clinics with a wall of protesters."[94] In the early 1980s, Francis and Frankie Schaeffer began to directly advise Republican politicians on wooing the Evangelical vote, including by persuading President Reagan to publish an article in the influential *Human Life Review*, which was subsequently turned into a book. The pro-life movement's strands had come together and were now centered in the White House.

---

[88] Schaeffer, *Crazy for God*, 285–286.   [89] See Dowland, *Family Values*, 17, 85, 96, 120–128.
[90] Schaeffer, *Crazy for God*, 289.   [91] Schaeffer, *Crazy for God*, 289.
[92] Schaeffer, *Crazy for God*, 325.
[93] See Kersch, "Constitutional Conservatives Remember the Progressive Era," in Skowronek, Engel, and Ackerman, editors, *The Progressives' Century*.
[94] Schaeffer, *Crazy for God*, 294–295. Schaeffer, *Christian Manifesto*; Francis Schaeffer, *A Time for Anger: The Myth of Neutrality* (Westchester, IL: Crossway Books, 1982); Ronald Reagan, "Abortion and the Conscience of the Nation," *Human Life Review* (Spring 1983).

OPERATIONALIZING THE EVANGELICAL VISION:
RELIGIOUS RIGHT LITIGATION CAMPAIGNS

Francis Schaeffer, his son Frankie, and Jim Buchfuehrer also played a critical role in moving the Christian Right into the courts and the country's legal culture more generally. The three met secretly with the televangelist and Christian Broadcasting Network (CBN) founder the Reverend Pat Robertson to arrange a contact with John Whitehead that led to the founding of The Rutherford Institute, "the 'Christian answer to the ACLU.'"[95] The Rutherford Institute, a pioneering Christian conservative cause litigation firm, was, of course, named for the very same Samuel Rutherford that Francis Schaeffer had lionized in his oeuvre, idiosyncratically insisting that Rutherford was the missing link that proved that Christianity was at the center of the Anglo-American legal tradition and, indeed, was the taproot of the rule of law itself. [96] In this story, besides

---

[95] Frankie Schaeffer, Buchfuehrer, Whitehead, and the Christian Reconstructionist Gary North were members of Rutherford's founding board. Schaeffer, *Crazy for God*, 315–316. Whitehead later served as co-counsel for Paula Jones in her sexual harassment lawsuit against President Bill Clinton. See www.rutherford.org/ (the site's banner trumpets the group as being "dedicated to the defense of civil liberties and human rights"). Within the movement, Whitehead's Rutherford model was soon followed by the Reverend Donald Wildmon's American Family Association Center for Law and Policy, available online at www.afa.net/; and Reverend Pat Robertson's American Center for Law and Justice, headed by Jay Sekulow (who currently serves also as a personal lawyer for President Donald Trump), available online at www.aclj.org/. Whitehead is a prolific author, often on constitutional topics. See John Whitehead, *Slaying Dragons: The Truth About the Man Who Defended Paula Jones* (Nashville, TN: Thomas Nelson, 1999); John Whitehead, *The Freedom of Religious Expression in Public Universities and High Schools*, 2nd ed. (Westchester, IL: Crossway Books, [1985] 1986); John Whitehead, *Stand and Fight: It's Time for a Second American Revolution* (Tyler, MN: Glass Onion/TRI Press, 2009). See also R. Jonathan Moore, *Suing for America's Soul: John Whitehead, The Rutherford Institute, and Conservative Christians in the Courts* (Grand Rapids, MI: William B. Eerdmans, 2007). In more recent years, The Rutherford Institute took some seemingly surprising turns, opposing, for example, the Iraq War and the USA Patriot Act, and defending the due process rights of War on Terror detainees José Padilla and Yaser Hamdi. Whitehead has, in some respects, turned away from politics, at least in its more statist ambitions. See John Whitehead, *God Is a Four-Letter Word* (Tyler, MN: Glass Onion/TRI Press, 2007). See Rob Boston, "Theocracy Rejected: Former Christian Right Leaders 'Fess Up': Frank Schaeffer, John Whitehead and Cal Thomas Have Repudiated the Theocratic Movement They Once Led. Here's Why," *Alternet* (March 10, 2008), accessed online January 20, 2015, at htttp://alternet .org/story/78818/theocracy_rejected%3A_former_christian_right_leaders_%27fess_up/? page=2. Ted Olson, "The Dragon Slayer: He Fights for Religious Liberty, Defends, the Civil Rights of Homosexuals, and Funded Paula Jones's Case against the President – the Enigmatic John Wayne Whitehead," *Christianity Today* 42 (December 7, 1998); Daniel Bennett, *Defending Faith: The Politics of the Christian Conservative Legal Movement* (Lawrence: University Press of Kansas, 2017), 19, 31, 140.

[96] Portions of the chapter that follow were previously published in Ken I. Kersch, "Constitutive Stories About the Common Law in Modern American Conservatism," in Sanford V. Levinson, Joel Parker, and Melissa S. Williams, editors, *Nomos LVI: American Conservatism* (New York: New York University Press, 2016), and are reprinted here by permission.

passing over (pagan) ancient Rome, Schaeffer, a few dismissive quips aside, almost completely ignored the (Roman Catholic) medieval constitutionalism he abhorred. He also all but wrote the religiously cagey John Locke out of the story and substituted the devoutly Christian Rutherford in his place, serviceably, given Rutherford's personal ties to John Witherspoon, The College of New Jersey (Princeton), and James Madison. This symbolically freighted distortion of history, now resident in The Rutherford Institute's very name, proved a useable past for a new group of politically involved and litigious right-wing Evangelical Christians.

There has been some excellent scholarship in recent years on the legal mobilization of Evangelical Christian conservatives; it is not my purpose to either repeat or try to add to that work in significant ways, although it is important to situate that mobilization at the *end* of an extended period of meaning-making culture work that over many antecedent years had laid the groundwork for that mobilization within the broader conservative movement.[97] It is important as well to note that Christian conservative legal advocacy groups were a distinctive type of legal mobilization. As Ann Southworth explained, "Advocates for social conservative groups are generally less inclined than lawyers for other constituencies to view politics as an arena for give and take and striking deals. Many religious conservatives view their organizations' goals as God's mandates rather than merely compelling policy objectives, and they are not inclined to compromise."[98] Amanda Hollis-Brusky and Josh C. Wilson's work has demonstrated the degree to which Evangelical and Fundamentalist Christian cause lawyers see their jobs less as ordinary political work and more as a religious calling.[99]

R. Jonathan Moore had earlier explained that in the late twentieth century, "Evangelical Protestants ... perceived themselves as defenders of the sacred spheres of family, church, and community, spheres increasingly and unjustifiably encroached upon by an out-of-control, hostile-to-religion

---

[97] See, e.g., Southworth, *Lawyers on the Right*; Hans Hacker, *The Culture of Conservative Christian Litigation* (Landham, MD: Rowman and Littlefield, 2005); Moore, *Suing for America's Soul*; Kevin den Dulk, "Prophets in Ceaser's Courts: The Role of Ideas in Catholic and Evangelical Rights Advocacy" (PhD dissertation, University of Wisconsin, 2001); Kevin den Dulk, "In Legal Culture, but Not of It," in Austin Sarat and Stuart Scheingold, editors, *Cause Lawyers and Social Movements* (Stanford: Stanford University Press, 2006); Amanda Hollis-Brusky and Josh C. Wilson, "Lawyers for God and Neighbor: The Emergence of 'Law as a Calling' as a Mobilizing Frame for Christian Lawyers," *Law and Social Inquiry* 39:2 (2014).

[98] Southworth, *Lawyers on the Right*, 105.

[99] Hollis-Brusky and Wilson, "Lawyers for God and Neighbor." This, of course, may be equally true of many, if not most, "cause lawyers," given that they have devoted their professional lives to a cause. That is, it is likely true almost by definition. Cause lawyers often practice law at a considerable financial sacrifice when compared to what they might earn in other areas of law. Lawyers for the NAACP LDF, the ACLU, and the Sierra Club most likely also see their legal work as involving a calling. That said, Hollis-Brusky and Wilson usefully document these dynamics within the litigation shops of the contemporary Christian Right.

government." In this, whatever their nominal affiliations or protestations to the contrary, many Evangelical conservatives especially were convinced that liberals (later, "progressives") were not "true" Christians. In many cases, they were even the enemies of Christianity, and Christians. Their objective as a newly mobilized political and legal community was no less than "to rehabilitate America's true religious character."[100] Evangelical and Fundamentalist Christian conservatives and other legally mobilizing members of the Reagan Era Religious Right were convinced that "history clearly demonstrated that the new nation's founders designed a constitutional framework dependent for legitimacy and success upon religion – specifically Christianity or the 'Judeo-Christian tradition.'" The Supreme Court, in decisions like *Engel* v. *Vitale*, *Abington* v. *Schempp, Roe* v. *Wade,* and *Bob Jones University* v. *United States* (1983) (and, later, the gay rights decisions of *Lawrence* v. *Texas* (2003) and *Obergefell* v. *Hodges* (2015)), had repudiated this truth and heritage and declared war on a Christian America.[101]

As Moore summarized it, many Evangelicals and Fundamentalists believed that "American courts systematically denuded American public life of religious activities and symbols during the last half of the twentieth century." These Evangelical and Fundamentalist Christians believed as follows:

---

[100] Moore, *Suing for America's Soul*, 5, 17. See also Dowland, *Family Values*.
[101] Moore, *Suing for America's Soul*, 24–25, 29–32; Dowland, *Family Values*. See also John Whitehead, *The Separation Illusion: A Lawyer Looks at the First Amendment* (Milford, MI: Mott Media, 1977). Many of these views were later picked up by the Evangelical Christian nationalist conservative author David Barton, who is widely read in key precincts of the contemporary popular American Right. Barton is currently active in Texas Republican politics, a supporter of his home state US Senator Ted Cruz, and a leader of "Project Blitz," a project of the Congressional Prayer Foundation (cpcfoundation.com), that is spearheading a campaign for state-level initiatives to promote discrimination against gays and lesbians under the guise of protecting religious liberty. Katherine Stewart, "A Christian Nationalist Blitz," *New York Times* (May 26, 2018) (www.nytimes.com/2018/05/26/opinion/project-blitz-christian-nation-alists.html). See David Barton, *The Myth of Separation: What Is the Correct Relation Between Church and State* (Aledo, TX: Wallbuilder Press, 1992); David Barton, *America's Godly Heritage* (Aledo, TX: Wallbuilder Press, 1993); David Barton, *Separation of Church and State: What the Founders Meant* (Aledo, TX: Wallbuilder Press, 2007); David Barton, *Original Intent: The Courts, the Constitution, and Religion* (Aledo, TX: Wallbuilder Press, 1996); David Barton, *The Jefferson Lies: Exposing the Myths You Have Always Believed About Thomas Jefferson* (Nashville, TN: Thomas Nelson, 2012); David Barton, *Restraining Judicial Activism* (Aledo, TX: Wallbuilder Press, 2003); David Barton, "The Image and the Reality: Thomas Jefferson and the First Amendment," *Notre Dame Journal of Law, Ethics, and Public Policy* 17 (2003): 399–459. Barton was invited to contribute to this academic "Symposium on Religion and the Public Square," hosted by right-wing Catholics at the University of Notre Dame, where his work – Barton holds only a B.A. in Christian Education from Oral Roberts University, and later had a best-selling book pulled by its publishers for historical inaccuracies – was presented alongside that of Douglas Kmiec, Kent Greenawalt, Francis Beckwith, and Richard Garnett, among others.

In ejecting religious conservatives from the nation's cultural center, the courts had unjustifiably attacked the very nature of American identity itself. As well, the courts assisted an increasingly secularist federal government in encroaching upon spheres of life once reserved to families and religious communities. While the courts busied themselves with stripping the public terrain of Christian totems, the federal government expanded its power over individual lives in an attempt to secularize all aspects of American life. This constituted a two-front war against religious conservatives, in their estimation, prosecuted by the very institutions that claimed to protect their freedoms.[102]

The Rutherford Institute's founder John Whitehead "believed strongly that Christianity belonged at the center of the American experience – historically, morally, and constitutionally. Near the end of the twentieth century, he thought that secularist forces were deliberately seeking to supplant Christianity." Whitehead had two goals in founding Rutherford: first, "to convince his fellow believers that secular humanism was indeed on the loose," and second, "to enable Christian resistance to secularism to take successful legal form."[103] Under the additional sway of Hal Lindsay's Christian apocalypse best seller *The Late Great Planet Earth* (1970) and radical Calvinist Rousas Rushdoony's (1916–2001) Christian Reconstructionism, as well as the ongoing influence of Francis Schaeffer, Whitehead melded current events with Biblical prophecy.[104] He "looked out at America and saw its conservative Christian subpopulation in need of a savior, one armed with the correct understanding of the Constitution and the courage to proclaim it and fight for it."[105] There was a strong dose of "originalism" in this vision, in the social movement, if not the legal academic

---

[102] Moore, *Suing for America's Soul*, 24.   [103] Moore, *Suing for America's Soul*, 37.

[104] Moore, *Suing for America's Soul*, 37, 58. Hal Lindsay, *The Late Great Planet Earth* (Grand Rapids, MI: Zondervan, 1970). Frankie Schaeffer later characterized the Christian Reconstructionists as "our version of the Taliban." He described them as "antitax, antigovernment libertarians (when it came to economics), but on social issues were working to replace secular law with Old Testament biblical law." Howard Ahmanson Jr., the heir to a banking fortune who later helped bankroll the Intelligent Design movement, helped found The Rutherford Institute, and served as a board member of the (West Coast Straussian) Claremont Institute, was a longtime adherent of Christian Reconstructionism. Schaeffer, *Crazy for God*, 333. See Rousas Rushdoony, *This Independent Republic: Studies in the Nature and Meaning of the American System* (Nutley, NJ: Craig Press, 1964); Rousas Rushdoony, *The Nature of the American System* (Nutley, NJ: Craig Press, 1965); Rousas Rushdoony, *Law and Liberty* (Vallecito, CA: Ross House Books, 1984). The Christian Reconstructionist Gary North melded Christian Reconstructionism with Austrian Economics – which I discuss at length in Chapter 3, "Stories About Markets." In the late 1960s through the 1970s, North, who has a PhD in history from UC-Riverside, wrote for *The Freeman* and worked for the Foundation for Economic Education (FEE), and, in turn, with Auburn, Alabama's Ludwig von Mises Institute. He is the founder of the Institute for Christian Economics. See Gary North, *An Introduction to Christian Economics* (Nutley, NJ: Craig Press, 1973); Gary North, *Inherit the Earth: Biblical Principles for Economics* (Arlington Heights, IL: Christian Liberty Press, 1987); Gary North, *Political Polytheism: The Myth of Pluralism* (Tyler, TX: Institute for Christian Economics, 1989).

[105] Moore, *Suing for America's Soul*, 38.

sense of the term: Whitehead invoked the Founders' constitutional understandings repeatedly in advancing his constitutional views and agenda. He was profoundly troubled that "America looks terribly disfigured when compared with the founders' original vision," that this once deeply religious nation, rooted in Biblical religion, had abandoned its founding ideals.

Prior to establishing Rutherford, Whitehead had taken his own scholarly stab at originalism in *The Separation Illusion* (1977), which sought to demonstrate the Founders' original understandings of the place of religion in America's constitutional order. While the presumption that Whitehead brought to this study might have been widespread among right-wing Evangelicals and Fundamentalists, others might find them highly idiosyncratic: in *The Separation Illusion*, Whitehead assumed, for instance, that everyone, including secularists, atheists, and agnostics, is, at his or her core, deeply religious. Everyone worships a God, in one form or another. If you don't worship the true (Christian) God, you, by default, ended up worshipping Man – that is, following popular ideas, wishes, and demands. This led to an amoral relativism and historicism and to a belief in the inherent rightness of political majorities (democracy). In the past, the worship of the people had led ineluctably to the horrors of the French Revolution, which, for its part, had led directly to communist totalitarianism. The time for choosing for America was now at hand: will it be God or Man?[106] As things then stood in the mid-1970s, Whitehead saw the United States moving headlong toward installing secular humanism as its all but official religious establishment. This posed a critical question for contemporary Americans: Who is lord – Our Lord Jesus Christ or the (Godless) State? On this question one could not be neutral: one had to choose sides.[107]

Whitehead had concluded *The Separation Illusion* with a ringing affirmation: Christianity is not just one worldview among many. It is *the* foundation. As such, it had, until very recently, been privileged in the United States, and rightly so; without a Christian foundation, morals become arbitrary, a mere matter of personal preference. If the bloody twentieth century had taught us anything, it was that the abandonment of the Christian foundation leads directly to Hitler and Stalin (Whitehead spoke repeatedly throughout *The Separation Illusion* about the "road to Auschwitz," not infrequently alluding to Supreme Court Justice Oliver Wendell Holmes Jr. along the way. The predominating contemporary understandings of law and the Constitution, Whitehead warned, were setting the United States on the road to totalitarianism.[108]

But there was an answer, and a hope. The United States had a constitutional heritage running from Samuel Rutherford, to John Witherspoon, to James

---

[106] Whitehead, *Separation Illusion*, 39, 42–47, 58, 66–67.
[107] Whitehead, *Separation Illusion*, 58, 66–67, 71. Whitehead was fond of quoting G. K. Chesterton: "When a man ceases to believe in God, he does not believe in nothing. He believes in anything." Moore, *Suing for America's Soul*, 91, n.15.
[108] Whitehead, *Separation Illusion*, 60–62, 88–89.

Madison, and beyond. We had a Declaration of Independence – which John Witherspoon, a clergyman, had solemnly signed – that put God's eternal Truth at its core. All that was required now was that Bible-believing Christians, the truest and most grounded of Americans, stand up, be counted, and fight.[109]

In the year he founded Rutherford, Whitehead published the book of which R. Jonathan Moore suggested Whitehead was most proud, *The Second American Revolution* (1982), which sold more than 100,000 copies and was also made into a documentary film.[110] Under the manifest influence of Rushdoony's Christian Reconstructionism, the book is an attack on the role that American courts have played in creating and advancing "the pagan state."[111]

The Second American Revolution provides a highly idiosyncratic, selective, and distorted – if, nevertheless, powerfully presented – account of American history and constitutionalism that opens with the assertion that an absolute, eternal, and fixed foundation is indispensible to government.[112] Repeating a major theme of *The Separation Illusion*, Whitehead announced that "man cannot escape his religiousness ... This principle is inherent in the Second

---

[109] Moore, *Suing for America's Soul*, 62–64, 72–75, 83–84, 94.

[110] Whitehead, *Second American Revolution*, 18 (Cover image: "The Spirit of '76," original painting in Selectmen's Room, Abbot Hall, Marblehead, Massachusetts). At Frankie Schaeffer's instigation, and in line with his conceptions, the book was also made into a film released by Frankie Schaeffer V Productions (Acknowledgments, n.p.). In the foreword to the book, Francis Schaeffer explains, "The government, the courts, the media, the law are all dominated to one degree or another by [the] elite. They have largely secularized our society by force, particularly using the courts ... If there is still an entity known as 'the Christian church' by the end of this century, operating with any semblance of liberty within our society here in the United States," he writes, "it will probably have John Whitehead and his book to thank," adding that this is "the most important book that I have read in a long, long time." See http://rutherford.org/ .

[111] See Rousas Rushdoony's *This Independent Republic: Studies in the Nature and Meaning of American History* (Nutley, NJ: Craig Press, 1964); Rousas Rushdoony, *The Nature of the American System* (Nutley, NJ: Craig Press, 1965); Rousas Rushdoony, *The Roots of Reconstruction, Law and Liberty* (Portland, OR: Ross House Books, 1971); and Rousas Rushdoony, *Institutes of Biblical Law*, Vols. 1–3 (Nutley, NJ: Craig Press, 1973). In 1965, Rushdoony founded the Chalcedon Institute, which is committed to the advancement of Reconstructionist Christianity. See http://chalcedon.edu/. "Post-Millennial" Reconstruction calls for the rule here and now, on earth, by the literal word of God, as set out in the Bible – particularly in the Old Testament. See generally Walter Olson, "Invitation to a Stoning: Getting Cozy with Theocrats," *Reason* (November 1, 1998). See also Frances Fitzgerald, *The Evangelicals: The Struggle to Shape America* (New York: Simon and Schuster, 2017), 340–347.

[112] See Neal Devins, "Book Review: *The Second American Revolution* by John W. Whitehead," *Hastings Constitutional Law Quarterly* 11 (Spring 1984): 505–522, concluding that Whitehead's thinking as expressed in the book "is alien to the values underlying American jurisprudence," that his history is "inaccurate," and that *The Second American Revolution* in the end is little more than "normative advocacy of the virtues of and the necessity for Christian life in a Christian state."

Commandment, prohibiting idolatry. In it the concern is not with atheism but with the fact that all men, Christian or not, seek something outside themselves to deify."[113] Since man is a deifying animal, in forming a society he faces a stark and momentous decision: he can either deify (worship) God or man. To deify man, including under the guise of the separation of church and state, is to commit the sin of idolatry. Thus, the state must be anchored in the belief in (a Christian) God. A state founded on the worship of God will be a Christian state. A state founded on the worship of man will be pagan.

There is no such thing as religious pluralism (in its "new," modern sense) consistent with Christianity, Whitehead explained. Since the truth is absolute, uniform, and Christian, religious pluralism is a step backward into pagan polytheism. Whitehead looked around at the contemporary United States and saw that "a new polytheism exists: the state tolerates many religions and, therefore, many gods ... The position of the American state is increasingly that of pagan antiquity," he warned, "in which the state as god on earth provides the umbrella under which all institutions reside." Whitehead insisted that the American Founders were clear about these matters and that they intended to institute a Christian state. The First Amendment's prohibitions on the establishment of religion and protection of religious liberty had been added to the body of the Constitution for one reason only: to ensure that the newly powerful national state would have no authority over the church and religion. The First Amendment's religion clauses were fashioned to protect "denominational pluralism – a healthy coexistence between the various Christian denominations." Whitehead explained, "[s]uch practical denominational pluralism is not to be confused with the new concept of pluralism, which commands complete acceptance of all views, even secular humanism": "The Principal religion to be protected by the First Amendment was Christian theism." Through its rulings, however, the Supreme Court has demoted Christianity from its historically preferred constitutional position.[114]

Although it forbade the establishment of a national church, the Constitution secured the "blessings of liberty" by licensing the states to be "openly Christian." As evidence for this, Whitehead cited the preambles and bodies of the various state constitutions at the time of the Founding, which, he noted, all clearly manifested the theistic grounding of their governments, all sovereign under the American federal system. Thus, "when the federal constitution was drafted, the principle of faith in God was presumed to be a universal for healthy civil government." The nation's Christian grounding was also evident in the text of the Seventh Amendment, which expressly incorporated the common law, "which applied biblical principles in judicial decisions," into the constitutional

---

[113] Whitehead, *Second American Revolution*, 86.
[114] Whitehead, *Second American Revolution*, 113, 96, 101, 103. See also Robert T. Handy, *A Christian America: Protestant Hopes and Historical Realities* (New York: Oxford University Press, 1984); Green, *Second Disestablishment*.

system. By incorporating the common law, Whitehead concluded, "the Constitution was acknowledging that a system of absolutes," accessible only through Biblical revelation, exists "upon which government and law can be founded."[115]

The American Founding, Whitehead explained, was a restoration of (Protestant) Christianity to its proper role in government after its influence had been attenuated through the corrosive effects of Roman Catholic theology. Echoing Francis Schaeffer, Whitehead argued that the modern crisis began with the work of Saint Thomas Aquinas, who had argued in error "that man could discover at least some truth without revelation." Fortunately, "the Reformation thinkers of the sixteenth century, notably Martin Luther and John Calvin, fought against Aquinas's concept of the Fall. They revived the old Christian suspicion of human reason and once again made the Bible the sole reference point for truth."[116]

Again, following Schaeffer, *The Second American Revolution* explained that the "fundamental principles" of the Reformation were bequeathed to the American colonists "without significant alteration" through the influence of *Lex Rex,* or *The Law and the Prince* (1644), written by the Scottish clergyman Samuel Rutherford: "Rutherford's assertion [was] that the basic premise of government and, therefore, of law must be the Bible, the Word of God rather than the word of any man." "All men, even the king," Rutherford argued, "were under the law and not above it." Following Schaeffer again, Whitehead elevated the significance of Rutherford to American political thought, over and above that of John Locke, and linked him, via John Witherspoon, to James Madison, and hence to the American Founding and Constitution. Whitehead, bizarrely, now went even further: he insisted that it had been the devout Rutherford who had first "established the principle of equality and liberty among men, which was later written into the Declaration of Independence."[117] William Blackstone, whose study of the common law (genuinely) had a major influence on the Founders and on nineteenth-century American law, was, Whitehead emphasized, likewise "a Christian, [who] believed that the fear of the Lord was the beginning of wisdom," as evidenced by his decision to open his *Commentaries* "with a careful analysis of the law of God as revealed in the Bible."[118] As Blackstone and the American Founders understood:

Law in the Christian sense implies something more than form. Law has content in the eternal sense. It has a reference point. Like a ship that is anchored, law cannot stray far

[115] Whitehead, *Second American Revolution*, 95, 96, 76, 21.
[116] Whitehead, *Second American Revolution*, 21.
[117] Whitehead, *Second American Revolution*, 28–30. Hayek alluded to Rutherford's *Lex Rex* in *The Constitution of Liberty* as "one of the polemical tracts of the period." Friedrich A. Hayek, *The Constitution of Liberty* (Chicago: University of Chicago Press, 1960), 169.
[118] Whitehead, *Second American Revolution*, 31.

from its mooring. If the anchor chain breaks, however, the ship drifts to and fro. Such is the current state of law in our country. Law in the true sense is bibliocentric, concerned with justice in terms of the Creator's revelation.[119]

"[B]ecause law establishes and declares the meaning of justice and righteousness," Whitehead continued, "law is inescapably religious": "Acts of the state that do not have a clear reference point in the Bible are ... illegitimate and acts of tyranny ...."[120]

Like legislative power, properly understood, judicial power in its true sense consisted of enacting into positive law principles that were already inherent in God's commands. Whitehead explained:

Essentially, common law is an age-old doctrine that developed by way of court decisions that applied the principles of the Bible to everyday situations. Judges simply decided their cases, often by making explicit reference to the Bible, but virtually always within a framework of biblical values. Out of these cases rules were established that governed future cases.[121]

"To some extent," Whitehead instructed his readers, "the common law has been present with us ever since the teachings of Moses, in that common law is essentially biblical principles adapted to local usage. It was an application of biblical principles – essentially the Ten Commandments – to the problems of everyday life."[122]

The common law, moreover, was Biblical not simply in substance but in process as well. For instance, "[t]he doctrine of stare decisis," he insisted, "is clearly based upon biblical principles."[123] Whitehead continued:

This precedent of precedents was based upon Christian principles as they had been expressed in judicial opinions. Past decisions provided a ground for deciding present cases because past decisions were developments of the implications of the basic principle that was based on biblical absolutes. Common law rules then were conceived as founded in principles that were permanent, uniform, and universal.[124]

---

[119] Whitehead, *Second American Revolution*, 73.
[120] Whitehead, *Second American Revolution*, 111, 153.
[121] Whitehead, *Second American Revolution*, 76.
[122] Whitehead, *Second American Revolution*, 77, 194. This lends heightened symbolic importance to the Supreme Court's later decisions holding that the First Amendment's Establishment Clause limits the public display of the Ten Commandments. *McCreary County* v. *American Civil Liberties Union*, 545 US 844 (2005); *Van Orden* v. *Perry*, 545 US 677 (2005). From the ideological perspective set out here, these decisions are read as plain evidence of the depth of the (liberal) Supreme Court's moral and constitutional corruption. Such decisions are "the false dictum of the absolute separation of church and state." Whitehead, *Second American Revolution*, 78. Needless to say, it is this vision that most likely helped inform the worldview of the disgraced former Chief Justice of Alabama (and failed US Senate candidate) Roy Moore, and his legions of supporters.
[123] Whitehead, *Second American Revolution*, 195.
[124] Whitehead, *Second American Revolution*, 195–196.

The Second American Revolution detailed how the English common law arose out of

[John] Wycliffe's contention that the people themselves should read and know the law of the Bible (hitherto the province of the clergy) and that they should ... govern as well as be governed by it. From this thesis ... emerged a set of principles based upon the Bible and applied by the courts ... known as the common law ... The common law became established in the English courts, and when the Constitution was being drafted, much of it was incorporated as part of that document.[125]

Whitehead explained that given that some of it was peculiar to the English system, English common law was not imported into the United States in its entirety. It was, however, "in its Christian form, substantially implanted in the American legal system."[126]

Whitehead argued that the United States was governed by three basic systems of law. The first was Fundamental Law, which is "clearly expressed in God's revelation as ultimately found in the Bible." The second was Constitutional Law, which provided "the form of civil government to protect the God-given rights of the people." The Constitution, he emphasized, "presupposes the Declaration and the higher, fundamental law to which the Declaration witnesses." Popular sovereignty governed in the sense that "[t]he people can base their institutions upon constitutional law, in conjunction with the higher or fundamental law ... Such biblical principles as federalism, separation of powers, limited authority, and liberty of conscience found in the Constitution" make sense only if we understand that the Constitution rests on the foundation of Fundamental Law. "They did not arise in a vacuum." The same is true for rights, which Whitehead defined as "a benefit or lawful-claim recognized by the law itself in recognition of principles of the biblical higher law."[127]

The third kind of law was composed of "laws enacted by the political body having legislative power" – Positive Law. Legislators, in Whitehead's account, did not make law: they pronounced it. "The very term legislator," Whitehead noted, meant "not one who makes laws but one who moves them – from the divine law written in nature or in the Bible into the statutes and law codes of a particular society. Just as a translator is supposed to faithfully move the meaning from the original language into the new one, so the legislator is to translate laws, not make new ones." Democracy and freedom are consistent with each other for Whitehead only in the sense that true freedom consists in enacting laws consistent with God's will. "In the last analysis," he insisted, "we would be far freer under an absolute monarch who saw his authority as subject

---

[125] Whitehead, *Second American Revolution*, 193.
[126] Whitehead, *Second American Revolution*, 197.
[127] Whitehead, *Second American Revolution*, 75, 116. For this reason, there can be no such thing as "gay rights" or a right to an abortion. Because they are inconsistent with God's law, they are not "rights." "Vice – homosexuality, prostitution – represents idolatry and can never be justified even if 'legalized' by the state. Attempts to do so repudiate the Second Commandment," at 79.

to God's law in the Bible and in nature than under a democratically elected assembly that took the arbitrary will of the majority as its highest value."[128]

Whitehead condemned "[m]odern legal scholars" who "have rejected the views of Blackstone because they have rejected faith in God and his reliance upon the Genesis account of creation and the origin of man and the universe." The seminal act of treachery in this regard was committed by Christopher Columbus Langdell, who, through his invention of the case method of law teaching at Harvard in the 1870s, had reimagined law along evolutionary scientific lines. "Langdell's real impact on law education," Whitehead wrote, "was his belief that basic principles and doctrines of the law were the products of an evolving and growing process over many years. Langdell believed that this evolution taking place in opinions written by judges. This meant that what a judge said was law, and not what the Constitution said."[129] In prelapsarian America, before Langdell's perspective came to dominate American legal education:

[T]he law had primarily been taught by practicing lawyers in law offices throughout the country. William Blackstone's *Commentaries* were often the basic legal treatise. The prevailing opinion was that the principles and doctrines of the law were unchanging; law was based on [biblical] absolutes ... All the student had to learn was to apply those ... Beginning with Langdell, however, law education shifted to the classroom, where students were taught that the principles and doctrines of the law were being developed in the appellate courts by judges ... Justice Hughes was merely echoing Langdell's philosophy when he remarked that "the Constitution is what the judges say it is.[130]

Langdell's views were reinforced by the scholarship of Oliver Wendell Holmes Jr.:

In Holmes's theory – summed up in the expression that the law is not logic but experience – law was the product of man's opinion, supported by the absolute rights of the majority. Thus, the principles of the common law, which had guided courts and governments for centuries before America was settled, were to be left in the dust of history for the concept of evolving law. As a consequence common law is virtually ignored in legal education today.[131]

Whitehead explained to his readers that they were currently living under a system ruined by the intellectual, moral, and historical corruptions of legal positivism. Such positivism, "unknown in early American law ... has resulted in a decline of

---

[128] Whitehead, *Second American Revolution*, 75–76.
[129] Whitehead, *Second American Revolution*, 47.
[130] Whitehead, *Second American Revolution*, 47.
[131] Whitehead, *Second American Revolution*, 193. Oliver Wendell Holmes Jr. has famously said, and argued, in *The Common Law* (Boston: Little Brown & Co., 1881) that "The life of the law has not been logic: it has been experience. The felt necessities of the time, the prevalent moral and political theories, intuitions of public policy, avowed or unconscious, even the prejudices which judges share with their fellow-men, have had a good deal more to do than the syllogism in determining the rules by which men should be governed. The law embodies the story of a nation's development through many centuries, and it cannot be dealt with as if it contained only the axioms and corollaries of a book of mathematics."

American liberties ... Justice itself has become a remote concept, which is the esoteric concern of a group of legal technicians and professionals who codify the concerns of almost every area of life in some form of state or bureaucratic regulation." Moreover, "with the rise of legal positivism and sociological law, the flexibility once reserved to the common law judge is given over to the legal technician – or the modern judge who sits without the Bible as his guide and who, in fact, is often openly hostile to the Bible and Christian principles."[132]

Today, law schools hide the truth from their students: "Very few attorneys even have an understanding of what the common law is." Whitehead called upon Christian law students to study the "true law." They had a duty to remind their professors "that much of law is still based on the Bible," to demand courses on Blackstone and the common law, and to commit themselves to the study of "the true legal roots of American society."[133]

The Second American Revolution called for a renewed commitment by judges as well. Whitehead reminded them, and us, that as the apostle Paul declares in Romans 13: 1–4, "all civil authorities are ministers of God."[134] As civil authorities, judges must employ higher law as their ultimate reference point. Courts must act as ministers of God, and, in this sense, are religious establishments.[135]

At one time, American judges understood that the United States is a Christian nation. Today, however, they proceed in accord with the whims of man. They are humanists – devotees of a pagan religion "opposed to any other religious system."[136] Christians have a high responsibility to act now to reclaim their country for Christ:

When a [pagan] state claims divine honors, there will always be warfare between Christ and Caesar, for two rival gods claim the same jurisdiction over man. It is a conflict between two kingdoms, between two kings, each of whom claims ultimate and divine powers ... [O]ur government has ... become a religion and is ... involved in a bitter conflict with the religion of Christ. Christianity and the new state religion of America cannot peacefully coexist.

In a state with Christian foundations, Whitehead concluded, "man's law must have its origin in God's revelation. Any law that contradicts biblical revelation is illegitimate."[137]

---

[132] Whitehead, *Second American Revolution*, 196, 200.
[133] Whitehead, *Second American Revolution*, 193, 170, 171.
[134] Whitehead, *Second American Revolution*, 85–86.
[135] Whitehead, *Second American Revolution*, 85–86. This theme has been emphasized recently by the (conservative) legal historian Philip Hamburger as well. Philip Hamburger, *Law and Judicial Duty* (Cambridge, MA: Harvard University Press, 2008).
[136] Whitehead, *Second American Revolution*, 40, 106. This is a major theme on the contemporary Right. See, for example, Robert P. George, *The Clash of Orthodoxies: Law, Religion, and Morality in Crisis* (Wilmington, DE: ISI Books, 2001).
[137] Whitehead, *Second American Revolution*, 18, 74.

CONCLUSION

Over the course of its postwar ascendency, the modern conservative movement publicly aligned itself, more exclusively as time went on, with the Republican Party, and with a menu of conservative-identified public policies. As it did so, of course, it defined itself not just as *for* a party and a set of policies, but *against* a competing party and policy agenda. To limit our understanding of modern conservatism to these more concrete political goals is to miss the underlying meanings that forge political identities, tie together what otherwise would at times be a motley, if not inconsistent or even contradictory, assortment of positions and programs and motivate political behavior. Much of the tenor of modern conservatism, especially beginning in the late 1970s into the 1980s – the Reagan Era, or New Right – was underwritten by the meanings made by Evangelical and Fundamentalist Christians. Over time, particularly under the influence of Francis Schaeffer, that tenor became increasingly civilizational and existential, in ways that echoed and harmonized with the themes of civilizational and existential struggle emphasized elsewhere on the Right by conservative Catholics, (key) Straussians (the decline of the West), anticommunists, and Austrian economists (the road to serfdom). Right-wing Evangelical and Fundamentalist Christians, in the tradition of religious warriors from time immemorial, were keen to distinguish friends from enemies. And they called for a crusade to redeem the nation from the Godless turn it had tragically taken and to restore its foundational Christian heritage and traditions, as enshrined in its Founding, its laws, and its Constitution. Abortion and the Supreme Court's decision in *Roe* v. *Wade* were crucial in significant part for the symbolic role they were accorded in framing the larger narrative of dispossession: the constitutional protection newly afforded to abortion did not simply institute and invite bad laws and policies but stood as Exhibit A in a much broader civilizational and existential account of the trajectory of the nation, which, as they would have it, now faced an epic choice between God and Man – as so memorably set out by Whittaker Chambers in *Witness* (1952) – and the need for constitutional redemption and restoration.

Looking back later on the critical role he played in helping his father mobilize the Christian Right in the late 1970s and 1980s, Frankie Schaeffer recalled of his erstwhile compatriots that "the threat of losing [their] faith … seem[ed] to infuriate them":

If life can't be tied up in a neat package, if you let those doubts begin to gnaw your guts, where will it end? It is no coincidence that about 99 percent of evangelical books are written to help people order their lives according to an invisible world when everything in the visible world is challenging faith. The title of almost every evangelical book could be, "How to Keep Your Faith in Spite of … " fill in the blank, college, art, science, philosophy, sex, temptation, literature, media, TV, movies, your homosexual tendencies, your heterosexual tendencies ... in other words, every breath you take.[138]

"Dad," he reported,

said there was a 'line of despair' that separated modern secular man from all who came before ... [T]he fruits of Christianity created the rule of law and human rights as we now understood them. For all the talk about the so-called Dark Ages and the evils of Christendom, from the Spanish Inquisition to the burning of witches in Salem, to the slave trade, the twentieth century – a virtual textbook experiment in godlessness – was the most inhuman and bloody of all centuries.[139]

The senior Schaeffer regularly animadverted against secularist sneering at the crimes of Christians that had dotted the history of Western civilization. "[B]efore secularists glibly critiqued religious and especially Christian culture," he countered, "perhaps they should take time to explain Marx, Lenin, Hitler, Stalin, and Mao, not to mention the Gulag and Auschwitz" – all the achievements of militant secularists. "On a good day, the social and political results of secularism made the horrors of Christendom look like a Sunday-school picnic, Dad said," reported the younger Schaeffer.[140]

While Christianity might have led some misguided souls to commit great evils, Christian culture, "unlike secularism ... had a self-correcting impulse." Wilberforce had fought to free the slaves. The common law of Christian England was the basis of Western and American freedoms. "[I]f the idea of biblical God-given absolutes was abandoned," the elder Schaeffer had warned, it is not clear "where a new morality would come from." In addition, "Since humankind did not like chaos ... either we would turn to authoritarian systems (some sort of technocratic elite), or we would be ruled by the 'tyranny of the majority, with no way to challenge the popular will, nothing higher to appeal to.'" This seemed to Schaeffer and his followers to be the path that was now being taken, under secularist control, by the formerly Christian United States.[141]

It is important to note that Schaeffer's influential framing was offered in the stream of time in both the political and constitutional development of the United States, and of the modern conservative movement. As noted earlier, Evangelical Christianity has a long history in the United States, and Fundamentalist Christianity dated back to the turn of the twentieth century. From an ideological perspective, the Schaeffer (and, indeed, the Whitehead) framings presented a mixed bag on the liberal-conservative spectrum. On what became known as culture war issues – chiefly, in the late 1970s and 1980s, abortion and a range of bioethics questions – Schaeffer's vision offered a veritable roadmap for the Right, a map that the movement largely followed that laid the foundation for its political and constitutional vision. At the same

---

[138] Schaeffer, *Crazy for God*, 33.   [139] Schaeffer, *Crazy for God*, 254–255.
[140] Schaeffer, *Crazy for God*, 254–255.   [141] Schaeffer, *Crazy for God*, 254–255.

time, Schaeffer took an explicit position on two other issues of considerable developmental significance, wealth and inequality and race. On the former, Schaeffer and Whitehead stuck to the "liberal" position, criticizing free market economics, at least in the late nineteenth-century form that other conservatives were effusively praising and campaigning to reestablish (in time, the movement rejected the Christian positions on these matters, theorizing them away through a new (Christian) theology of free market capitalism (discussed in Chapter 3, "Stories About Markets")). On the latter – which Schaeffer was offering, it should be noted, more than a decade after the passage of the Civil Rights Act of 1964 and the Voting Rights Act of 1965, and more than a quarter century after the Supreme Court's decision in *Brown* v. *Board of Education* (1954) – Schaeffer prominently criticized race discrimination, as had the Reverend Billy Graham before him. Like Schaeffer's economic position, this might have been considered liberal, except that Schaeffer played a major role in making it into a conservative position as well. Here, the conservative movement followed him and updated its developing understandings of itself as antiracist (in a particular way, and within a particular frame, of course). In this, Schaeffer's vision joined other antiracist streams within the movement, including the emergence in the mid-1960s of neoconservatism, a movement of ex-liberal Democrats, mostly from New York City, some of whom had actively participated in the civil rights movement and remained committed to what they saw as its initial understandings, and the redemptive West Coast Straussianism of Harry V. Jaffa, which focused on the promise of the equality of natural rights in the Declaration of Independence as redeemed by Abraham Lincoln in ending chattel slavery. What Schaeffer offered was a thoroughgoing update on racism within the modern conservative movement – especially among those who most needed it, like the Fundamentalists – to fold antiracism into the larger conservative story. From here on out, movement members could use the Schaefferist vision to help them see that it was actually liberals/progressives/secularists who were the real racists, while they – conservatives – stood in the shoes of the abolitionists, Lincoln, and Martin Luther King Jr. Using the abortion (and bioethics) issue, Schaeffer helped the modern Right think its way forward to a broader coalition that could win elections and national majorities.

6

Right-Wing Roman Catholic Stories

THE ROMAN CATHOLIC MORAL IMAGINATION AND THE AMERICAN CONSENSUS

At the height of the Cold War, an outsized – and, at times, bombastic – patriotic nationalism, underwritten by a civic religious commitment to "American values," united adherents of diverse faiths who had long eyed one another with suspicion, if not hostility.[1] The ostentatious patriotism of the country's Roman Catholics at mid-century was second to none and proved especially prominent because it coincided with a peak of Catholic influence on the tenor of American popular culture.[2]

The mid-twentieth century witnessed "a veritable Catholicization of the American imagination," in which a wide array of cultural products – books, movies, radio and television shows, and mass-circulation magazines – showcased a Catholic sensibility rooted in communalism and moral traditionalism. These ranged from Catholic convert Walker Percy's National Book Award–winning novel *The Moviegoer* (1962), a rumination on the dislocation of modern man questioning his increasing reliance upon science rather than religious faith to explain mysteries of existence, to the film *Knute Rockne, All-American* (1940), a heart-wrenching and inspirational story of University of Notre Dame football, starring Pat O'Brien as the Fighting Irish coach Rockne and the future president of the United States Ronald Reagan as

---

[1] Will Herberg, *Protestant, Catholic, Jew: An Essay in American Religious Sociology* (Garden City, NY: Anchor Books, 1960). Robert Wuthnow, *The Restructuring of American Religion: Society and Faith Since World War II* (Princeton: Princeton University Press, 1988).

[2] See Lizabeth Cohen, "Re-viewing the Twentieth Century through an American Catholic Lens," in R. Scott Appleby and Kathleen Sprows Cummings, editors, *Catholics in the American Century: Casting Narratives of US History* (Ithaca, NY: Cornell University Press, 2012), 55–57.

the star player, George Gipp: the film was just one of many in the era that
featured Catholic priests and nuns in starring roles.[3]

Earlier, in the 1930s, when popular culture began to serve as the "means by
which ethnic and class identities transformed the definition of national
communities," the commitments to God and country had positioned many
Catholic traditionalists as liberal political reformists: Catholics were a key
part of President Franklin Delano Roosevelt's New Deal Coalition. The more
communalist Catholic teaching, articulated in the public sphere most
prominently by "Monsignor New Deal" Father John A. Ryan (1869–1945),
indicted individualism and the free market as having precipitated the Great
Depression. Beginning in the 1940s, however, Catholic communalism and
traditionalism, with its emphasis on faith, home, and family, started to sound
anew in American conservatism, with an increasingly aggressive defense of
consensus values over reform.[4]

The most prominent postwar embodiment of this trend and turn was Roman
Catholic Bishop Fulton J. Sheen (1895–1979), whose rise to prominence began
with his nationally broadcast Sunday evening radio show *Catholic Hour* on
NBC during the 1930s and 1940s, a show that had been commissioned by the
network as a platform for explaining Catholicism to Americans in the aftermath
of the disturbing anti-Catholicism occasioning Al Smith's 1928 run for the
White House. The downstate Illinois native Sheen parlayed his success with
Catholic Hour into a hit early television show *Life Is Worth Living*

[3] *Knute Rockne: All-American* (Warner Bros., 1940) (d. William K. Howard/Lloyd Bacon).
The film positions the deeply Catholic University of Notre Dame as an icon and symbol of
Americanism. It is also contains one of the most famous rallying cries of underdogs onward to
victory, voiced in the film by its star Ronald Reagan's George Gipp, but relayed to the team by
Rockne himself after Gipp's early death: "The last thing George said to me, 'Rock,' he said,
'sometime when the team is up against it and the breaks are beating the boys, tell them to go out
there with all they've got and win just one for the Gipper.'" Because of his role in this film, Reagan
was known by George Gipp's nickname – "The Gipper" – for the rest of his life. See Anthony
Burke Smith, *The Look of Catholics: Portrayals in Popular Culture from the Great Depression to
the Cold War* (Lawrence: University Press of Kansas, 2010), 45. Father Charles Coughlin's anti-
Semitism did resonate, of course, with aspects of the Old Right, as featured, for instance, in the
Old Right outlet *The American Mercury*. But, at mid-century, the Old Right was not aborning but
passing.
[4] Smith, *Look of Catholics*, 1–6, 18–19. The populist, anti-modern, anti-Semitic, anti-communist
Catholic priest Father Charles Coughlin, based in Royal Oak, Michigan, once a New Deal
supporter turned implacable Roosevelt enemy, had a notable radio following in the crisis years
of the 1930s. But, as Alan Brinkley's study demonstrates, this was more reflective of malignant
trends of those times, as also exemplified by the Louisiana governor (and Southern Baptist) Huey
Long than of Catholics *per se*. Both men were hard to classify politically, supporting positions
that would today be classified, variously, as both on the Left and Right – though Coughlin's views
skewed increasingly Right over time. The virulent extremist Coughlin flamed out, and Long was
assassinated (1935). Alan Brinkley, *Voices of Protest: Huey Long, Father Coughlin, and the
Great Depression* (New York: Vintage Press, 1983). See also Donald Warren, *Radio Priest:
Charles Coughlin, the Father of Hate Radio* (New York: The Free Press, 1996).

(1952–1957), which premiered on the Dumont network and, in 1955, migrated to ABC. By the middle 1950s, Sheen, who had presided over the first televised religious service ever, had cultivated a viewership of 30 million and won an Emmy. In accepting the award in 1952, the same year he appeared on the cover of *Time* magazine, Sheen paid tribute to four authors who had made his achievement possible: Matthew, Mark, Luke, and John. The bishop was consistently voted in the nation's early Gallup polls to be one of the ten most admired men in America, rising in 1956 to third (only Dwight Eisenhower and Winston Churchill ranked higher). In time, Sheen was personally responsible for the conversion to Catholicism of Heywood Broun; Henry Ford II; the editor of the communist newspaper the *Daily Worker*, Louis Budenz; the former Soviet spy Elizabeth Bentley; and the playwright, socialite, and wife of the founder of Time, Inc., Clare Boothe Luce.[5]

Sheen, one of those "individuals for whom religion exists not as a dull habit, but as an acute fever,"[6] was a classically trained Thomist philosopher and theologian at the Catholic University of America with a unique ability to convey complex ideas in clear and popularly relatable ways.[7] Sheen's TV show amounted to a full-court press to popularize Thomism and sell it as the answer to the ills of modern America. He set the stage by convincing his viewers that they were living at the center of a momentous religious drama. In an "age of extremes," the charismatic Sheen argued, their understanding and choices were of immense significance, both to them personally and, indeed, to the future of the world. The cheerful, humorous, and learned Sheen's message consistently targeted what he took to be the flawed thinking of progressives and liberals, whom he suggested were blithely undermining Western civilization. Sheen described American society as a battleground for two great contending forces fighting for humanity's soul, one whose capital was in Moscow, and the other in Rome. Provided liberals did not sap its moral core and commitments, the United States had the potential to be "an instrument of virtue in the world." Everything was at stake. In the struggle against atheistic communism, the ultimate triumph would come only through a commitment to God, perfect moral clarity, and, in a Cold War context, a willingness to fight.[8]

In a time when Pope Pius X had recently insisted that Saint Thomas Aquinas serve as the sole model of Catholic intellectual life, the neo-medieval scholasticist

---

[5] Smith, *Look of Catholics*, 103, 125, 128, 135, 137. *Time Magazine* (April 14, 1952) [Sheen cover]. Later, Sheen hosted the nationally syndicated television show, *The Fulton Sheen Program* (1961–1968).

[6] William James, *The Varieties of Religious Experience: A Study in Human Nature* (New York: Modern Library, 2002 [1902]), 9.

[7] Sheen had earned a PhD in Greek, Roman, and medieval philosophy at the University of Louvain in Belgium. Timothy H. Sherwood, *The Rhetorical Leadership of Fulton J. Sheen, Norman Vincent Peale, and Billy Graham in the Age of Extremes* (Lanham, MD: Lexington Books, 2013), 17, 19.

[8] Smith, *Look of Catholics*, 135–150; Sherwood, *Rhetorical Leadership of Fulton J. Sheen*, 20.

Sheen wielded his Thomism as a sword against the beast of modernism – the engine of spiritual decline, as propagated by value-free empiricism and (the Godless) Karl Marx and Sigmund Freud. As he told this story to a mass audience in postwar America, Sheen made aggressive use of Roman Catholic symbolism, appearing on TV in full ecclesiastical regalia, and availing himself of emotional appeals to the Cross, the Sacred Heart, and the Blessed Virgin.[9]

For a growing population of Catholics newly entering the middle class and laboring under an intellectual inferiority complex, Sheen's living-room Thomism offered a narrative that melded the Church's emotional symbolism with a philosophical rigor that vastly surpassed that of the country's (shallow, dangerous) modernists, besides having the added virtue of being true.[10] In this, Sheen served as the popular voice of the postwar (Thomist) natural law revival, offered to counter the currents of modern social thought devoted to materialism, scientific positivisim, historicism, pragmatism, and psychology. While some versions of this thought – such as that of Jacques Maritain (1882–1973) and later (as will be discussed) John Courtney Murray (1904–1967) in the United States – were politically liberal and progressive, it was the conservative natural law theorists (or the conservative aspects of the thought of the liberal Thomists) who had the greatest influence on both the broader culture and the ascendant American Right. As the historian Anthony Burke Smith explained, these conservative Catholic thinkers "saw themselves as protecting transcendent, metaphysical truth and the spiritual foundation of culture against the corrosive effects of a skeptical, disenchanted, modern world."[11]

At the time, the notion that the Catholic Church was the natural home of the basic principles of US constitutional government was common enough in mainstream conservative sources.[12] Perhaps most notably, the Catholic Church's mid-twentieth-century bid for leadership in championing

---

[9] Smith, *Look of Catholics*, 127–131. On the growing authority and influence of value-free social science in this period, see generally Alan Petigny, *The Permissive Society: America, 1941–1965* (Cambridge: Cambridge University Press, 2009).

[10] Petigny, *Permissive Society*.

[11] Smith, *Look of Catholics*, 18; Sherwood, *Rhetorical Leadership of Fulton J. Sheen*, 24–25.

[12] An article by liberal attorney Harry Hogan in the *ABA Journal* in the late 1960s, for instance, explained, "Because the founding fathers believed in a certain kind of natural law, they were able to conceive of a limited government." The medieval Church played a formative role in forging the idea of limited (constitutional) government, performing "this watchdog function" as society's social conscience. Today, however, Hogan explained, "The churches are certainly not strong enough as institutions to reassume the medieval function of passing judgment on the state and standing up against it." In their stead, in the contemporary United States, "The Supreme Court, as a focus of the community's conscience, is the strongest institution to do the job." Conservative Catholics shared Hogan's framework but came to aggressively reject his institutional conclusion. Harry J. Hogan, "The Supreme Court and Natural Law," *American Bar Association Journal* 54 (June 1968): 570–573, 572–573. Hogan, a Princeton and Columbia Law School graduate with a PhD in history from George Washington University, had served in the Franklin Roosevelt and John F. Kennedy administrations and was director of government relations for the Catholic University of America.

traditionalist morality made the Church a special favorite of Henry Luce and his *Time* and *Life* magazines, which played a major role in reaffirming consensus morals in the 1950s. Luce's flagship magazines broadcast the message that American democracy was defined by a philosophy of limited government, foundationally premised on the existence of God.[13] As such, religious believers were the nation's sheet anchors. An editorial entitled "The American Moral Consensus" (1955) published by *Life*, for instance, was bannered by two visages, one of the great Chief Justice John Marshall, who stood, the magazine explained, for a moral vision imprinted on mankind by his "Creator," and the other of the Roman Catholic bishop and the first Catholic cardinal in the United States, James Gibbons, one of many Catholics leaders and thinkers, *Life* underlined, who had embraced the Constitution at the time of the nation's Founding. Notably, "The American Moral Consensus" was studded with quotations from Henry Luce's friend and golfing buddy, the Jesuit priest John Courtney Murray, SJ, who at the time was hard at work on his landmark statement of Catholic Americanism – and a Catholicized vision of American constitutionalism – *We Hold These Truths* (1960).[14]

The argument that American democracy was defined by a philosophy of limited government, foundationally premised on the existence of God was, of course, also advanced consistently by Fulton J. Sheen. In his lecture "How a Democracy Differs from a Totalitarian State," delivered as part of his *Life Is Worth Living* Series in 1956, Sheen rooted democracy, naturally enough, in "the people." He went on to explain, however, that the Declaration of Independence had made clear that Americans were a certain sort of people – people who held their "rights from God." The Declaration of Independence had

---

[13] The Luce media ethos anticipated the concerns of the New Right by celebrating the American success story premised on "a traditional social arrangement of home, family, and religion." This vision helped orient national understandings not simply through policy positions or even constitutional resistance but also through a politicization of traditionalist visions of the core institutions of civil society that it cast as symbols of true Americanism. Much of the earlier *laissez-faire*, anti–New Deal resistance, which the forward-looking Luce put behind him, was anchored in Victorian culture and the worldview of privileged, individualist Protestant elites. Luce took what can be characterized as a more Catholic-friendly vision of American conservatism rooted in moral traditionalism and unapologetic and, at times, lachrymose patriotism. In consonance with the views of many Catholics of his time, Luce's vision was not as categorically anti-statist, and he accepted that government should fulfill many roles. It also embraced a variety of pluralism that countered the long-standing discrimination that had condemned Catholics as outside of the circle of real Americans. Luce played a significant role in the process on the Right of placing conservative Catholics at the center of the national, and constitutional, project. Smith, *Look of Catholics*, 92, 103.

[14] "The American Moral Consensus," *Life* (December 26, 1955): 56–57; Smith, *Look of Catholics*, 115; Robert A. Orsi, "US Catholics between Memory and Modernity: How Catholics Are American," in R. Scott Appleby and Kathleen Sprows Cummings, editors, *Catholics in the American Century: Casting Narratives of US History* (Ithaca, NY: Cornell University Press, 2012), 17; John Courtney Murray, SJ, *We Hold These Truths: Catholic Reflections on the American Proposition* (New York: Sheed and Ward, 1960).

been an appeal made by the new Americans seeking "Divine Justice." The US Constitution was framed by these self-same "We the People" – children of God acting as self-governing worldly sovereigns. Sheen distinguished "the masses," whose interests were purportedly advanced by totalitarian states, from the American "people." "*People are made up of persons,*" Sheen reasoned, "A Person has sovereign worth because he has been created by God, because he has been redeemed by Christ, because he has rights which no state can take away from him." "*Masses,*" by contrast, "*are made up of individuals,*" Sheen explained. Unlike persons, "[i]ndividuals are material: for example, a stone is an individual, but it is not a person; a cow is an individual, but it is not a person; an orange is an individual, but it is not a person." Individuals, material as they are, have no rights, even to life. They can thus "be used as the dictator pleases." As such, it is the faith in God (and Christ) that distinguished free constitutional government in the United States from atheistic communism and other materialist totalitarian systems. Religious faith and constitutional patriotism were inextricable.[15]

---

[15] Fulton J. Sheen, "How a Democracy Differs from a Totalitarian State," in *Life Is Worth Living*, Fourth Series, 67–77 (New York: McGraw-Hill, 1956), 67, 71, 74–75, discussed in Sherwood, *Rhetorical Leadership of Fulton J. Sheen*, 26–29 [emphasis in original]. See also Sherwood, *Rhetorical Leadership of Fulton J. Sheen*, 35, drawing from, among other sources, Sheen's "The Role of Communism and the Role of America," in *Life Is Worth Living*, 263–71 (New York: McGraw-Hill, 1953), "The East and the West," in *Life Is Worth Living*, 92–100 (1956), and "US State Church Opposed by Sheen," *New York Times* (March 17, 1952), 15. The last quotes are from a Sheen sermon entitled "God and Country" (1952) holding, "We believe that religion and morality are indispensible supports of democracy and that religion and patriotism go together; We believe in the First Amendment to the Constitution of the United States; We believe that the best guarantee against totalitarianism is a deep religious faith among citizens; We want to keep the United States a leader of the world, and we believe that all God-believing people in the United States should unite to keep our country under Providence as the secondary cause [after God] for the preservation of the liberties of the world." For a more recent Sheen-like take on the Declaration of Independence by a leading conservative Catholic thinker, see Michael Novak, *God's Country: Taking the Declaration Seriously* (Washington, DC: American Enterprise Institute, 2000).

It is worth noting that a similar framework was in effect among conservative LDS/Mormons. Their sense of shared commitment to the Constitution and militant opposition to progressives who have betrayed it has, in recent years, served as common ground for these two faiths in the United States. While, as Aziz Rana has most recently shown, "constitution worship" has been common enough across American history, that worship is quite literally scriptural within the Church of Jesus Christ of Latter-Day Saints: the sanctity of the US Constitution is a tenet of the Mormon faith. A core scripture of the faith, *Doctrine and Covenants*, setting out revelations from God to the prophet (and LDS/Mormon Church founder) Joseph Smith (1805–1844) represents God as declaring "And for this purpose have I established the Constitution of this land, by the hands of wise men whom I raised up unto this very purpose" (*Doctrines and Covenants* 101:80). It further sets out the prayer: "Have mercy, O Lord, upon all the nations of the earth; have mercy upon the rulers of our land; may those principles, which were so honorably and nobly defended, namely, the Constitution of our land, by our fathers, be established forever" (*Doctrines and Covenants* 109: 54). The "Guide to the Scriptures" posted online by the LDS Church makes clear that "In the *Doctrine and Covenants*, 'the Constitution'

This basic understanding, and theology, formed the bedrock thought of a rising cohort of right-wing Catholics who were beginning to coalesce as some of the most influential thought-leaders of the postwar conservative movement. A *Who's Who* of first movers in postwar conservatism included devout conservative Catholics. These included *National Review* and Young Americans for Freedom (YAF) founder William F. Buckley Jr.; direct-mail pioneer and Heritage Foundation founder Paul Weyrich; Heritage Foundation founder and president (1977–2013) and Donald Trump champion Ed Feulner Jr.; the impresario behind Barry Goldwater's 1964 presidential run and his heavily constitutional campaign manifesto *The Conscience of a Conservative*, right-wing radio pioneer, and Notre Dame Law School dean Clarence Manion; the ghostwriter of *The Conscience of a Conservative* Brent Bozell Jr.; the

refers to the Constitution of the United States of America, which was divinely inspired in order to prepare the way for the restoration of the gospel" (www.lds.org/scriptures/). Ninety-six percent of Mormons believe *The Book of Mormon* is divinely inspired; 94 percent believe the US Constitution is. Mormons attribute their persecution and expulsion, leading to their forced migration to the Utah territory, to be a direct consequence of the abandonment of the Constitution. The conservative talk radio firebrand Glenn Beck, an LDS convert, tells an apparently apocryphal story about the Mormons marching into the Utah territory after their expulsion from the United States in a parade with the women bearing the Declaration of Independence and the men the Constitution. Peter Beinart, "Glenn Beck's Regrets," *The Atlantic Monthly* (January/February 2017), 16–19; Alexander Zaitchik, "Meet the Man Who Changed Glenn Beck's Life," *Salon* (September 16, 2009). On the sacralization of the Constitution, see Aziz Rana, "Progressivism and the Disenchanted Constitution," in Skowroenk, Engel, and Ackerman, editors, *Progressives' Century*; Michael Kammen, *A Machine That Would Go of Itself: The Constitution in American Culture* (New York: Knopf, 1986). See also Susan McWilliams, "Lost But Not (Yet) Forgotten: *America's Forgotten Constitutions* by Robert Tsai," *Tulsa Law Review* 52 (2016): 293–299.

Right-wing Mormons wielding the Constitution have made their own contribution to (at times the fringes of) the postwar Right. W. Cleon Skousen (1913–2006), an FBI veteran who had worked closely with Director J. Edgar Hoover (1935–1951), a Brigham Young University religion professor (1967–1978), John Birch Society member, and survivalist whose teachings had a transformational influence on Glenn Beck, emphasized in his influential book *The Five Thousand Year Leap: Twenty-Eight Great Ideas That Are Changing the World* (Washington, DC: The National Center for Constitutional Studies, 1981) that the United States was a Christian nation, founded on natural law. In 1972, Skousen founded The Freemen Institute, which was devoted to teaching about the Founding Fathers and the Constitution, and also founded George Wythe University to spread his message (The Freeman Institute's name was subsequently changed to the National Center for Constitutional Studies). Skousen's book *The Making of America: The Substance and Meaning of the Constitution* (Washington, DC: National Center for Constitutional Studies, 1985) was devoted to setting out the Founders' original understanding of the Constitution. His book (and, today, instructional DVD series) *The Miracle of America* (Washington, DC: National Center for Constitutional Studies, 1981) both set out those under-standings and the ways in which they have been corrupted since 1900. The National Center for Constitutional Studies is active today (www.nccs.net). George Wythe (1726–1806) was the first US constitutional law professor: he taught law at the College of William and Mary (where his students included John Marshall and Thomas Jefferson), signed the Declaration of Independence, and attended the Constitutional Convention as a delegate from Virginia.

crusading anti-communist Republican senator from Wisconsin Joe McCarthy, whom Buckley and Bozell teamed up to defend in *McCarthy and His Enemies*; the antifeminist activist Phyllis Schlafly; key leaders of the originalist movement in legal academia Antonin Scalia and (the Catholic convert) Robert Bork; Federalist Society leader and Republican Supreme Court appointments point man Leonard Leo; Contract With America bomb thrower and House Speaker Newt Gingrich (also, like Bork, a Catholic convert); the Princeton University Thomist politics professor Robert P. George; and Breitbart News founder and Donald Trump campaign chief Steve Bannon.[16] The modern conservative movement was shaped in significant ways by the postwar Catholic imagination.

THE "DEEP STORY" – SENSIBILITIES AND STORIES OF TRADITIONALIST CATHOLICS

The political and constitutional understandings of conservative Catholics in the postwar United States can only be understood to the extent that those understandings are embedded in the "deep story"[17] these co-religionists have told themselves about their lives, positions, and duties in the world and to God – that is, how they make meaning and meanings. In this, it is worth starting at the beginning.

In her 1957 memoir of growing up Catholic in Minnesota and Seattle, the novelist, essayist, and critic Mary McCarthy (1912–1989) isolated "two distinct strains" of the Irish Catholic tradition in which she had been reared, one decent and loving and the other nasty and vicious. "There was the Catholicism I learned from my mother and from the simple parish priests and nuns in Minneapolis, which was, on the whole, a religion of beauty and goodness, however imperfectly realized," McCarthy recalled, "Then there was the Catholicism practiced in my grandmother McCarthy's parlor ... a sour, baleful doctrine in which old hates and rancors had been stewing for generations, with ignorance proudly stirring the pot." Although "false magnanimity" was to be found everywhere among her co-religionists, she found "largeness of spirit" in short supply, leading her to wonder if perhaps "Catholicism is a religion not suited to the laity, or ... at any rate ... the American laity, in whom it seems to bring out some of the worst traits in human nature and to lend them a sort of sanctification."[18]

The vicious strain McCarthy identified was in considerable evidence among conservative Catholics in the postwar United States who, constituting themselves as a pressure group, aggressively menaced others by hurling charges of "hate," "poison," "filth," and "trash" and demanding purifying purges, redress, and rectification. "[T]he average Catholic," McCarthy observed of her co-religionists, "perceives no connection between religion and

---

[16] Southworth, *Lawyers on the Right*, 133.   [17] Hochschild, *Strangers in Their Own Land*.
[18] Mary McCarthy, *Memoirs of a Catholic Girlhood* (San Diego: Harvest Books, 1957), 21.

morality, unless it is a question of someone else's morality ... of the supposed pernicious influence of books, films, ideas, on someone else's conduct."[19]

Brimming with "meanness" arising out of "her blood-curdling Catholicism," Grandmother McCarthy was an exemplar of this disposition: combativeness was her "dominant trait." "The religious magazines on her table furnished her not with food for meditation but with fresh pretexts for anger; articles attacking birth control, divorce, mixed marriages, Darwin, and secular education were her favorite reading. The teachings of the Church did not interest her, except as they were a rebuke to others."[20] To the extent such Catholics tolerated those of different faiths, it was on the grudging basis of their having "partial truth."[21]

Given her experiences, Catholicism for Mary McCarthy entailed not so much the Church's theological doctrines as the feelings the faith had engendered in many of its adherents, including a fiery and self-righteous rage directed, all too often, at modernity itself. "To care for the quarrels of the past, to identify oneself passionately with a cause that became, politically speaking, a losing cause with the birth of the modern world," McCarthy observed, "is to experience a kind of straining against reality, a rebellious non-conformity that ... is rare in America, where children are instructed in the virtues of the system they live under, as though history had achieved a happy ending in American civics."[22] If McCarthy's description did not apply to all highly religious Catholics – many, including her other devout relatives, embraced modernity to varied degrees – it nevertheless described the constitution of many postwar Catholic conservatives.

When it came to constitutional understandings, Catholic traditionalists are oriented toward the conviction that any understanding of freedom, including one premised on rights, that does not conduce toward substantive moral ends is not "real" freedom but, rather, slavery – that is, enslavement to one's base, worldly passions or desires. Within this framework, rights are only cognizable to the extent they are genuinely liberating – that is, conducive to the realization of the good. Whether that is the case can be determined only by a consideration

---

[19] McCarthy, *Memoirs of a Catholic Girlhood*, 21–23; Orsi, "Between Memory and Modernity," 36–39.

[20] McCarthy, *Memoirs of a Catholic Girlhood*, 30–34, 50–51.

[21] McCarthy, *Memoirs of a Catholic Girlhood*, 19. See generally Orsi, "Between Memory and Modernity," 36. In the end, McCarthy arrived at the following conclusions about religious faith: "From what I have seen, I am driven to the conclusion that religion is only good for good people ... Only good people can afford to be religious. For the others, it is too great a temptation – a temptation to the deadly sins of pride and anger, chiefly, but one might also add sloth. My grandmother McCarthy, I am sure, would have been a better woman if she had been an atheist or an agnostic. The Catholic religion, I believe, is the most dangerous of all, morally (I do not know about the Moslem), because, with its claim to be the only true religion, it fosters that sense of privilege ... the notion that not everyone is lucky enough to be a Catholic." McCarthy, *Memoirs of a Catholic Girlhood*, 23.

[22] McCarthy, *Memoirs of a Catholic Girlhood*, 25.

of whether the rights serve desirable substantive ends – positive goods. From this perspective, rights are not about individual autonomy but are instrumental to the advancement of foundational, substantive goods.[23]

Given this orientation and disposition, it is understandable that the traditionalist Catholic Right emphasized the existence of absolute, unchanging foundations and obedience to the teachings of the Church regarding how we, individually and collectively, must live in consonance with those foundations. For these Catholic Rightists, an undiluted and unwavering certitude was the rock of the faith. Alienation or abandonment of that faith and its teachings brought chaos and evil. Fortunately, the (traditionalist) Church offered the permanence and certitude that only truth can provide.[24]

Catholic teaching, of course, did not necessarily align in policy terms with the agendas of postwar American conservatism: there are no shortage of Catholic injunctions regarding concern and responsibility for the poor and sick that might imply support for an expansive social welfare state. The alignment of traditionalist Catholicism with US political conservatism and, eventually, the Republican Party was built over time, not just politically but ideologically. Many conservative Catholics came to newly spurn the welfare state not by repudiating their Church's ethic of care, as they saw it, as did many libertarians (to say nothing of Ayn Rand devotees) – who were hyper-liberal individualists, after all[25] – but rather by arguing that when the ethic of care was instantiated in the state, it undercut the institutional strength and viability of

---

[23] See Robert P. George, *Making Men Moral: Civil Liberties and Public Morality* (New York: Oxford University Press, 1993); John H. Garvey, *What are Freedoms For?* (Cambridge, MA: Harvard University Press, 1996). See also Southworth, *Lawyers on the Right*, 103, who alludes to this understanding within the socially conservative precincts of mobilized contemporary conservative Christian cause lawyers. For classic statements from the obverse modern civil libertarian perspective emphasizing rights as aimed at individual autonomy, see, e.g., Thomas Emerson, *The System of Freedom of Expression* (New York: Random House, 1970); Ronald Dworkin, *Taking Rights Seriously* (Cambridge, MA: Harvard University Press, 1977).

[24] Traditionalist Catholics commonly argue that liberal Catholics are taking their political commitments from the broader liberal culture as it is evolving across time rather than from the unchanging Truths, as discerned by the Church. As such, liberal Catholicism is not genuine Roman Catholicism but rather a corruption of the Church's teachings: the traditionalists alone are the true defenders of the Faith.

[25] See, e.g., William Graham Sumner's classic statement: "A free man in a free democracy has no duty toward other men ... except respect, courtesy, and good-will ... Every man and woman in society has one big duty. That is, to take care of his or her own self." William Graham Sumner, *What Social Classes Owe to Each Other* (New York: Harper and Brothers, 1883), 39, 113. See also Rand, *Virtue of Selfishness*, 95, 112 ("The government was set to protect man from criminals – and the Constitution was written to protect man from the government. The Bill of Rights was not directed against private citizens, but against the government – as an explicit declaration that individual rights supersede any public or social power"; "The proper functions of a government fall into three broad categories, all of them involving the issues of physical force and protection of men's rights: *the police*, to protect men from criminals – *the armed services*, to protect men from foreign invaders – *the law courts*, to settle disputes among men according to objective laws."). [Emphases in original.]

non-governmental institutions that were firmly committed to teaching and practicing a communalist ethos underwritten by an ethic of care. Foremost among these institutions was the Roman Catholic Church.

Here, the UC-Berkeley sociologist Robert Nisbet's *The Quest for Community* (1953) served.[26] In a text that became a postwar movement classic, Nisbet argued that the rise of the modern social welfare state had significantly undermined the rich and expansive web of private/local/community-based intermediate associations that Alexis de Tocqueville had indelibly described as one of the wonders of the young, lightly governed United States. Once the state began to assume many of the functions traditionally served by these associations, which included churches, families, and civic organizations, these intermediate associations lost their *raison d'être*: they atrophied, if not disappeared. Into the vacuum flowed secularism and individualism, generating "moral and spiritual chaos."[27] In this period, many Catholic traditionalists began arguing that over time, government aid to the poor and sick undermined the Church and eroded the moral foundations of both society and individuals. In this way, they worked their way away from the views of Monsignor New Deal John A. Ryan and toward libertarians and others, including conservative Protestants, on the anti-statist American Right.[28]

---

[26] Robert Nisbet, *The Quest for Community* (New York: Oxford University Press, 1953).

[27] Nisbet, *Quest for Community*; Alexis de Tocqueville, *Democracy in America* (Chicago: University of Chicago Press, 2002) (Harvey Mansfield Jr. and Delba Winthrop, translators and editors).

[28] The most sophisticated intellectual work on this was done in the lead-up to the Reagan years by Michael Novak in *The Spirit of Democratic Capitalism* (New York: Simon and Schuster/American Enterprise Institute, 1982). See also Michael Novak, *The New Consensus on Family and Welfare: A Community of Self-Reliance* (Washington, DC: American Enterprise Institute, 1987); Michael Novak, *Business as a Calling: Work and the Examined Life* (New York: Free Press, 1996); Michal Novak, *The Catholic Ethic and the Spirit of Capitalism* (New York: Free Press, 1993); Michael Novak, *Writing from Left to Right: My Journey from Liberal to Conservative* (New York: Random House, 2014). See also Thomas E. Woods Jr., *The Church and the Market: A Catholic Defense of the Free Economy* (Lanham, MD: Lexington Books, 2005). See Thomas J. Sugrue, "The Catholic Encounter with the 1960s," in Appleby and Cummings, *Catholics in the American Century*, 74. For a precursor effort on the postwar Right to make the Christian case for the free market by a Congregationalist minister associated with the Foundation for Economic Education, see Edmund A. Opitz, *Religion and Capitalism: Allies, Not Enemies* (New Rochelle, NY: Arlington House, 1970). I discuss Opitz in Chapter 3 on "Stories About Markets." On Opitz, see Father Robert Sirico [President of the Acton Institute], "A Tribute to Edmund A. Optiz" (October 1, 1993) (fee.org). The Acton Institute describes itself "a think-tank whose mission is to promote a free and virtuous society characterized by individual liberty and sustained by religious principles" (https://acton.org/about/mission). Among other things, it publishes the journal *Religion & Liberty* and *The Journal of Markets and Morality*. Sirico, a member of both the Mont Pelerin Society and the Philadelphia Society, and a frequent commentator on the Christian Broadcasting Network and Fox News, is the pastor of a Catholic Church in Grand Rapids, Michigan. See Rev. Robert Sirico, *Defending the Free Market: The Moral Case for a Free Economy* (Washington, DC: Regnery, 2012).

This led to calls for constitutional restoration that were, if one understood the deep story, premised on Christian theological arguments. The stance, perhaps surprisingly, came to be adopted ecumenically on the postwar Right. *National Review*'s Will Herberg, who was Jewish, was among the most prominent voices on the Right calling for a return to (Judeo) Christian touchstones. "The secularist dessication of modern society is clear," Herberg thundered, "It is a massive socio-cultural trend that (humanly speaking) is not to be reversed." Herberg went so far as to proclaim, "*as a believing Jew,* I would rather live in a genuinely Christian society with all of its problems than in the present secularist society with all its freedoms."[29] Other non-Catholics like Irving Kristol and Wilson Carey McWilliams spoke in much the same vein, newly finding virtue in religious orthodoxy, a Catholic specialty, which they praised as a vital force in building a good community. In this way, conservative atheists, agnostics, and Jews (that is, non-Christians) came to a deeper appreciation of Christian clerics, whom they earlier might have considered a source of oppression.[30] While atheists and agnostics on the Old Right like Ayn Rand and Rose Wilder Lane had scorned both religious belief and theology and the notion that the United States had been somehow sponsored and sustained by God, as time went on such views became increasingly rare within the postwar conservative movement. Dogma, orthodoxy, and faith were increasingly appreciated, even by those within the movement who, more and more quietly, and even apologetically, remained nonbelievers.[31]

THE "MIND" OF THE CONSERVATIVE CATHOLIC: RUSSELL KIRK'S BROWNSON AND NEWMAN

Russell Kirk's book *The Conservative Mind* (1953) was a landmark and revelation to many during the heyday of a "liberal consensus" that had denied the existence of any homegrown US intellectual conservative tradition. At a time when the label "conservative" remained in bad odor as an embarrassingly

[29] Will Herberg, in L. Brent Bozell Jr., "Letters from Yourselves," *Triumph* 4:6 (June 1969): 17–19, 40, 18. [Emphasis in original]
[30] Nisbet, *Quest for Community*, 10, 46, 27–30. Such was the case with two figures (discussed later) important to the postwar Right who have histories, and continuing ties to, the postwar Left, Alasdair MacIntyre (who, in his fifties, converted to Catholicism and began teaching at the University of Notre Dame), and Wilson Carey McWilliams (who, although a Presbyterian, was fond of Catholic orthodoxy and communalism). See Wilson Carey McWilliams, "Critical Rebound: Why America Needs a Catholic Recovery," in Wilson Carey McWilliams, *The Democratic Soul: A Wilson Carey McWilliams Reader* (Lexington: University Press of Kentucky, 2011) (Patrick J. Deneen and Susan J. McWilliams, editors).
[31] Quoted in David Beito and Linda Royster Beito, "Selling Laissez Faire Antiracism to the Black Masses: Rose Wilder Lane and the Pittsburgh Courier," *The Independent Review* 15:2 (Fall 2010): 279–294, 292.

unthinking atavism, Kirk assembled an intellectual canon that encouraged conservatives to reimagine themselves as part of a long and rich *American* intellectual tradition. Two nineteenth-century Roman Catholic thinkers had important roles in Kirk's project, Orestes Brownson (1803–1876) and (the English) Cardinal John Henry Newman (1801–1890).

Kirk – a later, but fervent Catholic convert[32] – celebrated Brownson as a denizen of the US "prelapsarian" literary tradition that predominated before the "fall" ushered in by New England Transcendentalists like Ralph Waldo Emerson and Henry David Thoreau. Before Emerson, the sage of Mecosta, Michigan, taught, American writers like Washington Irving, Edgar Allan Poe, and James Fenimore Cooper had manifested a "conservatism of mind" marked by a "suspicion of democracy ... innovation [and a] ... love of old ways."[33] Kirk recounted the story of how Brownson's "restless mind" had sampled nearly all the dissenting ways in his time, including via stints as a Unitarian/Universalist minister and Owenite social reformer. Not finding what he sought, and profoundly unsatisfied, Brownson had "at length embraced orthodoxy with the fervor of a man who has found sanctuary." In 1844, possessed by a newborn "revulsion against private judgment," Brownson converted to Roman Catholicism, joining, Kirk rejoiced, "a community older than nations."[34] Calling Brownson "the most interesting example of the progress of Catholicism as a conservative spirit in America," Kirk used his introduction to Brownson's thought as preface to a call for a renewed commitment to the study of Roman Catholicism in America.[35]

In recounting the lessons of Brownson's conversion to the Church of Rome, Russell Kirk taught that in addition to being indispensible to eternal salvation, "[o]bedience, submission to God, is the secret of justice in society and tranquility in life." "[F]ree political institutions," Kirk affirmed, "can be secure only when the people are imbued with religious veneration." Kirk went on to describe Brownson as committed to the proposition that "[d]emocracy, more than any other form of government, rests upon the postulate of a moral law, ordained by an authority superior to human wisdom."[36] Protestantism had failed democracy: unlike Catholicism, it was predisposed to – and its history was one of – declension involving

first, the subjection of religion to the charge of civil government; second, the rejection of the authority of temporal government, and the submission of religion to the control of the faithful; third, individualism, which "leaves religion entirely to the control of the

---

[32] See generally Bradley Birzer, *Russell Kirk: American Conservative* (Lexington: University Press of Kentucky, 2018).

[33] Russell Kirk, *The Conservative Mind: From Burke to Eliot* (Chicago: Gateway Editions, Regnery Publishers, 1960 [1953]), 272.

[34] Kirk, *Conservative Mind*, 272.   [35] Kirk, *Conservative Mind*, 273.

[36] Kirk, *Conservative Mind*, 273.

individual, who selects his own creed, or makes a creed to suit himself, devises his own worship and discipline, and to no restraints but such as are self-imposed."[37]

In this final stage, "disintegration of the religious spirit is imminent ... for man is not sufficient unto himself, reason unaided cannot sustain faith, and Authority is required to preserve Christianity from degenerating into a congeries of fanatic sects and egotistical professions." "Under Protestantism," Brownson had observed, "the sect governs religion, rather than submitting to governance; the congregation bully their ministers and insist upon palatable sermons, flattering to their vanity." As such, "Protestantism cannot sustain popular liberty because 'it is itself subject to popular control, and must follow in all things the popular will, passion, interest, prejudice, or caprice.'"[38]

The modern spirit of which Protestantism was a part, Brownson had explained, spurned hierarchy, loyalty, and authority: indeed, what the modern spirit hated was "'not this or that form of government,'" but the very idea of *legitimacy* itself. It would set itself against *any* claim to legitimacy, absolute monarchy and democracy alike, if it made a bid for legitimacy. Moreover, the modern spirit set itself equally against (practical) reason through its assertion of "'the universal and absolute supremacy of man, and his unrestricted right to subject religion, morals, and politics to his own will, passion, or caprice.'" "This," the admiring Kirk explicated, "is fatal to democracy, for it stimulates insubordination and disorder, setting everything afloat" and destroying the "moral solidarity" that necessarily underwrites such a "delicate" a system of government. Crucially, Kirk explained to his fellow Americans, while popular religious feeling "conceivably may be absent in a monarchy or an aristocracy without ruining the social structure, [it] is indispensible to democracy."[39]

Kirk attested that reading Brownson had given him a deeper understanding of the truth that "[m]en's passions are held in check only by the punishments of divine wrath and the tender affections of piety." As such, "far from repressing liberty ... the sovereignty of God ... establishes and guarantees freedom." Thus, "authority is not the antagonist of liberty, but its vindicator." As a Church devoted to the sanctification and defense of authority, "Catholics, above all others, should be conservatives." The Roman Catholic Church, Kirk reassured readers, "has no desire to meddle in the affairs of government; it endeavors simply to expound the moral laws which just governments obey."[40]

Brownson had advanced a *constitutional* theory to complement his political theory, which Kirk also recounted in *The Conservative Mind*. Orestes Brownson had rejected the view that constitutions could be made at a moment in time, with their meanings fixed at the time of their founding;

[37] Kirk, *Conservative Mind*, 274, quoting Orestes Brownson, *Essays and Reviews*, 373–375
[38] Kirk, *Conservative Mind*, 274, quoting Orestes Brownson, *Essays and Reviews*, 379.
[39] Kirk, *Conservative Mind*, 274–275, quoting Orestes Brownson, *Essays and Reviews*, 307–308.
[40] Kirk, *Conservative Mind*, 275.

he argued instead for organicist understanding of constitutionalism. "Constitutions cannot be made," Kirk reported that Brownson had insisted, "they are the product of slow growth, the expression of a nation's historical experience, or they are mere paper . . . Constitutions must vary as the experience of the people who live under them has varied; and whatever form of government has been long established in a nation, that must be the best permanent framework for the national corporate life." Since they were native and deeply imbricated in the entire "tenor" of European society, Kirk's Brownson held that "monarchy and aristocracy ought to be perpetuated [in Europe]." But because the United States was founded and settled entirely by commoners, "republicanism" better suited this country. Given the distinctive history of the United States, Kirk taught that "the true American conservative will struggle to maintain the Republic in its purity, strictly obeying its laws, cleaving fast to its written Constitution." That said, Kirk's Brownson had wisely understood that "[n]o human institution is immutable": "constitutions must be mended and healed now and then." But the social reformer must recognize that his place is not to create but to develop and restore – "he cannot hack a new constitution out of raw humanity."[41]

Kirk acknowledged that the Roman Catholic Church's progress in the United States had been slower than Brownson had hoped. Nevertheless, Kirk observed in the 1950s, "it has been persistent": "What a triumphant Catholicism in America may be like – whether, as Tocqueville hints and Evelyn Waugh conjectures, it will be a Catholicism much altered and diluted by American materialism and democracy – the next few generations may begin to learn." Kirk instructed his fellow American conservatives to look to Brownson's sophisticated Catholic intelligence as they move toward "reconcile[ing] orthodoxy with Americanism."[42]

Russell Kirk also wrote Cardinal John Henry Newman into his canon of American conservatism by including a celebratory chapter on the leader of England's "Oxford Movement." Newman, a Catholic convert, had sought to restore Catholicism and medieval ritual to the Anglican country that, in his view, had tragically separated from the Church of Rome under Henry VIII. In *The Conservative Mind*, Kirk placed particular emphasis on Newman's unrelenting opposition to both pluralism and Benthamite utilitarianism. The passage of the Reform Acts in nineteenth-century England (1832–1884)

---

[41] Kirk, *Conservative Mind*, 275–276. Kirk ties Brownson's constitutional theory to that of the Savoyard counterrevolutionary, counter-Enlightenment political theorist, and ultramontane Catholic apologist, Count Joseph de Maistre (1753–1821). The organic character of Brownson's constitutional theory was Burkean, and Burke's *Reflections on the Revolution in France* (1790) had been an important influence on de Maistre. For an overview of de Maistre's thought on the United States, see Joseph Eaton, "'This babe-in-arms': Joseph de Maistre's Critique of America," in Carolina Armenteros and Richard A. Lebrun, editors, *Joseph de Maistre and the Legacy of Enlightenment* (Oxford: Voltaire Foundation, 2011).

[42] Kirk, *Conservative Mind*, 277.

had significantly expanded the franchise to the working and middle classes. Kirk explained that these democratizing reforms had unsettled Newman, informed, as they had been and as Newman believed, by religious nonconformism and secular rationalism, if not outright hostility to the established Church. Newman had read these developments toward a more broad-based democracy as a harbinger of "a secularizing process which, if not impeded, would end in the humanitarian pseudo-religion advocated by the Utilitarians." Expanding power to a broader swath of people, including the uneducated lower classes, who were newly empowered to work what they took to be, as the utilitarians would have it, "the greatest good for the greatest number," might ultimately lead to disestablishment – a threat to religious orthodoxy everywhere. Newman's measures of True and False, of Good and Evil, Kirk admiringly explained, were absolute: they had nothing to do with what untutored individuals thought conduced to their "happiness": the Church, of course, taught what made for genuine happiness – a human soul in harmony with its natural ends, as created by God and explicated by the teachings of his Church. Newman and his fellow "Tractarians" called for the restoration and revival of the corporate and sacramental Church by which religion would once again "'have to find a place for feelings of beauty, antiquity, and mystery, which the ruling theology had dismissed or ignored as worldly or unprofitable or profane.'"[43]

Kirk explained Cardinal Newman's argument that knowledge of all kinds, whether moral or physical, arose not out of mere facts alone but rather out of the way the meaning or significance of those facts was understood. This entailed a process of subtle, imperfect apprehension – what Newman had called the "Illiative Sense" – through which we relate the world to ultimate (ontological) Truths. "Without a foundation of first principles," Cardinal Newman had demonstrated, "science ... is worthless – a meaningless accumulation of unrelated facts." "Our first principles are not obtained," he underlined, "by heaping together data, after Bacon's method, and drawing inferences."

Life being what it is, humans must act in the world. The problem is that if we were to insist on proofs for everything, we would be paralyzed. As such, in the nature of things, man was forced to act on assumptions, feeling his way forward. Under the circumstances, it was a misimpression to hold that reason formed man's impressions and directed his actions. In truth, more than we realize, the assumptions we act on are premised on faith.[44] The Illiative Sense

---

[43] Kirk, *Conservative Mind*, 313–314, and 315, quoting Young, *Early Victorian England II*, 472. On the period and its politics, see Eric Hobsbawm, *Industry and Empire: The Birth of The Industrial Revolution* (New York: New Press, 1999).

[44] Kirk, *Conservative Mind*, 316–318, and 319, quoting Newman, *Discussions and Arguments*, 274–275. The fellowship of those committed to "first things" or "first principles" – as against those who are not (progressives, liberals, relativists) – is a trope of contemporary conservatism. See Hadley Arkes, *First Things: An Inquiry into the First Principles of Morality and Justice* (Princeton: Princeton University Press, 1986) (Arkes is a Jewish-born Straussian and Robert P. George compatriot who recently converted to Roman Catholicism and, shortly thereafter,

by which we make our way forward should be "corrected ... by reference to Authority," which Newman characterized as "a sort of filtered collective Illiative Sense, [which] provides the purgation of individual error."[45] Thus, as Kirk explained, Newman taught, "Without personal religion, secular knowledge commonly is a tool of unbelief."[46]

Newman was an intransigent opponent of religious and political liberalism, premised as both were on the principle of "private judgment," which, as he saw it, left often "grave questions according to the imprudent and fallible dictates of one's own petty personal understanding." For Newman, to proceed by private judgment was "an act of flagrant impiety, approaching diabolic possession, the sin of spiritual pride." Given man's position and circumstances, only the veneration of authority will serve.[47] Russell Kirk observed that it was hardly coincidental that Cardinal Newman, who considered "doubt ... a surly, envious, egotistic emotion, a bitter denial of everything but the sullen self" from which one learns nothing, was also our "noblest" proponent of liberal education. For "liberal education" is "liberal" under a "far more ancient and more pure ... [and] true understanding of liberty, which is freedom to live within the compass of God's ordinances, not freedom to doubt and demolish. Liberal education, in this sense and this sense only, is the intellectual training of free men."[48]

Newman traced the successful movement for universal, uniform, free, compulsory, secular, government-run schooling in England to Benthamite utilitarians: he considered the development yet another step in the march toward "the new consolidating socialism." Today, Kirk explained in his chapter on Newman in *The Conservative Mind*, "[t]he notions of Gradgrind, mingled with a Rousseauistic sentimentality, have come to dominate state-supported education in both Britain and America; and now that the age of passion is here, a part of the thinking public seems to be waking in alarm to the menace of quasi-education divorced from religious principle." "In America, at least," Kirk noted with some hope, "the parochial schools, and the universities endowed by religious bodies, are increasing in influence." "Whether they know

became a supporter of President Donald Trump. The conservative magazine *First Things*, published by the Institute of Religion and Public Life, describes itself, perhaps accurately, as "America's Most Influential Journal of Religion and Public Life" (www.firstthings.com). Founded by Father Richard John Neuhaus, who served as its longtime editor (1990–2009), it has since been edited by Catholic conservatives Joseph Bottum and (currently) R. R. Reno. Many of the most familiar luminaries of the modern Roman Catholic Right – Robert P. George, Mary Ann Glendon, Ryan T. Anderson, and Arkes, among others – serve on its advisory council (as did Michael Novak, until his death in 2017). In addition, the online journal *First Principles* (www .firstprinciplesjournal.com/journal/), offered by the Intercollegiate Studies Institute (ISI), bills itself as "the home of intellectual conservatism." In addition to other features, *First Principles* offers free online courses in Western Civilization, The American Experience, Free Markets and Civil Society, America's Security, Conservative Thought, and Higher Education.

[45] Kirk, *Conservative Mind*, 320.   [46] Kirk, *Conservative Mind*, 318.
[47] Kirk, *Conservative Mind*, 323.   [48] Kirk, *Conservative Mind*, 321–323.

it or not," he explained, these schools will "find in Newman the best expression of their educational theories."[49]

"People say to me, that it is but a dream to suppose that Christianity should regain the organic power in human society which it once possessed," Newman wrote (as quoted by Kirk) in *The Tamworth Reading Room* (1841), lamenting that that might very well be so. But the problem remains. If "the ascendency of Faith may be impracticable ... the reign of Knowledge is incomprehensible": "The problem for statesmen [nevertheless] is how to educate the masses." Let us be clear, Newman had emphasized: "[L]iterature and science cannot give the solution."[50]

ALLIED ANTI- AND AMBIVALENT MODERNS: ERIC VOEGELIN,
RICHARD WEAVER, AND LEO STRAUSS

Fulton Sheen's anti-modernism was hardly an exclusively Catholic phenomenon – though right-wing Catholicism lent medievalist anti-modernism a popular presence and influence in the broader political culture. Three non-Catholic elite conservative thinkers, Eric Voegelin, Richard Weaver, and Leo Strauss, joined the postwar Roman Catholic Right in reflecting at length upon a world in which political authority was rooted no deeper than in the sovereign individual self.

The Roman Catholic Church's story was fundamentally connected with the history of Western Europe, which, given the Reformation, from the Church's perspective could only be viewed in its broadest sense as a history of declension – as a history of the rejection of the medieval worldview in preference for liberal modernity and liberal modernity's subsequent ascendance. Catholics, more than most, remembered that there had been a time when the Church had been (gloriously) predominant in the West: it had ordered every aspect of European civilization's religious, political, and cultural life. The Church's teachings were held to be synonymous with "Truth" itself – not merely as the views of one religion among many, chosen by individuals, or not, according to what they had (idiosyncratically) decided best suited their sovereign selves.[51]

---

[49] Kirk, *Conservative Mind*, 328–329. The reference is to the character Thomas Gradgrind in Charles Dickens's novel *Hard Times* (1854), whose name has become a synonym for the character's core traits: a rigid and relentless insistence in life, against any claims of sentimentality or emotion, on the numbers and the cold, hard facts.

[50] John Henry Newman, "The Tamworth Reading Room" (1841), quoted in Kirk, *Conservative Mind*, 312.

[51] This sense of decline from the medieval consensus existed on the Catholic Right – indeed, constituted it – first with the counter-Reformation within the Church itself and then in the work of, among others, Joseph de Maistre, and of the French counter-Enlightenment more generally, which formed in reaction to the French Revolution. See Isaiah Berlin, "Joseph de Maistre and the Origins of Fascism," in Isaiah Berlin, *The Crooked Timber of Humanity:*

The descent of Western Europe into fascism, the Holocaust, and the Second World War in the 1930s and 1940s once again prompted those on the Right to search out the sources of the catastrophe. Their inclination was to find it in the philosophical presuppositions of modern Europe; their method was to identify the fatal philosophical wrong turn – the tragic metaphysical error – that had set civilization down this wicked road. As war loomed, a host of the most serious thinkers in this vein, Left, Right, and other, fled for their lives across the Atlantic to the United States, where they took up that task of identifying the "transformation in Western thinking that had prepared the unthinkable."[52]

One of the most prominent people to influence the postwar American Right was the emigré Viennese historian and Louisiana State University (LSU) English professor Eric Voegelin – as Mark Lilla colorfully put it, "a hothouse flower transplanted from the dark garden of German *Geschichte* to the land of the open road."[53] Voegelin, whom I introduced earlier in Chapter 2 on "The Alternative Tradition of Conservative Constitutional Theory," rooted the European cataclysm of the 1930s, Nazism, in the secularization of the modern West, and the fatal decision of the radical Enlightenment to distinguish the "transcendent City of God from the terrestrial City of Man," leaving man unanchored and unleashed. Man set himself, personally and politically, at the center of all things, "a Prometheus, believing himself a god capable of transforming anything and everything at will." This opened the door to all manner of political religions: Marxism, fascism, and nationalisms. Voegelin's argument, in essence, was that "[w]hen you abandon the Lord, it is only a matter of time before you start worshiping a Fuhrer."[54] A world without a foundation in religion would devolve ultimately into a hell on earth.[55]

The Catholic Right's answer, of course, was to call for Western civilization's return to the One True Faith. In a rub, however, Voegelin himself blamed Christianity for initiating key chapters of the decline into barbarism. Voegelin's first book in English, *The New Science of Politics* (1952), became a classic text of the modern American Right. There, Voegelin targeted "Gnosticism," – a movement that, first under Christianity and later secularized, "de-devined" temporal power. Voegelin then charted the subsequent progress of this corruption of Christian thought as it moved forward in time from England's Puritan Revolution, to Thomas Hobbes's materialism, to, crucially, the French Revolution. As time went on, Gnostic leaders moved from not only rejecting the divine but also to substituting man

Chapters in the History of Ideas (Princeton: Princeton University Press, 2013) (2nd ed.; Henry Hardy, editor); T. J. Jackson Lears, *No Place of Grace: Antimodernism and the Transformation of American Culture, 1880–1920* (Chicago: University of Chicago Press, 1981).

[52] Mark Lilla, *The Shipwrecked Mind: On Political Reaction* (New York: New York Review Books, 2016), 26.

[53] Lilla, *Shipwrecked Mind*, 27.   [54] Lilla, *Shipwrecked Mind*, 26–28.

[55] See Eric Voegelin, *Political Religions* (Lewiston, NY: E. Mellon Press, 1986) (trans. T. J. DiNapoli and E. S. Eastery III).

in its place – that is, to making man the new God. Men came to worship temporal goals and grew increasingly impatient about achieving them: they simply could not wait. At last they came to insist on no less than employing human means to establish heaven on earth – "immanentiz[ing] the eschaton."⁵⁶ Voegelin built out this basic argument by formulating a universal theory of political societies – Voegelin's proposed "new science of politics" – as being anchored in the symbols by which they order their institutions and public lives.⁵⁷

University of Chicago English professor Richard M. Weaver (1910–1963), a Kentucky-born Platonist who had studied with the coterie of southern agrarians and New Critics at Vanderbilt University before falling under Eric Voegelin's tutelage at LSU, added to the postwar conservative anti-modernist canon with his landmark manifesto *Ideas Have Consequences* (1948). Writing partly in reaction to World War II, Weaver too recounted a story of the steady decline of Western culture since the eclipse of medieval Europe by liberal modernity. *Ideas Have Consequences* culminated in a clarion call for a revival of "the chivalry and spirituality of the Middle Ages."⁵⁸

Weaver argued at length for "healing" and "restoration" through (with an allusion to Saint Peter) the reestablishment of society on the "rock" of "metaphysical right" – what Weaver called the "world of ought," anchored

---

⁵⁶ See Lilla, *Shipwrecked Mind*, 36–37.
⁵⁷ Eric Voegelin, *The New Science of Politics* (Chicago: University of Chicago Press, 1987)[1952]. See also Eric Voegelin, *Science, Politics, and Gnosticism* (Chicago: Regnery Gateway Editions, 1986)[1968].
⁵⁸ Richard M. Weaver, *Ideas Have Consequences* (Chicago: University of Chicago Press, 1984) [1948], 187. "There can be no doubt that the enormous exertions made by the Middle Ages to preserve a common world view – exertions which took forms incomprehensible to modern man because he does not understand what is always at stake under such circumstances – signified a greater awareness of realities than our leaders exhibit today." Weaver, *Ideas Have Consequences*, 21. Similar arguments were advanced by later conservative classics, particularly by Straussians like Allan Bloom. See, e.g., the discussion of the pursuit of the good and the significance of friendship at 30–31, in Bloom's *The Closing of the American Mind: How Higher Education Has Failed Democracy and Impoverished the Souls of Today's Students* (New York: Simon and Schuster, 1987). Books like Wendy Shalit's *A Return to Modesty: Discovering the Lost Virtue* (New York: The Free Press, 1999), Rochelle Gurstein's *The Repeal of Reticence: America's Cultural and Legal Struggles Over Free Speech, Obscenity, Sexual Liberation, and Modern Art* (New York: Hill and Wang, 1996), David Lowenthal's *No Liberty for License: The Forgotten Logic of the First Amendment* (Dallas, TX: Spence Publishing, 1997), and Harry Clor's, *Obscenity and Public Morality: Censorship in a Liberal Society* (Chicago: University of Chicago Press, 1969), whether consciously, coincidentally, or not, all later developed themes first set out in abbreviated form in *Ideas Have Consequences*. Similar concerns are at the core of Daniel Bell's *The Cultural Contradictions of Capitalism* (New York: Basic Books, 1976) (the difficult-to-classify Bell, often grouped as a neoconservative, famously defined himself as "a socialist in economics, a liberal in politics, and a conservative in culture"). To paraphrase what is often said about Plato's and Aristotle's influence on political philosophy, we might consider much of contemporary conservative thought to be little more than a set of footnotes on Richard Weaver's *Ideas Have Consequences*.

neither in the *demos* nor in material experience, but in eternal Truth.[59] That many would "not be at all happy with the political implications" of his conclusions, Weaver underlined, was irrelevant.[60] Bucking up those who would follow him down this hard but virtuous road, Weaver warned that in "asking for a confession of guilt and an acceptance of sterner obligation ... we are making demands in the name of the ideal or the suprapersonal, and we cannot expect a more cordial welcome than disturbers of complacency have received in any other age."[61]

The American-born Weaver joined Voegelin and the other European émigré philosophers working from the United States at mid-century in seeking "to analyze many features of modern disintegration by referring them to a first cause," to provide "a rigorous cause-and-effect analysis of the decline of a belief in standards and values" in the modern world. Weaver found the critical juncture – the fork in the road – in "a change that overtook the dominant philosophical thinking of the West in the fourteenth century, when the reality of transcendentals was first seriously challenged."[62] Weaver's culprits were various. The nominalism of William of Occam, which denied the existence of universals and insisted that universal terminology was a matter of convenient labeling, loomed large. "The practical result of nominalist philosophy," Weaver attested, "is to banish the reality which is perceived by the intellect and to posit as reality that which is perceived by the senses. With this change in the affirmation of what is real," he explained, "the whole orientation of culture takes a turn, and we are on the road to modern empiricism." "The denial of universals carries with it the denial of everything transcending experience," he continued, "The denial of everything transcending experience means inevitably ... the denial of truth ... [with] no escape from the relativism of 'man the measure of all things.'" The result is "a feeling of alienation from all fixed truth."[63]

The thought of Saint Thomas Aquinas marked another malign turning point. Thomas's error, Weaver argued, was to abandon the idealism and certitudes of Plato for the moderation and accommodationism of Aristotle. "In Thomism," Weaver wrote, "based as it is on Aristotle, even the Catholic Church turned away from the asceticism and the rigorous morality of the patristic father to accept a degree of pragmatic acquiescence in the world." Elsewhere, Weaver charged that "[t]he metaphysical right of religion went out at the time of the Reformation."[64]

Then there was modern scientific rationalism. Hobbes and Locke had erroneously "taught that man needed only to reason correctly upon evidence

---

[59] Matthew 16:18 ("And I say also unto thee, That thou art Peter, and upon this rock I will build my church; and the gates of hell shall not prevail against it").

[60] Weaver, *Ideas Have Consequences*, vi, 129–130.   [61] Weaver, *Ideas Have Consequences*, 11.

[62] Weaver, *Ideas Have Consequences*, v, 187.   [63] Weaver, *Ideas Have Consequences*, 3–4.

[64] Weaver, *Ideas Have Consequences*, 120, 131.

from nature." Once these views were ascendant, and then predominant, religion began to assume "an ambiguous dignity," and its future was in doubt. Early efforts to reconcile religion with scientific rationalism culminated in Deism, which Weaver spurned as a complacent denial of "antecedent truth" (it was the Deist Jefferson, he reminded readers, who had made the spurious appeal to "nature and Nature's God" in the Declaration of Independence). Then, of course, there was Darwinism, which positioned biological necessity as man's superintending motive. "Whereas nature had formerly been regarded as imitating a transcendent model and as constituting an imperfect reality," Weaver explained, "it was henceforth looked upon as containing the principles of its own constitution and behavior ... The expulsion of the element of unintelligibility in nature was followed by the abandonment of the doctrine of original sin."[65]

In light of all this, Weaver proclaimed on the very first page of *Ideas Have Consequences*, "There is ground for declaring that modern man has become a moral idiot": "For four centuries every man has been not only his own priest but his own professor of ethics, and the consequence is an anarchy which threatens even that minimum consensus of value necessary to the political state."[66] Liberal modernity was an abomination, and modern man "a parricide" who had defied "the order of nature" by "tak[ing] up arms against, and ... effectually slain, what former men have regarded with filial veneration." What's more, "[h]e has not been conscious of crime but has, on the contrary ... regarded his action as proof of virtue."[67]

The situation was dire:

There is no term proper to describe the condition in which [modern man] is now left unless it be "abysmality." He is in the deep and dark abysm, and he has nothing with which to raise himself. His life is practice without theory. As problems crowd around him, he deepens confusion by meeting them with *ad hoc* policies. Secretly he hungers for truth but consoles himself with the thought that life should be experimental.[68]

Ultimately, Weaver held that the predicament was rooted in a crisis of authority. Modern man's "decline can be represented as a long series of abdications. He has found less and less ground for authority at the same time he thought he was setting himself up as the center of authority in the universe; indeed, there seems to exist here a dialectic process which takes away his power in proportion as he demonstrates that his independence entitles him to power." The natural end of this, of course, was the tragedy of communism, a truly evil political system, where man is all – and nothing.[69]

Notwithstanding this damning assessment, Weaver, perhaps surprisingly, did have a few good things to say about the communists who, as fellow

---

[65] Weaver, *Ideas Have Consequences*, 4–6.   [66] Weaver, *Ideas Have Consequences*, 1–2.
[67] Weaver, *Ideas Have Consequences*, 170–171, 182.   [68] Weaver, *Ideas Have Consequences*, 7.
[69] Weaver, *Ideas Have Consequences*, 7, 11.

radicals, had at least gotten to the root of things. Unlike liberals, for whom Weaver reserved his supreme contempt, the communists at least knew that "[w]ithout the metaphysical dream it is impossible to think of men living together harmoniously over an extent of time. The dream carries with it an evaluation, which is the bond of spiritual community." "When we affirm that philosophy begins with wonder," he wrote, "we are affirming in effect that sentiment is anterior to reason. We do not undertake to reason about anything until we have been drawn to it by an affective interest."[70] "Reason alone," moreover, "fails to justify itself. Not without cause has the devil been called the prince of lawyers, and not by accident are Shakespeare's villains good reasoners. If the disposition is wrong, reason increases maleficence; if it is right, reason orders and furthers the good."[71]

Weaver was no patriot. The United States – a nation, after all, defined by its frontier experience, including its characterizing flight from restraints, forms, and formalities – chafed at hierarchy and authority. Weaver preferred Europeans, whom he adjudged more mature and adult. He shared their relative fastidiousness and refined sense of propriety. A believer in rank, order, and place, and a respecter of forms, Weaver looked to medieval Europe as the epitome of Western civilization's emphasis on authority and hierarchy, on awe and the veneration of the eternal. It is this context only, he observed, that makes possible the hero – who, he underscored, "can never be a relativist."[72]

---

[70] Weaver, *Ideas Have Consequences*, 18–19,122–123, 129–131. For a defense of orthodoxy influential among Catholic conservatives, see G. K. Chesterton, *Orthodoxy* (London: John Lane/Bodley Head, 1908). For an illustration of contemporary influence, see Tod Worner, "Books That Rocked My World: G.K. Chesterton's "Orthodoxy," *Word on Fire* (September 25, 2017) (www.wordonfire.org/resources/blog/books-that-rocked-my-world-gk-chestertons-orthodoxy/5588/. *Word on Fire* is the online right-wing–leaning Catholic web emporium of Word on Fire Catholic Ministries devoted to "Proclaiming Christ in the Culture." It is run by Bishop Robert Barron (WordOnFire.org).

[71] Weaver, *Ideas Have Consequences*, 19.

[72] Weaver, *Ideas Have Consequences*, 24–26. See generally Mary Douglas, *Purity and Danger: An Analysis of Concepts of Pollution and Taboo* (London: Penguin, 1966); Barrington Moore Jr., *Moral Purity and Persecution in History* (Princeton: Princeton University Press, 2000); Martha Nussbaum, *Hiding From Humanity: Disgust, Shame, and the Law* (Princeton: Princeton University Press, 2006). Weaver writes, "Our age provides many examples of the ravages of immediacy, the clearest of which is the failure of the modern mind to recognize obscenity … [which] is not connected with the decay of Puritanism. The word is employed here in its original sense to describe that which should be enacted off-stage because it is unfit for public exhibition." He explains, "it has been left to the world of science and rationalism to make a business of purveying of the private and the offensive. Picture magazines and tabloid newspapers place before the millions scenes and facts which violate every definition of humanity. How common is it today to see upon the front page of some organ destined for a hundred thousand homes the agonized face of a child run over in the street, the dying expression of a woman crushed by a subway train, tableaux of execution, scenes of intense private grief. These are the obscenities. The rise of sensational journalism everywhere testifies to man's loss of points of reference, to his determination to enjoy the forbidden in the name of freedom. All reserve is being sacrificed to titillation. The extremes of passion and suffering are served up to enliven the

Needless to say, like other critics of liberal individualism, including Roman Catholics, Left and Right, Weaver vehemently rejected the reduction of man to *homo economicus*. He held Darwinism responsible for the materialistic ravages of Gilded Age capitalism, which he strenuously condemned. "[T]he man of commerce is by the nature of things a relativist," Weaver damningly observed. "[H]is mind is constantly on the fluctuating values of the market place, and there is no surer way for him to fail than to dogmatize and moralize about things." Weaver had next to nothing in common – save, perhaps, a contempt for mass man – with contemporaneous apologists for tooth-and-claw capitalism like Ayn Rand.[73]

Relatedly, Weaver had nothing but contempt for the bourgeois consumer culture that had emerged on a large scale in the early twentieth-century United States, reaching its apotheosis in the postwar period.[74] That culture was causing "the steady obliteration of those distinctions which create society," which Weaver called "the most portentous general event of our time." It was inevitable, given his nature, that the mass of Western men were being ground up into the pabulum of a shallow, materialistic middle class: "Loving comfort, risking little, terrified by the thought of change, its aim is to establish a materialistic civilization which will banish threats to its complacency. It has conventions, not ideals; it is washed rather than clean." In contrast to later neoconservatives like Irving Kristol and Norman Podhoretz, and revisionist conservative Catholics like Michael Novak, himself sometimes classed as a neoconservative, who, writing in reaction to the 1960s counterculture and New Left, praised free markets and bourgeois values, Weaver condemned "the bourgeois ascendency and its corrupted world view," pronouncing it "the final

---

breakfast table or to lighten the boredom of an evening at home. The area of privacy has been abandoned because the definition of person has been lost; there is no longer a standard by which to judge what belongs to the individual man. Behind the offense lies the repudiation of sentiment in favor of immediacy." Weaver, *Ideas Have Consequences*, 28–29.

[73] Weaver, *Ideas Have Consequences*, 6, 32. See also Whittaker Chambers, "Big Sister Is Watching You" [review of Ayn Rand's *Atlas Shrugged*], *National Review* (December 28, 1957) ("For, if [as Rand would have it] Man's "heroism" [some will prefer to say: 'human dignity'] no longer derives from God, or is not a function of that godless integrity which was a root of Nietzsche's anguish, then Man becomes merely the most consuming of animals, with glut as the condition of his happiness and its replenishment his foremost activity. So Randian Man, at least in his ruling caste, has to be held 'heroic' in order not to be beastly. And this, of course, suits the author's economics and the politics that must arise from them."). *Ideas Have Consequences* makes additional arguments currently associated with the Left, including a lament concerning the alienation of labor in a capitalist society, a critique of modern media, a vehement critique of materialism and consumerism, and a decrying of the barbarity of nuclear weapons. Some of these positions are hardly surprising given Weaver's roots in the Southern Agrarian circles at Vanderbilt.

[74] Lizabeth Cohen, *A Consumer's Republic: The Politics of Mass Consumption in Postwar America* (New York: Knopf, 2003); Meg Jacobs, *Pocketbook Politics: Economic Citizenship in Twentieth Century America* (Princeton: Princeton University Press, 2005). See also Dwight Macdonald, "Masscult and Midcult II," *Partisan Review* (Fall 1960): 589–631.

degradation of the Baconian philosophy ... that knowledge becomes power in the service of appetite."[75]

Weaver was also an adamant critic of equality and democracy. "The comity of peoples in groups large and small," he argued, "rests not upon this chimerical notion of equality but upon fraternity, a concept which long antedates it in history because it goes immeasurably deeper in human sentiment." Fraternity roots people "in a network of sentiment, not of rights." "Equality," by contrast, "is a disorganization concept in so far as human relationships mean order. It is order without design; it attempts a meaningless and profitless regimentation of what has been ordered from time immemorial by the scheme of things." To be sure, he qualified, "[n]o society can rightly offer less than equality before the law":[76]

[B]ut there can be no equality of condition between youth and age or between the sexes; there cannot be equality even between friends. The rule is that each shall act where he is strong; the assignment of identical roles produces first confusion and then alienation ... Not only is this disorganizing heresy busily confounding the most natural social group-ings, it is also creating a reservoir of poisonous envy. How much of the frustration of the modern world proceeds from starting with the assumption that all are equal, finding that this cannot be so, and then having to realize that one can no longer fall back on the bond of fraternity![77]

It was in feudal Europe where things had been properly ordered, "before people succumbed to various forms of the proposal that every man should be king."[78]

A spurious commitment to equality has implications for the possibilities of democracy. "It is generally assumed that the erasing of all distinctions will usher in the reign of pure democracy," Weaver observed:

But the inability of pure democracy to stand for something intelligible leaves it merely a verbal deception. If it promises equality before the law, it does no more than empires and monarchies have done ... If it promises equality of condition, it promises injustice, because one law for the ox and the lion is tyranny ... When it was found that equality before the law has no effect on inequalities of ability and achievement, humanitarians concluded that they had been tricked ... The claim to political equality was supplemen-ted by the demand for economic democracy, which was to give substance to the ideal of the levelers. Nothing but a despotism could enforce anything so unrealistic, and this explains why modern governments dedicated to this program have become, under one guise or another, despotic.[79]

A spurious equality – what Weaver calls radical egalitarianism – is, as such, no friend of freedom. Some say that democratic equality is good because it allows

---

[75] Weaver, *Ideas Have Consequences*, 35, 38. This, at least, was a sentiment with which the UC-Berkeley Free Speech movement leader Mario Savio – educated in the left-wing, Jesuit, Catholic social justice tradition – might well have agreed. See Robert Cohen, *Freedom's Orator: Mario Savio and the Radical Legacy of the 1960s* (New York: Oxford University Press, 2014).

[76] Weaver, *Ideas Have Consequences*, 41–42.   [77] Weaver, *Ideas Have Consequences*, 42.

[78] Weaver, *Ideas Have Consequences*, 43.   [79] Weaver, *Ideas Have Consequences*, 44–45.

each to develop his diverse potentials. But, Weaver argued, one must look more deeply into this claim, with attention to "the nature of things." The implication here is that man is like a seed, "having some immanent design of germination, so that for his flowering he needs that liberty which is 'freedom from.'" He will then grow naturally, according to a plan, oriented from below, established solely by nature. But this metaphor positions discipline as "a force constraining what nature had intended," placing the highest value on freedom from. "That men are a field of wild flowers, naturally good in their growing," Weaver complained, however, "is the romantic fallacy." In the end, "[e]very attempt to find a way out of these dilemmas points to a single necessity; some source of authority must be found."[80]

Because the inequality of men is self-evident, hierarchies and diversities will break out everywhere. Democrats will make constant war on these hierarchies and diversities, with the aim of denying their truth, of erasing or suppressing them. This process is the origin of democratic society's strange "adulation of the regular fellow, the political seduction of the common man, and the deep distrust of intellectuals, whose grasp of principles gives them superior insight." An egalitarian democratic society "may even pay tribute to the exemplar of easy morals; for he is the 'good fellow,' who has about him none of the uncomfortable angularities of the idealist." It will be disinclined to recognize that "the primary need of man is to perfect his spiritual being and prepare for immortality," which requires the disciplined "education of the mind and the passions": "The growth of materialism, however, has made this a consideration remote and even incomprehensible to the majority." In such a world, Weaver lamented, "even in everyday speech the word *fact* had taken the place of *truth*."[81]

Turning to the US Constitution, Weaver emphasized the degree to which the American Founders (the Federalists especially), who recognized the insufficiency of majority rule without reference to an end, harbored serious reservations about democracy. Since democracy rested on no more than the sentiments of the moment, the Founders "labored long and with considerable cunning to perfect an instrument which should transcend even the lawmaking body." The Constitution, "which in the American system stands for political truth," was never understood to be immutable. But with its notoriously difficult Article V process for constitutional amendment, "[i]t was hoped that the surmounting of these would prove so laborious and slow that errors would be exposed and the permanent truly recognized. In this way they endeavored to protect the populace of a republic against itself."[82]

It is because the nation's constitutional Founders rejected both a romantic theory of human nature and a pure majoritarian democracy that their design is perpetually under siege from Jacobins of all stripes: "They regard it as a kind of

[80] Weaver, *Ideas Have Consequences*, 45, 50.
[81] Weaver, *Ideas Have Consequences*, 46, 49, 58.   [82] Weaver, *Ideas Have Consequences*, 47.

mortmain, and during the administration of Franklin Roosevelt its interpreters were scornfully termed, in an expression indicative of the modern temper, 'nine old men.'"[83] Weaver's call was to keep the faith.

Leo Strauss's *Natural Right and History* (1953), which, like Eric Voegelin's *The New Science of Politics*, was initially delivered in the Walgreen Foundation Lecture Series at the University of Chicago, similarly argued in defense of transcendent moral standards, which Strauss, like his mid-century compatriots, found to be deeply embattled.[84] *Natural Right and History* was marked by a profound sense of civilizational crisis, in which modern man, it seemed, was not only no longer able to reliably distinguish between right and wrong, ethically and politically, but also, in fact, no longer believed there was any true basis for the distinction. This was the crisis of moral relativism. It was manifested in the world of ideas, first, by a thoroughgoing historicism, the belief that meanings were meaningful only within, and did not transcend, their times. It was further manifested by the proliferation of positivism, which held fast to the sharp distinction the German sociologist Max Weber had drawn between facts and values, and insisted that a true social science be empirical, on the model of the "hard" sciences like chemistry and physics, and value-free. Strauss rooted the great crises of the twentieth century, from which, like Voegelin, he literally fled for his life, in these new, "modern" philosophical turns: he found the academic discipline of modern philosophy, as practiced by the likes of Husserl and Heidegger (Strauss had personally studied with both) to be wellsprings of the turn away from transcendence, and thus complicit in the modern predicament – and, by implication, in its atrocities. Strauss was passionate about the civilizational need for a re-grounding in transcendent truths. *Natural Right and History* set the broad outlines of what needed to be done.

The book turned to the history of political thought to undertake this needful recovery. In it, Strauss returned to the ethical and political thought of the premoderns – the ancients – to recover the concept of classical natural right. For Strauss, the ancient Greeks, and the works of Plato and Aristotle above all, were truly the best that has been thought and said: not only did they distinguish between true and false and right and wrong, but the best among them, the philosophers, devoted their entire lives to the rigorous and passionate search for truth and, so far as society was concerned, the supreme value: justice.

The critical juncture in the history of Western political thought involved the civilizational abandonment of the ancient pursuit of an understanding of

[83] Weaver, *Ideas Have Consequences*, 47–48.
[84] Leo Strauss, *Natural Right and History* (Chicago: University of Chicago Press, 1953). See also Leora Batnitzky, "Leo Strauss," *The Stanford Encyclopedia of Philosophy* (Summer 2016 edition), Edward N. Zalta, editor. For relatively brief summaries of the Straussian perspective from inside the movement, see Richard Sherlock, "The Secret of Straussianism," *Modern Age* 48 (2006): 208, 211; Mark C. Henrie, *Straussianism, First Principles* (May 5, 2011), www .firstprinciplesjournal.com/articles.aspx?article=871&theme=cotho&loc=b

transcendent truths, like justice, and the aspiration to live in consonance with
them, beginning with the political thought of Niccolo Machiavelli (*The Prince*
(1532)), and then Thomas Hobbes, who grounded their theories of political
power in the basest but most reliable of worldly human needs, the individual's
animal will to self-preservation. These modern understandings provided the
groundwork for the social contract theories of political authority found in the
landmark works of modern political thought, Hobbes's *Leviathan* (1651), John
Locke's *Second Treatise on Civil Government* (1689), and Jean-Jacques
Rousseau's *The Social Contract* (1762), which posited that political societies
are legitimately formed by individuals seeking to preserve, first, their lives *tout
court* (Hobbes), and then their individual liberties and estates (property) (Locke,
Rousseau). This thought formed the basis for modern liberal understandings of
political authority – governments are instituted by men to advance their liberty
and protect their rights – rather than to pursue truth or justice, understood
according to substantive and transcendent, rather than liberal, ends and, hence,
formed the basis for modern liberal democracies like the United States.

Strauss was not a reactionary – at least not in any clear sense. Unlike Weaver, he
did not call for a thoroughgoing return to an antecedent model. To the
consternation of the many who have tried to get a bead ever since on what he was
really after, Strauss framed the core questions and challenges and charismatically
and brilliantly argued that the answers we arrived at to those questions were of
immense importance, and likely would determine whether civilization itself would
live or die ... and then left it at that. Ever since, his students – and his enemies – have
fought vigorously over whether Strauss was a friend or foe of liberal democracy, and
whether he had really demurred on the critical issues or had merely hidden the
answers he had arrived at esoterically in his own work, as he argued his politically
dangerous philosopher progenitors had done in theirs.[85]

One thing Strauss was clear about in *Natural Right and History* was his
conviction that given their abandonment of the notion of transcendent truths
and their turn toward positivism, historicism, and relativism, the moderns and
liberal democrats seemed to him dangerously ill-equipped to arrive at
a compelling defense of their way of life when confronted by challenges from
those who, building upon the philosophical premises of Nietzsche and
Heidegger, believed only in the will to power. Historicists and relativists all,
modern liberals could offer no reason why their way of life was preferable to
that of, say, the Nazis and the communists, or why civilization would be any
worse off under Nazi or communist rule, since, after all, their guiding rule was
to each (in his own time, and according to his own preferences) his own. Strauss
believed that if, indeed, it *was* superior, the West needed to mount a coherent
defense of its own superiority. In this, he argued, Western civilization had

---

[85] See Leo Strauss, *Persecution and the Art of Writing* (New York: The Free Press, 1952);
Arthur Melzer, *Philosophy Between the Lines: The Lost Art of Esoteric Writing* (Chicago:
University of Chicago Press, 2014).

heretofore failed miserably. And in this regard, new directions in both Western philosophy and political science did not augur well.

For Strauss, the paths of modern philosophy and political science were, in many respects, the story not of progress but decline. In *Natural Right and History*, and in Strauss's many other writings, the question raised by the modern predicament – what is to be done? – is a portal into a profusion of arcane debates, initiated by Strauss and undertaken by a legion of his students and fellow travelers, as it happened, many of whom ended up as conservatives, Republicans, and conservative movement thought leaders; indeed, many Straussians, particularly of the "East Coast" variety, devoted themselves solely to academic political philosophy. These debates concerning "what is to be done" were presented in Straussian idioms. They raised questions concerning "the quarrel between the Ancients and the Moderns." To complicate things further, it was Strauss's view that some of the ancient rootedness in transcendent truth had been carried forward even into (liberal) modernity via revealed religion. This meant that moderns were enmeshed in the "theological-political predicament" – they were confronting the consequences not only of the abandonment of (ancient, classical) philosophy but also of the effects of early modern attempts to separate theology from politics (in this regard, Strauss and many later Straussians evinced an abiding interest in medieval Jewish, Islamic, and Christian religious thinkers who, early on, had grappled in rich ways with the relationship, as Strauss framed it, between "Reason [philosophy] and Revelation." It was via this intellectual route that many later conservative Straussians, although they might themselves actually (and, perhaps secretly, on the model of pagan Greek philosophers like Socrates) be unbelievers, came to place a surpassing value on the political role of religious faith in modern liberal democracies: such faith, especially among the masses, who needed it, brought the concern for and commitment to the transcendent, to right and wrong, true and false, as against historicism and relativism, into the modern world.

THE THOMIST MOMENT

For many Catholics, the self-evident answer to the problems of modernity and modern thought was the Church of Rome. Rome was in its ascendancy in the mid-century United States not just in popular culture but also in some of philosophy's most recondite precincts, which began to apply themselves to contemporary American political and legal problems.[86] There were both

---

[86] Papal Encyclicals, particularly in the late nineteenth century, were aimed directly at political issues such as the problems of capitalism, liberalism, democracy, disestablishment, concern for the poor, labor unions, and other public issues. In the early twentieth century, Father John A. Ryan advocated for progressive public policies using neo-scholastic argument – argument that is notably omitted in the excerpt from Ryan's thought provided, e.g., in Kramnick and Lowi's *American Political Thought: A Norton Anthology*.

progressive and conservative versions of neo-scholasticism – Thomism – in this period, with Charles Malick and Jacques Maritain on the Left (though, late in life, Maritain denounced Vatican II), and Clarence Manion and Fulton J. Sheen on the Right. The mid-century Thomists had set themselves to no less a task than the ultimate displacement of modern understandings of and within Western civilization by a wholesale return to the West's once dominant medieval framework. The neo-Thomists were convinced that Western civilization's turn to modernity had been a mistake. The time was ripe for a restoration of medieval scholasticism.

Earlier resistance to progressive legal thought such as sociological jurisprudence, legal realism, and in, due course, living constitutionalism emphasized the foundation of individual liberty in property rights guarantees, formal limitations on government powers, and concerns for the rule of law in a modern liberal legal/political order. The Catholic critique of progressive legalism, however, was different. Its unique standpoint found converts among prominent non-Catholics, including the influential Yale Law School dean Robert Maynard Hutchins.

Hutchins's intellectual trajectory is yet another instance of the postwar era's remarkable intellectual odysseys. While Hutchins had championed Legal Realism as a wunderkind law school dean at Yale, upon moving to the University of Chicago in 1930 to assume its presidency, he began to question the ability of empirical social science to solve important social problems – which directly challenged the academic approach that had been pioneered by the university's scholars, and at the time represented one of its signature contributions to American life. Hutchins's critique soon led him all the way to a foundationalism anchored in both Great Books (particularly the Great Books of Western civilization) and an Aristotelean/Thomist epistemology. University denizens ruefully reported that Hutchins and his new compatriot, the philosopher Mortimer Adler, talked incessantly about Saint Thomas Aquinas – to the point that many began to accuse Hutchins and Adler of plotting to convert the University of Chicago's students to Roman Catholicism. At the least, it was said, Hutchins was pushing for the restoration of the medieval university, giving rise to the quip that the University of Chicago was a former Baptist school where Jewish professors were teaching Catholic theology to atheists.[87]

Others variously elaborated the same basic framework. The University of Notre Dame philosopher Gerhart Niemeyer, an Eric Voegelin devotee and an increasingly orthodox Episcopalian (late in life, he was a Catholic convert), traced communism and Nazism to modernism, holding "ideology" to be one of modernism's most pernicious spawns. Niemeyer stumped for Christianity as the

---

[87] Beam, *Great Idea*, 59; See Harry Ashmore, *Unseasonable Truths: The Life of Robert Maynard Hutchins* (Boston: Little Brown, 1989). This clearly set the stage for the university, in time, becoming a Straussian redoubt.

only reliable antidote to modernism and its virulent ideologies. The active ingredient of Christianity as antidote was its commitment to truth, and its status as a carrier of our truth-anchored humanistic heritage.[88]

THE CATHOLIC RIGHT AND THE AMERICAN CONSENSUS: FROM A TROUBLED RELATION TO "ARTICLES OF PEACE" WITH LIBERAL AMERICA

> I see no way to sum up the offense of modern man except to say that he is impious.
>
> Richard Weaver[89]

Liberalism begins with the premise that legitimate political authority originates in the sovereign self. As noted earlier, and as Leo Strauss expounded upon at length, this modern view marked a major departure from ancient political thought, which rooted claims to governing authority in some transcendent conception of the Truth and the Good. In premodern political theory, the "saving absolute"[90] was sought in the gods, the divine, the teachings of the Church or of elders and the wise, or in the commands of divinely sanctioned monarchs.

For most of its history, the Roman Catholic Church rejected the premise that authority – including political authority – originated in the sovereign self. Over the course of modern history, this positioned the Roman Catholic Church as liberal modernity's most intransigent opponent. When confronted with an emerging modern world, the Catholic Church vehemently opposed not only

---

[88] Niemeyer taught at Notre Dame between 1955 and 1973: his son, incidentally, was educated at the Straussian strongholds Kenyon College and the University of Notre Dame Law School and is currently a federal judge, appointed to the bench by Ronald Reagan and the Fourth Circuit of Appeals by George H. W. Bush. Other non-Catholic political thinkers like Willmoore Kendall, an admirer of Leo Strauss, if not a Straussian, and Frederick Wilhelmsen, who taught at a Spanish University founded by Opus Dei (the University of Navarra in Pampalona), and ultimately landed at the far Right-Wing Roman Catholic University of Dallas. The University of Dallas is now the home to, among other denizens of the Catholic Right, the constitutional scholar Christopher Wolfe, who teaches in UD's Politics Department. Wolfe is the founder of the American Public Philosophy Institute (http://appii.org/), whose web banner is the US Constitution, and which holds, "The conviction upon which this institute is based is that twenty-first century America faces a profound moral crisis which manifests itself in a variety of deep social fissures and public policy problems." It declares its mission to "Promote a natural law public philosophy rooted in the principles of the American Founding – one that pursues freedom and prosperity grounded on the moral integrity of our social and political institutions." Luis Tellez, an Opus Dei cleric, serves on the institute's small (seven person) board of directors (right-wing Catholic Murrayist, Thomist constitutional law scholars Robert P. George and Gerald V. Bradley serve on its advisory council).

[89] Weaver, *Ideas Have Consequences*, 170. This quotation is published as an epigraph by permission of the University of Chicago Press.

[90] Letter, A. R. Ammons to Harold Bloom (1971), quoted in Helen Vendler, "American Expansion: The Innovation of A.R. Ammons," *Harper's Magazine* (August 2017), 70.

market capitalism but also democracy, religious liberty, church-state separation, the freedom of speech, and rights to bodily autonomy – the full panoply of "civil liberties." For orthodox Catholics, all worldly authority, including, ultimately, political authority, resided in the Church, which alone had effectively synthesized divine revelation and human reason in ways that were faithful to the sovereign God.

Conventional wisdom holds that it was only anti-Catholic bigots who doubted the compatibility of Roman Catholicism and Americanism. But in the postwar United States, a significant number of far right-wing Catholics – albeit in diminishing numbers as the years went on – entertained the very same doubts. A key dynamic of the trajectory of the Catholic Right involves a mass migration away from the position that Catholicism was incompatible with (liberal) Americanism toward a new position that, as fads, fashions, and threats rocked the world at mid-century, the Roman Catholic faith, rightly understood, stood firmly at its core.

Indeed, the relationship between the Church's teachings and America was perhaps *the* central question facing Catholic political and constitutional thinkers in the mid-twentieth century United States. Many on the Catholic Right, including those associated with the Catholic Right organ *Triumph*, had long since concluded that a hopelessly liberal America and an unwaveringly anti-liberal Roman Catholicism were foundationally inconsistent. When choices had to be made, Catholics had the high duty to choose the Church. The conservative anti-modernist Fulton J. Sheen, however, who, like those on far Catholic Right, fulminated against decline and yearned for a recovery of medieval Christendom's unities and certainties, took a somewhat chastened tack: instead of repudiating America, Sheen called on the United States to adopt and champion medieval Catholic understandings – on the grounds not that they were Catholic but that they were true. Both the ultramontane Right and Sheen's visions, however, remained transparently vexed and perplexed by the American problem.

Operating on a parallel track to Strauss and the Straussians, these anti-modernist – and, as such, at least implicitly anti-American – visions were challenged by a rising group of Catholic conservatives who began to newly adopt an affirming, patriotic position on the United States. This ascendant group of Catholics began to argue that America, at least as the Founders (and Abraham Lincoln) had understood it, was on all fours with the Roman Catholic faith and its doctrines and teachings and, put otherwise, that good Catholics could be good Americans. This emergent line was featured in *National Review*, where its faithful Catholic founder and editor William F. Buckley Jr. directly challenged the ultramontane counter-vision being propounded over at his brother-in-law Brent Bozell's magazine *Triumph*. "There are those [such as those writing for *Triumph*] who will not settle for anything less than a mutinous relationship between themselves and their society," Buckley's *National Review* observed, acknowledging that "[t]here are societies in which such a relationship is the only bearable relationship: such societies as Hitler's and the Communists." "We judge that reading of the proper posture of American dissidence to be incorrect," *National Review* answered, deeming it, moreover, for good measure, "to be anti-conservative": "We have got, in America, what we have got. It is not what we would have, but neither is it as bad as what we might have. To dismiss even contemporary America as one vast plot against the survival of our eternal souls is Manichean and boring."[91]

On this, *National Review* took a firm position. But as a magazine, it was not *National Review*'s place to elaborate the thesis. At about the same time, the heavy lifting of explaining precisely why good Catholics could be good Americans was undertaken by the (quasi) modernizing priest John Courtney Murray, SJ, in his landmark book *We Hold These Truths: Catholic Reflections on the American Proposition* (1960). Murray insisted in that book – whose argument I outlined Chapter 2 on "The Alternative Tradition of Conservative Constitutional Theory" (and briefly reprise here)[92] – that, as a pragmatic matter, at least, American Catholics should embrace the liberal pluralism of the contemporary United States on the grounds that, if rightly read as rooted in the natural law tradition of the opening pronouncements of the Declaration of Independence, that liberal pluralism was consistent with Catholic teaching.[93]

In many ways, as noted earlier, the Jesuit Murray was – and was considered in his time to be – an outspoken liberal (in the Nancy Pelosi, Joe Biden sense): he challenged not only the Church hierarchy but also the core convictions of the nation's most conservative lay Catholics. As the first major Catholic theologian to argue in a sustained way for the virtues of religious liberty, pluralism, the "distinction" between church and state, and the secular state,[94] Murray laid the basis for and played a major role in crafting the Church's Vatican II reforms that, in line with the views he had been advancing, modernized the Church's teachings.[95] At the very moment when the United States was electing its first Catholic president, Father Murray demonstrated through systematic philosophic argument starting with the principles articulated in the opening

---

[91] *National Review* editors, in L. Brent Bozell Jr., "Letters from Yourselves," *Triumph* 4:6 (June 1969): 17–19, 40, 40.

[92] In discussing Murray in what follows, I borrow again, as revised, from Ken I. Kersch, "Beyond Originalism: Conservative Declarationism and Constitutional Redemption," *Maryland Law Review* 71 (2011): 229–282.

[93] Murray, *We Hold These Truths*. See Wilfred McClay, "The Catholic Moment in American Social Thought," in R. Scott Appleby and Kathleen Sprows Cummings, editors, *Catholics in the American Century: Casting Narratives of US History* (Ithaca, NY: Cornell University Press, 2012), 149–151.

[94] Murray, *We Hold These Truths*, 59–60. All of which he celebrated through his extended reading of, and support for, the First Amendment.

[95] Murray was the primary drafter of Vatican II's Declaration of Religious Freedom. *See* Robert John Araujo, SJ, "Forming the Well-Formed Conscience," *Journal of Catholic Legal Studies*, 47 (2008) 219, 228.

lines of the Declaration of Independence that good Catholics could be good Americans. In this sense, Murray was a modernizer.[96]

That said, it is also easy to see why Murray has also, especially recently, become a touchstone for many contemporary conservatives, particularly those interested in the legacy of the American Founding and the American constitutional tradition.[97] The contemporary conservative intellectual historian Wilfred McClay has defiantly, and rightly, argued,

> It would require a monumental misreading of Murray to attribute to him anything like a full-scale capitulation to contemporary American political and cultural life ... Murray's Catholicism came first. Rather than trim Catholicism's sails to fit American democratic sensibilities, he argued for the possibility that one could affirm American democratic institutions on a basis entirely faithful to the Catholic distinctives – one that might constitute a deeper and more satisfactory basis for that affirmation and aim not to destroy the founders' work but to fulfill it by addressing its inadequacies.[98]

Peter Lawler, the contemporary Catholic conservative political theorist, set out the case in more detail, noting that it was Murray's conviction that "*only* the Catholic community," with its richer and deeper tradition and carefully cultivated systematic philosophy and theology, "could illuminate what was true and good about what our founders accomplished."[99] Who better than a Catholic theologian trained in natural law to explain to Americans the true

---

[96] Murray noted that people asked repeatedly whether Catholicism was compatible with American democracy. He answered, "The question is invalid as well as impertinent; for the manner of its position inverts the order of values. It must, of course, be turned round to read, whether American democracy is compatible with Catholicism." Murray offered the book as "the reflections of a Catholic who, in seeking his answer to the civil question, knows that the principles of Catholic faith and morality stand superior to, and in control of, the whole order of civil life." Murray, *We Hold These Truths*, ix–x. Murray continued: "The Catholic may not, as others do, merge his religious and his patriotic faith, or submerge one in the other. The simplest solution is not for him. He must reckon with his own tradition of thought, which is wider and deeper than any that America has elaborated. He must also reckon with his own history, which is longer than the brief centuries that America has lived. At the same time, he must recognize that a new problem has been put to the universal Church by the American doctrine and project in the matter of pluralism, as stated in the First Amendment. The conceptual equipment for dealing with the problem is by no means lacking to the Catholic intelligence." Murray, *We Hold These Truths*, xi. These convictions made Catholics (to borrow Albert Murray's label for African Americans) the "omni-Americans" – the group whose worldview most consistently exemplified the soul of the nation. See generally Albert Murray, *The Omni-Americans: Some Alternatives to the Folklore of White Supremacy* (New York: Outerbridge & Dienstfrey, 1970).

[97] See, e.g., Peter Augustine Lawler, "John Courtney Murray as Catholic, American Conservative," in Ethan Fishman & Kenneth L Deutsch editors. *The Dilemmas of American Conservatism* (Lexington: University Press of Kentucky, 2010); Wilfred McClay, "The Catholic Moment in American Social Thought," in Appleby and Cummings, editors, *Catholics in the American Century*.

[98] McClay, "Catholic Moment," 149–150.

[99] Peter A. Lawler, "Critical Introduction" to John Courtney Murray, *We Hold These Truths* (Lanham, MD: Rowman and Littlefield, 2005) [1960] [emphasis added].

meaning of the Declaration of Independence, as elaborated by its most profound and fervent proponent, Abraham Lincoln, "our most ambitious and philosophic president?"[100] "If veneration for the true accomplishment of our political Fathers is the standard of citizenship," Lawler argued, "those within the Catholic natural-law community of thought are the least alienated of Americans today."[101] "*Only* a Thomistic or natural-law understanding," Lawler said Murray had demonstrated, "can make sense of our framers' accomplishment."[102]

What's more, Peter Lawler argued for good measure, far from being divisive, the Thomist philosophical method provided a common ground for discussions between Evangelical Protestants, with their emphasis on revelation, and secular humanists, who prize reason. Since its animating purpose is to synthesize reason and revelation (or, as Straussians put it, "Athens and Jerusalem"), Thomism provided the best available framework for appreciating, understanding, and explicating the implications of the American Founding and the US Constitution – or, indeed, of the meaning and creed of the American nation itself.[103]

Murray's case was as follows. As befits a Thomist exegesis by a Jesuit (and as is indicated in his book's title), *We Hold These Truths* begins with a theorem or proposition – the Declaration of Independence's statement that "all men are created equal" (also, subsequently, "immortally asserted by Abraham Lincoln").[104] Murray pronounced this theorem or proposition to be, indisputably, the rock upon which the American nation was built. He then took up the question of its nature and implications.[105]

The next natural question for Murray – especially in a vibrant democracy, where all power tends to be claimed by the *demos* – was "Do we hold these truths because they are true, or are these truths true because we hold them?" Murray answered the former: the truths are held because they are true, not simply because, in a democratic, majoritarian, consensus spirit, most people happen to believe them. That the American proposition is true "is a truth that lies beyond politics; it imparts to politics a fundamental human meaning. I mean the sovereignty of God over nations as well as over individual men."[106]

---

[100] Lawler, "Critical Introduction," 3.   [101] Lawler, "Critical Introduction," 4.

[102] Lawler, "Critical Introduction," 13 (emphasis added). The Athens (reason) and Jerusalem (revelation) trope is also a major axis for Straussian political thought.

[103] Lawler, "Critical Introduction," 22. Murray states flatly, "Religious pluralism is against the will of God. But it is the human condition; it is written into the script of history. It will not somehow marvelously cease to trouble the City." It is also "the native condition of American society." Murray, *We Hold These Truths*, 23, 27. We must, he argues, deal with it. In this regard, Murray celebrated the First Amendment as providing serviceable "articles of peace." Lawler, "Critical Introduction," 56.

[104] Murray, *We Hold These Truths*, vii, 109.   [105] Murray, *We Hold These Truths*, viii–ix.

[106] Murray, *We Hold These Truths*, 98, 106–107, 28. It is a commitment to this principle, Murray continued, "that radically distinguishes the conservative Christian tradition of America from the Jacobin laicist tradition of Continental Europe," the latter of which worships the presumed autonomy of man, and his all-powerful individual reason.

As a nation firmly anchored in a commitment to God's sovereignty, it followed naturally for Murray that the nation "was conceived [by its Founders] in the tradition of natural law." This was the case whatever the religion (or lack of religion) of those Founders: as the Jesuit theologian explained, they built better than they knew. This made Thomas Aquinas "the first Whig," and natural law "the first structural rib of American constitutionalism." The American tradition of free government pivoted on the "profound conviction that only a virtuous people can be free." And, of course, we know that people are virtuous only when they are "inwardly governed by the recognized imperatives of the universal moral law."[107]

This had implications for the way that rights were to be understood within the American constitutional tradition. It is a simple fact, Murray averred, that "[t]he American Bill of Rights ... [is] the product of Christian history": "The 'man' whose rights are guaranteed in the face of law and government is, whether he knows it or not, the Christian man, who had learned to know his own personal dignity in the school of Christian faith."[108] As such, the content of those rights can only be defined and understood in light of the nature of the supreme Good, as set out in universal natural law. This places natural law philosophy at the center of the inquiry into the nature and proper application of the Bill of Rights.

While there is nothing inherently Catholic about natural law, Murray explained that the natural law tradition and, hence, the American constitutional tradition, found its "intellectual home within the Catholic Church." "Catholic participation in the American consensus," Murray proudly observed, "has been full and free, unreserved and unembarrassed, because the contents of that consensus – the ethical and political principles drawn from the tradition of natural law – approve themselves to the Catholic intelligence and conscience." While mainline Protestantism may have moved away from the old English and American tradition in this regard, its foundations are "native" to Catholics. On the fundamentals, the "Fathers of the Church and the Fathers of the American Republic" were of one mind.[109]

Catholics, Murray argued, had a special role to play in the modern context as guardians of the foundations of the American Republic. After all, no society without a substantive core can long survive. In the modern context of pluralism and democracy, the truths set out in the Declaration of Independence, as re-affirmed by Lincoln, articulated that core. Catholic natural law philosophy thus helps us understand and appreciate the nature of that core and its indispensability in the deepest possible way.[110]

Murray's understandings – which harmonize extensively with Straussianism – have evinced a special attraction for the contemporary Catholic

---

[107] Murray, *We Hold These Truths*, 31, 32, 36.   [108] Murray, *We Hold These Truths*, 39.
[109] Murray, *We Hold These Truths*, 41–43.
[110] Murray, *We Hold These Truths*, 41–43, 74–75.

Right.[111] These conservatives emphasize that other nations, most notably Hitler's Germany and Marxist totalitarian states like the Soviet Union, lacked a natural law grounding, premised on God's sovereignty, with results that led to some of the worst catastrophes in human history. The contemporary Murrayist Catholic Right and its allied Straussians suspect that secular progressives, in their denial of the natural law foundations of the American nation and its constitutional traditions, have more in common with America's greatest twentieth-century enemies than with its eighteenth-century Founders, whose principles were set out in the Declaration of Independence's opening lines, or its Constitution, as redeemed by Lincoln.[112]

That said, as the conservative movement has gained in strength and power in recent years, some significant voices on the Catholic Right have started to push back against the pragmatic accommodations John Courtney Murray had made with liberal, democratic pluralism in the early 1960s at the expense of traditional Catholic teaching. As such, they are, in significant ways, walking the contemporary Right back in the direction of *Triumph* and Sheen – albeit while retaining Murray's celebration of the Constitution, the Declaration of Independence, and the American national project. Since Murray's work was written to move America as close as possible to adopting a Catholic framework within its particular time and historical context, there is no reason to believe that, in more politically congenial times, right-wing Catholics will not bring American political and constitutional thinking in closer alignment with the timeless teachings of the Church.[113]

ROBERT BOLT'S A MAN FOR ALL SEASONS: OBEDIENCE AS DISSENT

One sign of the resonance of the Murrayist sensibility at mid-century was the breakout popularity of Robert Bolt's play *A Man for All Seasons* (play, 1960; film 1966) – a parable of liberation through obedience (the film version of Bolt's play, directed by Fred Zinnemann, was a sensation, winning six Academy

---

[111] See generally Welcome from Director Robert P. George, James Madison Program in American Ideals and Institutions (http://web.princeton.edu/sites/jmadison/welcome.html) (discussing the founding and mission of the program; The Witherspoon Institute (Princeton, New Jersey) (www.winst.org/people/staff.php). Both the Murrayist, Thomist Robert P. George's James Madison Program in American Ideals and Institutions (Princeton University) and the subsequently established Witherspoon Institute's inaugural scholarly conferences were devoted to the Declaration of Independence.

[112] See *Media Matters for America*, quoting Bill O'Reilly, *The Radio Factor* (Fox News Radio Nov. 28, 2005) (http://mediamatters.org/mmtv/200511300007) (comparing the modern American secular progressive movement to totalitarian regimes of the twentieth century and claiming that "[i]n every secular progressive country, they've wiped out religion … Joseph Stalin, Adolf Hitler, Mao Zedong, Fidel Castro, all of them. That's the first step. Get the religion out of there, so that we can impose our big-government, progressive agenda").

[113] See, e.g., Gerald V. Bradley, "*We Hold These Truths* and the Problem of Public Morality," *Catholic Social Science Review* 16 (2011): 123–132.

Awards, including the Oscars for Best Actor and Best Picture). Bolt's theme was the conflicting claims of natural and positive law. While hardly a novel theme in political and legal theory (it was the fulcrum, for instance, of Sophocles's *Antigone* (circa 442 B.C.), Thoreau's "On Civil Disobedience" (1849), and Martin Luther King Jr.'s "Letter from a Birmingham City Jail" (1963)), in Bolt's play, the dilemma was dramatized in one of the most famous incidents of Western (Catholic) history. *A Man for All Seasons* told the story of St. Thomas More's resistance to Henry VIII in the name of natural law and the Church in a way that appealed both to a general American audience in the age of the Rights Revolution but also to both right-wing Catholic traditionalists and left-wing Catholic "social justice" proponents (John Courtney Murray had threaded this same needle in *We Hold These Truths*).

The play was a paean to fidelity as dissent – about the heroism of summoning the courage to obey:[114] it defined freedom (as had Russell Kirk) as "submission to the will of God." Motivated by his Catholic faith and his ultimate obedience to Rome, More, England's lord chancellor, had refused to take an oath of loyalty to King Henry VIII in the Tudor monarch's battle with the pope seeking leave to divorce Catherine of Aragon so he could marry Anne Boleyn and, Henry expected, secure a male heir to the throne (the denouement led to the Church of England's dramatic split from the Church of Rome, and to More's beheading and subsequent canonization).

While, as noted, the theme of dissent in fidelity to conscience was hardly unique to Roman Catholicism, Bolt's play presented the conflict in a distinctively Catholic voice. The Catholic conception of conscience placed a heavy emphasis not on the unmediated inner light of the autonomous individual (formed by the individual *solo scripture*) but rather of a conscience properly "formed" by and under the tutelage and authority of the Church. To be sure, actual Catholics, including members of the clergy, arrived at different theological understandings of the commands of conscience as

[114] Robert Bolt, *A Man for All Seasons* (New York: Vintage Books, 1960). *A Man for All Seasons*, Columbia Pictures, 1966 (Fred Zinneman, director). Influential contemporary conservative Catholics have cast both Martin Luther King Jr. and Pope John Paul II in the position of St. Thomas More in Bolt's play and film of the mid-1960s – as great dissenters, whose faith was in the natural law of the Church of Rome (King is, of course, a stretch in this regard, but conservative "Declarationists" emphasize the Baptist King's citations of St. Thomas Aquinas and St. Augustine in his *Letter from a Birmingham City Jail* (1963)). Martin Luther King Jr., "Letter from a Birmingham City Jail," in Kramnick and Lowi, editors, *American Political Thought*; George Weigel, *Witness to Hope: The Biography of John Paul II* (New York: Cliff Street Books, 1999); George Weigel, *The End and the Beginning: Pope John Paul II – The Victory of Freedom, the Last Years, the Legacy* (New York: Doubleday, 2010). See Ken I. Kersch, "Beyond Originalism: Conservative Declarationism and Constitutional Redemption," *Maryland Law Review*, 71 (2011–2012): 229–282. Interestingly, Robert Bolt himself was an existentialist and atheist, and an admirer of Berthold Brecht and Albert Camus. Still, the book was plainly read by the devout at mid-century as a sort of existentialism for Catholics, a call to the courage of faith.

applied to concrete circumstances (in the Catholic tradition, careful consideration of the nuances of circumstance in applying the natural law constitute a major part of natural law thinking).[115] But, in the Church of Rome, meaning was determined more hierarchically, and dissent was more problematic. Conservative or orthodox Catholics, in particular, heavily emphasized obedience to the ecclesiastical hierarchy, truculently spurning "modern" interpretations of the natural law that suggested a belief in individual autonomy in the discernment of unchanging, objective truth. *A Man for All Seasons* can be easily read as lauding the courage it takes for the individual to give himself wholly to the organization, to abide by the commands of its hierarchy, to subsume himself within the group, to live as an exemplar of fidelity and faithfulness and, in so doing, to demonstrate both humility and courage. These resonant themes could only be a tonic to the many Catholics who, at the time, were aspiring to full acceptance as Americans in the face of the scorn of sophisticates like Paul Blanshard, John Dewey, and others, on the grounds of their purportedly sheep-like adherence to their faith – for their inability to think for themselves.[116] *A Man for All Seasons* took their obedience and Americanized it by recasting it as a form of dissent – a reconciliation of fidelity and dissent, moreover, that the play celebrated as a pillar of Western civilization.[117]

---

[115] The same was true of the Straussian applications of the classical virtue of prudence.

[116] See Kersch, *Constructing Civil Liberties*, 292–325.

[117] On the play's political resonance in its time, see Jonathan Imber, "A Man After Sixty Seasons," *The American Interest* (December 19, 2013). Bolt's *A Man for All Seasons* resonated with some prominent American jurists too, including Felix Frankfurter and, most pertinently, Robert Bork, under the sway of his relentlessly orthodox Catholic wife Mary Ellen, an ex-nun. Indeed, the man who, in conjunction with Mary Ellen, was most responsible for Bork's conversion to the Church of Rome (2003) – in the scarred aftermath of his failed Supreme Court appointment – the Opus Dei prelate Father C. John McCloskey III, upon Bork's death, remarked upon the affinity, venturing that "Bob, in his own way, was a man for all seasons." See Sophia Mason, "Judge Robert Bork, Conservative Icon and Catholic Convert, R.I.P," *National Catholic Register* (December 20, 2012); Edwin M. Yoder Jr., "'A Great American Life,'" *Washington Post* (November 16, 1982). Bork reflected on Bolt's play in a noted article in *First Things*, where he largely tracked the conservative reading of the play set out earlier. Robert H. Bork, "Thomas More for Our Season," *First Things* (June 1999). Along the way, in part reacting against what he took to be his own time's "rapid social and cultural unraveling," a time "when law [has] falter[ed], as it must when morality is no longer widely shared, [and thus] society and culture teeter on the brink of chaos," Bork admired More's holding of "the utmost respect for authority, hierarchy, and social discipline," opposition to the idea of "individual conscience," and More's "devotion to papal supremacy." Bork emphasized that "More's behavior may be seen as submission to external authority, a conscious and difficult *denial* of self" (emphasis in original), underlining "This was not disobedience but obedience." Bork ended by arguing that More's views "provide the sharpest contrast" to the "moral relativism" that had underwritten "modern constitutional adjudication" under the Rights Revolution, and its lawless judicial activism. See also Robert H. Bork, *The Tempting of America: The Political Seduction of the Law* (New York: Free Press, 1990), 354. When Clarence Thomas '71 returned to his (Jesuit, Catholic) *alma mater*, The College of the Holy Cross, to deliver the annual

THOMIST AND STRAUSSIAN SYNERGIES

As noted earlier, the theological understandings of the Murrayist Roman Catholic vision harmonized with the political-philosophical understandings of the Straussian school that was emerging in postwar America at about the same time. Both, after all, were essentially premodern, focused on the transcendent, grappling with the problem of liberal modernity, and seeking an acceptable reconciliation – if, indeed, one was possible – by adequately integrating, theologically or philosophically, the old with the new.

The Straussian Harry V. Jaffa's efforts were especially prominent in this regard: Jaffa's reading of the Declaration of Independence posits – as does Thomist Roman Catholic theology, which itself has origins in Aristotle – a unified and ultimate supreme Good. Jaffa argued that within the framework of the Declaration, the nature of particular rights, as with all other powers and limits on the powers of government, were comprehensible only as ordered in relation to this *summum bonum*. This frame of understanding provided a common ground for conservative Catholics and Straussians to think and reason together.[118]

Hanify-Howland Lecture in the spring of 2002, the college announced that "In addition to his lecture, Thomas will attend two seminars, during which students will discuss readings from *A Man for All Seasons* by Robert Bolt and *The Tempting of America* by Robert Bork." *Holy Cross Magazine* 36(1) (Winter 2002). Interestingly, the director of the film version of *A Man for All Seasons*, Fred Zinneman, had also directed the iconic Cold War parable *High Noon* (1952) (with Gary Cooper in the lead hero's role), which cast American patriotism in a similar light. At this formative moment of Catholic Americanization, these two films might be usefully considered together.

[118] Jaffa's first book, which immediately preceded *Crisis of the House Divided*, was a study of Thomas. Harry V. Jaffa, *Thomas and Aristotelianism: A Study of the Commentary by Thomas Aquinas on the Nicomachean Ethics* (Chicago: University of Chicago Press, 1952). Although seemingly recondite and out of view of the general public, bringing Evangelical Protestants (and favorably inclined others) into this intellectual circle oriented around the *summum bonum* and the requirements of teleology was a major agenda of conservatives working to forge and unite the modern Religious Right. On the level of basic rhetoric, of course, the foundations were already there in any of the legion statements emphasizing American providentialism, exceptionalism, or Christian roots. The non-Catholic Chief Judge John J. Parker of the US Court of Appeals for the Fourth Circuit – who lost a confirmation vote for an appointment to the Supreme Court by a single vote – to take one of thousands of examples, once offhandedly stated that "We believe that a natural law underlies the activities of human society, that it is based upon reason, that it is declared by the legislature and the courts and that when so declared it is binding upon everyone, the President, the Congress, the courts, as well as the general citizenry." John J. Parker, "Our Great Responsibility: We Must Lead the World to Freedom and Justice," *American Bar Association Journal* 44 (January 1958): 17–21, 17. For a political and legal profile of Parker, see Peter G. Fish, "A 'Freshman' Takes Charge: Judge John J. Parker of the United States Court of Appeals, 1925–1930," *Journal of Southern History* (2003): 59–113. If the debate was about means of apprehending the natural law and its nature, Catholics and Protestants disagreed vehemently – and venomously. But if the issue was about God as source of law versus a positivism holding man to be its source instead, or of Christian or, in time, of religious foundations more generally versus secularism, Protestants and Catholics (and later conservative Jews) could unite around a commitment to natural law.

Jaffa made the connection himself, explicitly. Drawing a parallel between the American Founders and seminal Catholic thinkers, Jaffa noted early on in *Crisis of the House Divided* that "whatever their differences," Thomas Aquinas and Thomas Jefferson

shared a belief concerning the relation of political philosophy to political authority that neither shared with the last ten presidents of the American Political Science Association ... [B]oth believed it was the task of political philosophy to articulate the principles of political right, and therefore to teach the teachers of legislators, of citizens, and of statesmen the principles in virtue of which political power becomes political authority.[119]

Unlike modern social scientists, contemporary relativists, and other positivist progressive/liberals, both Aquinas and Jefferson were committed to the proposition that there are objective standards of right and wrong. Following Aquinas in this regard, Jefferson had held firm, Jaffa said, to the conviction that democratic politics, properly understood, involved at its core the advancement of a unified and ultimate Good: "the laws of nature mentioned in the Declaration." Everything followed from that, and all must be considered in this light.[120]

On this, one of Jaffa's most vehement critics, the southern traditionalist M. E. Bradford, objected that Jaffa was attempting to understand America through the lenses of systematic philosophy – treating the country as standing for a philosophical "proposition" from which all else followed logically, philosophically, and theologically. Bradford pointed out that this was, to say the least, a passing strange way to think about a concrete, rooted country, with its own history, rules, folkways, and traditions. It was also, he argued emphatically, profoundly pernicious – a dangerous way of thinking about the United States, and American politics.

RIGHT RIGHTS ONLY: THE CASE OF THE MID-CENTURY ROMAN CATHOLIC CENSORSHIP AND WAR ON "DISORDERED SEXUALITY"

For the properly formed orthodox Catholic, the world is not a pluralistic "aggregate or collection of higher and lower things and principles," but "an absolutely unitary fact." The nature of this unity is accessible metaphysically through the teachings of the faith – the theology of the Church. Practices that do not fit within this metaphysical unity are held "objectively disordered." This framework set the backdrop of the legions of mid-century Catholics who rallied to the war on "dirt" or "filth" – the dissemination of crude sexual materials.

---

[119] Jaffa, *Crisis of the House Divided*, 9. The conservative Catholic Peter Lawler described the American Founding as a case of "accidental Thomism." Peter Lawler, "What Was Said by ME at Georgetown," *First Things* (February 7, 2011) (www.firstthings.com/blogs/postmoderncon-servative/2011/02/07/what-was-said-by-me-at-georgetown).

[120] Jaffa, *Crisis of the House Divided*, 11.

These "might be, and may always have been," but they nevertheless constituted "an independent portion that had no rational or absolute right to live with the rest, and which we might conceivably hope to see got rid of at last."[121]

Catholic spirituality and ritual, in marked contrast to Protestant spirituality and ritual, place a particular emphasis on the corporeal – blood, excrement, and such – most apparently in the image of the crucifix, to which Protestants, in their abstracting, spare approach to purity, were appalled and which they rejected. If the Protestant obsession with purity – which, of course, was just as pronounced – was more about distance and denial of disgust, the Catholic apprehension led to the immediate, visceral engagement with it: like Mary McCarthy's grandmother they were determined to wade into the muck to fight it tooth and claw. The battle with the (repulsive, disgusting) Devil was real; it was here, and now – and on.[122]

Right-wing Catholics were among the modern conservative movement's most uncompromising and relentless moralists. As William James said of the ilk, "Official moralists advise us never to relax our strenuousness. 'Be vigilant, day and night,' they adjure us; 'hold your passive tendencies in check; shrink from no effort; keep your will like a bow always bent.'" Far from solving the problem, though, James observed that this orientation could lead to increasing frustration-unto-rage. For the official moralists will soon "find that all this conscious effort leads to nothing but failure and vexation in their hands, and only makes them twofold more the children of hell they were before.

---

[121] James, *Varieties of Religious Experience*, 149.

[122] "Evil ... is pure abomination to the Lord, an alien unreality, a waste element, to be sloughed off and negated, and the very memory of it, if possible, wiped out and forgotten. The ideal, so far from being co-extensive with the whole actual, is a mere *extract* from the actual, marked by its deliverance from all contact with this diseased, inferior, and excrementitious stuff ... Here we have the interesting notion ... of there being elements of the universe which may make no rational whole in conjunction with the other elements, and which, from the point of view of any system which those other elements make up, can only be considered so much irrelevance and accident – so much 'dirt,' as it were, and matter out of place," James, *Varieties of Religious Experience*, 150. See also Douglas, *Purity and Danger*; Moore, *Moral Purity and Persecution*. This battle regarding the simultaneous attraction and repulsion to "filth" is at the core of landmark American Catholic allegories of postwar America, such as Martin Scorsese's film *Taxi Driver* (Columbia Pictures, 1976), in which the protagonist, Travis Bickel (played by Robert DeNiro), an ex-Marine and Vietnam veteran, is powerfully drawn sexually to a teenage prostitute (Jody Foster) and, at the same time, profoundly disgusted by her, and by the moral depravity of New York City in the 1970s (and, implicitly, by his own unrelenting attraction to her and fascination with the city's swirling perversity that surrounds him). "All the animals come out at night – whores, skunk pussies, buggers, queens, fairies, dopers, junkies, sick, venal," Bickel says, "Someday a real rain will come and wash all this scum off the streets." Both the director Scorsese and the screenwriter Paul Schraeder had deeply religious upbringings, with Scorsese initially studying for the priesthood, and Schrader raised by strict Calvinist parents in Grand Rapids, Michigan who forbade him from seeing any films until he was an adult, just before he matriculated at Calvin College, where he minored in theology. *Taxi Driver* ends in a crescendo of shocking political violence.

The tense and voluntary attitude becomes in them an impossible fever and torment"; ultimately, "[t]heir machinery refuses to run at all when the bearings are made so hot and the belts so tight."[123]

Postwar conservative Catholics were particularly inflamed by disordered sexuality and were leaders in a crusade to cleanse disgusting sex and sexualities from the American polity. This had nothing to do with freedom, pluralism, and church-state separation. As right-wing Catholics saw it, Catholic theology on "properly ordered" sexuality was premised not on the particulars of their faith but rather on reason as applied to the world as it was (that is, reason, as applied to nature) by their own stable of highly trained ecclesiastical thinkers. Their views on properly ordered sexuality were not, as they saw it, one view among many, or a view peculiar to Catholics: they were an objectively true, reasoned deduction from the laws of nature. In this regard, orthodox, traditionalist Catholicism's conclusions pertaining to a properly ordered sexuality were the result of proofs undertaken in obedience to ironclad laws, like the proofs of algebra or geometry. Although others might need tutoring in what reason taught, there was no reasonable justification for tolerating (sexually disordered) filth, whether practiced, produced, or purveyed.

The idea of "to each his own" was, many believed, a corruption to which the Reformation had opened the door. Since Catholic teaching was universal – not simply a teaching of the faith, governing only the faithful – there were few qualms among orthodox, right-wing Catholics about imposing their views on the broader American polity. The glory of the Church, after all, was its objective knowledge of the distinction between right and wrong, and its willingness to go all out, the prejudices of the day notwithstanding, to champion the former and vanquish the latter.[124]

Even as John Courtney Murray was drawing up his "articles of peace" with liberal modernity, Catholic traditionalists continued to reject the view that individual rights claims were appropriately premised on claims to individual autonomy. To be sure, those on the Catholic Right who operated within a premodern medievalist framework in rejecting liberalism *in toto* also rejected individualism *per se*. But for the Murrayist Catholics – and even for ostensibly orthodox medievalists who decided, uneasily, to remain Americans in spite of themselves – an additional step in the argument was necessary. That step involved demonstrating that the claimed "right" was, in fact, no right at all

---

[123] James, *Varieties of Religious Experience*, 124. They become Travis Bickel – see previous footnote.

[124] As noted in Chapter 5 on "Evangelical and Fundamentalist Christian Stories," many conservative evangelicals at least initially held the Catholic Church itself partly responsible for the nation's – and, indeed, Western civilization's – moral decline. Francis Schaeffer fixed the foundational problem in the Church's theological reliance on what he took to be corrupted human reason (corrupted by the Fall – by original sin). Extensive intellectual/political work was required on the Right to bridge this gap: the opposition to abortion and later gay rights provided a platform for this work.

because, despite being claimed on behalf of the individual self, it did not benefit but actually harmed the claiming self, with the harm "objectively" demonstrable through a reasoned teleological inquiry that posited, *ex ante*, an objectively demonstrable *summum bonum*. To be sure, individuals might claim that having a particular "right" and freely exercising it was in their own self-interest. But they were often – objectively, demonstrably – mistaken. As such, as Fulton Sheen explained, any claims grounded in appeals to individual rights, including constitutional rights of free expression, amounted to almost "a war against the self in opposition to modern people's supposed selfishness."[125] In the modern context, in the end, these claims involved little more than willful assertions of animal desire. Any assertion that they were good for the individual self was perverse.[126]

Catholics sought to impose these teachings on the faithful. As the dissenting mid-century Catholic writer Thomas Joseph Sugrue (1907–1953) explained in the early 1950s, "Within the [American Church] ... there has developed a system of supervision and censorship for literature, the arts and entertainment; the Catholic is told by his diocesan newspaper what books he may read, what plays and movies he may see."[127] Sugrue found this bad enough. But the "real danger," he testified, "lies in the attempt which is made to fasten them on the non-Catholic population" through relentless, and often vicious, means.[128] "Catholic groups and organizations badger newspaper and magazine editors," Sugrue complained, "Any mention of anything Catholic must be favorable or the heat is on: an unfavorable comment brings hundreds of letters abusing the author of the comment and threatening the editor with boycott of his publication ... [and additionally threatening] to knock the block off anyone who spoke slightingly of the Pope."[129]

---

[125] Smith, *Look of Catholics*, 134.

[126] This is the form taken by all arguments concerning individual rights and liberties made by contemporary Catholic (natural law) constitutional theorists such as Princeton's Robert P. George and the Catholic University of America president (and former Notre Dame Law School professor and Boston College Law School dean) John Garvey: all rights claims are assessed by backward deduction from a preexisting substantive end involving a timeless "good." It is precisely this form of reasoning that John Dewey critiqued, and which, in significant part, the American pragmatists formulated their understandings against.

[127] Thomas Sugrue, *A Catholic Speaks His Mind on America's Religious Conflict* (New York: Harper and Bros., 1952). Kirkus Reviews said of the book: "Adding more fuel to the fires of controversy over the position of Catholicism in American life, this little book is likely to be angrily denounced by Catholics and gleefully praised by Protestants. Both reactions will issue out of a superficial and mistaken interpretation of the basic thesis of the book. However, the ordinary reader will not get beyond the fact that a practising Catholic of real standing in the literary world openly and sharply criticizes the drive of the Catholic Church for social and political power in America." *Kirkus Reviews* (March 26, 1952).

[128] Thomas Sugrue, "Let's Get Together: A Catholic Layman Speaks His Mind," *Reader's Digest* 60:362 (June 1952): 23–26, 23, reprinted, condensed, from *Christian Herald* (January & February 1952).

[129] Sugrue, "Let's Get Together," 24–25.

In the postwar United States, both the Church and Catholic civic organizations like the Knights of Columbus were at the forefront of the country's censorship efforts. Some proudly donned the mantle. Others, particularly clerical leaders publicly advancing and justifying the Church's position, insisted that banning smut and filth was not "censorship" at all: within their teleological framework anchored by an *ex ante* posited *summum bonum*, there was no "right" (under the First Amendment or otherwise) to do what is wrong. To the well-formed Catholic mind, any such rights claim was not only pernicious but also spurious.[130]

Perhaps the Church's greatest postwar cultural and public policy success story was the Legion of Decency's successful spearheading of the nation's regime of film censorship. With its leadership in establishing Hollywood's Movie Production (or "Hays") Code, the Church had finally arrived as a major influence on American politics and culture. For a country that had historically described such inclinations as "puritanical," the Church of Rome had at long last assumed its rightful position as the nation's preeminent – that is, most vigilant – moral guardian.[131] Attacking Hollywood as a moral sewer, the Legion of Decency recruited Boston College Jesuit priest Daniel Lord, SJ, to draft "the Code." Wielding threats of boycotts and other forms of condemnation, protest, and retaliation, the Legion then successfully lobbied the film industry to adopt it.

Getting Lord on board was a coup for the Legion. As one of the faith's most prolific and popular mid-century voices, Lord had penned innumerable pamphlets and columns, including a nationally syndicated weekly column

---

[130] Whitney Strub, *Perversion for Profit: The Politics of Pornography and the Rise of the New Right* (New York: Columbia University Press, 2011), 47. See generally, Frank Walsh, *Sin and Censorship: The Catholic Church and the Motion Picture Industry* (New Haven: Yale University Press, 1996); Gregory D. Black, *Hollywood Censored: Morality Codes, Catholics, and the Movies* (Cambridge: Cambridge University Press, 1994); Thomas Patrick Doherty, *Hollywood's Censor: Joseph I. Breen and the Production Code Administration* (New York: Columbia University Press, 2007); Marjorie Heins, "The Bishops Go the Movies: The Miracle: Film Censorship and the Entanglement of Church and State," *Conscience* (Spring 2003). The entry for "Censorship of Books" in the *Catholic Encylopedia* (1907–1912) reads: "In general, censorship of books is a supervision of the press in order to prevent any abuse of it. In this sense, every lawful authority, whose duty it is to protect its subjects from the ravages of a pernicious press, has the right of exercising censorship of books." "Censorship of Books," in the [Original] *Catholic Encyclopedia: An International Work of Reference on the Constitution, Doctrine, Discipline, and History of the Catholic Church* (New York: Robert Appleton Co., 1907–1912) (16 vols.), 519–520.

[131] Smith, *Look of Catholics*, 11, 34, 37. For the story of the collapse of this regime with the arrival of the "New Hollywood" directors like Robert Altman, Francis Ford Coppola, Martin Scorsese, Mike Nichols, John Boorman, John Schlesinger, William Friedkin, Michael Cemino, Robert Towne, Terrence Malick, Hal Ashby, and others, see also Peter Biskind, *Easy Riders, Raging Bulls: How the Sex-Drugs-and-Rock 'N' Roll Generation Saved Hollywood* (New York: Simon and Schuster, 1999).

("Along the Way") and a youth column for *Our Sunday Visitor*.[132] Although
criticized in Jesuit circles for peddling an oversimplified, popularized, and non-
intellectual message unbefitting an Ignatian, through his leadership of the
Sodality of the Blessed Virgin Mary at Catholic educational institutions and
his emotive religiosity aimed at mass publics in the emergent mass media age,
Lord garnered the attention and admiration of tens of thousands of Catholics –
in particular, of Catholic youth. Through the adept deployment of catchphrases
and songs, pageants, and cartoons, Lord indefatigably promoted the themes of
the (transnational) Catholic Action movement: Eucharistic and Marian
devotion, modest dress and irreproachable conduct, respect for family and
authority, anti-secularism and staunch anticommunism, and a commitment to
expanding the Church's influence on the broader society. Lord wrote the
Catholic Action Movement's theme song "For Christ the King" ("An army of
youth flying the standards of Truth / We're fighting for Christ the Lord / Heads
lifted high, Catholic Action our cry / And the Cross our only sword"), which
many mid-century Catholic schoolchildren would always remember. Lord was
also a major figure in early twentieth-century Catholic literary revival that
propagated a set of distinctively Catholic literary works. In all of this, Lord's
public Catholicism, which was doctrinally orthodox but looked beyond the
rectory outward to the world, endeavored to remake the world in a way that
would be hospitable to orthodox Catholics and evangelize for the expansion
along the way of their ranks.[133]

Lord argued that because movies played a major role in forming public
morals in the modern United States, the film industry had a special
responsibility for instilling respect for traditional morality. This meant that
films should treat the society's institutional instillers of morals – religion,
family, men in authority – with respect and, indeed, deference: movies should
always convey a moral message, and never a subversive one. With that end in
mind, the Production Code would require that in American movies, illicit
behavior would always be punished.[134]

---

[132] Founded in Indiana in 1912 by Father John Francis Noll (later named a bishop and an
archbishop) to combat anti-Catholicism and affirmatively serve and promote the faith, *Our
Sunday Visitor* is still published today (www.osv.com/).
[133] Like many orthodox Catholics of the period, at least, Lord confounded the categories of
"liberal" and "conservative" by campaigning simultaneously for film censorship, economic
justice, and racial fairness. Endes, "Dan Lord, Hollywood Priest" (http://dawneden
.blogspot.com/2009/03/i-found-out-all-of-sudden-that-life.html). Lord's papers are housed at
Georgetown University. See Black, *Hollywood Censored*, 37–49. Thomas Patrick Doherty, *Pre-
Code Hollywood: Sex Immorality, and Insurrection in American Cinema, 1930–1934*
(New York: Columbia University Press, 1999); Doherty, *Hollywood's Censor*. Pope Benedict
XVI issued a formal affirmation and appreciation of the then 140-year-old Catholic Action
Movement in 2008. Press Release, Vatican Information Service (May 6, 2008).
The organization remains active today (http://catholicsinaction.org/camovement/).
[134] Smith, *Look of Catholics*, 32–33.

When the Supreme Court handed down its pioneering *Roth* v. *United States* (1957) decision, written by the liberal Catholic Justice William Brennan, upholding an obscenity prosecution but, in so doing, setting out a new more speech-protective doctrinal test, the editors of the Jesuit magazine *America* – who misunderstood the decision's implications by placing too much weight on its immediate result rather than its doctrinal new departure – openly celebrated *Roth* as a victory for partisans of censorship (like the Church).[135] It was not long, however, before it became clear that, so far as things orthodox conservative Catholics cared about were concerned, the Supreme Court was moving in sharply different directions. When the speech-protective *MANual Enterprises, Inc.* v. *Day* (1962) and the *Engel* v. *Vitale* (1962) decisions striking down state-sponsored public school prayer were handed down, few were more outraged than the Catholic media – with one such outlet headlining its report, with a nod to Sidney Hook: "Prayer, No; Obscenity, Yes."[136]

THE RIGHT-WING CATHOLIC CONSTITUTIONALISM OF NOTRE DAME'S CLARENCE "PAT" MANION

Among the thousands who thrilled to Daniel Lord, SJ's message was the influential conservative crusader, impresario, constitutional scholar, dean of the University of Notre Dame Law School, and founder of the Notre Dame's Natural Law Institute (1947), Clarence "Pat" Manion.[137] Until recently, Clarence Manion, at whose wedding Daniel Lord had officiated, was an all-but-forgotten figure in the development of mid-century political and constitutional conservatism.[138] If he were only known for having encouraged Barry Goldwater to run for president, to write *The Conscience of a Conservative* (1960) (ghostwritten by L. Brent Bozell Jr., as Manion had arranged), and for publishing and tirelessly promoting that book, Manion's place in the history of the modern conservative movement should have been secure. There was, however, much more.

Born in Henderson, Kentucky, to a fervently Catholic mother who "never missed Mass a day in her life," and "steeped in Irish tradition and Catholic

---

[135] Strub, *Perversion for Profit*, 62.

[136] Strub, *Perversion for Profit*, 67. See Powe, *Warren Court and American Politics, 186–190; Roth* v. *United States*, 354 US 476 (1957); *MANual Enterprises, Inc.* v. *Day*, 370 US 478 (1962); *Engel* v. *Vitale*, 370 US 421 (1962). See Sidney Hook, *Heresy, Yes – Conspiracy, No* (New York: The John Day Co., 1953).

[137] Manion's Natural Law Institute began publishing the *Natural Law Forum* in 1956, a cynosure of the American Thomist revival. The *Natural Law Forum* changed its name in 1970 to the *American Journal of Jurisprudence* and is currently edited by Catholic Right scholars John Finnis and Gerald V. Bradley. As previously mentioned, Finnis was Supreme Court Justice Neil Gorsuch's mentor and PhD advisor. The *American Journal of Jurisprudence* is still published today (http://scholarship.law.nd.edu/ajj/).

[138] Manion is extensively discussed in Hemmer, *Messengers of the Right* (2016).

roots," Manion, who was educated at Catholic schools through law school at Notre Dame, joined the university's faculty in 1924, where he served simultaneously as law professor and pep rally leader.[139] It was rumored that at one point Manion, a lifelong Democrat, was on track to be appointed to the Supreme Court by Dwight Eisenhower, who was searching for a nationally prominent Catholic for the position. But Manion had a falling out with Eisenhower over Ike's penchant for executive agreements and assertions of broad national authority over the states. In the end, the appointment went instead to New Jersey Supreme Court Justice, and Manion's fellow Irish Catholic, William J. Brennan Jr.[140]

Manion, an America First Committee veteran, was pro–states rights, a crusading anticommunist (he coined the phrase "Godless communism"), a Bricker Amendment champion (the amendment, a major constitutional issue in the 1950s, would have expressly prevented treaties from altering the terms and understandings of the US Constitution), and a loyal supporter of "Mr. Republican" Robert A. Taft. Beginning in the 1930s, Manion published a number of books, including, *Lessons in Liberty: A Study of God in Government* (1939), which assailed legal positivists for holding man-made laws to be the source of American constitutional rights, and *The Key to Peace* (1950), which argued that the nation's strength was premised on its faith in God and the Constitution, which itself was premised on limited government and individual freedom. *The Key to Peace* was celebrated by right-wing outlets as a landmark statement: it inspired the establishment of "Key to Peace Clubs" with members committed to affirming the "real Americanism" propounded in Manion's book and launched a speaking tour for the author in which Manion emphasized the pillars of real Americanism: the Constitution, the Declaration of Independence, and the Ten Commandments.[141] Starting in 1954, following conservative radio pioneers like Paul Harvey, H. L. Hunt (*Life Line*), and the ex-FBI agent and conservative firebrand Dan Smoot (publisher of the commie-hunting *The Dan Smoot Report*), along with right-wing radio preachers like Billy James Hargis (*Christian Crusade*) and Carl McIntire (*Twentieth Century Reformation Hour*), Manion reached a mass

[139] Hoplin and Robinson, *Funding Fathers*, 88–90.
[140] Hoplin and Robinson, *Funding Fathers*, 92–97.
[141] The term "Americanism" was in much more widespread use at the time in the United States for what would, beginning in the mid-1950s, begin to proudly be called "conservatism." Clarence Manion, *Lessons of Liberty: A Study of God in Government* (Notre Dame, IN: University of Notre Dame Press, 1939); Clarence Manion, *The Key to Peace: A Formula for the Perpetuation of Real Americanism* (Chicago: Heritage Foundation, 1950); Hemmer, *Messengers of the Right*, 20–25, 31. See also Clarence Manion, *Let's Face It! Adopted from the Manion Forum Broadcasts, 1955* (South Bend, IN: Manion Forum, 1956); Clarence Manion, *The Conservative American: His Fight for National Independence and Constitutional Government* (New York: Devin-Adair, 1964).

national audience with his Sunday evening radio show, *The Manion Forum of Opinion* (launched October 3, 1954).[142]

Frustrated by the direction of the Republican Party under Eisenhower (and after the premature death of Robert Taft in 1953, and the implosion of Joseph McCarthy (1954) in the Army-McCarthy hearings), Manion turned to the then relatively unknown Arizona Senator Barry Goldwater, telling him, "[y]ou and your valiant, patriotic coterie in Congress may fight on for Constitutional Government as indeed you must, but neither you nor all the Senators put together can possibly change the prevailing Socialist weather in Washington until you change the political climate by putting an unadulterated American in the White House who believes in Constitutional Government."[143] Manion was the prime mover in drafting Goldwater as the standard-bearer for the Republican Party's fighting conservatism, one that was anchored in an appeal to constitutional government, rightly understood.

Goldwater initially resisted Manion's overtures. But he gave his blessing to a move to form a "Committee of 100" as a foundation for a Draft Goldwater movement. Manion soon became convinced that that movement would benefit from a short book in which the Arizona senator could lay out his political and constitutional philosophy and place it before the nation. For this, Manion took his own books – where, in clear and accessible prose, he had forthrightly stated his creed – as the model. He suggested the title *The Conscience of a Conservative*, arranged for the book's publication, and subsequently, with evangelical fervor, for its widespread distribution to libraries, bookstores, Republican members of Congress, and its advertisement from coast to coast in American newspapers.[144]

A PROPRIETARY CHURCH AGAINST "GODLESS COMMUNISM"

Before Vatican II in the early 1960s and even after it, many Catholics proudly, even truculently, considered the Roman Catholic faith not simply their faith, or one faith among many, but as the cornerstone of Western civilization.[145]

---

[142] In the first broadcast, Manion declared, "We need first to revive our American faith and then to defend it with determination." Hemmer, *Messengers of the Right*, 45–46, 108–113; Heather Hendershot, *What's Fair on the Air? Cold War Right-Wing Broadcasting and the Public Interest* (Chicago: University of Chicago Press, 2011).

[143] Hoplin and Robinson, *Funding Fathers*, 102 [quoting Manion].

[144] Hoplin and Robinson, *Funding Fathers*, 101–115; Hemmer, *Messengers of the Right*, 158–161.

[145] For a recent statement, see Thomas E. Woods Jr., *How the Catholic Church Built Western Civilization* (Washington, DC: Regnery, 2005). Woods is also the author of, among other books, Thomas E. Woods Jr., *The Politically Incorrect Guide to American History* (Washington, DC: Regnery, 2004); Thomas E. Woods Jr., *The Church Confronts Modernity: Catholic Intellectuals and the Progressive Era* (New York: Columbia University Press, 2004); and Thomas E. Woods Jr., *The Church and the Market: A Catholic Defense of the Free Economy* (Lanham, MD: Lexington Books, 2005). The jacket description of the books touts Woods, whose PhD degree is broadcast on the book's cover, as a scholar's scholar, holding

In confronting what Clarence Manion had called "Godless Communism," the proprietary Church saw itself as facing down an existential threat menacing its grand civilizational achievement. As Manion's newly coined characterization suggested, and Whittaker Chambers, William F. Buckley Jr., and other conservatives emphasized, the foundational fact about communism from which all else followed was its Godlessness. The Catholic Right understood itself to be squared off in an existential death match against the atheistic Soviet Union, with the Western civilization it had built at stake. To be vehemently and unrelentingly anticommunist, in what amounted a fight for world domination, was to live life as a true hero – a defender of the faith.[146]

This Rightist Roman Catholic framing was inscribed in the biography of *National Review* founder William F. Buckley Jr. himself, the postwar movement's peerless impresario. William's father, Will, a Texas oilman (later relocated to Connecticut), had been legal counsel to Mexico's Huerta government before and during the Mexican Revolution. The revolutionaries, who called for levies on the nation's oil companies, had called the family's beloved Church a "cancerous tumor" on the nation. As Mexico's anticlerical Left wrested power from Huerta, Will Buckley joined an underground movement seeking to shelter the country's priests and secret Church property, while defending (the) religious freedom (of Catholics). When the revolutionaries got around to confiscating the American oilman's property, and much of his wealth, the senior Buckley gathered his family and fled the country. Will remained a fervent anticommunist ever after. Given their experiences and beliefs, the Buckleys saw no daylight between communism's assault on private property and the free market and its crusade against God and his universal Church.[147]

During the postwar period, conservative Catholic politics increasingly emphasized this consonance between God and the free market, in the process forging new ties with traditionally anti-Catholic Evangelicals and with American business leaders, who were also active at the time in touting the virtues of the market.[148] With this relatively new departure, American Catholics joined long extant streams of American traditions opposed to collectivism, socialism, and Bolshevism. But these streams of thought and opinion had tended, in more typical liberal fashion, to focus on the collectivist

"four Ivy League degrees." Woods also published a new edition of Orestes Brownson's *The American Republic* for Regnery. Orestes Brownson, *The American Republic* (Washington, DC: Gateway Editions/ Regnery, 2003) (Thomas E. Woods Jr., editor).

[146] See Sugrue, "Catholic Encounters with the 1960s," 73; Orsi, "Between Memory and Modernity," 33–35, 37–39; Susan Jacoby, *Alger Hiss and the Battle for History* (New Haven: Yale University Press, 2009), 38. See also Daniel Peris, *Storming the Heavens: The Soviet League of the Militant Godless* (Ithaca, NY: Cornell University Press, 1998).

[147] Hoplin and Robinson, *Funding Fathers*, 59–62.

[148] See Kevin M. Kruse, *One Nation Under God: How Corporate America Invented Christian America* (New York: Basic Books, 2015).

threat to property rights – that is, on individual autonomy and freedom. The Catholic Right, by contrast, framed the issue of the rejection of markets as a repudiation of God, and a rejection of truth, in ways that portended the impending collapse of the West.[149] Far from remaining a fringe sensibility, mainstream media outlets like Henry Luce's *Time* magazine championed the Catholic anticommunist frame, casting the pope, the Vatican, and (in the United States) Cardinal Spellman as leading the West in its cultural war with the Soviets. This frame, of course, helped reconstruct Catholics, long considered suspect as outsiders potentially loyal to a foreign sovereign, as the nation's most grounded and uncompromising defenders – the rock upon which American freedom was built.[150] Inspiring stories of faithful Catholics bravely standing up to communism around the world were a staple of conservative magazines.[151] By 1954, the Cold War's peak, communism's Godlessness was being emphasized as never before, making its way into the nation's mission statement itself, as learned and voiced by every child, when the words "under God" were added to the Pledge of Allegiance originally penned with no reference to God in 1892.

THE KENNEDY BID AND CATHOLIC AMERICANISM

For many Americans, Massachusetts Senator John F. Kennedy's bid for the presidency raised in the most concrete way the question about whether a faithful Catholic could be a loyal American. The problem for many non-Catholics was not so much the Church's position on particular public policy

[149] In the United States, there was a long tradition of Christian socialism. Proponents of the Social Gospel like Walter Rauschenbusch and socialists like Eugene V. Debs had repeatedly invoked God in their politics, and, in the case of the Social Gospel, found the primary motivation for their politics in Christ's teachings. It was thus a new departure for conservatives to insist that socialism was, by its very nature, Godless or anti-Christian. See generally Kramnick and Lowi, eds., *American Political Thought*.

[150] Smith, *Look of Catholics*, 89–90, 105. I again borrow the concept of omni-Americans from Albert Murray, *The Omni-Americans*.

[151] See, e.g., Michael Scully, "Don Pepe's Private War Against Communism," *Reader's Digest* 56:338 (June 1950): 112–116 [reprinted, condensed, from *The Christian Science Monitor* (May 3, 1950)]. This was the same frame that made many conservative American Catholics so worshipful of Pope John Paul II, the Polish cleric who stood down the communists. See, e.g., George Weigel, *Witness to Hope: The Life of John Paul II* (New York: Cliff Street Books, 1999) and George Weigel, *The End and the Beginning: Pope John Paul II – The Victory of Freedom, the Last Years, the Legacy* (New York: Doubleday, 2010). Weigel, a frequent contributor to *National Review*, is the William E. Simon Chair in Catholic Studies at the conservative Washington think tank Ethics and Public Policy Center, which he formerly led. (The center is bannered on its website as "Defending American Ideals Since 1976" (https://eppc.org/). Robert P. George said of him: "George Weigel is a giant. George, God bless you for everything you do, not only for this organization, not only for the Church, not only for the country, but truly for humanity." Ethics and Public Policy Center Fortieth Anniversary Gala (https://vimeo.com/163860708) (keynoted by Speaker of the House Paul Ryan).

issues but the nature and structure of the Church itself – its (medieval) monarchial form, with a pope in the role of a king, sitting on the throne of a sovereign state (first officially recognized as such by FDR), and a rigid ecclesiastical hierarchy. If a faithful Catholic were obedient to the pope, sitting as king on his throne in the Holy See, could he also be loyal to the United States and its Constitution? What would happen in a case of conflict? And what did democracy mean to an orthodox Catholic? Democracy, perhaps even the very idea of self-government, was natural to Protestants. Indeed, in the modern world, they could claim to be its chief architects and champions. Protestants, after all, gathered voluntarily to form their own churches. After collective discussion, each church voted to select its own minister. In a parallel, if not progenitor, of democratic accountability, if a chosen church (as an institution) or minister (as an elected agent and leader of an institution) was not serving its members' needs or betrayed their convictions, the congregations would remove and replace their current minister with one who better served their needs and reflected their concerns and beliefs, or they would vote with their feet by withdrawing and forming a new church. In Catholicism, by contrast, the Church was a global unity; exit was not an option. Parishioners did not choose priests: they were assigned by bishops, operating under the direct hierarchical aegis of Rome. Lay input was minimal, and often highly unwelcome. Given these differences, many American Protestants harbored serious concerns that Catholicism was incompatible with democracy, and the Church was incapable of forming democratic citizens: the Catholic Church, simply put, was un-American.

And this is to say nothing of the problems with Roman Catholic theology. The belief in *solo scriptura* – that the Bible is the literal word of God, accessible to all directly, without the intermediary of a priest or the commands of a clerical hierarchy – was at the core of the Reformation. Catholics continued to insist, however, that God's commands could not be understood outside the teachings of the Church. These teachings, moreover, constituted an elaborate theology honed within the Church's elite scholastic precincts over the course of its centuries-long history. Given these real and important differences and this history, many on each side of the US Protestant-Catholic divide had long viewed the other as no less than heretical.

Since the American colonies had been founded and settled largely, if not exclusively, by Protestants – and, mostly, members of Protestant sects that had dissented from the established Church of England – and since the United States had been governed by Protestants ever since, Catholics had their work cut out for them with the Kennedy bid for the White House. Although, given geographic expansion and mass immigration over the course of the nineteenth and early twentieth centuries, Catholics had risen to enough prominence in American life to have seen one of their own, New York Governor Al Smith, secure the Democratic nomination for the presidency in the 1920s, anti-Catholic prejudice had played a major role in that campaign, especially in the South and Midwest, and in Smith's dispiriting defeat.

Not surprisingly, as Kennedy's bid for the White House took flight, many Catholic intellectuals joined the Murrayist project of publicly reconciling Catholicism not only with Americanism but with the Constitution – and, specifically, with the First Amendment. Writing for *Reader's Digest*, the Reverend John O'Brien, a University of Notre Dame theologian, appealed to the facts on the ground of American history, explaining that "[f]rom the earliest days of the Church in this country, Catholics have supported separation." Indeed, as Catholics were a religious minority in the United States, O'Brien characterized the Catholic "stake in separation as higher than the stake of most other religious groups." While he stipulated that "it is axiomatic that error has no rights against truth," O'Brien allowed that "men are, nevertheless, free to embrace error rather than truth, though they must pay the inevitable penalty for doing so."[152] The implication that non-Catholics, although damned to hell, would not be repressed politically – of necessity, given the minority status of American Catholics – might have reassured some. But the argument that "we won't repress you because, under current conditions, we can't" was hardly a winner for most. Father O'Brien's piece was paired with an article written by two Protestant ministers who expressed serious, ongoing concerns about the Church.

John F. Kennedy himself did not adopt O'Brien's tack. In a now famous speech to the Greater Houston Ministerial Association (1960), Kennedy firmly opposed the allocation of federal funds to sectarian schools and declared himself against appointing a US ambassador to the Vatican. While this pleased the assembled Protestant ministers, they nevertheless noted with concern that Kennedy had been roundly assailed by the Catholic press for taking precisely those positions. The ministers underlined that the Catholic Church in the United States and elsewhere had regularly opposed on principle both church-state separation and religious freedom.[153] While the ministers thus thought well of Kennedy, they were worried nevertheless.

The Reverend James Pike, the Episcopal bishop of California, however, offered a less ambivalent defense of the Catholic Kennedy in both *Life* and *Reader's Digest*. In doing so, Pike distinguished the positions of the Catholic Church from those of Catholic Americans. Pike observed that while the official Catholic position on the relationship between church and state "is at great variance with the ideals of most Americans," that position is "only rarely asserted by American Roman Catholics."[154] After providing a detailed

---

[152] Rev. John A. O'Brien, "The Religious Issue in This Campaign," *Reader's Digest* 77:461: September 1960): 65–70, 65, 67 [reprinted, condensed, from *Look* (February 16 and May 10, 1960].

[153] Rev. Dr. Eugene Carson Blake and Bishop G. Bromley Oxnam, "A Protestant View," *Reader's Digest* 77:461 (September 1960): 68–70, 69, 70.

[154] The Right Reverend James A. Pike, "Should a Catholic Be President?" *Reader's Digest* 76:455 (March 1960): 37–41, 37 [reprinted, condensed, from *Life* (December 24, 1959)].

account of traditional Catholic theology on these matters, Pike contrasted it with John Courtney Murray's "American Interpretation." Murray, Pike recounted, had explained that the Church's traditional position on these matters was situational and historicized: it had been "directed against a particular evil of a particular time – i.e. 19th century European liberalism with its threat to the Church." "American democracy," Murray had argued, was "a horse of another color." "[W]hether consciously or unconsciously," Pike was convinced that the American interpretation was "doubtless" the one held by most American Catholics. If a Catholic president, like most American Catholics, held to Murray's American Interpretation, there would be no problem. Accordingly, Pike urged his fellow Americans in casting their votes to "be loyal to the spirit expressed in the Constitutional inhibition against a religious test for public office."[155]

A PROCLAMATION OF CO-BELLIGERENCE: EVANGELICALS AND CATHOLICS TOGETHER

Toward the end of the twentieth century, conservative Catholics loomed ever larger in the conservative movement's effort to unify the religiously diverse strands of the Religious Right under the Constitution's banner. Groups and institutions were formed to build the personal, intellectual, and political alliances necessary for the task. These frequently used a shared commitment to the Constitution to help forge a common ground. Among the earliest of these organizations was the Institute for Religion and Democracy (IRD) (founded in 1981), which adopted a Murrayist template in its effort to expand – would "restore" – the influence of orthodox Christianity on the broader political culture. The IRD bore the clear imprint of right-wing Catholic leadership: at one time or another, its board members have included Mary Ellen Bork, Robert P. George, Fred Barnes, Michael Novak, George Weigel, and the late Father Richard John Neuhaus (Mark Tooley, the group's current president, is a Catholic-educated Methodist). While many of those working for the IRD are Protestants, they are closely aligned with the Catholic Right's goal of pushing the Protestant churches in a sharply more orthodox direction.[156]

---

[155] Pike, "Should a Catholic Be President?" 40–41.
[156] Theird.org . The ecumenical coalition forged in significant part under Right-wing Roman Catholic leadership, it should be underlined, included right-wing (Orthodox or Conservative) Jews like Rabbi David G. Dalin, a Robert P. George crony, who wrote a serviceable book for Regnery defending the Catholic Church against the charges it had colluded with the Nazis, as did Vatican advisor and University of Mississippi Law Professor Ronald J. Rychlak, also a Robert P. George compatriot, and Straussians, including the late Peter Augustine Lawler, an idiosyncratic (for Straussians) hipster Murrayist – recipient of the Richard Weaver Prize for Scholarly Letters – who melded Catholic political thought with Straussian teachings. See David G. Dalin, *The Myth of Hitler's Pope: How Pope Pius XII Rescued Jews from the Nazis* (Washington, DC: Regnery 2005). Dalin's book is advertised as an expose on "the newly

In the early 1990s, Catholics like New York's Cardinal John O'Connor, Fordham University's Father Avery Dulles, SJ, Bishops Frances George and Carlos Sevilla, Father Richard John Neuhaus, theologians Michael Novak of the American Enterprise Institute and George Weigel of the Ethics and Public Policy Center, and Harvard Law School Professor Mary Ann Glendon joined Evangelical Protestants like the Reverend Pat Robertson, the University of Notre Dame's Mark Noll (then at Wheaton College in Illinois), Southern Baptist Convention head Richard Land, born-again Watergate criminal Charles Colson, conservative cause lawyer William Bentley Ball, and Campus Crusade for Christ founder Bill Bright in drafting, promulgating, or officially endorsing (variously) the manifesto/declaration *Evangelicals and Catholics Together: The Christian Mission in the Third Millennium* (1994).[157]

While pronouncing that "[a]s Christ is one, so the Christian mission is one," *Evangelicals and Catholics Together* simultaneously affirmed "legitimate diversity," holding that "one mission can be and should be advanced in diverse ways." Basking in the potential of Christian power, the manifesto noted the following:

As we near the Third Millennium, there are approximately 1.7 billion Christians in the world. About a billion of these are Catholics and more than 300 million are Evangelical Protestants. The century now drawing to a close has been the greatest century of missionary expansion in Christian history. We pray and we believe that this expansion has prepared the way for yet greater missionary endeavor in the first century of the Third Millennium.

---

resurrected, widely accepted, yet utterly bankrupt smearing of Pope Pius XII, whom Jewish survivors of the Holocaust considered a righteous gentile." It received the high praise of a blurb from AEI's Michael Novak, declaring, "This is a stunning book. I wish I had known more of this material years ago." See also Ronald J. Rychlak, *Hitler, the War, and the Pope* (Huntington, IN: Our Sunday Visitor Press, 2000). These books answered the penetrating but seriously flawed work of British journalist John Cornwell in *Hitler's Pope: The Secret History of Pius XII* (New York: Viking Press, 1999). For a reliable account of the actual (complicated/troubled) relationship, in broader context, starting with the relationship of the Church to the rise of Italian fascism, see David I. Kertzer, *The Pope and Mussolini: The Secret History of Pius XI and the Rise of Fascism in Europe* (New York: Random House, 2014). See also David I. Kertzer, *The Popes Against the Jews: The Vatican's Role in the Rise of Modern Antisemitism* (New York: Knopf, 2001) (taking a longer view, and providing a fuller picture). Yet another Robert George protégé, the Jewish Daniel Mark, a political science professor at Villanova University specializing in constitutional law, has served – virtually from the moment he defended his PhD. thesis at Princeton directed by George – as a commissioner of the United States Commission on International Religious Freedom (www.uscirf.gov/). Mark – a young fledgling assistant professor – was appointed to the Commission by House Speaker Paul Ryan (R). Robert George himself is a former commissioner and chair of the USCIRF (appointed by Speaker of the House John Boehner (R)). Mark is now Chairman of the Commission. Mary Ann Glendon, among others, has also served as a Republican appointee to the body, which is bipartisan, as have Richard Land, Leonard Leo – a leader of The Federalist Society – and former UN ambassador and, now, Donald Trump national security advisor, John Bolton.

[157] *First Things* 43 (May 1994): 15–22 (drafted beginning in September 1992).

Those numbers might be impressive, but the manifesto emphasized that the challenge was dire: "At the same time, in our so-called developed societies, a widespread secularization increasingly descends into a moral, intellectual, and spiritual nihilism that denies not only the One who is the Truth but the very idea of truth itself": "With Paul and the Christians of the first century, we know that 'we are not contending against flesh and blood, but against the principalities, against the powers, against the world rulers of this present darkness, against the spiritual hosts of wickedness in the heavenly places'" (Ephesians 6). Disunion among believers only hurt the cause and emboldened the wicked. "As Evangelicals and Catholics," the manifesto declared, "we dare not by needless and loveless conflict between ourselves give aid and comfort to the enemies of the cause of Christ." A functional political alliance was imperative: "The love of Christ compels us and we are therefore resolved to avoid such conflict between our communities and, where such conflict exists, to do what we can to reduce and eliminate it." The manifesto continued: "As we are bound together by Christ and his cause, so we are bound together in contending against all that opposes Christ and his cause" and "As Evangelicals and Catholics, we pray that our unity in the love of Christ will become ever more evident as a sign to the world of God's reconciling power."

The manifesto was clear that in drawing closer together, Evangelicals and Catholics would forswear the wishy-washy ecumenicalism that their progenitors had strenuously condemned in mainline mid-century liberal Protestantism. The late twentieth-century signatories, they made clear, were made of stronger stuff. "We do not deny but clearly assert that there are disagreements between us," they affirmed. But "[m]isunderstandings, misrepresentations, and caricatures of one another . . . are not disagreements. These distortions must be cleared away if we are to search through our honest differences in a manner consistent with what we affirm and hope together on the basis of God's Word."

The statement then set out at length a political – and constitutional – vision and agenda. This started with "first things," the signatories proclaiming that

[t]ogether we contend for the truth that politics, law, and culture must be secured by moral truth. With the Founders of the American experiment, we declare, 'We hold these truths.' With them, we hold that this constitutional order is composed not just of rules and procedures but is most essentially a moral experiment. With them, we hold that only a virtuous people can be free and just, and that virtue is secured by religion. To propose that securing civil virtue is the purpose of religion is blasphemous. To deny that securing civil virtue is a benefit of religion is blindness.

Alas, there has been a falling away:

Americans are drifting away from, are often explicitly defying, the constituting truths of this experiment in ordered liberty. Influential sectors of the culture are laid waste by relativism, anti-intellectualism, and nihilism that deny the very idea of truth. Against such influences in both the elite and popular culture, we appeal to reason and religion in contending for the foundational truths of our constitutional order.

Religious liberty was crucial in taking the fight to the enemy. "[W]e contend together for religious freedom," the manifesto proclaimed:

We do so for the sake of religion, but also because religious freedom is the first freedom, the source and shield of all human freedoms. In their relationship to God, persons have a dignity and responsibility that transcends, and thereby limits, the authority of the state and of every other merely human institution. Religious freedom is itself grounded in and is a product of religious faith ... Today we rejoice together that the Roman Catholic Church – as affirmed by the Second Vatican Council and boldly exemplified in the ministry of John Paul II – is strongly committed to religious freedom and, consequently, to the defense of all human rights. Where Evangelicals and Catholics are in severe and sometimes violent conflict ... we urge Christians to embrace and act upon the imperative of religious freedom. Religious freedom will not be respected by the state if it is not respected by Christians or, even worse, if Christians attempt to recruit the state in repressing religious freedom. In this country, too, freedom of religion cannot be taken for granted but requires constant attention.

Consistent with Vatican II's Murrayist vision, the proclamation "strongly affirm[ed] the separation of church and state." But it "just as strongly protest[ed] the distortion of that principle to mean the separation of religion from public life." It added,

We are deeply concerned by the courts' narrowing of the protections provided by the "free exercise" provision of the First Amendment and by an obsession with "no establishment" that stifles the necessary role of religion in American life. As a consequence of such distortions, it is increasingly the case that wherever government goes religion must retreat, and government increasingly goes almost everywhere. Religion, which was privileged and foundational in our legal order, has in recent years been penalized and made marginal.

Evangelicals and Catholics Together called for "a renewal of the constituting vision of the place of religion in the American experiment." "Religion and religiously grounded moral conviction is not an alien or threatening force in our public life," it insisted:

For the great majority of Americans, morality is derived, however variously and confusedly, from religion. The argument, increasingly voiced in sectors of our political culture, that religion should be excluded from the public square must be recognized as an assault upon the most elementary principles of democratic governance. That argument needs to be exposed and countered by leaders, religious and other, who care about the integrity of our constitutional order.

The manifesto then recurred to the backstory of its genesis in the fight against the Supreme Court's abortion rights decision in *Roe* v. *Wade* (1973):

The pattern of convergence and cooperation between Evangelicals and Catholics is, in large part, a result of common effort to protect human life ... With the Founders, we hold that all human beings are endowed by their Creator with the right to life, liberty, and the pursuit of happiness. The statement that the unborn child is a human life ... is not a religious assertion. It is a statement of simple biological fact. That the unborn child has a right to protection, including the protection of law, is a moral statement supported by moral reason and biblical truth. We, therefore, will ... multiply every effort ... to secure the legal protection of the unborn. Our goals are: to secure due process of law for the unborn, to enact the most protective laws and public policies that are politically possible, and to reduce dramatically the incidence of abortion.

Their cause, they said, is also one of women's rights: "As the unborn must be protected, so also must women be protected from their current rampant exploitation by the abortion industry and by fathers who refuse to accept responsibility for mothers and children. Abortion on demand, which is the current rule in America, must be recognized as a massive attack on the dignity, rights, and needs of women."

Indeed, its implications were even larger. "Abortion is the leading edge of an encroaching culture of death," *Evangelicals and Catholics Together* taught:

The helpless old, the radically handicapped, and others who cannot effectively assert their rights are increasingly treated as though they have no rights. These are the power-less who are exposed to the will and whim of those who have power over them. We will do all in our power to resist proposals for euthanasia, eugenics, and population control that exploit the vulnerable, corrupt the integrity of medicine, deprave our culture, and betray the moral truths of our constitutional order.

Our public schools, the manifesto continued, are on the front lines of these fights. "In public education," it declared, "we contend together for schools that transmit to coming generations our cultural heritage, which is inseparable from the formative influence of religion, especially Judaism and Christianity":

Education for responsible citizenship and social behavior is inescapably moral educa-tion. Every effort must be made to cultivate the morality of honesty, law observance, work, caring, chastity, mutual respect between the sexes, and readiness for marriage, parenthood, and family. We reject the claim that ... "tolerance" requires the promotion of moral equivalence between the normative and the deviant. In a democratic society that recognizes that parents have the primary responsibility for the formation of their chil-dren, schools are to assist and support, not oppose and undermine, parents in the exercise of their responsibility.

In the current context, this means "a comprehensive policy of parental choice in education," which "is a moral question of simple justice." Because "[p]arents are the primary educators of their children; the state and other institutions should be supportive of their exercise of that responsibility. We affirm policies that enable parents to effectively exercise their right and responsibility to choose the schooling that they consider best for their children."

The manifesto also condemned "the widespread pornography in our society, along with the celebration of violence, sexual depravity, and antireligious bigotry in the entertainment media." "In resisting such cultural and moral debasement," it proclaimed, "we recognize the legitimacy of boycotts and other consumer actions, and urge the enforcement of existing laws against obscenity." As for the First Amendment, the statement rejected "the self-serving claim of the peddlers of depravity that this constitutes illegitimate censorship. We reject the assertion of the unimaginative that artistic creativity is to be measured by the capacity to shock or outrage. A people incapable of defending decency invites the rule of viciousness, both public and personal."

The statement, moreover, affirmed the indispensability of "a vibrant market economy" to a "free society." While insisting that "Christianity is not an ideology and therefore does not prescribe precisely how that balance is to be achieved in every circumstance," the statement "affirm[ed] the importance of a free economy not only because it is more efficient but because it accords with a Christian understanding of human freedom. Economic freedom, while subject to grave abuse, makes possible the patterns of creativity, cooperation, and accountability that contribute to the common good."

As had Robert Nisbet and Alexis de Tocqueville before it, the statement conveyed a steadfast support for the claims of civil society's core intermediate institutions of church, family, and voluntary associations. It emphasized that "The state is not the society, and many of the most important functions of society are best addressed in independence from the state." Special emphasis was placed on "[t]he role of churches in responding to a wide variety of human needs, especially among the poor and marginal" and on generally advancing "both personal well-being and the common good." The most important institution of all, the statement emphasized, was the family: "Laws and social policies should be designed with particular care for the stability and flourishing of families." The manifesto held government largely responsible for "the crisis of the family in America" where, "as a result of well-intended but misguided statist policies," many families ended up as "virtual wards of the government."

In concluding, the manifesto characterized itself as "a partial list of public responsibilities on which we believe there is a pattern of convergence and cooperation between Evangelicals and Catholics." It emphatically "reject[ed] the notion that this constitutes a partisan 'religious agenda' in American politics." It characterized itself, rather, as a set of proposals oriented to the common good, discussable on the basis of public reason. "While our sense of civic responsibility is informed and motivated by Christian faith," the proclamation closed, "our intention is to elevate the level of political and moral discourse in a manner that excludes no one and invites the participation of all people of good will."

CONCLUSION

Reviewing Supreme Court Justice Abe Fortas's book *Concerning Dissent and Civil Disobedience* (1968) in the late 1960s, the far Right Catholic magazine *Triumph* pronounced it "remarkable" that, in setting out the problem of resisting unjust laws, Justice Fortas had made "no reference to immutable principles or to absolute standards." Shocked by Fortas's presumed legal positivism, the magazine stridently condemned Fortas for making "no room for the law that even judges must obey, the law of God, the only law in which freedom is found." For liberals like Fortas, apparently, as *Triumph* would have it, law had been "reduced to ... five to four" – a simple majority vote of fallible human beings. Inexcusably, Fortas had failed to explain that not only the Constitution but also the nation's foundational English common law inheritance, "the basis of the law of most of our 50 states," was rooted in God's law. "[E]ven if their instincts were dulled by the Enlightenment," the magazine lectured, "our own Founding Fathers ... had no intention of abolishing common law and its prescriptive force" – the real meat of American law, which dealt with "the real problems of the citizen – with conduct, with guilt, with punishment, in everyday situations." "The Constitution was not the basic law of the land, as popularly supposed. It was rather a super-law, a crowning appendage" to the common law. It, and federal law more generally, was there only to deal "with violations of the limited authority conferred on the federal government."[158]

Perhaps surprising, *Triumph* argued that the adoption of the Fourteenth Amendment in the Civil War's aftermath had manifestly changed things for the worse: it had altered what had heretofore been "an essentially positivist arrangement addressed to the narrow sphere of politics" to a document that "now assumed primacy over the Natural Law that had been embodied in the common law." As a consequence, "[t]he prescriptive force of common law ... was now *subject* to the Bill of Rights. What is more, the Bill of Rights itself was soon to become – not the unchanging 'rights of Englishmen' – but the *ipse dixit* of five men": "[W]hen this happened, the traditional concept of justice disappeared." We were left with the husk of an "un-Christian" legal positivism.[159]

Enough was enough. A year later, *Triumph*'s founder Brent Bozell decided that he had had enough with the United States and its congenital liberal individualism: Bozell had decided that it was fundamentally incompatible with Catholic teaching. He decamped to Francisco Franco's fascist Spain, which he found infinitely more congenial to the teachings of the Universal Church. On the way out the door, Bozell denounced the Republican Party (insufficiently Catholic), *National Review* (insufficiently Catholic), and the

---

[158] Hippolytus, "Is Abe Fortas A Sensible Social Necessity?" *Triumph* 3:10 (October 1968), 11–14, 11–13. See also Ken I. Kersch, "Constitutive Stories About the Common Law in Modern American Conservatism," in Sanford Levinson, Joel Parker, and Melissa Williams, editors, *NOMOS: American Conservatism* (New York: New York University Press, 2016).

[159] Hippolytus, "Abe Fortas," 11. See also Michael Lawrence, "An Inaugural Address," *Triumph* 4:1 (January 1969): 11–14. Abe Fortas, *Concerning Dissent and Civil Disobedience* (New York: New American Library, 1968).

Roman Catholic Church (insufficiently Catholic). At long last, of necessity outside the United States, Bozell could live his faith.[160]

The great majority of US Catholic conservatives, however, took a different path. Instead of denouncing America's (Founding) liberal modernity as fundamentally incompatible with the Roman Catholic faith, they moved to reimagine and re-narrate the nation's history – including the history of its Founding, its Constitution, and its political and legal development – as, if even consciously unawares, anchored in the commitments and principles of the Catholic faith. Not only did right-wing Catholics learn to see themselves as the peerless guardians of American principles and values, rightly understood, but many went on to argue that *only* a Roman Catholic framework could fully illuminate the American Founders' achievement at a level of sufficient intellectual and moral depth to render their achievement fully comprehensible. As such, instead of leaving America like Bozell, they would take it upon themselves to redeem it.[161]

In a country whose Founders and Founding were most deeply rooted in an at times unorthodox and often vehemently anti-Catholic Protestantism – and, perhaps surpassingly, Enlightenment liberalism – the degree to which Roman Catholicism has played a critical role in the supposedly Founder-worshipping modern Right is perhaps surprising. A single Opus Dei cleric, C. John McCloskey III, converted many pillars of the contemporary political and legal Right to the Roman Catholic faith, including Robert Bork, Robert Novak, Newt Gingrich, Sam Brownback, Lawrence Kudlow, the Right to Life activist Bernard Nathanson, the constitutional historian Herman Belz, and the Straussian constitutional theorist Hadley Arkes. Most of the Supreme Court's current justices, liberal and conservative alike, are Roman Catholics (the non-Catholics are Jews: there are no Protestants on the current Court). Many

---

[160] Hemmer, *Messengers of the Right*, 201. See L. Brent Bozell Jr., "Letters from Yourselves," *Triumph* 4:6 (June 1969): 17–19, 40, 17; L. Brent Bozell Jr., "Letter to Yourselves," *Triumph* (March 1969); L. Brent Bozell Jr., "Letter to Yourselves," *Triumph* (April 1969). See generally L. Brent Bozell Jr., *Mustard Seeds: A Conservative Becomes a Catholic* (Front Royal, VA: Christendom Press, 2004).

[161] A number of prominent conservatives, including Jeffrey Hart, John Chamberlain, Will Herberg, and Gerhart Niemeyer, directly engaged Brent Bozell at the time in the pages of *Triumph*, challenging his claim that because the country's ideological bloodstream had been fatally poisoned by liberalism, conservative politics in the United States could never satisfactorily substitute for a Christian politics. Hart, for one, agreed with Bozell that "a viable conservatism must be religious," and, what's more, "that it must be Catholic." But he remained hopeful that such a conservatism had a future in the contemporary United States. See L. Brent Bozell Jr., "Letters from Yourselves," *Triumph* 4:6 (June 1969): 17–19, 17, 40. While the fascist Spain option is off the table, this debate is by no means a thing of the past: indeed, it has recently been rekindled – see, e.g., the devoutly Catholic conservative University of Notre Dame political scientist Patrick Deneen's *Why Liberalism Failed* (New Haven: Yale University Press, 2018) (thrust) versus the devoutly Catholic conservative University of Notre Dame political scientist Vincent Phillip Muñoz's "Defending American Classical Liberalism," *National Review* (June 11, 2018) (parry).

leading thinkers of the Religious Right like Harvard Law School's Mary Ann Glendon, the University of Notre Dame's (and Oxford University's) John Finnis (the supervisor of Supreme Court Justice Neil Gorsuch's PhD thesis), Amherst College's Hadley Arkes, and Princeton's Robert P. George are conservative Catholics. George, in particular, a Murrayist Thomist, has served as an intellectual impresario of the nation's far Right. Through relentless fundraising and the sponsorship, and shaping, and vetting of scholarship and constitutional studies programs, like Princeton University's James Madison Program in American Ideals and Institutions – a Catholic redoubt – and Princeton, New Jersey's Witherspoon Institute (spearheaded by George and headed by an Opus Dei cleric), conservative American Catholics have played a major role in forging the program of co-belligerence that has united the once theologically divided factions of the modern Religious Right and immensely strengthened their political and legal influence.

In seeking to redeem the American constitutional project in a way that fully honored Catholic understanding and the faith – that is, objective Truth – the United States the Catholic Right reimagined and re-narrated could never be wholly modern. But, in the nature of things, it remained (strategically? temporarily? permanently?) poised, in the Catholic historian Robert Orsi's characterization, "between memory and modernity."[162]

Traditionalist Roman Catholicism had long been understood, not least by Catholics themselves, like Bozell, as out of place in American culture, from its Protestant, liberal, Enlightenment Founding forward. Indeed, American Catholics understood themselves as out of place not simply on the basis of their often atypical ethnicities and national origins but also "specifically because what was most fundamental to being Catholic – loyalty to the pope, obedience to authority, love of the Virgin Mary, and devotional practices addressed to the saints ... [which] stuck Americans as pagan, premodern, and perverse." The faith's preoccupations – "sainthood, martyrdom, and bodily mortification," a "devotional culture" involving ongoing interaction with the supernatural and, more generally, the "mingling of the human and the nonhuman" – were alien to mainstream American culture. These were what Orsi described as constituting Roman Catholic "memory" – the culture and traditions of the premodern Catholic Church. The modern strand of American Catholicism, Orsi argued, was long in the making and never fully completed. From John Gilmary Shea (1824–1892), to the Catholic University of America's Commission on American Citizenship (1938), to the heroic bodily sacrifices made by American Catholics during the fight against Godless communism during the Cold War, as told in Father John F. Donovan's *The Pagoda and the Cross* (1967), Father Harold W. Rigney, SVD's *4 Years in Red Hell* (1956), and the imprisonment in communist Hungary of Cardinal Mindszenty, to John

---

[162] Orsi, "Between Memory and Modernity," in Appleby and Cummings, *Catholics in the American Century.*

Courtney Murray's *We Hold These Truths* (1960), and the founder and Constitution-venerating Roman Catholic conservatives of today, Catholic prelates, writers, scholars, and lawyers assiduously crafted new, assimilative "civic narratives aimed to show how Catholics fit into the American story." Infused by the "sacred memory" of the Church, these narratives went beyond the parameters of civic stories to "[reframe] the American narrative as a recognizably Catholic drama of heroic holiness, suffering, and sacrifice."[163]

Orsi rightly observes that "[t]he ethos of U.S. political conservatism from the 1980s to the present owes much to this Catholic inheritance" (in this regard, among others, Orsi mentions Supreme Court Justices Antonin Scalia and Clarence Thomas, and might have also mentioned Robert Bork and Samuel Alito). Much of the emotional tenor of today's populist constitutional Right, moreover, as expressed, for instance, by Steve Bannon and Bill O'Reilly – and their predecessors like Father Charles Coughlin, Wisconsin Senator Joseph McCarthy, and Patrick Buchanan – is, even more precisely, genealogically and quintessentially Irish-American Catholic. As Orsi explains, this disposition partakes of and feeds "a vein of violence and anger [that] runs through the language of U.S. Catholic citizenship and public life ... marked by stories of the North American martyrs and also by the realities of violence in working class Catholic neighborhoods, by memories of persecution of priests in Ireland and by the humiliations of class in the United States."[164] This refusal to "be purified for modernity," the "Catholic askewness to the modern," remains alive and well – and, indeed, is powerfully ascendant – in contemporary conservatism, including in its efforts to refashion the nation's constitutive understandings, the membership of the Supreme Court, and the future of American constitutional law.[165]

---

[163] Orsi, "Between Memory and Modernity," in Appleby and Cummings, *Catholics in the American Century*, 12, 14–15, 18–21, 23, 25–27, 31, 33. John M. Donovan, *The Pagoda and the Cross: The Life of Bishop Ford of Maryknoll* (New York: Charles Scribner's Sons, 1967); Rev. Harold W. Rigney, SVD, *4 Years in Red Hell* (Chicago: Regnery, 1956). See generally, Smith, *Stories of Peoplehood*; Smith, *Political Peoplehood*.

[164] In illustrating the prevalence of this vein of the American Irish Catholic disposition, Orsi alludes to what he calls the "clerical noir" genre in mid-twentieth-century American popular culture that featured truculent "deeply pious, self-abnegating, and self-punishing" but patriotic Catholic priests, "canny about the nasty ways of the world, impatient with the niggling scruples of democracy, and comfortable with booze and the company of thugs and cops," related with a homoerotic undercurrent, and fed by an "[a]rrogance, intolerance, self-righteousness, and cruelty" that evinced a simultaneous superiority and sense of victimhood. Orsi, "Between Memory and Modernity," 37.

[165] Orsi, "Between Memory and Modernity," 36–38, 40–41. See also Sugrue, "Catholic Encounter with the 1960s," 74–75. Robert H. Bork, *Slouching Toward Gomorrah: Modern Liberalism and American Decline* (New York: HarperCollins, 1996).

Conclusion

The Development of Constitutional Conservatism

After years of marginality and irrelevance during the heyday of American liberalism, when it was variously ignored, diagnosed, dismissed, and denounced, movement conservatism – which, from its inception, rallied for constitutional restoration and redemption – at long last won governing power with Ronald Reagan's election as president. The movement conservative Reagan promised to finally deliver what his predecessor, Barry Goldwater, had only promised – "a choice, not an echo": the restoration of constitutional government in the United States.

Even with a commanding victory, however, the task would not be easy. While dismissed by many as little more than a B-movie actor with a degree from a flyspeck college in his native downstate Illinois – a marked contrast to the pedigreed Ivy Leaguer Robert A. Taft, who might have assumed some version of Reagan's role had he not succumbed to cancer in 1953 – the autodidact Reagan, who had read broadly in many of the magazines and books I have canvassed in this book, was deeply versed in the modern conservative movement's political and constitutional thought. As a former labor union leader and two-term governor of one of the nation's largest states, moreover, Reagan also had a sense of political institutions. A child of the Great Depression and lifelong admirer of Franklin Delano Roosevelt, Reagan had ambitions not simply of election to the nation's highest office or the passage of landmark legislation, but also, like his hero Roosevelt, of regime-changing institutional and constitutional transformation.

By the time Reagan took office, this push for constitutional restoration and redemption – which had been discussed, theorized, and vigorously debated throughout the postwar period by a broad-ranging cohort of philosophically, theologically, and legally inclined conservative thinkers wielding diverse understandings and presumptions and diverse senses of cultural, religious, and professional identity and mission – was whittled down to the focused objective of appointing reliably conservative judges to the federal bench, including the US Supreme Court. Over the course of his pre-presidential career, which spanned the heyday of American liberalism, Reagan spoke frequently about the Constitution, and about appointing judges who would faithfully apply and enforce it. When it came time for him to institute his long-stated objective of constitutional restoration and redemption, Reagan, after some fumbling beginnings under his first attorney general William French Smith, turned to his long-term aide Edwin Meese III, whom he moved from the White House to the top position in the Justice Department, to translate this broadly articulated objective into a targeted plan for practical implementation and enforcement.

Most of the excellent scholarship on the rightward movement in the nation's constitutional law published in recent years has focused on this final, most proximate stage of (conservative) American constitutional development: the founding of The Federalist Society in 1982 (in which Meese participated) and the agenda-setting initiatives of the Meese Justice Department (1985–1988), including the pronouncement of a doctrinal and interpretive fighting faith, a judge-centered, jurisprudentially oriented "originalism," and the establishment of a disciplined system for vetting and appointing federal judges who adhered to it. These mattered – a lot. But they were never the alpha and omega of what modern movement conservatives had truly thought or believed about the Constitution during the heyday of American liberalism, even as they moved toward assuming the reins of power in the 1970s and 1980s. They were, rather, the narrowed and tightly focused game plan – emphasizing a repeatedly reiterated, on-message focus on "judicial restraint" and deference to legislative majorities – for the opening moves in a much larger struggle aimed more broadly at political, institutional, and cultural transformation. This struggle, even as it pertained to constitutional objectives, extended well beyond theories about the hermeneutic responsibilities of life-tenured judges in a tripartite political system in reading (even) a foundational legal text. These broader movement objectives, it is particularly worth noting now, never went away.

Given that bigger picture, to treat the story of the ascent of constitutional conservatism as chiefly involving the triumph of The Federalist Society is to be transfixed by the iceberg's tip while overlooking the hulking mass looming below. For movement conservatives *outside the law schools* – that is, for most movement conservatives – conservative constitutional theory and thought have always been deeply embedded in conservative political thought and conservative political identities more generally – as, of course, had been the progressive/liberal constitutional thought that underwrote the Progressive/ Liberal New Deal/Great Society regime. For liberals inclined to conspiracy theories centered on the mobilized legal elites of The Federalist Society, the news is actually a whole lot worse than they may have imagined. The mobilization for the restoration and redemption of constitutional government in the United States in its modern form, as conservatives understood it, dates way back, in ways that are strikingly wide, arrestingly deep, and, as far as liberals should be concerned, disturbingly ambitious. To all this, liberal responses charging conservative judges with being "judicial activists" and not deferring to "majoritarian legislatures" are laughably inapposite.

In all this, it seems to me, liberals are still punching in the dark. They do not know much about conservative *constitutional* thought from the 1930s forward because, as they saw it, they had said goodbye to all that in the late 1930s: it was pointless, reactionary, and irrelevant; it had nothing to do with the future and its problems and aspirations. For all they knew, outside The John Birch Society and the White Citizens Councils, it had ceased to exist. This general ignorance was only reinforced by the professionalization of constitutional thought during the heyday of American liberalism – by its domestication into a form of elite, regime-enforcing professional knowledge, as something practiced or "done" by law professors in the nation's law schools and, in turn, implemented by the nation's (liberal) judges. Since however much they spoke and wrote about the Constitution – and they wrote and spoke a lot about the Constitution – conservatives – political scientists, political philosophers, independent scholars, practicing lawyers, journalists, theologians, and social movement actors, even those with PhDs and those who would go on to win Nobel Prizes – were not speaking and writing as credentialed *legal academic* professionals, they were, by definition, not really doing "constitutional theory." When it came to the courts and their intimate associates in legal academia and the broader legal culture, legal liberals called the tune and set the agenda, all the while policing the "boundary conditions" of what counted as serious, and relevant, constitutional ideas, scholarship, and thought.

Liberals were jarred awake, to be sure, by Ronald Reagan's election and his bid to appoint originalist judges to the federal bench, including the Supreme Court. They *could* and *did* see and understand the rather late-in-the-game appearance of The Federalist Society, conservative legal mobilization, and law school–style originalism in the 1980s. To them, *that*, at least, was legible. And why shouldn't it be? It was written in big letters in their own language. It was spoken by the types of people they knew (more or less) in a language and idiom they could understand, in a way that had addressed their own historical preoccupations and concerns. This late-stage conservative bid for power was taking place, after all, on the liberals' home turf: it was launched from within the elite institutions liberals controlled and played by the rules of the game that liberals had set since the Progressive Era. Those rules provided that points in the constitutional theory game were to be awarded for winning drives in theoretical debates about the duty and powers of countermajoritarian judges problematically exercising their judicial review powers as against the ostensibly majoritarian claims of legislatures. The extensive scholarly and popular focus on legalist originalism as advanced by the likes of Robert Bork, Antonin Scalia, and The Federalist Society as the core conservative understanding of the Constitution channeled scholarly attention to judges – the outsized preoccupation of most law professors – and foregrounded themes of textual interpretation and fidelity and judicial role and duty.

As the Right has steadily gained political power since the 1980s, however – including the power to appoint judges and shape law – the great hulking mass of conservative constitutional thought that did not focus disproportionately on judges and was deeply embedded in the substance of conservative political thought more generally began vying with the originalist legalism of Bork, Scalia, and The Federalist Society for a starring role on the constitutionalist Right, a role that, in their own way within the movement – if not, to be sure, in the law schools – conservative constitutionalists had never actually relinquished. *This* constitutionalist Right had never limited itself to instructing judges in the "matter of interpretation" and in institutional role, but was deeply engaged in telling stories to movement members and would-be recruits about who they were and their critical role in the American national story as founders, citizens, cultural and constitutional centurions, and constitutional redeemers.

As these redemptionist and restorationist themes have moved to the center of right-wing movement politics in recent years, they have underwritten increasingly vigorous challenges to New Deal/Rights Revolution constitutional understandings, including radical challenges to the entire "administrative state" and to long-settled understandings of the substance of constitutional rights.[1] It may soon be the case that we will not be able to understand even conservative judges and their approach to textual interpretation and judicial role and duty without an appreciation for the deeper restorationist or redemptivist visions in which they have long been embedded, and their elaborately constructed historical memories, principles, and philosophies.[2]

DEVELOPMENT

There is no denying that conservative legal mobilization and legal academic originalist constitutional theory have played critical roles in the trajectory of the modern Right. But it is essential to contextualize and situate that influence. Its greatest accomplishments registered at a certain stage in the postwar Right's developmental trajectory. Legal mobilization, after all, only makes sense strategically when there is at least some prospect of influencing a cohort of

---

[1] See Gillian Metzger, "The Supreme Court, 2016 Term – Foreword: 1930s Redux: The Administrative State Under Siege," *Harvard Law Review* 131 (2017): 1

[2] Post and Siegel, "Originalism as a Political Practice." See also Logan Sawyer III, "Why the Right Embraced Rights," *Harvard Journal of Law and Public Policy*, 40:3 (2016): 729–757; Logan Sawyer III, "Principle and Politics in the New History of Originalism," *American Journal of Legal History* 57 (2017): 198.

sympathetic judges. As that judicial cohort expands and becomes increasingly self-confident – and, presumably, increasingly legitimate and legitimized – the arguments movement claimants make to that cohort of judges will change. The judges will be increasingly asked by mobilized conservatives to draw on their newfound power to actively constitutionalize ideological *substance* instead of passively performing institutional deference (to legislatures, e.g., or executive agencies). Put otherwise, the movement and its professional judges will have moved from a loose alliance to full *substantive* alignment.

From its wilderness years during the heyday of American liberalism, the fledgling postwar American conservative movement expressed a profound sense of dispossession and repeatedly called for constitutional restoration and redemption. If this call was originalist, it was so in a broader, more philosophical, and more contested way than the law school–based, legalist originalism that later became synonymous with conservative constitutionalism. Far from being a weaponized conspiracy by an ideologically streamlined group, however, the alternative tradition of conservative constitutional theory in these wilderness years reflected both the movement's intellectual diversity and its political pluralism. Such was the state of the Right's all-but-invisible constitutional theory in the heyday of American liberalism.

But time moved forward, and things happened. The polity, the conservative movement, and the nation's political parties changed. The movement's constituency – and eventually the Republican Party, within which the movement was an outsider insurgency – altered. So too did the conservative movement's relation to political and, subsequently, academic/institutional power. These developments were reflected in shifts in relative prominence and influence of different strands and strains of the postwar movement's diverse and pluralistic constitutional theory. Following the passage of the Civil Rights Act of 1964, the passage of the Voting Rights Act of 1965, and the successes of the civil rights movement more generally, neo-confederate constitutional argument was increasingly driven to the fringes. During the turmoil and divisions of the long 1960s and the launching of Lyndon Johnson's Great Society, a cohort of ex-liberal intellectuals, the neoconservatives, joined the movement and were soon wielding an intellectual influence disproportionate to their relatively small numbers.

For all intents and purposes, as noted earlier, there were at that time no conservative constitutional theorists in the legal academy.[3] But beginning in the mid-to-late 1960s, a cohort of influential *liberal* constitutional theorists, mostly born in the 1920s, who had never relinquished the hostility to activist judges inculcated in them by their progressive mentors like Felix Frankfurter, found themselves increasingly read and praised by conservative movement participants. When this elite cohort of legal academics, schooled in

---

[3] To be sure, there must have been legal scholars who were conservatives. But they did not produce conservative constitutional theory.

Progressive Era critiques of activist courts and judges and the promise of unimpeded majoritarian democracy, was confronted with the liberal activist Warren Court in the 1950s and 1960s, it marshaled the old progressive/ Frankfurtian critique of the "problem" of countermajoritarian courts in which they had been reared. For their efforts in championing this *procedural* commitment to a (mostly) restrained and deferential judiciary, these liberals, like Felix Frankfurter himself, found themselves being spoken of as "conservative" or "neoconservative" – a designation that, given their still strongly held progressive/liberal *substantive* commitments, they, also like Frankfurter, futilely disavowed. It was this challenge to the Warren Court, and the relatively narrow constitutional theory that underwrote it, that was soon adopted by the fledgling legalist wing of an ascendant conservative movement – by, for example, Robert Bork and Antonin Scalia – and became the basis for the proceduralist originalism that trumpeted the claims of democratic majorities and criticized the extensive exercise of judicial review by activist courts and judges. By dint of this developmental trajectory, the old progressive constitutional theory became the new conservative constitutional theory. The Federalist Society was founded by an up-and-coming set of conservative law students at Yale and the University of Chicago law schools in large part to discuss and promote this new legal proceduralist originalism. When, at long last, with the election of Ronald Reagan, conservatives – going from outsiders to insiders – took power, these young law students, now graduated, nabbed prime federal court clerkships for the likes of Reagan appointees Robert Bork and Antonin Scalia, and high positions in the Meese Justice Department, setting the stage for distinguished academic careers. Many others followed. And from the 1980s forward, originalism ascended to a respected status as one of the touchstone, professionally approved (albeit hotly disputed) legal academic constitutional theories.

But the story did not end there either. Once in power, and once conservatives were appointed to the bench and secured prestigious academic appointments, the attraction to conservatives of the proceduralist appeal for judicial deference to majorities began to wane. At an earlier stage in the movement's developmental trajectory, the deferential proceduralist stance aligned with the movement's substantive commitments. But now that the judges were increasingly their own people rather than agents of the political opposition, this was no longer the case.

But along with the conservative movement in the courts, the conservative movement in the executive (the White House, the Justice Department), and the conservative movement in the law schools, the conservative movement in the Republican Party was also changing. With Reagan's triumph, movement conservatives had at long last seized control of the party, along with the political power to implement their substantive political and constitutional vision. And, as it happened, a major engine driving this final step in the movement's long march from the wilderness to power was a co-belligerent Religious Right, especially, at the time, Evangelical and Fundamentalist Christians, many of whom had heretofore been Democrats. This group, of course, had almost no active ties to either the New York City–based neoconservatives or the elite law students who had founded The Federalist Society. This motley assortment, aflame with their own concerns and ambitions for law, the courts, and the Constitution, now found themselves fledgling political bedfellows.

By the 1980s, the racism and segregationism of Fundamentalist Christians (especially) was at long last a nonstarter on the mainstream movement Right. Even the more passive indifference to racism among Evangelical Christians was now embarrassing – a rebuke to their stance and self-conception as uncompromising moralists. It was here that the sort of entrepreneurial culture work discussed by the political scientists Adam Sheingate, Victoria Hattam, and Joseph Lowndes was especially needed. Conservative Christians like Francis Schaeffer took the lead in formulating a new constitutional positioning that would actively condemn racism and shunt the old neo-confederatism to the side. They did so by elevating a new set of "culture war" issues – abortion, most importantly, but subsequently bioethics and gay rights – to the front lines of the moral crusade. Although Schaeffer, like perhaps most of his Evangelical and Fundamentalist co-religionists at the time, loathed Roman Catholicism, his newfound fixation on abortion – which, as we have seen, he initially resisted strenuously on the ground that it was "a Catholic issue" – set in motion a rapprochement with pro-life Catholics that served as a foundation for a broadly based, co-belligerent Religious Right in which conservative Catholics, and even LDS/Mormons (long considered beyond the pale), were increasingly welcomed as equal partners. As it happened, while they had had virtually no previous contact with Evangelical and Fundamentalist Christians, The Federalist Society counted plenty of conservative Catholics (and Jews too) among its founders and early membership. These elite proponents of legalist originalism may have, consistent with their training at Yale, the University of Chicago, and elsewhere, (initially) opposed *Roe* on proceduralist/majoritarian judicial restraint grounds. But they did not seem to have reservations about allying themselves with those whose aversion to *Roe* may have arisen out of substantive theological commitments – and convictions concerning an apocalyptic civilizational crisis. It was an "incompletely theorized agreement," to be sure, but for the time being – and onward to today – it was apparently good enough.[4]

---

[4] Cass R. Sunstein, "Incompletely Theorized Agreements in Constitutional Law," *Social Research* 74 (Spring 2007): 1–24. See also John S. Dryzek and Simon Niemeyer, "Reconciling Pluralism and Consensus Political Ideals," *American Journal of Political Science* 50 (July 2006): 634–649. Conservative Roman Catholic Federalist Society members in some, and perhaps even most, cases may have shared the theological commitments of the Evangelicals and Fundamentalists concerning abortion – commitments that had, after all, largely originated in Catholic doctrine. But they had, at least until recently, been socialized and educated that such religious beliefs and theological commitments were no proper business of law, especially constitutional law, and should largely be confined to the private sphere.

The Evangelical and Fundamentalist Christians who played a key role in sweeping Ronald Reagan into power – the so-called Moral Majority – told deep constitutive stories about the American Founders, the US Constitution, and the contemporary United States. In doing so, they repeatedly analogized their newly launched culture war crusades to nineteenth-century crusades against chattel slavery, in the process nicely positioning themselves as the legatees of Frederick Douglass, Abraham Lincoln, and (the Christian minister) Martin Luther King Jr., and casting liberal/progressive proponents of abortion, gay rights, and the right to die as pro-slavery and anti–civil rights. Successful bridges were built under the auspices of a newly declared culture war to the already anti-abortion, anti–gay rights, and anti–right to die Catholics – who had long been considered liberals when economic issues had been foregrounded – and also to the (always pro–civil rights, circa 1964–1965) neoconservatives, who, in the wake of the tumultuous late 1960s, were increasingly emphasizing the contributions that religious faith, moral discipline, and strong families had made to the promotion of a healthy social order.

An alliance with free market proponents required that many Evangelical and Fundamentalist Christians start thinking in new ways about government regulation of the economy. As Kevin Kruse has shown, some of that had been there from the beginning, particularly among successful Christian businessmen. But, for what was not, a new set of Evangelical, Fundamentalist, and right-wing Roman Catholic theologians set themselves to work, quieting any remaining critiques of the effects of anti-regulatory free market capitalism as culture war issues moved to the fore. All of this was wrapped up in an overarching story of the crisis of Christian civilization – manna to the Religious Right, and to some conservatives generally, across the postwar period – on the verge of succumbing to an existential threat launched by the secularlists, humanists, positivists, historicists, and nihilists who supported abortion, socialism, and gay rights. To date, nearly half a century after President Reagan's election, this political, and constitutional, coalition has held.

CURRENT TRENDS: VICARIOUS ABOLITIONISM AND THOMIST NATIONALISM

If the call for constitutional restoration or redemption had been a motivating and unifying rallying cry of the modern conservative movement during the heyday of American liberalism, this book has shown that it nevertheless came in several versions, each underwritten by different – if, after some serious culture work, ultimately compatible – constitutive stories about where the country has been, where it is, and where it could or is likely to go. There are, after all, different ways of telling the story of how the Constitution came into being and why; what it was, did, and does; how it was used, respected, honored, lost, abandoned, or betrayed; how it succeeded or failed, proved durable, workable, distorting, hopeless, or malign; who it helped or hurt, served, advanced, privileged, marginalized, or oppressed; when any of these things happened, or did not; who deserves credit, honor, or blame; and what these imply or teach about the contemporary and future problems and possibilities of individuals, the nation, and humanity. Progressives and liberals told these stories, or demurred, in a family of ways. So too did conservatives. Each, in so doing, constructed a distinctive – and alternative – constitutional consciousness.

For conservatives, as this book has also shown, redemption was a keynote. Needless to say, the idea, in the United States, is highly freighted. Historically, it has perhaps been most commonly been used in two contexts, one regional and the other religious, which only compounds the concept's embeddedness. "Redemption" has long been the term used to describe the process by which, in the aftermath of the Confederacy's defeat in the Civil War, military occupation, and "Reconstruction," the southern states sought to regain their powers of home rule with the primary aim of reestablishing white supremacy. It is a familiar charge on the contemporary liberal-left that modern conservatism is little more than a push to, in essence, revive and restore the Old Confederacy, reeking of white supremacism, White Citizens Councils, and constitutionalist resistance to civil rights.[5] Especially given the revival of an avowed and explicit white supremacism on the Right in recent years – with the winking approval from a Republican president who has, notwithstanding, consistently enjoyed widespread popularity among Republican voters, including, and especially, white Evangelical and Fundamentalist Christians – it is easy enough to double-down on these charges.[6] Doing so, however, would lead one off the scent of one of the most significant trends in the development of the constitutional consciousness of the contemporary American Right: the perhaps surprising degree to which its denizens have come to associate themselves not with racism but with *anti-racism*. Indeed, as I have argued at various points in this book in my discussions of the stories told by Evangelical and Fundamentalist Christians, right-wing Roman Catholics, and West Coast Straussians, this shift in movement self-understanding was an inflection point for the broader movement's turn away from constitutional resistance to civil rights after the passage of the Civil Rights Act of 1964 and the Voting Rights Act

---

[5] For both acknowledgment of the resistance and added subtleties concerning the developmental path forward, see Christopher W. Schmidt, "Litigating Against the Civil Rights Movement," *University of Colorado Law Review* 86 (2015): 1173–1220. See also Nancy MacLean, "Neo-Confederacy Versus the New Deal: The Regional Utopia of the Modern American Right," in Joseph Crespino and Matthew Lassiter, editors, *The Myth of Southern Exceptionalism* (New York: Oxford University Press, 2010); Christopher W. Schmidt, "Beyond Backlash: Conservatism and the Civil Rights Movement," *American Journal of Legal History* 56 (2016): 179–194.
[6] See George Hawley, *Making Sense of the Alt-Right* (New York: Columbia University Press, 2017); Carol M. Swain, *The New White Nationalism in America: Its Challenge to Integration* (New York: Cambridge University Press, 2002).

of 1965 and toward a new chapter in its history of constitutional resistance in the culture wars of the 1970s and 1980s.[7]

It is significant but all too rarely noticed that, in recent years, movement conservatives who speak, write, and think about the Constitution, especially on the Roman Catholic, Evangelical, and Fundamentalist Christian Right, have become second to none in repeatedly and aggressively denouncing chattel slavery. Indeed, for those who care to look, it can sometimes seem that slavery, abolitionism, Frederick Douglass, and Abraham Lincoln are now the *major scholarly interest* of the constitutionalist Right in the age of the culture wars.[8] While this strident – and, I would underscore, *vicarious* – abolitionism on the Right seems to strangely co-exist with a palpable indifference to the concerns of contemporary African Americans on issues such as the carceral state, police brutality, voting rights, and the racism of President Trump (among others), within the context of the developmental trajectory of the constitutionalist Right, it is *not* surprising and makes a lot of sense: the second-to-none commitment of the contemporary culture wars Right to abolishing chattel slavery serves a key theoretical point for right-wing Roman Catholics,

---

[7] Hunter, *Culture Wars.*

[8] As a major theme of the contemporary Right, the examples are legion, and too many to list. They are the primary focus, among many others, of the work of Justin Buckley Dyer, Lucas Morel, and Allan Guelzo. See, e.g., Justin Buckley Dyer, *Natural Law and the Antislavery Constitutional Tradition* (New York: Cambridge University Press, 2012); Justin Buckley Dyer, *Slavery, Abortion, and the Politics of Constitutional Meaning* (New York: Cambridge University Press, 2013); Lucas Morel, editor, *Lincoln and Liberty: Wisdom for the Ages* (Lexington: University Press of Kentucky, 2015); Lucas Morel, "Lincoln, God, and Freedom: A Promise Fulfilled," in Harold Holzer and Sara Gabbard, editors, *Lincoln and Freedom: Slavery, Emancipation, and the Thirteenth Amendment* (Carbondale: Southern Illinois University Press, 2007); Allan Guezlo, *Abraham Lincoln: Redeemer President* (Grand Rapids, MI: Wm. B. Eerdmans Publishing Co., 1999). See also, e.g., Hadley Arkes, "Lincoln, Nietzsche, and the Constitution," *First Things* (April 2000); John Burt and Diana Schaub, "A CRB Discussion of Abraham Lincoln and Moral Conflict," *Claremont Review of Books* (February 19, 2014) (online edition) www.claremont.org/crb/basicpage/a-crb-discussion-of-abraham-lincoln-and-moral-conflict/; James G. Basker, "Freedom's March," *Claremont Review of Books* (September 9, 2011) (reviewing Seymour Drescher, *Abolition: A History of Slavery and Antislavery*, www.claremont.org/crb/basicpage/freedoms-march/). Peter W. Schramm, "Douglass and Lincoln," *Claremont Review of Books* 9:1 (Winter 2008/2009). Discussions of Lincoln, Douglass, and the evils of chattel slavery, moreover, are currently one of the most common touchstones of right-wing articles and debates on all manner of contemporary intellectual and policy issues. The point stands despite the fact that Abraham Lincoln, was not an abolitionist but was, more precisely, anti-slavery. Frederick Douglass, another hero of the modern Right, was, of course, an abolitionist and, moreover, unlike the Garrisonians and like Lincoln, made his case by appealing to the stated principles of the nation's Constitution, especially as he held them to be foundationally underwritten by those proclaimed near the opening of the Declaration of Independence. The consideration of the Declaration and the Constitution side-by-side allows for all manor of debates about strategy, prudence, conscience, resistance, and statesmanship in the face of great moral evil (read, today: abortion rights and gay rights), and the presumed liberal/progressive effort to excise God and his laws from the American political and constitutional tradition.

Evangelical and Fundamentalists Christians, and West Coast Straussians about belief, faith, and morals – an issue largely irrelevant to the earlier civil rights era conservative constitutional resistance of the 1950s and 1960s. Vicarious abolitionism has been the rocket fuel the contemporary constitutionalist Right has used to launch and fight the culture wars.

In this, black people – except to the extent that they are themselves conservative Christians – are largely irrelevant: they represent, rather, a starting point, a philosophical first premise. In the contemporary right-wing constitutional consciousness, black people stand as signifiers for the proposition that there is such thing as clear, absolute, moral right and wrong (see chattel slavery). As such, the fire-breathing abolitionism of the contemporary Right serves as a bludgeon to pummel liberals – or, rather, progressives – who, presumably, are thoroughgoing positivists, utilitarians, historicists, secularists, cultural relativists, and nihilists. On what firm philosophical grounds, after all, the argument and assertion go, could these progressives/ liberals hold chattel slavery to be morally wrong? "None whatsoever!" says the contemporary Evangelical and Fundamentalist Christian, Roman Catholic, and Straussian Right. If this is the deep story and the mobilized historical memory, as these right-wing thought-leaders see it, then we as a nation are facing the crisis of the house divided in a new guise. Other strands and strains of the conservative movement like libertarians and business conservatives, of course, continue to exist. But, as I write, this particular constitutive story has moved to the center of the contemporary conservative movement. And we would be remiss not to note that, in this drama, conservatives are cast in the roles of Frederick Douglass and Abraham Lincoln, while the liberals and progressives are cast as Roger Brooke Taney, the infamous author of *Dred Scott*, and the slavery-accommodating Illinois Senator Stephen A. Douglas ... if not worse.

While most people might think that chattel slavery in the United States – and the courageous Christian abolitionists who opposed it – are confined to the American past, the contemporary American Right is broadcasting far and wide that no one has stood more courageously against slavery than today's right-wing Roman Catholics, Evangelical and Fundamentalist Christians, and West Coast Straussians, with the late Professor Harry V. Jaffa (who provided the *ur*-text) leading the way, with an assist from the anti-slavery[9] Murrayist Thomist Catholic Robert P. George and the anti-slavery Straussian Catholic convert Hadley Arkes, and a host of lesser lights. To be sure, they had been too young to serve and fight in the first war. But they can relive it in their writings and ride into battle once again,[10] by massing against contemporary manifestations of positivism, utilitarianism, historicism, secularism, cultural relativism, and

---

[9] And anti-masturbation.
[10] Or, alternatively, if the analogy is Nazism – and it often is – bunker down with Churchill during the Blitz.

nihilism that had (so they seem to believe) laid the foundations for chattel slavery, and chattel slavery's contemporary legacy in the push for progressivism and abortion rights and gay rights.

The vicarious abolitionism prominent and ascendant on the contemporary culture wars constitutional Right had been complemented by a conjointly ascendant Murrayist Thomist nationalism. As should be plain from this book's chapters on "The Alternative Tradition of Conservative Constitutional Theory" and "Right-Wing Roman Catholic Stories," this form of constitutionalist nationalism, as practiced by Princeton's Robert P. George and others, is a revival of that advanced at mid-century in Father John Courtney Murray's *We Hold These Truths* (1960) – albeit in a different context, for different ends, and, arguably, in a very different spirit.

John Courtney Murray's nationalist constitutional theory – which, in its time, sounded in "vital center" liberalism, in conjunction with the Catholic Church's Vatican II reforms – was fashioned as part of the push in the 1950s and 1960s for full Catholic civic integration into the American political project at the time the nation (for many, with great misgivings) was electing its first Roman Catholic president. President Kennedy's own path to civic integration and national leadership as a Catholic entailed a full assent to mainstream Rights Revolution constitutional liberalism, as most emphatically expressed in the much-noted speech Kennedy delivered as a presidential candidate to the Greater Houston Ministerial Association. Father John Courtney Murray's contemporaneous constitutional liberalism was also a document of assent, but with a subtext. Whereas Kennedy seemed to truly believe in the separation of church and state, the sacrosanct nature of individual liberties, and democracy (he was, as the Episcopal Bishop James Pike repeatedly pleaded at the time, a modern American), the Jesuit Murray's assent to the American political project was a much more intricate and subtle affair. While trumpeting his assent to modern liberalism, Murray nevertheless made it perfectly clear to his careful – but perhaps not his casual – readers that that assent was offered only temporarily as an agreement under current conditions to sign onto "articles of peace" with liberal modernity. These articles of peace, Murray suggested, would of course remain in force for the foreseeable future – until the time that (an un-liberal/anti-liberal) Roman Catholic truth – that is, Truth – could be restored to its rightful place in the affairs of men. Once that happened, Murray intimated, all bets were off.

In its time and context, this more worrisome argument of Murray's, the subtext of *We Hold These Truths*, was largely ignored, since, besides being quite subtly expressed, it was irrelevant. In the context of the subsequent rise of the Religious Right and the outbreak of the culture wars, however, as contemporary conservative constitutionalists have recognized, it is anything but. With the prospect of right-wing Christian rule at hand, Murray's Thomist nationalism has been transformed from shield to sword.

At the time it was published in 1960, *We Hold These Truths* was taken to be a major leap forward in the liberalization and Americanization of the Catholic Church. As such, it was largely opposed by the Catholic Right of its day. By the late twentieth century, by contrast, the Catholic Right was coming to appreciate more and more the degree to which Father Murray had carefully made space for the triumph of their own understandings of Truth, as discerned by the Church, but had set aside for another day any hopes for imposing them via constitutional law. Murray, they saw, had demurred on the question of how to get from here to there. With the successful mobilization of the Religious Right in the late 1970s and early 1980s and, in turn, its capture of the Republican Party, however, the Catholic Right was coming to appreciate that, since the time Murray had written, the ball had been advanced far down field surprisingly quickly. Finding themselves unexpectedly first-and-goal, the intellectual leaders of the contemporary Christian Right realized that it was time to stop arguing technical points of constitutional theory with a feckless secular liberal enemy and devote their full time and efforts to forging a new constitutional Christian theology aimed at solidifying, first, a unified Christian Right, and then a unified Right, *tout court*, whose constitutional understandings had been fundamentally remade under conservative Christian auspices.

Today, that project is at the heart of much of modern conservative constitutional thought and theory, which is why, in recent years, that thought and theory – most of which remains unknown to most Americans, including elite American constitutional law scholars – has assumed such a palpably theological cast. John Courtney Murray's challenge – asking what is to be done about Truth in a nation that seems so apparently steeped in liberal modernity – has become the ground on which the more intellectually ambitious and influential precincts of the modern constitutionalist Right – the Evangelicals, Fundamentalists, Pentecostals, Mormons, Straussians, and Roman Catholics – now meet as part of the co-belligerent constitutional "resistance." Libertarians, (non-Straussian) neoconservatives, business conservatives, and old-school Federalist Society legalists are positioned somewhat outside this increasingly vocal constitutionalist core. But they have been acknowledged by the rising powers, and, so far, fairly successful efforts have been made within the coalition to work together and find constitutionalist common ground.

Given their long history of religious enmity, one might have thought that Evangelical and Fundamentalist Christians (and other right-wing Protestants and LDS/Mormons) might not be especially receptive to newly rooting their efforts to remake – they would say "renew" or "restore" – American constitutionalism in Thomist Roman Catholic theology. Recent statements from key figures on the intellectual Christian Right, however, suggest otherwise. The politically engaged Evangelical historian Mark Noll – formerly of Wheaton College but now at the University of Notre Dame – for instance, has prominently lamented his own faith tradition's lack of a rigorously systematic philosophy, which he has contrasted with that of the Church of Rome.[11] The active reconstruction of historical memory has played a critical role in this process. The scholarly division of each branch of the contemporary Religious Right, for instance, has undertaken significant work that has sought to re-narrate the history of the nineteenth-century legal and constitutional order – to which they are campaigning to return – on its own terms, but in ways that are self-consciously compatible with the stories being told by their now co-belligerent compatriots: Evangelicals and Fundamentalist Christian legal scholars, for instance, can advocate the return to the aggressive enforcement of morals laws by emphasizing what they take to be the Christian foundations of the common law (as I have detailed in Chapter 5 on "Evangelical and Fundamentalist Christian Stories"), while right-wing Thomist Roman Catholic constitutional theorists can reach the same destination via a teleological-philosophical reading of constitutional rights, as rooted in Murrayist readings of the Declaration of Independence. In this regard, Roman Catholic constitutionalists now sing the praises of the once largely presumed and un-theorized nineteenth-century US Protestant moral order – and, for good measure, of the role that Godly Evangelical Christians played at the same time in ending chattel slavery[12] – while Evangelicals like Mark Noll, in return, sing the praises of the admirably more systematic theology of the Catholics, who have methodically and brilliantly articulated precisely why, although they had never been able to adequately articulate it before, their moral positions are indeed right. As the right-wing Roman Catholic theologians/constitutional theorists with whom they are now communing have explained, they are right not simply because their understandings are commanded by Scripture but also because they are the only reasonable positions to take. This Roman Catholic explication has brought the added bonus of making it perfectly clear (to right-wing Evangelical and Fundamentalist Christians, at least) that in joining with their right-wing Catholic brethren in imposing those understandings on the country – in writing them into constitutional law – they are *not* imposing their religious views on others – as theocrats, that is – but simply following the path of moral logic to which any reasonable person must assent.

[11] See Mark A. Noll and Carolyn Nystrom, *Is the Reformation Over? An Evangelical Assessment of Contemporary Roman Catholicism* (Grand Rapids, MI: Baker Academic, 2005) (winner of the *Christianity Today* Book Award (2006)).

[12] In truth, it was mostly *northern* Evangelical Christians. But, as one would predict, the distinction between the northern Evangelical abolitionists who opposed chattel slavery and the many (white) *southern* Evangelical Christians who fervently enlisted Scripture *in justifying and defending it* is a distinction on which the contemporary Christian Right, rooted in the South, chooses not to dwell. John Patrick Daly, *When Slavery Was Called Freedom: Evangelicalism, Proslavery, and the Causes of the Civil War* (Lexington: University Press of Kentucky, 2002); "Why Did So Many Christians Support Slavery?" *Christianity Today* (https://www.christianitytoday.com/history/issues/issue-33/why-christians-supported-slavery.html).

What disagreement remains on the Christian and Straussian constitutionalist Right – and it does remain – about the appropriate underlying political and constitutional theory currently serves as fodder for a lively series of academic debates taking place among friends and compatriots in a rapidly proliferating number of symposia, roundtables, and conferences and in a publication boom in scholarly books and articles on these themes. Within this "interpretative community"[13] of scholars – and the politicians, lawyers, journalists, and activists who are being influenced by them – the underlying understanding and premise is that in the battle for the control of the nation and its constitutional law, whatever their disagreements, they clearly stand on one side of the battle lines and their liberal/progressive/relativist/positivist/historicist/nihilist/anti-American antagonists stand on the other. In this way, the stories told by the contemporary movement's vicarious abolitionists and Thomist nationalists about constitutional redemption and restoration have knitted them together and helped define the "us" and "them" of contemporary American politics.

What does any of this have to do with originalism – the focus of almost all of the discussion of and writings on conservatives and the Constitution since at least the early 1980s? Nothing ... and everything. "Nothing" in the sense that, aside from its legal academic Old Guard, the contemporary conservative movement does not retain any proceduralist commitment to the view that, with the exception of clear and rare cases, unelected, life-tenured judges have any institutional duty to defer to the constitutional assumptions and understandings of the nation's majoritarian, democratically elected legislatures.[14] "Everything" in the sense that the entire project is steeped in the conviction that liberals and progressives have abandoned and betrayed the constitutional commitments forged by the nation's Founders and ratified by "We the People," and that it is the duty and calling of contemporary conservatives to restore "The Founders' Constitution," and, in so doing, *Make America Great Again*.

THE TRUMP GAMBIT

> 2016 is the Flight 93 election: charge the cockpit or you die. You may die anyway. You – or the leader of your party – may make it into the cockpit and not know how to fly or land the plane. There are no guarantees. Except one: if you don't try, death

---

[13] Stanley Fish, *Is there a Text in this Class? The Authority of Interpretive Communities* (Cambridge, MA: Harvard University Press, 1980).
[14] On the "old" or "preemptive" originalism, see Jamal Greene, "On the Origins of Originalism," *Texas Law Review* 88 (2009): 1; Jamal Greene, "Selling Originalism," *Georgetown Law Journal* 97 (2009): 657; Whittington, "The New Originalism"; Kersch, "Ecumenicalism Through Constitutionalism." If one considers these purportedly proceduralist commitments of the likes of Robert Bork, Edwin Meese, and Antonin Scalia, among others, as strategic and instrumental – as, in fact, not truly institutionalist/proceduralist, but, in truth, substantive, motivated not by a theory of a fixed relation of courts to legislatures, but rather at cabining, or even reversing, the Warren Court Rights Revolution – however, the matter looks rather different.

is certain. To compound the metaphor, a Hillary Clinton presidency is Russian Roulette with a semi-auto. With Trump, at least you can spin the cylinder and take your chances.

Publius Decius Mus [Michael Anton][15]

The presidential election of 2016 posed a serious dilemma for an American Right that had, most recently with the Tea Party movement, placed a commitment to constitutional redemption at the center of its political mobilization. As Christopher Schmidt has detailed, the Tea Party's vision of constitutional restoration and redemption was "akin to a fundamentalist religious revivalism, with the text of the Constitution serving the role of scripture." The Tea Party's constitutional populism was fed by a heightened, and heavily moralized, sense of national crisis.[16] That vision's central tenets in what they held to be a time of crisis were as follows:

One, the solutions to the problems facing the United States . . . can be found in the words of the Constitution and the insights of its framers. Two, the meaning of the Constitution and the lessons of history are . . . readily accessible to American citizens who take the time to educate themselves. Three, all Americans, not just lawyers and judges, have a responsibility to understand the Constitution and act faithfully toward it. And four, the overarching purpose of the Constitution is to ensure that the role of government, and particularly the federal government, is a limited one; only by following constitutionally defined constraints on government can individual liberties be preserved.[17]

With the nation's first black president in the White House and what seemed to be the country's first woman president in the wings, the sense of crisis on the American Right reached an apotheosis of sorts with the publication of Michael Anton's "The Flight 93 Election" in the online edition of the (West Coast Straussian) *Claremont Review of Books*.[18] There, analogizing the choice facing Republican voters in the Trump-Clinton contest to the choice facing passengers on the Al Qaeda–hijacked United Airlines Flight 93 on September 11, Anton – who holds advanced degrees from the "Great Books" St. John's College in Annapolis, Maryland, and the Straussian Claremont Graduate University – argued, against a list of "Never Trump" conservatives that included the neoconservatives David

---

[15] Publius Decius Mus [Michael Anton], "The Flight 93 Election," *The Claremont Review of Books* (September 5, 2016) (online edition) (www.claremont.org/crb/basicpage/the-flight-93-election/). This quotation is published as an epigraph by permission of *The Claremont Review of Books*.

[16] See generally Jan-Werner Müeller, *What Is Populism?* (Philadelphia: University of Pennsylvania Press, 2016).

[17] Christopher W. Schmidt, "The Tea Party and the Constitution," *Hastings Constitutional Law Quarterly* 39 (Fall 2011): 193–252, 194, 198. As Schmidt points out, the TV host Glenn Beck's "9–12 Project" of about the same time championed similar tenets. See also Christopher W. Schmidt, "Popular Constitutionalism on the Right: Lessons from the Tea Party," *Denver University Law Review* 88 (2011): 523.

[18] Publius Decius Mus, "The Flight 93 Election." The influential right-wing radio talk show host Rush Limbaugh read Anton's article aloud in its entirety on his show.

Frum and William Kristol and other high-profile thought-leaders like Ross Douthat and Reihan Salam, that "constitutionalist conservatives" were facing a crisis so dire that even likely death was preferable to submission. The core of Anton's article chastised anti-Trump conservatives – "Conservatism, Inc. . . . keepers of the *status quo*" – as traitors to the cause and the movement who, it was now apparent to Anton, had never taken the nation's constitutional crisis seriously; if they had, Publius Decius Mus thundered, they would recognize that "*we are headed off a cliff*" and know exactly what to do: pull the lever for Donald Trump, the only "hope for a restoration of our cherished ideals."[19]

Whatever might be Trump's many, freely admitted personal failings and potential weaknesses as candidate and president – Anton characterized the pugnacious New York City real estate developer, reality television star, libertine, and vulgarian as "worse than imperfect" – Anton insisted that "[i]f conservatives are right about the importance of virtue, morality, religious faith, stability, character and so on in the individual; if they are right about sexual morality or what came to be termed 'family values'; if they are right about the importance of education to inculcate good character," they had to vote for Trump: he at least promised to throw his body against the gears, and the positions he had adopted on the core conservative issues were at least right.[20]

While shocking some, the vivid, last-ditch, hell-bent framing offered by Anton – subsequently a member of President Trump's national security team before leaving to join Hillsdale College's Allan P. Kirby Jr. Center for Constitutional Studies and Citizenship[21] – analogizing progressives and liberals to 9/11 terrorists intent on taking down the nation motivated and inspired others. Appeals of a similar vein and tenor were hardly new on the American Right. The theme of existential threat and impending civilizational collapse, which I have alighted upon throughout this book, were a staple of, among others, conservatives who had rejected – and were enraged by – modernity.[22] In the American context, the intellectual historian Michael Wreszin charted similar reactions, for instance, in the late-career Henry Adams (1838–1913) and in the conservative libertarian iconoclast Albert Jay Nock (1870–1945), the latter of whom was driven by American societal decline to

---

[19] Emphasis in original.
[20] For subsequent reflections in a similar vein, see Charles R. Kesler, "Thinking About Trump," *The Claremont Review of Books* 18:2 (Spring 2018); Charles R. Kesler, "So What if Trump Breaks Norms?" *New York Times* (August 28, 2018).
[21] Eliana Johnson, "Trump's Top National Security Spokesman to Leave White House," *Politico* (April 18, 2018); Rosie Gray, "The Populist Nationalist on Trump's National Security Council," *The Atlantic* (March 24, 2017). Hillsdale's Kirby Center website banners and posts an online guide entitled "The Founders' Compass: A Guide to America's Constitutional Crisis" (https://kirbycenter.hillsdale.edu/).
[22] Mark Lilla, *The Shipwrecked Mind: On Political Reaction* (New York: New York Review Books, 2011). For recent examples, see Deneen, *Why Liberalism Failed*; Ross Douthat, *To Change the Church: Pope Francis and the Future of Catholicism* (New York: Simon and Schuster, 2018).

wish for death ("I say let's go fast and straight and get it over with").[23] Nock ended his days attacking those who were criticizing Adolf Hitler, a man Nock praised for at least recognizing a civilizational crisis fomented in his homeland by outsiders and, the many obstacles he faced notwithstanding, at least committed to getting down to serious business. Nock dismissed the strident attacks on – he was careful to stipulate, the seriously problematic – Hitler to "liberal propaganda." "[T]he leadership of a wretched lunatic," Nock maintained, "was preferable in the circumstances to none at all."[24] At one time a harsh critic of the American Constitution, Nock in time married his attack on Hitler's critics to a call for the restoration and redemption of American constitutional government.[25]

The West Coast Straussian Michael Anton was certainly right, at least, that the Trump ascendency directly implicated the question of the seriousness of the constitutional conservatives who had long argued that "The Founder's Constitution" had not merely been mistakenly applied and interpreted but also illegitimately abandoned and betrayed. Those on the constitutionalist Right emphasizing mistake and error over abandonment and betrayal – in fact, if not always in word – were unlikely to make the Trump gambit. And in the context of Donald Trump's ascendency, Michael Anton insisted on calling their bluff. Like Albert Jay Nock before him, Anton insisted that the nation's constitutional crisis and the crisis of Western civilization were, in their essentials, one and the same. On this core point, Anton asked, were other self-styled constitutional conservatives with him or against him? If they spurned Trump, Anton argued, they failed the test of true believers in the gravity of the national and civilizational crisis.

---

[23] Wreszin, *Superfluous Anarchist*, 144. See The Doors, "The End" (Elektra, 1967). The Doors song "The End" can be read as fixing the moment when the quest for total freedom becomes a death wish: as such, as Joan Didion observed, it "suggest[s] some range of the possible just beyond the suicide pact." The Doors' music, and The Doors themselves, but particularly their lead singer Jim Morrison, signified for Didion the American West's final frontier – both geographically, perched on the edge of the Pacific Ocean, the last solid ground for the pioneers moving West, and civilizationally. The homicidal drama recounted in Morrison's lyrics was sung on the edge of the cliff of the liberationist 1960s, overlooking the abyss where the promise of total freedom portended a free fall into nihilism. Joan Didion, *The White Album* (New York: Simon and Schuster, 1979). While Thomas Hobbes (in *Leviathan*) may have considered the fear of death as the one hard fact to be counted upon in the organizing of political life, Morrison, in "suggest[ing] some range of the possible just beyond the suicide pact," was intimating that transcendence of the fear of death – and moral resistance to killing – is the final frontier of human liberation. In a similar vein, in his "Flight 93 Election" article in *The Claremont Review of Books* – which portended its own "End," the point of inflection where the dream becomes the nightmare – it was far from clear whether Anton was calling upon conservatives to thwart terrorists or become them.

[24] Albert Jay Nock, *Journal of These Days*, November 19, 1932, March 30, 1933, September 28, 1933, December 18, 1933, pp. 84, 150, 256, 298, quoted in Wreszin, *Superfluous Anarchist* at 141. See also Lilla, *Shipwrecked Mind*.

[25] Wreszin, *Superfluous Anarchist*, 92, 146.

As it turned, and turns, out, many on the intellectual Right failed Anton's test. The intellectual Right split. But a certain subset of those thinkers – right-wing Evangelical and Fundamentalist Christians, conservative Roman Catholics, and West Coast Straussians (not all, but in droves) – was with him. The heavily moralized stories these groups had long told and continue to tell in the postwar United States about civilizational and constitutional decline and crisis spoke to them in the age of Trump, as they had for the full run of the past half century or more. Of even greater significance was that those stories seemed to have been adopted by rank-and-file Republican voters, among whom, over two years since his election, President Trump's support continues to hover at nearly 90 percent.

Whether they are self-professed originalists in their constitutional theory did not determine whether conservative constitutional thinkers were pro-Trump or anti-Trump. By the early twenty-first century, originalism had long since become the official constitutional theory of the American conservative movement; a handful of idiosyncratic exceptions aside, no self-professed movement conservative was against it. What *was* determinative was the nature and tenor of their conviction that the US Constitution had been transgressed or abandoned, and the nature and tenor of their call for a course correction, restoration, and redemption. Those, by contrast, were determined not by some abstract and professed commitment to "original meanings" or "The Founders' Constitution," but by the way in which those commitments were underwritten, or not, by the deep constitutive stories that diverse intellectual strains and identity-based sub-communities of the conservative movement told and were telling themselves about constitutional betrayal, abandonment, restoration, and redemption that I have presented at length in this book. Put otherwise, they were not determined by the abstract ideas themselves, but by the emotional architecture and constructed historical memory into which the particular policy and constitutional arguments were fitted or, to enlist another metaphor, the vessels in which they were carried and conveyed. Those, Michael Anton correctly observed, dictated what particular conservatives thought and felt about the threats that liberals and progressives posed to the nation, and the gravity of the constitutional crisis.[26]

---

[26] For the statement of "Originalists Against Trump," which includes William Baude, Steven Calabresi, Richard Epstein, Richard Kay, Benjamin Kleinerman, Michael Stokes Paulsen, Jeremy Rabkin, Stephen D. Smith, Ilya Somin, Michael Uhlmann, Keith Whittington, George F. Will, and Michael Zuckert, see https://originalistsagainsttrump.wordpress.com/2016-statement/. For a statement scholars and intellectuals in support of Trump, including Hadley Arkes, William Bennett, John C. Eastman, Bruce Frohnen, Charles Kesler, John R. Lott, Ken Masugi, Ronald Pestritto, Alfred Regnery, Ralph Rossum, Ronald Rotunda, Ronald Rychlak, Thomas G. West, Newt and Callista Gingrich, and Bradley C. S. Watson, see https://scholarsandwriters-foramerica.org/. First in this latter group's list of stated commitments, presumably promised by Trump, is to the restoration of "constitutional governance."

To the extent that they closely identify the nation's "constitutional crisis" with a moralized vision of an impending crisis of Western civilization, portending an imminent collapse – as, apparently, a large number of right-wing Evangelical and Fundamentalist Christians, Roman Catholics, and Straussians do – "the counterinsurgency" or "the rejectionists"[27] (the other side of the coin of restoration) will be the wave of the future on the American Right. Depending, perhaps, on the success of the public policy side payments made to those within the movement less inclined to moral apocalyptic understandings (like many libertarians, business conservatives, the disrespected rural and white working class, and miscellaneous Republican others), those views might capture much of the governing apparatus of the deeply polarized nation.

FROM MOVEMENT VISION TO LEGAL DOCTRINE?

As this book has shown at length – and my two future books on this general subject will further demonstrate – originalist claims notwithstanding, neither American conservatism nor the positions movement conservatives have taken on constitutional issues have been fixed or static. As a political disposition or theory, to be sure, "conservatism" might have some core of common ideas, principles, and commitments.[28] But, in the United States especially – where, as Milton Friedman and Friedrich Hayek, among others, have rightly recognized, it was thoroughly admixed from its inception with "liberalism–"[29] the disposition and theory's range of application were unusually flexible, and vast. To complicate matters further, the country's conservative (Republican) and liberal (Democratic) political parties, whatever their ideological predispositions, are not political theory seminars: they are political organizations aimed at winning elections and assuming and holding political power. And success in winning elections and assuming and holding political power require an ear for, and deft skill at, reading a perpetually changing political context, with a keen eye for both its current opportunities and latent possibilities. Given the constitutional and political architecture of the United States, successfully reading that changing context and the opportunities and possibilities it provides requires an attentiveness to the possibilities for assembling a winning coalition. Over the course of the twentieth century, and on into the twenty-first, the nature and priorities of the Republican Party, like those of the Democratic Party, changed over time in line with its perceived need to both maintain and expand its (group-based) political coalition and its mass appeal to voters.[30]

---

[27] Bradley C.S. Watson, "The Hundred Years' War," *The Claremont Review of Books* 18:1 (Winter 2018).

[28] For a recent statement, see Roger Scruton, *Conservatism: An Invitation to the Great Tradition* (New York: Horsell's Morsels, Ltd., 2017).

[29] See also Clinton Rossiter, *Conservatism in America* (New York: Alfred A. Knopf, 1955).

[30] See David Karol, *Party Position Change in American Politics: Coalition Management* (New York: Cambridge University Press, 2009).

There has been considerable talk lately among political scientists and others about how the Republican and Democratic Parties today go about this business in fundamentally different ways. The Democrats in recent years, it is said, do it largely without ideas by simply tallying up the support of a diverse set of interests and identities. The Republicans, by contrast, have based their modern mobilization on (a presumably shared) set of broad and perpetually reiterated set of principles and ideational commitments.[31] Among the many things that I hope this study has done is to raise questions about this understandable but ultimately deceptive dichotomy.

Putting aside for the moment the Democrats – other than to note in passing, as my late teacher Theodore J. Lowi did long ago, that the notion that the mechanical assembly of choices of a vast field of group interests would ultimately yield "the public good," on the model of the invisible hand of economic markets, which underwrote the modern New Deal/Great Society social welfare and administrative state, *is itself an idea*[32] – it seems passing strange, especially in light of the history I have provided here, to consider the Republicans to be *primarily* about principles and ideas, and not about assembling a politically mobilized coalition of diverse interests and identities. The posited dichotomy, moreover, seems fundamentally false. The Republicans certainly were a party of principles and ideas, perhaps – though far from obviously – more so than the Democrats with whom, in the heyday of American liberalism, they were vying for political power. But to the extent that they were the party of principles and ideas, they used, revised, and perpetually reworked these principles and ideas in ways that would help bring in and secure the loyalty of a coalition of concrete interests and fervent political identities: to a significant extent, the claims made by interests and identities preceded the principles and ideas, just as it did with the purportedly unprincipled and idea-less Democrats. The Republicans, of course, as I have shown in this book, used ideas to help unite potentially disparate groups and interests. What the Republicans did do better than the Democrats, however, was convey a sense that, in fact, they had not done so – that they had not changed with the times, that their principles and commitments were fixed and timeless, and that they stood arm and arm with the nation's Founders and the plain meaning and original understanding of the US Constitution. Their great success, put otherwise, was in convincing enough Americans that the Democrats were the party of special interests and "identity politics," and that *they* were the party of ideas and principles.

This will have direct consequences for the future of American constitutional law – including as, perhaps now for generations, it will be expounded by the

---

[31] See Matt Grossmann and David A. Hopkins, *Asymmetric Politics: Ideological Republicans and Group Interest Democrats* (New York: Oxford University Press, 2016); Mark Lilla, *The Once and Future Liberal* (New York: HarperCollins, 2017).

[32] Theodore J. Lowi, *The End of Liberalism: The Second Republic of the United States* (New York: W. W. Norton, 1969).

conservative Supreme Court, where the purportedly neutral, principled, and consistent application of the law of the land is the ostensible coin of the realm. Just how movement conservative principles and ideas about the Constitution – in fact, the developmental product of more than a half century of culture work undertaken to unite a political coalition of diverse interests and identities – will be translated by right-wing judges into what is, after all, a recondite and quasi-autonomous realm of legal/constitutional doctrine, however, is far from clear. The recent contention over whether Donald Trump should appoint Brett Kavanaugh, the Yale-educated Federalist Society stalwart, or the University of Notre Dame Law School's right-wing Roman Catholic Amy Coney Barrett to the Supreme Court was less about how either of the two contenders would "vote" on the Court – all evidence is that they would mostly vote alike – but about the terms and nature of this translation.[33]

It is notable, but all-to-rarely noted, that Donald Trump's first appointment to the Supreme Court, Neil Gorsuch – the first Supreme Court Justice in American history to hold a PhD in addition to a law degree – was reportedly pushed in the Trump White House by the aggrieved, Catholic-raised, Evangelical Christian Vice-President Mike Pence,[34] and trained by one of the Catholic Right's most influential Thomist legal philosophers, John Finnis of Oxford and the University of Notre Dame. It is also notable that the Straussians, political philosophers and not lawyers who, in most of the earlier period I chronicle here, did their constitutional theorizing outside of the legal world in political science departments, are now venturing into the direct training of lawyers and judges.[35] All of these recent developments speak to the nature of what seems to be the impending translation, in overturning *Roe* and beyond.

---

[33] This is something that California Senator Dianne Feinstein awkwardly – and, for the Christian Right, notoriously – grasped during Barrett's appointment hearings for the US Court of Appeals for the Seventh Circuit. Adam Liptak, "Two Judges Exemplify the Choice Trump Faces in a Supreme Court Pick," *New York Times* (July 3, 2018) (www.nytimes.com/2018/07/03/us/politics/trump-supreme-court-judges-kavanaugh-barrett.htm) (Senator Feinstein said to Barrett: "You have a long history of believing that your religious beliefs should prevail. The dogma lives loudly within you."). Brett Kavanaugh is *also* a conservative Catholic. But, at least prior to his Supreme Court confirmation hearing, when he turned belligerently tribal, Kavanaugh's faith, it seemed, was not the point. For Barrett it is very much the point. The Religious Right is heavily invested in having any opposition to her sort of translation stigmatized as anti-Catholic/anti-Christian bigotry, and a blow against "religious liberty."

[34] Meghan O'Gieblyn, "Mike Pence's Persecution Complex," *Harper's Magazine* (May 2018).

[35] The West Coast Straussian Claremont Institute's John Marshall Fellows program launched in 2012 is devoted to training early career law students, law clerks, and lawyers (www.claremont.org/page/john-marshall-fellowship/). Similarly, the Straussian (and right-wing Catholic) Hadley Arkes's new venture, The James Wilson Institute on Natural Rights and the American Founding, declares in its mission statement that "The James Wilson Institute's Mission is to restore to a new generation of lawyers, judges, and citizens the understanding of the American Founders about the first principles of our law and the moral grounds of their own rights," and, elsewhere on its website, that "Our main objective is to restore a moral coherence to our jurisprudence." (https://jameswilsoninstitute.org/).

It is not clear, going forward, how much of the Supreme Court's conservative jurisprudence – its language of justification – will continue to hew to Federalist Society scripts or rather reflect, either directly or subtextually, the vicarious abolitionism and Thomist nationalism that has been so prominent in recent years on the constitutionalist American Right. As an increasingly right-wing Court is feeling its oats and moving beyond the restraintist posture championed back in the day by the likes of Robert Bork, Raoul Berger, Antonin Scalia, and Edwin Meese, the deep stories that conservative Roman Catholics, Evangelical and Fundamentalist Christians, Straussians, and other conservative constitutional theorists have told across the entire postwar period about the nation's political and constitutional trajectory, and aligned conservatives told about communism and markets, are likely to work their way into, and drive the development of, constitutional law – just as progressive and liberal stories about the nation's political and constitutional trajectory drove constitutional development during the heyday of American liberalism.[36]

It is also not clear how much resistance to what seems a likely tilt toward the constitutive stories – to say nothing of the concrete policy positions – of the conservative movement's Evangelical and Fundamentalist Christians and its moralist Straussians might ultimately be resisted by both movement libertarians and law school originalists who lack Christian theological impulses, either generally or in relation to law. As noted earlier, many of these libertarians and law school originalists have at least spurned Donald Trump himself, if not, to be sure, his Supreme Court picks. To date, the originalist and rights aegis under which this rising species of right-wing constitutional thought has been packaged and branded – and its hostility to government power, especially at the national level – seems to have provided enough "overlapping consensus" or grounds for "incompletely theorized agreement"[37] to keep these diverse conservative groups satisfactorily on the same team. At some point, however, they may be forced to ask how complicit their parallel insistence on a rigid textualism and legalist originalism has become in the broader Right's restorationist and redemptivist project, as anchored not simply in a set of interpretive principles but also in a host of deeply constitutive, and politically incendiary, stories about American political identity and nationalism.

In this regard, constitutional law is not simply "a matter of interpretation." It does not only involve, as many legalists would imagine it, the application of

---

[36] See, e.g., Herbert Croly, *The Promise of American Life* (New York: The MacMillan Company, 1909); Theodore Roosevelt, *The New Nationalism* (New York: The Outlook Company, 1910); Woodrow Wilson, *The New Freedom: A Call for the Emancipation of the Generous Energies of a People* (New York: Doubleday, Page and Company, 1913).

[37] I borrow from John Rawls and Cass Sunstein, respectively. See Ken I. Kersch, "Constitutive Stories About the Common Law in Modern American Conservatism," in Sanford Levinson, Joel Parker, and Melissa Williams, editors, *NOMOS: American Conservatism* (New York: New York University Press, 2016).

a legal text to a relatively delimited real-world bilateral dispute brought to a triadically structured court of law for judicial resolution.[38] In the United States, at least, constitutional law is heavily implicated not just in the critical matter of how we live together and what our government does but also in our understanding of who we are and what we want to be. The two are inextricable: a country whose politically divided citizenry tell radically different stories about their past will be hard pressed to imagine a shared future.[39]

Perhaps this is no more than par for the course for our sometimes robust, and even angry, constitutional democracy. But the history of what we commonly describe as our unbroken and successful constitutional tradition includes much violence and, indeed, civil war. Drawing on deep constitutive stories, the contemporary Right has ratcheted up the confrontation significantly. We should at least be conscious of, and knowledgeable about, what is happening. We no longer have the luxury of assuming that the battle over the past is not, in a very immediate sense, a fight for the nation's future.

---

[38] See Martin Shapiro, *Courts: A Comparative and Political Analysis* (Chicago: University of Chicago Press, 1981). Antonin Scalia, *A Matter of Interpretation – Federal Courts and the Law* (Princeton: Princeton University Press, 2018) (2nd ed.), with a new introduction by Akhil Reed Amar and a new afterword by Steven Calabresi.

[39] See Laila Parsons, "Separate But Unequal," *Times Literary Supplement* (April 20, 2018), citing Edward Said, and, in the absence of a shared version of the past, describing contemporary historians' enlistment of paired, side-by-side narratives to recount contemporary Israeli/Palestinian history.

Index